Comparative Politics
NOTES AND READINGS

COMPARATIVE POLITICS

Notes and Readings

Edited by

ROY C. MACRIDIS

Professor of Political Science

and

BERNARD E. BROWN

Associate Professor of Political Science

both of

State University of New York at Buffalo

.

REVISED EDITION

1964

THE DORSEY PRESS

Homewood, Illinois

———————

REVISED EDITION
First Printing, August, 1964

Library of Congress Catalog Card No. 64–24700

PRINTED IN THE UNITED STATES OF AMERICA

Preface

THIS VOLUME is an introduction to current developments in the field of comparative government and politics. In recent years political scientists, in addition to undertaking descriptive analysis of institutions, have sought to interpret politics in terms of key analytic concepts. It is our hope that this volume will encourage students to generalize about political systems, the way in which they function, and the historical, social, and other factors which account for similarities and differences. But the study of politics is also an unrelenting quest (in Aristotle's terms) for the highest good. The student should attempt to relate his knowledge about the functioning of political systems to the issues of our time.

In the three years since the appearance of the first edition of this volume, a great number of studies seeking to refine methods and concepts and to generalize about political behavior have attested to the vitality of comparative politics. In bringing out this revised edition, we have tried to adhere to our original purpose: to present the student with comparative studies that offer a comprehensive view of the field. It is our hope that students of comparative politics will continue to find here the building blocks for a general theory of political systems.

Regretfully, it was necessary to eliminate many of our original selections in order to keep this book down to a reasonable size for both publisher and student. In making final choices, our primary concern was to present representative selections of readings, rather than favor one approach to the exclusion of all others. We are, of course, grateful to the publishers or authors for granting their kind permission to reprint.

We should also like to acknowledge the many helpful suggestions given us by Professor Arthur L. Kalleberg, University of Missouri; Professor Theodore McNelly, University of Maryland; and Professor R. J. Richardson, Tulane University, New Orleans; who commented in detail on the First Edition of *Comparative Politics*.

We owe special thanks to many friends and colleagues for their valuable suggestions. Our thanks also go to Mrs. Hannelore Todd, secretary of the Department of Political Science at the State University of New York at Buffalo, and to Mrs. Margaret Hodge for help with innumerable clerical and editorial tasks. Kathy, Peter, and Stephen Macridis did not help very much, but they were fun to have around during our editorial conferences.

The task of writing all introductory essays and notes, and selecting materials, was shared by the two editors. They alone are jointly responsible for the final product.

R. C. M.
B. E. B.

Buffalo, New York
· April, 1964

List of Authors

(Note: Pages in brackets refer to contributions in this volume)

GABRIEL ALMOND. Professor of Political Science, Stanford University. Author, *The American People and Foreign Policy* (1950); *The Appeals of Communism* (1954); co-editor, *The Politics of Developing Areas* (1960); co-author, *The Civic Culture* (1963).

ARISTOTLE. (384–327 B.C.). A good one-volume collection is the Modern Library edition, *Introduction to Aristotle,* edited by Richard McKeon.

SAMUEL H. BEER. Professor of Government, Harvard University. Author, *The City of Reason* (1949); *Treasury Control* (1956); co-editor, *Patterns of Government* (1958).

KARL DIETRICH BRACHER. Professor of Political Science and Modern History at the University of Bonn (Germany). Author, *Die Auflössung der Weimarer Republik* (3rd ed., 1960); co-author, *Die Nationalsozialistiche Machtergreifung* (1960).

RALPH BRAIBANTI. Professor of Political Science, Duke University. Co-editor, *Traditions, Values and Socio-Economic Development* (1961); and *Administration and Economic Development in India* (1963).

CRANE BRINTON. McLean Professor of Ancient and Modern History, Harvard University. Author, *The Jacobins* (1930); *Nietzsche* (1941); *The United States and Britain* (1948); *English Political Thought in the Nineteenth Century* (1949); *Ideas and Men* (1950).

BERNARD E. BROWN. Associate Professor of Political Science, State University of New York at Buffalo. Author, *American Conservatives* (1951); *New Directions in Comparative Politics* (1962); Co-author, *The De Gaulle Republic* (1960).

JAMES BRYCE (1838–1922). British historian, statesman and diplomat. Author, *The Holy Roman Empire* (1864); *The American Commonwealth* (1888); *Studies in History and Jurisprudence* (1901).

ZBIGNIEW BRZEZINSKI. Professor of Government, Columbia University. Author, *The Permanent Purge* (1956); *The Soviet Bloc* (1960); *Ideology and Power in Soviet Politics* (1962); co-author, *Totalitarian Dictatorship and Autocracy* (1957).

TAYLOR COLE. Provost of Duke University. Author, *The Canadian Bureaucracy* (1949); co-author, *Responsible Bureaucracy, a Study of the Swiss Civil Service* (1932); editor, *European Political Systems* (1954).

PHILIP E. CONVERSE. Associate Professor of Political Science, University of Michigan. Co-author, *The American Voter* (1960).

ALDO DAMI. Professor, University of Geneva. Author, *Les Nouveaux Martyrs, Destin des Minorités* (1936); *Dernier des Gibelins, Réflexions hétérodoxes sur la Politique* (1960).

KARL W. DEUTSCH. Professor of Political Science, Yale University. Author, *Nationalism and Social Communication* (1953); *The Nerves of Government* (1963); co-author, *Political Community and the North Atlantic Area* (1957); *Germany Rejoins the Powers* (1959).

GEORGES DUPEUX. Professor, Faculty of Letters and Human Sciences, University of Bordeaux. Author, *Le Front populaire et les élections de 1936* (1959); *Aspects de l'histoire sociale et politique du Loir-et-Cher* (1962).

MAURICE DUVERGER. Professor, Faculty of Law, University of Paris. Author, *The French Political System* (1958); *Political Parties* (2d ed., 1959); and numerous other works.

DAVID EASTON. Professor of Political Science, University of Chicago. Author, *The Political System* (1953).

NEIL ELDER. Lecturer in Political Science, University of St. Andrews (Scotland).

RUPERT EMERSON. Professor of Government, Harvard University. Author, *State and Sovereignty in Modern Germany* (1928); *Representative Government in Southeast Asia* (1955); *From Empire to Nation* (1960).

CARL J. FRIEDRICH. Eaton Professor of the Science of Government, Harvard University. Author, *Constitutional Government and Democracy* (2d ed., 1951); *Inevitable Peace* (1947); *Man and His Government* (1963), etc.

EVERETT E. HAGEN. Professor of Economics and Senior Staff Member, Center for International Studies, Massachusetts Institute of Technology. Author, *The Economic Development of Burma* (1956); *On The Theory of Social Change* (1962); co-author, *The Sioux on the Reservation* (1960); editor, *Planning Economic Development* (1963).

GUNNAR HECKSCHER. Professor of Political Science, University of Stockholm. Author, *The Study of Comparative Government and Politics* (1957); *Démocratie efficace* (1957); and many works in Swedish.

H. STUART HUGHES. Professor of History, Harvard University. Author, *Oswald Spengler: A Critical Estimate* (1952); *The United States and Italy* (1953); *Consciousness and Society* (1958); *Contemporary Europe: A History* (1961); and *An Approach to Peace* (1962).

SAMUEL P. HUNTINGTON. Professor of Government, Harvard University. Author, *The Soldier and the State* (1957); editor, *Changing Patterns of Military Politics* (1962).

ELDON L. JOHNSON. Former President of the University of New Hampshire. Author of numerous articles in professional and law journals.

GEORGE McT. KAHIN. Professor of Government and Director of the Southeast Asia Program, Cornell University. Author, *Nationalism and Revolution in Indonesia* (1952). Editor, *Major Governments of Asia* (1958); and *Governments and Politics of Southeast Asia* (1959).

MARTIN L. KILSON. Lecturer on Government, Harvard University.

OTTO KIRCHHEIMER. Professor of Government, Columbia University. Author, *A Constitution for the Fourth Republic* (1947); *Political Justice* (1961).

HAROLD J. LASKI. (1893–1950). Late Professor at the London School of Economics. Author, *A Grammar of Politics* (1925); *Parliamentary Government in England* (1939); *The American Democracy* (1948); *Reflections on the Constitution* (1951), etc.

HAROLD D. LASSWELL. Professor of Law and Political Science, Yale University. Author, *Psychopathology and Politics* (rev. ed., 1960); *Politics—Who Gets What, When, How* (1936); *The Analysis of Political Behavior* (1949); *The Future of Political Science* (1963).

DANIEL LERNER. Professor of Sociology, Massachusetts Institute of Technology. Author, *The Passing of Traditional Society* (1958); *The Human Mean-*

ing of the Social Sciences (1959); co-author, *France Defeats the E.D.C.* (1957); co-editor, *The Policy Sciences* (1951).

WERNER LEVI. Professor of Political Science, University of Hawaii. Author, *Fundamentals of World Organization* (1950); *Free India in Asia* (1952); *Modern China's Foreign Policy* (1953); *Australian Outlook on Asia* (1959).

MARION J. LEVY, JR. Professor of Sociology, Princeton University. Author, *The Family Revolution in Modern China* (1949); *The Structure of Society* (1952).

SEYMOUR M. LIPSET. Professor of Sociology, University of California. Author, *Agrarian Socialism* (1950); *Political Man* (1960); *The First New Nation* (1963); co-author, *Union Democracy* (1956).

LESLIE LIPSON. Professor of Political Science, University of California. Author, *The American Governor* (1939); *The Politics of Equality* (1948); *The Great Issues of Politics* (1960).

VAL R. LORWIN. Professor of History, University of Oregon. Author, *The French Labor Movement* (1954).

C. B. MACPHERSON. Professor of Political Economy, University of Toronto. Author, *The Political Theory of Possessive Individualism* (1962).

ROY C. MACRIDIS. Professor of Political Science, State University of New York at Buffalo. Author, *The Study of Comparative Government* (1955); co-author, *The De Gaulle Republic* (1960); editor, *Foreign Policy in World Politics* (rev. ed., 1961); *Modern Political Systems: Europe and Asia* (1962).

M.I.T. STUDY GROUP. Among those participating in the preparation of the report on "The Transitional Process" were: FRANCIS M. BATOR, DONALD L. M. BLACKMER, RICHARD S. ECKAUS, EVERETT E. HAGEN, DANIEL LERNER, MAX F. MILLIKAN, ITHIEL DE SOLA POOL, LUCIAN W. PYE, PAUL N. ROSENSTEIN-RODAN and W. W. ROSTOW.

R. T. MCKENZIE. Reader in Sociology, London School of Economics and Political Science. Author, *British Political Parties* (rev. ed., 1962).

JEAN MEYNAUD. Professor at the Universities of Geneva and Lausanne. Author, *Les Groupes de Pression en France* (1958); *Introduction à la Science Politique* (1959); *Destin des Idéologies* (1961); *Nouvelles études sur les Groupes de Pression en France* (1962).

ROBERT MICHELS (1876–1946). Italian economist and sociologist. Author of *Political Parties* (1914), and numerous other works in Italian and German.

JOHN STUART MILL (1806–73). Noted English philosopher and essayist. A convenient collection of his political writings is the Everyman edition of *Utilitarianism, Liberty, and Representative Government*.

BARRINGTON MOORE, JR. Senior Research Fellow, Russian Research Center, Harvard University. Author, *Soviet Politics: The Dilemma of Power* (1950); *Political Power and Social Theory* (1959).

FRANZ L. NEUMANN (1900–1954). After a career as a lawyer and professor in Germany, he lived in England and then the United States. Late Professor of Government at Columbia University. Author of *Behemoth: The Structure and Practice of National Socialism* (1944); and *The Democratic and the Authoritarian State* (1957).

L. VINCENT PADGETT. Associate Professor of Political Science, San Diego State College.

GUY J. PAUKER. Research Associate, RAND Corporation. Author, *Role of the Military in Indonesia* (1961).

DON K. PRICE. Professor of Government and Dean of the Faculty of Public Administration, Harvard University. Author, *The New Dimension of Diplomacy* (1951); *Government and Science* (1954); editor, *The Secretary of State* (1960).

LUCIAN W. PYE. Professor of Political Science, Massachusetts Institute of Technology. Author, *Guerrilla Communism in Malaya* (1956); *Politics, Personality, and Nation Building: Burma's Search for Identity* (1962); editor, *Communications and Political Development* (1963).

RICHARD ROSE. Lecturer in Government, University of Manchester (England). Co-author, *British General Election of 1959* (1960) and *Must Labour Lose?* (1960).

DONALD C. ROWAT. Professor of Political Science, Carleton University (Ottawa). Editor, *Basic Issues in Public Administration* (1961).

HUGH SETON-WATSON. Professor of Russian History, School of Slavonic and East European Studies, University of London. Author, *The East European Revolution* (1950); *The Decline of Imperial Russia* (1952); *Neither War Nor Peace* (1960); *From Lenin to Khrushchev* (1960), etc.

KALMAN H. SILVERT. Professor of Government, Dartmouth College, and Director of Studies, American Universities Field Staff. Author, *A Study in Government: Guatemala* (1957); editor, *Expectant Peoples* (1963).

ROBERT C. TUCKER. Professor of Politics, Princeton University. Author, *Philosophy and Myth in Karl Marx* (1961).

ROBER9 E. WARD. Professor of Political Science, University of Michigan. Author, *Japanese Political Science* (1961); co-author, *Village Japan* (1959); editor, *Five Studies in Japanese Politics* (1957) and *Modern Political Systems: Asia* (1963).

MAX WEBER (1864–1920). German sociologist. Among his works in English translation are: *The Protestant Ethic and the Spirit of Capitalism; The Theory of Social and Economic Organization* (1947); and *From Max Weber*, edited by H. H. Gerth and C. W. Mills (1952).

Table of Contents

Part One–Problems of Comparative Analysis
INTRODUCTORY ESSAY

I

Political Systems

THIS VOLUME is prepared on the basis of a general conception: a political system is, above all, a mechanism for the making of decisions. It is endowed with legitimacy, that is, the decisions made by the various organs of government are expected to be widely obeyed.

Decisions involve compromises among many conflicting points of view held by social groups, parties, associations, interest organizations, and regions. On the one hand, we have the governmental organs that make decisions—the legislature, the executive, the courts, and the bureaucracy. On the other hand, there are the social and economic forces and groupings, and the beliefs and values held by the members of the society about their political system. This suggests a threefold distinction: (1) the government; (2) the "social and cultural configuration," that is, social classes, economic groups, ethnic groups, regions, interest groups and their mode of action; and (3) the pattern of values and ideologies relating specifically to political authority, permissive areas of governmental action, and the role and position of individuals and associations.

It is the interplay between social configuration, ideology, and the governmental organs that constitutes the dynamics of politics—the making of decisions. Social and economic groups, molded and patterned in accordance with the ideas men hold, press their claims upon the government. Interest groups and political parties function as conveyor belts between interest claims and governmental decisions. Political leadership sifts these claims, often provides for compromise, and articulates them in the form of pledges or decisions. It is not impossible, especially when conflicts assume a high level of intensity and when opposing sides are evenly balanced, for a political system to find itself in a situation where no decision can be made. The system is at a state of stalemate, or to use the expression often employed to characterize the French parliamentary system under the Third and Fourth Republics, "immobility."

The efficiency of a political system can be gauged in terms of its ability

1

to make decisions that are widely accepted. In a democratic system this can be determined by the response such decisions elicit among the social groups, interest groups, and voluntary associations. In a totalitarian system the test is ultimately the same.

An efficient system maintains a balance between change and stability. Change is the result of constant claims that arise from the social groups because of evolving technical and economic conditions. Emerging social groups inevitably put forward demands as they gain access to positions of influence and power. Throughout the nineteenth century, for instance, the general theme of political change was associated with the claims of the lower-middle classes and the workers (in some cases the slaves and serfs) for suffrage and political participation. As societies industrialize, these same groups organize in order to facilitate the translation of their newly acquired political influence into immediate socioeconomic benefits. Efficiency therefore depends upon the nature of governmental response to the demands from groups. If existing institutions prove incapable of meeting these demands, the new groups may attempt to gain power by revolutionary means, which has disruptive effects upon the whole system.

From this point of view there is no guarantee that a democratic system is more efficient than a totalitarian one. The latter must provide some way (for example, through the ruling party) for significant groups to be heard. The former may find that its representative institutions no longer adequately translate claims of equally strong and competing groups into decisions or provide a satisfactory synthesis. In both systems leadership plays an important role. Basically, a leader decides in favor of certain groups and at the expense of other groups. But he cannot impose a policy which is out of line with the existing balance of forces. In fact a democratic society may become the victim of its own philosophy. By creating organs that register accurately the demands of all groups and by attempting to satisfy all of them, it may give to each a "veto power" over decisions and thus founder in stalemate.

The most persistent challenges to a political system derive from economic and technological modernization. In underdeveloped countries modernization involves literally the restructuring of society—the inculcation of new norms of behavior, the training of skilled bureaucrats, and drastic action on the basis of newly established goals. Modernization at the political level involves the identification of the masses of the people with these goals. Disciplined effort is indispensable because of the lack of available resources. These societies must rely upon their most plentiful and therefore cheapest commodity—human labor—whose effective utilization requires sacrifice and unremitting toil. In western Europe, the Protestant religion, it has been suggested by Max Weber, provided the philosophy that broke down the barriers of feudal and medieval society, secularized human motivation, and supplied incentive that made possible the Industrial Revolution. Ideologies and values in the underdeveloped societies are now undergoing similar transformations. Will these nations follow the European pattern of economic individualism, or the Communist type of collective effort with emphasis on coercion and indoctrination? Their choice will largely determine the nature of their emerging political institutions.

Problems of modernization are naturally different for the societies that have already attained a high level of industrialization. The crucial problem in economically advanced systems is to maintain a constant rate of economic growth, to develop technology rapidly and effectively in order to increase the productivity of labor, and to make the benefits of increased productivity available to all in the form of better living conditions and welfare. The government is compelled to provide a wide range of services and to enforce social justice by means of income distribution.

To summarize: We have suggested that in a political system conflicting claims and demands are translated into accepted decisions. The claims are made by social groups. The manner in which conflicts are expressed depends to a great degree upon the nature of ideologies and values concerning political authority. The links between the social structure and the governmental organs are political parties, interest groups, and other associations. It is the role of political leadership to articulate interests and conflicts, achieve a synthesis in the form of policy, and carry it out through the governmental organs. An efficient government is able to provide for change in a stable fashion—that is, without recourse to violence on the part of important groups. It must also be able to survive as a system in the midst of competing nation-states.

An examination of all these propositions requires comparative analysis and study.

II

The Comparative Approach

The study of comparative government is in a state of flux. Traditionally, it has been preponderantly descriptive rather than problem solving, explanatory, or analytic in its method. It did not lend itself to the development of theories and the testing of hypotheses and the compilation of significant data. It was limited to the description of the forms of government of foreign political systems.

Recently there has been an increasing awareness of the shortcomings of the traditional approach, leading to an attempt to develop a more systematic orientation. The need has been felt to broaden our approach both horizontally (by including as many political systems—Western and non-Western—as possible) and vertically (by attempting to relate the political process to broad social and economic conditions). There has been a growing concern to be more "scientific." Science aspires to the establishment of universal patterns of behavior and requires the testing of hypothetical propositions. This means that the testing should be made against as many systems as possible in the light of common analytical categories.[1]

The new approach is more probing and systematic. It is probing in that it attempts to go behind the façade of political institutions; it is primarily concerned with the social configuration, the interest group universe, political parties, ideological attitudes as they shape and condition political behavior, and elite structure. It is systematic in seeking to discover "relations" between politics and the contextual elements of a system.

But a systematic approach requires an over-all view or theory of politics. Political science has therefore borrowed extensively from sociological theory. For example, politics has been viewed by some analysts as a system of interaction between actors (individuals and groups) for the purpose of realizing specific goals. A political system must perform certain indispensable (or requisite) functions in order to survive. Certain institutions are also indispensable (or requisite) structures for the performance of these functions. Structures differ from one system to another and undergo profound modifications under the impact of diverse factors—war, industrialization, economic changes, new aspirations, and new demands.

The study of politics (as for Aristotle) becomes the study of a "system" linked organically with social structure, traditions and ideologies, culture, and the environment within which it operates. It may then be possible to discern significant similarities and differences which mere description of the legal forms of a state does not suggest. Establishment of *correlations* between political, economic, cultural, and social phenomena provide a perspective in terms of which the dynamics of change may be understood and broad generalizations made. In essence, this is the application of scientific method to the study of political phenomena. Hypotheses and theories about the political process are elaborated into a rational system and then examined critically in the light of available evidence.

The analytical approach, then, strives toward a definition of a political system, identifies the most important structures through which a system functions, and studies differences and similarities. It purports to establish general propositions about political behavior. As in natural science generalizations are stated in the form of hypotheses involving a series of conditions. For instance, it could be posited that if there are no serious ideological conflicts in a society and if there is a majority electoral system, then two parties will develop. It can be posited that industrialization and prosperity will, all other conditions being held in check, lead to a decrease in conflict about issues and the development of a political system concerned with the solution of concrete problems. It may be posited that economic policies endangering the status of certain social groups will provoke a strong movement of protest on the part of the threatened groups, who will seek to protect themselves even by violence—or that

---

[1] See Roy C. Macridis, *The Study of Comparative Government* (New York: Random House, 1955), especially pp. 15–17 and Bernard E. Brown, *New Directions in Comparative Politics* (London: The Asia Publishers, 1962), Chapter 1.

groups denied participation in the political system will, all other things being equal, seek to gain status and influence also by violence.

These hypotheses can be tested against reality and accordingly qualified, modified, or rejected. Field work and empirical observation are therefore indispensable for comparative study as for all forms of scientific inquiry. This kind of analysis will add to our knowledge of the conditioning factors whose presence or absence account for the validation or the rejection of our hypothesis. For instance, if we propose that wherever there is *A* (for example, a majority electoral system) then *B* (a two-party system) will follow and find that in one system this obtains but in another it does not, then we have to seek the reasons for this disparity. We do so by finding a series of other factors $(X, X_1, X_2, X_3, X_4, X_5,$ etc.). Our hypothesis then will be qualified to read *A* will follow *B* *provided* factors X_2 (religious differences), X_3 (regionalism) or X_4 (ethnic groups) or others, depending upon field observation, obtain. In this manner a comprehensive explanation accounting for the differences between two systems may be given.

It is at this point that comparative analysis becomes both challenging and at the same time frustrating for the student. Rarely if ever can we provide a coherent and satisfactory generalization explaining the differences between systems. Historical and other factors give nations characteristics that are unique, that is to say, cannot be duplicated. In fact we shall find it virtually impossible to verify any hypothesis or to develop any generalization that is valid for *all* political systems. It is necessary to lengthen the chain of conditioning factors (X's) for each political system in order to take into account individual and idiosyncratic factors. The proposal to develop general laws seems to bog down in a never-ending explanation for unique situations. Some observers contend that there are no universally valid laws. In despair they conclude that the indeterminacy and uniqueness of political behavior does not permit generalization.

It would be a serious mistake to accept this point of view. Comparative analysis can at the very least identify and perhaps explain uniqueness, which is of crucial importance. Unless we start with general concepts and hypotheses, we are not able even to draw distinctions let alone account for them. How can we tell what is unique without knowing what is general? Power, for instance, is manifested in many ways and contains many elements—religion, property, birth, administration, and so on. But these different manifestations can be distinguished, related, and understood only in terms of some general concept of power.

The Range of Comparison

The range of comparison will usually be determined by the theoretical scheme, by the formulation of a *problem* or the study of *a given area*. In all cases two crucial questions must be confronted: How do we compare? What do we compare?

Comparison may be attempted between segments of the political process in various systems, or between certain institutions, or between political systems as such, in order to clarify issues which preoccupy us. Let us take the multiparty system in France. The historian of French political institutions will describe the origin, development, ideologies, and characteristics of the French multiparty system. The student of comparative politics faced with the same problem would ask rather: What are the conditions for the existence of a multiparty system? Are they institutional?—social?—sectional?—ideological? Once the conditions have been identified, then comparison with other multiparty structures will show the relevance of some but not others, that is, comparative study may disprove the relationship between certain conditions and multipartism. We may find, for instance, that analogous sectional conditions in the United States have not produced a multiparty system—or that similar electoral systems exist in both two-party and multiparty systems.

Through comparison it is possible to explain the nature of a phenomenon like a multiparty system in the light of a chain of conditioning factors, such as sectionalism, proportional representation, the cabinet's inability to dissolve parliament, and so on. The chain of conditioning factors that we find in France cannot be reproduced historically or experimentally in any other country. But this in no way lessens the need for suggesting relationships among conditioning factors for the purpose of analysis and empirical investigation. Nor does it mean that because France or Country X or Y are unique they cannot be the subject of comparison. France is indeed unique, but in an analytical sense the conditions of multipartism are general categories permitting comparison of France with other political systems. Every suicide is unique. But as Emile Durkheim demonstrated, the conditions under which people commit suicide can be analytically identified in terms of a number of broad categories.

We compare, therefore, in order to discover the conditions under which certain phenomena take place. Conditions or, more precisely, a series of conditions are hypothetically related to the phenomenon we study. The task of empirical observation is to test the validity of such hypothetical formulations. By so doing we enrich our knowledge of the factors that account for a given phenomenon until we are able to generalize about them. The presence or absence of some or others will enable us to make tentative judgments about political developments and occurrences.

Comparison may be either *static* or *dynamic*. In the first instance, we undertake an anatomy, so to speak, of political systems. Structures are described and related. In this connection classificatory tables are useful in that they suggest analogies and differences. Structures, however, must be identified in terms of the particular function they perform in a system. This is much more difficult than it may seem to be. It is essential to discern the *overt* from the *covert*, and the *manifest* from the *latent* functions. For instance, though there are striking structural analogies between the electoral systems of the Soviet Union and the United States, their functions are wholly dissimilar. Elections in the United States are an integral part of the process of arriving at decisions over which the body politic is divided. In the Soviet Union, on the other hand, elections are used to express loyalty to the regime, and to rally the people around the policy of their leaders. Their function is roughly that of a patriotic celebration.

Dynamic comparison is the study of the performance of various systems. We not only identify structures through which certain functions are performed but also account for the structural variations between systems. Ultimately an effort may be made to trace out consequences of alternative courses of action, or predict in the light of a chain of conditioning factors. This last stage is indeed the most significant but at the same time the most difficult to reach.

The Problem Approach in Comparative Studies

The study of a problem in comparative terms may be conducted at several different levels of abstraction. For instance, the study of political instability as a "problem" would be at a high level of generalization. On the other hand, the study of political instability in parliamentary systems would involve less sweeping concepts and a more limited range of observation and variables. Finally, the study of cabinet instability in its relation to electoral systems would deal with even narrower concepts and more strictly defined variables.

Three types of problem approaches may be distinguished:

1. The "middle-range theory problem" approach.
2. The "policy-oriented problem" approach.
3. The "narrow-gauge theory problem" approach.

The Middle-Range Approach. This approach requires a theoretical scheme involving a fairly high degree of generalization and abstraction but remains below the level of a comprehensive scheme of politics. In the words of Robert K. Merton, theories of the middle range are "theories intermediate to the minor working hypotheses evolved in abundance during the day-to-day routines of research, and the all-inclusive speculations comprising a master conceptual scheme from which it is hoped to derive a very large number of empirically observed uniformities of social behavior."[2] The problem is significant and not trivial or narrow, yet is "researchable." It is possible, that is, to test out the theory by examining relevant data. Its flexibility and adaptability to modest levels of empirical research at manageable levels is its greatest merit. Many of the selections in this volume are illustrative of the "middle-range" approach, for example, Samuel Beer's theory concerning the relationship between

[2] Robert K. Merton, *Social Theory and Social Structure* (Glencoe, Ill.: The Free Press, 1949), p. 5.

organized interests and political systems, or Otto Kirchheimer on ideological trends in industrialized societies.

A Policy-Oriented Approach. A second type of approach, put forward recently by a number of authors, is the presentation and selection of problems for policy purposes.[3] Both in their selection and in their study, problems are related to the requirements of policy making. They are chosen because of a "conflict situation" or a "high degree of tension." They are studied for the purpose of suggesting "solutions" through which the causes of tensions may be removed and conflict lessened. An examination of racial relations in major urban centers in the United States, for instance, is in a sense comparative and attempts to elicit information and data that may guide policy makers. Insecurity and its manifestations under various political and economic systems is a problem that can also be studied comparatively and again is formulated because of the observable signs of tension. Studies of revolution undertaken comparatively may shed light upon the relevant factors that bring about violent action on the part of certain groups. They may be undertaken either for the purpose of studying this phenomenon as such or for the purpose of working out a policy to prevent its recurrence.

The problem approach has the great advantage of orienting research empirically along multiple avenues without being tied down to premature theoretical schemes. Also, it is perhaps inevitable that political scientists should concern themselves with contemporary crises. But one of the dangers is oversimplification. Conflict and tensions are the result of many factors situated in a time dimension. Suggested policies may provoke new tensions or have unanticipated consequences unless they are carefully thought out in the light of the many existing factors.

Narrow-Gauge Theory Approach. Narrow-gauge theory involves the selection of a problem that has a limited range of variables. It fulfills some of the same functions as middle-range theory but can be used only for the study of phenomena in similar social contexts. For this reason narrow-gauge hypotheses are fruitful mainly in suggesting broader theories.

The most familiar narrow-gauge hypotheses are those used for the study of Western political systems. Invariably they are "disproved" and as a result abandoned. To give an illustration: Does the power of dissolution create well-disciplined parties which in turn account for cabinet stability? The question as formulated obviously relates to the parliamentary systems of Great Britain and western Europe. Observation reveals that there is a missing link—the electoral system. Hence, the question may be rephrased in the following terms: Does the power of dissolution in a single-member district system bring about party discipline and cabinet stability? On the basis of comparative study an affirmative or negative answer is unwarranted. No two parliamentary systems of western

---

[3] See Daniel Lerner and Harold Lasswell (eds.), *The Policy Sciences* (Stanford, Calif., 1951).

Europe satisfy the requirements of this proposition. Even if they did, stability or instability might still be caused by other factors.

Nonetheless, the narrow-gauge theory approach is extremely useful. Through a process of disproof rather than proof it trains students to think in terms of hypotheses and their verification. By eliminating irrelevant causes, students learn how to relate politics to social, economic, and cultural factors.

The most fruitful work in the field of comparative politics in recent years has resulted from analysis of middle-range theory problems. It should be emphasized, however, that the study of the issues and crises of our century is not necessarily to be shunted aside in favor of an exclusive preoccupation with theoretical constructs and model building. It would be unfortunate, indeed self-defeating, if students of politics confined their attention only to problems which can be formulated on a low or middle level of abstraction, or if all lines of political inquiry were to be dictated by the research tools at our disposal. The political scientist should be concerned not only with predictability but also desirablity and the social conditions under which desired goals can be realized. The examination of such goals in terms of ethical postulates is also the task of the political scientist. Unless we resign ourselves to acceptance of any state which happens to exist, and to any goals sought by a group, then ethics will always constitute a legitimate subject of political inquiry. In this volume, however, we are deliberately focusing our interest on the political process and system.

III

The Search for New Definitions

Awareness of the need for a more systematic approach to the study of politics, coupled with a new appreciation of the interrelationship between social and political structures, has played havoc with the old descriptive definitions and classifications. Traditionally, a state has been described as a community of people living in a given territory with a government. Wherever there is a stable relationship between governors and governed there is a state. Thus, both Ecuador and the United States are examples of "states." But the classic definition does not tell us what to look for and where to look in order to find out how and why these two states are different. The use of categories like ideology, social configuration, and government as a decision-making mechanism aids the student to understand similarities and differences.

The United States is an industrial society; Ecuador is agrarian. In the one, effective participation in politics is widespread; in the other, it is extremely limited. In the one, there is a clear differentiation between the bureaucrat, the soldier, the priest, or the producer; in the other, the differentiation is blurred. In the one, literacy is very high; in the other, literacy is low. In the one, people constantly make demands through a number of clearly discernible institutions—interest groups, parties, and legislatures; in the other, emerging aspirations are not clearly channeled in an orderly way. All these differences constitute the real "stuff" of politics.

Most scholars writing in the field of comparative politics today have abandoned the traditional classification of governments—as put forth by Aristotle and Montesquieu, for example—in terms of monarchy, aristocracy, democracy, mixed governments, and separation of powers. Even the distinction between totalitarian systems and constitutional democracies is not wholly satisfactory. The structure of political power is only one of many interrelated factors.

A profusion of new schemes for classifying governments has been suggested in recent years. Many stem from Max Weber's distinction between three types of authority: traditional, rational, and charismatic. Gabriel Almond in his article, "Comparative Political Systems," distinguishes between four major kinds of systems: consensual (primarily Anglo-American), fragmented (continental Europe), totalitarian (communist and fascist), and preindustrial. David Apter refers to political systems as dictatorial, indirectly and directly representational, and oligarchical. A group of authors from the Massachusetts Institute of Technology, in a report prepared for the Senate Committee on Foreign Policy, identify the following types among the erstwhile colonies: traditional oligarchies, modernizing oligarchies, and potentially democratic societies. James Coleman refers to "terminal colonial democracy" and "colonial or racial oligarchy." In addition, he describes "stable and unstable" systems, and "underdeveloped and developing" societies. There are "transitional" societies in which Daniel Lerner tells us that we must look for a cluster of interrelated phenomena—industrialization, urbanization, literacy, participation in mass media, role differentiation, and empathy. Karl W. Deutsch develops an impressive listing of variables in order to differentiate systems on the basis of diverse combinations. Finally, the terms "Western" and non-Western" are on everybody's lips today.

The "boundaries" of the field of politics have become blurred. In identifying the component elements of a system, Gabriel Almond lists the following "input" (primarily political) functions: political socialization and recruitment, interest articulation, interest aggregation, and political communication. The "output" (or governmental) functions are more familiar even if the terms appear to be new. They are rule making, rule application, and rule adjudication. Professor Lasswell goes a step further in describing the functions of a political system as follows: intelligence, recommendation, prescription, invocation, application, appraisal, and termination. David Easton is more parsimonious. He holds that the main functions of a political system are demands, supports, and authoritative decisions—the latter determining the proper boundaries of politics. Samuel Beer discusses a political system with reference to its "political culture," the "pattern of power," the "pattern of interests," and the "pattern of policy."[4]

We are, therefore, as was said at the outset, in a state of flux. We are uncertain of the boundaries of political science in its relation to other social sciences and in disagreement over the significant components of political systems. But a state of flux is not necessarily a state of confusion. It may rather be an indication of healthy curiosity and intellectual ferment. The discipline is maturing as it attempts to relate political and social factors, explain behavior, and clarify problems. Description of the institutions and policies of states continues to be of crucial importance. But they are properly viewed only as parts of the "political system."

---

[4] The works referred to include: Max Weber, *The Theory of Social and Economic Organization* (New York: Oxford University Press, 1947), pp. 324–91; Gabriel A. Almond, "Comparative Political Systems," *Journal of Politics,* August, 1956 (reproduced below); David Apter, "A Comparative Method for the Study of Politics," *American Journal of Sociology* (November, 1958), pp. 221–37; Gabriel A. Almond and James S. Coleman, *The Politics of Developing Areas* (Princeton, N.J.: Princeton University Press, 1960), Daniel Lerner, *The Passing of Traditional Society* (Glencoe, Ill.: The Free Press, 1958); Karl W. Deutsch, "Towards an Inventory of Basic Trends and Patterns in Comparative and International Politics," *American Political Science Review,* March, 1960 (reproduced below); Harold D. Lasswell, *The Decision Process* (Bureau of Governmental Research, University of Maryland, 1956); David Easton, "An Approach to an Analysis of Political Systems," *World Politics* (April, 1957) (reproduced below); and Samuel Beer, *Patterns of Government* (New York: Random House, 1958), pp. 3–51.

Chapter 1. Classic Contributions

Introductory Note

FROM THE moment the difference in the ways and manners of men living in societies was observed, "comparison" was unavoidable. Aristotle and Plato drew upon the differences of the Greek city-states to develop a classification of political systems. Aristotle (384–327 B.C.) in his *Politics* put forward three criteria for the distinction of political systems: (1) the number of citizens participating in the making of decisions, (2) the existence or absence of legal restraints, and (3) the "ethos" of the ruling class. On this basis he distinguished "normal" and "corrupt" systems: monarchy, aristocracy, and democracy under law (polity); tyranny, oligarchy, and majoritarian democracy (without restraints). These terms continue to be used by many political scientists.

The most significant contribution of Aristotle, however—one that is "rediscovered" today, notably by Seymour Lipset in his *Political Man* (1960) was his emphasis upon groups and classes and the balance and stability that ensues from a system in which property as an instrument of power is widely shared. The state is an association of associations, a "community of communities," as he put it, with diverse occupational and social groups, all of which ought to be allowed a share of political power and participation. Collective judgment was superior to that of the king, and less amenable to passions and error.

The Romans—notably Polybius (201–120 B.C.) and Cicero (106–43 B.C.) —took up the Aristotelian categories but considered them in formal and legalistic terms. Power was defined as the ability to command, lodged in a state. In order to prevent abuses the state was to be divided into separate organs—executive, legislative, and judicial.

Concern with comparative study reappears at the end of the fifteenth century with Machiavelli (1469–1527) in his *Prince* (1513) and *The Discourses* (1519). He drew from the manifold experiences of the Italian city-states and from his wide reading of history. Political behavior was explained in terms of one basic category—power. The technique of government was that of securing, maintaining, and extending power. How could this be done? Only by understanding human nature and by drawing as many examples as possible from the past. Human nature is selfish, timid yet power driven, seeking gratification—both physical and psychological. History can give us guidance to successful rulership. But the conclusions reached are always tentative and conditional. Though Machiavelli is the first to describe the art of government by invoking parallel situations, that is, by comparing, he is also prone to attribute events to factors that by themselves cannot be studied in a scientific manner: the courage of the Prince, his upbringing, the "wisdom" of his councilors, and very often sheer luck—*fortuna*. In every parallel situation therefore there are always imponderables. The art of statecraft is highly contingent and the prescriptions that Machiavelli doles out for the Prince are fraught with so many "ifs" and "buts" as to make any generalization difficult.

Montesquieu, in the eighteenth century, was far more conscious of the need of relating politics to social factors—groups, economic classes, education, tradition, and ideology—than perhaps anybody before his time with the exception of Aristotle. In his *Spirit of Laws* (1748) there is a consistent effort to devise classification of political systems in terms that relate political power to a broader context. But it was with John S. Mill (1806–73) and Edward A. Freeman (1823–92) that we have the first efforts not only to compare political systems but also to develop a method of comparison. Mill's inverse deductive or historical method and his law of correspondence call for generalizations (logical propositions that one state of things will follow from another) and empirical verification. Both his *Considerations on Representative Government* (1861) and his *System of Logic* (1848), (especially the whole of Chapter X from which excerpts are given) can be read with profit. He was heavily indebted to French sociologists and historians like Condorcet and Auguste Comte, particularly the latter's *Cours de Philosophie Positive* (6 vols. 1830–42).

The last important representative of the classical tradition was James Bryce (1838–1922). He begins with a theory of human nature which is supposed to be constant, and then studies political systems in order to discover the variations and deviations brought about by historical, social, and economic conditions. His *Modern Democracies* (1921) is a typical illustration of the use of the concept of human nature.

The "classic" contribution to the development of a method of comparative government is therefore very limited. Machiavelli, to be sure, uses experience and observation to reach conclusions about political behavior. But his method partakes more of the nature of alchemy than chemistry. In the nineteenth century sociologists, historians, and economists suggested theoretical generalizations—Jeremy Benthan (1748–1842), Adam Smith (1723–90), Auguste Comte (1798–1857), Alexis de Tocqueville (1805–59), Karl Marx (1818–83), Henry Maine (1822–88), Vinogradoff (1854–1925), Emile Durkheim (1858–1917). They either used an abstract deductive method or, as with de Tocqueville, a historical approach. It is only recently that they began to influence appreciably the students of politics. The latter remained primarily concerned with what Edward Sait called in his book *Political Institutions* (which is still worth reading) "excogitation." A rich body of political philosophy was developed. They were also concerned with law, law making, and policy making and to an even greater extent with history—describing the ways in which institutions evolved and sometimes searching for the ultimate causes of historical change.

The study of politics as a manifestation of behavior reflecting a great number of factors, some of which could be related in a systematic fashion in order to find regularities, has been revived in the last few decades. The way was shown primarily by sociologists and anthropologists who tried to imitate natural science by suggesting propositions about human behavior that could be tested, or at the very least by observing, describing, and cataloguing it.

Readings

1. THE PREVALENCE OF THE POLITICAL*

Aristotle

As, IN an inquiry into every other subject, it is necessary to separate the different parts of which it is compounded, till we arrive at their first elements, which are the most minute parts thereof; so by the same proceeding we shall acquire a knowledge of the primary parts of a city and see wherein they differ from each other, and whether the rules of art will give us any assistance in examining into each of these things which are mentioned. . . .

. . . When many villages so entirely join themselves together as in every respect to form but one society, that society is a city, and contains in itself, if I may so speak, the end and perfection of government: first founded that we might live, but continued that we may live happily. For which reason every city must be allowed to be the work of nature, if we admit that the original society between male and female is; for to this as their end all subordinate societies tend, and the end of everything is the nature of it. For what every being is in its most perfect state, that certainly is the nature of that being, whether it be a man, a horse, or a house: besides, whatsoever produces the final cause and the end which we desire, must be best; but a government complete in itself is that final cause and what is best. Hence it is evident that a city is a natural production, and that man is

---

* From *Politics*, translated by John Warrington, copyright translation, J. M. Dent & Sons, Ltd., 1959. Everyman's Library edition. Reprinted by permission of E. P. Dutton & Co., Inc.

naturally a political animal, and that whosoever is naturally and not accidentally unfit for society, must be either inferior or superior to man: thus the man in Homer, who is reviled for being "without society, without law, without family." Such a one must naturally be of a quarrelsome disposition, and as solitary as the birds. The gift of speech also evidently proves that man is a more social animal than the bees, or any of the herding cattle: for nature, as we say, does nothing in vain, and man is the only animal who enjoys it. Voice indeed, as being the token of pleasure and pain, is imparted to others also, and thus much their nature is capable of, to perceive pleasure and pain, and to impart these sensations to others; but it is by speech that we are enabled to express what is useful for us, and what is hurtful, and of course what is just and what is unjust: for in this particular man differs from other animals, that he alone has a perception of good and evil, of just and unjust, and it is a participation of these common sentiments which forms a family and a city. Besides, the notion of a city naturally precedes that of a family or an individual, for the whole must necessarily be prior to the parts; for if you take away the whole man, you cannot say a foot or a hand remains, unless by equivocation, as supposing a hand of stone to be made, but that would only be a dead one; but everything is understood to be this or that by its energic qualities and powers, so that when these no longer remain, neither can that be said to be the same, but something of the same name. That a city then precedes an individual is plain, for if an individual is not in himself sufficient to compose a perfect government, he is to a city as other parts are to a whole; but he that is incapable of society, or so complete in himself as not to want it, makes no part of a city, as a beast or a god. There is then in all persons a natural impetus to associate with each other in this manner, and he who first founded civil society was the cause of the greatest good; for as by the completion of it man is the most excellent of all living beings, so without law and justice he would be the worst of all, for nothing is so difficult to subdue as injustice in arms: but these arms man is born with, namely, prudence and valour, which he may apply to the most opposite purposes, for he who abuses them will be the most wicked, the most cruel, the most lustful, and most gluttonous being imaginable; for justice is a political virtue, by the rules of it the state is regulated, and these rules are the criterion of what is right.

Since it is now evident of what parts a city is composed, it will be necessary to treat first of family government, for every city is made up of families, and every family has again its separate parts of which it is composed. When a family is complete, it consists of freemen and slaves; but as in every subject we should begin with examining into the smallest parts of which it consists, and as the first and smallest parts of a family are the master and slave, the husband and wife, the father and child, let us first inquire into these three, what each of them may be, and what they ought to be; that is to say, the herile, the nupial, and the paternal. Let these then be considered as the three distinct parts of a family: some think that the providing what is necessary for the family is something different from the government of it, others that this is the greatest part of it; it shall be considered separately; but we will first speak of a master and a slave, that we may both understand the nature of those things which are absolutely necessary, and also try if we can learn anything better on this subject than what is already known. Some persons have thought that the power of the master over his slave originates from his superior knowledge, and that this knowledge is the same in the master, the magistrate, and the king, as we have already said; but others think that herile government is contrary to nature, and that it is the law which makes one man a slave and another free, but that in nature there is no difference; for which reason that power cannot be founded in justice, but in force. . . .

DIFFERENT FORM OF POLITICAL SOCIETIES

The reason for there being many different sorts of governments is this, that each state consists of a great number of parts; for, in the first place, we see that all cities are made up of families: and again, of the multitude of these some must be rich, some poor, and others in the middle station; and that, both of the rich and poor, some will be used to arms, others not. We see also, that some of the common people are husbandmen, others attend the market, and others are artificers. There is also a difference between the nobles in their wealth, and the dignity in which they live: for instance, in the number of horses they breed; for this cannot be supported without a large fortune: for which reason, in former times, those cities whose strength consisted in horse became by that means oligarchies; and they used horse in their expeditions against the neighbouring cities; . . . Moreover, besides the difference of fortune, there is that which arises from family and merit; or, if there are any other distinctions which make part of the city, they have been already mentioned in treating of an aristocracy, for there we considered how many parts each city must necessarily be composed of; and sometimes each of these have a share in the government, sometimes a few, sometimes more.

It is evident then, that there must be many forms of government, differing from each other in their particular constitution: for the parts of which they are composed each differ from the other. For government is the ordering of the magistracies of the state; and these the community share between themselves, either as they can attain them by force, or according to some common equality which there is amongst them, as poverty, wealth, or something which they both partake of. There must therefore necessarily be as many different forms of governments as there are different ranks in the society, arising from the superiority of some over others, and their different situations. And these seem chiefly to be two, as they say, of the winds: namely, the north and the south; and all the others are declinations from these. And thus in politics, there is the government of the many and the government of the few; or a democracy and an oligarchy: for an aristocracy may be considered as a species of oligarchy, as being also a government of the few; and what we call a free state may be considered as a democracy: as in the winds they consider the west as part of the north, and the east as part of the south: and thus it is in music, according to some, who say there are only two species of it, the Doric and the Phrygian, and all other species of composition they call after one of these names; and many people are accustomed to consider the nature of government in the same light; but it is both more convenient and more correspondent to truth to distinguish governments as I have done, into two species: one, of those which are established upon proper principles; of which there may be one or two sorts: the other, which includes all the different excesses of these; so that we may compare the best form of government to the most harmonious piece of music; the oligarchic and despotic to the more violent tunes; and the democratic to the soft and gentle airs.

2. HOW WE COMPARE*

John Stuart Mill

GENERAL CONSIDERATIONS ON THE SOCIAL SCIENCE

1. NEXT AFTER the science of individual man comes the science of man in society; of the actions of collective masses of mankind, and the various phenomena which constitute social life.

If the formation of individual character is already a complex subject of study, this subject must be, in appearance at least, still more complex; because the number of concurrent causes, all exercising more or less influence on the total effect, is greater, in the proportion in which a nation, or the species at large, exposes a larger surface to the operation of agents, psychological and physical, than any single individual. If it was necessary to prove, in opposition to an existing prejudice, that the simpler of the two is capable of being a subject of science; the prejudice is likely to be yet stronger against the possibility of giving a scientific character to the study of Politics, and of the phenomena of Society. It is, accordingly, but of yesterday that the conception of a political or social science has

---

* From Book VI, Chapter VI, "General Considerations on the Social Sciences," and Chapter X, "Of the Inverse Deductive, or Historical Method," *A System of Logic* (1848).

existed anywhere but in the mind of here and there an insulated thinker, generally very ill prepared for its realisation: though the subject itself has of all others engaged the most general attention, and been a theme of interested and earnest discussions, almost from the beginning of recorded time. . . .

No wonder that when the phenomena of society have so rarely been contemplated in the point of view characteristic of science, the philosophy of society should have made little progress; should contain few general propositions sufficiently precise and certain for common inquirers to recognise in them a scientific character. The vulgar notion accordingly is, that all pretension to lay down general truths on politics and society is quackery; that no universality and no certainty are attainable in such matters. What partly excuses this common notion is, that it is really not without foundation in one particular sense. A large proportion of those who have laid claim to the character of philosophic politicians have attempted, not to ascertain universal sequences, but to frame universal precepts. They have imagined some one form of government, or system of laws, to fit all cases; a pretension well meriting the ridicule with which it is treated by practitioners, and wholly unsupported by the analogy of the art to which, from the nature of its subject, that of politics must be the most nearly allied. No one now supposes it possible that one remedy can cure all diseases, or even the same disease in all constitutions and habits of body.

It is not necessary even to the perfection of a science that the corresponding art should possess universal, or even general rules. The phenomena of society might not only be completely dependent on known causes, but the mode of action of all those causes might be reducible to laws of considerable simplicity, and yet no two cases might admit of being treated in precisely the same manner. So great might be the variety of circumstances on which the results in different cases depend, that the art might not have a single general precept to give, except that of watching the circumstances of the particular case, and adapting our measures to the effects which, according to the principles of the science, result from those circumstances. But although, in so complicated a class of subjects, it is impossible to lay down practical maxims of universal application, it does not follow that the phenomena do not conform to universal laws.

2. All phenomena of society are phenomena of human nature, generated by the action of outward circumstances upon masses of human beings: and if, therefore, the phenomena of human thought, feeling, and action, are subject to fixed laws, the phenomena of society cannot but conform to fixed laws, the consequence of the preceding. There is, indeed, no hope that these laws, though our knowledge of them were as certain and as complete as it is in astronomy, would enable us to predict the history of society, like that of the celestial appearances, for thousands of years to

come. But the difference of certainty is not in the laws themselves, it is in the data to which these laws are to be applied. In astronomy the causes influencing the result are few, and change little, and that little according to known laws; we can ascertain what they are now, and thence determine what they will be at any epoch of a distant future. The data, therefore, in astronomy, are as certain as the laws themselves. The circumstances, on the contrary, which influence the condition and progress of society, are innumerable, and perpetually changing; and though they all change in obedience to causes, and therefore to laws, the multitude of the causes is so great as to defy our limited powers of calculation. Not to say that the impossibility of applying precise numbers to facts of such a description, would set an impassable limit to the possibility of calculating them beforehand, even if the powers of the human intellect were otherwise adequate to the task.

But, as before remarked, an amount of knowledge quite insufficient for prediction may be most valuable for guidance. The science of society would have attained a very high point of perfection if it enabled us, in any given condition of social affairs,—in the condition, for instance, of Europe or any European country at the present time,—to understand by what causes it had, in any and every particular, been made what it was; whether it was tending to any, and to what, changes; what effects each feature of its existing state was likely to produce in the future; and by what means any of those effects might be prevented, modified, or accelerated, or a different class of effects superinduced. There is nothing chimerical in the hope that general laws, sufficient to enable us to answer these various questions for any country or time with the individual circumstances of which we are well acquainted, do really admit of being ascertained; and that the other branches of human knowledge, which this undertaking presupposes, are so far advanced that the time is ripe for its commencement. Such is the object of the Social Science. . . .

THE METHOD OF SOCIAL SCIENCE

There are two kinds of sociological inquiry. In the first kind, the question proposed is, what effect will follow from a given cause, a certain general condition of social circumstances being presupposed. As, for example, what would be the effect of . . . abolishing monarchy, or introducing universal suffrage, in the present condition of society and civilization in any European country, or under any other given supposition with regard to the circumstances of society in general: without reference to the changes which might take place, or which may already be in progress, in those circumstances. But there is also a second inquiry, namely, what are the laws which determine those general circumstances themselves. In this last the question is, not what will be the effect of a given cause in a certain state of society, but what are the causes which produce, and the phenomena which characterize, States of Society generally. In the solution of this question consists the general Science of Society; by which all the conclusions of the other and more special kind of inquiry must be limited and controlled.

In order to conceive correctly the scope of this general science, and distinguish it from the subordinate departments of sociological speculation, it is necessary to fix with precision the ideas attached to the phrase, "A State of Society." What is called a state of society, is the simultaneous state of all the greater social facts, or phenomena. Such are, the degree of knowledge, and of intellectual and moral culture, existing in the community, and in every class of it; the state of industry, of wealth and its distribution; the habitual occupations of the community; their division into classes, and the relations of those classes to one another; the common beliefs which they entertain on all the subjects most important to mankind, and the degree of assurance with which those beliefs are held; their tastes, and the character and degree of their æsthetic development; their form of government, and the more important of their laws and customs. The condition of all these things, and of many more which will spontaneously suggest themselves, constitute the state of society or the state of civilization at any given time.

When states of society, and the causes which produce them, are spoken of as a subject of science, it is implied that there exists a natural correlation among these different elements; that not every variety of combination of these general social facts is possible, but only certain combinations; that, in short, there exist Uniformities of Coexistence between the states of the various social phenomena. And such is the truth: as is indeed necessary consequence of the influence exercised by every one of those phenomena over every other. It is a fact implied in the *consensus* of the various parts of the social body.

States of society are like different constitutions or different ages in the physical frame; they are conditions not of one or a few organs or functions, but of the whole organism. Accordingly, the information which we possess respecting past ages, and respecting the various states of society now existing in different regions of the earth, does, when duly analyzed exhibit such uniformities. It *is* found that when one of the features of society is in a particular state, a state of all the other features, more or less precisely determinate, always coexists with it. . . .

It is one of the characters, not absolutely peculiar to the sciences of human nature and society, but belonging to them in a peculiar degree, to be conversant with a subject matter whose properties are changeable. I do not mean changeable from day to day, but from age to age: so that not only the qualities of individuals vary, but those of the majority are not the same in one age as in another.

The principal cause of this peculiarity is the extensive and constant reaction of the effects upon their causes. The circumstances in which mankind are placed, operating according to their own laws and to the laws of human nature, form the characters of the men; but the men, in their turn, mould and shape the circumstances, for themselves and for those who come after them. From this reciprocal action there must necessarily result either a cycle or a progress. . . .

But, while it is an imperative rule never to introduce any generalizations from history into the social science unless sufficient grounds can be pointed out for it in human nature, I do not think any one will contend that it would have been possible, setting out from the principles of human nature and from the general circumstances of man's position in the universe, to determine *à priori* the order in which human development must take place, and to predict, consequently, the general facts of history up to the present time. The initial stages of human progress—when man, as yet unmodified by society, and characterized only by the instincts resulting directly from his organization, was acted upon by outward objects of a comparatively simple and universal character—might indeed, as M. Comte remarks, be deduced from the laws of human nature; which moreover is the only possible mode of ascertaining them, since of that form of human existence no direct memorials are preserved. . . .

If, therefore, the series of the effects themselves did not, when examined as a whole, manifest any regularity, we should in vain attempt to construct a general science of society. We must in that case have contented ourselves with that subordinate order of sociological speculation formerly noticed, namely, with endeavoring to ascertain what would be the effect of the introduction of any new cause, in a state of society supposed to be fixed; a knowledge sufficient for most of the ordinary exigencies of daily political practice, but liable to fail in all cases in which the progressive movement of society is one of the influencing elements; and therefore more precarious in proportion as the case is more important. But since both the natural varieties of mankind, and the original diversities of local circumstances, are much less considerable than the points of agreement, there will naturally be a certain degree of uniformity in the progressive development of man and of his works. . . . History accordingly does, when judiciously examined, afford Empirical Laws of Society. And the problem of general sociology is to ascertain these, and connect them with the laws of human nature by deductions showing that such were the derivative laws naturally to be expected as the consequences of those ultimate ones. . . .

The Empirical Laws of Society are of two kinds; some are uniformities of coexistence, some of succession. . . .

In order to obtain better empirical laws, we must not rest satisfied with noting the progressive changes which manifest themselves in the separate elements of society, and in which nothing is indicated but the relation of the fragments of the effect to corresponding fragments of the cause. It is necessary to combine the statical view of social phenomena with the dynamical, considering not only the progressive changes of the different elements, but the contemporaneous condition of each; and thus obtain empirically the law of correspondence not only between the simultaneous states, but between the simultaneous changes, of those elements. This law of correspondence it is, which, after being duly verified *à priori*, will become the real scientific derivative law of the development of humanity and human affairs.

In the difficult process of observation and comparison which is here required, it would evidently be a very great assistance if it should happen to be the fact, that some one element in the complex existence of social man is preëminent over all others as the prime agent of the social movement. For we could then take the progress of that one element as the central chain, to each successive link of which, the corresponding links of all the other progressions being appended, the succession of the facts would by this alone be presented in a kind of spontaneous order, far more nearly approaching to the real order of their filiation than could be obtained by any other merely empirical process.

Now, the evidence of history and the evidence of human nature combine, by a most striking instance of consilience, to show that there is really one social element which is thus predominant, and almost paramount, among the agents of the social progression. This is, the state of the speculative faculties of mankind; including the nature of the speculative beliefs which by any means they have arrived at, concerning themselves and the world by which they are surrounded.

It would be a great error, and one very little likely to be committed, to assert that speculation, intellectual activity, the pursuit of truth, is among the more powerful propensities of human nature, or fills a large place in the lives of any, save decidedly exceptional individuals. But notwithstanding the relative weakness of this principle among other sociological agents, its influence is the main determining cause of the social progress; all the other dispositions of our nature which contribute to that progress, being dependent upon it for the means of accomplishing their share of the work. Thus (to take the most obvious case first), the impelling force to most of the improvements effected in the arts of life, is the desire of increased material comfort; but as we can only act upon external objects in proportion to our knowledge of them, the state of knowledge at any time is the impassable limit of the industrial improvements possible at that time; and the progress of industry must follow, and depend upon, the progress of knowledge. The same thing may be shown to be true, though it is not quite so obvious, of the progress of the fine arts. Further, as the strongest propensities of human nature (being the purely selfish ones, and those of a sympathetic character which partake most of the nature of selfishness) evidently tend in themselves to disunite mankind, not to unite them—to make them rivals, not confederates; social existence is only possible by a disciplining of those more powerful propensities, which consists in subordinating them to a common system of opinions. The degree of this subordination is the measure of the completeness of the social union, and the nature of the common opinions determines its kind. But in order that mankind should conform their actions to any set of opinions, these opinions must exist, must be believed by them. And thus, the state of the speculative faculties, the character of the propositions assented to by the intellect, essentially determines the moral and political state of the community, as we have already seen that it determines the physical.

These conclusions, deduced from the laws of human nature, are in entire accordance with the general facts of history. Every considerable change historically known to us in the condition of any portion of mankind, has been preceded by a change, of proportional extent, in the state of their knowledge, or in their prevalent beliefs. As between any given state of speculation, and the correlative state of everything else, it was almost always the former which first showed itself; though the effects, no doubt, reacted potently upon the cause. Every considerable advance in material civilization has been preceded by an advance in knowledge; and when any great social change has come to pass, a great change in the opinions and modes of thinking of society had taken place shortly before. Polytheism, Judaism, Christianity, Protestantism, the negative philosophy of modern Europe, and its positive science—each of these has been a primary agent in making society what it was at each successive period, while society was but secondarily instrumental in making *them,* each of them (so far as causes can be assigned for its existence) being mainly an emanation not from the practical life of the period, but from the state of belief and thought during some time previous. The weakness of the speculative propensity has not, therefore, prevented the progress of speculation from governing that of society at large; it has only, and too often, prevented progress altogether, where the intellectual progression has come to an early stand for want of sufficiently favorable circumstances.

From this accumulated evidence, we are justified in concluding, that the order of human progression in all respects will be a corollary deducible from the order of progression in the intellectual convictions of mankind, that is, from the law of the successive transformation of religion and science. The question remains, whether this law can be determined; at first from history as an empirical law, then converted into a scientific theorem by deducing it *à priori* from the principles of human nature. As the progress of knowledge and the changes in the opinions of mankind are very slow, and manifest themselves in a well-defined manner only at long intervals; it cannot be expected that the general order of sequence should be discoverable from the examination of less than a very considerable part of the duration of the social progress. It is necessary to take into consideration the whole of past time, from the first recorded condition of the human race; and it is probable that all the terms of the series already past were indispensable to the operation; that the memorable phenomena of the last generation, and even those of the present, were necessary to manifest the law, and that consequently the Science of History has only become possible in our own time.

3. THE METHOD OF COMPARISON*

James Bryce

THE CONTRAST between the rapid progress made during the last two centuries in the study of external nature and the comparatively slow progress made in the determination of the laws or principles discoverable in the phenomena of human society is usually explained by the remark that in the former success was attained by discarding abstract notions and setting to work to observe facts, whereas in the latter men have continued to start from assumptions and run riot in speculations. As respects politics, this explanation, though it has some force, does not cover the whole case. . . .

The fundamental difference between the investigation of external nature and that of human affairs lies in the character of the facts to be observed. The phenomena with which the chemist or physicist deals—and this is for most purposes true of biological phenomena also—are, and so far as our imperfect knowledge goes, always have been, now and at all times, everywhere identical. Oxygen and sulphur behave in the same way in Europe and in Australia and in Sirius. But the phenomena of an election are not the same in Bern and in Buenos Aires, though we may call the thing by the same name; nor were they the same in Bern two centuries ago, or in Buenos Aires twenty years ago, as they are now. The substances with which the chemist deals can be weighed and measured, the feelings and acts of men cannot. Experiments can be tried in physics over and over again till a conclusive result is reached, but that which we call an experiment in politics can never be repeated because the conditions can never be exactly reproduced, as Heraclitus says that one cannot step twice into the same river. Prediction in physics may be certain: in politics it can at best be no more than probable. If vagueness and doubt surround nearly every theory or doctrine in the field of politics, that happens not so much because political philosophers have been careless in ascertaining facts, but rather because they were apt to be unduly affected by the particular facts that were under their eyes. However widely and carefully the materials may be gathered, their character makes it impossible that politics should ever become a science in the sense in which mechanics or chemistry or botany is a science. Is there then no way of applying exact methods to the subject, and of reaching some more general and more positive conclusions than have yet secured acceptance? Are the materials to be studied, viz. the acts and thoughts of men, their habits and institutions, incapable of scientific treatment because too various and changeful?

The answer is that there is in the phenomena of human society one "Constant," one element or factor which is practically always the same, and therefore the basis of all the so-called "Social Sciences." This is Human Nature itself. All fairly normal men have like passions and desires. They are stirred by like motives, they think upon similar lines. When they have reached the stage of civilization in which arts and letters have developed, and political institutions have grown up, reason has become so far the guide of conduct that sequences in their action can be established and their behaviour under given conditions can to some extent be foretold. Human nature is that basic and ever-present element in the endless flux of social and political phenomena which enables general principles to be determined. And though the action of individual men may often be doubtful, the action of a hundred or a thousand men all subjected to the same influences at the same time may be much more predictable, because in a large number the idiosyncrasies of individuals are likely to be eliminated or evened out. Politics accordingly has its roots in Psychology, the study (in their actuality) of the mental habits and volitional pro- clivities of mankind. The knowledge it gives is the knowledge most needed in life, and our life is chiefly spent in acquiring it. But we are here concerned only with the political side of man, and have to enquire how to study that particular department of his individual and collective life.

Two other differences between the Natural and the Human Sciences need only a word or two. The terms used in the latter lack the precision which belongs to those used in the former. They are not truly technical, for they do not always mean the same thing to all who use them. Such words as "aristocracy," "prerogative," "liberty," "oligarchy," "fac- tion," "caucus," even "constitution" convey different meanings to differ- ent persons. The terms used in politics have, moreover, contracted associations, attractive or repellent, as the case may be, to different persons. They evoke feeling. An investigator occupied in the interpretation of history is exposed to emotional influences such as do not affect the enquirer in a laboratory. . . .

Human nature being accordingly a factor sufficiently constant to enable certain laws of its working to be ascertained, though with no such precision and no such power of prediction as is possible in the physical sciences, how is it to be studied?

The best way to get a genuine and exact first-hand knowledge of the data is to mix in practical politics. In such a country as France or the United States a capable man can, in a dozen years, acquire a comprehension of the realities of popular government ampler and more delicate than any which books supply. He learns the habits and propensities of the average citizen as a sailor learns the winds and currents of the ocean he has to navigate, what pleases or repels the voter, his illusions and his prejudices, the sort of personality that is fascinating, the sort of offence that is not forgiven, how confidence is won or lost, the kind of argument that tells on the better or the meaner spirits. Such a man forms, perhaps without knowing it, a body of maxims or rules by which he sails his craft, and steers, if he be a leader, the vessel of his party. Still ampler are the opportunities which the member of an Assembly has for studying his colleagues. This is the best kind of knowledge; though some of it is profitable only for the particular country in which it has been acquired, and might be misleading in another country with a different national character and a different set of ideas and catchwords. Many maxims fit for Paris might be unfit for Philadelphia, but some might not. . . . When he extends his enquiry to other countries than his own, the abundance of materials becomes bewildering, because few books have been written which bring together the most important facts so as to provide that information regarding the conditions of those countries which he needs in order to use the materials aright.

These data, however, do not carry us the whole way towards a comprehension of democratic government in general. The student must try to put life and blood into historical records by what he has learnt of political human nature in watching the movements of his own time. He must think of the Past with the same keenness of interest as if it were the Present, and of the Present with the same coolness of reflection as if it were the Past. The English and the Americans of the eighteenth century were different from the men of to-day, so free government was a different thing in their hands. There are, moreover, differences in place as well as in time. Political habits and tendencies are not the same thing in England as in France or in Switzerland, or even in Australia. The field of observation must be enlarged to take in the phenomena of all the countries where the people rule. The fundamentals of human nature, present everywhere, are in each country modified by the influences of race, of external conditions, such as climate and the occupations that arise from the physical resources of the country. Next come the historical antecedents which have given, or withheld, experience in self-government, have formed traditions of independence or submission, have created institutions which themselves in turn have moulded the minds and shaped the ideals of the nations.

This mode of investigation is known as the Comparative Method. That which entitles it to be called scientific is that it reaches general conclusions by tracing similar results to similar causes, eliminating those disturbing influences which, present in one country and absent in another, make the results in the examined cases different in some points while similar in others. When by this method of comparison the differences between the working of democratic government in one country and another have been noted, the local or special conditions, physical or racial or economic, will be examined so as to determine whether it is in them that the source of these differences is to be found. If not in them, then we must turn to the institutions, and try to discover which of those that exist in popular governments have worked best. All are so far similar in that they are meant to enable the people to rule, but some seek this end in one way, some in another, each having its merits, each its defects. When allowance has been made for the different conditions under which each acts, it will be possible to pronounce, upon the balance of considerations, which form offers the best prospect of success. After the differences between one popular government and another have been accounted for, the points of similarity which remain will be what one may call democratic human nature, viz. the normal or permanent habits and tendencies of citizens in a democracy and of a democratic community as a whole. This is what we set out to discover. The enquiry, if properly conducted, will have taught us what are the various aberrations from the ideally best to which popular government is by its very nature liable.

It is this method that I have sought to apply in investigating the phenomena each particular government shows, so as to indicate wherein they differ from or agree with those found in other governments. Where the phenomena point to one and the same conclusion, we are on firm ground, and can claim to have discovered a principle fit to be applied. Firm ground is to be found in those permanent tendencies of mankind which we learn from history, *i.e.* from the record of observations made during many centuries in many peoples, living in diverse environments, physical and historical. The tendencies themselves take slightly diverse forms in different races or peoples, and the strength of each relatively to the others varies. These diversities must be noted and allowed for; but enough identity remains to enable definite conclusions of general validity to be attained.

So expressed and considered in their application to practice, these conclusions have a real value, not only to the student but also to the statesman. Many an error might have been avoided had a body of sound maxims been present to the minds of constitution makers and statesmen; not that such maxims could be used as necessarily fit for the particular case, but that he who had them before him would be led to weigh considerations and beware of dangers which might otherwise have escaped him. Some one has said, There is nothing so useless as a general maxim. That is so only if you do not know how to use it. He who would use it well must always think of the instances on which it rests and of the instruction these may be made to yield. Its use is to call attention. It is not a prescription but a signpost, or perhaps a danger signal.

The conclusions obtained by these methods of investigation are less capable of direct application to practice than are those of the exact sciences. However true as general propositions, they are subject to many qualifications when applied to any given case, and must be expressed in guarded terms. The reader who may be disposed to complain of the qualified and tentative terms in which I shall be obliged to express the results which a study of the phenomena has suggested will, I hope, pardon me when he remembers that although it is well to be definite and positive in statement, it is still better to be accurate. I cannot hope to have always attained accuracy, but it is accuracy above everything else that I have aimed at.

Chapter II. Concepts and Theories

Introductory Note

THE ROLE of a "concept" is to suggest a special analytical category in terms of which a political system can be studied. Some writers consider a political system to be a state of conflict and competition between influential groups; they are prone, as a result, to emphasize the concept of power and study political manifestations as power phenomena. Others study the personality structure and the actors and gauge the functioning of the system in terms of its outlets or its inhibitions. Some emphasize what might be called a cultural configurative approach—in which personality, satisfaction of economic needs, ideals, and symbols are interwoven and patterned to form different structural types of government and authority. Still others study those who control the instrumentalities of power—formal and informal—and concentrate on *elites*. Attention may also be focused upon *role*—the particular positions individuals hold in the social and political system and the perception they have of their positions, or upon *political culture*—a complex of attitudes and orientations through which the individual comprehends his political environment and acts within it. Related research has dealt with problems and processes of the assimilation or socialization of the individual within a given political culture.

Concepts, when related to each other, lead to the development of a theory. Theory purports to isolate and connect the most significant variables of political dynamics. A scientific theory can be readily related to social variables and tested by observation and comparison. For example, Marx developed theories that are cast readily in the form of causal relations. The given modes of production determined the total political and ideological configuration of a society. This interpretation became and, to some extent, continues to remain, despite its many errors and contradictions, one of the most prevalent modes of thinking not only in Europe but also in the United States and England. In the United States, Charles A. Beard (1874–1948) in a number of his works—notably in his *Economic Interpretation of the Constitution* (1913)—stressed the economic basis of politics. Harold Laski's *Parliamentary Government in England* (1938) reflects the same influence.

In contrast, Max Weber was more concerned with the development of a comprehensive analytical scheme rather than the establishment of causal

30

hypotheses. His work, particularly with reference to the nature of political systems, the modes of economic organization, types of authority and legitimacy, and the nature of bureaucracy, is typological rather than explanatory. He has had a great impact—thanks mainly to the efforts of Professor Talcott Parsons—upon contemporary sociological and political theory in the United States. The Weberian influence is evident in the writings of Parsons, notably *Essays on Sociological Theory, Pure and Applied* (1949), *Social Systems* (1951), and *Toward a General Theory of Action* (1958); and also in Robert K. Merton's *Social Theory and Social Structure* (1949); and Marion Levy's *The Structure of Society* (1952), to mention only a few.

Political scientists have become increasingly concerned with the use of concepts. In studying the types of poltical authority, the changing character of traditional societies, the characteristics of bureaucracy and "ideologies," they found a number of the Weberian categories useful and fruitful. Works by Gabriel A. Almond—notably his *The Politics of the Developing Areas* (1960); Snyder, Bruck, and Sapin, *Decision-Making: A Frame of Reference* (1954); David Easton, *The Political System* (1953), David Apter, *The Gold Coast in Transition* (1955), and Harry Eckstein, *Pressure Group Politics* (1960)—reflect this great concern with conceptualization and the influence of Weber in particular. The essay we reproduce in Chapter III by five sociologists is a succinct statement of this kind of social analysis. They view a "system" as a pattern of interrelations in which functions and the structures through which they are performed are clearly distinguished. This is referred to as "structure-function" analysis.

In the readings included here are only a sample of the most significant concepts that have been advanced for comparative study of political systems. Mention, therefore, might be made of some other trends which, regretfully, had to be omitted for lack of space. Professor Richard Snyder's studies of decision making, for example, have proved fruitful for the comparative study of foreign policy making. In the voluminous literature on national character, the student will find stimulating observations in Ernest Barker, *The Character of England* (1947), Margaret Mead, *And Keep Your Powder Dry* (1943); Geoffry Gorer and John Rickman, *The People of Great Russia* (1949); Ruth Benedict, *Chrysanthemum and the Sword* (1946); and André Siegfried's works on France. We have also been compelled to omit illustrations of the comparative method in philology and ethnography, and the rich contributions of historians. Among the latter, Alexis de Tocqueville's works on the *Old Regime* (1856) and *Democracy in America* (1835, 1840, 2 vols.) are rewarding. A good modern example of the utility of historical analysis in understanding the development of political systems is Louis Hartz's *The Liberal Tradition in America* (1955). A comprehensive treatment of political culture and socialization may be found in Gabriel Almond and Sidney Verba, *The Civic*

Culture (1963). For a fine synthesis see also Robert Dahl, *Political Analysis* (1963).

Readings

A. Personality

4. INNOVATIONAL AND AUTHORITARIAN PERSONALITIES*

Everett E. Hagen

THE INTERRELATIONSHIPS between personality and social structure are such as to make it clear that social change will not occur without change in personalities. We can more readily analyze changes in the personality type that is typical in traditional societies, authoritarian personality, if we probe that personality type further. We may understand it better if we delineate a contrasting case.

In discussing social change, Riesman has described tradition-directed and autonomous individuals, and in exploring the problems of colonial control Mannoni has referred to personalities dominated by a dependency complex and an inferiority complex respectively.[1] In the discussion below, the reader familiar with Riesman and Mannoni will be reminded of both pairs of contrasts, but neither seems to me to delineate fully the contrasting personality types that are typical of traditional and creative societies respectively. Hence instead of using the terminology of either author, I shall refer to "authoritarian" and "innovational" personalities.

I am using the term "innovational personality" rather than "creative personality" since the latter seems less descriptive. It will be well to begin the discussion by making clear the relationship between creativity and innovation.

CREATIVITY AND INNOVATION

Innovation consists of organizing reality into relationships embodying new mental or aesthetic concepts, the new relationships serving the pur-

---

* From Chapter 5, *On the Theory of Social Change* (Homewood, Ill.: The Dorsey Press, 1962). Reprinted by permission of The Dorsey Press. Footnotes abridged by the editors.

[1] David Riesman, *The Lonely Crowd* (New Haven, Conn.: Yale University Press, 1950), and O. Mannoni, *Psychologie de la Colonisation* (Paris, Ed. du Seuil, 1950), translated into English by Pamela Powesland as *Prospero and Caliban: The Psychology of Colonization* (New York: Frederick A. Praeger, Inc., 1956).

pose of the innovator better than the old. Analytically, and also in time sequence, innovation involves two steps: arriving at a new mental conception, and converting it into action or into material form.[2]

In technological innovation the second step may involve only design or rearrangement of some items of physical equipment or it may involve the organization of a group of human beings into a going concern that carries out a new concept. In the latter case it is entrepreneurship; the concept of entrepreneurship seems always to include the management of other human beings.

In the limiting case the process consists of the first step alone; the individual may solve a problem mentally without any overt action. Perhaps the mathematician most closely approaches this limit, his only material craftsmanship being that of writing down his concepts. In technical innovation, however, putting flesh on the idea is of the essence of the process.

Arriving at the new conception may be termed the creative act, and sometimes the term "innovation" is reserved for the second step.[3] However, the implication that putting flesh on the concept is not creative is illusory, for a concept of new productive equipment or a new method of organization of human beings is hardly complete when it is only an idea in the mind. The purely mental concept probably virtually never anticipates correctly all the properties the human or physical material will exhibit when it is being reshaped. Creative adjustment and revision will be necessary as the idea is worked out overtly. Sometimes, of course, the further creativity required is very little. I have suggested that in the adaptation of Western technical methods to optimum use in underdeveloped economies it is great.

There is no such thing as innovation in the abstract. Innovation is always innovation in some specific field, involving some specific materials or concepts, or relationships of some sort to other persons. Some types of innovation will involve overcoming resistances by other persons; others will not. Some will involve managing a large organization; others, working in isolation. Some will involve experiencing smells or dirt; others will not. Some will have an aura of learned or sacred activity; others of practical work. And so on. An individual will enjoy one or another type of activity

---

[2] The concept can hardly be put into overt form until after it has been conceived. The act of conception may be unconscious, however, and the innovator may not know that he has arrived at a new concept until he has produced a new artifact or a new organization. Conceivably, also, the innovator may arrive at a new result by trial and error, and only when he sees the results analyze the operation and realize the relationships responsible for the results. The statement in the text ignores this case.

[3] Either the first step or both may also be termed "problem-solving." Insofar as a problem has been solved previously and one merely repeats a known solution, one's activity is not problem solving. But any activity, mental or overt, that is not purely random is problem solving in some degree. Even walking down a familiar street involves some new elements. Innovation or creative activity, more strictly defined, is performing activity that involves problem solving in a high degree.

or relationship in the degree to which its various aspects satisfy his various attitudes. An individual will not innovate in a sphere in which, on balance, he finds dissatisfaction in working. Thus, in addition to creativity, attitudes favorable to working in one or another field are necessary for innovation in that field. . . . I shall discuss the general characteristics of creativity at some length and pay only brief attention to the added characteristics of personality that cause creativity to be exercised in one field rather than another.

INNOVATIONAL PERSONALITY

The Quality of Creativity

When it is stated that innovation requires creativity, the reader should not assume that the term "creativity" refers to genius. Creativity exists in varying degrees; the man who conceives of an improvement in a can opener as well as the man who conceives of the theory of relativity is creative. Technological progress results from the actions of men characterized by varying degrees of creativity. The discussion of creativity refers, therefore, not merely to the limiting case of genius but to the quality of creativity in general, in whatever degree it may be found in a given individual.

The major qualities that constitute creativity are easy to list imprecisely: openness to experience, and, underlying this, a tendency to perceive phenomena, especially in an area of life that is of interest to the individual, as forming systems of interacting forces whose action is explainable; creative imagination, of which the central component is the ability to let one's unconscious processes work on one's behalf; confidence and content in one's own evaluations; satisfaction in facing and attacking problems and in resolving confusion or inconsistency; a sense that one has a duty or responsibility to achieve; intelligence; energy; and, often, related to several of these, a perception that the world is somewhat threatening and that one must strive perpetually if one is to be able to cope with it. The type of creative personality that is driven by a sense that the world is threatening sometimes seems to belong to a different category from the person characterized by some of the other qualities listed. I shall discuss first the ideal or pure type of unanxious creative person, and then indicate how the sense of living in a threatening world qualifies the characteristics described.

Poincaré has suggested the "capacity to be surprised" and Carl R. Rogers "openness to experience" as essential to creativity.[4] I would judge that the meaning of the two is almost identical. What is referred to is an unconscious alertness that leads the individual to note that some aspect of

---

[4] Poincaré's phrase is quoted by Erich Fromm in Harold H. Anderson (ed.), *Creativity and Its Cultivation* (New York: Harper & Bros., 1959), p. 48. "Scientific genius," said Poincaré, "is the capacity to be surprised." Rogers' phrase is in *ibid.*, p. 75. Several essays in this interesting volume are pertinent to the present discussion.

an everyday phenomenon differs from the expected and to appreciate the significance of the difference. This is the capacity that leads an individual to note that, contrary to the body of scientific authority in his time and the conclusions of common sense, bodies fall at the same rate regardless of their weight if air resistance is the same; to have his curiosity aroused by the fact that iron filings adhere to a coil of wire as an electrical current passes through it; to observe that some men with paralyzed limbs handle them in ways that suggest that the paralysis of function begins at a point at which there is no physiological reason for it to begin—to note such a thing and say to himself, "What an interesting force must have caused that! I wonder what its implications are."

Basic to this quality of observation is assurance in one's own evaluation of experience, freedom from a tendency to take a generally accepted evaluation for granted and overlook facts inconsistent with it. Basic to it also is a tendency to assume that one can understand experience. The creative individual has a sense, deeper than any rational acceptance of cause and effect, that the world is orderly; that every phenomenon of life or of some large area of experience is part of a system whose operation can be understood and explained; that if he approaches the sphere of life in which he is interested it will respond dependably, even though perhaps in a complex fashion, so that if he has enough information he will be able to understand the response. If the world were not orderly, or if the individual were not confident and content in his ability to understand its order, he would not be unconsciously alert to unexpected aspects of phenomena, for they would contain no lessons for him.

Openness to experience, then, refers to a capacity to note phenomena that are starting points for new analyses. Creative imagination refers to a tendency to leap far afield from a starting point, to note relationships where others had not thought to find them. In part it is the product simply of superior innate intelligence, of a mind which can hold many factors in simultaneous consideration and analysis. But it is more than this. It embraces two kinds of mental activity. One is the capacity to use an interesting or unsatisfactory situation as a springboard from which one's imagination roams, apparently uncontrolled and seemingly undirected, in varying associational bypaths, regressions, and far reaches, then returns to the matter at hand either with a workable conception for the reconstruction or transformation of the unsatisfactory situation or with a novel analytical model of the significance of the observed fact. Conscious movement from one step of analysis to the next is at a minimum; the individual does not ask consciously whether the wandering is pertinent to the problem.

The other is the capacity to let one's purely unconscious processes work for one without any conscious awareness or acknowledgment of the activity and to admit the results to consciousness. Unaware that his mind has been working on the problem, the individual finds that a solution, an appropriate ordering, an explanation has come to him. Visualization occurs as he wakes from sleep, when he has been daydreaming, on rare occasions in a dream while sleeping, or perhaps while he walks his dog. "It came to me," the scientist sometimes says, or, "As the problem returned to my mind, I saw how it could be done." Subsequently he demonstrates to himself the logic of the solution. The solution was presumably reached by a sequence of logical steps or chain or association of thoughts (how else could it have been reached?), but these were unconscious, or, sometimes, in more precise psychological terminology, preconscious.

Such creative imagination is often stressed as a part of literary or, more generally, aesthetic creativity. But there is ample evidence from biographies of scientists that it is important in their creative achievement also. There is less evidence concerning strictly technological creativity, but it is reasonable to suppose that this is because of absence of documentation rather than because of a difference in the creative process.

These two aspects of creative imagination have two important elements in common: the unconscious processes of the individual are productive rather than distractive in nature, and the individual is unafraid or little afraid of them. The aspect of a problem that some individuals react unconsciously to is a sense of frustration at not having an answer at hand. As a defense against that sense of frustration, the individual, if he lets himself go, experiences fantasies of magic achievement, crushing victories over persons who have slighted him, sexual conquest, the attainment of position so high that all of his wishes are gratified, and the like. Even if he does not let himself go, such fantasies occur in his unconscious processes. The unconscious processes of some individuals, on the other hand, react to the substance of a problem or surprising phenomena at hand, and aid in logical and imaginative analysis of it. When the individual "floats," his mind rearranges elements of thought in bold ways but ways which, when he returns to the details of reality, are fruitful. Every individual responds in some degree in both ways. Creative individuals are those who primarily respond productively.

The individual who responds with unacceptable fantasies may shut them out from his conscious mind, but he senses dimly the emotional surges within him and fears what is going on in his unconscious. Finding impulses in himself which he regards as evil or foul or dangerous, he is afraid of letting his unconscious processes come to the surface for fear that dangerous or evil or vile urges will appear. Hence his unconscious processes are not only primarily unproductive; even insofar as they are productive, they are unavailable to him. The results do not appear in his conscious mind. The creative individual, on the other hand, is not afraid of his unconscious processes, and their results appear in his conscious mind. In the technical terms of psychoanalysis, he can "regress in the service of the ego."[5]

More than other individuals, he understands his unconscious motiva-

[5] Ernst Kris, *Psychoanalytical Explorations in Art* (New York: International Universities Press, 1952).

tions.[6] It is commonly recognized that ability to understand one's unconscious motivations is an important element in artistic and especially literary creativity; one understands others and can portray them only to the degree that one understands oneself. It is less well recognized that the same understanding of self may be conducive to understanding of the physical world as well. The man who understands something of his unconscious motivations understands his interaction with phenomena outside him as a system in which there is causality. He is self-conscious; he watches his own behavior as an observer. This understanding seems to be the model for the individual's perception of the external world as a system and subject to analysis, the perception which gives him openness to experience, which makes him wonder creatively why some everyday phenomenon is as it is.

Such an individual is somewhat detached from himself and from his society. To some degree all that goes on is something he watches from the outside. This detachment seems to be an integral part of creativity. It does not imply lack of interest in the world or of concern about it. In fact, it is often peculiarly associated with a sense of moral obligation, of responsibility for society and the world.

This sense of detachment has often been observed in creative workers in science as well as in literature and art. It must also be associated with technological innovation. It is difficult to see how any person can manipulate the world about him, put its elements together in new ways to obtain new order, except as he sees it as a system outside himself, detached from himself. Even the tinkerer who merely improves a machine must see the machine as a system to be analyzed rather than simply taking it for granted as an instrument if he is to be free to conceive of changes in it. The business administrator, whose function is to manipulate other men, often gives little overt evidence of this detachment; yet his understanding of how other men function is evidence of such understanding of himself, which again is a symptom of this detachment.

Because the creative individual assumes that the world will respond dependably to his judicious initiative, he does not feel threatened by unresolved situations. He has no need to turn to the judgment of others for reassurance or relief from anxiety, for the facing of unresolved situations arouses little anxiety within him. He trusts his own evaluations of them. His "locus of evaluative judgment" is within himself. This does not mean that he is always sure that he is right, but only that he does not have anxiety about his own observations and evaluations. Knowing that the comments of others may suggest new avenues of approach or added relationships in a complex problem which has no one solution, he may turn to them, but as instruments to help him, not for reassurance.

---

[6] Which include passive, so-called "feminine" needs, needs to be dependent and to be nurtured, needs for aesthetic gratification. These needs are greater in him, as measured by psychological tests, than in the average person.

He feels satisfaction at the prospect of testing his capacities against a problem and is drawn toward the attempt. If the solution does not readily appear, and the problem is of relevance to his interests, it remains a matter on a shelf in his mind, and he will anticipate the possibility of realizing a solution later.

Because he is not afraid of problems or of the world, he has a tolerance for recognizing apparently contradictory or discrepant facts. He will not unconsciously and conveniently ignore one of them because the discrepancy alarms him. But, because he perceives the world as orderly, he assumes that two discrepant facts, both having been verified as true, are not really contradictory but are part of a higher order whose nature he does not yet realize. Their apparent inconsistency, like any problem, is therefore a challenge to him, and he feels satisfaction in seeking a higher order within which they will both rest comfortably. He feels a need to place them in a logical or pleasing relationship. Too simple order is uninteresting and somewhat unpleasant to him. He may have some fondness for disorder and conflicting logic since they suggest to him that a higher order is available.

As his experience and confidence in his ability grow, he will lose interest in simpler problems and will seek to attack more and more difficult ones, or sometimes merely different ones. The former trend is manifested by a painter who as his career proceeds passes from simple symmetry to balance of colors and forms so complex that the picture is confusing to the novice but brings the greatest aesthetic pleasure to the individual whose comprehension has grown until he can appreciate it, and the latter in a painter who moves from simple realism to impressionism to expressionism toward abstraction, as Rembrandt did. It is also readily noticeable in the other arts and in literature. In business the process is one of moving up the ladder to positions which are more difficult as well as more responsible.

In mathematics the peak of creativity usually comes early; almost all of the great mathematicians made their most original contributions before the age of thirty, whereas in some other fields creative activity reaches its peak later in life. The difference seems to be associated with some degree of difference in the locus of the creative process. In mathematics the immediate creative act is more largely unconscious; the new concept presents itself to the conscious mind in largely finished form; whereas in many other fields a greater element of conscious judgment enters. Perhaps almost no one has within him more than one great new view of the world. In a field unrelated to the complex facts of life, one in which abstract logical relationships alone constitute the materials, one may encompass the known logic and realize his new view in his twenties. Then, his mind being drawn thereafter to the area which proved so satisfying, he spends the rest of his life tidying up and making minor advances here and there. However, in fields in which the complex details and relationships of real life are pertinent to the creative act, accumulation of knowledge by strengthening the basis for judgment provides increasing grist for one's unconscious (as well as conscious) processes to work on as the years pass, and creativity matures later in life.

The innovator not only feels pleasure in solving problems; he also feels a duty to achieve. The avowed goal of economic innovators, the purpose which they have felt it their duty to serve, has varied greatly among societies, but the sense of duty is a constant. Often this sense is religious in nature. The doctrine that the specific religious dogma of the Protestant Dissenters is peculiarly associated with innovational activity is obsolete,[7] but a number of scholars observing economic growth in various societies have noted that innovators in the early stages of growth seem to be characterized by a common ethic which is appropriately termed religious in nature, whatever their religious dogma. They feel a personal responsibility to transform the world that far transcends a profit motive.

To these qualities should be added intelligence and energy. Intellectual capacity is in part inherited, and no doubt innate capacity is higher among innovators than among the population in general. In part, however, the intellectual capacity of innovators is due to the qualities described above. An individual with a given intellectual endowment will use it the more effectively the greater the degree to which he perceives the world as an orderly system, the greater his contentedness in his own judgment and reactions, the greater his satisfaction in attacking problems or in resolving inconsistencies, and the less the degree to which his energy has to be used to suppress unacceptable impulses within himself. The person with lack of these attitudes toward the world will be inhibited from attempting to use his capacities. But these attitudes are not simply the products of high innate intelligence; they derive primarily from conditions of the individual's environment as he grows up, and especially in childhood, that are quite independent of his innate capacities.

Much the same factors determine the individual's level of energy. No doubt there are innate or, more broadly, constitutional determinants of energy just as there are of intelligence. The individual who is constitutionally endowed with an ampler than average reserve of energy stands a better than average chance of accomplishing creative deeds. But to a large degree the ability to draw on a great store of energy seems to depend on an individual's freedom from doubt and mistrust of himself, on his sense that the world is orderly and will respond dependably and pleasingly to his initiative. It is as though, not having to use his energy in conflicts within himself, he has it available to direct toward the world outside him.

The creative individual is not necessarily a happy man who faces problems with pure pleasure. Rather, most creative individuals are driven to creative activity by an incessant anxiety; their perception of the world

---

[7] Perhaps it never was held by scholars. Max Weber in *The Protestant Ethic and the Spirit of Capitalism*, trans. Talcott Parsons (New York: Charles Scribner's Sons, 1956), at times seems to argue this thesis but then backs away from it.

as a threatening place leaves them only while they are active, then returns to drive them on again. Yet in other individuals anxiety is associated with rage that provokes urges and fantasies which persist in the unconscious and cause an individual to seal over his unconscious processes for fear of what he will find in them. (The anxiety is also largely unconscious; if questioned, the individual would probably deny its existence.) The two types of personality must be distinguished.

An individual acquires persisting anxiety if in his early life he faces a sequence of situations important to him that he cannot resolve satisfactorily or can resolve satisfactorily only by repeated attempts and with great difficulty—hunger, pressure on him to walk, and so on. The anxiety-creating situations may, however, be of two types which convey to the child differing perceptions of the world. He may become anxious because persons important to him, for example, his mother, seem willing to hurt him. If so, combined with his anxiety will be rage directed at her and fantasies of revenge. However, he must suppress these from consciousness since his mother is so important to him that he dares not admit that he hates her. He then seals over his unconscious processes, and their inaccessibility to him prevents him from being creative, or greatly cripples his creativity.

Suppose, however, that his experiences of infancy and early childhood give him a firm and satisfying impression of the loving nurturance of his mother, but that repeatedly he is unable to achieve as she seems to wish him to. He may then feel that the fault must lie in him, and there may become built into him anxiety that he may not accomplish enough, anxiety that drives him all his life to achieve in order to regain fleetingly that temporary feeling of security conveyed by his mother's praise and caresses. In this case, little rage and hatred may be provoked in him, and his unconscious processes will remain accessible to him. Given the other necessary qualities, he becomes the anxious creative individual.

Of course the perceptions sketched here as arising from his relationship to his mother may arise also in relationships to other persons important to him in early life.

He may not be quite as open to experience as the unanxious creative individual because he is more fearful of experience. The accessibility of his unconscious processes to him may be somewhat less than to the unanxious individual, since the tensions of his childhood may have caused some reactions in him which were fearful or unacceptable and had to be repressed permanently. But these handicaps to creativity are compensated for by his incessant scanning of the horizon and by the great energy which he is incessantly driven to exert in defense against his anxieties.

Indeed, innovational activity is always a reaction to some degree of anxiety. The individual who is not in the least pushed toward creative activity as a relief from anxiety but is only drawn toward it by the great pleasure it gives him is an ideal case; he does not exist in life. Creativity does not require complete access to one's unconscious processes, complete confidence in one's own judgment, and so on. It requires only somewhat more of these qualities than characterizes the average person. Moreover, some types of innovation may require only a moderate degree of creativity combined with dogged determination or a high degree of motivation to dominate other men. Thus the characteristics of creativity described may not be high in some economic innovators. Often, however, they are greater than appears on the surface, especially since in business it is often desirable to keep one's inner life to oneself and to cast an image of oneself as a highly conventional extrovert. . . .

AUTHORITARIAN PERSONALITY

Against the foil of this description of creative personality, it is possible to enrich the discussion of authoritarian personality . . . for many characteristics of the creative individual. For that reason they may be outlined in a few paragraphs. Authoritarian personality is not the only type of uncreative personality; what is described here briefly is not uncreative personality in general but one specific type.

One gains an understanding of most of the facets of authoritarian personality if one assumes that as a child the authoritarian individual acquired no perception of the phenomena around him as elements in systems whose operation is amenable to analysis and responsive to his judicious initiative. Instead he must have gained two other impressions of the world that were overwhelmingly important in disciplining his later behavior. One of these is a perception of the world as arbitrary, capricious, not amenable to analysis, as consisting of an agglomeration of phenomena not related by a cause-and-effect network. The other is that the caprice of the world is not accidental but the play of willful powers far greater than his which serve their own purposes and disregard his unless he submits his will to theirs. These perceptions, we must assume, because the experiences which gave rise to them were very painful, have been pressed down out of his conscious mind; but he retains them in his unconscious, and they guide his adult behavior.

These perceptions breed in him a fear of using his initiative, an uncertainty concerning the quality of his own judgment, a tendency to let someone else evaluate a situation in order to avoid frustration and anxiety. Out of these perceptions also grows uneasiness at facing unresolved situations. Rather than rely on his own analysis to solve problems of the physical world or his relations to other individuals, he avoids pain by falling back on traditional ways of behavior that his parents and other earlier authorities taught him, and by relying on the judgment or will of individuals superior to him in authority or power.

To an individual guided by such perceptions it would seem to serve no satisfying purpose to be open to experience. Since phenomena and the forces that control them seem arbitrary to him, there are no useful deductions to be drawn from them. Moreover, a novel phenomenon would be disturbing since if it posed a problem it would arouse the anxiety associated with prospective initiative on his part. Hence for both positive and negative reasons he wears blinders to the interesting details of the world. He finds it safer to rely on traditional rules or on the judgment of older, wiser, and superior persons.

The painful experiences which gave rise to these perceptions must have created hatreds in him which shocked those around him. We shall see . . . that they also tend to arouse in him both doubt of his manliness and homosexual inclinations and desires. He presses these fears and unacceptable urges out of his conscious mind and seals over his unconscious processes as best he can because he is uneasy about what thoughts and fears they include. Hence his unconscious processes are inaccessible to him. In addition, they would not be useful if they were accessible, for instead of reactions to the phenomena he has currently observed they consist of the inadmissible impulses and desires which he has repressed and which are activated anew by the anxiety created by facing a problem.

But rage and pain, though repressed, are still within him. He dared not express his rage against the superior authorities who early in life directed him arbitrarily, but once he is an elder in the community, or a father, or even an older brother, he can somewhat satisfy his aggressiveness by his dominance over his inferiors. Moreover, as he moves to successive positions of authority at successive stages in his life the anxiety he feels in ambiguous situations causes him to insist that his own authority not be questioned, just as it earlier required that he submit his judgment to superior judgment and will. Thus each traditional adult individual in traditional society presents strong resistance to the questioning of authoritative decisions or traditional ways. That resistance is an important obstacle to change.

In sum, then, the member of a traditional society is uncreative for several reasons. He perceives the world as an abitrary place rather than an orderly one amenable to analysis and responsive to his initiative. His unconscious processes are both inaccessible and uncreative. He resolves his relationships with his fellows primarily on the basis of ascriptive authority. He avoids the anxiety caused by facing unresolved situations in the physical word by reliance on the judgment of authority. . . .

B. Elites

5. THE ELITE CONCEPT*

Harold D. Lasswell, Daniel Lerner, and C. Easton Rothwell

THE ELITE concept fills a blank in the language of science and policy. Words standing close to it already have rather definite meanings. A "leader," for instance, is ordinarily understood to be a prominent and active person. All leaders collectively are the "leadership." What is lacking is a term to cover both the leadership and the strata of society from which leaders usually come. Consider Winston Churchill. No one hesitates to call him a leader and to recognize that he has been part of the leadership of England for a long time, even though he was not always a leader. Nevertheless, even when too young to take part in public affairs, Churchill belonged to the political elite of his country, since he was born into one of the ruling families.

The concept of the elite is classificatory and descriptive, designating the holders of high positions in a given society. There are as many elites as there are values. Besides an elite of power (the political elite) there are elites of wealth, respect, and knowledge (to name but a few). Since we need a term for persons who are elite in relation to several values we speak of "*the* elite" (the elite of society). In democratic countries the political elite is recruited from a broad base. Elites in nondemocratic societies, on the contrary, spring from a narrow base, often from a few families.

It is true that the term elite has not been popular in democratic countries. In recent years Fascist, Nazi, and other nondemocratic movements have seized upon the word and given it a special twist for use as a weapon in the struggle for power. The elite, they say, is composed of persons with superior fitness to rule. They will and *ought* to rule. It is obvious, however, that no "ought" has scientific standing, since science is entirely concerned with "is." A scientist (and a democrat) can treat as a hypothesis the statement that individuals of great energy have an advantage in the struggle for power. Empirical connections between biology and power, however, cannot be transmogrified into a doctrine of "right to rule" which legitimately claims the sanction of science.

We need not take the fact too tragically that the term elite has often

* Reprinted from *The Comparative Study of Elites: An Introduction and Bibliography* by Harold D. Lasswell, Daniel Lerner, and C. Easton Rothwell, with the permission of the publishers, Stanford University Press. Copyright 1952 by the Board of Trustees of the Leland Stanford Junior University.

been misappropriated for doctrinal purposes, rather than left pure and free for the social sciences. A fact of life for social scientists is that many of the most convenient key words have "halo" effects arising from use in nonscientific circles. It is impracticable to expunge all halo words from the lexicon of the political and social sciences. It would be necessary to discard "democracy," "conservative," "liberal," "radical," "power," "political," "science," and a host of other terms. The only effective caution against halo effects is to develop scientists who are enough at home with the verbal tools of their craft to avoid being taken in by extraneous meanings. Any new word introduced in place of elite would soon need laundering since whatever refers to a high position comes, by a process of generalization, to have normative connotations. The "high" is equated with "very desirable.". . .

The Political Elite

The first step in clarifying the elite concept is to provide a working definition of power. In the older vocabulary of political science, power was often talked about in terms of will. In response to current pressure to substitute "behavioristic" for "subjective" terms, words like "decision-making" have come into vogue. The "decision process" appears to combine subjective and behavioristic connotations, and to imply phases of initiation, consideration, enactment, and enforcement. A decision can be defined as a severely sanctioned choice.

A heavy deprivation is expected to be imposed, or is imposed, against a deviationist. The deprivation involves any or all values. For example, there can be severe reductions of power (loss of office, disenfranchisment, loss of citizenship); of wealth (fines, confiscation); or of life itself (capital punishment). When statutes, ordinances, and awards are flouted or disregarded, they are not true decisions; we speak of them at best as presumptive decisions. Power we can now define as sharing in decisions. (Obviously the degree of sharing can range from near zero to near 100).

If we could define a decision as "what officials decide" the task of locating leaders would be simple. Unhappily those who are called officials do not always make the severely sanctioned choices, and the severely sanctioned choices are not necessarily made by persons called officials. Hence we distinguish between "authority" and "control," since the king who reigns may not rule, and the elected governor may be subservient to the unelected boss. Authority aways carries with it some modicum of control, however tenuous; control may have no shred of authority. When expectations concerning who "ought" coincide with who "does," authority and control can be reached at the same address.

Another complication arises from the difference between "actual" and "potential" power. The problem is acute when a revolutionary movement is coming to full tide, but has not risen high enough to sweep ancient landmarks downstream. The usual criteria reveal that the traditional holders of power are greatly restricted in scope. But it is not yet clear how to estimate potential power, since the success of the revolution remains in doubt. In quieter times the discrepancies between power currently exercised and power which is potential are less great.

The search for the political elite may well begin with what is conventionally known as the government. *Conventionally* speaking, government is the institution which is so named by the members of the community in question. *Functionally*, however, only the institution which makes the severely sanctioned choices can qualify. Since the true decision-makers are not necessarily known at the beginning of research the investigator can select government in the conventional sense as a convenient starting point.

The first research operation is to identify the individuals who have held a given position during a selected period. It is then possible to calculate the rate of *personal circulation*, which is the number of individuals occupying the post per unit of time.

The second problem is to determine the rate of *social circulation*, which refers to the social and personal characteristics of those passing through a specified position during a given interval. We are interested in the continuity (or discontinuity) of the social circulation. If everybody moves up a notch when his superior dies, the continuity of recruitment is complete. It is attained by providing for immediate succession. Continuity can also be realized by modes of recruitment which prescribe more remote succession, as when a process of election picks individuals outside the immediate and formal hierarchy. Discontinuity occurs when the method of replacing personnel is changed, or when it yields a personnel with novel traits.

In deciding whether new types of leaders are appearing we look into social class characteristics. An analysis of the House of Commons which included seven general elections, for example, showed that the percentage of members coming from titled families was high and stable (40 percent). Other ties with the social structure are examined, such as wealth, occupation, and enlightenment (to mention only a few possibilities). We also consider the types of personality from which generals, legislators, judges, and other political personnel are recruited.

Having found the social circulation we can determine the *representativeness* of community leadership. During the past sixty years, for instance, over half of the presidents' cabinets have been lawyers (55 percent). However, less than 1 percent of the gainfully employed in the general population are lawyers and judges. It is typical for the parliaments of Western powers to underrepresent certain elements in the population, such as manual workers, clerks, farmers, women, and young people.

We also consider the *flexibility* with which a given leadership adapts to the changing composition of the community, or to varying levels of social

crisis. From an analysis of social circulation through important governmental posts in New York, we know that during such crises as wars,
officeholders are recruited to an increasing degree from among the
wealthy. During intercrisis periods the wealthy return to private life,
leaving the field clear to persons originating in lower income groups.

Further insight into the elite comes with the calculation of *interlocking*
among positions. During the Fascist period in Italy it made sense to pay
particular attention to the interlocking of various organs of government
with the Fascist party, since it was possible to explain which agencies were
rising or falling in influence on this basis. (When persons or positions are
described as rising or falling in influence, it is a matter of specifying the
amount of *vertical mobility* involved.)

Which time periods are the most suitable for elite studies? Even though
no consensus exists, it is often assumed that "about a generation" is meant.
But the boundaries of a generation are not fixed. We might arbitrarily
choose a year to mark "coming of age." If we take the twentieth or
twenty-first year, a century divides conveniently into five generations.
This pace is prehaps too fast, since the oncoming wave of twenty-
year-olds does not press upon or begin seriously to displace the elder
generation until after more age and experience have been acquired. By the
mid-thirties enough influence has been amassed to penetrate some important posts. Hence the convention of counting three generation per
century has sometimes been adhered to. In crises, however, old ways of
doing things rapidly grow obsolete, and leaders are superannuated at a
faster rate than usual. During quiet times, on the contrary, a given
personnel persists longer than usual.

No one clock serves the multifarious purposes of research on elites.
Some inquiries are better served by gathering data by regular intervals of
time and studying "chronological generations." For other research tasks a
"functional generation" is more illuminating, since it is described according to varying phases of social adjustment. A functional example is the
"revolutionary generation" of 1917, meaning the leaders who appeared
during the first seizure and defense of power, and under whose direction
the initial steps were taken toward industrializing Russia. The "Stalinist
generation" is another functional case, referring to those in top positions
after Stalin entrenched himself in command of the Party.

Among the personal and social characteristics of an elite which are
worthy of separate examination must be included the means by which the
active members of a ruling class reach the very top positions, or, contrari-
wise, fail. Not all members of a ruling class, as implied before, take an
active role, or even an interest in politics. The point comes out plainly if
we inspect a sample of 100 families of the British peerage in which the title
has descended without interruption between 1800 and 1900. No less than
thirty-one of these elite families were without known political activity.
This was counterbalanced by the thirty-four families, two-thirds or more

of whose members were active in politics. Since this sample was confined to the peers themselves, it is reasonable to assume that the degree of political interest has been understated rather than overstated.

The systematic study of elites calls for information about the values which are employed by the active members as the *bases* of authority and control. (We speak of base values as the means; power, in this case, is the "scope" value sought.) Individuals born into the upper classes in any social structure that endures during their lifetimes are in possession of many assets of potential political importance. We know that an upper-class position typically carries the advantage of intimacy with the powerful, and a tradition (which is one form of enlightenment) about the strategy and tactics of rule. Besides, there is comparatively ready access to prestige, income, and other values.

We must specialize our examination of the active power elite by taking note of the instrumentalities upon which they rely in advancing themselves, and the usual ladder of rise (and decline). What is involved are the skills (and the associated knowledge) utilized by the active and successful. Following current usage, it is convenient to classify the instruments of policy in a fourfold scheme according to the degree of reliance upon the manipulation of symbols or upon nonsymbols. Diplomacy and propaganda depend upon words (and word equivalents). In diplomacy, the words are exchanged among elites (or elite members), while propaganda is addressed to large audiences of the rank and file. Economic and military policy usually involve the management of material resources and the coordination of human effort. We think of bargaining in the market and the management of production as representative economic skills, and military and police activity as specializations relating to violence. The negotiations of the diplomat and the bargaining of the businessman may both be "horse trading," as Bismarck put it, but they usually occur in a setting where the traders bear different relations to the horse.

Our conception of the "world revolution of our time" includes a number of hyoptheses about the skills of elites and the design of the ladder climbed by the proficient. We shall emphasize the shifting correlation of influence among specialists on bargaining, violence, and symbols. Among the symbol specialists we pay particular heed to those who are devoted to propaganda, or to such bureaucratic skills as the management of mass parties or the administration of official agencies. We look closely at the members of professions for which systematic training is requisite, such as law, and the more impressionistic intellectual activities which are closely connected with the humanistic tradition. We also consider the relationship between those engineering and technical skills which are connected with industrial methods of production, and the skills of the artisan and the peasant, which stem from a pre-industrial epoch. Among the symbol specialists we inquire into the relative influence of those who specialize upon sacred symbols and pastoral work, and the ones who deal in secular symbols and social work. Our investigation must ultimately ramify through all branches of the healing arts and sciences, where the "medicine men," old and new, find their place in the sun or shade. Questions of this kind will be particularly rewarding when we examine the way in which folk cultures adjust themselves to the industrial pattern.

Because of the stress so often put upon the social origins of an elite, and upon the path by which active members of an elite rise to the top, it is sometimes lost sight of that origins are no infallible guide to eliteship. The essential condition to be fulfilled is *accountability*. To be accountable is to be influenced. We are acquainted with the wide range of devices evolved by representative governments in their long struggle to control the executive, and to keep all members of the active elite accountable to the passsive elements of the ruling class. The devices include popular election of officials at frequent intervals; short official terms; initiative, referendum, recall; freedom of press; freedom to organize opposing (loyal) parties; freedom from coercion during campaigns and at the ballot box; separation of authority between branches of government; federation and devolution; substantive and procedural protections of the individual and of private associations from executive arbitrariness.

There is no body politic in which the active elite is wholly unaccountable to large circles within the community, and even to the community as a whole. Where means of peaceful influencing are not at hand, and deprivations are widespread, attempts at enforcing accountability are likely to end in coercion, whether in the form of assassination, uprising, sabotage, or civil disobedience.

In what has gone before we have put the principal emphasis upon obtaining facts about the origins, skills, and accountability of elites. It is impossible to contemplate information of the kind we have been discussing without drawing inferences about the *perspectives* of elites. No one is at a loss to predict some of the dominant attitudes of an elite whose members have had experience in police work, and more especially in political police service, and whose numbers have been frequently decimated by peasant uprisings, assassination, and related means. Nor are we at a total loss for ideas about the outlook of an elite whose most active members come from old, landed aristocracy, and who have rarely been the target of anything more serious than campaign epithets. However, we cannot verify these hypotheses short of conducting a direct examination of the utterances of elites. More than that, we cannot rationally infer from facts such as the nature of the skills employed by a revolutionary elite that the revolutionists necessarily possess a comprehensive theory of world history which is avowedly Marxian. We must turn to the direct scrutiny of elite utterances (and of the flow of communication through the body politic) to enlighten us on these and many other points. . . .

Modern methods have provided us with research tools capable of being applied to the problem. One general hypothesis is that the realistic sub-divisions of the elite have been recruited from those who have been in a position to acquaint themselves with emerging trends. This means that the focus of attention of the "realist" diverges from that of the "fantast." We may find that tutors or playmates, or travel abroad, give occasion for a new set of expectations, demands, or even identifications. However, this is not enough to explain all, since members of ruling groups can be exposed to similar opportunities without revising what they believe. Not only exposure but the pattern of predispositon at the time of exposure must be taken into account. We know that predispositions are screens to sift out the novel and disturbing, and to re-edit the current stream of incoming stimuli into old familiar grooves. The problem, thus narrowed, remains: what factors explain why some persons remain open to new and challenging experiences to which others (whose backgrounds are interchangeable in terms of class structure and culture) remain untouched? Much remains to be learned by intensive studies directed at the realistic and the fantasy sub-elites of a given ruling class.

The most intensive research on elites can focus directly on the question of distinctive elite practices. It is a question of the perspectives and operations revealed by the decision process. By proper methods it is possible to ascertain the "code" of an elite, and to describe the values and objectives sought; the base values typically relied upon; and the detailed patterns of expectation, identification, and operation which are present. A scientific observer will take into consideration the principles and maxims made articulate among the decision-makers. In addition, the analyst will examine the mode of conduct displayed in typical circumstances, estimating the degree of elaboration and the intensity of all manifestations. Hence the "code" of an elite summarizes both conscious perspectives and unconscious demands, identifications, and expectations. The measure of intensity is the degree in which the total personality is involved. (By far the most thorough work of this kind is by Nathan Leites on the Politburo.)

In studying elites a word of caution may not be amiss. In the literature there are frequent references to the "pyramid" of power. It should be clear that nothing inherent in the geometry of power restricts power to the pyramid. In innumerable situations, nevertheless, the pyramid is a faithful image of the prevailing pattern. When compared with the small elite cluster, other groups fall away toward the broad bottom layer of impotence or indifference. But power is not always concentrated in a few hands. When effective participation is widely dispersed it is more accurate to redraw the pyramid into a squat figure resembling a "flat-top" or a western "mesa." The group at the very bottom of the heap may be small, rather than large, so that the bottom of the pyramid must be pinched together and the whole figure redrawn nearer to the shape of a carrot. In any case the significant point is that elite patterns are to be discovered by research and not settled by arbitrary definition.

What has been said about the concept of the political elite can be summed up as follows: *The political elite comprises the power holders of a body politic. The power holders include the leadership and the social formations from which leaders typically come, and to which accountability is maintained, during a given generation. In other words, the political elite is the top power class.* Obviously it does not include all members of the body politic unless everyone shares equally in the decision process. The extent of power sharing must be determined in every situation by research, since there is no universal pattern of power. We speak of an *open elite* when all or a very considerable number of the members of a body politic are included. A *closed elite*, on the other hand, embraces only a few. A ruling caste is a ruling class closed to all save certain families.

C. Political Culture

6. COMPARATIVE POLITICAL SYSTEMS*

Gabriel A. Almond

WHAT I propose to do in this brief paper is to suggest how the application of certain sociological and anthropological concepts may facilitate systematic comparison among the major types of political systems operative in the world today.

At the risk of saying the obvious, I am not suggesting to my colleagues in the field of comparative government that social theory is a conceptual cure-all for the ailments of the discipline. There are many ways of laboring in the vineyard of the Lord, and I am quite prepared to concede that there are more musical forms of psalmody than sociological jargon. I suppose the test of the sociological approach that is discussed here is whether or not it enables us to solve certain persistent problems in the field more effectively than we now are able to solve them.

Our expectations of the field of comparative government have changed in at least two ways in the last decades. In the first place as American interests have broadened to include literally the whole world, our course offerings have expanded to include the many areas outside of Western Europe–Asia, the Middle East, Africa, and Latin America. Secondly, as our international interests have expanded and become more urgent, our

* From *The Journal of Politics,* Vol. 18 (1956), pp. 391–409. By permission of the *Journal* and the author.

requirements in knowledge have become more exacting. We can no longer view political crises in France with detached curiosity or view countries such as Indo-China and Indonesia as interesting political pathologies. We are led to extend our discipline and intensify it simultaneously.

It would simply be untrue to say that the discipline of comparative government has not begun to meet both of these challenges. As rapidly as it has been possible to train the personnel, new areas have been opened up to teaching and research; and there has been substantial encouragement to those who have been tempted to explore new aspects of the political process both here and abroad and to employ new methods in such research. It is precisely because of the eagerness and energy with which these challenges have been met that the field is now confronted with the problem of systematic cumulation and comparison. What appears to be required in view of the rapid expansion of the field are more comparative efforts in the tradition of Finer and Friedrich, if we are to gain the maximum in insight and knowledge from this large-scale research effort.

The problem to which this paper is a tentative and provisional answer is the following. With the proliferation of courses and special studies of specific "governments" and groupings of governments on an area or other bases, is it possible to set up and justify a preliminary classification into which most of the political systems which we study today can be assigned? The classifications which we now employ are particularistic (e.g., American Government, British Government, the Soviet Union, and the like); regional (e.g., Government and Politics of the Far East, Latin America, and the like); or political (e.g., the British Commonwealth, Colonial Government, and the like); or functional (e.g., the comprehensive comparative efforts limited to the European-American area, such as Finer and Friedrich, and the specific institutional comparisons such as comparative parties, and comparative administration).

Anyone concerned with this general problem of classification of political systems will find that all of the existing bases of classification leave something to be desired. Dealing with governments particularistically is no classification at all. A regional classification is based not on the properties of the political systems, but on their contiguity in space. The existing structural classifications, such as democracy-dictatorship, parliamentary-presidential systems, two-party and multi-party systems, often turn out to miss the point, particularly when they are used in the strikingly different political systems of the pre-industrial areas. There may be a certain use therefore in exploring the possibilities of other ways of classifying political systems. What is proposed here is just one of these ways, and because of the uneven state of our knowledge is necessarily crude and provisional.

In my own efforts to stand far off, so to speak, and make the grossest discriminations between types of empirical political systems operative in the world today, I have found a fourfold classification to be most useful: the Anglo-American (including some members of the Commonwealth), the Continental European (exclusive of the Scandinavian and Low Countries, which combine some of the features of the Continental European and the Anglo-American), the pre-industrial, or partially industrial, political systems outside the European-American area, and the totalitarian political systems. This classification will not include all the political systems in existence today, but it comes close to doing so. It will serve the purpose of our discussion, which is not that of testing the inclusiveness of this classification but rather the usefulness of sociological concepts in bringing out the essential differences between these political systems.

The terms which I shall use in descriminating the essential properties of these classes have emerged out of the Weber-Parsons tradition in social theory.[1] I shall try to suggest why I find some of these concepts useful. First, a political system is a system of *action*. What this means is that the student of political systems is concerned with empirically observable behavior. He is concerned with norms or institutions in so far as they affect behavior. Emphasizing "action" merely means that the description of a political system can never be satisfied by a simple description of its legal or ethical norms. In other words, political institutions or persons performing political rôles are viewed in terms of what it is that they do, why they do it, and how what they do is related to and affects what others do. The term *system*[2] satisfies the need for an inclusive concept which covers all of the patterned actions relevant to the making of political decisions. Most political scientists use the term *political process* for these purposes. The difficulty with the term *process* is that it means any patterning of action through time. In contrast to *process*, the concept of *system* implies a *totality* of relevant units, an interdependence between the interactions of units, and a certain stability in the interaction of these units (perhaps best described as a changing equilibrium).

The unit of the political system is the rôle. The rôle, according to Parsons and Shils, ". . . is that organized sector of an actor's orientation which constitutes and defines his participation in an interactive process."[3] It involves a set of complementary expectations concerning his own actions and those of others with whom he interacts. Thus a political system may be defined as a set of interacting rôles, or as a structure of rôles, if we understand by *structure* a patterning of interactions. The advantage of the concept of *rôle* as compared with such terms as *institutions*, *organizations*, or *groups*, is that it is a more inclusive and more open concept. It can include formal offices, informal offices, families, electorates,

---

[1] See in particular Max Weber, *The Theory of Social and Economic Organization*, trans. by A. M. Henderson and Talcott Parsons (New York: Oxford University Press, 1947), pp. 87 ff.

[2] See David Easton, *The Political System: An Inquiry into the State of Political Science*, (New York: Alfred Knopf, 1953), pp. 90 ff.

[3] Talcott Parsons and Edward A. Shils (eds.), *Towards a General Theory of Action* (Cambridge: Harvard University Press, 1951), p. 23.

mobs, casual as well as persistent groupings, and the like, in so far as they enter into and affect the political system. The use of other concepts such as those indicated above involves ambiguity, forced definitions (such as groups), or residual categories. Like the concept of system it does not prejudice our choice of units but rather enables us to nominate them on the basis of empirical investigation.

While there appear to be certain advantages in these concepts of political system and rôle for our purposes, they confront the political scientist with a serious problem. While he intends the concept to have a general application, Parsons appears to have had before him in elaborating the concept the model of the primary group—family, friendship, and the like—and not complex social systems, the units of which are collectivities and not individual actors. In this sense the sociological concept of system and of rôle can only be a beginning of a conceptual model of the political system. The job of developing additional concepts necessary to handle macrocosmic social systems such as political systems—national and international—is still to be done.

My own conception of the distinguishing properties of the political system proceeds from Weber's definition—the legitimate monopoly of physical coercion over a given territory and population.[4] The political systems with which most political scientists concern themselves all are characterized by a specialized apparatus which possesses this legitimate monopoly, and the political system consists of those interacting rôles which affect its employment. There are, of course, simpler societies in which this function of maintenance of order through coercion is diffuse and unspecialized; it is combined with other functions in the family and other groupings. While these systems are also properly the subject matter of political science, there are few political scientists indeed with the specialized equipment necessary to study them.

It may be useful to add a few comments about this definition of politics and the political in order to avoid misunderstanding. To define politics as having this distinguishing property of monopolizing legitimate coercion in a given territory is not the same thing as saying that this is *all* that government does. It is the thing that government does and that other social systems ordinarily may not do legitimately. Other social systems may employ other forms of compulsion than physical coercion. Some indeed may legitimately employ physical coercion on a limited scale. But the employment of *ultimate, comprehensive,* and *legitimate* physical coercion is the monopoly of states, and the political system is uniquely concerned with the scope, the direction, and the conditions affecting the employment of this physical coercion. It is, of course, clear that political systems protect freedoms and provide welfare, as well as impose order backed up by physical compulsion, but even their protection of freedom and their

[4] *From Max Weber: Essays in Sociology,* trans. by H. H. Gerth and C. Wright Mills (New York: Oxford University Press, 1946), p. 78.

provison of welfare is characteristically backed up by the threat of physical compulsion. Hence it seems appropriate to define the political system as the patterned interaction of rôles affecting decisions backed up by the threat of physical compulsion.

The task of describing a political system consists in characterizing all the patterned interactions which take place within it. It takes us beyond the legal system into all the rôles which occur and involves our defining these rôles in action or behavioral terms. The concept of system implies that these rôles are interdependent and that a significant change in any one rôle affects changes in the others, and thereby changes the system as a whole. Thus the emergence of pressure groups in the present century produced certain changes in the party system and in the administrative and legislative processes. The rapid expansion of executive bureaucracy was one of the factors that triggered off the development of legislative bureaucracy and pressure group bureaucracy. Changes in the rôle of political communication have transformed the electoral process, the behavior of parties, the legislature, the executive. The concepts of system and of interdependence lead us to look for these changes when any specific rôle changes significantly. It suggests the usefulness of thinking at the level of the system and its interdependence rather than in terms of discrete phenomena or only limited bilateral relationships, or relationships occurring only within the formal-legal rôle structure.

The fourth concept is *orientation to political action*. Every political system is embedded in a set of meanings and purposes. We speak of "attitudes toward politics," "political values," "ideologies," "national character," "cultural ethos." The difficulty with all these terms is that their meanings are diffuse and ambiguous. The concepts of orientation to action and of the pattern variables are useful since they at least attempt logical distinctness and comprehensiveness. It is not essential for my purposes to go into the modes of orientation of action, or into the "pattern variables" in detail. Parsons and Shils tell us that any orientation to politics involves three components: the first is perception, or *cognition;* the second is preference, involvement, or affect (*cathexis*); the third is evaluation or choice through the application of standards or values to the cognitive and affective components. By *cognition* is meant the knowledge and discrimination of the objects, events, actions, issues, and the like. By *cathexis* is meant the investment of objects, issues, etc., with emotional significance, or affect. By *evaluation* is meant the manner in which individuals organize and select their perceptions, preferences, and values in the process of establishing a position *vis-à-vis political action.*[5]

Every political system is embedded in a particular pattern of orientations to political action. I have found it useful to refer to this as the *political culture*. There are two points to be made regarding the concept

---

[5] Parsons and Shils, *op cit.*, pp. 58 ff.

of political culture. First, it does not coincide with a given political system or society. Patterns of orientation to politics may, and usually do, extend beyond the boundaries of political systems. The second point is that the political culture is not the same thing as the general culture, although it is related to it. Because political orientation involves cognition, intellection, and adaptation to external situations, as well as the standards and values of the general culture, it is a differentiated part of the culture and has a certain autonomy. Indeed, it is the failure to give proper weight to the cognitive and evaluative factors, and to the consequent autonomy of political culture, that has been responsible for the exaggerations and over-simplifications of the "national character" literature of recent years.

The usefulness of the concept of political culture and its meaning may perhaps be conveyed more effectively through illustration. I would argue that the United States, England, and several of the Commonwealth countries have a common political culture, but are separate and different kinds of political systems. And I would argue that the typical countries of continental Western Europe, while constituting individual political systems, include several different political cultures which extend beyond their borders. In other words, they are political systems with fragmented political cultures.

In an effort to overcome understandable resistances to the introduction of a new term, I should like to suggest why I find the concept of political culture more useful than the terms we now employ, such as *ideology* or *political party*. As I understand the term *ideology*, it means the systematic and explicit formulation of a general orientation to politics. We need this term to describe such political phenomena as these and should not reduce its specificity by broadening it to include not only the explicit doctrinal structure characteristically borne by a minority of *militants*, but also the vaguer and more implicit orientations which generally characterize political followings. The term *political party* also cannot serve our purpose, for we are here dealing with a formal organization which may or may not be a manifestation of a political culture. Indeed, we will be gravely misled if we try to force the concept of party to mean political culture. Thus the commonly used distinctions between one-party, two-party, and multi-party systems simply get nowhere in distinguishing the essential properties of the totalitarian, the Anglo-American, and the Continental European political systems. For the structure we call *party* in the totalitarian system is not a party at all; the two parties of the Anglo-American system are organized manifestations of a homogeneous political culture; and the multi-parties of Continental European political systems in some cases are and in some cases are not the organized manifestations of different political cultures.

But the actual test of the usefulness of this conceptual scheme can only come from a more detailed application of it in developing the special properties of the classes of political systems to which we earlier referred.

THE ANGLO-AMERICAN POLITICAL SYSTEMS

The Anglo-American political systems are characterized by a *homogeneous, secular* political culture. By a secular political culture I mean a multi-valued political culture, a rational-calculating, bargaining, and experimental political culture. It is a homogeneous culture in the sense that there is a sharing of political ends and means. The great majority of the actors in the political system accept as the ultimate goals of the political system some combination of the values of freedom, mass welfare, and security. There are groups which stress one value at the expense of the others; there are times when one value is stressed by all groups; but by and large the tendency is for all these values to be shared, and for no one of them to be completely repressed. To a Continental European this kind of political culture often looks sloppy. It has no logic, no clarity. This is probably correct in an intellectual sense, since this balancing of competing values occurs below the surface among most people and is not explicated in any very elegant way. Actually the logic is complex and is constantly referred to reality in an inductive process. It avoids the kind of logical simplism which characterizes much of the Continental European ideological polemic.

A secularized political system involves an individuation of and a measure of autonomy among the various rôles. Each one of the rôles sets itself up autonomously in political business, so to speak. There tends to be an arms-length bargaining relationship among the rôles. The political system is saturated with the atmosphere of the market. Groups of electors come to the political market with votes to sell in exchange for policies. Holders of offices in the formal-legal rôle structure tend to be viewed as agents and instrumentalities, or as brokers occupying points in the bargaining process. The secularized political process has some of the characteristics of a laboratory; that is, policies offered by candidates are viewed as hypotheses, and the consequences of legislation are rapidly communicated within the system and constitute a crude form of testing hypotheses. Finally, because the political culture tends to be homogeneous and pragmatic, it takes on some of the atmosphere of a game. A game is a good game when the outcome is in doubt and when the stakes are not too high. When the stakes are too high, the tone changes from excitement to anxiety. While "fun" is frequently an aspect of Anglo-American politics, it is rarely a manifestation of Continental European politics; and, unless one stretches the definition, it never occurs at all in totalitarian politics.

RÔLE STRUCTURE IN THE ANGLO-AMERICAN POLITICAL SYSTEMS

The rôle structure in this group of political systems is (1) highly differentiated, (2) manifest, organized, and bureaucratized, (3) characterized by a high degree of stability in the functions of the rôles, and (4) likely to have a diffusion of power and influence within the political system as a whole.

With regard to the first point, each one of the units—formal governmental agencies, political parties, pressure groups and other kinds of voluntary associations, the media of communication, and "publics" of various kinds—pursues specialized purposes and performs specialized functions in the system. As was already pointed out, each one of these entities is more or less autonomous—interdependent, but autonomous. Certainly there are striking differences in this respect as between the United States and the United Kingdom, but their similarity becomes clear in contrast to the other major types of systems which will be described below. Secondly, this rôle structure is manifest and on the surface. Most of the potential "interests" have been organized and possess bureaucracies. Thirdly, there is in contrast to some of the other systems a relatively high degree of stability of function in the various parts of the structure. Bureaucracies function as bureaucracies, armies as armies, parliaments as parliaments. The functions are not ordinarily substitutable as among these various institutions and organizations, in contrast to some of the other systems. This is another way of saying that the political division of labor is more complex, more explicit, and more stable. There are, of course, striking differences between the British and American versions in these respects. For the American system is at the same time more complex and less stable than the British. There are, for example, many more pressure groups and types of pressure groups in the United States for reasons of size, economic complexity, and ethnic and religious heterogeneity. Furthermore there is more substitutability of function in the American system, more policy-making by pressure groups and the media of communciation, more intervention in policy-making through the transient impact of "public moods." But again if we are comparing the Anglo-American system with, for example, the pre-industrial or partially industrial systems, the British and American systems will stand out by virtue of their similarities on the score of complexity, manifestness, and stability of rôle structure.

Finally the Anglo-American type of political system is one in which there is diffusion of power and influence. This is only partially expressed in the formal legal phraseology of a democratic suffrage and representative government. There is an effective as well as a legal diffusion of power, resulting from a system of mass communciations, mass education, and representation by interest groups. Here again the British and American versions differ sharply in terms of formal governmental structure, the relations between parties and pressure groups, and the system of communication and education. The net result is a more centralized, predictable rôle structure in Britain than in the United States.

THE PRE-INDUSTRIAL POLITICAL SYSTEMS

The political systems which fall under this very general category are the least well-known of all four of the classes discussed here. But despite our relative ignorance in this area and our inability to elaborate the many sub-types which no doubt exist, a discussion of this kind of political system is analytically useful since it presents such a striking contrast to the homogeneous, secular political culture, and the complex and relatively stable rôle structure of the Anglo-American political system.

The pre-industrial—or partially industrialized and Westernized—political systems may be best described as mixed political cultures and mixed political systems. Nowhere does the need for additional vocabulary become clearer than in the analysis of these systems; for here parliaments tend to be something other than parliaments, parties and pressure groups behave in unusual ways, bureaucracies and armies often dominate the political system, and there is an atmosphere of unpredictability and gunpowder surrounding the political system as a whole.

Some clarity is introduced into the understanding of these systems if one recognizes that they are embedded in mixed political cultures. What this means is that as a minimum we have two political cultures, the Western system with its parliament, its electoral system, its bureaucracy and the like, and the pre-Western system or systems. In countries such as India there are many traditional political cultures which intermingle with the Western system. What kind of amalgam emerges from this impingement of different political cultures will depend on at least five factors: (1) the type of traditional cultures which are involved; (2) the auspices under which Westernization has been introduced (e.g., Western colonial powers, or native élites); (3) the functions of the society which have been Westernized; (4) the tempo and tactics of the Westernization process; (5) the type of Western cultural products which have been introduced. As a consequence of this impingement of the Western and traditional political cultures, there is a third type of political culture which frequently emerges in this type of system; what in Max Weber's language may be called a charismatic political culture. It often happens as a consequence of the erosion of a traditional political culture that powerful forces are released—anxieties over the violation of sacred customs and relationships, feelings of rootlessness and directionlessness because of the rejection of habitual routines. The impact of the Western rational system on the traditional system or systems often creates a large potential for violence. One of the typical manifestations of this conflict of political cultures is the charismatic nationalism which occurs so frequently in these areas and which may be in part understood as being a movement toward accepting a new system of political norms, or a movement toward reaffirming the older traditional ones, often both in peculiar combinations. To overcome the resistance of habitual routines backed up by supernatural sanctions, the new form of legitimacy must represent a powerful affirmation capable of breaking up deeply ingrained habits and replacing earlier loyalties. Thus, at the minimum, we must have in these political systems the old or the traditional political culture, or cultures, the new or the Western-rational political culture, and transitional or resultant political phenomena of one kind or another. Needless to say, this typical mixture of political cultures presents the most serious problems of communication and coordination. We are dealing with a political system in which large groups have fundamentally different "cognitive maps" of politics and apply different norms to political action. Instability and unpredictability are not to be viewed as inescapable consequences of this type of mixture of political cultures.

RÔLE STRUCTURE IN THE PRE-INDUSTRIAL POLITICAL SYSTEMS

These characteristics of the pre-industrial political systems may be brought out more clearly and systematically in an analysis of the political rôle structure which is more or less characteristic.

There is first a relatively low degree of structural differentiation. Political interest often tends to be latent and when it emerges into politics often takes the form of spontaneous, violent action. Political parties are unstable; they fragment and consolidate, appear and disappear. There is ordinarily only a rudimentary specialized system of communciation. Unless there is a bureaucracy left by a Western colonial power, the bureaucratic structure may be only partially developed.

Secondly, because of the absence of a stable and explicit rôle structure, there is likely to be a high degree of *substitutability* of rôles. Thus bureaucracies may take over the legislative function, and armies may and often do the same. A political party may pre-empt the policy-making function, or a mob may emerge and take the center of the policy-making stage for a brief interval. In other words, in contrast to the Anglo-American political systems, there is no stable division of political labor.

A third and most important aspect of these political systems is the mixing of political rôle structures. Thus there may be a parliament formally based on a set of legal norms and regulations; but operating within it may be a powerful family, a religious sect, a group of tribal chieftains, or some combination of these. These are elements of the traditional rôle structure operating according to their own traditional norms. The student of these political systems would be greatly misled if he followed Western norms and expectations in describing such a decision making system. What would be corruption in a Western parliament would be normatively oriented conduct in a "mixed parliament" of the kind often found in the regions outside of the Western-European American area.

Thus such concepts as mixed political culture and mixed political rôle structures may prepare the field research more adequately than the accepted political science theory and terminology; for in going to Indonesia or Thailand he will not only have in mind the Western conception of political process and system and a conception of the appropriate rôles of legislatures, bureaucracies, parties, pressure groups, and public opinion, but will rather look for the particular pattern of amalgamation of these rôles with the traditional rôles. His intellectual apparatus would enable him to grapple more quickly and more adequately with political phenomena which he might otherwise overlook, or treat as pathologies.

TOTALITARIAN POLITICAL SYSTEMS

The totalitarian political culture gives the appearance of being homogeneous, but the homogeneity is synthetic. Since there are no voluntary associations, and political communication is controlled from the center, it is impossible to judge in any accurate way the extent to which there is a positive acceptance of the totalitarian order. One can only say that in view of the thorough-going penetration of the society by a centrally controlled system of organizations and communications, and the special way in which coercion or its threat is applied, the totalitarian system, in contrast to the others, tends to be non-consensual. This is not to say that it is completely non-consensual. A completely coercive political system is unthinkable. But if one were to place the totalitarian system on a continuum of consensual-non-consensual it would be located rather more at the non-consensual end of the continuum than the others described here. Unlike the other systems where some form of legitimacy—whether traditional, rational-legal, or charismatic—underlies the acquiescence of the individual in the political system, in the totalitarian order the characteristic orientation to authority tends to be some combination of conformity and apathy. This type of political system has become possible only in modern times, since it depends on the modern technology of communication, on modern types of organization, and on the modern technology of violence. Historic tyrannies have no doubt sought this kind of dominion but were limited in the effectiveness of their means. Totalitarianism is tyranny with a rational bureaucracy, a monopoly of the modern technology of communciation, and a monopoly of the modern technology of violence.

ROLE STRUCTURE IN TOTALITARIAN POLITICAL SYSTEMS

I believe Franz Neumann in his *Behemoth*[6] was one of the first students of totalitarianism who rejected the *monocratic* model as being useful in understanding these systems. He spoke of the peculiar shapelessness of the

---

[6] Franz Neumann, *Behemoth: The Structure and Practice of National Socialism* (New York: Oxford University Press, 1942), pp. 459 ff.

Nazi régime, of the fact that there was no stable delegation of power among the bureaucracy, party, the army, the organizations of big business, and the like. He concluded, as you recall, that there was no state under the Nazis. I believe what he meant to say was that there was no *legitimate* state. Later students of totalitarianism such as Hannah Arendt,[7] Merle Fainsod,[8] Carl Friedrich,[9] Alex Inkeles,[10] and Barrington Moore, Jr.,[11] have been led to similar conclusions about totalitarianism in general, or about Soviet totalitarianism. Hannah Arendt has painted the most extreme picture, which, while an exaggeration, is useful analytically. She urges that the "isolation of atomized individuals provides not only the mass basis for totalitarian rule, but is carried through at the very top of the whole structure." The aim of this process of atomization is to destroy solidarity at any point in the system and to avoid all stable delegations of power which might reduce the freedom of manoeuver of those at the very center of the system. "As techniques of government, the totalitarian devices appear simple and ingeniously effective. They assure not only an absolute power monopoly, but unparalleled certainty that all commands will always be carried out; the multiplicity of the transmission belts, the confusion of the hierarchy, secure the dictator's complete independence of all his inferiors and make possible the swift and surprising changes in policy for which totalitarianism has become famous."[12]

There are thus at least two distinctive characteristics of the totalitarian rôle structure: (1) the predominance of the coercive rôles, and (2) the functional instability of the power rôles—bureaucracy, party, army, and secret police. The predominance of the coercive rôle structure is reflected in its penetration of all of the other rôle structures. Thus all forms of organization and communication become saturated with a coercive flavor. This predominance of coercion is reflected in the celebrated definition of the state as "bodies of armed men" in Lenin's *State and Revolution*. It is also reflected in the doctrine of the "potential enemy of the state," a conception under which almost any behavior may be arbitrarily defined as disloyal behavior. This eliminates the predictability of the impact of coercion and renders it an omnipresent force, however limited its application may be in a quantitative sense.

The functional instability among the power rôles has as its main

---

[7] Hannah Arendt, *The Origins of Totalitarianism* (New York: Harcourt, Brace and Company, 1951), p. 388.

[8] Merle Fainsod, *How Russia is Ruled* (Cambridge: Harvard University Press, 1953), pp. 354 ff.

[9] Carl J. Friedrich (ed.), *Totalitarianism* (Cambridge: Harvard University Press, 1954), pp. 47 ff.

[10] Alex Inkeles in *ibid.*, pp. 88 ff.

[11] Barrington Moore, Jr., *Terror and Progress USSR: Some Sources of Change and Stability in the Soviet Dictatorship* (Cambridge: Harvard University Press, 1954), pp. 154 ff.

[12] Arendt, *op. cit.*, p. 389.

purpose the prevention of any stable delegation of power, and the consequent diffusion of power and creation of other power centers. This pattern was apparently quite marked in the development of the Nazi régime and has been observable in the uneasy balance established in the Soviet Union between party, bureaucracy, army, and secret police. In the nature of the case there must be a stabler delegation of power among the economic allocative rôles, but even these rôles are penetrated by the coercive rôle structure and manipulated within limits. A third class of rôles is illustrated by the electoral process and the representative system, as well as the practice of "self-criticism" in the party. While there is a set of norms under which these activities are supposed to influence power and policy-making, they are rather to be understood as mobilizing devices, as devices intended to create a façade of consent.

THE CONTINENTAL EUROPEAN POLITICAL SYSTEMS

We refer here primarily to France, Germany, and Italy. The Scandinavian and Low Countries stand somewhere in between the Continental pattern and the Anglo-American. What is most marked about the Continental European systems is the fragmentation of political culture; but this fragmentation is rather different from that of the non-Western systems. For in the non-Western systems we are dealing with mixed political cultures involving the most striking contrasts. The Western political culture arising out of a very different development pattern is introduced bodily, so to speak, from the outside. In the Continental European systems we are dealing with a pattern of political culture characterized by an uneven pattern of development. There are significant survivals, "outcroppings," of older cultures and their political manifestations. But all of the cultural variations have common roots and share a common heritage.

In view of this developmental pattern it may be appropriate to speak of the Continental European systems as having political subcultures. There is indeed in all the examples of this type of system a surviving pre-industrial sub-culture (e.g., the Catholic *Ancien Régime* areas in France, Southern Italy, and the Islands, and parts of Bavaria). The historical background of all three of these systems is characterized by a failure on the part of the middle classes in the nineteenth century to carry through a thoroughgoing secularization of the political culture. Thus another political sub-culture in these political systems constitutes remnants of the older middle classes who are still primarily concerned with the secularization of the political system itself. A third group of political sub-cultures is associated with the modernized and industrialized parts of these societies. But because they emerged in an only partially secularized political culture, their potentialities for "political market" behavior were thwarted. As major political sub-cultures there are thus these three: (1) the pre-industrial, primarily Catholic components, (2) the older middle-class components, and (3) the industrial components proper. But the political culture is more complex than this. Since in the last century the political issues have involved the very survival of these sub-cultures, and the basic form of the political system itself, the political actors have not come to politics with specific bargainable differences but rather with conflicting and mutually exclusive designs for the political culture and political system. This has involved a further fragmentation at the level of ideology and political organizations. Thus the pre-industrial, primarily Catholic element has both an adaptive, semi-secular wing and an anti-secular wing. The middle classes are divided into conservative wings in uneasy alliance with clerical pre-republican elements, and left-wings in uneasy friendship with socialists. Finally, the industrial workers are divided according to the degree of their alienation from the political system as a whole. The organized political manifestations of this fragmented political culture take the form of "movements" or sects, rather than of political parties. This means that political affiliation is more of an act of faith than of agency.

Perhaps the most pronounced characteristic of the political rôle structure in these areas is what one might call a general alienation from the political market. The political culture pattern is not adapted to the political system. For while these countries have adopted parliaments and popular elections, they are not appropriately oriented to these institutions. The political actors come to the market not to exchange, compromise, and adapt, but to preach, exhort, convert, and transform the political system into something other than a bargaining agency. What bargaining and exchanging does occur tends to take the form of under-the-counter transactions. Thus demoralization (*"transformism"*) is an almost inescapable consequence of this combination of political culture and system. In contrast, the normatively consistent, morally confident actor in this type of political system is the *militant* who remains within the confines of his political sub-culture, continually reaffirms his special norms, and scolds his parliamentarians.

This suggests another essential characteristic of this type of rôle structure, which places it in contrast to the Anglo-American. There is not an individuation of the political rôles, but rather the rôles are embedded in the sub-cultures and tend to constitute separate sub-systems of rôles. Thus the Catholic sub-culture has the Church itself, the Catholic schools, propaganda organizations such as Catholic Action, Catholic trade unions, or worker organizations, a Catholic party or parties, and a Catholic press. The Communist sub-culture—the sub-culture of the political "alienates" —similarly has a complete and separate system of rôles. The socialist and "liberal" sub-cultures tend in the same direction but are less fully organized and less exclusive. Thus one would have to say that the center of gravity in these political systems is not in the formal legal rôle structure but in the political sub-cultures. Thus "immobilism" would appear to be a normal property of this kind of political system, and it is not so much an "immobilism" of formal-legal institutions as a consequence of the condition of the political culture. Needless to say, this portrayal of the Continental European political system has been exaggerated for purposes of contrast and comparison.

Two other general aspects of the rôle structure of these countries call for comment. First, there is a higher degree of substitutability of rôles than in the Anglo-American political systems and a lesser degree than in the non-Western systems. Thus parties may manipulate pressure groups in the sense of making their decisions for them (the Communist case); interest groups such as the Church and Catholic Action may manipulate parties and trade unions; and interest groups may operate directly in the legislative process, although this last pattern occurs in the Anglo-American system as well. The "immobilism" of the formally political organs often leads to a predominance of the bureaucracy in policy-making.

A second general characteristic, which is a consequence of the immobilism of the political system as a whole, is the ever-present threat of what is often called the "Caesaristic" breakthrough. As in the non-Western area, although the situations and causes are different, these systems tend always to be threatened by, and sometimes to be swept away by, movements of charismatic nationalism which break through the boundaries of the political subcultures and overcome immobilism through coercive action and organization. In other words, these systems have a totalitarian potentiality in them. The fragmented political culture may be transformed into a synthetically homogeneous one and the stalemated rôle structure mobilized by the introduction of the coercive pattern already described.

*   *   *   *   *

In conclusion perhaps the point might be made that conceptual and terminological growth in the sciences is as inevitable as the growth of language itself. But just as all the slang and neologisms of the moment do not find a permanent place in the language, so also all of the conceptual jargon which the restless minds of scholars invent—sometimes to facilitate communication with their colleagues and sometimes to confound them—will not find its permanent place in the vocabulary of the disciplines. The ultimate criterion of admission or rejection is the facilitation of understanding, and this, fortunately enough, is not in the hands of the restless and inventive scholar, but in the hands of the future scholarly generations who will try them out for "fit." If I may be permitted to conclude with a minor note of blasphemy, it may be said of new concepts as it was said of the salvation of souls . . . "there shall be weeping and gnashing of teeth, for many are called but few are chosen."

D. Power

7. APPROACHES TO THE STUDY OF POLITICAL POWER*

Franz L. Neumann

POLITICAL POWER AND PSYCHOLOGY

POLITICAL POWER is an elusive concept. It embraces two radically different relations: control of nature, and control of man. Power over nature is mere intellectual power. It consists in man's understanding of the lawfulness of external nature for the ultimate purpose of subjecting external nature to man's needs. It is this accumulated knowledge which is the basis of the productivity of any given society. This power is powerless. It does not involve control of other men.

Political power is social power focused on the state. It involves control of other men for the purpose of influencing the behavior of the state, its legislative, administrative and judicial activities. Since political power is control of other men, political power (as contrasted with power over external nature) is always a two-sided relationship. Man is not simply a piece of external nature; he is an organism endowed with reason, although frequently not capable of, or prevented from, acting rationally. Consequently, those who wield political power are compelled to create emotional and rational responses in those whom they rule, inducing them to accept, implicitly or explicitly, the commands of the rulers. Failure to evoke emotional or intellectual responses in the ruled compels the ruler to resort to simple violence, ultimately to liquidation.

The two-sided character of political power already marks political science off from natural science. It makes it impossible (even if it were desirable) to measure power relationships as one measures the behavior of external nature. The variations of the power relationships are numberless. One may classify and describe them, but one cannot measure them.

Political power is not comparable to the category of energy in physics. Nor is power the sole category of political science. Politics is not merely the art of getting something in a certain way regardless of the what and of the how. The trend to equate politics with power politics goes back to Machiavelli and appears to have become the predominant trait of American and, perhaps, of modern political science in general. Politics is viewed as a purely technical concern. "Values" (the term is used only provisionally) are then mere personal preferences; valid if they work, invalid if they fail. History is then quite meaningless. It is an indifferent repetition of the endless struggle of "in-groups" versus "out-groups." It is thus reduced

* From *The Political Science Quarterly*, Vol. LXV, No. 2 (June, 1950), pp. 161–80. By permission.

to mere chronology, a file of illustrative materials for so-called hypotheses or, at best, is governed by what Machiavelli called Fortuna, the luck of the participants in the struggle.

The theoretical basis of this approach to politics and political science is usually psychological, as Machiavelli has already developed it. Men are the same throughout history. They have certain stable traits, and all, or almost all, are equipped with "power drive," an uncontrollable and irrational impulse for power. From this assertion are then derived such facile half-true generalizations as the famous statement of Lord Acton: "Power tends to corrupt, absolute power corrupts absolutely."

This is not to imply that the psychology of power has no place in political science. Its significance is great, but not decisive. Its contribution is twofold. First, it leads to the realization that the optimistic theories of human nature are one-sided and thus false. Man, although endowed with reason, frequently knows not—or is not permitted to know—what his true interests are. This rediscovery of ancient truths is particularly the merit of the materialistic psychology of Freud. Secondly, psychological techniques permit us to describe in concrete and convincing terms the personality structures most capable of exerting or of suffering power. But psychology cannot go beyond concretization and description. It cannot supply a theory of political power. The action of each man is as much the result of the environment as it is the manifestation of a personality structure. Indeed, personality itself is historically conditioned. To the psychologist, the environment is a mere "stimulus" of the individual act. To the political scientist, it is one element in the total setting of political power.

The present orientation of psychology, besides, tends to make it simply a technique of rule, of maintaining and strengthening power relationships, an instrument of manipulation of the masses by the élite.

The rejection of the psychological approach involves in its positive aspect the view that politics (and thus history) is not simply a struggle of power groups for power, but an attempt to mold the world according to one's image, to impress one's view upon it. The historical process has a meaning. Provisionally, we may accept the traditional pre-positivistic formulation that politics is the struggle of ideas as well as of force. . . .

THE SIGNIFICANCE OF POLITICAL POWER

No society in recorded history has ever been able to dispense with political power. This is as true of liberalism as of absolutism, as true of laissez faire as of an interventionist state. No greater disservice has been rendered to political science than the statement that the liberal state was a "weak" state. It was precisely as strong as it needed to be in the circumstances. It acquired substantial colonial empires, waged wars, held down internal disorders, and stabilized itself over long periods of time.

But the methods applied by those who wield power and the scope of its application vary, of course. And it is precisely this problem that is of major significance for the political scientist. Formally, the methods range from the marginal case of killing to the marginal case of education. Three basic methods are at the disposal of the power group: persuasion, material benefits, violence. Violence is probably most effective as a short-range method, but little effective as the principal method of maintaining power over long periods since it compels the group (particularly under modern conditions) to intensify the methods of violence and to extend it to larger sections of the ruled. The most efficient (that is, cheapest form) is, of course, persuasion. Yet all three, persuasion, benefits, violence, are always present in all forms of government. And it is precisely the mixture of the three elements which constitutes another major problem for the political scientist. I shall attempt to clarify the meaning by the formulation of some sociological generalizations.

Sociological Generalization 1

The significance of persuasion grows with the growing complexity of society. It is, perhaps, legitimate to consider persuasion, as a rule, to be merely a form of violence, "violence committed against the soul" as the French historian of Catholic England under Henry VIII formulated it. Through persuasion, the rulers achieve a marked degree of habituation of the ruled so that their reactions assume an almost automatic character. The success of persuasion will, however, depend upon the scope and duration of the propaganda and the skills by which stereotypes are produced. There is little doubt that persuasion is a more efficient and cheaper exercise of political power than the employment of large police forces, armies and militias.

Sociological Generalization 2

The increasing complexity of society requires that the rulers increasingly utilize arcana, secret techniques of rule. The struggle for power is a real struggle aiming at the control of the state machine. In any struggle, however, tactical decisions can be effectively made only in secret. Secrecy, in turn, can be preserved only by small numbers. It is this very fact that necessitates the rise of oligarchies within mass movements. Max Weber and Robert Michels (and probably many others) have drawn attention to this phenomenon, and Max Weber, besides, correctly stressed the superiority of small over large numbers because of the significance of secrecy for any rule designed to be more than temporary. It is precisely for this reason that the rule of the few becomes particularly marked in those mass organizations which, more than other movements, are essentially devoted to democracy: the trade unions and the social democratic (labor) parties. The reason is obvious. The opponents of these movements are usually numerically few, but individually powerful, subjects who are thus able to keep their strategic and tactical decisions secret. The mass organization, faced with such opposition, must, in turn, resort to the construction of forms of rule which also permit secrecy. Aristocratic rule thus becomes a sociologically necessary implementation of democratic movements.[1] It is, therefore, no accident that the growth of oligarchies within mass movements was first studied in the example of the German Social Democratic party.

Lenin made a virtue of this necessity. His vanguard theory of leadership frankly replaces the traditional democratic conception of social democracy by an aristocratic one.

Sociological Generalization 3

The higher the state of technological development, the greater the concentration of political power. The legal conception of ownership is quite irrelevant for an analysis of this phenomenon. It matters not who owns a technical unit: an individual, a corporation, a state, any other organized society. The social organization of large technical units may, of course, be a coöperative one. In every social group which is based on struggle, however, the organization will, of necessity, be hierarchic. The larger the size, the more hierarchic it becomes. Growing hierarchic trends lead to concentration of power at the top. The relation between social and political power will be analyzed at a later place.

Sociological Generalization 4

With the growing complexity of society and its increasing industrialization, the significance of political power in the social process grows. Concentration of power (in the economy, in society, in culture) makes for more rigidity. A process of social petrifaction sets in and prevents the system from achieving a semiautomatic balance. The equilibrium, once disturbed, can be restored only through active intervention of the political power. Control of the state then becomes more precious than ever before.

Sociological Generalization 5

The same trend also produces a greater separation of political power from social power—a phenomenon that shall concern us later.

Some or all of these generalizations are subject to challenge. They are not meant to be exhaustive, but merely point the direction to a proper study of political power. That they produce uneasiness is to be expected. At first sight it seems difficult to reconcile them with the theory of democracy. If by democracy is understood that mixture of diverse elements, of Locke and Rousseau, St. Augustine and St. Thomas, which is usually called "democratic theory," a reconciliation of those realistic trends with the doctrine is, indeed, impossible. We are not now concerned

---

[1] That it may become, not its implementation, but its negation should be kept in mind.

with the problem of democratic theory. For the present it suffices to say that an adequate democratic theory will have to deal with these problems.

ROOTS OF POLITICAL POWER

Three questions have to be faced in the analysis of the roots of political power: the conceptual framework has to be established; the institutional setting to be clarified; and the historical process to be understood which leads to a change in institutions and different attitudes toward power and to a different political behavior. For the ancient historians, this was no problem. Political power derived squarely from economic power, particularly from the control of land. Changes in ownership, the emergence of new modes of production, and so on, created new sources of political power and thus made for conflicts. Modern historians dealing with this period of history have not hesitated to restate the problem in the same way as the ancients stated it.

As we shall directly show, modern capitalist economy has rendered this whole subject problematical. And, despite the fact that the issue is so crucial, analysis has been hindered by senseless taboos. The older insights have been lost or hidden and are rarely brought fully into the open. Thus, the classical approach has been restated in modern times by Marx's interpretation of history (that this did not originate with him—and is not "Marxist"—he himself admitted). Yet since it is fashionable to reject Marxism root and branch sight unseen so to speak—the student precludes himself from a clear understanding of the relationship between economic power and political power.

The approach is facilitated by the establishment of certain categories of relationships.

1. The ancient conception. Here—and this follows already from what has been said—although the source of political power is economic power, political power permeates all social activities and all spheres of life. The economic power position merely provides the motor of political power which then includes all power relationships.

2. The feudal conception. In the ideal-typical form, political power does not exist. It is merely a function of an economic power position: the ownership of land. From it flow judicial, military, religious, legislative and administrative powers.

3. The capitalist conception. It is only in this period that a real problem arises: the independence of political power and yet its interconnection with economic power. Political power (the theoretical construction has been perfected by Hobbes) is a separate activity, carried out in a separate institution: the state. The state has the monopoly of coercive power which it exercises in a separate institutional framework. At the same time, however, this separate institution is intrinsically connected with society in the service of which it operates. It is this conception of political power

that unites Locke and Hobbes, and distinguishes both from Rousseau. Both separate political power from social power; both connect them. Hobbes believes it necessary to maximize political power in order to serve society; Locke maintains that only by its minimizations can society be served. Both, however, admit of exceptions. In Hobbes's theory, political power will be destroyed if it fails to serve its social function (the social contract lapses); Locke, through the institution of the prerogative and federative power, maximizes political power if it is necessary for the good of the commonwealth. What Hobbes and Locke did not clearly state is that the two are not only functionally but genetically connected; that is, economic power is the root of political power. The first systematic analysis of this relationship stems from St. Simon's analysis of the French Revolution and then spreads rapidly into French and English historiography and sociology.

From this general view of Hobbes and Locke it follows that whatever freedom society, and particularly economic activity, is to have, it has for the sake of maintaining a stable political order. There is thus no "pure" economic power and no "pure" political activity. Economics is as much as instrument of politics as politics is a tool of economics. The mythological conception of the laissez-faire state ought finally to be destroyed.

If this general view is accepted, the translation of economic power into social power and thence into political power becomes the crucial concern of the political scientist.

The Political Party

The single most important instrument for the translation of social power into political power is the political party. The reason for the supreme position of the party lies in the very nature of democracy. The party permits the presentation of particular and, quite frequently, very egoistic interests as national interests. At the same time, however, it prevents the total domination of national interests by particular interests. The function of the political party in democracy is thus ambiguous. The democratic process compels each social group to strive for mass support. Each group, therefore, must present its egoistic interests as universal. Politics in a democracy, the struggle for political power, thus becomes far more ideological than in any previous period in history. What was obvious for the ancients, and clear to the feudal system, becomes hidden in the democratic process. But the valuable side of this process must equally not be forgotten. The very need to appeal to social groups larger than the immediate interest group compels adjustment of various interests. Politics becomes more democratic.[2]

Private Property

Social power, in turn, either is derived from private property or is against it. The legal meaning of private property comprises two radically

---

[2] It is this fact that Marxists usually overlook.

different conceptions: power over an external piece of nature (or an absolute right) and power over other men derived from power over nature. It is only the second meaning of private property with which the political scientist is concerned: with proprietorship in the means of production. This type of property gives power—power in the labor market, in the commodity market, and in the political market of the state.

The three power functions of property are usually (and particularly in Europe where political and social life is more petrified than in the United States) institutionalized in three types of organization: for the labor market, the employer's association; for the commodity market, the cartel; for the political market, the territorial form of the chambers of commerce and the functional form of the trade associations.

As against property, the trade unions (in Europe) attempt to organize the labor markets and the political markets by the collective power of organized labor, sometimes in one organization, sometimes in several. Consumers' and producers' co-operatives, however, affect only slightly the power of property in the commodity market.

Studies of these organizations and the devices by which their power is translated into political power are vital to the political scientist. Large numbers of individual studies of pressure groups exist, but a really sophisticated, comparative analysis is still lacking. The translation of these economic power positions differs from country to country and from historical situation to historical situation. The relative strength of the competing economic groups is far more important for the analysis of political power than the study of the political institutions proper. There are countries (like Germany and England) where the agents and managers of the economic organizations enter parliaments directly; there are others (like the United States) where the influence is more indirect. There are countries (like Germany and England) where trade unions are political as well as industrial bodies; there are others (like France and the United States in certain situations) where they apparently abstain from politics.

The devices and forms for the translation of economic power into political power thus vary considerably and yet patterns are discernible which ought to be more sharply defined on a comparative basis. A high degree of knowledge of problems of social stratification and economic organization is thus indispensable for the political scientist.

The Ascendance of Politics and of Bureaucracies

The classical relationship between economics and politics changes. It now appears as if political power has begun to emancipate itself from its economic roots and, indeed, tends to become a base for the acquisition of economic power. In general, bureaucratization is believed to be the manifestation of that trend which culminates in doctrines of managerial rule: private and public managers eliminating property owners and parliaments. The trend toward bureaucratization has unquestionably two roots: the transformation of parliamentary democracy into mass democracy; and the transition of a predominantly competitive economy into a predominantly organized economy. While these trends are known and progress under our very eyes, they do not necessarily involve an assumption of political power by bureaucracies. The growth of the scope and number of bureaucratic structures may merely indicate that the social groups which rule now need more and more bureaucracies in order to cope with the exercise of political power. But the equation of a larger number of bureaucrats with increase of their power is due to the inability (or unwillingness) to distinguish sharply three different problems involved in what is called "bureaucratization"; namely, bureaucratic behavior, bureaucratic structure, and bureaucratic power.

Bureaucratic behavior (roughly equated here with routine performance as against initiative or creative performance) is, of course, spreading. No sphere of activity is exempted from it. Whether it is beneficial or not shall not be discussed here. We should merely remember the tremendous extent to which our comforts depend on routine performances. Moreover, it is untrue that the decisions of the bureaucrats (public or private) are exclusively routine decisions. Many, indeed, are creative ones, not derived from precedent or standing rules, but highly discretionary and thus essentially lawmaking in character. Finally, bureaucratic organization, that is, hierarchies where commands are channeled from above to below and responsibility goes from below to above, is not confined to public life. The facts are obvious.

Though the growth of bureaucratic behavior, with the increase in the number of bureaucratic structures, is a continuous process, it does not thereby follow that power (private or public) has shifted to the bureaucracies. No abstract answer can be given; only empirical investigations can reveal whether shifts in power have taken place. Such investigations are, unfortunately, rare.

The Soviet Union presents a clear-cut marginal case where political power not only has made itself supreme but has become the fount of whatever economic power positions exist. Nazi Germany, on the other hand, exhibited a transitional case. It is undisputed that the Nazi party rose to power with the financial and political assistance of German big-business leaders who doubtless hoped to use the party for the promotion of their own interests. But the party, once having achieved power, emancipated itself from business control, and its political power became autonomous. The party then went further and attempted to create economic power positions for itself. Clearly the new political power was seeking to give itself an economic base. This, indeed, is the significance of the Goering combine, the expanding enterprises of the Labor Front and the S.S., and the acquisitions resulting from Aryanization and Germanization. The war, which made it inadvisable to carry out sweeping institutional changes, interrupted the process. But it is quite safe to assume that, had there been no war or had the Nazis been victorious, the Soviet pattern would have prevailed.

The reactions to the ascendant rôle of political power are, as a rule, hostile. Most notable is the attempt to ascribe this phenomenon to democracy. This is, of course, essentially correct. For, as we have indicated, the attitude of democracy toward political power is undoubtedly positive. Yet more is meant by that statement which by no means is a mere scientific one but has definite political undertones and overtones. It is implied that the growing political power will, by its inner dynamics, be abused and will ultimately lead to a totalitarian system. In this, modern criticism resumes the traditionalist critique not of political power but of democracy. Maistre and Bonald are resurrected. Proceeding from the shaky psychology of the essential evilness of man, they assert the inevitable transformation of democracy into mob rule, which, in conjunction with the modern trend of state interventionism, must culminate in totalitarianism. The remedy is some kind of aristocratic rule. A second reaction believes bureaucracy to be inimical to liberty and attempts to protect democracy by identifying it with individual liberty against the state.

Both reactions base themselves on what they call the tradition of Western civilization, the kernel of which is allegedly hostility to political power as expressed in constitutionalism. This is only a partial truth and, therefore, false. The tradition of Western civilization is more complex. . . . Certainly, one may say that Rousseauism is a more important element in the political tradition of democracy than the essentially self contradictory and arbitrary doctrines of Locke and of the natural law. That political power (whether democratic, aristocratic, or monarchic) can be abused is beyond doubt; but it is doubtful that abuses can be effectively checked by constitutionalism. The problem of modern democracy is much less the fencing of political power than its rational utilization and provision for effective mass participation in its exercise.

IDENTIFICATION OF POLITICAL POWER

In the Soviet Union, there is little doubt where political power resides. In Nazi Germany, after June 1934, it was equally clear that the monopolistic party concentrated all political power. In a liberal democracy (and in constitutional systems generally) the identification of political power is extremely difficult. Our contention that political power has its roots in economic power can merely provide a frame within which the analyses have to be made; for we deliberately stated: "Social power . . . is derived from private property or is against it." Since the distribution of the "for" and "against" varies, the empirical sociological analyses of this interrelationship are the crucial concern of the political scientist.

Constitutional law helps but little. The form of government may or may not truly express the distribution of power. The doctrine of separate powers may or may not express the fact that social forces are as balanced as are the political institutions. As a rule, they are not. Constitutional law merely supplies the frame for the exercise of political power but does not indicate its holder or its functions. All traditional legal conceptions are negative ones. They limit activities but do not shape them. It is this very character of law which grants to the citizen a minimum of protection. This applies specifically to the conception of external sovereignty, a term which we have so far avoided. It does not indicate the owner of sovereign power nor the use to which this power may or can be put; it merely delimits the power of one territorial unit from any other. The conception of property is fashioned in exactly the same way. It does not reveal the object of property nor its social function; it merely protects man's control of an external piece of nature. Constitutional law, secondly, indicates the form in which political power may be legitimately exercised. While the significance of both aspects of constitutional law may not be underestimated, empirical sociological studies of the locus of political power are indispensable.

There are, however, situations which may reveal in a flash, so to speak, where political power resides. There are emergency situations such as stages of siege, martial law, and so on. It is for this reason that Carl Schmitt, the famous Nazi constitutional lawyer, stated in his pre-Nazi period: "Sovereign is he who decides the emergency situation." While not accepting the implications of Schmitt's doctrine of sovereignty, it is clear that the study of such emergency situations will yield valuable hints as to where political power actually resides in "normal" periods. Such a marginal situation existed in Nazi Germany on June 30, 1934. Up to that date, it could be very doubtful whether political power rested with the party alone, or with a combination of party, army, business, and so on. The liquidation of the Röhm group, of the generals, and of others made it, however, abundantly clear that the party had succeeded in monopolizing political power.

Such studies have been neglected. They are carried out mostly in terms of constitutional law, but rarely in political-sociological categories.

POLITICAL POWER AND FREEDOM

I stressed initially that political power is neither comparable to the concept of energy in physics nor the sole conception of political science. Yet the original formulation, power vs. idea, is too ideological. If history were a conflict between power groups and ideas, ideas would be invariably defeated. Politics is certainly the conflict between power groups, and the conflicts may be resolved by victory and defeat or by conciliation, that is, compromise. But one group may, in its struggle for power, represent more than a particular interest; it may indeed represent the idea of freedom, the idea crucial to political theory. If, for example, you analyze immigration legislation and come to the conclusion that business groups pressured for its liberalization in order to secure cheaper labor power, you have indeed done part of your tasks as political scientists, but only part of it. Of equal importance is the analysis of the rôle of immigration legislation in the historical development of the United States. The task of political theory is thus the determination of the degree to which a power group transcends its particular interest and advocates (in Hegelian terms) universal interests.

This determination is by no means easy. In fact, the distinction between ideology and truth becomes increasingly difficult. Some of the difficulty lies in the ideological character of politics in a democracy (discussed above), but, in the last resort, it results from the tremendous weight of power on what is called public opinion. Every political system impresses the mores of the ruling group upon the population. The greater the tensions, the more stringent the impositions become. The individual then resorts to many forms of dissimulation; and, in certain periods of history, it is the liar who becomes the hero. The lie (in its many forms) becomes the protection of the individual against a universalized system of propaganda. It is for this reason that I am skeptical of the value of the various highly developed techniques of measuring attitudes, particularly attitudes which may challenge the basic foundation of a contemporary society. George Orwell, in his otherwise brilliant performance, *1984*, overlooks the fact that compulsion operates wherever political power exists . . .

Chapter III. Comparison of Total Systems

Introductory Note

WE HAVE already dealt with some basic concepts and theories—power, elites, structure-function, personality, and the like. These are all attempts to interpret a political system from a specific and significant point of view. But emphasis on one or another of the manifold characteristics of political behavior does not constitute a general theory—or a "model" of political behavior. In his *Study of Comparative Government* (1955), one of the editors of the present volume suggested four categories that could be useful for comparative study: the deliberative process and decision making; the power configuration—with particular reference to group conflict; the ideology—traditions, ideas, etc., about political authority; and the organization of political authority (that is, the structure of government). Professor Samuel H. Beer has proposed a somewhat similar scheme in his *Patterns of Government* (1958). A political system is characterized by a political culture—a "pattern" of ideas and traditions about the nature and purpose of authority; a "pattern" of power with primary emphasis on political power; an interest "configuration"—with groups being of major importance, and, finally, a "pattern" of policy—that is, the flow and character of decisions made by a political system. Many such definitions and theories have been propounded. Among the very recent works particularly worth consulting are: Daniel Lerner, *The Passing of Traditional Society* (1958); Seymour Lipset, *Political Man* (1960); Barrington Moore, Jr., *Terror and Progress—USSR* (1954), especially the last chapter. Relevant theories and concepts can be found in Emile Durkheim, *The Social Division of Labor in Society* (1933); Max Weber, *A Theory of Social and Economic Organization* (1947); Talcott Parsons, *The Social System* (1951); David Easton, *The Political System* (1953); and Harry Eckstein and David Apter, *Comparative Politics: A Reader* (1963), particularly the introductory and concluding chapters.

In recent writings two issues have received much attention. The first is the question of area studies. What are the common characteristics in terms of which one geographic entity can be singled out as an area? How is it to be studied? Some feel that an area specialist must completely immerse himself within the system he is studying and attune himself to its political culture. Others consider an area to be at most a convenient label. According to this view, area studies and area research centers serve primarily as research sites or laboratories for comparative study and data collection. Cutting across the controversy about the meaning of areas is the old problem of method. Those who emphasize analysis and data collection have developed impressive techniques of describing "national profiles" (as in the essay by Karl Deutsch reproduced below). A recent pioneering effort in this direction is Arthur S. Banks and Robert B. Textor, *A Cross-Polity Survey* (1964) in which polities are compared and scaled in relation to over 60 variables.

Readings

A. System Analysis

8. THE FUNCTIONAL PREREQUISITES OF A SOCIETY*
D. F. Aberle, A. K. Cohen, A. K. Davis, M. J. Levy, Jr., and F. X. Sutton

A COMPARATIVE social science requires a generalized system of concepts which will enable the scientific observer to compare and contrast large bodies of concretely different social phenomena in consistent terms. A promising step in furthering the development of systematic social analysis is a tentative formulation of the functional prerequisites of a society. Functional prerequisites refer broadly to the things that must get done in any society if it is to continue as a going concern, i.e., the generalized conditions necessary for the maintenance of the system concerned. The specific structural arrangements for meeting the functional prerequisites differ, of course, from one society to another and, in the course of time, change in any given society.[1]

This paper offers (1) a definition of a society on the most general level; (2) a statement of four generalized conditions, the complete realization

---

* Reprinted from "The Functional Prerequisites of a Society," in *Ethics*, Vol. LX, No. 2 (January, 1950), pp. 100–111, by D. F. Aberle, A. K. Cohen, A. K. Davis, M. J. Levy, Jr., and F. X. Sutton. By permission of the University of Chicago Press. Copyright 1950 by the University of Chicago Press.

[1] Thus all societies must allocate goods and services somehow. A particular society may change from one method, say business enterprise, to another, say a centrally planned economy, without the destruction of the society as a society but merely with a change in its concrete structures.

We seek to avoid the limitation inherent in defining the function of a social element solely in terms of its contributions to the survival or maintenance of the particular system of which it is a component. Structure analysis, which has recently undergone notable development, is prone to focus attention on static equilibriums. We consider *what* must be done in *any* society and hope our effort may be of use in considering the alterations that take place in *how* things are done in a society while that society persists.

of any one of which would terminate the existence of a society as defined; (3) a list of the functional prerequisites of a society. It seeks to justify the inclusion of each prerequisite by the demonstration that in its hypothetical absence the society could not survive, since at least one of the four conditions terminating a society would occur. There is no reason to believe that the list of functional prerequisites offered here is definitive. It is subject to revision with the growth of general theory and with experience in its application to concrete situations.

Any formulation of functional prerequisites depends for its categories on the theory of action employed. Our theory of action uses the concept of an actor whose orientation to his situation is threefold: cognitive, affective, and goal-directed. The actor is an abstraction from the total human being. Many of the qualities of the human being constitute part of the situation, the set of means and conditions, within which the actor operates.

Though the definition of the functional prerequisites of a society logically precedes the development of a scheme of structural prerequisites—which tell *how* the functional prerequisites may be met—in actuality the theoretic development of the two approaches is indivisible.

1. A DEFINITION OF A SOCIETY

The unit we have selected for analysis is a *society*, such as a nation, tribe, or band, and not any social system in general. The statement of the functional prerequisities of *any social system*—a monastery, a church, or a town, for example—would be on too general a level for the present discussion, though it may be an important task. Futhermore, once the functional prerequisites of a society are outlined, it becomes easier to state those of other types of social systems, often by dropping certain prerequisites from the list, since most of these other types of systems are parts of a society (or result from the interrelations of two or more societies) and depend for their perpetuation on the existence of a society.

A society is a group of human beings sharing a self-sufficient system of action which is capable of existing longer than the life-span of an individual, the group being recruited at least in part by the sexual reproduction of the members.

The identity and continuity of a society inhere in the persistence of the system of action in which the actors participate rather than in the particular set of actors themselves. There may be a complete turnover of individuals, but the society may survive. The individuals may survive, but the society may disintegrate. A system may persist in a situation while its component relationships change. Its persistence inheres in the fact that it maintains its separation from the situation, i.e., it inheres in the *integrity* of the organism, not in its fixity or unalterable character.

A system of action always exists in a situation. In the case of a society this situation includes the nonhuman environment and, in almost every case, it includes other societies. The viability of a social system and its recognition as a society within the terms of this definition depend upon the particular set of conditions in which it function. Study of the system itself cannot alone determine whether the system meets the criteria of the definition. What is crucial is that a social system contain successful arrangements for meeting the chronic and recurrent features of its milieu.[2]

"Longer than the life-span of an individual" reminds us that a society must be able to replace its members with effectively socialized individuals from the maturing generation. The requirement of sexual reproduction excludes from consideration such groups (monasteries, cliques) as depend *solely* on types of recruitment other than sexual. But a society may be recruited in part by nonsexual means, e.g., by immigration and conquest.

The heart of the definition is "self-sufficient system of action."[3] Its full meaning will be developed in the exposition of the functional prerequisites and in the next paragraphs.

A number of questions are bound to arise in the reader's mind as to the application of the definition to particular social systems and as to the basis on which the decision is to be made as to whether such systems fall within the definition of a society. We emphasize that the definition is an ideal type. *A concrete aggregate is a society in so far as it approaches the generalized model.* The following examples, though not definitive, suggest the way in which the definition may be applied.

A society is not a culture. Culture is socially transmitted behavior conceived as an abstraction from concrete social groups. Two or more *societies* may have the same *culture* or similar cultures. Though the Greek city-states shared similar culture patterns, each possessed a self-sufficient structure of action and is hence to be considered a separate society. One society may be composed of groups with some marked differences in culture. The union of agricultural, industrial, and pastoral groups in a single structure of action is an example. We discuss below the limits as to the amount of diversity possible and the conditions under which such diversity may occur without the disintegration of the society.

To some degree two different societies may possess overlapping personnel and even structural elements without losing their identity as

---

[2] This point receives further treatment below. A social system need not be copperplated to meet the definition of a society. Natural catastrophe may terminate a concrete society. Such an event does not represent a failure to meet the functional prerequisites but is rather to be considered the result of a change in the nonhuman environment beyond the limits assumed here as the setting of a society. Many concrete societies have been assimilated by the expansion of groups with which these societies had had little or no previous contact. This, too, represents an alteration in the situation of the society beyond the limits within which it had been meeting its functional prerequisites.

[3] "System" and "structure" will be used interchangeably throughout the remainder of this treatment.

distinct societies. The fact that Englishmen live in the United States as diplomats and traders and function, in effect, as actors in both systems, does not destroy the identity or the self-sufficiency of the United States or of Great Britain as action-systems.

To be considered a society, a group need not be self-sufficient with respect to resources. It is the structure of action that must be self-sufficient. Thus, the United States is a society. While imports and exports are necessary to its maintenance, arrangements for foreign trade are part of its self-sufficient structure of action. It is this, and not the group of individuals, that is self-sufficient. Hence Chinese-American trade does not make China and America parts of a larger society. Trade relationships are limited and relatively unstable. Their existence does not involve the two aggregates in the same self-sufficient structure of action. For parallel reasons the British Empire and the United Nations are not societies but associations.

A series of difficult decisions about the relationships of various social systems can be resolved by the introduction of a point of crucial differentiation. When a social aggregate is not capable of providing a structure, structures, or parts of structures which can meet the functional prerequisites in question, it is not to be considered a society. Thus, occupied Japan does not constitute part of American society, since in the absence of American forces Japan would seem to be able to continue control and the legitimized use of force. A group of American Indians governed by the United States for a sufficient length of time may lack the crucial structures necessary for continued existence as an independent entity and therefore be considered part of American society, in spite of an important cultural variation. An American town does not constitute a society because of its thorough participation in American political, economic, value, and other structures. The early Mormon settlement in Utah, however, did constitute a society. . . .

We assume that social change characterizes all societies. Change may be gradual and peaceful or characterized by severe conflicts. In either case there may be profound structural changes. Societies may split or merge peacefully or violently. In all these instances a society of some sort exists. Whether it is considered the same society or a new one depends on the relation between the level of the structural change and the level of analysis. The changes in question may be analyzed in terms of this frame of reference. We may examine the way in which a society meets it's functional prerequisites, the points of tension (those functional prerequisites least effectively met), and the responses to those strains. We do not assume the perfect integration of any society.

We have omitted from our definition any statements regarding territoriality. Action, it has been pointed out, always takes place in a situation, one feature of which is a spatial dimension. The existence of two societies intermingled during a civil war, or any such example, does not negate considerations of spatiality, which are always an essential background feature of any society.

II. FOUR CONDITIONS TERMINATING THE EXISTENCE OF A SOCIETY

The realization of any of the following conditions terminates the existence of a society—the existence of the structure of action, though not necessarily of the members.

A. *The biological extinction or dispersion of the members.*—To arrive at this condition, a society need not lose all its members but need only suffer such losses as to make inoperative its structure of action. Analyses of such conditions may be made at this level in terms of fertility, morbidity, and migration rates, without reference to the highly complex factors underlying them.

B. *Apathy of the members.*—Apathy means the cessation of individual motivation. This condition affects some individuals to some extent in all societies and large numbers in a few societies. That migrant Polynesian laborers have died of nostalgia is well known. It is claimed that whole societies in Melanesia have withered away from ennui. In these cases, physical extinction is merely an extreme consequence of the cessation of motivation.

C. *The war of all against all.*—This condition appears if the members of an aggregate pursue their ends by means selected only on the basis of instrumental efficiency. Though the choice of means on this basis may result at times in co-operative combinations, these combinations are by definition subject to immediate dissolution if, for example, exploitation or annihilation becomes more advantageous for any one member. Hence a state of indeterminate flux, rather than a system of action, exists. The use of force is efficient only for limited purposes. Force is a sanction, but never the essence, of a society. A society based solely on force is a contradiction in terms that raises the classical question, *Quis custodiet ipsos custodes?*

D. *The absorption of the society into another society.*—This entails the partial loss of identity and self-sufficiency of the total action-system but not necessarily the extinction of the members.

The more fully these four conditions are realized, the more indeterminate is the structure of action, a condition also induced when the rate of social change is very rapid. Hence we may hypothesize that fluctuations in the vital indices, in apathy, and in coercion are to some extent functions of the rate of social change. In fact, revolutions (extreme social change) are characterized by increases in mortality, morbidity, apathy, force, and fraud. The faster the change, the greater the stress, two manifestations of which are force and/or apathy. Viewing coercion as a response to stress should help us to put the discussion of the role of force in social systems on a nonideological basis.

III. THE FUNCTIONAL PREREQUISITES OF A SOCIETY

The performance of a given function is prerequisite to a society if in its absence one or more of the four conditions dissolving a society results. This can be demonstrated clearly in some cases. Less clearly, but still convincingly, the nonfulfilment of certain other functions can be shown at least to foster one or more of the conditions negating a society. No specific action-pattern is prerequisite to the existence of our ideal-typical society. We are concerned with *what* must get done in a society, not with *how* it is done.

A. *Provision for adequate relationship to the environment and for sexual recruitment.*—This includes modes of adapting to, manipulating, and altering the environment in such a way as (*a*) to maintain a sufficient number and kind of members of the society at an adequate level of functioning; (*b*) to deal with the existence of other societies in a manner which permits the persistence of the system of action; and (*c*) to pattern heterosexual relationships to insure opportunities and motivation for a sufficient rate of reproduction. In the absence of these provisions, the group will suffer biological extinction through the death of the members or failure to reproduce or it will suffer absorption into another social system. . . .

A society must adapt to, manipulate, and alter its situation. Among the features thus dealt with may be chronically threatening aspects of the situation. In a dry region a society may employ techniques of food storage, irrigation, or nomadic migration. If neighboring societies are hostile, an army may be essential and the society thus dependent on the deliberate hazarding of some of its members' lives. The existence of Murngin society depends partly on the destruction of a portion of its adult males by chronic warfare. Resistance is only one possible response to hostile neighbors. Certain "men-o-bush" tribes of New Guinea make but little resistance to raids. These raids, however, do not threaten to extinguish the society. Only if they do can such a passive adaptation be said to be inadequate to meet the functional prerequisite.

The inclusion of such apparently disparate features as maintenance of the organism, defense, and provision for sexual reproduction under one heading is by no means arbitrary. From the point of view of a social system, the nonhuman environment, the biological nature of man, and the existence of other societies are all part of the situation of action. To none of these aspects of the situation is passive adaptation the only mode of adequate relationship. Thus the biological basis of society itself is molded. Individuals have constitutional differences, but the latter are variously evaluated and dealt with by societies. The biological birth-growth-death cycle is a dynamic process in its own right, yet societies both adapt to it and modify it in a number of ways. In noting the necessity for a society to meet certain biological prerequisites, we remark also upon the great plasticity of individuals. It is scarcely necessary to remark that, concretely, societies alter their modes of relationship to their situations; that technological changes occur, sometimes through loss, more often by invention and diffusion.

B. *Role differentiation and role assignment.*—This signifies the systematic and stable division of activities. We will treat under other headings role-learning and the sanctions perpetuating the role structure.

In any society there are activities which must be regularly performed if the society is to persist. If they are to be done dependably, these extensive and varied activities must be broken down and assigned to capable individuals trained and motivated to carry them out. Otherwise everyone would be doing everything or nothing—a state of indeterminacy which is the antithesis of a society and which precludes getting essential activities carried out. The universal problems of scarcity and order are insoluble without legitimized allocation of property rights and authority, and these, in turn, are unattainable without reasonably integrated role-differentiation. While a given individual is often the locus of several roles, he can never combine all the roles of his society in himself. Age and sex differences impose a degree of role-differentiation everywhere; in some societies class and occupation are additional bases of differentiation. Arguments for specialization based on differential ability, while of great force in complex societies, have no clear bearing on societies so simple that any technique can be learned by any individual who is not feeble-minded. Whatever the society, activities necessary to its survival must be worked out in predictable, determinate ways, or else apathy or the war of each against all must prevail. Without reliable provision for child-rearing activities and without their assignment to specific persons or groups, the society invites extinction, since children at birth are helpless. The absence of role-differentiation and of role-assignment thus makes for three of the conditions negating a society. A system of role-differentiation alone is useless without a system of selection for assigning individuals to those roles.

Mention should be made of one particular type of role-differentiation that is a requirement for any society, namely, stratification. Stratification is that particular type of role-differentiation which discriminates between higher and lower standings in terms of one or more criteria. Given the universality of scarcity, some system of differential allocation of the scarce values of a society is essential. These values may consist of such desiderata as wealth, power, magic, women and ceremonial precedence. That conflict over scarce values may destroy a society will be shown in another connection below. Our present point is that the rank order must be legitimized and accepted by most of the members—at least by the important ones—of a society if stability is to be attained. Allocation of ranks may be on the basis of ascribed or achieved qualities or both.

Role-differentiation implies organization. Precedence in specialized activities must be correlated to some extent with rank order. Coercive sanctions and initiative must be vested in specified status-positions. Some individuals will thus receive more than others. These privileges are usually made acceptable to the rank and file by joining to the greater rights of the elite a larger share of responsibilities. The Brahmins stand closer to other-worldly nonexistence than do the members of any other Hindu caste, but they also have to observe the most elaborate ritual obligations. The Trobriand chief enjoys a multiple share of wealth and wives; he must also finance community enterprises and exhibit at all times more generosity than anyone else. . . .

C. *Communciation.*—Evidence from deaf-mutes, "wolf children," and bilinguals shows that speech, the basic form of communication, is learned and that only rudimentary communication is possible in the absence of shared, learned linguistic symbols. Without learned symbolic communication only a few highly general emotional states—e.g., anger, sexual passion—in one individual can evoke an appropriate response in another; only a few skills may be conveyed by imitation.

No society, however simple, can exist without shared, learned symbolic modes of communication, because without them it cannot maintain the common-value structure or the protective sanctions which hold back the war of each against all. Communication is indispensable if socialization and role-differentiation are to function effectively. That each functional prerequisite thus depends in part on other functional prerequisities does not vitiate our argument so long as the functional prerequisites are logically separable. But they need not be empirically distinct activities, since any action-system may contribute to several functional prerequisites.

In a simple society, where relationships are exclusively face-to-face, shared speech forms suffice. In complex societies, other than oral communication is necessary for the system as a whole, though not for subsystems. Thus, in China, writing facilitates the survival of the society despite local dialect differences too great to permit oral communication without bilingual intermediaries. Clearly, no modern society could survive without writing. Thus, communication requires language, a medium of communication, and channels.

D. *Shared cognitive orientations.*—In any society the members must share a body of cognitive orientations which (*a*) make possible adaptation to and manipulation of the situation; (*b*) make stable, meaningful, and predictable the social situations in which they are engaged; and (*c*) account for those significant aspects of the situation over which they do not have adequate prediction and control in such a way as to sustain and not to destroy motivation.

If the first criterion were not met, biological existence would be impossible. If the second were not, interpersonal and intergroup relations could not exist. Private definitions of social situations or the absence of such definitions could lead only to mutually incompatible actions and the war of each against all. In no society are all conditions predictable and controllable; so the frustration of expectations is a chronic feature of social life. Without a reasonably determinate explanation of such areas of existence, the individual would exist in an unstructured world and could not avoid psychological disorganization. In the absence of shared orientations, serious clashes would ensue.

Cognitive orientations must be shared, but only in so far as the actors are involved in the same situation of action. A housewife may not distinguish a colonel from a corporal; a soldier may not appreciate that he is using his hostess' "wedding silver." They must agree, however, that a foot is "so long" and that that gentleman is a "policeman." But though a farmer may pray for rain and an aviator rub a rabbit's foot for good weather with no resultant difficulties between them, both must define the American political system in a roughly similar fashion if they are to vote.

E. *A shared, articulated set of goals.—* To phrase this prerequisite in terms of ultimate ends of action produces a vague and not very useful formulation. . . . It is equally difficult to operate in terms of motivations, since these are exceedingly diverse and are intricately articulated with the social structure. Our statement in terms of goals seeks a middle ground and is couched in the terms most suitable for considering a system of action.

Because there is role-differentiation in every society, we must consider a set of goals rather than a common goal. The facts of scarcity and of differential individual endowment, features of all societies, also make it necessary to speak of a set of goals. It is the range of goals, however narrow, that provides alternatives for individuals and thus reduces one serious source of conflict in societies. (The possibility of universally sought goals in a society is not ruled out.)

The goals must be sufficiently articulated to insure the performance of socially necessary activities. They must not include too much action which threatens the existence of a society. A cult of sexual abstinence, if universalized, would terminate the society. The goals must be shared to some degree, though this will vary with the differentiation of the society. Finally, the goals of one individual must be meaningful to another in so far as they share a common structure of action.

There will be both empirical and nonempirical goals. Some goals may be mutually incompatible without being destructive to the society. Without an articulated set of goals the society would invite extinction, apathy, or the war of all against all.

F. *The normative regulation of means.—*This functional prerequisite is the prescription of means for attaining the socially formulated goals of a society and its subsystems. It complements but does not overlap the functional prerequisite of "effective control of disruptive behavior." The "normative regulation of means" defines positively the means (mostly noncoercive) to the society's goals.

That these means must be stated clearly for the sake of order and the effective functioning of the society follows from (*a*) the nature of other functional prerequisites and (*b*) the *anomie* that must result from the lack of recognized legitimized means. First, role-differentiation specifies *who* is to act, while the common articulated set of goals defines *what* is to be done. The normative regulation of means tells *how* those goals may be won. Second, the absence of normative regulation of means invites apathy or the war of each against all. Without socially prescribed means, a goal must be either devalued or forcibly seized. As the loss of a bolt may cause a great machine to beat itself to pieces, so the absence of normatively regulated means operates cumulatively to destroy the social structure.

Especially in ritual and initiatory activities must procedures be normatively specified. The content of prescriptions may vary greatly among societies; what is indispensable is simply that socially accepted directives for ceremonial and symbolic action exist. This point emphasizes the necessity for the category of normative regulation of means, in addition to the effective control of disruptive behavior. Moreover, there are often alternative, noncoercive ways of realizing goals, and they must be differentially evaluated for the sake of order, or else some must be ruled out.

G. *The regulation of affective expression.*—In any society the affective states of the members must be mutually communicable and comprehensible. Furthermore, not every affect can be expressed in every situation. Some must be suppressed or repressed. Lastly, there are affects which must be produced in the members if the social structure is to survive. All these aspects are included in the regulation of affective expression.

In the absence of the first of these conditions, stability of expectations between individuals is destroyed, and apathetic or destructive reactions will occur. This is true alike of states of anger and of affection, of love, lust and the like. Without comprehensibility and communicability, mutually inappropriate responses in affectively charged situations can only result in the destruction of the relationship. In a love affair, if one member's expression of affection has the intended meaning of a flirtation, while to the other it signifies willingness to consummate the affair, the relationship is headed for a crisis. The same state of affairs with respect to the expression of affect in an entire society is clearly incompatible with the continuation of that society. This is not a matter of a lack of a shared cognitive frame of reference; rather, the conflicts are potentially explosive because of the emotional involvement. The cues that make affective expression comprehensible range from obvious and subtle linguistic behavior to posture, facial expression, gesture, and tone of voice. Many of these cues are not consciously recognized by the actors themselves.

In the face of regulated competitive, co-operative, and authority relationships, some of which are entailed in any conceivable system of role-allocation, taken together with disturbances of expectation and scarcity situations, no society can survive if it permits complete latitude of affective expression in all situations. The ungoverned expression of lust and rage leads to the disruption of relationships and ultimately to the war of all against all.

Finally, a society must not only structure the way in which affects are expressed and restrict certain forms of emotional expression; it must actively foster some affects. Unless we adopt the view that all relationships in all societies can be rational and contractual in character, we must take the position that some relationships depend on regulated affects for their perpetuation. In the absence of the production of appropriate affects, the family, for example, would not survive. The question of what affects must regularly be produced in any society is closely related to the way other functional prerequisites are fulfilled. In American society the urban middle-class conjugal family depends heavily on the establishment of strong affective ties between spouses. The American family system in meeting the demands of a highly mobile society is deprived of certain bases of stability which other family systems possess, and the mutual affection of spouses becomes of correspondingly greater importance.

H. *Socialization.*—A problem is posed for any society by the fact that its structure of action must be learned by new members. To each individual must be transmitted so much of the modes of dealing with the total situation—the modes of communication, the shared cognitive frame of reference, goal-system, attitudes involved in the regulation of means, modes of expression, and the like—as will render him capable of adequate performance in his several roles throughout life, both as respects skills and as respects attitudes. Socialization thus is a different concept from the maintenance of the child in a state of biological well-being.

Furthermore, socialization includes both the development of new adult members from infants and the induction of an individual of any age into any role of the society or its subsystems where new learning is required.

A society cannot persist unless it perpetuates a self-sufficient system of action—whether in changed or traditional form—through the socialization of new members, drawn, in part, from the maturing generation. Whatever the defects of any particular mode of socialization, a universal failure of socialization means the extinction of the society, through a combination of all four of the terminating conditions mentioned previously.

One individual cannot become equally familiar with all aspects of his society; indeed, he may remain completely ignorant of some. But he must acquire a working knowledge of the behavior and attitudes relevant to his various roles and identify to some degree with such values as are shared by the whole society or segments thereof wherever his behavior articulates with that of other members of the society. A Brahmin and an Untouchable learn some skills and attitudes unknown to each other. Both, however, must learn that the Hindu world is made up of castes and that this is the way things should be.

I. *The effective control of disruptive forms of behavior.*—Prominent among disruptive modes of behavior are force and fraud. The extent to which such behavior will occur is dependent on the way that various other functional prerequisites are met: role-allocation, goal-system, regulation of means and of expression, and socialization being the more obvious cases in point. All these functional prerequisites, it is clear from the preceding argument, tend to prevent the occurrence of disruptive behavior. In addition to, and separate from, these is the effective control of such behavior when it occurs. To understand why this functional prerequisite is necessary, we must ask: Why would not a perfectly integrated society exist in its absence?

The answer lies in three conditions inherent in any society: scarcity of means, frustrations of expectations, and imperfections of socialization. That many of the desiderata of life are ultimately scarce needs no emphasis. Since sexual objects are differentially evaluated by a society, those few at the top of the scale tend to be sought by a large number of the opposite sex. Wealth, however defined, is basically scarce for the mass of individuals everywhere. Force and fraud are often the most efficient methods of acquiring scarce values. Indeed, only scarce values can be objects of rationally directed coercive effort. To argue that society without coercion and deceit can exist, one must first demonstrate the absence of scarcity. Frustration of expectations is inevitable for many individuals in any society so long as there are such universal realities as unexpected consequences of purposive behavior, scarcity, and uncertainty.

Imperfect socialization results, among other things, in evasions of the normatively prescribed paths of action. Together with frustrations of expectations, it results in explosive outbursts of anger and violence. Thus, both rationally directed exercise of force and fraud and less rational outbursts of emotion continually press to disrupt stable social relationships. If resort to these disruptive behaviors is restricted only by opportunity, the war of all against all will ultimately result. (Some disruptive action may also tend in the direction of an apathetic breakdown. This does not alter the nature of the argument.)

The system of goals tells *what* must be done; the normative regulation of means prescribes *how*. It also includes pre- and proscriptions regarding the use of force and fraud. In addition, however, the society must have techniques for handling those who, for reasons outlined, use these disruptive means or are subject to these outbreaks. The form of control and the degree of efficiency may vary greatly. What type of action is directly destructive of a society depends on the nature of the society: patricide in a society founded on patriarchal clans, violation of property rights in a property-emphasizing society, and so on. Conversely, some societies can tolerate forms of these behaviors that others cannot. Chuckchee social structure, for example, withstands a high homicide rate.

IV. CONCLUSION

This treatment makes no claim to be final. Our list of functional prerequisites can be elaborated and altered by the reader by making explicit the elements we have left implicit. At present, a statement of the functional prerequisites of a society is primarily useful as a contribution to general social theory rather than as a tool for analyzing individual societies. It should be especially useful for constructing a general system of structural prerequisites that will tell us how the functional prerequisites may be met, and this in turn may lead to a more comprehensive and precise comparative sociology.

Even at the present stage, however, the authors have found this approach useful as a point of reference for analyses of societies and their subsystems, and for suggesting inadequacies in the analysis of given societies and in the empirical data available. It directs attention to features of social systems, relationships among institutional structures, and implications for social change which might otherwise be overlooked.

9. THE ANALYSIS OF POLITICAL SYSTEMS*
David Easton

1. SOME ATTRIBUTES OF POLITICAL SYSTEMS

IN AN EARLIER work I have argued for the need to develop general, empirically oriented theory as the most economical way in the long run to understand political life. Here I propose to indicate a point of view that, at the least, might serve as a springboard for discussion of alternative approaches and, at most, as a small step in the direction of a general political theory. I wish to stress that what I have to say is a mere orientation to the problem of theory; outside of economics and perhaps psychology, it would be presumptuous to call very much in social science "theory," in the strict sense of the term.

Furthermore, I shall offer only a Gestalt of my point of view, so that it will be possible to evaluate, in the light of the whole, those parts that I

* From "An Approach to the Analysis of Political Systems," *World Politics*, Vol. 9, No. 3 (April, 1957), pp. 383–400. By permission.

do stress. In doing this, I know I run the definite risk that the meaning and implications of this point of view may be only superficially communicated; but it is a risk I shall have to undertake since I do not know how to avoid it sensibly.

The study of politics is concerned with understanding how authoritative decisions are made and executed for a society. We can try to understand political life by viewing each of its aspects piecemeal. We can examine the operation of such institutions as political parties, interest groups, government, and voting; we can study the nature and consequences of such political practices as manipulation, propaganda, and violence; we can seek to reveal the structure within which these practices occur. By combining the results we can obtain a rough picture of what happens in any self-contained political unit.

In combining these results, however, there is already implicit the notion that each part of the larger political canvas does not stand alone but is related to each other part; or, to put it positively, that the operation of no one part can be fully understood without reference to the way in which the whole itself operates. I have suggested in my book, *The Political System*,[1] that it is valuable to adopt this implicit assumption as an articulate premise for research and to view political life as a system of interrelated activities. These activities derive their relatedness or systemic ties from the fact that they all more or less influence the way in which authoritative decisions are formulated and executed for a society.

Once we begin to speak of political life as a system of activity, certain consequences follow for the way in which we can undertake to analyze the working of a system. The very idea of a system suggests that we can separate political life from the rest of social activity, at least for analytical purposes, and examine it as though for the moment it were a self-contained entity surrounded by, but clearly distinguishable from, the environment or setting in which it operates. In much the same way, astronomers consider the solar system a complex of events isolated for certain purposes from the rest of the universe.

Furthermore, if we hold the system of political actions as a unit before our mind's eye, as it were, we can see that what keeps the system going are inputs of various kinds. These inputs are converted by the processes of the system into outputs and these, in turn, have consequences both for the system and for the environment in which the system exists. The formula here is very simple but, as I hope to show, also very illuminating: inputs—political system or processes—outputs. These relationships are shown diagrammatically in Figure 1. This diagram represents a very primitive "model"—to dignify it with a fashionable name—for approaching the study of political life.

Political systems have certain properties because they are systems. To

----
[1] New York, 1953.

present an over-all view of the whole approach, let me identify the major attributes, say a little about each, and then treat one of these properties at somewhat greater length, even though still inadequately.

(1) Properties of identification. To distinguish a political system from other social systems, we must be able to identify it by describing its fundamental units and establishing the boundaries that demarcate it from units outside the system.

(a) Units of a political system. The units are the elements of which we say a system is composed. In the case of a political system, they are political actions. Normally it is useful to look at these as they structure themselves in political roles and political groups.

(b) Boundaries. Some of the most significant questions with regard to the operation of political systems can be answered only if we bear in mind the obvious fact that a system does not exist in a vacuum. It is always immersed in a specific setting or environment. The way in which a system works will be in part a function of its response to the total social, biological, and physical environment.

The special problem with which we are confronted is how to distinguish systematically between a political system and its setting. Does it even make sense to say that a political system has a boundary dividing it from its setting? If so, how are we to identify the line of demarcation?

Without pausing to argue the matter, I would suggest that it is useful to conceive of a political system as having a boundary in the same sense as a physical system. The boundary of a political system is defined by all those actions more or less directly related to the making of binding decisions for a society; every social action that does not partake of this characteristic will be excluded from the system and thereby will automatically be viewed as an external variable in the environment.

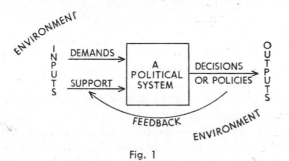

Fig. 1

(2) Inputs and outputs. Presumably, if we select political systems for special study, we do so because we believe that they have characteristically important consequences for society, namely, authoritative decisions. These consequences I shall call the outputs. If we judged that political systems did not have important outputs for society, we would probably not be interested in them.

Unless a system is approaching a state of entropy—and we can assume that this is not true of most political systems—it must have continuing inputs to keep it going. Without inputs the system can do no work; without outputs we cannot identify the work done by the system. The specific research tasks in this connection would be to identify the inputs and the forces that shape and change them, to trace the processes through which they are transformed into outputs, to describe the general conditions under which such processes can be maintained, and to establish the relationship between outputs and succeeding inputs of the system.

From this point of view, much light can be shed on the working of a political system if we take into account the fact that much of what happens within a system has its birth in the efforts of the members of the system to cope with the changing environment. We can appreciate this point if we consider a familiar biological system such as the human organism. It is subject to constant stress from its surroundings to which it must adapt in one way or another if it is not to be completely destroyed. In part, of course, the way in which the body works represents responses to needs that are generated by the very organization of its anatomy and functions; but in large part, in order to understand both the structure and the working of the body, we must also be very sensitive to the inputs from the environment.

In the same way, the behavior of every political system is to some degree imposed upon it by the kind of system it is, that is, by its own structure and internal needs. But its behavior also reflects the strains occasioned by the specific setting within which the system operates. It may be argued that most of the significant changes within a political system have their origin in shifts among the external variables. Since I shall be devoting the bulk of this article to examining some of the problems related to the exchange between political systems and their environments, I shall move on to a rapid description of other properties of political systems.

(3) Differentiation within a system. As we shall see in a moment, from the environment come both energy to activate a system and information with regard to which the system uses this energy. In this way a system is able to do work. It has some sort of output that is different from the input that enters from the environment. We can take it as a useful hypothesis that if a political system is to perform some work for anything but a limited interval of time, a minimal amount of differentiation in its structure must occur. In fact, empirically it is impossible to find a significant political system in which the same units all perform the same activities at the same time. The members of a system engage in at least some minimal division of labor that provides a structure within which action takes place.

(4) Integration of a system. This fact of differentiation opens up a major area of inquiry with regard to political systems. Structural differen-

tiation sets in motion forces that are potentially disintegrative in their results for the system. If two or more units are performing different kinds of activity at the same time, how are these activities to be brought into the minimal degree of articulation necessary if the members of the system are not to end up in utter disorganization with regard to the production of the outputs of interest to us? We can hypothesize that if a structured system is to maintain itself, it must provide mechanisms whereby its members are integrated or induced to cooperate in some minimal degree so that they make authoritative decisions.

II. INPUTS: DEMANDS

Now that I have mentioned some major attributes of political systems that I suggest require special attention if we are to develop a generalized approach, I want to consider in greater detail the way in which an examination of inputs and outputs will shed some light on the working of these systems.

Among inputs of a political system there are two basic kinds: demands and support. These inputs give a political system its dynamic character. They furnish it both with the raw material or information that the system is called upon to process and with the energy to keep it going.

The reason why a political system emerges in a society at all—that is, why men engage in political activity—is that demands are being made by persons or groups in the society that cannot all be fully satisfied. In all societies one fact dominates political life: scarcity prevails with regard to most of the valued things. Some of the claims for these relatively scarce things never find their way into the political system but are satisfied through the private negotiations of or settlements by the persons involved. Demands for prestige may find satisfaction through the status relations of society; claims for wealth are met in part through the economic system; aspirations for power to find expression in educational, fraternal, labor, and similar private organizations. Only where wants require some special organized effort on the part of society to settle them authoritatively may we say that they have become inputs of the political system.

Systematic research would require us to address ourselves to several key questions with regard to these demand.

(1) How do demands arise and assume their particular character in a society? In answer to this question, we can point out that demands have their birth in two sectors of experience: either in the environment of a system or within the system itself. We shall call these the external and internal demands, respectively.

Let us look at the external demands first. I find it useful to see the environment not as an undifferentiated mass of events but rather as systems clearly distinguishable from one another and from the political system. In the environment we have such systems as the ecology, economy, culture, personality, social structure, and demography. Each of these constitutes a major set of variables in the setting that helps to shape the kind of demands entering a political system. For purposes of illustrating what I mean, I shall say a few words about culture.

The members of every society act within the framework of an ongoing culture that shapes their general goals, specific objectives, and the procedures that the members feel ought to be used. Every culture derives part of its unique quality from the fact that it emphasizes one or more special aspects of behavior and this strategic emphasis serves to differentiate it from other cultures with respect to the demands that it generates. As far as the mass of the people is concerned, some cultures, such as our own, are weighted heavily on the side of economic wants, success, privacy, leisure activity, and rational efficiency. Others, such as that of the Fox Indians, strive toward the maintenance of harmony, even if in the process the goals of efficiency and rationality may be sacrificed. Still others, such as the Kachins of highland Burma, stress the pursuit of power and prestige. The culture embodies the standards of value in a society and thereby marks out areas of potential conflict, if the valued things are in short supply relative to demand. The typical demands that will find their way into the political process will concern the matters in conflict that are labeled important by the culture. For this reason we cannot hope to understand the nature of the demands presenting themselves for political settlement unless we are ready to explore systematically and intensively their connection with the culture. And what I have said about culture applies, with suitable modifications, to other parts of the setting of a political system.

But not all demands originate or have their major locus in the environment. Important types stem from situations occurring within a political system itself. Typically, in every on-going system, demands may emerge for alterations in the political relationships of the members themselves, as the result of dissatisfaction stemming from these relationships. For example, in a political system based upon representation, in which equal representation is an important political norm, demands may arise for equalizing representation between urban and rural voting districts. Similarly, demands for changes in the process of recruitment of formal political leaders, for modifications of the way in which constitutions are amended, and the like may all be internally inspired demands.

I find it useful and necessary to distinguish these from external demands because they are, strictly speaking, not inputs of the system but something that we can call "withinputs," if we can tolerate a cumbersome neologism, and because their consequences for the character of a political system are more direct than in the case of external demands. Furthermore, if we were not aware of this difference in classes of demands, we might search in vain for an explanation of the emergence of a given set of internal demands if we turned only to the environment.

(2) How are demands transformed into issues? What determines

whether a demand becomes a matter for serious political discussion or remains something to be resolved privately among the members of society? The occurrence of a demand, whether internal or external, does not thereby automatically convert it into a political *issue*. Many demands die at birth or linger on with the support of an insignificant fraction of the society and are never raised to the level of possible political decision. Others become issues, an issue being a demand that the members of a political system are prepared to deal with as a significant item for discussion through the recognized channels in the system.

The distinction between demands and issues raises a number of questions about which we need data if we are to understand the processes through which claims typically become transformed into issues. For example, we would need to know something about the relationship between a demand and the location of its initiators or supporters in the power structures of the society, the importance of secrecy as compared with publicity in presenting demands, the matter of timing of demands, the possession of political skills or know-how, access to channels of communication, the attitudes and states of mind of possible publics, and the images held by the initiators of demands with regard to the way in which things get done in the particular political system. Answers to matters such as these would possibly yield a conversion index reflecting the probability of a set of demands being converted into live political issues.

If we assume that political science is primarily concerned with the way in which authoritative decisions are made for a society, demands require special attention as a major type of input of political systems. I have suggested that demands influence the behavior of a system in a number of ways. They constitute a significant part of the material upon which the system operates. They are also one of the sources of change in political systems, since as the environment fluctuates it generates new types of demand-inputs for the system. Accordingly, without this attention to the origin and determinants of demands we would be at a loss to be able to treat rigorously not only the operation of a system at a moment of time but also its change over a specified interval. Both the statics and historical dynamics of a political system depend upon a detailed understanding of demands, particularly of the impact of the setting on them.

III. INPUTS: SUPPORT

Inputs of demands alone are not enough to keep a political system operating. They are only the raw material out of which finished products called decisions are manufactured. Energy in the form of actions or orientations promoting and resisting a political system, the demands arising in it, and the decisions issuing from it must also be put into the system to keep it running. This input I shall call support. Without support, demands could not be satisfied or conflicts in goals composed. If demands are to be acted upon, the members of a system undertaking to pilot the demands through to their transformation into binding decisions and those who seek to influence the relevant processes in any way must be able to count on support from others in the system. Just how much support, from how many and which members of a political system, are separate and important questions that I shall touch on shortly.

What do we mean by support? We can say that A supports B either when A acts on behalf of or when he orients himself favorably toward B's goals, interests, and actions. Supportive behavior may thus be of two kinds. It may consist of actions promoting the goals, interests, and actions of another person. We may vote for a political candidate, or defend a decision by the highest court of the land. In these cases, support manifests itself through overt action.

On the other hand, supportive behavior may involve not external observable acts, but those internal forms of behavior we call orientations or states of mind. As I use the phrase, a supportive state of mind is a deep-seated set of attitudes or predispositions, or a readiness to act on behalf of some other person. It exists when we say that a man is loyal to his party, attached to democracy, or infused with patriotism. What such phrases as these have in common is the fact that they refer to a state of feelings on the part of a person. No overt action is involved at this level of description, although the implication is that the individual will pursue a course of action consistent with his attitudes. Where the anticipated action does not flow from our perception of the state of mind, we assume that we have not penetrated deeply enough into the true feelings of the person but have merely skimmed off his surface attitudes.

Supportive states of mind are vital inputs for the operation and maintenance of a political system. For example, it is often said that the struggle in the international sphere concerns mastery over men's minds. To a certain extent this is true. If the members of a political system are deeply attached to a system or its ideals, the likelihood of their participating in either domestic or foreign politics in such a way as to undermine the system is reduced by a large factor. Presumably, even in the face of considerable provocation, ingrained supportive feelings of loyalty may be expected to prevail.

We shall need to identify the typical mechanisms through which supportive attitudes are inculcated and continuously reinforced within a political system. But our prior task is to specify and examine the political objects in relation to which support is extended.

(1) The Domain of Support

Support is fed into the political system in relation to three objects: the community, the regime, and the government. There must be convergence of attitude and opinion as well as some willingness to act with regard to each of these objects. Let us examine each in turn.

(a) The political community. No political system can continue to operate unless its members are willing to support the existence of a group that seeks to settle differences or promote decisions through peaceful action in common. The point is so obvious—being dealt with usually under the heading of the growth of national unity—that it may well be over-looked; and yet it is a premise upon which the continuation of any political system depends. To refer to this phenomenon we can speak of the political community. At this level of support we are not concerned with whether a government exists or whether there is loyalty to a constitutional order. For the moment we only ask whether the members of the group that we are examining are sufficiently oriented toward each other to want to contribute their collective energies toward pacific settlement of their varying demands. . . .

(b) The regime. Support for a second major part of a political system helps to supply the energy to keep the system running. This aspect of the system I shall call the regime. It consists of all those arrangements that regulate the way in which the demands put into the system are settled and the way in which decisions are put into effect. They are the so-called rules of the game, in the light of which actions by members of the system are legitimated and accepted by the bulk of the members as authoritative. Unless there is a minimum convergence of attitudes in support of these fundamental rules—the constitutional principles, as we call them in West-ern society—there would be insufficient harmony in the actions of the members of a system to meet the problems generated by their support of a political community. The fact of trying to settle demands in common means that there must be known principles governing the way in which resolutions of differences of claims are to take place.

(c) The government. If a political system is going to be able to handle the conflicting demands put into it, not only must the members of the system be prepared to support the settlement of these conflicts in common and possess some consensus with regard to the rules governing the mode of settlement; they must also be ready to support a government as it undertakes the concrete tasks involved in negotiating such settlements. When we come to the outputs of a system, we shall see the rewards that are available to a government for mobilizing support. At this point, I just wish to draw attention to this need on the part of a government for support if it is going to be able to make decisions with regard to demands. Of course, a government may elicit support in many ways: through persuasion, consent, or manipulation. It may also impose unsupported settlements of demands through threats of force. But it is a familiar axiom of political science that a government based upon force alone is not long for this world; it must buttress its position by inducing a favorable state of mind in its subjects through fair or foul means.

The fact that support directed to a political system can be broken down conceptually into three elements—support for the community, regime, and government—does not mean, of course, that in the concrete case support for each of these three objects is independent. In fact we might and normally do find all three kinds of support very closely intertwined, so that the presence of one is a function of the presence of one or both of the other types. . . .

(2) Quantity and Scope of Support

How much support needs to be put into a system and how many of its members need to contribute such support if the system is to be able to do the job of converting demands to decisions? No ready answer can be offered. The actual situation in each case would determine the amount and scope required. We can, however, visualize a number of situations that will be helpful in directing our attention to possible generalizations.

Under certain circumstances very few members need to support a system at any level. The members might be dull and apathetic, indifferent to the general operations of the system, its progress or decisions. In a loosely connected system such as India has had, this might well be the state of mind of by far the largest segment of the membership. Either in fact they have not been affected by national decisions or they have not perceived that they were so affected. They may have little sense of identification with the present regime and government and yet, with regard to the input of demands, the system may be able to act on the basis of the support offered by the known 3 per cent of the Western-oriented politicians and intellectuals who are politically active. In other words, we can have a small minority putting in quantitatively sufficient supportive energy to keep the system going. However, we can venture the hypothesis that where members of a system are putting in numerous demands, there is a strong probability that they will actively offer support or hostility at one of the three levels of the system, depending upon the degree to which these demands are being met through appropriate decisions.

Alternatively, we may find that all the members of a system are putting in support, but the amount may be so low as to place one or all aspects of the system in jeopardy. Modern France is perhaps a classic illustration. The input of support at the level of the political community is probably adequate for the maintenance of France as a national political unit. But for a variety of historical and contemporary reasons, there is considerable doubt as to whether the members of the French political system are putting in anything but a low order of support to the regime or any particular government. This low amount of support, even though spread over a relatively large segment of the population, leaves the French political system on somewhat less secure foundations than is the case with India. There support is less widespread but more active—that is, quantitatively greater—on the part of a minority. As this illustration indicates, the amount of support is not necessarily proportional to its scope.

It may seem from the above discussion as though the members of a political system either put in support or withhold it—that is, demonstrate hostility or apathy. In fact, members may and normally do simultaneously engage in supportive and hostile behavior. What we must be interested in is the net balance of support.

IV. MECHANISMS OF SUPPORT

To this point I have suggested that no political system can yield the important outputs we call authoritative decisions unless, in addition to demands, support finds its way into the system. I have discussed the possible object to which support may be directed, and some problems with regard to the domain, quantity, and scope of support. We are now ready to turn to the main question raised by our attention to support as a crucial input: how do systems typically manage to maintain a steady flow of support? Without it a system will not absorb sufficient energy from its members to be able to convert demands to decisions.

In theory, there might be an infinite variety of means through which members could be induced to support a system; in practice, certain well-established classes of mechanisms are used. Research in this area needs to be directed to exploring the precise way in which a particular system utilizes these mechanisms and to refining our understanding of the way in which they contribute to the making of authoritative policy.

A society generates support for a political system in two ways: through outputs that meet the demands of the members of society; and through the processes of politicization. Let us look at outputs first.

(1) Outputs as a Mechanism of Support

An output of a political system, it will be recalled, is a political decision or policy. One of the major ways of strengthening the ties of the members to their system is through providing decisions that tend to satisfy the day-to-day demands of these members. Fundamentally this is the truth that lies in the aphorism that one can fool some of the people some of the time but not all of them all of the time. Without some minimal satisfaction of demands, the ardor of all but the most fanatical patriot is sure to cool. The outputs, consisting of political decisions, constitute a body of specific inducements for the members of a system to support that system.

Inducements of this kind may be positive or negative. Where negative, they threaten the members of the system with various kinds of sanctions ranging from a small monetary fine to physical detention, ostracism, or loss of life, as in our own system with regard to the case of legally defined treason. In every system support stems in part from fear of sanctions or compulsion; in autocratic systems the proportion of coerced support is at a maximum. For want of space I shall confine myself to those cases where positive incentives loom largest.

Since the specific outputs of a system are policy decisions, it is upon the government that the final responsibility falls for matching or balancing outputs of decisions against input of demand. But it is clear that to obtain the support of the members of a system through positive incentives, a government need not meet all the demands of even its most influential and ardent supporters. Most governments, or groups such as political parties that seek to control governments, succeed in building up a reserve of support. This reserve will carry the government along even though it offends its followers, so long as over the extended short run these followers perceive the particular government as one that is in general favorable to their interests. One form that this reserve support takes in Western society is that of party loyalty, since the party is the typical instrument in a mass industrialized society for mobilizing and maintaining support for a government. However, continuous lack of specific rewards through policy decisions ultimately leads to the danger that even the deepest party loyalty may be shaken. . . .

Thus a system need not meet *all the demands* of its members so long as it has stored up a reserve of support over the years. Nor need it satisfy even *some of the demands* of all its members. Just whose demands a system must seek to meet, how much of their demands, at what time, and under what conditions are questions for special research. We can say in advance that at least the demands of the most influential members require satisfaction. But this tells us little unless we know how to discover the influentials in a political system and how new sets of members rise to positions of influence.

The critical significance of the decisions of governments for the support of the other two aspects of a system—namely, the political community and the regime—is clear from what I have said above. Not all withdrawal of support from a government has consequences for the success or failure of a regime or community. But persistent inability of a government to produce satisfactory outputs for the members of a system may well lead to demands for changing of the regime or for dissolution of the political community. It is for this reason that the input-output balance is a vital mechanism in the life of a political system.

(2) Politicization as a Mechanism of Support

It would be wrong to consider that the level of support available to a system is a function exclusively of the outputs in the form of either sanctions or rewards. If we did so conclude, we could scarcely account for the maintenance of numerous political systems in which satisfaction of demands has been manifestly low, in which public coercion is limited, and yet which have endured for epochs. Alternately, it might be difficult to explain how political systems could endure and yet manage to flout or thwart urgent demands, failing thereby to render sufficient *quid pro quo* for the input of support. The fact is that whatever reserve of support has been accumulated through past decisions is increased and reinforced by a complicated method for steadily manufacturing support through what I shall call the process of politicization. It is an awkward term, but nevertheless an appropriately descriptive one.

As each person grows up in a society, through a network of rewards and punishments the other members of society communicate to and instill in him the various institutionalized goals and norms of that society. This is well known in social research as the process of socialization. Through its operation a person learns to play his various social roles. Part of these goals and norms relate to what the society considers desirable in political life. The ways in which these political patterns are learned by the members of society constitute what I call the process of politicization. Through it a person learns to play his political roles, which include the absorption of the proper political attitudes.

Let us examine a little more closely something of what happens during the process of politicization. As members of a society mature, they must absorb the various orientations toward political matters that one is expected to have in that society. If the expectations of the members of society with regard to the way each should behave in specific political situations diverged beyond a certain range, it would be impossible to get common action with regard to the making of binding decisions. It is essential for the viability of an orderly political system that the members of the system have some common basic expectations with regard to the standards that are to be used in making political evaluations, to the way people will feel about various political matters, and to the way members of the system will perceive and interpret political phenomena.

The mechanism through which this learning takes place is of considerable significance in understanding how a political system generates and accumulates a strong reserve of support. Although we cannot pursue the details, we can mention a few of the relevant dimensions. In the first place, of course, the learning or politicization process does not stop at any particular period for the individual; it starts with the child and, in the light of our knowledge of learning, may have its deepest impact through the teen age. . . .

In the second place, the actual process of politicization at its most general level brings into operation a complex network of rewards and punishments. For adopting the correct political attitudes and performing the right political acts, for conforming to the generally accepted interpretations of political goals, and for undertaking the institutionalized obligations of a member of the given system, we are variously rewarded or punished. For conforming we are made to feel worthy, wanted, and respected and often obtain material advantages such as wealth, influence, improved opportunities. For deviating beyond the permissible range, we are made to feel unworthy, rejected, dishonored, and often suffer material losses. . . .

In the third place, the means used for communicating the goals and norms to others tend to be repetitive in all societies. The various political myths, doctrines, and philosophies transmit to each generation a particular interpretation of the goals and norms. The decisive links in this chain of transmission are parents, siblings, peers, teachers, organizations, and social leaders, as well as physical symbols such as flags or totems, ceremonies, and rituals freighted with political meaning.

These processes through which attachments to a political system become built into the maturing member of a society I have lumped together under the rubric of politicization. . . .

When the basic political attachments become deeply rooted or institutionalized, we say that the system has become accepted as legitimate. Politicization therefore effectively sums up the way in which legitimacy is created and transmitted in a political system. And it is an empirical observation that in those instances where political systems have survived the longest, support has been nourished by an ingrained belief in the legitimacy of the relevant governments and regimes.

What I am suggesting here is that support resting on a sense of the legitimacy of a government and regime provides a necessary reserve if the system is to weather those frequent storms when the more obvious outputs of the system seem to impose greater hardships than rewards. Answers to questions concerning the formation, maintenance, transmission, and change of standards of legitimacy will contribute generously to an understanding of the way in which support is sufficiently institutionalized so that a system may regularly and without excessive expenditure of effort transform inputs of demand into outputs of decision.

That there is a need for general theory in the study of political life is apparent. The only question is how best to proceed. There is no one royal road that can be said to be either the correct one or the best. It is only a matter of what appears at the given level of available knowledge to be the most useful. At this stage it appears that system theory, with its sensitivity to the input-output exchange between a system and its setting offers a fruitful approach. It is an economical way of organizing presently disconnected political data and promises interesting dividends.

B. Area Study

10. AREA STUDY AND COMPARATIVE POLITICS*

Roy C. Macridis and Richard Cox

The Area Study and Comparative Politics

ONE APPROACH to the study of comparative politics is the more systematic and precise use of the *area concept*. The members of the group felt that

* From "Research in Comparative Politics," *The American Political Science Review*, Vol. XLVII, No. 3 (September, 1953). By permission.

the concept has been abused in the organization of university studies. The expression "world areas," though of some use, lacks operational clarity and consistency. It was agreed also that the concept of area has been somewhat indiscriminately associated with the following concepts either separately or in combination: (1) geographic: the definition of an area simply because of the geographic propinquity of certain states, i.e., Western Europe, or the Far East; (2) historical: the definition of an area in the light of a common historical task and common historical experience; (3) economic: the definition of an area in the light of comparable economic conditions and needs; and (4) cultural: the definition of an area in the light of common cultural heritage or common experience of cultural inter-actions between two or more cultures.

It was generally felt that all of the above definitions are for the political scientist unsatisfactory. Neither geographic, historical, economic, nor cultural similarities constitute prima facie evidence of the existence of similar political characteristics. But if the concept of an area is to be operationally meaningful for the purpose of comparison, it should correspond to some uniform political patterns against which differences may be studied comparatively and explained.

The definition of an area on the basis of culture was considered to be worth detailed discussion. It was suggested that though primarily used by the anthropologists it might be adapted to the needs of the political scientists. Its use promises the following advantages for the political scientist:

1. A greatly heightened awareness of the multiple connections between the sphere of politics and other aspects of a culture, which may be described as a feeling for total context and for the overall integration and patterning of cultures.

2. An incentive to the adoption of an inter-disciplinary approach and the utmost possible utilization of the knowledge and skills of allied disciplines. It thus attempts to raise the student's methodological equipment to a level and potency more compatible with the dimensions of his problems.

3. A framework for political comparison across national and cultural boundaries far more realistic and meaningful than that supplied by the partial and out-of-context institutional framework generally utilized.

4. An awareness of the shortcomings of political explanations couched in terms of single-factor and proximate level causality and an impulsion to go more deeply into the complex ranges of social causality.

5. Some aid in avoiding the purely descriptive approach to political institutions and some incentive towards its replacement by a problem-oriented approach.

6. As effective a counterbalance to the irrational effects of ethnocentrism as a determinant of "proper" areas of interest and terms of appraisal as has been discovered.

Granting these advantages, however, it was pointed out that the concept of culture has been used by anthropologists as a static device for classifying cultural types and arranging data primarily in respect to primitive cultural units over a large and disparate geographic area. Furthermore, the concept of culture as used by other social scientists, e.g., ethnographers, becomes ambiguous and comes perilously close to being identifiable with the national characteristic or the "gestalt" or "ethos" approaches, which are operationally unacceptable to political scientists.

To make the concept operationally meaningful, therefore, for political science, it was suggested that an attempt be made to define areas with reference to "political traits" or "trait complexes" or "problem configuration patterns," in terms analogous to those used by the anthropologists when they break down the concept of culture into "traits" or "trait complexes." Such an approach to the definition of an area has not, as yet, been undertaken, despite its promise for comparative study. First, the very search for common political traits and problem configuration patterns will call for classification and conceptualization. Secondly, once similar traits or patterns have been distinguished and have been related to certain geographically delimited units, the area concept will be of great value, since certain political processes will be compared between units within the area against a common background of similar trait configuration. In this sense it was felt that future research should be directed towards developing in great detail classificatory schemes within areas. With the help of such a scheme the study of differences would be made far more manageable. For instance, it was felt that in Latin America the following problems offer the prospect of a fruitful intra-area comparison:

1. Political instability and "revolution."
2. Constitutional problems—the relation of written constitution to the actual operation of government in Latin American states.
3. Dictatorship—the typical character of Latin American dictatorships, and their differences from the European brand of totalitarianism.
4. Militarism—the extent and nature of military rule in Latin American politics.
5. Regionalism and particularism—the reasons underlying politically centrifugal tendencies.
6. International politics—the major factors which affect the role played by Latin American states in world politics and in international organizations.

Similar types of problems could easily be suggested for the Middle East, Scandinavia, and Western Europe.

Another general definition of an area which might be of use to political scientists included five operational criteria: (1) inter-action of values and ideas (culture); (2) physical proximity; (3) economic relations; (4) political interaction of power relations and power groups; and (5) strategic considerations. These criteria have the advantage of pointing to the most important factors that enter into the area concept. The political scientist, however, has to relate them to similarities and dissimilarities in the observable political processes and attempt to explain them through the formulation of hypotheses.

11. THE CONFIGURATIVE APPROACH*

Gunnar Heckscher

RECENTLY, a general criticism has been levelled against area studies as lacking in 'clarity and consistency.' It has been argued that 'the concept of an area is . . . operationally meaningful for purposes of comparison' only if it corresponds 'to some uniform political pattern against which differences may be studied comparatively and explained.' The idea of using geographical, historical or cultural definitions of the areas to be studied by political scientists is thereby rejected.

It is submitted that a criticism of this type, as it stands, is manifestly unreasonable. It is true that there has often been a considerable amount of abuse and a lamentable lack of clarity in using the area concept. But how should we know about 'uniform political patterns' until we have made our comparisons in the form of area studies? Moreover, it should be remembered that the idea of an area is only an auxiliary concept. In one sense, no definite areas exist, since not only 'political patterns' but also all other social and cultural patterns are eternally both similar and dissimilar wherever we go. In fact, it is not seriously important if the delimitation of the area in question proves a little dubious. We are only dealing with one approach to comparison. . . .

In determining the areas to be studied, much is, in fact, to be said for an approach quite contrary to that of the critics just quoted. Probably both the easiest and the most fruitful method is to choose a criterion *outside* the realm of political science and to examine to what extent 'uniform *political* patterns' can be found where the existence of uniform geographical, historical, economic, cultural or other pattern has already been established. This may mean that we simply start from geographical concepts and study the similarities and dissimilarities of contiguous countries; but on the whole historical development, economic structures and social patterns, in so far as they can be established, seem to present the best bases for our choice. More important than geographic contiguity, is for instance, whether the countries studied have the same or similar religions Protestant, Moslem, etc., 'areas'—or whether they have for some time formed part of the same political unit. Thus, the word 'area' is, in fact, not very appropriate. We shall continue to use it here, but with the reservation that area terms such as that of 'the Middle East,' 'the Far East,' 'the Northern countries,' etc., are meaningful only if it is understood that the main basis of the concept is not to be found in the geographical field but rather in general historical and cultural development and structure.

---

* From *The Study of Comparative Government and Politics* (London: George Allen & Unwin Ltd., 1957). Reprinted by permission.

The critics just quoted also made a strong diatribe against what they called 'parochialism.' It is difficult not to agree with them at this point. When they say that 'the study of comparative government has been primarily parochial in its emphasis upon Western systems,' they are speaking no more than the truth. There are a number of perfectly good explanations and excuses, but on the whole it is true that only a limited number of countries have been studied, and equally true that it is necessary to go farther and include new areas. 'New areas,' it might be submitted, however, can be defined only as areas not previously studied. It is not certain that those areas necessarily have anything in common beyond the 'novelty' of not having been studied before. In principle, that would be correct. But in fact, the areas and countries which have been the object of study are primarily those belonging to Western Europe, the United States and the British Commonwealth; and consequently there is considerable reason to believe that we shall be able to find at least one more characteristic common to most of those who have been formerly left out. The majority of such regions fall under the conventional heading of 'underdeveloped' countries. In choosing its fields of study, political science has tended to take those which were by Western standards 'interesting,' that is, relatively highly developed. This should not be taken to mean that *all* highly developed countries have been the object of comparative study. But on the whole, when we speak of 'new' areas to be studied, we think chiefly of Asiatic, African and South American regions. To study these is important not only on general principles but also because of what we can learn about the validity of our criteria and the specific characteristics of the West in extending our studies to these 'new' areas.

In any case, whether areas are 'new' or 'old,' it can hardly be denied that area studies give the problems of comparative government in a nutshell. In the first place, the configurative approach is indispensable; and in the second place, the number of variables, while frequently still very large, is at least reduced in the case of a happy choice of area. Consequently, while area studies are of the very essence of comparative government, they also are more manageable than studies of an institution covering, or attempting to cover, the whole field.

What problems should be introduced into an area study? We may begin with some general observations. As usual when attempting synthesis, we have to take stock of *what* we know, as well as of what we do *not* know and of *how* we know the things which have come within our knowledge. In the case of comparative studies, this is particularly important. Comparison, furthermore, must take place both between different countries, etc., *within* the area to be studied, and *between* that area and others of which some knowledge has previously been acquired.

Secondly, we begin as usual with the 'superficial,' descriptive approach. Then follows the need for explanation, which in turn gives more depth to the study. We try to ascertain the mechanics of politics (whether or not they are democratic politics); the legislative procedure; the administrative structure; existing forms of self-government; etc. The next step is to investigate parties and other organised groups, as much as other forces behind the mechanism: social, cultural and economic. And that, finally, leads us to an inter-disciplinary approach.

A number of fundamental concepts and problems are involved in our study. Individual area studies cannot give an answer to all these questions. On the other hand, the answers are subject to influence from the general concepts of the student. The result of a study is always to some extent determined by the subjective attitude of the researcher in such respects, but area studies illustrate some of the difficulties of this type with special clarity.

To give an example: it is asked whether we can speak of a 'unity of human society.' Some authors assume that we can, others hold opposite views, and undoubtedly area studies organised on one or the other assumption will be to some extent different in character. But in any case, whatever the original attitude of the student, the study itself will contribute to the establishment of an attitude in this respect on the part of whoever follows it.

A similar general question is whether we are primarily interested in similarities or in differences. Obviously, both are important. But if we assume similarity, regarding difference as the exception, this will create an approach rather different from the one found if we assume uniqueness and regard every fundamental similarity as a fact requiring special explanation. . . .

An enumeration of some areas which could be studied on a comparative basis shows how far we have fallen short of satisfactory results even in the case of 'old' areas. . . . Proper comparative studies are largely missing in the case of the Western European continent which might be studied as a whole or divided up into a number of areas. To mention some examples of such areas, we have those of France and Belgium, that of the Benelux states, that of Germany and Austria, that of Scandinavia and Finland, that of Spain, Portugal and Italy. The dominions within the British Commonwealth have been studied by several authors, and the comparative approach has not been altogether lacking. Still, much remains to be done, especially in view of the rather rapid and partly unexpected development which has taken place after World War II. Another interesting area is provided by the 'satellite states' in Europe, i.e. by the non-Russian 'popular democracies.' A comparison between them, and perhaps in particular a comparison between a number of such states on one hand and the Soviet Union and its component republics on the other, would undoubtedly be illuminating. . . .

But comparison within the 'old' areas is obviously not enough. The concepts may be developed there, but we cannot be quite sure of their applicability until we have gone beyond the 'parochial' field. Passing to the 'new' areas, it can hardly be denied that there are certain salient points which require more emphasis there than in the case of Western countries. Whether or not we adhere to the principle of the 'unity of human society,' at least in the initial stages we have to be aware of the fact that our concepts are largely based on the circumstances of the West and that we must therefore exercise particular care when passing beyond that orbit.

In the first place . . . the 'total fabric of society' is particularly important with regard to the study of Asia or other regions of a similar cultural structure. Thus, the problems of politics cannot be isolated even to the limited extent possible in the case of Western studies. Political instability is a more serious problem than in the West. Frequently political institutions have been created overnight; also, states themselves may be only in the process of emerging. Under such circumstances, the durability of the state itself and of its basic institutions is a fundamental problem. The maintenance of government (of *any* sort of government) may prove more important than the political structure. (On the other hand, it could be argued that the doubtful durability of states is a reason for an area approach to political studies; the alternative is to study states individually, and this may have its disadvantages if the states themselves are not sufficiently permanent.)

12. NATIONAL PROFILES*

Karl W. Deutsch

A SIMPLE technique for surveying the inventory of variables and countries by means of "country profiles" would be as follows: (1) List in a fixed sequence a number of variables—say, ten—of presumed interest. (2) Assign a ten-place number to each country, with one digit corresponding to each variable. (3) Obtain the distribution for each variable, and divide all countries by rank for this particular variable into five classes, according to some suitably chosen intervals. (4) Assign a number to each class, beginning with 0 for the lowest, and ending with 4 for the highest class. (5) Write the class number for each variable into the appropriate digit of the "country profile" number. (6) Match the country profiles for two or more countries which you wish to compare for some purpose of political analysis. (7) Observe the distribution of all country profiles, or of all such profiles for a particular group of countries. Many possible profiles will

* From "Toward an Inventory of Basic Trends and Patterns in Comparative and International Politics," *The American Political Science Review*, Vol. LIV, No. 1 (March, 1960). By permission of the American Political Science Association.

have no countries in them; a few profiles may correspond to several countries.

A possible set of such variables and coding classes might be the following:

1. Gross national product (GNP):　Code: 0. under $1 billion
　　　　　　　　　　　　　　　　　1. $1–4.9 billion
　　　　　　　　　　　　　　　　　2. $5–24.9 billion
　　　　　　　　　　　　　　　　　3. $25–124.9 billion
　　　　　　　　　　　　　　　　　4. $125 billion and above

2. Per capita gross national product　Code: 0. under $100
　　(gnp):　　　　　　　　　　　　　1. $100–299
　　　　　　　　　　　　　　　　　2. $300–599
　　　　　　　　　　　　　　　　　3. $600–899
　　　　　　　　　　　　　　　　　4. $900+

3. Population (P):　　　　　　　　Code: 0. under 1 million
　　　　　　　　　　　　　　　　　1. 1–9.9 million
　　　　　　　　　　　　　　　　　2. 10–39.9 million
　　　　　　　　　　　　　　　　　3. 40–99.9 million
　　　　　　　　　　　　　　　　　4. 100+

4. Population increase (P') av. p. a.:　Code: 0. zero or decline
　　　　　　　　　　　　　　　　　1. 0.1–0.9%
　　　　　　　　　　　　　　　　　2. 1.0–1.9
　　　　　　　　　　　　　　　　　3. 2.0–2.9
　　　　　　　　　　　　　　　　　4. 3+

5. Work force in non-agricultural　Code: 0. 0–9%
　　occupations (P_{na}), % (from　　1. 10–29 (*e.g.*, Thailand, Turkey, In-
　　United Nations, *World Social Sur-*　　dia)
　　vey, 1957, [henceforth cited as　2. 30–49 (*e.g.*, Egypt, Brazil, Mexico)
　　WSS], p. 92):　　　　　　　　3. 50–74 (*e.g.*, Spain, Japan, USSR,
　　　　　　　　　　　　　　　　　　Italy, Argentina)
　　　　　　　　　　　　　　　　　4. 75+ (*e.g.*, France, Germany, Aus-
　　　　　　　　　　　　　　　　　　tralia, US, UK)

6. Share of population in towns of　Code: 0. 0–9% (*e.g.*, Haiti, Pakistan)
　　20,000 or more (P_{u20}), % (WSS,　1. 10–19 (*e.g.*, Guatemala, India, Yu-
　　p. 115):　　　　　　　　　　　　goslavia)
　　　　　　　　　　　　　　　　　2. 20–29 (*e.g.*, Iran, Brazil, Mexico,
　　　　　　　　　　　　　　　　　　Finland, Egypt, 1947)
　　　　　　　　　　　　　　　　　3. 30–39 (*e.g.*, Venezuela, Cuba,
　　　　　　　　　　　　　　　　　　France, Canada)
　　　　　　　　　　　　　　　　　4. 40+ (*e.g.*, Japan, US, Germany,
　　　　　　　　　　　　　　　　　　Argentina, UK)

7. Literacy: % literate in population　Code: 0. 1–9% (*e.g.*, Ethiopia)
　　15 and above (lit):　　　　　　1. 10–19 (*e.g.*, Nigeria, Iraq, Paki-
　　　　　　　　　　　　　　　　　　stan, India)
　　　　　　　　　　　　　　　　　2. 20–39 (*e.g.*, Turkey, South Korea)
　　　　　　　　　　　　　　　　　3. 40–59 (*e.g.*, Portugal, Malta,
　　　　　　　　　　　　　　　　　　Burma, Brazil)
　　　　　　　　　　　　　　　　　4. 60+ (*e.g.*, Ceylon, Cyprus, Yugo-
　　　　　　　　　　　　　　　　　　slavia, Hungary, US, UK)

8. Daily newspaper circulation per 1000 population (n) (WSS, p. 86 ff.):

Code:
0. 1–9 (*e.g.*, Burma, India, Pakistan, Indonesia)
1. 10–49 (*e.g.*, Egypt, Tunisia, Bolivia, Ghana, Philippines)
2. 50–99 (*e.g.*, Lebanon, Spain, Brazil, Venezuela, Greece)
3. 100–199 (*e.g.*, Italy, Bulgaria, Hungary, Argentina, Cuba)
4. 200+ (*e.g.*, Japan, USSR, France, Germany, US, UK)

9. Voting participation of population 20 and above (V_a), %:

Code:
0. 1–4%
1. 5–9
2. 10–29
3. 30–49
4. 50+

10. Calory intake above or below estimated requirements (cal), % + or −:

Code:
0. Below −10% (*e.g.*, Ceylon, India, Philippines, Peru)
1. −3 to −10% (*e.g.*, Japan, Pakistan, Brazil, Mexico)
2. −2 to +2% (*e.g.*, Cyprus, Egypt)
3. +3 to +10% (*e.g.*, Argentina, Uruguay)
4. Above +10% (*e.g.*, Italy, France, USSR, US, UK)

11. Crude death rates per 1000 population (p_d) (UN *Demographic Year Book*, 1957, Table 8, 1956 data, or nearest year, pp. 186–199):

Code:
0. 25 and above (*e.g.*, India, No. Rhodesia native population)
1. 20–24.9 (*e.g.*, Ghana, Brazil)
2. 15–19.9 (*e.g.*, Egypt, Sudan, Tunisia, Guatemala, Ecuador)
3. 10–14.9 (*e.g.*, France, Germany, Indonesia, Mexico, Ceylon, UK)
4 Below 10 (*e.g.*, Japan, Australia, Argentina, USSR, US)

In addition to the "measurement profile" just discussed, we might obtain "rating profiles," based on combined data and judgments as to partly qualitative characteristics relevant for the political performance of governments in national and international affairs. Some such characteristics might be coded as follows:

1. Sovereignty:

Code:
0. Dependent
1. Sovereign only after 1945
2. Sovereign only after 1930
3. Sovereign only after 1890
4. Sovereign before 1890

2. Western impact

Code:
0. No major Western impact (*e.g.*, Nepal)
1. Some impact, but sovereign (*e.g.*, Japan)
2. Western colonial relationship after 1900 (*e.g.*, India)
3. Western colonial relationship only before 1900 (*e.g.*, Brazil)
4. Western (*e.g.*, Sweden)

3. Constitutional stability:

Code: 0. No current constitution, neither formal nor effective
1. Current formal constitution but not effective
2. Current effective constitution (written or unwritten), but only after 1945
3. Current effective constitution (written or unwritten), but only after 1890
4. Current effective constitution (written or unwritten) older than 1890

4. Political homogeneity:

Code: 0. Extreme opposition (*i.e.*, secessionist or revolutionary) has 50% or more of vote, or of politically active population
1. Extreme opposition has 30–49%
2. Extreme opposition has 10–29%
3. Extreme opposition has 5–9%
4. Extreme opposition has less than 5%

5. Ethnic and racial homogeneity: Code for same percentages as 4, above.
6. Linguistic homogeneity: Code for same percentages as 4, above.
7. Religious homogeneity: Code for same percentages as 4, above.
8. Sectional homogeneity (% population in politically self-conscious geographic sections, *e.g.*, US South).   Code for same percentages as 4, above.

9. Voting system:

Code: 0. No voting at all
1. Only plebiscite-type voting, with single party and no effective primary
2. Single party with effective primary
3. Multi-party system with ban on extreme parties (*e.g.*, Communists, nationalists, etc.)
4. Multi-party system without limitation on parties

10. Freedom of group opposition:

Code: 0. No autonomous groups tolerated ("totalitarianism")
1. Autonomous groups tolerated informally and outside politics
2. Informal autonomous groups effective in politics ("authoritarianism")
3. Autonomous groups free to organize in politics, but restricted in opposing government ("authoritarian constitutionalism")
4. Autonomous groups free to enter politics and to oppose government

An example for both the "measurement profile" and the "rating profile" for the United States might look like this:

MEASUREMENT PROFILE

A. Digit	1	2	3	4	5	6	7	8	9	10	11
B. Category	GNP	gnp	Pop	P'%	w_{na}%	P_{u20}%	lit%	n_a	V_a	cal%	P_d
C. Data	387	2243	168	1.8	87	43	98	339	50+	+12	9.4
D. Code	4	4	4	2	4	4	4	4	4	4	4

This could be written more conveniently M 4442–44444–44. The first group of digits would indicate levels of income, population and population growth; the second group would indicate levels of social mobilization and voting participation; and the last two digits would suggest levels of nutrition and of health.

RATING PROFILE

A. Digit	1	2	3	4	5	6	7	8	9	10
B. Category	Sov.	West.	Constit. Stab.	Extreme Pol. Opp.	Racial Minor.	Ling. Min.	Relig. Min.	Sect. Min.	Voting System	Group Org.
C. Data	Before 1890	Itself West.	Before 1890	0–5%	10%+	0–5%	10–30%	10–30%	Free	Free
D. Code	4	4	4	4	2	4	2	2	4	4

This rating profile could be written conveniently as R 4444–2422–44. The first four digits identify the United States as an old independent and very stable Western nation; the second group of digits suggests its pluralistic rather than homogeneous character; and the last two digits identify its substantially free voting system and group politics. Measurement profiles for a number of countries are given in Table 1.

TABLE 1

A PRIMITIVE TYPOLOGY: SOME COUNTRY PROFILES
TYPED BY CLASSES OF SIZE AND WEALTH

1955 GNP per cap.	*1956 Pop. (millions)*				
	Under 1	1–10	10–40	40–100	100+
$900		Switz. 2412-x344-43	Canada 3423-4344-44	*Fr. 3431-3344-43	US 4442-4444-44
		N.Z. 1413-xx44-44		UK 3431-4444-43	
		Aust. 2413-4444-44			
		Swed. 2411-4344-44			
		Belg. 2411-4444-43			
		Norway 1412-xx44-44			
		Finl. 1412-x244-44			
		Denm. 1411-x444-44			
$600–900		Venez. 1314-x332-14	Neth. 2322-4444-44	Ger.F.R. 3332-4444-43	USSR 43xx-3344-44
			*Czech. xx22-xx43-x4		
			*Poland xx23-xx43-x4		
$300–600	*Israel 0214-xx43-x4		Argen. 2222-3443-34	Italy 2231-3x43-43	
	Austria 1211-3444-x3				
$100–300	Port. 1111-xx32-x3	Yugo. 2122-x141-33	Brazil 2133-2232-11		
	*Iraq 111x-xx11-x1	Mex. 2123-xx31-13	*Indon. 2132-xx10-x3		
	*Guat. 0114-x121-x2	Turk. 2123-1121-3x	Japan 2132-3444-14		
	*Ghana 0112-xx21-x1	Spain 2121-3x42-x4			
		Phil. 1122-xx41-04			
		*Egypt 1123-2211-22			
		*Thail. 1122-1x30-x4			
		*Iran 112x-x210-x4			
under $100	*Jordan 0013-xx10-x4	Ethio. 002x-xx00-xx	*Pakistan 1032-1010-13	India 3042-111000	
	*Bolivia 0012-xx21-x3	*Burma 1022-xx30-x1		*China 3043-xx3x-x2	
		*Niger. 1022-xx10-x3			

Categories: Coded in profiles as explained in the text, above. Note that statistics of voting participation have been omitted.

* Drastic change of regime since December 31, 1945.

x = Data not available.

Part Two—Political Dynamics

INTRODUCTORY ESSAY

The Group Universe

THE PURSUIT of power—the capacity to command the actions of others—by individuals and groups is a universal phenomenon. However, political power must be understood not only in terms of influence or domination, but also authority. Those who make decisions must be accorded this right by the community.

The process whereby groups compete for positions and advantage takes place in all political systems, and hence can be studied functionally and comparatively. Group analysis has the merit of bringing the student directly into the heart of the political process—social conflict and its resolution. By studying the "interest group universe" in a given political system, we gain a good insight into the distribution of power in that society and the manner in which interests are organized and expressed.

However, there is considerable disagreement among students of politics over the precise meaning of key concepts in group analysis. Arthur Bentley held that politics is action, through groups, aiming at the realization of interest. Group activity is thus identifiable with interest activity. David Truman states that an interest group is characterized by "a shared attitude." A political interest group is one that "makes claims through or upon the institutions of government." According to Lasswell and Kaplan, an interest group is "an interest aggregate," and a group is "an organized aggregate." They then distinguish between special interest groups and general interest groups, expediency interest groups, and principled groups. Charles Hagan attempts to reduce problems of political science to "their simplest terms and the smallest number of explanatory principles," by defining a group as "activity of human beings."[1]

Thus, for some, "interest" and "group" are identified; for others, they are distinctive. "Interest" may mean material and economic interest with every individual or group attempting to maximize advantages in a rational manner. Or it may designate activity (like lobbying or "pressure") for

---

[1] The works of the authors cited are: Arthur F. Bentley, *The Process of Government* (Chicago, 1908); David Truman, *The Governmental Process* (New York, 1953); H. D. Lasswell and A. D. Kaplan, *Power and Society* (New Haven, 1950); Charles Hagan, "The Group in Political Science," in *Approaches to the Study of Politics* (Evanston, Ill., 1958).

the accomplishment of any given purpose. The term "group" is also used in several ways. It sometimes designates a specific formal pattern of action (like AFL–CIO or Farm Bureau), and sometimes refers loosely to social groupings (church, party, family, state).

One fruitful approach for comparative study is to give the term "interest" the broadest possible meaning by considering it in functional terms, as an all-pervasive activity in all societies. This ubiquitous force manifests itself differently in different societies. In some systems interest is articulated through "interest" or "pressure" groups; in others through the political parties or administration. Comparative analysis can be conducted by studying the diverse patterns of interest articulation. Interest groups can be considered in terms of their size, membership, leadership, organization, relations with political parties, and means used to mobilize public opinion, gain access to the state, and influence decisions.

One of the striking features of industrialized societies is the development and proliferation of specialized groups. In a modern society they represent every conceivable social, economic, religious, and professional interest. The largest and most powerful groups, speaking on behalf of the major social classes, are the business, labor, and agricultural organizations. It is a major function of every modern political system to provide these associations or interest groups with the opportunity to gain access to the policymakers and make known their proposals or demands.

Reconciliation of the demands of interest groups and, broadly speaking, of social forces, is perhaps the most serious single challenge confronting any political system. We are not referring here to the demands, say, of trade unions and management for a minimum wage fixed at a particular level, though this kind of conflict is quite intense. We refer rather to the attitude of social groups towards the political process itself, the acceptance of the "rules of the game" by all the players. For example, there is a complex network of specialized associations in both Great Britain and France. In both countries we find powerful trade unions, business groups, churches, and associations of farmers, veterans, teachers, and so on. Some French groups are more powerful than their opposite numbers in Britain (for example, farmers, small merchants, lay Catholics) and vice versa (British trade unions and business groups are more highly organized than their counterparts in France). Yet the basic attitudes of the groups are significantly different. In spite of their political rivalry, expressed through support of the Labor and Conservative Parties, the trade unions and management groups in Great Britain accept a commitment to parliamentary institutions. With a few minor exceptions, they are willing to work within the existing system in order to realize their goals, and do not turn against it when they lose. The habits of compromise are solidly established in British society. The actors abide by fundamental rules which are embodied in the constitutional system.

In France, however, the same economic or social interests are *not* in agreement upon the values of the state or on political procedures to be used in the resolution of group conflicts. The labor and business groups are fundamentally hostile to each other, and constantly strive to change the rules of the game or the system itself so as to secure a more advantageous position. The most powerful trade union in France, the General Confederation of Labor, is Communist controlled and Communist oriented. That is, the industrial proletariat in France largely expresses its demands through a union and a party which reject the system. Important elements of the business community, on the other hand, not only distrust the workers, but wish to introduce a "strong" state to deal with them. The parliamentary system is held in low repute by other important interests as well. Political debates and meetings are marked by verbal and physical violence. In practice the disaffected groups are generally unable to overthrow the system, and accept it provisionally. Compromise is difficult to achieve and breaks down altogether during political crises. There is a distinct tendency to change the rules of the game (usually by promulgating a new constitution) whenever the balance shifts and one constellation of groups or forces gains the upper hand. Thus, one of the most important questions to pose about a political system is the attitude of the principal organized groups towards each other and towards the system itself.

Political Parties

Max Weber's definition of party is useful for placing the subject in broad social and historical perspective. "The term political party," he suggested, "will be employed to designate an associative type of social relationship, membership in which rests on formally free recruitment. The end to which its activity is devoted is to secure power within a corporate group for its leaders in order to attain ideal or material advantages for its active members. These advantages may consist in the realization of certain objective policies or the attainment of personal advantages or both." As Weber uses the term, a "party" can exist in any corporate group—unions, fraternal orders, churches, university faculties, and corporations. It can be oriented towards personal interest or towards broad policy. When the rules of the corporate group provide for campaigns and elections, the parties coalesce around interests. Political victory in party terms means that its adherents, in assuming direction of the state, can realize party proposals. Political parties thus tend to be complex social institutions holding together those who have a common program and those who strive for power and personal advantage.[2] In a sense they are specialized associations *within* specialized associations and become more complex, organized, and bureaucratic as a society approaches the "modern" type.

---

[2] See Max Weber, *The Theory of Social and Economic Organization* (Oxford University Press, 1947), pp. 407–12.

It is therefore understandable that political parties were not studied systematically until the modern period, when they were fully developed. John Stuart Mill's treatise *On Representative Government,* written in 1861, contained an extensive plea for proportional representation but no analysis of parties. Insofar as parties were brought under scrutiny, they were generally denounced as expressions of factionalism. In a classic criticism of political parties, James Bryce expressed his fear that insofar as parties are permitted to run the government a community falls below the level of ideal democracy. "In the ideal democracy every citizen is intelligent, patriotic, disinterested. His sole wish is to discover the right side in each contested issue, and to fix upon the best man among competing candidates. His common sense, aided by a knowledge of the constitution of his country, enables him to judge easily between the arguments submitted to him while his own zeal is sufficient to carry him to the polling booth. . . ." But, Bryce continues, the electorate is *not* informed or interested. Hence, politicians discover the advantages of organization. "Organization and discipline mean the command of the leaders, the subordination and obedience of the rank and file; and they mean also the growth of a party spirit which is in itself irrational, impelling men to vote from considerations which have little to do with a love of truth or a sense of justice."[3]

Most students of political parties at the turn of the century, like Bryce, were concerned with the shortcomings and deficiencies of the political parties: with bossism, corruption, and the inability of the parties to put forward coherent programs and implement them once in power. M. I. Ostrogorski's classic treatise on *Democracy and the Organization of Political Parties* emphasized especially the sordid side of politics—above all, the politicians' craving for spoils. The thesis argued by Bryce and Ostrogorski concerning American parties was strengthened by Robert Michels' study of the German Social Democratic Party. From the viewpoint of comparative analysis Michels' work marked an advance, since his "iron law of oligarchy" could be construed as a general theory in the light of which all political parties may be examined. Bryce, Ostrogorski, and Michels, taken together, offered a full-fledged theory of parties and their role in democracies. They fully documented the growth of mass political parties with complex structures in the United States, Britain, and Germany. They assumed that democracy somehow involves meaningful participation by the masses in the making of important decisions. They agreed that parties were controlled by a handful of politicians and leaders. Democracy therefore becomes less and less feasible as parties become more and more complex.

Theory regarding the role of parties in a democracy has undergone sweeping change in the past 30 years. The widespread view of parties as

---

[3] From James Bryce's preface to M. Ostrogorski, *Democracy and the Organization of Political Parties* (New York, 1902).

destructive of democracy has given way to an almost equally widespread view that parties are indispensable to the operation of democratic institutions. American political scientists were especially affected by the New Deal, which seemed to demonstrate the potential utility of political parties in mobilizing public support for a program of social reform. Also, the hostile reaction to the Nazi regime included searching appraisal of the one-party system. In defense of Western democracy against the challenge of fascism and communism, it was discerned that democracy was bound up somehow with the existence of at least two parties. The previously despised parties were elevated to positions of great prestige by political philosophers and researchers.

Stress was laid upon the role of parties in the democratic process by such writers as A. D. Lindsay, R. M. MacIver, C. J. Friedrich, Joseph Schumpeter, and Walter Lippmann, to name but a few.[4] They argued that a distinctive element of democracy, as contrasted with fascism and communism, was the existence of an opposition. But it is not sufficient to grant an abstract right of opposition to individuals. To be effective, opposition must be enabled to organize, that is, form a party. In the absence of parties, there would be no check upon the egoistic impulses of the rulers. Also, the masses can participate effectively in government only through the agency of parties. Thus, parties organize the "chaotic public will," educate the private citizens to public responsibility, connect government with public opinion, and select the political leadership. In answer to Michels' criticism of oligarchy, it has been argued that even oligarchical parties may serve democratic purposes—provided that there is free competition among the parties.[5] Thus, Gwendolyn Carter concludes her survey of parties in the Commonwealth: "Political parties . . . are not only an aid to democracy but an essential element in making it possible." Similarly, E. E. Schattschneider on the American parties: "The major parties have become the crucial and competing channels of policy formulation in our national democracy." And Maurice Duverger contends that in all advanced societies, "liberty and the party system coincide."[6] The contrast with Bryce, Ostrogorski, and Michels is complete!

However, the pervasive crisis of parliamentary democracy since World War II has been reflected in a revival of criticism of political parties. This is especially the case in countries where large social groups have not been fully integrated into the political system, as evidenced by massive support

---

[4] See A. D. Lindsay, *The Modern Democratic State* (New York, 1947); R. M. MacIver, *The Web of Government* (New York, 1947); Carl J. Friedrich, *Constitutional Government and Democracy* (Boston, 1946); Joseph Schumpeter, *Capitalism, Socialism and Democracy* (New York, 1947); and Walter Lippmann, *Public Opinion* (New York, 1945).

[5] See the argument in R. T. McKenzie, *British Political Parties* (London, 1955).

[6] See contributions by Gwendolyn Carter and E. E. Schattschneider in Sigmund Neumann (ed.), *Modern Political Parties* (Chicago, 1956), pp. 103, 215; and M. Duverger, *Les partis politiques*, (Paris, 1954), p. 465.

for antiparliamentary parties. In France, for example, there is now an extensive literature critical of the role played by parties in the democratic process. Among the major contributors to this critical literature are such Gaullist intellectuals as Louis Vallon and Michel Debré, and of course, General de Gaulle himself.[7]

In many developing nations, political parties have fallen into disrepute. In many countries, as in Burma, Turkey, South Korea, Pakistan, and Egypt, the army seized power professedly in order to defend the national interest against the corrupt parties. In India, disciples of Mahatma Gandhi urge the conversion of Congress into a national movement and the creation of a "party-less democracy." Ben Bella declared after coming to power that the "Front" ruling Algeria must never degenerate into a mere party. It would be simple to consider all criticism of parties as manifestations of a dictatorial impulse. But most students of developing nations recognize that in fact there are genuine difficulties in transferring democratic institutions from Europe and North America to the rest of the world. Democracy does not appear appropriate in societies where the overwhelming majority of the people is illiterate and therefore not in a strong position to judge intelligently between candidates and programs. Different kinds of questions about both parties and democracy are raised: how the elite is recruited, what role is played by the party in mobilizing the masses and breaking up the traditional society, what kind of values are held by the educated elite, and so on. The trend in interpreting the democratic nature of parties in developing nations is to assess their role in the transition from traditional to more modern forms of social organization. Mass participation in politics is one of the social conditions of democratic government. In some cases the party asserts a monopoly of power in order to create a modern society with the support, even if without the understanding of the peasantry. In other cases, the party seeks to preserve the power of a traditional group. Dominant parties may seek to crush opposition, or may tolerate criticism and respect an independent judiciary. Theory concerning the role of parties in a democracy is thus being modified in the light of the experience of the developing nations.

Groups and Parties

The political party is the most important single link between groups, the people, and the government in a democracy. Through the party, leadership is able to reach out into the masses for support and new sources of strength, while the masses in turn are able to focus criticism and make demands upon it. The party, if backed by a majority of the electorate,

---

[7] Louis Vallon, *Le dilemne français* (Paris, 1951); Michel Debré, *Ces Princes qui nous gouvernent* (Paris, 1957); *La République et ses problèmes* (Paris, 1952); and *La République et son pouvoir* (Paris, 1950). Also, General de Gaulle, *Discours et Messages* (Paris, 1946).

co-ordinates the multifarious functions of the government in order to achieve coherently stated aims. A minority party gives like-minded individuals and groups an opportunity to rally their forces, develop a program, and prepare for the day when power might be wielded or at least shared.

But the mass party also characterizes modern dictatorships. In the Soviet Union the Communist Party attempts to co-ordinate the activities of all major interests in the nation; while in Great Britain the majority party recognizes the right of other parties to seek the support of the electorate. Yet in both countries the party remains the most important instrument used by social groups in their quest for power. In a dictatorship the over-riding task of the party is to mobilize the masses. This is the dominant trend also in developing nations, where a small, educated elite is determined to bring about modernization. Even in parliamentary democracies parties must be able to generate widespread popular support for the policies of the executive, or else the regime is in serious trouble. Totalitarian parties in particular secure the adherence of masses of people by offering them an opportunity to gratify social impulses, but democratic parties likewise engage in some of the same activities. Most studies of totalitarian parties have emphasized the role of the party as an instrument of the leadership, while most studies of democratic parties stress the role of the party in limiting the leadership and permitting popular participation in the decision-making process. Yet, all parties may be viewed and compared in both ways. As Avery Leiserson points out, the party is a strategically critical concept for understanding *any* developed political system. "The political party, or party system, provides the major connective linkage between people and government, between separate, formal agencies and officials of government, and between official and nonofficial (extragovernmental) holders of power."[8]

Thus, groups organize, present their claims to the parties, and are in turn courted by party leaders. Decision makers are themselves members of parties and are dependent upon the support of groups for maintenance in office. The delicate process of compromising pressures must take place somewhere within the political system: Is it within the single party, or the major party of a two-party system, or a parliamentary assembly? Does the nature of the relationship between leaders and followers in British, American, French, and Russian parties reveal differences or similarities? If we compare parties as regards function, we may discover that social conflict is expressed and resolved in different ways in these countries. Comparative study of party structure may reveal the existence of common organizational trends in all party systems.

Analysis of the parties will also furnish valuable clues to the degree of

---

[8] Avery Leiserson, *Parties and Politics* (New York, 1958), p. 35.

consensus in any particular society, to the quality of its political leadership, and the prospects for stability. If party leadership is capable of mobilizing widespread social support for dynamic policies, then the organized groups are probably participating effectively in the system. But if parties are faction ridden and unable to provide a firm lead, there are probably deep-lying social divisions.

Classification of Party Systems

Classification is a first step in comparison since it enables the observer to select for analysis the like elements of various political systems. It is especially important to place parties in historical perspective because of the great differences between early and modern forms. Parties existed, in Max Weber's sense of the term, in Greece and Rome and throughout the Middle Ages. But the ancient parties were really loose factions held together by common loyalty to a leader. There was no organization of voters within a political structure, and no party system as such. The modern parties are distinguished from classical parties in that they are stable associations organizing opinion and voters.

The parties of the nineteenth century were primarily intended to *represent* interests and permit like-minded individuals to collaborate for political purposes. They were especially suitable for societies with limited suffrage and a widespread consensus regarding the underlying values of the state. A new type of party, termed by Sigmund Neumann the "party of integration,"[9] came into being in the twentieth century. The rationale of the party is no longer purely political. Some socialist parties (particularly the German Social Democratic Party) developed into virtually states within the state, with their own cultural, social, sport, and educational institutions. In self-defense, parties of the right and center also tried to become massive, though with less success, as in Britain after 1900 and France after 1944. Communist movements developed a highly effective technique of uniting forceful leadership and mass support in such a way that the former had a monopoly on decision-making power. A new twist was added by the Fascists, who mobilized a popular militia for use in street fighting.

Parties of Interest and Parties of Principle. Political parties are frequently classified according to the means employed in appealing to the electorate and organizing opinion. Some commentators distinguish between parties of interest and parties of principle, or parties of personalities and parties of program, "broker" parties and "missionary" parties. American parties would thus be considered examples of interest appeal and personalities, while British and continental parties would be programmatic. Yet this classification does not fully explain modern trends. American parties reflect ideological orientations, and continental parties represent

---

[9] Sigmund Neumann, editor, *Modern Political Parties* (Chicago, 1956), p. 404.

interests and may be led by forceful personalities. As Sigmund Neumann has persuasively argued:

The reality of modern politics represents a much more complex picture than is suggested by the simple array of insiders and outsiders, of parties of patronage and parties of principles, of expediency, interests and Weltans-chauung, of personages and programs. Such precise but utterly imaginary partitions fail to reveal the inner dynamics and tensions of a functioning de-mocracy. In fact, it is the inexhaustible mixture of all these elements that comprises the life of modern political parties—and perhaps escapes any rigid classification.[10]

Degree of Centralization. A more useful scheme of classification is in terms of degree of centralization and discipline. Robert Michels, in his classic study of *Political Parties,* argued that the dominance of the leadership characterizes *all* mass parties, including those whose ideology is militantly democratic. Michels raised a significant problem of democratic theory. Democracy obviously involves some kind of control over the rulers by the people. Every democracy is run by political parties. But who runs the parties? To what extent can the leaders be controlled by those who hold subordinate positions in the organization?

In dictatorial systems the parties are always highly centralized and serve as admirable instruments of co-ordination and control. Democratic parties vary greatly as regards the relative power of local units, members, national agencies, and leaders. American parties, for instance, are federa-tions of state political organizations. There is no formal chain of command. National leadership results from coalitions among local party leaders, not from the directives of a powerful center. "The organization of the party on a national scale," Pendleton Herring has observed, "is most accurately envisaged in terms of a network of personal relations."[11] British parties, on the other hand, are national organizations with local branches. In both the Conservative and Labor Parties decision making is vested in the leaders.[12]

The French parties run the gamut, from the British (indeed, Soviet) model to the American. Three levels of party centralization can be discerned: (1) a high degree of centralization and discipline—Communists and, to a lesser extent, Gaullists; (2) a moderate degree of centralization and discipline—Socialists and Popular Republicans; (3) a large degree of decentralization and lack of discipline—Radical Socialists, Independents, and smaller groups on the Right.

In the French Communist Party relations between local units and national bodies are proclaimed to be "democratic"—that is, each local unit elects delegates to the next highest organization, and all delegates are urged to "discuss" party policy. The impression is carefully cultivated

---

[10] *Ibid.*, p. 401.

[11] P. Herring, *Politics of a Democracy* (New York, 1940), p. 204.

[12] The structure of power in the British parties is examined at length in R. T. McKenzie's article, reproduced below, pp. 229–38.

that "democratic centralism" enables the party to act as a unity, on the basis of widespread debate within the party ranks. In practice, however, "democratic centralism" vests plenary control of the party in the leadership and confines the role of militants to the execution of policy.

A significant attempt has been made by Gaullists to introduce a large measure of discipline and centralization into their organizations. From 1948 to 1953 all power within the Rally of the French People was concentrated in the hands of the president of the party, General de Gaulle. It turned out that General de Gaulle could not impose his will on all the deputies who were elected to the National Assembly in 1951 as Gaullists, and the party disintegrated within two years. When brought back to power in 1958, General de Gaulle dissociated himself from *all* political parties, including the newly formed Union for the New Republic. After the UNR's unexpected electoral success, De Gaulle discouraged the efforts of Léon Delbecque and Jacques Soustelle to create a well-disciplined mass party. The UNR is only a pale image of the former RPF as regards leadership, organization, and program. The party presents the curious spectacle of absolute devotion to a man who refuses to be its leader!

The French Socialists (SFIO) and Popular Republicans (MRP) have organized themselves along traditionally democratic and parliamentary lines. Local units or sections are united as federations within each department, and the federations send delegates to a national congress. Regional units enjoy a fair degree of autonomy in both parties. In preparation for each national congress, policy statements by national leaders are circulated among the federations and debated by the membership. The SFIO and MRP, then, occupy a middle ground in regard to intensity of organization. Each has a fairly cohesive leadership, which is freely criticized by militants and dissidents, but which in the last analysis may take disciplinary action against those who would disrupt the party. The moderate and rightist parties in France have relatively few active members, and are run almost exclusively by parliamentarians.

The two large parties of the Federal Republic of Germany are structurally similar to the British parties. Leadership in both is concentrated and personalized. The Social Democratic Party holds an annual conference, which selects an executive committee. While the executive committee controls the deliberations of the national conference, it is itself dominated by the chairman. The Christian Democratic Union is somewhat less centralized, but leadership here is also concentrated in the hands of one individual, the chairman of the party's executive.

The degree of centralization and discipline within parties largely determines the "style" of the political process, that is, the level of the political system at which compromises are made, the cohesion of parliamentary groups, and the nature of electoral appeals. Yet in all parties there is a sharp distinction between the leadership and the followers. It would be inaccurate to claim that only in highly centralized parties of the Communist and Fascist type are the members unable to control policy.

The Number of Parties

The most popular classification of party systems is in terms of the number of parties in the field. According to this scheme we distinguish between one-party, two-party, and multiparty systems. Each type has certain characteristic features. The greatest difference is between the one-party system and all the others, for this corresponds usually to the difference between dictatorships and democracies.

One-Party Systems. The leading example of a one-party system is the Soviet Union. The Communist Party of the Soviet Union is a governing party, not one which seeks to govern in competition with other parties. It is highly centralized, and above all tolerates no organized opposition. The monolithic character of the Communist Party was shaped in the early years of the twentieth century when the followers of Lenin won out over the more moderate Russian Socialists, who wanted a labor party in the Western democratic tradition. Lenin developed his thesis in the pamphlet, *What Is to Be Done?* The Revolution would not be spontaneous, Lenin warned, but would rather have to be planned by a strongly disciplined party of professional revolutionaries. It would bring "from the outside" a knowledge of revolutionary tactics which the workers could not possibly acquire from everyday factory experience. As for "democracy" within the party, Lenin held:

> . . . "broad democracy" in Party organization, amidst the gloom of autocracy and the domination of gendarme selection, is nothing more than a *useless and harmful toy*. It is a useless toy because, as a matter of fact, no revolutionary organization has ever practiced *broad* democracy, nor could it, however much it desired to do so. It is a harmful toy because any attempt to practice the "broad democratic principles" will simply facilitate the work of the police in making big raids, it will perpetuate the prevailing primitiveness, divert the thoughts of the practical workers from the serious and imperative task of training themselves to become professional revolutionaries to that of drawing up detailed "paper" rules for election systems.

The fundamental task, then, is to plan, engineer, and maintain the Revolution without capitulating to the trade union demands of the workers whose support the party seeks.

In the first few years of Bolshevik rule, opposition groups proliferated within the party. Lenin stressed the need for establishing iron unity. The Central Committee was instructed to abolish all "fractionalism," that is, "the appearance of groups with special platforms and with the ambition to form in some degree a unit and to establish their own group discipline." In theory, individuals are free to criticize party leaders ("democratic centralism"); but any attempt to *organize* opposition constitutes a violation of party rules against "fractionalism."

Ever since, the party has firmly maintained its ban on fractionalism, which in effect makes it impossible for members to rally support against the policies of the leadership. But the main function of the Communist Party within the Soviet system is not one of debate and criticism. It is rather implementation of the decisions made by the political leadership, and co-ordination of all social and economic activities for that purpose.[13]

In most of the developing nations, there is also a tendency towards a one-party system. It is not always brought about by suppression of minority opinion, however. For example, the Indian Congress Party dominates the national and state legislatures, even though it receives less than a majority of the popular vote as a whole, because the opposition parties are hopelessly fragmented. The emerging native leaderships in these nations are driving above all for rapid economic and social moderni-zation. Debate and criticism seem to be irrelevant, since the course of action to be followed is clearly marked out. The masses have to be taken out of their tribes and villages, and put to work at the immense task of creating a modern nation. Throughout the new nations the educated class is sharply set off from the illiterate masses, and runs the state in a paternalistic fashion. The "one-party dominant" system is characteristic of the nations of Asia, Africa, the Middle East, and Latin America.

Two and Multiparty Systems. It is always difficult to explain the origins of social and political institutions. While Catholics, workers, peasants, and others have created special political parties for themselves throughout most of Europe, in the United States and Britain correspond-ing elements in the population seem capable of working together within the same party. Yet social diversity is perhaps even greater in the United States and Britain than in many nations with multiparty systems, like Switzerland or Denmark.

Perhaps the key element in the crystallization of party systems is the timing of political and class conflict. In Britain the cleavage between supporters and opponents of the king paralleled a division between the land owning and commercial classes; the foundation was thus provided for a clear-cut fight between two parties only, the Whigs (backed by the middle class and supporting Parliament) and the Tories (rooted in the landed aristocracy and favoring the king).

In the United States the desire to retain or capture the all-important prize of the presidency provided the impetus for the early party conflict between Federalists and Republicans (1789–1816), then between Whigs and Democrats (1830–1856), and finally Republicans and Democrats (since 1865). Once established, the two-party mold became increasingly

---

[13] On the early conflict between Lenin and the moderates within the Russian Social Democratic Party, see the first volume of E. H. Carr, *The Bolshevik Revo-lution* (New York, 1951). The Lenin citation from *What Is to Be Done* may be found in *Essentials of Lenin* (London: Lawrence & Wishart, 1947), Vol. I, p. 245. For the structure of the Communist Party, see Merle Fainsod, *How Russia Is Ruled* (Cam-bridge, Mass., 1953), especially Chapter V.

set and was adapted to changing circumstances. In Britain and the United States all important social forces agreed on the *form* of the state by the late eighteenth century; thus a universally accepted governmental system was at the disposal of the nation in resolving the social and class conflicts arising from the Industrial Revolution.

Throughout most of Europe the nineteenth century was marked by conflict between a landholding aristocracy attached to monarchy, and a rising commercial and professional middle class seeking to limit monarchical government by means of parliamentary checks. In France the decision in favor of an anticlerical republic in 1789 was never accepted by the conservative rightists, who succeeded several times in restoring a monarchy. By the end of the nineteenth century, while the outlines of the constitutional system were still unsettled, the country was convulsed by social conflicts resulting from the Industrial Revolution. The absence of a generally accepted and stable state made it impossible for the society to deal effectively with these conflicts. Widespread popular discontent permitted Communist and Fascist movements to make considerable headway in the twentieth century, thereby further splintering the party system.

Viewed functionally, the differences between the two-party and multi-party systems are not as great as it may appear. Every modern industrial society, we noted, is composed of constellations of interests—industrial, financial, business, retail, agricultural, shipping, labor, and so on. Political parties usually bring those interests together and reconcile their disagreements. The parties in Britain and the United States bind large coalitions of interests. They seek to win the allegiance of the "undecided" or independent voters. If the parties were to appeal exclusively to workers or to the middle classes they would become permanent minorities. A two-party system generally forces the leaders of the large parties to co-operate and compromise, and fixes responsibility for a legislative program upon the majority party.

The continental parties, on the other hand, reflect regional, group, or ideological points of view. They compromise their differences first at the electoral stage, then in Parliament. In a sense, the counterpart of Anglo-American parties on the European continent are electoral *groupements* and parliamentary coalitions. Comparative study of the ways in which organized groups influence parties, and have their claims reconciled, is thus essential in order to gain an understanding of any given political system.

It should be pointed out, finally, that a party system is not the outcome of reasoned discussion of advantages and disadvantages, but of historical processes. The French traditionally seek to balance off their potentially dangerous and highly centralized administration with a sensitive, responsive, and ever-changing National Assembly. French politicians under the Third and Fourth Republics were skillful at the process of forming coalitions which assured a degree of compromise and yet checked attempts at dictatorship. Some multiparty systems (as in Switzerland, Denmark, Norway, Sweden, Holland, and Belgium) produce a high degree of governmental stability. On the other hand, a two-party system does not automatically eliminate sharp social conflicts. The question of home rule for Ireland and the American Civil War so stirred passions that the operation of the two-party system was completely disrupted. Whenever the democratic process is rejected by powerful groups, regardless of the nature of the party system, government does not function effectively.

Political Ideologies

The term "ideology" was first popularized by Napoleon when he used it in a derogatory fashion to refer to intellectuals opposing his policies. It was taken up by Marx and Engels, who distinguished between the material basis of society and the "superstructure" (including ideology, religion, legal systems, etc.) which rests upon it. Law, politics, morality, and religion in the Marxist view reflect the interests of the class in power.

At the other extreme from the Marxist theory of ideology is the view that ideas command interests. Even an observer as sympathetic to Marxism as Karl Mannheim suggested the existence of a "utopian" mentality, which does not derive from the life situation of the individual concerned. "A state of mind is utopian when it is incongruous with the state of reality within which it occurs." Thus, a businessman could develop ideas that transcend the reality of his economic or class interests. The modification is important. It admits the possibility that ideas might not emerge directly out of interests. Max Weber has argued cogently that some key belief systems—Protestantism, for example—may permit transformation of an existing reality. In encouraging thrift and hard work, Protestant ideology undermined feudal society and paved the way for the emergence of capitalist production.[14]

The controversy between the theorists of "ideology" and "utopia" has perhaps obscured a central feature of the political process: that generally ideologies are related to economic and social groups. In all political systems there is an understandable tendency for individuals and groups to define and defend their interests in universal or idealistic terms. Every group attempts to rationalize its position or program, even if only for tactical reasons. The alcohol-producing groups in France present themselves before the general public as defenders of certain "ideals" or principles. For example, they claim that wine contributes to the good life, home distilling of alcohol is a precious advantage for millions of "little" people, beet cultivation is essential to the national defense, and so on. In a general way, all major social groups tend to identify themselves with the nation as a whole. Thus, what's good for business (or even a single firm, like General Motors) is good for the country; the workers are the sole

[14] See Karl Mannheim, *Ideology and Utopia* (New York, 1949), and Max Weber, *Protestant Ethic and the Spirit of Capitalism.*

creators of value; and a sturdy peasantry is the backbone of the nation. These transparent rationalizations are usually recognized as such by politicians and the public alike.

Political Ideas and Movements. Each of the major social classes in a modern society also tends to associate itself with a particular interpretation of politics. This is not to say that all workers or businessmen or farmers think and vote alike, but merely that certain voting and ideological trends may usually be discerned. The clash of social forces is generally paralleled by a somewhat more complex clash of political ideologies. Socialism, conservatism, liberalism, and communism are all connected in some fashion with social classes, but these ideologies are not necessarily rationalizations of class interests. There are also ways of looking at the world in terms of key analytic concepts, *attempts to change reality* and not merely to justify it.

The comparative study of ideology involves the identification of specific ideologies in various countries, and tracing them to dominant social groups. What is the nature of conservative, or communist, or socialist ideology in different nations? The student should attempt to compare these ideologies in terms of content (for example, conservatism in Britain and the United States, or communism in Europe and Asia), and relationship to groups. Communism in an advanced country like France may receive major support from the industrial workers; in an underdeveloped country, where there is no proletariat, it may be primarily an intellectual or agrarian movement. Attention might be focused on particular groups, like the working class in the United States and continental Europe, and comparison made between their ideologies. The nature and intensity of ideological conflict should also be studied comparatively, since this is a fairly reliable indicator of stability or instability, consensus or lack of consensus, in a political system. Generalizations concerning groups and ideologies will reveal both differences and similarities, which can be explained only in terms of "conditioning factors," such as development of habits of compromise, dynamism of political leadership, effectiveness of political parties, viability of the economy, and so on. Certain social groups are of particular importance during periods of rapid political change, for example, the intellectuals. In short, virtually every significant part of the political system can be explored by using the relationship between groups and ideologies as an interpretive tool.

Chapter IV. Group Theory

Introductory Note

THE EARLY literature on groups shared many of the characteristics of studies of political parties. Groups, like parties, were either ignored, treated casually, or considered a dread disease. The first major theoretical discussion of groups was A. F. Bentley's *Process of Government* (1908). It was a serious attempt to view groups analytically, without condemnation and exhortation as a primary goal. But his book had little immediate influence. It was not until the 1920's that monographs began to appear on groups, and most were case studies of individual groups or of conflict situations involving group pressures. Mention may be made of Peter Odegard's book on *The Anti-Saloon League* (1928), E. P. Herring's *Group Representation before Congress* (1929), E. E. Schattschneider's *Politics, Pressures and the Tariff* (1935), the work of Belle Zeller and Dayton McKean on the state legislatures of New York and New Jersey (1938), Oliver Garceau's *Political Life of the American Medical Association* (1941), Avery Leiserson's *Administrative Regulation* (1942), and Stephen K. Bailey's *Congress Makes a Law* (1946). Although some of these writers were concerned with the theoretical implications of group analysis, most were drawn to the study of groups because it was "reality." Group study reflected disenchantment with the formal and juridical study of political institutions.

The most important single analytic work since Bentley is David Truman's *The Governmental Process* (1951). While most early writers sought to expose and condemn groups, Truman perceived them as vital parts of the political system. "Without some working conception of the political role of interest groups, their function, and the ways in which their powers are exercised," he wrote, "we shall not be able adequately to understand the nature of the political process."

Up to the time of the publication of *The Governmental Process* most monographs were by Americans and on American groups. Indeed, there was long an impression that lobbies and pressure groups were peculiarly American phenomena. In the early 1950's interest groups were discovered by European political scientists. The outpouring of literature on European interest groups has been torrential, as evidenced by: Jean Meynaud, *Les Groupes de Pressions en France* (1958) and *Nouvelles études sur les Groupes de Pression en France* (1962); Samuel E. Finer, *The Anonymous*

129

Empire (1958); Allen Potter, *Organized Groups in British Politics* (1961); and in Henry Ehrmann, (ed.), *Interest Groups on Four Continents* (1958). Thirty years ago the literature on interest groups was so sparse that comparison of American and European groups was virtually impossible. Today, the literature on interest groups both in and outside the United States is so vast that comparison is unavoidable. The expansion of our substantive knowledge of interest groups is by itself of considerable theoretical importance, since it is now more feasible to check hypotheses concerning political behavior.

A number of significant attempts have been made to apply group theory to comparative study. Professor Almond's "Research Note: A Comparative Study of Interest Groups and the Political Process," reprinted below, is perhaps the most stimulating of these analytic efforts. The reader is also referred to the suggestive article by Joseph LaPalombara, "The Utility and Limitations of Interest Group Theory in Non-American Field Situations," *Journal of Politics*, February, 1960; the excellent symposium in *The Annals* (September, 1958), "Unofficial Government, Pressure Groups and Lobbies," and also H. Eckstein, *Pressure Group Politics* (1960).

We have already discussed some of the advantages of the group approach, and also some of the drawbacks, particularly the lack of widely accepted definitions. Study of groups is a means, perhaps the best single means, of approaching and understanding any political system. Groups constitute the raw material, the "stuff" of politics. Description of groups, their internal organization, access to decision makers and the way in which they exert influence is extremely important in the comparative analysis of political systems. But the student should also remember that groups cannot be understood in a vacuum. They must be related to the social structure, culture, and political institutions of a nation. The universe of comparative analysis should consist of as large a number of relevant factors as is possible—not only parties and interest groups, but social groups, ideologies, values, and policy decisions. In the final analysis, a theory of groups must be part of a larger theory of the political system.

Readings

13. INTEREST GROUPS AND THE POLITICAL PROCESS*
Gabriel A. Almond

THE GENERAL OBJECTIVES

COMPARATIVE analyses of political institutions have thus far been confined to formal governmental institutions, and to political party and electoral systems. Dissatisfaction with these formal comparisons is widespread in view of the generally appreciated fact that formally similar governmental and party systems often function in radically different ways. And the search for explanation of the formally similar but differently functioning political systems has turned to vague residual categories such as "social structure," "national character," "consensus" or its absence, and "public opinion.". . .

We turn to the comparative study of interest groups not with the hope that these rather than parties or governmental institutions will yield *the principles* of discrimination between types of political systems, but rather with the expectation that the systematic examination of interest groups in their complex interrelations with public opinion, political parties and formal governmental institutions will enable us to differentiate more accurately between political systems as *wholes*. In other words, the growing concern among scholars with interest groups and public opinion is the consequence of a search for a more complete and systematic conception of the political process as a whole, rather than a search for an approach which is an *alternative* to the present emphasis on formal governmental institutions. . . .

The kinds of interest groups which are present in a society, the specificity or diffuseness of their demands, their conceptions of the political arena and of the "rules of the game," the ethos which they bring with them into the political process—these are the "raw materials" of politics—the unaggregated demands—which some set of mechanisms must transform into political personnel and public policy.

These general observations about interest groups not only suggest their importance as a subject of study, but set certain specifications in research design if the maximum value of a comparative study is to be attained. A good research job on interest groups in a particular country which may make possible meaningful comparisons with other countries, must examine

* From "Research Note: A Comparative Study of Interest Groups and the Political Process," *The American Political Science Review*, Vol. LII, No. 1 (March, 1958). By permission. [This article is a summary of the work of the Committee on Comparative Politics of the Social Science Research Council.]

the interest group system in its relations with the social structure and culture on the one hand and the other parts of the political structure on the other. In identifying the interest group system in any particular country this broad functional approach will prevent us from identifying interest groups with any particular kind of structure. The function of articulating and transmitting group interests may be performed in one system typically by the well organized and bureaucratized "pressure groups" familiar in the West, or it may be performed in another system, typically through an informal and intermittent process of communication between and among class and status groups such as large landholders or businessmen, and cliques of bureaucrats and/or army officers. If it is possible to state the theme of the comparative study in the form of a single question it might be: What form does the articulation of political interests take in various societies, and how are these interests transmitted to other parts of the political and governmental structure, and translated into choices of political personnel and public policy? . . .

INTEREST GROUPS AND PUBLIC OPINION

One of the central problems in interest group theory is the relation between manifest and latent interests. To what extent can organized, overt interests be taken as reflecting the interest tendencies of the general population? The phenomena of the mob in non-Western countries, of riots in totalitarian countries, of "Caesarism," "Poujadism," and "incivisme," in the European area suggest that popular attitudes and tendencies are a separable factor in the political process, the properties of which cannot be inferred from the existing organized tendencies and from electoral behavior. Any characterization of a political system would be incomplete if it was confined solely to a description of current organizational patterns and processes. Latent interest may not only result in future changes in organization and process, it establishes an atmosphere which affects the contemporary operations of the political process. . . . The ways in which interest groups conceive of their audiences, and the ways in which they represent their interests to the public should throw light on the functioning of the political system as a whole. For example, French business associations are different from the American in that they do not engage openly and on a large scale in public "informational" activities. This may reflect a general condition of fragmentation in political communication in France, a condition of distrust and alienation among interests. . . .

INTEREST GROUPS AND POLITICAL PARTIES

In the Anglo-American type of political system the functions of political parties and interest groups are sharply differentiated. Interest groups articulate political demands in the society, seek support for these demands among other groups by advocacy and bargaining, and attempt to transform these demands into authoritative public policy by influencing the choice of political personnel, and the various processes of public policy-making and enforcement. Political parties tend to be free of ideological rigidity, and are aggregative, *i.e.*, seek to form the largest possible interest group coalitions by offering acceptable choices of political personnel and public policy. Both the interest group systems and the party systems are differentiated, bureaucratized, and autonomous. Each unit in the party and interest group systems comes into the "market," so to speak, with an adjustive bargaining ethos. Furthermore, the party system stands between the interest group system and the authoritative policy-making agencies and screens them from the particularistic and disintegrative impact of special interests. The party system aggregates interests and transforms them into a relatively small number of alternative general policies. Thus this set of relationships between the party system and the interest group system enables choice among general policies to take place in the legislature, and assures that the bureaucracy will tend to function as a neutral instrument of the political agencies.

We might take as our second type a model summarizing the properties of the political systems which are to be found in Asia, the Middle East and Latin America in which neither parties nor interest groups are fully differentiated. Associational interest groups such as trade unions and business associations may exist in the urban Westernized parts of the society, but in the village and the countryside interest organization takes the form of lineage, caste, status, class and religious groups, which transmit political demands to the other parts of the political structure by means of informal communication. In one version of this class of systems parties tend to be *ad hoc* coalitions without permanent bureaucracies, and without grass roots organization. They exist primarily in election periods and in effect cease to exist in the intervals between. Given such weak and non-aggregative party systems the capacity of the legislatures to formulate alternative policy choices may be seriously impaired, as is their capacity to control the bureaucracies. In many of these political systems the significant political groups are neither the parties, nor the associational interest groups, but elements or cliques within the bureaucracy, and the army; and cliques, informal groupings and powerful families formed within such non-associational interests as religious communities, the large landowners, the business community, and the like. The political process consists of the informal communication and flow of influence between these informally organized interests, and groups within the bureaucracy and the army.

The instabilities of this type of political system arise out of the fact that the agencies for the articulation, communication, and aggregation of interests are incomplete and unrepresentative, as well as out of the fact that the demands transmitted into the political system from interest groups are vague, diffuse, and of radically unlike content and intensity. Latent interests, lacking overt and organized channels of expression may suddenly break into the political arena. The information available to influential groups and individuals about the expectations and attitudes of the various interests in the society cannot be complete or accurate. Hence, calculation is impossible, and the flow of political interaction involves under-reaction and over-reaction, violence and apathy, alternations of periods of political latency, with sudden and violent shifts in power.

Given the basic instability of this general class of political systems, authoritarian stabilizations are a frequent event. Indeed, in many of them the developmental pattern is one of a shift from an unstable pluralism to authoritarianism, and then back again, or a shift from the authoritarianism of one clique to that of another. Authoritarianism may be based on control of the army either by a clique of army officers, or a clique of bureaucrats controlling the army, or by a coalition of both. Still another pattern is one in which the desire on the part of a controlling group to secure its own power and destroy opposition, or to mobilize the society for industrialization and national expansion, leads to the formation of an authoritarian party which actually penetrates the countryside. In some cases as in Turkey and in India the objectives of the ruling groups and of the dominant party are tutelary. That is, the function of the party is not only control and mobilization, but also political acculturation, the preparation of the ground for the emergence of a Western-type associational system and of a Western-type party system with a coherent, responsible, and loyal opposition.

Thus, it should be quite clear that there are many kinds of non-Western political systems. They all appear to have in common (1) a fragmented political culture as a consequence of Westernization, in many cases added on to an indigenous cultural heterogeneity, (2) poor political communications and a high degree of interest latency which renders political calculation difficult if not impossible, and (3) a party system which is incapable of aggregating and synthesizing interest demands into a small number of political alternatives either of personnel or of public policy. On a scale of political differentiation one would have to say that certain kinds of structures such as associational interest groups, the mass media of communication, and the kind of party system common in the West and essential for the functioning of a modern mass-suffrage parliamentary system, are present at best in only a limited degree. On a scale of functional specialization one would have to say that in the absence of fully developed associational interest groups, party systems, and modern media of communication, the functions of interest articulation, aggregation, communication and transmission are largely performed by bureaucratic or army cliques, traditional structures such as lineage or status groupings, and by mobs, street demonstrations and the like, which serve as one of the agencies by means of which latent interests are articulated and transmitted.

A third type of political system is exemplified by France and Italy and by the Germany of the Weimar Republic. Contemporary Germany appears to be moving in the direction of an autonomous interest group system and an aggregative two-party system; toward the Anglo-American model, in other words. In the French and Italian political systems parties and interest groups are organized and bureaucratized, but they are not autonomous systems. They interpenetrate one another and consequently fail to realize the two-stage pattern of the political process characteristic of the English and American systems. There are some parties which more or less control interest groups (*e.g.*, the Communist party and the Communist dominated trade unions, and to a lesser extent the Socialist parties and the Socialist trade unions). There are some interest groups which more or less control other interest groups and parties (*e.g.*, the Church, the Catholic trade unions, and the Catholic parties, business interest groups, and the center and right wing parties, and the like).

When parties control interest groups they inhibit the capacity of interest groups to formulate pragmatic specific demands; they impart a political-ideological content to interest group activity. When interest groups control parties they inhibit the capacity of the party to combine specific interests into programs with wider appeal. What reaches the legislative process from the interest groups and through the political parties thus are the "raw," unaggregated demands of specific interests, or the diffuse, uncompromising, or revolutionary tendencies of the Church and the movements of the extreme right or left. Since no interest group is large enough to have a majority, and the party system cannot aggregate different interests into a stable majority and a coherent opposition, the electoral and legislative processes fail to provide alternative, effective choices. The result is a legislature penetrated by relatively narrow interests and uncompromising ideological tendencies, a legislature which can be used as an arena for propaganda, or for the protection of special interests, by veto or otherwise, but not for the effective and timely formulation and support of large policy decisions. And without a strong legislature, special interests and ideological tendencies penetrate the bureaucracy, and undermine its neutral, instrumental character.

A fourth type of political system is exemplified by the Scandinavian and Low Countries. These systems appear to differ from the French and Italian in two respects. First, the party systems tend to be aggregative (*e.g.*, the Scandinavian Socialist parties, the Belgian Socialist and Catholic parties). Second, the relations between parties and interests appear to be more consensual, which makes stable majority and opposition coalitions possible. Thus, though the party systems fail to aggregate interests as thoroughly as in the British case, the public policy-making function of the legislature is not undermined to the same extent as in the French and Italian cases. What appears to happen in the Scandinavian and the Low Countries is that the function of interest aggregation and general policy formulation occurs at both the party and parliamentary levels. The parties are partly aggregative of interests, but "majority-minority" aggregation takes place finally in the coalition-making process in the legislature. This coalition-making process may be organized by parties in the formation of cabinets and the enactment of legislation or it may take the form of interest coalitions organized around issues of public policy. The capacity for stable majority-minority party coalitions and for relatively flexible issue-oriented interest coalitions is dependent upon the existence of a basic political consensus which affects both parties and interest groups. These appear to be the properties of the so-called "working multi-party systems.". . .

The relation between political parties and interest groups could be viewed as a continuum with substantial autonomy at one limit and sub- and super-ordination at the other. The relationship patterns which exist in historical political systems always involve two-way flows of influence, which differ from one another in the dominant direction of the flow and the different patterns which are occasioned by different kinds of issues. Thus the extreme case of the Communist Party–Communist trade union dominance still involves a flow of information and influence from trade union to party, but the dominant direction of the flow is from party to trade union. In the case of the church and Catholic parties the flow of influence varies from country to country, and even among regions within countries. In addition, in certain areas of policy Catholic parties may be relatively free of church influence, or may even influence the church to take a position consistent with or supportive of that of the party. In Germany, for example, the fact that the CDU has both Protestant and Catholic support seriously limits the power of the Catholic church to intervene in party policy-making. In other legislative fields, the freedom of Catholic parties may be sharply circumscribed by a rigid church position, as in the field of educational subsidies and the like. In other policy areas, *e.g.*, social-economic, there may be more give and take in the relations between church and Catholic party.

These considerations suggested that analysis of the flow of influence between parties and interest groups would require not only an examination of the interconnections through financing, interlocking memberships and directorates, sharing of ideological beliefs and the like, but would also require a judicious use of case study methods to discover the way in which different kinds of legislative issues affected the flow and pattern of influences between interest groups and parties. . . .

INTEREST GROUPS AND THE LEGISLATIVE PROCESS

Interest groups tend to seek out the important points of access in the legislative process; the points where legislative policy is initiated, and where revision, vetoing, and favorable action are possible. Hence, the constitutional separation and distribution of powers, legislative organization and procedure, the characteristics of the electoral system and the parliamentary party organization, set the problem of interest group access in the legislative process. Thus, the American system of federalism, and separation of powers, creates a different interest group "target structure" than does the British parliamentary-cabinet system. The American federal system produces a party structure with its center of gravity at the state level. This kind of decentralized party organization limits the possibilities of congressional party discipline and hence opens the legislative process to interest group penetration. The susceptibility of the legislature to interest group penetration is enhanced by the American single-member district electoral system which frequently exposes the legislator to the effective pressure of interests which may be especially concentrated in his constituency. In addition, the American separation of powers system grants a powerful and independent role in legislation to both the House and Senate. And since relatively large collegial bodies are, other things being equal, less able to aggregate interests and protect themselves against interest penetration than Cabinet-dominated parliaments, this aspect of American constitutional structure contributes significantly to interest group action in the legislative process. If we consider this constitutional and statutory structure on the one hand, and the economic, regional, ethnic, and religious composition of the American population on the other, it is hardly surprising that the penetration of the legislative process by interest groups in the United States is greater than in the United Kingdom. There, a unitary constitution, and a Cabinet-dominated parliament make possible a disciplined parliamentary party system which protects the legislative process from effective interest group penetration. The main targets of interest groups are the upper levels of the parliamentary and extra-parliamentary party structure where power is concentrated, and the bureaucracy. And because of the cohesion of the party system and the concentration of legislative power in the Cabinet, the impact of any single interest group—with the exception of the trade unions—is quite limited.

France presents yet another problem of interest group access. In the United States aggregation and synthesis of interests is performed by the party system and a powerful presidency responsible to a national constituency. France has neither a powerful executive nor an aggregative party system. A culturally and politically fragmented society choosing its legislators by means of proportional representation produces a legislature capable of producing only weak and unstable coalitions. The standing committees of the *Assemblée* are in many cases colonized by powerful interests. The net effect of this situation is a legislative process which can only rarely enact significant "national-interest" legislation, but which regularly and characteristically protects and subsidizes special interests. Still a fourth type of legislative interest group pattern is to be found in the Scandinavian countries where a stronger executive and a more aggregative party system limits the impact of interest groups in the legislative process.

These characteristics of constitutional, legislative, and party structures affect not only the tactics of interest groups, but the very goals and objectives which they can reasonably attain. A disciplined party system and a powerful executive forces interest groups to direct their energies to the upper levels of the executive and the bureaucracy where only moderate claims, well supported with technical information, become possible. A non-aggregative and undisciplined party system as in France opens up the legislative process to covert interest group domination of legislative committees and agencies, or to propagandistic interest group maneuvers of which "Poujadism" is only an extreme instance.

These hypotheses about patterns of interest-group-legislative relations in the European area suggest the importance of a careful analysis of the functioning of the constitutional, legislative, electoral, and party systems as they relate to interest group access. In other words, the aim of research in interest-group-legislative relations will be to determine the extent to which the parliamentary parties, or extra-parliamentary legislative institutions such as the American Presidency, are able to maintain independence of interest groups and relative freedom to legislate or influence legislation (a) by combining several interest groups in their support, and (b) by establishing and maintaining the discipline of the parliamentary party as a means of withstanding interest group pressures. . . .

COMPARISON OF WESTERN AND
NON-WESTERN INTEREST GROUPS

. . . Every independent society makes political choices, *i.e.*, broad policy decisions which are backed up by severe sanctions. In making and enforcing these political decisions all societies have some way of articulating and communicating political demands, aggregating these demands, translating them into choices of political personnel and public policy, executing these decisions in specific cases, and testing the appropriateness of these specific actions. In studying interest groups comparatively the participants in the study are primarily concerned with the structures, institutions and processes by means of which these functions are accomplished. Research conclusions as to which structures and processes perform which functions in different societies, and how they perform them, will provide the basic materials for comparative analysis.

Not only are these functions performed in all independent political systems—Western and non-Western—but the structures and processes which perform them in both areas overlap to a considerable extent. The West is more like the non-West than we sometimes think. Even in the most differentiated and specialized political systems in the West, such interest groups as families, status groups, and religious communities affect the political process. And in most of the non-Western countries—however "underdeveloped"—the beginnings of functionally specialized political parties, and associational interest groups such as trade unions and trade associations, may be found. Even in the field of political communication the highly elaborated mass communication systems of Western societies should not obscure the fact that informal and face-to-face communication is still a political factor of enormous importance.

In still another respect Western and non-Western systems are alike. While it is true in general that Western political structures are more specialized than the non-Western, there is much "multi-functionalism" in the West. Thus in a country such as France political parties and interest groups are not sharply differentiated from one another. And in all countries the structural specialization of policy-making and administration is by no means complete, nor can it ever be complete. If it is peculiar to non-Western countries that bureaucracies are penetrated by interest groups and ideological tendencies, this situation differs only in degree from the Western pattern where rationality, responsibility, and neutrality are only partially realized at best.

14. GROUPS AND GROUP THEORY*

Roy C. Macridis

WITHOUT ATTEMPTING to enter into a detailed discussion it would seem to me that group analysis is (epistemological labels may be used without implying any guilt by association) a crude form of determinism. Interest is the primary propelling force and every action is based upon sharing of interest. Power configuration is basically the configuration of competing and struggling interests organized into groups. Ideology, values, the state, the formal organization of political decision-making, and the content of decisions are determined by the parallelogram of group forces. Perhaps this may be an oversimplification, but I do not think that it does violence to the scheme of group analysis. It is interesting, for instance, that not only concern with the state recedes into the background in the writings of all proponents of the group theory, but also the role of ideology, of extra-economic and non-rational motivational patterns, and of the political system as an independent factor influencing group behavior.

But while Marx with his class theory and its deterministic underpinnings provided a broad theory of history and development through which man would ultimately be able to shed interest in order to attain freedom—that is, while Marxist determinism led progressively to higher stages of consciousness and perception of the environment, group theorists anchor man's life into the perennial group conflict which by their very nature groups can never transcend. Not only our lives remain intolerably and unredeemably "nasty and brutish," but our theoretical universe in

* From *The Journal of Politics* (February, 1961). By permission.

terms of which we can explain behavior becomes unduly restricted. Interest is the propelling force and man is forever destined to live in an environment that mirrors interest. It may be argued that group theory is "realistic" and, furthermore, that the "group" is a far more useful concept analytically than "class." I doubt it very much—first, because group analysis as I have noted has normative implications and second and more important, because the concepts of "interest" and "group" are fuzzy analytically, perhaps just as much as that of the "class."

But the above criticisms involve philosophic questions that are highly controversial. What is more important for our discussion is that group theory puts exaggerated demands upon empirical research and data collection. If an understanding of a political system at a given moment depends upon the study of the total configuration of interests the task of the political scientist becomes stupendous. We have to study every and all interest groups, index them and measure carefully and constantly the increments of power and influence they generate before we can make any statements about the most meaningful aspects of politics—the resolution of conflict and policy-making, including foreign policy. We would have to elaborate precise units of power in order to assess and reassess continuously group power. But such a measurement would involve so many variables that meaningful measurement and quantification would become hopeless. . . . Where then do we start and even more important where do we stop indexing and measuring group power and interaction: business interests, economic interests, labor interests, religious interests, local interests, bureaucratic interests, organized interests, to say nothing of potential groups that hide in their bosom potential interests that are ready to blossom forth? How many of them do we study and exactly for what purpose? The index of power at any given moment would be inaccurate unless we measure the potential counter-power that can be generated by the potential groups. How can we tell exactly under what conditions groups will compromise? What can we learn about the perception that groups have of other groups or the total group configuration? How can we measure the adherence of groups to the "rules of the game" that in all political systems curb, limit and often shape group action? What I am saying, of course, is that group analysis may prove to be both self-defeating and misleading. We cannot know the power configuration in a society unless we have studied all groups as they interact, and when we do so we still do not know why groups interact in one manner rather than another.

Finally, group analysis seems to beg rather than answer the very questions it purports to ask—to give us an explanatory frame of reference in terms of which we can account for differences and uniformities in political behavior and action. This is the central problem of comparative analysis. Group theory assumes the existence of organized groups or interests that can be defined in objective terms; labor, business, and agriculture are some of the more obvious and frequently studied ones. It is further assumed that their members have a common perception of the interest involved which accounts for the very formation of the group and its organization and articulation. So far so good. Descriptive and comparative study immediately presents us with extreme variations in the organization, cohesiveness, membership strength, forms of action and patterns of interaction among these groups. It reveals some striking differences in the manner in which interest groups in various political systems relate to the political parties and the political processes.

To attempt to explain such differences in terms of a group theory is impossible. Why are, for instance, agricultural groups so well organized under the National Farmers Union in England, to which more than 90 per cent of the farmers belong, but dispersed and relatively unorganized in the United States and France? Why are more than 85 per cent of all manufacturing concerns in England represented in their national association while not more than 6 per cent are so represented in the United States? Why do more than 50 per cent of the British workers belong to trade unions which are almost all represented in their peak organization, the TUC, while in France membership remains low and articulation of labor interest dispersed in at least four Trade Union organizations? Why is it that in England interest groups avoid large publicity campaigns and center their attention on the Party and the Cabinet, while in the United States interest groups perform important publicity and propaganda functions through the media of communications and center their efforts on the electorate and the legislature, primarily, while French interest groups shy publicity and center their activities upon the legislature and the administration?

A number of answers can be given to these questions in the form of propositions to be carefully investigated, but I submit none of them are researchable in terms of group analysis. The answers are often given (without adequate evidence, to be sure) in terms of other categories: the American political system *with multiple foci* of decision-making, for instance, makes the legislature and more particularly individual legislators more susceptible to pressure either directly or indirectly; *the diffusion of power* in the political party in the United States makes any effort to control or influence the Party unrewarding for pressure groups; the same applies for France, where it is often pointed out that "interest" and "interest groups" are divided and sub-divided and lose their "objective" or "real" interest *because of political reasons*. The workers, the farmers, the teachers have no spokesmen and no cohesive and disciplined interest articulation because they are divided into a number of "political" or "ideological" families. As for group interaction, again the differences are striking: in some cases, groups interact within a given political party and compromise their differences; in other cases, compromise is made outside of the political parties, or is not made at all, leading to immobility; elsewhere compromise is made impossible by virtue of the fact that interests are "colonized" by ideological parties so that interest groups mirror the ideological divisions of the society instead of causing them.

In all cases the reasons advanced for a given pattern of group organiza-tion, action and interaction derive from categories other than group analysis would suggest: the formal organization of power; the cohesiveness or dispersal of political power; the two-party or multi-party configura-tion; the "climate of public opinion"; the intensity of consensus or lack of same in given political systems. . . .

Let me further illustrate the shortcomings of group analysis as an explanatory theory by borrowing from the conclusions of authors inter-ested in comparative study or who did field work in foreign political systems. Professor Ehrmann writes in his introduction to *Interest Groups on Four Continents:* "The political system, as well as the social structure, will often decide whether claims raised in the name of special interests will be successful or not; it may determine the "style" used by pressure groups when raising their demands."[1] Professor Lavau, after indicating in detail the fragmentation of many French interests because of ideological reasons, points out that "This hostile ideological and moral climate surrounding pressure groups in France reacts in turn upon their be-havior. . . ." He indicates that some pressure groups if *not politicized* play an aggregative and integrative role that the French political parties do not play. This is, for instance, the case with some peak organizations that include a variety of professional groups. "Since it is (their) function to arbitrate or mediate possible conflicts between different member or-ganizations, this role confers upon (them), in the eyes of the administra-tion and the politicians, a considerable dignity."[2] In fact one of the most pervasive efforts of the French interest groups is to liberate themselves from a divided political culture and be able to organize their membership on the basis of interest alone. That they fail more often than they succeed is an indication of the importance, and what is more, the independence, of political and ideological factors. Professor Sam Finer accepts Beer's emphasis upon the British "consensus" and the general agreement of the British leadership on a number of policy issues as a factor that shapes and structures group action. He adds that such beliefs are brought together in English political life by the myth of "public interest" which provides a yardstick in terms of which interest claims are judged. The image of the national interest acts as a cohesive force. Professor Beer in an excellent analysis points to the parallel development in Great Britain of well organized and integrated political parties with well organized national interest groups.[3] For the purpose of our discussion this parallelism between interest organization and party organization is striking and one cannot

---

[1] Henry Ehrmann, *Interest Groups on Four Continents* (1959), p. 1.

[2] *Ibid.*, pp. 61 and 78.

[3] Samuel Beer, "Group Representation in Britain and the United States," *Annals* (September, 1958). [Reproduced below.]

avoid the impression that British interests gradually evolved a pattern of
organization and cohesiveness *that corresponds* to and *parallels* the highly
centralized and cohesive political system; that perhaps their "style" of
action was conditioned by the cohesiveness of the political culture and the
organization of political parties very much as the dispersion of the French
interest groups may well have been shaped by the diversity of the French
political culture and multi-partism. Joseph LaPalombara,[4] points out
bluntly that many interest groups in Italy (and the same applies to
France) operate within the political sub-cultures of the system (communist, catholic, socialist, etc.) resulting in an enormous proliferation
(and the same applies to France) of pressure groups. Writing for the
Swedish pressure groups Gunnar Heckscher points out that ". . . there
is hardly any point at which this term (politics of compromise) seems
more definitely warranted than with regard to interest organizations: an
equilibrium is maintained chiefly through the willingness of each of them
to make concessions in order to achieve important results. . . ." But why?
Because "the pluralistic character of the Swedish society is openly
accepted on all sides."[5] Back we come to the general values of the
community in terms of which the role of pressure groups and pressure
group action and interaction can be explained. Jean Meynaud, in his
comprehensive study of French pressure groups in France[6] comes very
close to a very important theoretical insight, when he points out that the
fragmentation of parties like the fragmentation of the groups has its origin
in the divisions in the public mind. Political ideologies and religious
considerations destroy the unity that would result from objective professional and interest considerations. A number of organizations mushroom
within the same professional sector because of ideological reasons. One
might hypothesize indeed that this parallelism between the political
system and the interest configuration is true everywhere. *Wherever the
political governmental organization is cohesive and power concentrated in
certain well established centers the pressure groups become well organized
with a similar concentration of power and vice versa.*

Despite its reputed advantage of concreteness, groups appear to be as
elusive as some of the much criticized terms used in the past—such as the
state, consensus, social structure, national character, or class; implicitly
accepting the power theory, group analysts tend to embrace a theory of
group determinism in which interest groups appear to be the most
significant actors within a system with the individual, on the one hand,
and the state on the other, receding in the background; from the standpoint
of research in a political system group analysis compels the student, if he

---

[4] "The Utility and Limitations of Interest Group Theory in Non-American Field
Situations," *Journal of Politics* (February, 1960).

[5] "Interest Groups in Sweden," in *Four Continents, op. cit.,* p. 170.

[6] Jean Meynaud, *Les Groupes de Pression en France* (1959), particularly Chapters
i and v.

is to gain a solid view of a system, to study all groups and all patterns of group interaction—no clear-cut discrimination of what is relevant and what is not being offered. Indeed, when David Truman brings the potential groups into the picture any discriminating feature that group analysis might offer goes to the winds; finally, and what is very revealing, researchers who start with a group orientation finish by admitting the inadequacy of their approach—they tell us that in order to understand how groups behave and how they interact, we must study the political system, the overall behavior patterns, the values and beliefs held by the actors, the formal organization of authority, the degree of legitimacy, etc., etc. Without realizing it, they reverse their theoretical position. They start with the groups only to admit the primacy of the political phenomenon and suggest that in order to explain group behavior we must start with what group behavior purported to explain—the political system!

*   *   *   *   *

The road to theory in comparative politics is a long one. Group theory claims that it is more "comprehensive" and "operational" in that it directs the student to the study of concrete and observable entities—the groups—and leads him immediately to the promised heaven of data-accumulation and explanation. When the real test of the utility of the theory comes, however—field work—groups prove to be just as stubborn in yielding their secrets as other structures and units of a system. Their pulsating reality often proves to be nothing but a ghost that haunts the field worker from one interest group office and organization to another, from one interest group publication to another. In some cases, especially in the underdeveloped systems where interest articulation is weak, the office may be vacant. Even where interest articulation and interest groups pulsate with life and vigor the student soon discovers that the "interest universe" overlaps with the political universe; that it is indeed enmeshed with the political universe in which tradition, values, habits, styles and patterns of leadership and the governmental organization must be carefully studied before we begin to understand the system as a whole. The dichotomy between "interest" and "government" appears increasingly tenuous and the student has often to study the latter in order to understand better not only the manifestations and actions but also the motivation and organization of the former. He is soon forced to the conclusion that "interest" like any other activity in a system is conditioned by secular forces that have shaped the political culture of the community and that the best way to a theory of comparative politics is at this stage a comprehensive comparative look at the main features of a political system—political culture, social configuration, leadership and governmental institutions. It is only such an approach, which requires a good understanding of the historical dimension of any and all political systems, that may help us differentiate between political systems and isolate those factors that may account for the diversities and similarities we observe.

Chapter V. Groups in Action

Introductory Note

THE STUDY of groups in various political systems lends itself to a comparison of some of the most significant aspects of politics. Specific social groups may be identified in several political systems, and comparison made in terms of their ideologies, memberships, and activities. Labor groups are especially important since they arose at about the same historical period in both Europe and North America, and are the inevitable product of industrialization everywhere. At a certain stage of industrialization, the working class may constitute the largest single group in the society, though evidence suggests that factory workers become less numerous in relation to the managerial and middle classes at a further stage of industrial development. What can account for the striking differences in the political orientation and action of organized labor in Europe, the United States, and Asia?

Business groups are also of great significance, partly because of their historical role as agents of transition from feudalism to the modern era and partly because of the influence they continue to exert. The bourgeois, commercial, and industrial classes had often to reach an accommodation with the landholding aristocracy, and then to effect a compromise with the working class.

The intellectuals as a social group are, as we shall discuss later, of key importance in any society, since it is their role to justify or sustain the authority of the rulers. Unrest among the intellectuals is a sure sign that the foundations of the regime are being eroded. The military in many nations play a recognizable political role—by influencing foreign and budgetary policy, and occasionally by seizing control of the state.

The study of groups in action thus offers clues to the configuration of the social structure, and provides an indispensable body of knowledge for testing out general theories about the functioning of political systems.

Some of the more suggestive recent studies on organized groups include: Henry Ehrmann, *Organized Business in France* (1958); Robert A. Brady, *Business as a System of Power* (1943); Joseph Berliner, *Factory and Manager in the USSR* (1957); Gabriel Almond, "The Political Attitudes of German Business," *World Politics* (January, 1956), pp. 157–86; H. J. Spiro, *The Politics of German Co-Determination* (1958); George Lichtblau, "The Politics of Trade Union Leadership in South Asia," *World Politics* (October, 1954), pp. 84–101; Val Lorwin, *The*

French Labor Movement (1954); Samuel P. Huntington, *The Soldier and the State* (1957); J. J. Johnson (ed.), *The Role of the Military in Underdeveloped Countries* (1962); and Edward Shils, "The Intellectuals in the Political Development of the New States," *World Politics* (April, 1960).

Readings

15. GROUP REPRESENTATION IN BRITAIN AND THE UNITED STATES*

Samuel H. Beer

WE USUALLY think of Great Britain as a country of strong parties and weak pressure groups; the United States as a country of weak parties and strong pressure groups. I wish to suggest some contrary views: that not only are British parties strong, but so also are British pressure groups; that in comparison both American parties and pressure groups are weak. The terms "strong" and "weak" cry out to be defined. The meanings I give them derive from a historical development—the rise of "collectivism"— that has similarly affected both parties and pressure groups.

What are the consequences for policy? Strong parties can more readily resist pressure groups. They can also more readily yield them what they want. On the other hand, the dispersion of power may simply produce a self-defeating war of all against all in which even the special interests suffer. Centralized power at least creates the possibility of deliberate and orderly solutions.

THE COLLECTIVIST ECONOMY

The virtue of centralized power is worth examining if for no other reason than that the opposite doctrine holds so high a place in liberal democratic thought. Liberals and Radicals in both Britain and America have applied the doctrine of dispersed power to both the economy and the polity. In the Smithian model of the economy, for instance, the wealth of the nation and the satisfaction of consumers' wants will be maximized if the market is free. No unit, not even government, is to exercise "market power." Once power is removed, rational and voluntary exchange will result and along with it other desirable consequences in the allocation of resources and the satisfaction of the consumer.

Very similar is the Liberal-Radical model of the polity. Remove

* From *The Annals of the American Academy of Political and Social Science*, Vol. 319 (September, 1958), pp. 130–40. By permission.

Burke's "established" aristocracy and all other agents of power that had historically guided the political process; reduce society to its individual, rational atoms; then, power removed, reason will reign. A free, competitive marketplace of ideas, automatic and self-regulating like the marketplace of the laissez-faire economy, will test the truth of opinions. Upon opinions so tested, popular government will base public policy.

In both the British and American economies in the nineteenth century, the market conditions required by the self-regulating model did actually exist in very great degree. And in both, to no inconsiderable extent, these conditions still exist. But in the past two generations or so, certain structural changes have taken place—reaching a further point of development in Britain than in the United States—that depart radically from this model. These developments, which we may call "collectivism," can be summarized under four headings. One is the tendency to a concentration of economic power among a few large buyers or sellers in a particular industry or complex of industries. Along with the increase in size of units has gone a change in internal structure that is referred to by terms such as bureaucracy and managerialism. Moreover, where such large units have grown up, they tend to deal with one another by a process of "bargaining"—or perhaps it is better to say, "collective bargaining." Finally, while bargaining tends to be confined to the relations of producers—whether business firms or trade unions—in their dealings with the mass of ultimate consumers, large units have learned to shape, even to create, the very "wants" that presumably they have come into existence to satisfy.

COLLECTIVIST PARTIES

In the polity as in the economy, there have been similar tendencies toward collectivism. By this I do not mean the increase in government intervention—the rise of the welfare state and the controlled economy. I mean rather that in the political structure have occurred certain changes analogous to those changes in economic structure summarized above. Starting from these contrasting models of the polity, the self-regulating and the collectivist, we may compare the distribution of power in Britain and the United States. It would appear that, as economic collectivism has proceeded farther in Britain than in the United States, so also has political collectivism.

We may look first at the relative number of units and their internal structure. Examined in the light of these criteria, both British parties and pressure groups present striking contrasts with the American models. While in both polities there are two major parties, the loose and sprawling parties of American politics make the British appear highly concentrated. In the American party, power is dispersed among many units—for example, personal followings or state and local machines—with the result that only occasionally and for limited purposes, such as nominating a Presiden-

tial candidate, does the national party act as a unit. In terms of density—
that is, the per cent of eligibles organized as party members—American
parties exceed British. But if we apply a measure of intensity, such as payment of dues, it is clear that British parties have mobilized the electorate
far more highly than have American. In the British party, moreover, this
membership is brought together for unified action by an elaborate and effective system of articulation, in particular active representative bodies extending from bottom to top and a bureaucratic staff running from top to
bottom. There are still semiautonomous centers within the party that a
perfected merger would obliterate. But to an American, a British party is
a highly unified social body, remarkably well equipped for co-ordinated
action: we think, for instance, of the fact that all candidates must be approved by a central-party agency and that they will all run on the same
platform. No doubt, the most striking expression of this power of united
action is the extent of party voting in the House of Commons. Judged
even by Lowell's strict criteria, party voting has been on the increase for a
hundred years and today reaches nearly one hundred per cent.[1]

Along with such concentration, and perhaps making it possible, goes a
high measure of political homogeneity. (I do not mean social homogeneity, for, measured by nonpolitical criteria, the British are a very
heterogeneous people.) This political homogeneity in the electorate as a
whole is reflected in what students of voting behavior call the "nationalizing" of British politics. When political opinion moves, it moves in
unison throughout the country: in a general election the "swing" from
one party to the other is much the same in every constituency. In the
United States . . . voting has also tended in this direction. Sectionalism
and the number of one-party states are on the decline. But—as 1956
illustrates—nothing like the uniformity of swing in British voting has been
reached.

In spite of mass membership and representative bodies, however, the
internal structure of the British party gives great power to central party
leaders—far more, of course, than that possessed by American leaders. It is
rather as if the Congressional caucus of post–Federalist days had been
imposed upon the Jacksonian party system. In both British parties, as
R. T. McKenzie has shown, the leaders of the parliamentary party, and
especially the Leader, are dominant.[2] That is a loose description and needs
must be, since the Leader's power is complex and certainly far from
dictatorial. He must continually practice "the art of management,"
appeasing a dissident faction, finding a formula, keeping up party morale.

[1] Lowell counted as a party vote a division in which at least 90 per cent of one
party voted in favor and at least 90 per cent of the other party voted against. A. L.
Lowell, "The Influence of Party upon Legislation in England and America," *Annual
Report of the American Historical Association for 1901*, Vol. 1 (Washington, 1902),
pp. 319–542.

[2] R. T. McKenzie, *British Political Parties* (New York: St. Martin's Press, 1955),
passim.

Indeed, he is a "manager"—a modern-day manager committed to party principle, of course, but by his function compelled above all to think of the continuation of the organization.

COLLECTIVIST PRESSURE GROUPS

Turning from parties to pressure groups, we find that in Britain as in the United States, the center of the stage is occupied by organizations based on the great economic interest groups of modern society, especially the big three of business, labor, and agriculture. Given the nature of public policy, which affects these interests so often and so intimately, pressure groups claiming to speak for them are bound in turn to influence policy making more frequently and on the whole more effectively than pressure groups of other types.

In Britain as well as the United States, in addition to such "self-oriented" pressure groups, we must also deal with what S. E. Finer calls "promotional" groups.[3] Among the former we may classify such organizations as the Federation of British Industries, the Trades Union Congress, the National Farmers Union, the British Medical Association, the National Union of Teachers, the British Legion, the National and Local Government Officers' Association. The "promotional" groups include the Howard League for Penal Reform, the National Council for Civil Liberties, the Peace Pledge Union, the Campaign for the Limitation of Secret Police Powers. As compared with the self-oriented groups, writes Finer, the latter "do not represent 'interests' in the same sense at all. They represent a cause, not a social or economic 'stake' in society."[4]

Such a broad distinction in the character of goals tends to have important consequences for structure and behavior. The promotional group, for instance, tends to be open to all like-minded persons, while the self-oriented group has, so to speak, a fixed clientele. By and large the self-oriented group can more readily extract money and work from its members on a continuing and regularized basis. It may also be less subject to splintering and more capable of continuous, unified action. At least in part for such reasons, the more powerful pressure groups of the British polity are self-oriented groups, based on a vocational interest, bureaucratic in structure, and continuing over a long period of time. While some form of group politics has long flourished in the British as in other polities, this modern, collectivist type has emerged only in recent generations. There is some sense in saying that one line of development in the history of British pressure groups has been from the promotional to the self-oriented, vocational type. Possibly a similar development has taken place in the United States, although here the third party has often played the role of

---

[3] S. E. Finer, *Anonymous Empire: A Study of the Lobby in Great Britain* (London: Pall Mall Press, 1958), p. 3.

[4] *Ibid.*

the promotional group in Britain. We might also find that the promotional group remains a more important feature of the American polity than of the British.

Farm, Labor, and Business Organizations

Concentration and bureaucracy characterize British pressure groups as well as parties. Hardly without exception the big vocational pressure groups in Britain have a higher index of density and concentration. There, for instance, the National Farmers Union is the only significant organization of farmers and includes 90 per cent of its potential membership. In the United States, of course, only a fraction—no more than 30 per cent—of all farmers are organized and these are divided among three main groups and various minor ones. While absolute numbers are much smaller in Britain, we must remember that British agriculture is highly diversified as to crops, size of farms, and location. Yet through the NFU British farmers speak with one voice to a degree rarely achieved by farmers in the United States. No doubt this is true because to no small extent the organization is run from the top. In Bedford Square is a large and able bureaucracy and at its head stands one of the ablest managers in modern Britain, Sir James Turner—sometimes known as the "Sacred Bull of British Agriculture."

In the field of trade unions, just a little less than half the total working force has been organized, while in the United States the figure is around a quarter. To one peak organization, the TUC, nearly all unions are affiliated and it has been the undisputed spokesman for organized labor for generations. Its permanent secretary, even when Walter Citrine held the post, has never occupied the position of, say, a Gompers. The heads of the Big Three,[5] however, have as prominent a political role as our Reuther, Meany, and Lewis. The British labor leaders of this generation are more likely to have worked their way up the bureaucratic ladder by long and able management than to have emerged from heroic struggles for the right to organize or for better contracts. Contrary to popular impression and in strong contrast with American experience, the strike has almost ceased to be an instrument of labor-management relations in Britain since as far back as 1932. If by bureaucracy, however, we mean fulltime paid staff, then British unions generally are far less well endowed than American. The reluctance of the rank and file to pay dues sufficient to employ such staff—and to pay substantial salaries to any permanent official—seriously handicaps British unions.

In the field of business, in Britain as in the United States the basic unit of political action is the trade association. Comparison is made a little easier if we consider only national manufacturing trade associations. Of these there are 1,300 in Britain and some 950 in the United States. Density

---

[5] The Transport and General Workers' Union; the National Union of General and Municipal Workers; the Amalgamated Engineering Union—which among them include 30 per cent of all unionists affiliated to the TUC.

is high: a sample survey showed that 90 per cent of larger firms and 76 per cent of smaller firms in Britain belong to such associations. Concentration among manufacturing trade associations is considerably greater in Britain. The peak association is the Federation of British Industries (FBI) which represents, through its affiliated trade associations and directly through member firms, some 85 per cent of all manufacturing concerns employing ten or more workers. In the United States, on the other hand, the National Association of Manufacturers has never represented more than 6 per cent of all manufacturing concerns. If the same base as that used for the FBI were taken, however, there is reason to think that the NAM figure would be more like 20 per cent to 25 per cent. The contrast would still be striking.

BARGAINING IN THE POLITY

So much for the briefest sort of sketch of collectivism in the structure of the British polity. Let us turn to the modes of interaction of these massive unit actors, in particular the political party and the pressure group.

What we have called bargaining is a principal trait of the relationships of large producers in the collectivist economy. Its essence is that each of the negotiating units is highly dependent on the other as a seller or as a buyer. In a free market, on the other hand, each seller can turn to other buyers and each buyer to other sellers and none have significant market power. In bargaining, however, each unit has substantial market power; hence, the ultimate decision is made as a result of negotiations in which each gauges his offers in the light of expectations about the possible offers of the other.

A similar kind of decision making occurs where a party enjoys large power over the authority of government, while a pressure group with which it deals enjoys similar power over something—such as votes—that the party wants. Such a situation is very different from one in which government authority is dispersed among many elected officeholders and voting power among an unorganized electorate. In the latter situation, there is a kind of bidding for votes on one side and for promises or policies on the other that has a limited, but real, analogy with the economic free market. Where the centralized party in office confronts the massively organized pressure group, decisions are made quite differently. Indeed, some who have sat in on the Annual Price Review between the National Farmers Union in Britain and the Ministry of Agriculture have reported that the proceedings and the way in which a settlement is reached resemble nothing so much as collective bargaining. For both the farmers and the ministry there is a range of outcomes that would be better than no agreement at all. Each opponent pretty well knows what this range is. No wonder it has sometimes taken four months for a decision to be reached!

Consultation with interests is a feature of all modern Western democratic governments. Some years ago Leiserson, writing of representative advisory committees, traced their origin to "the delegation of discretionary rule-making powers under legislative standards to administrative agencies executing various types of social legislation."[6] Leiserson's statement, broadened somewhat, is a generalization valid for not only American, but also for Western European government: increasing government intervention for such purposes as social reform, economic stability, and national defense has led to the grant of rule-making power to administrative agencies and to increasing participation of interested groups in decision making at that level.

Different stages in this development, however, can be distinguished, depending upon how far the scope of policy has been expanded and the polity has become collectivist. The extent to which power has been mobilized and unified on each side—on the side of the party in power and on the side of the pressure group with which it deals—will determine whether bargaining predominates in the relationship. In the United States, we find administrative consultation on a vast scale both in Washington and in the state capitols. In Britain, a more collectivist polity, the situation is better described as "quasi-corporatism."

It is against the background of this power pattern that we must examine the emphasis that British pressure groups give to the various points in the process of decision making. The formal structure of authority—British parliamentary government as compared with the American separation of powers—will play its role. But we must recall that a hundred years ago Britain also had parliamentary government, yet pressure groups then gave far more attention to the legislature than they do now.

ADMINISTRATIVE CONSULTATION

In each polity we may distinguish four main phases of policy making: at elections, in the legislature, within the party, and at the administrative level. British pressure groups exert their major influence at the administrative level, taking this to include both ministerial and official contacts. Perhaps their second most important point of influence is within the party. In contrast American pressure groups, by and large, concentrate on the first two points: the electorate and the legislature.

There are, of course, many variations within these two broad patterns. A very important difference may result from the character of the power base of a group. There is a kind of power—and this is particularly important in Britain—that is created by the expansion of policy itself. "The greater the degree of detailed and technical control the government seeks to exert over industrial and commercial interests," E. P. Herring wrote, "the greater must be their degree of consent and active participa-

[6] Avery Leiserson, *Administrative Regulation: A Study in Representation of Interests* (Chicago: University of Chicago Press, 1942), p. 162.

tion in the very process of regulation, if regulation is to be effective or successful."[7] This generalization, I should think, holds for most Western democracies and surely for Britain. There, certain types of control exercised in recent years—price control, materials allocation, tariffs, import control, and the encouragement of exports and productivity are only some of the more striking examples—simply could not be enforced effectively without the substantial co-operation of the groups concerned. The group's technical advice is often well-nigh indispensable. But co operation—something more than grudging consent to "the law"—is a further necessity. Our farm programs with their referenda and farmer-elected committees recognize this necessity. But in Britain the far wider scope of regulation and planning—even after the various "bonfires of controls"—gives this power factor far greater weight.

A few examples: The farmers—meaning in effect the NFU—are represented on a set of local committees that have had important administrative duties under various agricultural programs, and the chance that the NFU might encourage these farmer representatives to withdraw from the committees has been a force in the annual price reviews. When the Conservatives in denationalizing part of the transport industry in 1956 dismantled the government haulage (that is, trucking) system, a standby scheme was organized by the industry itself. The Labour government's limitation of advertising expenditure was policed by the organized adver tisers, and its important anti-inflationary effort to restrain both dividends and wage increases was carried out—and with remarkable success—on a voluntary basis by organized business and labor.

Neither the British nor the American system of consultation between government and pressure groups has been fully described. Some rough impressions, modestly intended, may be in order. In both countries the central device is the representative advisory committee. British examples range from high level bodies such as the Economic Planning Board, the National Joint Advisory Council of the Ministry of Labour, the National Production Advisory Council on Industry, on which the relevant peak organizations, the FBI, BEC and TUC, are represented, to the multitude of advisory committees of the main economic departments to which trade associations send representatives. The latter are connected with the system of "sponsoring" departments which grew up during and after World War II and which means today that every industry and every branch of it, no matter how small, has a sponsoring department or section of one, somewhere in the government machine. Apart from such committees, although often around them, a regular system of informal consultation has grown up. Private and public bureaucrats continually call one another on the telephone or meet for luncheon and discuss a problem on a first-name basis. Often several departments and several groups are concerned.

---

[7] E. Pendleton Herring, *Public Administration and the Public Interest* (New York: McGraw-Hill Book Co., 1936), p. 192.

On the American side, the immense documentation on advisory committees in the federal government that was assembled by a subcommittee of the Government Operations Committee in 1957 has not yet been analyzed by political scientists.[8] But it is clear that from the time of the National Recovery Administration, the use of this device, from being relatively rare, has immensely increased. The number of advisory committees associated with government departments at the center—and in addition to many more at the local or regional level—runs into the hundreds. One major set established by statute are in the Department of Agriculture—for instance, the Commodity Stabilization Committees. Of the remainder, the vast majority it seems are associated principally with the defense effort—procurement, development, standards, stockpiling, and so on—and consist of industry advisory committees. In comparison with similar British industry advisory committees, the American appear to depend less on trade associations, the result at least in part of the Defense Production Act of 1950 that requires that nonmembers as well as members of trade associations be included. The peak associations—the NAM and United States Chamber of Commerce—also play a much less prominent role than their British counterparts not being represented, as such, on even the Business Advisory Council. Certainly trade unions are not called in for advice so frequently or on so broad a front in the United States as in Britain. The TUC alone, for instance, is represented on some 60 committees touching all aspects of social and economic problems.

Of the broad character of the power relationship we can speak with confidence: the American executive possesses far less actual power than the British. Quite apart from the degree of delegated powers in this country, the political independence of Congress and the exercise of administrative oversight by Congressional Committees mean that the group interested in influencing policy must give great attention to the legislature. Some years ago Blaisdell found that pressure groups, while concerned with the administration, focused their attention principally upon Congress.[9] Broadly this must still be the case, although it would be interesting to know how far the defense effort may have shifted the balance.

PRESSURE ON PARTIES

At the Democratic National Convention in 1956 the number of trade-union officials sitting as delegates ran into the hundreds, while at the

---

[8] *Advisory Committees* (Parts I–V), subcommittee of the House Committee on Government Operations, 84th Congress, 2d Session (1956); Hearings before the same subcommittee on H.R. 3378, 85th Congress, 1st Session (1957); H.R. Report 576 on H.R. 7390, 85th Congress, 1st Session (1957).

[9] Donald C. Blaisdell, *Economic Power and Political Pressures*, Monograph 26, T.N.E.C., Investigation of Concentration of Economic Power, 76th Congress, 3rd Session (Washington, 1941), pp. 57 and 70.

Republican convention there was no more than a scattering. Generally, however, in both national and state parties in the United States, the connection of pressure groups and parties is less close than in Britain. We do not have the formal affiliation of the trade union movement with one party. But the more important difference arises from the fact that American parties are so poorly unified that they do not provide an effective channel for influencing the use of government authority. In Britain, on the other hand, the party ranks second—although perhaps a poor second—to the administration as an object of pressure.

Where the power is, there the pressure will be applied. Where we see the pressure being applied, therefore, we shall probably find the seat of power. Judged by this rule, the central organs of the British party, especially the parliamentary party, are far more powerful than the party's representative assemblies. Pressure groups do not openly descend on a British party conference as they do on the platform hearings of an American party convention. Their representatives, however, may be present and spokesmen for various special interests—farmers, trade unionists, veterans, teachers, old-age pensioners, advertising men with a concern for commercial broadcasting—will take up a good deal of time at a party conference.

The important point of influence, however, is the parliamentary party —its regular, full meetings and its specialized committees—and to a lesser extent the party's central office. We are familiar with the way leaders of the Labour party while in power or in opposition will frequently consult with the trade unions on pending decisions. There is also an active alignment, if not formal affiliation, of organized business with the Conservatives. During the passage of the bill nationalizing transport in 1946–47, for instance, the Conservative opposition tabled several hundred amendments. Where had they come from? In practice the party's Parliamentary Secretariat—a body of party employees, not MPs acted as intermediary between the transport committee of the parliamentary party and the various pressure groups, especially the General Council of British Shipping, the Dock and Harbors Association, and a joint committee of the Federation of British Industries, National Union of Manufacturers, and the Association of British Chambers of Commerce.

Inseparable from these channels of influence is one of the, to an American, most curious phenomena of British politics. He is the "interested MP"—that is, the member who is connected with an outside interest group by direct personal involvement, such as occupation or ownership of property, or by membership or office holding in an outside organization speaking for an interest group. Today and for generations the House of Commons through the personal involvement of its members has represented a far wider range of interests than has the American Congress, notoriously inhabited by lawyers.

In Britain such personal involvement was a principal way in which

interest groups of the nineteenth century made themselves heard in
government. Of more importance in today's collectivist polity is the
member connected with an outside organization. The MPs sponsored and
subsidized by the trade unions are the best-known examples. But there is
also a host of others: a joint Honorary Secretary of the Association of
British Chambers of Commerce, the Chairman of the Howard League for
Penal Reform, a Director of the Society of Motor Manufacturers and
Traders, the President of the British Legion, the Secretary of the National
Tyre Distributors Association—there seems to be hardly a member who
fails to note some such connection in his biography in the *Times' House
of Commons*. Perhaps some Congressmen also have similar connections.
Amid their wide membership in churches, fraternal organizations, and
"patriotic" groups as recorded in the *Congressional Directory*, however,
they fail to mention them.

Perhaps, as S. E. Finer has suggested, the absence of such interested
members from the Congress is one reason why American pressure groups
must make up the deficiency by hiring lobbyists in such large numbers.
For the interested MP is an active lobbyist within the legislature. His
principal role is played within the parliamentary party, but his activity in
the House itself is more observable. He may speak openly as the representative of a group, as the President of the British Legion often does in
forwarding the Legion's campaign to increase disability pensions. He is
more likely to be effective at the amendment stage of a finance or other
bill when, briefed by his association, he suggests changes, which perhaps
at the same time are being urged on the Minister and civil servants by
officers or staff of the pressure group.

INFLUENCING PUBLIC OPINION

Herring long ago observed how American pressure groups direct great
attention to influencing public opinion: not only to win support for some
immediate objective, but also to build up generally favorable attitudes.
This he found to be a trait of the "new" lobby, and it is not irrelevant
that this technique arose along with the development of modern mass-
advertising methods and media. A major difference in Britain is that the big
vocational pressure groups rarely mount such public campaigns. In the
nineteenth century, this was not so. Beginning late in the century,
however, this propagandist function seems more and more to have passed
to political parties. Today and for many years now, the parties, in contrast
with the pressure groups, have virtually monopolized communication
with the voters as such—that is with the general public as distinguished
from communication by a pressure group with its clientele.

This differentiation of function in political communication has gone
very much farther in Britain than in the United States. A striking feature

of nearly all the vocational pressure groups there is the extent to which they urge their demands simply and frankly as special interests. There is a significant contrast, I think, with American pressure groups which tend to base their claims on some large principle of social philosophy or national policy—as, for example, in the vast public-relations program of the NAM.

Yet the public campaign has sometimes been used by the big pressure groups of British politics and its use may be on the increase. Examples are the antinationalization campaign launched by the Road Haulage Association in 1946–47; Tate and Lyle's famous "Mr. Cube" campaign against the nationalization of sugar refining in 1949–50; and in general the growing use of Aims of Industry, a public-relations agency founded to defend and advocate free enterprise. Lesser efforts have been pressed by the National Union of Teachers and the British Legion. If this practice grows greatly, one might well expect it to weaken the position of the parties.

Such a development—which I do not expect—could have great consequences for the British polity. For without in any degree being cynical, one must acknowledge the large part played by British parties in creating the present political homogeneity of the British electorate—the national market for their brand-name goods. The British party battle is continuous and highly organized and so also is the stream of propaganda directed at the voter. Through it the party voter is strengthened, if not created, and the tight party majority in the legislature prepared. Even more important, the framework of public thinking about policy, the voter's sense of the alternatives, is fixed from above. Popular sovereignty in the polity has been qualified by the same means that have qualified consumers' sovereignty in the economy.

In this Americans are not likely to find much cause for self-congratulation. We will hardly say that we are more free of political propaganda. As in other aspects of the American power pattern, the difference is that the centers from which this weighty influence emanates are far more dispersed and unco-ordinated. Is this necessarily to our advantage? Some words of E. P. Herring's suggest an answer:

A democracy inclines toward chaos rather than toward order. The representative principle, if logically followed, leads to infinite diversity rather than ultimate unity. . . . Since the "voice of the people" is a pleasant fancy and not a present fact, the impulse for positive political action must be deliberately imposed at some strategic point, if democracy is to succeed as a form of government.[10]

---

[10] Herring, *op. cit.* (note 7 *supra*), p. 377.

16. PRESSURE POLITICS IN THE FIFTH REPUBLIC*

Bernard E. Brown

". . . ce qui a été fait ne sera pas changé. Nous n'en sommes plus où on en était hier . . . . Quand il s'agit d'un domaine d'intérêt national, le pouvoir ne recule pas."

General Charles de Gaulle, 10 November 1959.

THE THESIS of an inverse ratio between strength of the government and power of pressure groups is venerable. It has gained widespread acceptance among American political scientists, since it seems to explain the susceptibility of individual congressmen to pressure group demands, and the relative independence of the president. Some observers discern in this difference between Congress and the president an argument in favor of cabinet government along British lines. Other critics are content merely to ask for greater centralization of the political parties in the United States, which would have the same happy result as the introduction of a cabinet system: pressure groups would be drawn to a central point, and would therefore find it difficult to have their way.[1]

The advent of the Fifth Republic offers a unique opportunity to test the validity of these observations. One of the chief advantages claimed for the new regime by its founders is that the strengthened executive is better able to withstand the egoistic pressures and demands of organized interest groups. Conforming to the ideas of General de Gaulle and Michel Debré, a president chosen by a restricted electoral college (in the future by universal suffrage) now enjoys autonomous political power, while the position of the cabinet has been improved. Restrictions have been placed upon parliament as regards the procedure for voting censure, length of sessions, control over its agenda and role of the standing committees. In practice, decision-making power has been concentrated in the presidency ever since General de Gaulle's inauguration as president in January, 1959. Without entering into the polemical debate over the merits and demerits

---

* Reprinted from the *Journal of Politics* (August, 1963). Footnotes are abridged. By permission.

[1] See, for example, the argument in favor of party centralization in Elmer Schattschneider, *Party Government* (New York, 1942), especially Chapter 8; and "Towards a More Responsible Two Party System," supplement to the *American Political Science Review*, Vol. 44 (September, 1950). For a critique of these claims regarding the relative power of pressure groups in the United States and Britain, see: Samuel Beer, "Group Representation in Britain and the United States," *Annals of the American Academy of Political and Social Science* (September, 1958), and J. Roland Pennock, "Responsible Government, Separated Powers, and Special Interests: Agricultural Subsidies in Britain and America," *American Political Science Review* (September, 1962).

of these innovations, it is instructive to see what has happened to the pressure groups in these changed circumstances. Are they less important, as important or more important under the Fifth Republic than under the Fourth?

In order to answer that question definitively it will be necessary to undertake a large number of monographic studies of both individual groups and the decision-making process. It will probably be many years before sufficient information is available to satisfy the exigencies of the theorist and historian. However, at the time of this writing the Fifth Republic has been functioning for over four years, and a certain amount of experience is available for appraisal—tentative and limited as it may be. It may be possible to discern some trends by focusing attention on key groups. Fortunately, we now have at our disposal a new edition of the basic work on French pressure groups by Jean Meynaud, the leading authority on the subject. On the very first page of the 1962 edition the reader is warned that it is too soon to measure the impact of the changes brought by the Fifth Republic. Although it is not impossible to note signs of adaptation or continuity, Meynaud observes, our description or judgment of recent events may be distorted by political bias. But Professor Meynaud is far too modest. In the course of his new survey of French pressure groups a vast amount of material is presented—and there are both "description and judgments" which highlight the changes ushered in by the Fifth Republic.[2]

From Meynaud's survey it is evident that in many respects the pattern of pressure group activities has been altered under the new regime. Organized groups now pay less attention than formerly to parliament, its specialized committees, and the political parties—for the simple and understandable reason that the role played by these agencies in the policy-making process has diminished. Thus, notes Meynaud, a number of important measures have been virtually imposed upon a hostile or unwilling parliament, for example the creation of an independent nuclear striking force. In other cases parliament has been utterly unable to obtain even partial satisfaction in areas where once it ruled supreme—as in its failure in November, 1959, to reestablish pensions for veterans. The decline of parliament would therefore appear to mean, inevitably, a decline of pressure groups. "It is clear," says Meynaud, "on the whole, that this diminution of the prerogatives of the assemblies compels the groups to direct their interventions towards the centers of power whose influence has been maintained or is on the ascendant."

The major "ascendant power" in the Fifth Republic has been the

[2] Jean Meynaud, *Nouvelles études sur les groupes de pression en France* (Paris, 1962) and his earlier work, *Les groupes de pression en France* (Paris, 1958). In a recent article, however, Professor Meynaud specifically undertakes the task of contrasting and evaluating the role of pressure groups under the Fourth and Fifth Republics. See, "Les groupes de pression sous la V° République," *Revue Française de Science Politique* (September, 1962), pp. 672–97.

president, who appears to be in a strong position with regard to the pressure groups. General de Gaulle has apparently adopted policy concerning Algeria, national defense, the budget, and price-levels without even consulting organized interests. On several occasions he has proudly noted his independence of interest groups. In a letter of March 18, 1960, to Chaban-Delmas, explaining his refusal to convoke a special session of parliament demanded by a majority of the deputies for a debate on agricultural policy, General de Gaulle wrote: "Fully cognizant of the capital importance of the subject which the signatories justly believe should be considered by the public powers as soon as possible, it seems beyond question to me that their claims, as formulated, result largely from urgent demands on the part of the leaders of a professional group. Now, whatever may be the representativeness of this group as regards the particular economic interests which it defends, it is nonetheless—according to the law—bereft of all authority and of all political responsibility." Whatever the merits of the constitutional question raised by General de Gaulle's refusal to convoke parliament, the letter of March 18 is a significant indication of the chief of state's deep hostility towards organized groups.

Perhaps the best example of the Fifth Republic's firm stand with regard to pressure groups is the financial reform of December, 1958. As Meynaud points out, all the devaluations from 1936 to 1957 failed because the government was unable to impose collective discipline upon the producers and trade unions. Each devaluation was followed by inflation. In 1958 the government was able to resist the demands of the groups temporarily hurt by devaluation, and consequently was able to achieve a sound fiscal reform. "Technically," observes Meynaud, "the operation was and remains a success." Thus, the framers of the Fifth Republic seem to be vindicated by the success of the 1958 reform—a strong state was able to defend the general interest against the egoistic groups.

However, a note of caution is sounded by Meynaud throughout his book: group pressures result from the very movement of social life. Transformation of institutions does not annul the pressure or activities of groups; the latter merely search and use other techniques. "In order to bring about a radical change, it would be necessary to modify completely the social constitution of the country: at this price only would it be possible to establish a different system of relations between socio-economic forces and the public powers." Indeed, in a number of respects there are some striking *similarities* between the Fourth and Fifth Republics as regards the role of pressure groups.

In spite of the hard line taken by the government since 1958 towards pressure group claims, on numerous occasions concessions have been made: regarding the interpretation of "exterior signs of wealth" in calculating income taxes; charges for drugs under the national health service; increase of the minimum wage; reestablishment of some veterans

pensions which had been eliminated as part of the fiscal reform of 1958;
revival of the agricultural price index; and the promise to hold a round
table on the problems of viticulture. Meynaud speculates that the regime
may have been compelled to make these and other concessions because of
the need to secure widespread support for General de Gaulle's Algerian
policy—and for the Republic itself, in view of the uprisings of January,
1960 and April, 1961.

In many respects interest groups have the same opportunity for
exercising influence under the Fifth Republic as under the Fourth. There
are approximately five thousand assorted advisory councils, committees or
agencies in which organized groups participate. A number of these agencies
perform price fixing and other official functions, so that the groups may
make suggestions and argue their case *within* the government. The
existence of an Economic and Social Council with only minor modifications under the Fifth Republic provides yet another legal outlet for group
activities and influence. Most important of all, those organized groups
which had ready access to the administration under the Fourth Republic
continue to enjoy the same privilege under the Fifth. Both before and
since 1958 certain departments within the civil service have tended to be
receptive to the viewpoint of various groups (business, labor, farmer,
secular organizations, teachers, bankers, veterans, and so on). That is, the
groups not only compete with each other in a conflict arbitrated by the
government; to a certain extent the administration as well as the parliament
is caught up in the struggle and becomes a part of it. Criss-crossing
relations among civil servants, parliamentarians, party leaders and organized groups continue, though the exact balance among them has doubtless
shifted. By and large the wealthier groups, especially those able to present
well documented studies to buttress their claims, have a distinct advantage
over such poor or noisy groups as the home distillers. The fact that a
number of top civil servants resign their posts and take jobs with both
large enterprises and professional organizations (the practice of "pantou-
flage") facilitates the dialogue.

Before attempting to draw further conclusions about the role of
pressure groups in the Fifth Republic, it might be instructive to study a
few selected groups in more detail. Attention will here be drawn to three
groups or sets of groups concerning which considerable information is
available for the period before 1958: the alcohol lobby, the secular and
religious organizations, and the army.

THE STATE AND THE GROUPS: THREE CASES

The Alcohol Case

The nature of the alcohol problem in France is now so well known that
it needs no extensive description here. Briefly, for many years the *Service
des alcools* has purchased far more alcohol (distilled primarily from beets,

apples, molasses and wine) than the economy could absorb. In effect the state monopoly was a device whereby the alcohol producing groups (in particular the wealthy and powerful beetgrowers) compelled the rest of the nation in large part to subsidize their activities. Although most of the alcohol purchased by the state eventually was sold to industry, a portion of these stocks were used in the manufacture of alcoholic beverages. To make matters worse, a large number of people (from two to three million) enjoyed the historic right to distill ten liters of pure alcohol a year without payment of tax—and in fact at least twice that amount was distilled and put into circulation fraudulently. Overproduction of alcohol coincided with the existence of a serious problem of alcoholism. However, the two to three million home distillers, the 150,000 beetgrowers, the winegrowers, the proprietors of bars, and the commercial distillers constituted a powerful political force with a direct interest in maintaining the alcohol statute. Several cabinets under the Fourth Republic experienced great difficulty in attempting to bring about needed reform.

Under the Fifth Republic it appears that the basic problem of huge deficits and overproduction has been solved—though other problems are bound to arise as the Common Market takes shape. In 1958 and 1959 the *Régie* actually showed a modest profit, which was used to facilitate the conversion of apple orchards from alcoholic to non-alcoholic production. A number of measures were also adopted by both parliament and the cabinet to meet the menace of alcoholism: a decree of 30 August 1960 finally suppressed altogether the principle of tax exemption for home distillers—but maintained it as a personal right only for those who actually enjoyed that right in 1959–60 and for their "surviving mate." The privilege of home distilling will therefore be progressively restricted. A decree of 29 November 1960 also envisages measures to limit the number of bars in order to reduce temptation in the vicinity of hospitals, youth centers, and the like. On the surface, then, it appears that the Fifth Republic has successfully withstood the pressure of the alcohol lobbies, and resolved one of the problems which had plagued the Fourth Republic.

In all fairness, however, this judgment should be modified somewhat. The determination of the state to place the *Service des alcools* on a paying basis—that is, to put an end to the huge deficits resulting from subsidy of alcohol producers—dates at least from 1956, if not earlier. The Mendès-France government, by a decree of 13 November 1954, determined to abolish the privilege of the home distillers within one year—though every parliament thereafter succeeded in postponing its application. In 1956 the Socialist Finance Minister, Paul Ramadier, ordered an end to the practice of adding alcohol to gasolene. Above all, a vast program was launched to inform the public of the waste involved in the alcohol statute and also of the dangers of alcoholism. Given the decision of the financial experts that alcohol production could no longer be subsidized, reform was inevitable, and indeed some key measures were taken under the Fourth Republic. The Debré government had as much trouble in securing approval from parliament for its decrees against the home distillers as had any of its predecessors. The debate in the National Assembly in December, 1959, was as raucous and as shameful as any under the Fourth Republic. Most of the deputies defended the distillers and denied that their activities were responsible for alcoholism. A number of amendments to the government bill were voted which watered down the original proposal. M. André Liautey, former deputy and leader of the distillers' organization, was ordered to leave the public gallery because he was giving signals openly to the deputies! In the confusion following the debate, the distillers even believed that they had won a victory by securing a condemnation of the 1954 Mendès-France decree. The government measure was later defeated by a vote of 155 to 55 in the Senate. Finally, in July, 1960, the National Assembly voted a text authorizing the government to take measures against alcoholism, which provided the legal basis for the decrees of 29 November 1960 limiting the right of distillation. However, the distillers and their defenders put up a fine fight in parliament, comparing favorably with their efforts before 1958. Indeed, the situation as regards the home distillers was roughly comparable both before and after 1958. The distillers, because of their numbers and geographic distribution, enjoyed wide support among the parliamentarians. But, they had a bad press and were resolutely opposed by the financial and health experts. Their privileges were chipped away by a combination of executive decrees, technocratic pressure, and hesitant parliamentary compliance. The influence of the distillers has declined under the Fifth Republic, but that decline has been gradual rather than sharp.

A similar observation can be made about the wealthiest and most powerful of the alcohol groups—the General Confederation of Beetgrowers (CGB). Under the Fourth Republic the beetgrowers were active politically, and probably were instrumental in the overthrow of the René Mayer cabinet in 1953 (though obviously their opposition was only one element in a complex political situation). Under the Fifth Republic the influence of the CGB has been greatly reduced—but again, the decline began before 1958. Under both Republics the beetgrowers enjoyed the support of a large bloc of deputies, who acted on their behalf in debate and in negotiations with the civil service. The beetgrowers also may count on receiving a sympathetic hearing from the minister of agriculture. Traditionally, the minister attends the annual session, and a dialogue takes place between him and the president of the CGB. The minister invariably assures his listeners that their interests are understood and vigorously defended. But the beetgrowers are unable to make any headway at all with the finance minister or the director of the *Service des alcools*—who are unalterably opposed to the accumulation of huge deficits simply in order to encourage beet culture.

The Debré cabinet made a firm resolve to rationalize the alcohol industry, and this inevitably led to measures against the beetgrowers. One of the key moves was the creation of a committee in November, 1959, headed by Jacques Rueff and Louis Armand, with the task of proposing reforms to eliminate obstacles to economic expansion. The committee's findings regarding the beet industry were hardly to the liking of the CGB. It held that the fixing of quotas for sugar limited competition and checked expansion, and termed the manufacture of alcohol from beets "economic incoherence." The committee's recommendation would have the effect of converting beet production largely into sugar—or even reconverting the land altogether to other culture. The pattern of relations between the beetgrowers and the government was about the same under both the Fourth and Fifth Republics—a network of friendly contacts with parliamentarians and the minister of agriculture, but hostility on the part of most civil servants and especially the financial departments.

The long-range problem confronting the CGB is painfully evident: consumption of beet alcohol by industry will decline because of technological developments. In 1961 chemical industry spokesmen announced that within a few years they would be able to do without alcohol altogether—indeed, must do so in order to meet competition within the Common Market. The *Service des alcools* thereupon informed the CGB that it must prepare for a large reduction in purchases of beet alcohol.

These developments have led to a change in the tactics of the CGB. Inasmuch as the challenge is mainly from the technical and financial experts within the administration, the CGB is strengthening its own technical and research agencies. It has presented its principal demands in a form most likely to appeal to economists and civil servants. It now calls for a "sugar law," that is, a comprehensive statute or decree which would establish a target for production, a favorable price and a "trustworthy" administration. In a sense, the proposed sugar law (or five-year charter) reflects the new tactics adopted by many groups under the Fifth Republic. The emphasis is on a rational, long term plan, calculated in terms bound to appeal to civil servants. However, the chances of reversing the long range trend towards a rationalized economy are now slight—not only because of the stronger executive in the Fifth Republic, but also because of pressure within the Common Market. The decline in political influence on the part of the alcohol groups is due to a variety of reasons, and not merely to the advent of a new regime.

The Religious Schools Case

A slight change in the nature of pressure-group activity is also evident as regards the emotion-laden issue of relations between the state and privately run (in practice predominantly Catholic) school systems. The advocates and opponents of state aid to private schools are organized in powerful pressure groups: the *Ligue française d'enseignement* (which claims over two million adherents of member organizations), and the *Secrétariat d'Études pour la liberté de l'enseignement* (an apex organization, headed by Edouard Lizop, which includes representatives of the Catholic parents and teachers associations). In 1951 an intense battle over the question of subsidies resulted finally in the passage of the *loi Barangé*— a professedly temporary measure granting subsidies to both public and private schools, but a clear victory for the private school defenders. A key role in the drafting of the bill, and in planning parliamentary tactics, was played by the *Secrétariat*.

The Debré government expressed the hope in 1958 that issues could be "depoliticized." It was argued that pragmatic solutions should be worked out wholly apart from ideological considerations, making possible eventually a new national consensus. State aid to private schools was one of the divisive issues which the prime minister was determined to resolve. Roger Frey, Minister of Information, commented: "In the atomic age, this scholastic quarrel is completely outdated." The technique of "depoliticization" used by the government was to appoint a special committee, headed by Pierre-Olivier Lapie (a former socialist deputy) to take testimony from leading educational and political figures, and to make recommendations. The committee formula had been used under the Fourth Republic as well. In spite of pressure from both the *Secrétariat* and the *Ligue*, the Debré government refused to introduce legislation or in any way commit itself before receiving the Lapie committee's report. The Ministry of National Education drew up a bill on the basis of the committee's recommendations. After considerable discussion within the cabinet, and a stormy debate in parliament, a text finally was passed by a vote of 427 to 71 (the opposition including 10 Communists, 44 Socialists, 8 Radicals, 3 UNR, 2 Independents and 4 non-inscrits). The Senate likewise approved, after hearing the prime minister call for an end to the quarrel: "It is fitting that the present legislature mark an epoch in the history of public education and of school pacification, that pacification which we could have inscribed in the very title of our bill. It is necessary that the France of the second half of the twentieth century place itself above slogans which no longer represent anything." The solution offered by the Debré law of 31 December 1959 was to present private schools with four alternatives: to demand full incorporation into the state system; to maintain complete independence from the state (without subsidies); to negotiate a contract of "association"; or to negotiate a "simple contract." Both contracts would require various degrees of state supervision or control, but with the state paying the salaries of private school teachers and meeting other expenses.

In the debates leading to both the Barangé law of 1951 and the Debré law of 1959 the *Secrétariat* and the *Ligue* were exceedingly active. In both 1951 and 1959 the *Ligue* and the *Secrétariat* mobilized public opinion, worked actively with friendly deputies, and exerted considerable pressure on the cabinet. The chief channel of action for the *Secrétariat* remained the Parliamentary Association for the Liberty of Education (APLE), which played such an important role in 1951. Immediately after the results of the 1958 election were known, the APLE issued a press communique: it had received 323 signed membership forms from newly elected deputies, "which now guarantees a majority of more than two-thirds of the deputies from the Metropolis desirous of applying a rapid solution to the scholastic problem." Within a short time the Association boasted a membership of 380 deputies and 160 senators. The executive committee elected early in the parliamentary session included an Independent (Boscary-Monsservin), a UNR (Durbet) and an MRP (Thibault). The APLE formed a kind of brain trust, in collaboration with the *Secrétariat*, which functioned throughout the session. In view of their healthy majority in the Assembly, the friends of private schools viewed the coming debate with confidence.

The *Ligue's* political position after the 1958 election was precarious. It took no stand in either the referendum or the election—hardly surprising since its main support comes from such divergent groups as the Communists, Socialists and Radicals. Immediately after the election the General Council of the *Ligue* issued a moderately worded plea for "scholastic peace," by which it meant, naturally, an end to the "outmoded system of confessional separation." When the government's intention became clear, however, the *Ligue* was defiant. Albert Bayet, the *Ligue's* president, vowed to defend *laïcité* to the end. "From now on the motto of the *laïques* is the very same that, for four years, they opposed to the alleged government of Vichy: *Résistance!*" The brute fact remained: over two-thirds of the deputies had joined the Parliamentary Association for Liberty of Education. The only recourse for the *laïques* was to mobilize public opinion. A plan of action was drawn up, with the cooperation of the secular political parties and trade unions, for a series of political campaigns and mass rallies. But the secular forces were hopelessly outnumbered in parliament, and lacked the support of the government and the president of the Republic. Only a few ministers (notably Chatenet and Jeanneney), and some civil servants within the Ministry of National Education, could be counted on.

There was one important difference between the 1951 and 1959 situations: the Barangé law was virtually drafted in the office of the *Secrétariat*, and parliamentary strategy was also planned there. The Pleven cabinet in 1951 in effect invited the Assembly to work out its own solution, within certain broad limits. But the Debré government in 1959 jealously guarded the right to draft and present a text. In his declaration of 23 July 1959 to the National Assembly, the prime minister affirmed that "the responsibility of taking a decision devolves upon only the public powers, that is to say, government and Parliament." As for the "interested organizations" (obviously the *Secrétariat* and the *Ligue*): "if they want to be wise, they should remain quiet." And he added that even if they were unable to do so, they would have no influence whatsoever upon the government.

But neither side remained quiet. The laïques stepped up their public campaign, and the friends of the private schools continually pressured the government to go beyond the terms of the Lapie report. In spite of the prime minister's resolve to adopt a purely governmental measure, during the course of the debate he was compelled to make some significant concessions to the advocates of state subsidies. The original version of the government bill was opposed by Lizop, who declared at a press conference that private schools would refuse to negotiate contracts under the conditions stipulated in the bill—which he feared would lead ultimately to the simple incorporation of private schools into the state system. The prime minister thereupon accepted an amendment which eliminated confusion concerning the right of Catholic teachers to profess their religious doctrines—and the Minister of Education, M. Boulloche, promptly resigned. The president of the APLE, M. Boscary-Monsservin, announced that the bill was now satisfactory in view of the "clarification."

Since December, 1959 the *Secrétariat* has become a defender of the status quo, while the secular organizations have taken the offensive. In 1960 a campaign was begun for a mass petition demanding repeal of the Debré law. On 19 June 1960 a great rally was held at Vincennes, where the petitions were consolidated into one document, with almost eleven million signatures. The *Ligue* has vowed to take its vengeance, and to bring about the nationalization of private schools at the first opportunity. But it suffers one great weakness: even if the secular parties regain their representation in a future parliament, the divisions between Radicals and Socialists on the one hand, and Communists on the other, would make effective collaboration unlikely.

Thus, viewing the process whereby the Debré law came into being, it appears that the organized groups played a smaller *direct* role than in 1951. Perhaps a major reason was the determination of the government to resolve the "scholastic problem" by granting subsidies and establishing some state control. The views of the President of the Republic were crucial: as early as 1950 General de Gaulle had expressed himself in favor of state aid to parents so that they might educate their children in the manner considered appropriate by them. It was not only difficult for the *Secrétariat* to intervene directly in the law-making process in 1959—it was in a sense unnecessary. The government did the work for the organization. The *Ligue* could not intervene for the simple reason that the secular parties had virtually had their representation wiped out in the 1958 election. Hence, it may be concluded that the strengthening of the executive under the Fifth Republic did in fact result in a shift of tactics on the part of the secular and religious organizations. But both groups continued to act upon public opinion, organize friendly deputies, and gain the ear of the executive. The *Secrétariat,* in particular, had the opportunity to work *within* the parliamentary majority and the cabinet—tactics which proved remarkably effective.

The Army

Let us now consider a third type of pressure group active under both republics: the army. Professor Meynaud has excluded the army from his survey of pressure groups, arguing that the participation of the military establishment in politics should be viewed as an attempt to conquer or seize power. For our purposes, however, it would be useful to view the army as an organization whose members at times develop and act upon political attitudes. In this respect they share at least some of the characteristics of pressure groups, especially as regards the distribution of power between the state and those with claims upon the state. General de Gaulle himself considered the "weak state" under the Fourth Republic to be the principal cause of a general loss of national integrity, leading to egoism on the part of special groups and "trouble" in the armed forces. As he put it in his press communiqué of May 15, 1958: "The degradation of the State leads infallibly to the estrangement of the associated peoples, uneasiness in the army, the disintegration of the nation, the loss of independence." The army wants only to obey. But to obey requires the existence of a chief, a commander, a source of authority and of orders. The Fourth Republic did not give a firm lead—because of ministerial instability, the weakness of the executive, and divisions within parliament and public opinion. In General de Gaulle's view, the Fifth Republic remedied this defect. A strong executive, far above political bickering, is able to define a coherent national policy. The army's duty is to carry out that policy, fully confident that the objectives are consistent with national honor. In his address to army officers at Strasbourg in November, 1961, General de Gaulle declared: "Once the state and the nation have chosen their road, military duty is marked out once and for all."

But it did not work out that way. Within a period of twenty months—from the announcement of the self-determination policy in September, 1959 to the putsch of April, 1961—there were four major conspiracies, all involving the army to some degree: in October, 1959 an uprising in Algeria was to coincide with a coup d'état in Paris—but the action was called off at the last minute; in January, 1960 barricades went up in Algiers, but the government succeeded in surmounting the crisis; in December, 1960 an attempt was made to draw the army into opposition during De Gaulle's visit to Algeria; finally in April, 1961 four retired generals took command of a full-fledged military insurrection. After the collapse of the putsch, the Secret Army Organization (OAS) carried on a permanent conspiracy against the Gaullist regime, and received considerable support from army officers and veterans. As two well-known journalists put it, perhaps in exaggerated fashion, military opposition under the Fifth Republic replaced political opposition under the Fourth Republic.[3]

If anything, the army's political role was even greater after De Gaulle's return than before; the putsch of 1961 was an initiative of elements within the army, whereas in 1958 the army followed the lead of civilian insurgents. Important elements within the army were opposed to any policy envisaging independence for Algeria or political negotiations with the rebels, whether that policy emanated from a weak prime minister or a strong president of the Republic. Military intervention in politics was precipitated not by the weakness of the government in Paris, but rather by the development of a political consciousness on the part of a portion of the officer corps and within certain élite formations. Insofar as the army can be viewed as a pressure group, its relations with the state are far more complex than intimated by those who criticized the shortcomings of the Fourth Republic.

CONCLUSION

In its dealings with organized groups, the Gaullist regime has proclaimed its determination to vest policy making power entirely in the hands of the state. The prime ministers and the president have all spoken harshly of those groups—army officers as well as home distillers, beet-growers and butchers—who seek to influence political decisions. It should be pointed out, however, that hostility to pressure groups is not specifically Gaullist. A profound tradition in France, going back to Rousseau and the Jacobins, condemns all intermediary bodies between the individual and the state.

In fact the pressure groups have not been reduced to impotence under the new regime. The position of the groups has undergone a complex evolution since 1958. Some groups have clearly declined, others have merely changed their tactics and continue to enjoy considerable influence, while still others have become more powerful. In general, those groups which relied principally on contacts with parliamentarians have lost ground. However, the Fifth Republic continues to be a parliamentary system, that is, the cabinet is responsible to the National Assembly, and even the home distillers can still put up a good fight when given the opportunity. In addition, those groups which enjoyed close relations with the Left parties have also suffered, since the Communists, Socialists and Radicals fared poorly under the single-member-district system. The main losers are the trade unions and secular organizations. The shift of power to the prime minister, president and civil service has generally brought, not a diminution of pressure group activity, but rather a corresponding shift in

---

[3] See Jacques Fauvet and Jean Planchais, *La Fronde des généraux* (Paris, 1961), p. 7.

tactics or techniques. Thus, the friends of the religious schools, as well as agricultural and business spokesmen, found themselves within the majority or the cabinet. It was no longer necessary, then, to apply pressure noisily; there was rather an opportunity to press for political or administrative action from the inside. In those areas of policy which were taken over by the president of the Republic himself, pressure groups were in some cases completely frozen out (like the associations in favor of European unity). However, some financial, business and religious groups enjoyed exceptional opportunities to gain the ear of the decision maker through various loyal "companions." The most profound change of style was brought about by the increased importance of the civil service. Wealthy organizations hired researchers, economists and even ex-civil servants in order to present their case to the appropriate department in the most effective possible manner. According to one acute observer, the growing power of financial interests and technocrats is a striking feature of the Fifth Republic. He contends that increasingly there is a dialogue between the "men of the big lobbies" and the technocrats, who speak the same language and usually come from the same social class.[4]

The creation of more centralized political institutions in 1958 thus did not in itself bring about a reduction in the power of pressure groups. It rather compelled the groups to adapt and respond to a new situation, as a result of which their influence in many cases actually increased. Political structure may well determine *how* groups press their claims and *which* groups are to be favored. But there is no simple equation between centralization of political power and subordination of pressure groups to that power.

17. ARMIES AND POLITICAL MODERNIZATION*
Lucian W. Pye

ONLY A FEW years ago it was generally assumed that the future of the newly emergent states would be determined largely by the activities of their Westernized intellectuals, their socialistically inclined bureaucrats, their nationalist ruling parties, and possibly their menacing Communist parties. It occurred to few students of the underdeveloped regions that the military might become the critical group in shaping the course of nation-building. Now that the military has become the key decision-making

---

[4] P. Viansson-Ponté, "Vers une nouvelle France," *Le Monde*, 9 May 1962.

* From "Armies in the Process of Political Modernization," in J. J. Johnson (ed.), *The Role of the Military in Underdeveloped Countries* (Princeton University Press, 1962), pp. 69–89. Essay and footnotes abridged by the editors. Reprinted by permission of the Princeton University Press.

element in at least eight of the Afro-Asian countries, we are confronted with the awkward fact that there has been almost no scholarly research on the role of the military in the political development of the new states.

LACK OF KNOWLEDGE OR DOCTRINE

The trend of recent years toward increased authoritarian rule and army-dominated governments raises questions which seem only to emphasize the limitations of our knowledge. Is it true, as we have always supposed, that any encroachment of the military into civilian rule is a blow to liberal government and civil liberties? Or is it possible that military rule can, in fact, establish the necessary basis for the growth of effective representative institutions? Have events reached such a state in parts of Asia that we should welcome army rule as the least odious of possible developments and probably the only effective counterforce to communism? We seem to be confronted by two conflicting images of the politician in uniform. The first, derived largely from Latin America and the Balkans, is that of administrative incompetence, inaction, and authoritarian, if not reactionary, values. The second and more recent is that of a dynamic and self-sacrificing military leadership committed to progress and the task of modernizing transitional societies that have been subverted by the "corrupt practices" of politicians. How is it possible to tell in any particular case whether army rule will lead to sterile authoritarianism or to vigorous development?

To answer such questions is to explore two relatively unknown and overlapping areas; Western scholarship has been peculiarly inattentive to the sociology of armies, on the one hand, and to the processes of political development and nation-building, on the other. Only in recent years, as Professor William T. R. Fox observed, has the Western scholar's bias against the military been weakened to the point where he is prepared to go beyond the field of civil-military relations and recognize the entire range of national security problems as a respectable province of scholarship. Given the hesitation with which we have approached the study of the primary functions of armies it is not surprising that so little systematic thought has been given to the political sociology of armies and the roles that military institutions play in facilitating the processes of industrial and political development. It is hardly necessary to document the fact that we have limited knowledge about the nature of political development in transitional societies and the processes that produce the emerging political institutions. Without greater knowledge of these developments we lack perspective for viewing the rise of authoritarian practices and the emergence of military rule in transitional societies.

Our lack of knowledge about such important matters is probably less significant than the fact that we also lack an appropriate doctrine that, in lieu of tested knowledge, might serve to guide our policy. To put the matter bluntly, for all our commitment to democratic values, we do not know what is required for a society to move from a traditional and authoritarian basis to the establishment of democratic institutions and representative institutions.

When this problem has arisen in the past with respect to colonialism, our typical response has been anti-intellectual and antirational: colonial powers should relinquish their authority, and then an automatic and spontaneous emergence of democratic practices and institutions could be expected. Unfortunately, with the passing of colonialism we find we have little advice to give to the leaders of the newly emergent countries who are struggling to realize democratic ways. We have no doctrine to offer them, no strategies for action nor criteria of priorities, no sense of appropriate programs nor sets of hypotheses for explaining the paths to representative government. At best we have been able to piece together some concepts and considerations taken from embryonic theories of economic growth and have suggested that they might serve as guiding principles.

In contrast to our own bemusement, those interested in establishing other types of social and political systems—and most particularly, of course, the Communists—have a clearer sense of design and of priorities to guide their efforts. More often than not we have found that instead of developmental concepts and strategic plans we can offer only statements about the nature of democratic values and our vision of end-goals of political development. By stressing ends rather than the means we have inadvertently tended to highlight the extent to which the newly emergent states have failed to realize in practice their aspirations. In so doing we have contributed to the growing feeling of insecurity common to most of the leaders of such countries. These are generally men who, despite their bold exteriors, are inwardly plagued with self-doubts and uncertainties about their ability to run a country. Without clear notions as to the stages that must be passed through if their transitional societies are to realize free institutions, these leaders are in danger of thinking that the gap between current performance and democratic ideals means that their peoples are doomed to failure.

Our lack of doctrine for building a tolerably free society is most conspicuous with respect to the proper role of authority in government. How should the machinery of state, usually inherited from an essentially authoritarian colonial regime, be employed to ensure political development? Can these essentially coercive instruments of the state, which in a democratic order are the servants of the popular will, be utilized to guide a tradition-bound people to democratic values and habits of thought? Or is the result of any such efforts, no matter how well intended, likely to be a drift toward what is essentially an authoritarian order decorated with democratic trimmings? It would seem that these questions might serve as an appropriate beginning for a search for both a doctrine of political tutelage and a better understanding of the role of the military in the process of political modernization.

An underlying assumption behind much of Western political thought is that political institutions are above all else the products of the dynamic forces peculiar to a particular society and thus reflect the distinctive values and the styles of action common to that society. It is acknowledged, of course, that once institutions are established they tend to become dynamic and hence influence the values and the expectations of the population. There is thus an assumption of a circularity of relationships or a state of equilibrium. The fundamental view, however, is still that the dynamics of the system lie within the society as a whole and that it is the institutions which must be responsive. Governmental institutions can display initiative, but fundamental change originates within the society.

When we turn to the newly emergent countries this model no longer seems appropriate. For in these societies the historical pattern has been the introduction of institutions from outside, with a minimum concession to the values and behavior of the people. These fundamentally authoritative structures have thus tended to be shaped according to foreign standards. Rather than responding to indigenous values they have often proved to be the dominant factor in stimulating further changes throughout the society.

These considerations suggest that it might be useful to organize our analysis of the political role of the army, first, with respect to the political implications of the army as a modern institution that has been somewhat artificially introduced into disorganized transitional societies; and second, with respect to the role that such an army can play in shaping attitudes toward modernity in other spheres of society. By such an approach we may hope to locate some of the critical factors for explaining why it is that the military has been a vigorous champion of progress and development in some countries and a retarding influence in others. We may also hope to gain a basis for judging the probable effectiveness of armies in promoting national development and eventually democratic practices.

THE ARMY AS A MODERN ORGANIZATION

In large measure the story of the underdeveloped countries is one of countless efforts to create organizations by which resources can be effectively mobilized for achieving new objectives. This is the problem of establishing organizations that, as rationalized structures, are capable of relating means to ends. The history of much of the Western impact on traditional societies fits comfortably within this theme, for the businessman, planter, and miner, the colonial administrator, the missionary, and the educator each in his own way strives to fit modern organizations into tradition-bound societies. Similarly, the story of the nationalists and of the other Westernized leaders can be treated on essentially identical terms, for they too try to change the habits of their people by creating modern organizations.

Needless to say, there are not many bright spots in this history, and it is open to question as to who has been the more tragically heroic or comically futile: the Westerners struggling to establish their organizations in traditional societies, or the nationalist politician and the indigenous administrator endeavoring to create a semblance of order out of chaos. On balance, the attempts to establish military organizations seem to have been noticeably the most successful.

It would be wrong to underestimate the patient care that has gone into developing and training colonial armies, and in the newly independent countries the military have been treated relatively generously in the allocation of scarce resources. But in comparison to the efforts that have been expended in developing, say, civil administration and political parties, it still seems that modern armies are somewhat easier to create in transitional societies than are most other forms of modern social structures. The significant fact for our consideration is that the armies created by colonial administration and by the newly emergent countries have been consistently among the most modernized institutions in their societies. Viewed historically, some of these armies have been distinguished: the Indian Army, the Malay Regiments, the Philippine Scouts, the Arab Legion, the Gurkha Regiments, and the King's Own African Rifles, to mention only the more celebrated ones.

It would take us too far afield to explore the relative advantages military leaders have in seeking to establish armies in transitional societies. We need only note that there is a paradoxical relationship between ritualized and rationalized modes of behavior that may account for the ease with which people still close to a traditional order adapt themselves to military life. Viewed from one perspective, a military establishment comes as close as any human organization can to the ideal type for an industrialized and secularized enterprise. Yet from another point of view, the great stress placed on professionalism and the extremely explicit standards for individual behavior make the military appear to be a more sacred than secular institution. If discipline is needed to minimize random and unpredictable behavior, it is also consonant with all the demands that custom and ritual make in the most tradition-bound organization.

For these reasons, and for others related to the hierarchic nature of the organization, the division between traditional and rationally oriented behavior is not very great within armies.[1] Indeed, in any army there is

[1] It is significant that the most common weaknesses of civil bureaucracies in the new countries—like exaggerating the importance of procedure to the point of ritualizing the routine, and the lack of initiative and of a pragmatic and experimental outlook—are not as serious drawbacks to smooth functioning of military establishment. On the contrary, the very qualities that have hobbled civil administration in these countries have given strength and rigidity to their military establishments.

always a struggle going on between tradition and reason. Historically, during periods of little change in the state of military technology the tendency has been for the nonrational characteristics to become dominant. Given this inherent conflict in any military organization the question arises as to why the forces of custom and ritual do not readily dominate the armies of the newly emergent countries, and so cause them to oppose the forces of change. In societies where traditional habits of mind are still strong one might expect the military to be strongly conservative. Such was largely the case in the West during the preindustrial period. By contrast, in most of the newly emergent countries armies have tended to emphasize a rational outlook and to champion responsible change and national development.

This state of affairs is largely explained by the extent to which the armies in these countries have been influenced by contemporary Western military technology. In particular, nearly all of the new countries have taken the World War II type of army as their model.[2] In so doing they have undertaken to create a form of organization that is typical of and peculiar to the most highly industrialized civilization yet known. Indeed, modern armies are essentially industrial-type entities. Thus the armies of the new countries are instinct with the spirit of rapid technological development.

The fact that these new armies in preindustrial societies are modeled after industrial-based organizations has many implications for their political roles. One of their characteristics is particularly significant: the specialization that modern armies demand in skills and functions is only distantly related to the command of violence. There has generally been a tremendous increase in the number of officers assigned to staff functions as contrasted with line commands. As the armies have striven to approximate their ideal models they have had to establish all manner of specialized organizations and departments that require skills that are either in short supply or nonexistent in their societies. The Burmese Army, for example, in addition to its engineer and signal corps has special sections on chemical warfare, psychological warfare, and even a historical and archaeological section. All the new armies have attempted to introduce specialized training schools and advanced techniques of personnel management and procurement. Consequently, numbers of the more intelligent and ambitious officers have had to be trained in industrial skills more advanced than those common to the civilian economy.

The high proportion of officers assigned to staff functions means that large numbers of officers are forced to look outside their society for their

---

[2] World War II was in itself a decisive event in the birth of many of these countries and, of course, the availability of large quantities of surplus equipment and arms made it realistic to aspire to a modernized army. American military aid has contributed to making the military the most modernized element in not only recipient countries, but also in neighboring countries which have felt the need to keep up with technological advances.

models. The fact that army leaders, particularly the younger and more ambitious, generally come from those trained in staff positions means that they are extremely sensitive to the needs of modernization and technological advancement. This kind of sensitivity bears little relationship to the command of physical violence and tests of human endurance—in short, to the martial spirit as we customarily think of it. In consequence the officers often find that they are spiritually in tune with the intellectuals, students, and those other elements in society most anxious to become a part of the modern world. They may have little in common with the vast majority of the men they must command. In this respect the gap between the officer class and the troops, once largely a matter of social and economic class (as it still is to some degree), has now been widened by differences in the degree of acculturation to modern life.

It should be noted that these revolutionary changes in military life have significantly influenced the status of the military profession in different societies and hence have had an interesting effect on relative national power. Cultures that looked down on the military at an earlier stage of technology now accord high prestige to the same profession as it has raised its technology. For example, when armies depended entirely on human energy and animal power the Chinese placed the soldier near the bottom of the social hierarchy; with present levels of advanced military technology the soldier is now near the top of the social scale in both Communist and non-Communist China. The change has been more in the nature of the military profession than in basic Chinese cultural values. Conversely, peoples once considered "martial" may now show little interest in, or aptitude for, the new kind of soldiering.

Above all else, however, the revolution in military technology has caused the army leaders of the newly emergent countries to be extremely sensitive to the extent to which their countries are economically and technologically underdeveloped. Called upon to perform roles basic to advanced societies, the more politically conscious officers can hardly avoid being aware of the need for substantial changes in their own societies.

It might seem that those occupying positions in other modern-type organizations in underdeveloped societies would also feel much the same need for change. To whatever extent this may be so, three distinctive features of armies seem to make them somewhat more dynamic in demanding changes.

First of all, armies by nature are rival institutions in the sense that their ultimate function is the test of one against the other. All other organizations operate within the context of their own society; although their initial inspiration may have come from abroad, their primary focus is on internal developments. The civil bureaucracy, for example, can, and indeed has to, deal with its domestic problems with little regard for what other bureaucracies in other countries are doing. The soldier, however, is constantly called upon to look abroad and to compare his organization with foreign ones. He thus has a greater awareness of international standards and a greater sensitivity to weaknesses in his own society.

Second, armies for all their concern with rationality and becoming highly efficient machines are relatively immune to pragmatic tests of efficiency on a day-to-day basis. Armies are created for future contingencies, and in many underdeveloped countries these contingencies have never had to be faced. Even in countries such as Burma and Indonesia, where the army is forced to deal with internal security problems, the effects have been mainly to increase the resources available for building up the army according to the ideal model, with remarkably few concessions being made to practical needs. Other modernized organizations in underdeveloped societies have to cope with more immediate and day-to-day problems; hence they must constantly adjust themselves to local conditions. They cannot adhere as rigidly as armies can to their Western prototypes. Just as Western armies have often existed in a dream world of planning for types of wars that never occur, so armies of underdeveloped countries can devote themselves to becoming modernized and more "efficient" with little regard to immediate reality. Members of other modern-type organizations may desire to see social change in their society, but they are likely to be more conscious of the need to accommodate their ambitions to existing conditions.

Finally, armies always stand at some distance from their civilian societies and are even expected to have ways of their own, including attitudes and judgments, that are remote if not completely apart from those of civilian life. Thus again armies of the newly emergent countries can feel somewhat divorced from the realities of a transitional society and focus more on the standards common to the more industrialized world. In consequence they are often unaware of the difficulties inherent in modernizing other segments of their society. Within their tradition all problems can be overcome if the right orders are given.

ARMIES AS MODERNIZING AGENTS

. . . The relationship between armies and civilian leaders varies, of course, according to the circumstances of historic development. . . . Broadly speaking, however, it is helpful to distinguish three different general categories of such relationships.

There are first those patterns of development in which the military stand out because in a disrupted society they represent the only effectively organized element capable of competing for political power and formulating public policy. This situation is most likely to exist when the traditional political order, but not necessarily the traditional social order, has been violently disrupted and it becomes necessary to set up representative institutions before any of the other modern-type political organizations have been firmly established. The outstanding example of this pattern of development is modern China from the fall of the Manchu dynasty in 1911 to the victory of the Communists. Indeed, it is possible to think of this period as one dominated by a constant struggle to escape from the grim circumstances that obtained when only military organizations survived the fall of the traditional systems. Hence the military became the only effective political entity. Thereafter nothing could be done without them, and yet the military could do little without effective civilian institutions. Comparable situations seem to exist at present in some Middle Eastern countries where Western influence brought a commitment to republican institutions but left the army as the only effective modern political structure in the entire society.

A second category includes those countries where the military, while formally espousing the development of democracy, actually monopolizes the political arena and forces any emerging civilian elite to concentrate on economic and social activities. In many ways this arrangement is reminiscent of the Belgian variety of colonialism. At present, the most outstanding example of this form of rule is Thailand.

A third major category, which is probably the largest, consists of those countries in which the organization and structures essential to democratic government exist but have not been able to function effectively. The process of modernization has been retarded to such a point that the army, as the most modernized organization in the society, has assumed an administrative role and taken over control. In these cases there is a sense of failure in the country, and the military are viewed as possible saviors.

Before turning to our case studies, it is appropriate to note briefly some of the broader implications of the role of the armies in transitional countries—particularly in terms of international stability. The ways in which new societies are being created will have profound significance for the entire world. At the same time it is unrealistic to conclude that the army's role in the new countries is determined only by domestic developments. The nature of the contemporary international order and the focus of Western policies have had a profound influence on military institutions throughout the underdeveloped areas.

There has been a tendency in some quarters to regard the trend toward military rule as favorable to American policy interests. In particular, army rule has been welcomed as promising greater political stability and firmer policies against communism. Unfortunately, in the past we have generally been poor judges of leadership in the new countries. In fact, we have been so anxious to wish the new countries well that we have not been very realistic in appraising their national leadership. We have often placed faith in, and indeed lionized, men who are mediocre by any standard of measurement. The fault is more serious than just a misplaced sense of charitableness, for by refusing to employ realistic standards of judgment we encourage the lack of realism and even quackery in the political life of many of these countries.

In seeking a realistic estimate of the potential role of the military in the political development of particular countries it is also necessary to avoid being excessively influenced by ideological considerations which may be relevant only in advanced societies. We have in mind, in particular, the Western stereotype of the military as a foe of liberal values. This bias, for example, tends at present to take the form of seeing "military aid" as a threat to economic and political development and of assuming that only "economic aid" can make a positive contribution to such form of development. In some cases military aid has in fact made substantial contributions to road building, health facilities, communication networks and the like, all of which have directly facilitated economic growth. In other cases it has been equally clear that our military aid has seriously retarded economic development by diverting an excessive amount of the nation's energies into unproductive channels. The point is only that in our thinking about the newly emergent countries we must avoid stereotypes and expect many paradoxes.

If we are able to do so, we will be less surprised to note, for example, that it has been through the military that we have best been able to establish effective relations with the most strongly neutralist nations in Southeast Asia. With both Burma and Indonesia we have had considerable difficulties in almost every dimension of our relationships. Recently, however, it has appeared that we have been able to develop more genuine and straightforward relations with their military than with any other political element. Out of these relations have come further possibilities for cooperation. Thus, rather ironically, after the Burmese terminated our program of economic assistance to them, it was possible to reestablish such assistance only by first providing them with military aid. In this way confidence was reestablished and the stage set for their reacceptance of economic aid.

This particular example may, in fact, point up a most important consideration about armies in the new countries. For the various reasons which we have mentioned the army is often the most modernized public organization in an underdeveloped country, and as a consequence its leaders often feel more self-confident and are more able to deal frankly and cordially with representatives of industrialized countries. Military leaders are often far less suspicious of the West than civilian leaders because they themselves are more emotionally secure. This sense of security makes it possible for army leaders to look more realistically at their countries. All of these considerations make it easier for the military leaders to accept the fact that their countries are weak and the West is strong without becoming emotionally disturbed or hostile toward the West. Since these leaders seem to have less need to avoid realities, they are in fact easier people with whom to deal and to carry on straightforward relations.

It is important, however, to note from the example that it is possible, and indeed it is essential, to expand a narrow relationship with the military into a much broader one. Military aid has had to become economic aid.

Satisfactory relations with the military can become a dead end, just as military rule itself can become sterile if it does not lead to an interest in total national development.

This is only to say that while it may be possible to find in the armies of underdeveloped countries an element of stability, we should not confuse this with political stability for the entire society. The military may provide an opportunity and a basis for cooperation, but the objective must remain the development of stable representative institutions and practices. In planning for this objective it is essential to conceive of it as involving far more than just the efficient administration of public policies. It is necessary to keep in mind that in the past the West has come to these societies largely in the guise of administrators. This was the nature of colonialism, and we have tended to step into this role with our emphasis upon economic aid. In cooperating with the military we again are essentially strengthening this role of the administrator. In most underdeveloped countries there is at present a genuine need to improve the standards of public administration. In fact, unless such improvements take place they will be able to realize few of their national goals. However, there is a deeper problem, and this is the problem of developing effective relations between the administrators and the politicians. The disturbing fact is that we can with relative ease help people perform administrative roles, but we have not been particularly successful in devising ways of training people to the role of the democratic politician. In many respects this difficulty is the heart of the problem in our relations with the new countries.

This leads us to the conclusion that the military in the underdeveloped countries can make a major contribution to strengthening essentially administrative functions. If the new countries are to become modern nation-states they will have to have a class of competent administrators. They will also have to have responsible and skilled politicians. In cooperating with the military in these countries we should therefore recognize that they can contribute to only a limited part of national development. In particular, in assisting them to raise standards in the realm of public administration, we should also make certain that our assistance does not lead to a stifling of an even more basic aspect of political development: the growth of responsible and representative politicians.

18. THE DESERTION OF THE INTELLECTUALS*

Crane Brinton

WE COME to a symptom of revolution well brought out in Lyford P. Edwards's *Natural History of Revolution*, and there described as the

* Reprinted with permission of Prentice-Hall, Inc., from *The Anatomy of Revolution* by Crane Brinton. Copyright © 1952 by Prentice-Hall, Inc.

"transfer of the allegiance of the intellectuals." Although the word "desertion" has perhaps unfortunate moral overtones, the shorter phrase "desertion of the intellectuals" is so much more convenient that we propose to use it, rather than the longer one, in this study.

We must, however, be clear as to what we are talking about before we attempt to use the desertion of the intellectuals as a symptom. Intellectuals we may define without undue worry over preciseness as the writers, artists, musicians, actors, teachers, and preachers. Further subdivision into the small group of leaders who initiate, or at least stand prominently in the public eye, and the larger group who grind over material they get from the leaders, is not of major importance here. What is important, and somewhat puzzling, is the general position of the intellectuals in our Western society since the Middle Ages. Clearly we must not posit agreement among its intellectuals before we decide that a given society is reasonably stable. Even in the thirteenth century, in which so many of our contemporary thinkers find an enviable unanimity as to fundamentals of belief, the amount of bickering among the intellectuals was in reality very considerable. There were rebels and prophets aplenty throughout the Middle Ages. In modern times we expect the intellectuals to disagree among themselves, and certainly to disagree with the non-intellectuals, the vulgar, the Philistines, the Babbitts—or whatever other name the intellectuals may coin for them. Moreover, for a number of reasons, writers, teachers, and preachers are to a large degree committed by their function to take a critical attitude toward the daily routine of human affairs. Lacking experience of action under the burden of responsibility, they do not learn how little *new* action is usually possible or effective. An intellectual as satisfied with the world as with himself would simply not be an intellectual.

Here, as so often in the social sciences, and indeed in the natural sciences, we are dealing with a question where quantitative and qualitative differences shade most confusingly one into the other. Our distinction between the two is actually no more than a matter of convenience, a complex mental image of the investigating mind.

Quantitatively, we may say that in a society markedly unstable there seem to be absolutely more intellectuals, at any rate comparatively more intellectuals, bitterly attacking existing institutions and desirous of a considerable alteration in society, business, and government. Purely metaphorically, we may compare intellectuals of this sort to the white corpuscles, guardians of the bloodstream; but there can be an excess of white corpuscles, and when this happens you have a diseased condition.

Qualitatively, we may discern a difference of attitude, partly, no doubt, produced by the numbers and unity of these intellectuals in attack, but partly produced by a subtler reality. Victorian England, for instance, was a society in equilibrium, an equilibrium that looks in retrospect a bit unstable, but still an equilibrium. Here Carlyle upbraided a generation addicted to Morison's Pills instead of to heroes, Mill worried uncomfortably over the tyranny of the majority, Matthew Arnold found England short of sweetness and light, Newman sought at Rome an antidote for the poison of English liberalism, Morris urged his countrymen to break up machines and return to the comforts of the Middle Ages, and even Tennyson was worried over his failure to attain to anything more useful than a high, vague, and philosophical discontent.

Many, though by no means all, Victorian intellectuals were in disagreement among themselves, united apparently in nothing but a profound dislike for their environment. If, however, you look at them carefully you will find a curious agreement that not too much is to be done right away to remedy matters. Moreover, as Mr. Alan Brown has pointed out significantly in his study of the Metaphysical Society, they could actually meet together in Victorian comfort to discuss their differences. It is not, as we are told so often of the scholastic intellectuals of the Middle Ages, that these Victorians were in agreement on fundamental metaphysical and theological assumptions. They weren't in any such agreement. It is rather that they were in agreement about the less dignified but in some ways more important routines and habits of daily life, and they did not expect the *government* to change such matters.

The difference between the intellectual atmosphere of a group like the Victorians, writers who cannot be said as a whole to have deserted, and a group which has deserted, will be clear in a moment if we look at that famous group in eighteenth-century France which stood at the center of the great Enlightenment. One has first the impression of immense numbers of intellectuals, great and small, all studying matters political and sociological, all convinced that the world, and especially France, needs making over from the tiniest and more insignificant details to the most general moral and legal principles. Any of the testbooks will give you the roll—Voltaire, Rousseau, Diderot, Raynal, d'Holbach, Volney, Helvétius, d'Alembert, Condorcet, Bernardin de St. Pierre, Beaumarchais—rebels all, men leveling their wit against Church and State or seeking in Nature a perfection that ought to be in France. You will hardly find active literary conservatives like Sam Johnson or Sir Walter Scott, or even literary neutrals, men pursuing in letters a beauty or an understanding quite outside politics. Even the now almost forgotten opponents of the *philosophes*, even the pessimists who deny the doctrine of progress, are doctrinaire intellectuals, as unreasonable devotees of *la raison* as the radicals.

Literature in late eighteenth-century France is overwhelmingly sociological. If you look in the yellowing remains of French eighteenth-century journalism, if you try to reconstruct the chatter of salons and clubs, you will find the same chorus of complaints and criticisms of existing institutions, the same search for Nature's simple plan of perfection in politics. There is both a bitterness and a completeness in this chorus of complaint that you will not find in Victorian complaints. Statistically, one might establish the fact that there were proportionately more intellectuals "against the government" in eighteenth-century France than in nine-teenth-century England. But the difference goes beyond statistics, and into what we have called the qualitative difference. The French have a tone, at once more bitter and more hopeful, quite different from the Victorians. That this is not altogether a national difference will be clear to anyone reading the pamphlet literature of the age of Milton. Then the English intellectuals had deserted, as they had not under Victoria.

Russia, too, is a clear example of this desertion of the intellectuals. There is certainly much more than political propaganda in the series of novelists who have made Russian literature a part of the education of us all. But there is unmistakably political and social criticism of Czarist Russia even in the work of the most detached and Olympian of them, Turgenev. The impression one gets from even a cursory view of Russian intellectual life in the nineteenth and early twentieth centuries is unmistakable; to write or teach in those days meant being against the government. It did not in those days necessarily mean to be Marxist. Indeed, Marx bulked far less heavily in the lives of prerevolutionary Russia intellectuals than did the writers of the Enlightenment and the nineteenth-century romantic philosophers.

America is not so neat an instance. In Boston, for instance, in the 1760's and 70's, a good many of the kind of people we are discussing— "intellectuals" will have to do—were as firmly as many such people are now against so un-Bostonian an activity as sedition. It is clear that Harvard was by no means unanimous against the Crown, let alone in favor of the democratic machinations of her distinguished alumnus, Sam Adams. But if the literary and journalistic output in the colonies between 1750 and 1775—and even if we include the sermons—could be statistically assigned as either for or against the actual policies of the imperial government, there seems little doubt as to the very considerable balance against these policies. The Enlightenment, especially through Locke and Montesquieu, had come to the American colonies. The natural and inalienable rights of man were in this country, as in Europe, concepts introduced by intel-lectuals.

England may seem at first sight an exception to the desertion of the intellectuals. Lovelace, Suckling, even Donne seem hardly preoccupied with sociology. Yet at a second glance it is quite clear that English literature under the first two Stuarts is far from being the chorus of loyal praise it was in the days of Elizabeth I. A glance into Professor Grierson's *Cross Currents in English Literature in the Seventeenth Century* will show how much that literature was a dissolvent of the merry England of the Renaissance. Even more important is the fact that in those days there were no real newspapers. The pamphlet took their place. Now the pamphlet literature of the early seventeenth century in England, quanti-tatively enormous, even by modern standards, is almost wholly preoccupied with religion or politics—better, religion *and* politics—and is about as good an example of the desertion of the intellectuals as could be found. Indeed, as Professor Gooch has written, in the reign of James I "proclamation followed proclamation against the sale of 'Seditious and Puritan books,' and there was 'much talk of libels and dangerous writings.' "

There is such talk now, in the United States, in the mid-twentieth century. This simple statement should remind us of the difficulties of diagnosis of impending revolutions, of the need of considering all aspects of the syndrome, and not a single aspect, not even that fascinating one we have called here "desertion of the intellectuals." For one can make a case for the statement that from about 1900 on there has been desertion of the intellectuals in the United States. Yet the United States does not seem in this century ripe for revolution, does not seem to be a society in marked disequilibrium. Perhaps twentieth-century American intellectuals, like the Victorians we have just considered, are protesting from a sound background of basic agreement with their own Babbitts. Yet there is a bitterness in many American writers, a sense of being out of things in a country run by nonintellectual businessmen, which one does not quite feel even in the Matthew Arnolds, the Morrises, the Carlyles. American intellectuals tend to cling together as a class against other classes, which perhaps is why they show no signs of being about to inspire a revolution. We must not, however, be here led astray into the difficult and still poorly understood problems of *Wissenssoziologie* involved in the behavior of the intellectual classes of contemporary America. Sufficient that from Dreiser and Lewis to Hemingway, Farrell, and Mailer most of our widely read writers have been hostile to things as they are in the United States, and yet things as they are have remained quite unthreatened by revolutionary overturn.

To what did our successfully revolutionary intellectuals desert? To another and better world than that of the corrupt and inefficient old regimes. From a thousand pens and voices there are built up in the years before the revolution actually breaks out what one must now fashionably call the foundations of the revolutionary myth—or folklore, or symbols, or ideology. Some such better world of the ideal is contrasted with this immediate and imperfect world in all the ethical and religious systems under which Western men have lived, and notably in Christianity. It is not quite accurate to assert that for medieval Christianity the other, ideal world is safely put off to heaven. Yet it is clear that with the Reformation and the Renaissance men began to think more earnestly about bringing part of heaven, at any rate, to this earth. What differentiates this ideal world of our revolutionaries from the better world as conceived by more pedestrian persons is a flaming sense of the immediacy of the ideal, a feeling that there is something in all men better than their present fate, and a conviction that what is, not only ought not, but need not, be.

Perhaps, indeed, it is the lack of any such immediate better world in the minds of American intellectuals that explains why they are not playing now the kind of role the Voltaires and the Lockes played in the eighteenth century. American intellectuals have never really shared the Marxian dream; their dream—witness Parrington—has been the old eighteenth-century dream, which nowadays cannot be really revolutionary.

We shall later meet these revolutionary ideals in their fully developed forms. Here we need only notice that in the writings and preachings of the English Puritans—and to a lesser extent the constitutional lawyers—in those of the eighteenth-century *philosophes*, in those of the nineteenth- and twentieth-century Marxists, the evil, and indeed illegitimate, existing regime is very effectively contrasted with the good, and indeed inevitable, rule of right to come. In England, America, and in France, the essential principle to which men appealed against present conditions was nature, with its clear and simple laws. Ship Money in England, Stamp Act in America, patents of nobility in France, were all contrary to the law of nature. Even in England and America, where there was also much appeal to rights to be found in Magna Charta or the common law, the final appeal was always to a law of nature "engraved in the hearts of men." As the Puritan Henry Parker wrote in England, the common courts were "furnished only with rules of particular justice, which rules being too narrow for so capacious a subject [the relation of Crown to People] we must refer to those that the original laws of nature hold out to us." By the eighteenth century this kind of language had become almost universal among intellectuals. That nature always counseled what the intellectuals in revolt wanted is an observation we must in these days feel bound to make. It seems likely, however, that for most of those who appealed to her nature was as definite and explicit as God had once been, and as dialectical materialism was to be.

For the Russian writers and agitators of the Czarist regime, nature did not play quite so prominent a part. Not that nature is lacking in the pages of Tolstoy and his fellows, and the contrast between "artificial" society and "natural" instincts was not disdained even in Socialist propaganda. For the liberals, a rather heady mixture of advanced Western thought from the Rennaissance to Darwin gave them enthusiasm rather than firm standards. But the official ideology of the successful radicals in Russia was Marxism, and Marxism finds that the existence of capitalists, the rule of the bourgeoisie, is altogether natural. Only, its destruction by the proletariat is also natural, and this destruction is determined by forces quite beyond capitalistic control. The inevitable march of economic forces would then for the Marxists accomplish what the English Puritan expected from God and the French *philosophe* from nature and reason. The essential thing all these prerevolutionary agitators have in common, the essential ingredient, intellectually at least, in the revolutionary myth, is this abstract, all-powerful force, this perfect ally.

One special point is here worth our attention for a moment. Not only does God, nature, or dialectical materialism make the victory of the present underdog certain. The present upperdog can be shown—perhaps for propaganda purposes *must* be shown—to have acquired his preponderance by an accident, or a particularly dirty trick, while God or nature was temporarily off duty. Thus in the English Revolution the royalists and indeed the gentry as a whole were labeled "Normans," descendants of a group of foreign invaders with no right to English soil. John Lilburne, the Leveller, goes so far as to assert that the whole common law was a badge of slavery imposed upon the free people of England by the Norman Conquest. American hatred of absentee British government hardly needed such artifical fanning. The French were told by no less a person than Siéyès that all their trouble came from the usurpations of the Franks over a thousand years ago. French noblemen in 1789 were descendants of barbarous Germans, while French commoners were descendants of civilized Gauls and Romans. Revolution was but restoring the conditions of 450 A.D. Marxism explained the exploiting class without recourse to such pseudo-historical notions. And yet there is plenty of reference in Russian revolutionary agitation to the usurpation of land by the nobles, to their Varangian, or Tartar, or Western, or at any rate foreign origins. Present evil as well as future good needs the strengthening force of what Sorel called the "myth."

Finally, a great deal of energy has been expended on the question as to whether this revolutionary ideology "causes" revolutionary action, or whether it is merely a sort of superflous decoration with which the revolutionists cover their real acts and real motives. Most of this discussion is in the highest degree futile, since it is based on a crude notion of causation altogether untenable in fruitful scientific work beyond a very simple level. There is no more point disputing whether Rousseau made the French Revolution or whether the French Revolution made Rousseau than in disputing whether egg or chicken came first. We note that in our prerevolutionary societies the kind of discontents, the specific difficulties about economic, social, and political conditions that hardboiled moderns focus on are invariably accompanied by a very great deal of writing and talking about ideals, about a better world, about some very abstract forces tending to bring about that better world. It is, indeed, the *expression* of ideas, rather than particular ideas—which may vary enormously in different revolutions—that makes the uniformity. We find that ideas are always a part of the prerevolutionary situation, and we are quite content to let it go at that. No ideas, no revolution. This does not mean that ideas *cause* revolutions, or that the best way to prevent revolutions is to censor ideas. It merely means that ideas form part of the mutually dependent variables we are studying.

Chapter VI. Party Systems

Introductory Note

IN HIS influential book, *Political Parties*, Maurice Duverger points out that the one-party, two-party, and multiparty systems tend to correspond to the major types of contemporary regimes. Thus, dictatorships are characterized by the single party, and democracies by either a two or multiparty system. The two-party system is frequently held up as a model form, permitting the majority to govern and the minority to criticize. Multiparty systems are usually considered less stable, but offer the voter a greater choice of alternatives. However, in recent years this classification has come under attack. Mention has already been made of studies dealing with the party systems of developing nations. Some observers have suggested that one-party systems may serve as transitional forms, making possible the creation of a more democratic regime at a later time. Mexico is frequently cited as an instance where one-party rule is compatible with democracy because debate can take place within the dominant party.

The customary distinction between two and multiparty systems has also been questioned, particularly with regard to France and Scandinavia. French political scientists have called attention to the agreements (electoral alliances and cabinet coalitions) between parties of the same political family, which provides a measure of coherence. Thus, François Goguel speaks of the "party of order" and the "party of movement" in interpreting the conflict among the various parties of the Third Republic, in his *La Politique des partis sous la IIIe République* (1946). In runoff elections under the Third and Fifth Republics the French voter has frequently been presented with a choice between only two or three serious candidates. Similarly, students of Scandinavia have pointed out that these multiparty systems are capable of sustaining dynamic and stable governments. The parties form coalitions in the same way that wings of a major party in Britain or the United States come to agreement on a common policy or leader. It may be more fruitful to view party systems in terms of the nature of the national consensus, that is, whether or not the major parties (within either a two or multiparty system) and in turn the major social groups on which they are based, share the same attitudes towards basic values and goals and the means by which they are to be attained.

For a good treatment of the one-party systems in the developing nations: Gwendolyn Carter (ed.) *African One Party Systems* (1962); Ruth Schachter, "Single Party Systems in West Africa," *American Political Science Review* (June, 1961); and the article by Martin L. Kilson, "Authoritarian and Single Party Tendencies in African Politics," *World Politics* (January, 1963), reproduced in Part Four, below. Non-Western parties are described generally in G. Almond and J. Coleman, *The Politics of Developing Areas* (1960). See also Myron Weiner, *Party Politics in India* (1957). An excellent collection of essays on the principal party systems of the world may be found in Sigmund Neumann (ed.), *Modern Political Parties* (1956). The Swedish multiparty system receives special attention in Dunkwart Rustow, *The Politics of Compromise* (1955). The literature on the French multiparty system is abundant. See for example David Thomson, *Democracy in France* (1956); Philip Williams, *Politics in Postwar France* (1954); and Edward M. Earle (ed.), *Modern France* (1951). Two important recent books on the theory of parties are: Maurice Duverger, *Political Parties* (1951) and Avery Leiserson, *Parties and Politics* (1958).

Readings

19. TERROR AND PROGRESS*

Barrington Moore, Jr.

"NEVER BEFORE has the unity of Soviet society been so monolithic . . . as at the present time," said Georgii Maksimilionovich Malenkov, Chairman of the Council of Ministers, on August 8, 1953. Ordinarily this ritual formula might have no more impact on a Soviet audience than the minor interruption of a radio commercial on an American audience, forced to hear that "this year's Buick is even better than last year's." But to the Soviet delegates, assembled from all parts of the USSR for a special session of the Supreme Soviet, Malenkov's words must have had a certain piquancy lent by the immediately preceding events. Only a few weeks earlier the newspapers had briefly informed the Soviet public that Malenkov had brought about the arrest of Lavrentii P. Beriya, chief of the dreaded secret police and perhaps the most powerful of Malenkov's rivals in the "monolithic" society.

The frequency with which the claim of unity is repeated would be enough to evoke skepticism about its truth, even if there were no other

* Reprinted by permission of the publishers from Barrington Moore, Jr., *Terror and Progress—USSR*. Cambridge, Mass.: Harvard University Press. Copyright, 1954, by the President and Fellows of Harvard College.

evidence to the contrary. At the same time the Soviet dictatorship has survived many phases of growth and change, through invasion and bloody intrigues among its leaders, for the better part of two generations. Unity of a sort there seems to be. How is it brought about? How are the activities of millions of Soviet citizens related to one another, their billions of daily choices coördinated to produce a living society? It is inconceivable that the highest leadership with all its turmoil is merely an excrescence upon the larger society or that the latter can pursue its daily life undisturbed by the storms and lighting flashes at the top.

In any society order of some kind must exist in the way people get their living, reproduce themselves, guard against danger, or carry on other activities necessary for group existence. Methods of achieving this ordering of the separate choices of individuals show great variation. The American sociologist, William Graham Sumner, writing in the early years of this century, put a heavy stress on the importance of deeply rooted popular custom, rules that nobody makes, that are not enforced by any courts, but that nevertheless guide a substantial segment of human behavior. His work was an important part of a larger stream of thought that influenced people to look away from kings and battles as the moving springs of history and to search among mass phenomena for the explanation of the past and the present. Perhaps we have looked too hard and too long in this direction alone. In a small society with a simple technology such customary rules may be all that is necessary to solve the problem of order. Cases are known where a tribal chieftain or a set of institutions we would recognize as political are evidently unnecessary for the society to exist.

The situation in the USSR could scarcely be more different. Perhaps no government can maintain itself without some support in popular sentiment and custom. But these factors are definitely not the crucial ones in bringing about an ordered relationship in the behavior of the some 200 million human beings who make up the population of the Soviet Union. Especially in the form that it has taken in the USSR totalitarian dictatorship may be regarded as a substitute for other forms of coördination with a stronger groundwork in popular consensus.[1] For about the past twenty years Soviet society has been one enormous bureaucracy. The state has swallowed society. The behavior of nearly every adult male during his waking hours is heavily determined by his place within this bureaucracy, which confronts him with a set of alternatives in such a way as to make many of the choices among them obligatory. The same is true of course for the many Soviet women who are gainfully employed. As for children and housewives, the alternatives they face and the choices they make in daily life reflect rather closely the position of the breadwinner in this

---

[1] The reasons for the erosion of this consensus in Russia and the rise of a substitute form constitute fascinating historical and sociological problems about which specialists are far from agreed. But we cannot look into these questions here.

bureaucratized society. It is bureaucratized in the sense that the decisions of any adult are made within the framework of other decisions, reached at a higher level in an all-embracing administrative system. The peasant, the soldier, the worker, the artist, and the scientist play their roles in accordance with a web of decisions that ultimately originate in, or are approved by, the Presidium (formerly the Politburo), the highest organ of the Communist Party of the Soviet Union.[2] The Party Presidium now constitutes the most important single device through which the actions of Soviet citizens are connected with one another. Though by no means the only such device, it can be regarded as an indispensable one, for if it suddenly ceased to perform its functions, the entire fabric of Soviet society could be expected to disintegrate with astonishing rapidity.

If it is agreed that under the Bolshevik system the Party Presidium is the most important institution that gears together the various parts of Soviet society, we seem to be up against a blank wall of ignorance about this body that bars any hope of further analysis. It is quite true that we know extremely little about the process through which decisions are reached in the Kremlin. Nor will ingenuity carry us very reliably or very far in any attempt at long-distance mind-reading. But we do know quite well what the major decisions taken by the Kremlin have been. The record of Soviet policy at home and abroad is plain for all to see, even if valuable details that might alter our interpretation are sometimes missing. Furthermore we can see at least the major outlines of the chief problems that in an objective sense now confront the Kremlin leadership. The situation that they face does not have a completely random and unlimited number of possible outcomes. Even if we cannot predict what their exact response to the situation will be, it may be possible, through analysis of the situation and its component parts, to specify the range of alternatives and at the same time to indicate some of the consequences of different choices. This is a very different procedure, it may be noted, from merely projecting past trends into the future.

In regard to the situation facing the Party Presidium in the second half of the twentieth century, it is important to point out that the major decisions concerning the fundamental nature of the Soviet system are already a matter of history. Through rapid industrialization, the collectivization of agriculture, dictatorship within the Party, and the use of organized terror, Stalin succeeded in organizing and focusing the energies of Russian society in a manner that withstood the deep wounds of armed invasion and revealed itself capable of considerable expansion beyond the boundaries of the old Russian empire. These crucial decisions were made

---

[2] The name of the Politburo was changed to Presidium at the Nineteenth Congress of the Communist Party in the fall of 1952. The name of the Party was also changed from All-Union Communist Party (Bolshevik) to Communist Party of the Soviet Union. The term "Party Presidium" will be used to avoid confusion with the Presidium of the Supreme Soviet.

during the late twenties and early thirties. Though important internal problems remain, some of which are in a sense the consequence of Stalin's success, it does not seem likely that his followers, even if they quarrel further among themselves, will again try to remake Russian society on so grand a scale.

For the past twenty years the major problems confronting the top leadership of the Communist Party of the Soviet Union have concerned not the internal structure of their own system, but the relationship of that system to the outside world. In turn their appraisal of the situation abroad enters in as a major component of decisions that affect the life of every Soviet citizen. How many hours a Ukrainian miner or Central Asiatic peasant will work next year, and how much he will receive for this work, depends heavily on the leaders' appraisal of political trends in Washington, London, Paris, and other key centers. Particularly during the decade between the victory at Stalingrad and Stalin's death Soviet policy reflected a chain of commitments that derived from its increasingly expansionist foreign policy. This policy required the maintenance of a large body of men under arms, an emphasis on heavy industry at the expense of the general population's standard of living, ever greater pressure to extract the last ounce of produce from the peasantry through the machinery of the collective farms, and strict enforcement of conformity of all groups by means of terror and propaganda. No one link in this chain of commitments can be readily singled out as the causal one. Nor does the Kremlin enjoy a completely free hand in adapting to this set of dynamic relationships or in trying to control them. Both Moscow and Washington form parts of a larger system of world politics that has certain dynamic tendencies and properties of its own. Since the closing years of World War II these properties have manifested themselves in the form of intense rivalry between the two strongest powers, the United States and the USSR.

Despite the limitations on their freedom of action, stemming both from the large arena of world politics and from internal causes, the new Soviet leaders have shown several signs of an attempt to break free of the chain of commitments that characterized the last years of the Stalinist era. A policy that is new in certain important respects has been launched and to some extent carried out, in spite of dramatic internal struggles. Its goal seems to be to reduce commitments and to seek popularity, both at home and abroad, without making the amount or kind of concessions that would threaten vital and hard-won political gains. In other words, it may be interpreted as a minor retreat, executed to consolidate positions already held. . . .

On the whole, it seems most improbable that under the present leadership severe changes will be made in the general functions and structure of the Soviet control system, which has proved itself effective despite actual and potential weaknesses. Before probing for these soft spots and examining the sources of stability within this apparatus, it is necessary to sketch briefly, mainly for the nonspecialist in Russian affairs, the form and functions of this complicated system.

In general, the Soviet leadership has at its command three main instruments of control which it can use to enforce its decisions and to focus the energies of the Soviet population in the desired directions. One of these is the Party. The second is composed of the secret police and the military forces, which together constitute the instruments of violence. The third channel of control is, in a sense, a residual category, which many citizens of the USSR and the official press often lump together under the term "Soviet apparatus." It includes three major elements: (1) ministries administering economic activities (such as transport, coal, oil, chemicals, metallurgy, etc.), together with ministries directing noneconomic activities, such as the newly created Ministry of Culture and the Ministry of Health; (2) those agencies whose primary tasks are to check up on the economic performance of other ministries and to execute the technical, rather than the policy-making, aspects of drawing up economic plans (for example, the Ministry of Finances, the Ministry of State Control, and the State Planning Commission); and (3) the hierarchy of soviets, extending from the village, town, and city soviets to the Supreme Soviet, which are in essence appendages of the Party organization and also of the ministries in Moscow, although certain minor local administrative functions are carried out with relative freedom from central Party direction.

This threefold system of control—through the Party, the instruments of violence, and the Soviet apparatus—is superimposed on the patchwork of territorial divisions which constitute the USSR: the sixteen Soviet Socialist Republics (sometimes called Union Republics), of which the largest is the Russian Soviet Federated Socialist Republic (RSFSR); the approximately one hundred and sixty-odd *oblasts*, economic regional units into which each Soviet Socialist Republic is ordinarily divided; and the smallest territorial and administrative units, the *raions*, which exist in both the countryside and the city. Unlike many formal provisions in Soviet legal documents on Russian political structure, these territorial arrangements form the basis of real behavior. They are key administrative divisions around which a host of economic and political activities are organized.

The Party organization follows this territorial scheme. While Party communications from the center in Moscow sometimes skip the Union Republic organizations and go directly to the oblast, the Union Republics, particularly the larger ones, are also significant administrative units. At the 1952 Congress, Nikita S. Khrushchev, then on the road to becoming a major figure in Party organizational questions, suggested the inclusion in the Party statutes of a clause to the effect that the *obkom* (Party oblast committee) and central committee in a Union Republic systematically inform the Moscow Central Committee about their work by furnishing it with reports at set intervals. Though such a clause did not appear in the new statutes, it represents standard operating procedure that has existed for some time. Also in the interests of stricter control, Khrushchev suggested the creation of a secretariat, not to exceed three persons in number, in the obkom and central committee of a republic. This provision, which was adopted, also reflects the factual situation that major responsibility for events in a specific area rests on the shoulders of the Party secretary.

Refugees who were in a position to be familiar with these matters report that, as a rule, the nucleus of power at the oblast level is composed of the Party secretary, the oblast administrator for the secret police, and the representative of the economic ministry concerned with tasks in the area in question. At the raion level a corresponding arrangement probably exists, although printed confirmation of this point has not come to my attention. In some areas a military representative may also participate in local decision-making. All such officials are of course Party members.

The functions performed by the three major instruments of control are necessary in any complex industrial society if that society is to continue in existence. The first function, which may be labeled the politically positive one, consists of eliciting the kind of behavior from the population that the regime desires. The Party is the major agent in this area of control. Part of this work is done through formal education, which attempts to inculcate a set of attitudes, as well as to transmit knowledge and skills. Another part is done through the establishing of unequal material rewards or incentives for different kinds of work. Both the educational system and the system of differential incentives are under the close and continuous supervision of the Communist Party. On a number of occasions the highest Party authorities have intervened in these matters to establish major policies, scrapping old ones and adopting new ones that they considered necessary. Still another part of the politically positive function is performed by the Party's elaborate propaganda apparatus and through the control and deliberate manipulation of all media of mass communication. At the individual level, the Party member himself is of course supposed to serve as a living model of the desired behavior in all walks of life. Finally, the network of Party organizations indicates by suggestion and exhortation, as well as by direct command, the policy and behavior expected of organizations and individuals.

By their politically positive pressures the Soviet leaders seem to be aiming at enough spirited and intelligent support from the population so that at least minor officials, Party or non-Party, can be counted upon to do the right thing at the right time within the area of discretion that must of necessity be left to them. This hope has undoubtedly diminished with the passage of time and has been replaced with a more cynical and manipulative attitude, also a strong tradition in Bolshevik thinking. There are still, nevertheless, very strong traces in major public statements of the belief that only a certain irrational perversity, the relic of capitalist society and capitalist psychology, prevents segments of the population from accepting socialism with spontaneous enthusiasm. Thus, the politically positive strand of control represents a vast attempt to impose a new consensus, a new set of ideals, and a new social framework on a structure in which the sources of cohesion had already been partly destroyed in pre-Revolutionary times by the forces of industrialism and liberalism.

The positive function of eliciting certain kinds of behavior shades over into the negative one of preventing people from engaging in other kinds of behavior. Between these two, but closer to the negative pole, one finds compulsion used to make people do something, as well as to prevent them from doing something. The gradations along this continuum involve subtle distinctions that need not detain us here. Any society has to have negative means to channel and control behavior. Their extent, nevertheless, is an indication of the failure of the positive ones. In the development of the Soviet system, as positive methods failed to produce the required results, Lenin and Stalin found themselves compelled to resort more and more to terror and violence. In this connection it must be emphasized that the choice was not between using terror and permitting the disintegration of Russian society. Rather it was between using terror as a major instrument to create and then consolidate a new social system, or else letting power go by default. By the late twenties the forces of recovery and reintegration were growing stronger in Russian society. Since these forces were growing from the ground up in a way that threatened Bolshevik power, terror had to be used to destroy them and impose a new order, a process most clearly seen in the collectivization of agriculture. Later, terror had to be used within the Party itself, again to consolidate the power of the top leadership, perhaps essentially that of only one man, Stalin himself. A parallel growth of the importance of the instruments of violence may be observed in the Politburo's relationship with the outside world. Communist parties have not come to power anywhere outside Russia itself without prior military action.

The purpose of both positive and negative political controls in the Soviet Union, as elsewhere, is to enforce political decisions. A political decision, like any other, is a choice among alternatives. Can one point to any general criterion according to which the major political decisions made by the Soviet leaders appear to have been made? The maintenance of their own power has been suggested as an answer to this question, particularly by W. W. Rostow in his *Dynamics of Soviet Society*. Such an answer is, I believe, correct as far as it goes. Indeed the maintenance of pure and simple power does appear to have been the overriding criterion of major Bolshevik decisions, to which the leaders have been quite willing to sacrifice any literal adherence to Marxist doctrine. They are likewise relatively little concerned about questions of economic efficiency and general material welfare when such considerations conflict with the demands of keeping themselves in power, though they may continue to claim that, in the long run, their system will produce greater material welfare than any other.

Nevertheless power does not constitute a sufficient answer to this question. Power cannot be pursued as the one and only goal of any ruling group, in isolation, as it were, from other values. In modern times the pursuit of power requires the use of technological instruments that are quite complex. It also requires the creation of very complex human instruments: armies, bureaucracies, industrial systems, and devices for feeding and servicing these instruments. In turn the efficient manipulation of these human groups demands consideration of the forces of traditional beliefs and behavior which impede or resist social changes. Ingrained peasant traditions, as well as the more recently established industrial patterns of evasion and conservatism, constitute factors which the dictatorship cannot afford to ignore. . . .

Both the human and the material instruments have certain minimum technical requirements as to the way in which they must be used. If these technical requirements are neglected by those in search of power, their search will fail. In this respect power is limited by the autonomy of the instruments that must be used in its pursuit. Military strategy has its own technical requirements and autonomy that cannot be neglected by the most brilliant political strategist. Likewise, any industrial system requires discipline and punctuality from its labor force, some regularity in the availability of supplies of raw materials, means for distributing the finished product, and other functional arrangements that turn out to be very much the same in Magnitogorsk as in Detroit. Scientific research also is clearly an activity that has certain technical requirements in its successful pursuit.

For these reasons, even such thoroughly politically minded rulers as the Bolsheviks cannot make all of their decisions according to political criteria alone. Every decision of any consequence must take into account these instrumental or technical requirements as well. In any concrete issue that arises at any level of the Soviet bureaucratic hierarchy one criterion of a "good" decision will of course be: does the decision contribute to the power of the dictator? But another element that the Bolsheviks are forced to consider in trying to find a "good" decision is: does the decision meet the technical requirements of the situation? Naturally the reconciliation of these criteria is often far from easy. The technical requirements of a "good" decision demand therefore still a third instrument of control. The economic and noneconomic ministries, or the "Soviet apparatus," perform this control function. . . .

Here it is sufficient to point out certain general characteristics of the control system as a whole. Positive and negative political controls, as well as the technical ones, are by no means clearly allocated to various agencies, all of which stay neatly within their tables of organization. Instead, the system is one in which distinct lines of authority and sharp divisions of function are generally conspicuous by their absence. The confusion and overlapping stem partly from the speed with which the Soviet bureaucracy was constructed. They derive in addition from the dictatorship's need to fragment authority, lest one or the other levers of control develop into a power in its own right.

On this account one finds certain similarities in the structure and operation of a wide variety of Soviet institutions, ranging from a military unit, through a factory and collective farm, to even a scientific laboratory or a university. Three important officials will usually be found representing each of the three control functions. The Party secretary and the secret police officer, with his network of informers, serve as the positive and negative political controls. Technical control functions are performed by the cadre officer in the military unit, the manager in the factory, the chairman in the collective farm (where one or the other agents of political control may be missing), and by the director of a scientific laboratory or the rector of a university.

Such is the basic pattern of the Soviet dictatorship. . . .

Without too great distortion one can say that the growth of the Soviet system since 1917 has been characterized by the rise of the technical and politically negative lines of control, with which the politically positive one has had to compromise in order to retain its dominant position. The Party man has had to change from agitator to political administrator and give ground to both the engineer-administrator and the policeman. It is equally apparent that the last two have not been able to shake off the Party any more than the Party has been able to dispense with their services.

20. MEXICO'S ONE-PARTY SYSTEM*

L. Vincent Padgett

BECAUSE MEXICAN politics since the Revolution of 1910–17 have operated mainly within the framework of a one-party system and because in the past strong men have sometimes occupied the presidency, writers in the United States have tended to treat the system as authoritarian. Emphasis upon presidential rule and the corollary explanation of the role of the Revolutionary Party as nothing more nor less than an instrument of presidential domination have served to create an oversimplified picture of presidential power. . . .

THE THREEFOLD ROLE OF THE OFFICIAL PARTY

If the "official" or Revolutionary Party has not been an instrument for shaping the dominant power pattern into a monolithic structure, what has

* From "Mexico's One Party System: A Re-Evaluation," *The American Political Science Review*, Vol. 51, No. 4 (December, 1957). By permission.

been its socio-political function? The answer has more than one side since the party's role has in fact been threefold. The three aspects have formed the parts of a complete whole. But for analytical purposes they should be treated separately.

In the first place, the party has obviously had an electoral function. For election purposes it has served as a procedural device in the formalization of candidacies for public office, and it has organized the election campaigns for the persons nominated. Most important, however, has been its usefulness as a symbol of mutual interest. The party banner has become an emotional solvent for diverse economic groups and conflicting personal ambitions. As a symbol, it is the external manifestation of the rational conviction that the rewards of unity in terms of control of public office outweigh the occasional temporary disadvantages suffered from interpersonal or intergroup disagreements within the Revolutionary sector. The symbol seems to have become so venerated that it offers a reason in itself for unified electoral operations. Thus, during the election of 1952 when Avelino Navarro A., president of a District Committee, . . . sent a letter to the agrarian secretary of the party Central Executive Committee and expressed real dissatisfaction with party nominees for deputy and senator, the official's answer was couched in terms of the loyalty and unity of interest symbolized by the party emblem:

. . . I feel I should point out that regardless of whoever may be designated to run as candidates for deputies and senators, our obligation as members of the *Partido Revolucionario Institucional* is to uphold the party candidates. We should strive to prevent any division among the *campesinos* which might occur because none of our friends was nominated. . . .

It is noteworthy that in answering Navarro the Secretary of Agrarian Action did not try to defend the choices that were made. Instead he appealed to the values of unity and electoral success for the Revolutionary group as a whole as reflected in the triumph of its presidential candidate.

A second aspect of the party's total function has been its liaison role within the Revolutionary association. Daily throughout the year party committees work to facilitate the flow of information and the reconciliation of conflicting interests among the various groups and leaders associated in the revolutionary circle at a given level of government. In concrete, operative terms this has meant that the party central committee has been responsible for furthering understanding and a sense of common cause among federal legislators, state governors, the President and his cabinet, national committees of labor, peasant, professional, industrial, commercial and small property groups. On any typical weekday—between the hours of 10:00 and 2:00 in the afternoon and 4:00 and 8:00 in the evening—the central offices of the party in Mexico City teem with government officials, legislators, and interest group leaders who find there a kind of lodge or meeting place for exchanging confidences, swapping political gossip, sounding attitudes of colleagues and patching up differences.

Similarly, at the state level the party regional committees have worked for exchange of views and compromise of differences within the net of relationships involving functional groups, executive and legislature as well as the *ad hoc* groups of ordinarily apolitical persons which frequently emerge to demand civic improvements or redress of grievances. Day-to-day activity in the regional committee offices is not so great as in the party offices in the Federal District, but at election time it would be difficult to find a busier place than the headquarters of the regional committee in any one of the state capitals. The weakest point of party operation in terms of the liaison function has been at the municipal level where lack of finances and the consequent tendency to function on a part-time basis have limited the effectiveness of the party municipal committees.

The third aspect of the party's threefold role has been its operation as an intermediary between government and people. In this connection the party has acted as a channel of communication and an agency of mediation between policy makers in the executive branch of government, municipal, state and national, on the one hand and the majority and minority points of view at the grassroots on the other. . . .

THE ROLE OF THE PARTY AND THE IDEOLOGICAL BIAS OF THE POLITICAL ELITE

When a party system of government—two or more parties or coalitions of parties approximately equal in strength and share of electoral success—is lacking, the choice of means by which the political elite seek to maintain their power position becomes extremely important. The vital question is whether reliance will be placed primarily upon physical and psychological coercion or upon persuasion and compromise. In Mexico there has been a growing tendency toward the latter. This tendency has gathered strength from the expansion of literacy, the private ownership of mass media of communication, the constantly improving highway network—and particularly from the way decision-makers have interpreted their role, the value system of their countrymen and the history of the Mexican nation since Independence. These ideological factors are central to an understanding of "why" the party's role has developed as it has.

In the first place the self-ideal of those holding power has not been essentially authoritarian in character. The concept of an elite meriting unlimited discretion as the right of total omniscience has been lacking. Claims to legitimacy, in other words, have not been advanced in terms of a political theology centering upon revealed, universal truth as the single means for achieving social salvation. Instead, those who have aspired to and held power have emphasized the principles of free choice and majority rule as determined by elections. Practice has sometimes fallen short of ideological prescriptions, but theory has not been devoid of significance on that account since accepted norms have made room for political pluralism as a social value to be sought rather than stamped out.

Of particular significance has been the sense assigned the symbol "democracy" in the value system of the average Mexican. Democracy has not signified the institutions of party government nor the elaborate procedural-judicial arrangements for guaranteeing individual rights so characteristic of Anglo-Saxon political organization. As defined in Mexico, democracy has been less concrete, less rationalized and less closely tied to the institutional context. Primary emphasis has rested upon liberty in the more general and very basic sense of the capacity of the individual to move about, to associate freely, to discuss, to criticize—in summary to assert that independence without which there can be no dignity for the person. Liberty has been an ideological current running side by side with that of authoritarianism in the heritage of Spanish thought which has molded the Mexican value system. The institutional patterns by which rights for the individual have been secured in the United States and Western Europe have not taken root in a large way, but this should not obscure the fact that the concept of personal liberty has been familiar, deepbedded, and emotionally potent.

A second emphasis evident in the Mexican definition of democracy, particularly since the Revolution, has involved the execution of social and economic reforms for the purpose of raising the living standard of the poverty-ridden rural and urban masses. The rights of urban and rural labor to organize and strike, the land reform program, the social welfare and security measures, and the efforts to reduce illiteracy all have been manifestations of the social justice bias of Revolutionary democracy. But it has never been assumed that social justice precludes individual liberty, as has been the case with the political doctrine of some other revolutionary regimes of the twentieth century.

As a matter of fact, a prime conditioning factor in the development of the political institutions of Mexico has been the close interrelationship of these two emphases in Revolutionary ideology. Both facets have been treated as necessary parts of a whole. This was clearly pointed up by Adolfo Ruiz Cortines when he spoke to the people of Puebla as the candidate of the Revolutionary Party during the presidential campaign of 1952:

. . . reaffirming our purpose to take care . . . that Mexico shall follow without pause the path of dignity, of social justice and of unceasing progress . . . the Revolutionary administrations consolidate more each time the public liberties which are the root of our *mexicanism:* the liberty of belief, of thinking and of writing, of criticism of government, of association and all the rest which dignify man and the citizen and which our Great Charter consecrates. Such liberties we shall never set aside.

The ideological commitment with regard to liberty, particularly important for purposes of this study, has interlocked with the interpretation of Mexican history officially set forth and widely accepted in terms of personal conviction on the part of the political elite themselves. On the one hand the Revolutionary regime has been presented to the people as the logical, historical link in the heritage of popular revolutions led by heroes of other eras—such giant symbols of the folk struggle for liberty and self-determination as Padre Hidalgo, José María Morelos, and Benito Juárez. Also included have been such latter day prophets as Francisco Madero and Emiliano Zapata—even Lázaro Cárdenas. The stories and myths surrounding these leaders have formed the historical bases of the argument for legitimacy. On the other hand, in the process of forging the institutions of the Revolutionary regime the members of each succeeding administration have themselves been affected in their thinking and in their actions by the historical symbols which have been invoked as instruments for achieving and maintaining power.

This latter factor has been central to the creation of a widespread conviction in Revolutionary circles to the effect that the ideal of liberty in the Mexican system of values has made it difficult in the past to establish a lasting system of rule based upon organized, arbitrary coercion of the Mexican masses. It has been accepted as gospel that the Wars of the Reform and the defeat of the French puppet Maximilian in the nineteenth century as well as the overthrow of the Porfirio Díaz regime in 1910 and the ensuing years of bloody revolution all had among their primary causes the Mexican sentiment with regard to liberty.

Taken from this point of view, the lesson of history for those who wish to maintain their dominant power position in the Mexican political system has been clear enough, namely, ways and means must be found to prevent a sense of discontent and personal injustice from becoming widespread among Mexican citizens. In metaphorical terms, one way to remove the fuse from the political dynamite has been to institutionalize devices by which dissident groups can articulate their grievances and aspirations and have them considered.

Under the stimulus of this felt need the Revolutionary Party has been developing into something more than an electoral mechanism, symbol of unity for diverse groups and agent of intra-association communication for the various elements of the dominant power group in their relationships with each other. The party has become all these things; but, from the standpoint of stability within the Mexican political system and citizen participation in the molding of policy, the emerging function of the party as an instrument of mediation between government and people has been most important. For this latter aspect of the party's role reflects the understanding of Revolutionary leaders as to the importance of individual liberty, dignity and differences in the minds of the Mexican people. It reflects the recognition of the fact that the only course by which the

existing power pattern can be maintained without threat of rebellion on
the one hand or resort to organized control of social action in a total sense
on the other must be the development of multiple points of access by
which citizen and official can meet to adjust differences and reach new
understandings. An "official" party need not necessarily be an instrument
of imposition. It may be a device for bridging the gap between authoritarianism and representative democracy.

21. THE TWO-PARTY SYSTEM IN BRITISH POLITICS*
Leslie Lipson

I

BRITAIN MAY fairly be called the classic home of two-party government.
This claim is justifiable because of some characteristics for which the
system, as employed in Britain, is distinctive. Chief among these is its long
duration. Although there is room for disagreement among historians about
the time and circumstances of its birth, it would be difficult to deny that
two-party government was established earlier, has lasted longer, and at the
present time is probably more firmly rooted there than in any contemporary state. Indeed, the practice of simplifying the complexities of
politics into a contest for office between a pair of major claimants has
endured in Britain through a catalogue of changes which would assuredly
have wrecked a less effective system. In that country it has survived the
evolution from an oligarchy of aristocrats to a democracy of the whole
people; the transfer of power from monarchy to parliament and then from
parliament to cabinet; the rise of large-scale industry with its social
aftermath; the switch in economic policy from mercantilism to laissez
faire and from this to state planning; and withal, the expansion and
subsequent shrinkage of Britain's international might.

Especially in recent decades, moreover, both major parties have developed a strength of organization and tightness of discipline, to which
New Zealand offers the nearest parallel inside the British Commonwealth
and no similar approximation exists outside. For this reason, Britain, whose
two powerful parties differ so sharply from the plethora of groups in
France, also stands in contrast to the United States. What we have in this
country can more accurately be described as two party systems rather
than a two-party system. In the election of Senators and Representatives
and in the conduct of congressional business, the size and diversity of the

* From *The American Political Science Review*, Vol. XLVII, No. 2 (June, 1953).
By permission of the American Political Science Association.

United States have fostered a multiplicity of groups more akin to the politics of France than of Britain. Every four years, however, in order to capture the presidency, these groups amalgamate into two large and loose coalitions—like federal unions within a federal union. But even during a presidential election the cohesiveness of the Democrats and Republicans is far from matching that of the Conservatives and Laborites.

Many studies have been made of parties which examine their structure and organization, the interests they represent, and the programs they espouse. Also plentiful, because of the controversies surrounding proportional representation and because of the political experiences of various European nations, are discussions about the pros and cons of having two parties or many. Relatively less attention has been paid, however, to the problem of explaining why one or the other system emerges and survives and to that of detecting the circumstances which accompany and may cause the respective systems. With this problem, as it relates to Britain, the present article is concerned. It is written in the belief that a science of politics needs to devote more attention to the diagnosis of causation and that the comparative study of government can offer the best approach to its elucidation. The study of a single country, as is evident, can lead to conclusions which are valid for it alone and do not in themselves warrant a wider application. But such conclusions will suggest hypotheses for testing in other contexts, so that, when these are checked by a comparative method, a reliable body of argument can be pieced together.

The pitfalls on the way are, of course, many and deep. Frequently in efforts to analyze causal relationships there is much that consists of assertion rather than evidence; of assumed, instead of established, connections; and of effects mistaken for causes. Moreover, there is the danger in a complex situation of seeking the simple explanation of a single cause and believing one has found it. If these traps are successfully avoided, it should be possible to state, with more certainty than can be done at present, what conditions are responsible for the generation and operation of each type of party system; whether the causes that sustain it are identical with those from which it initially derived; whether similar factors, reproduced in like combination in different places, always yield the same results; and whether the same consequences may sometimes flow from dissimilar causes.

To avoid misunderstanding, a few preliminary clarifications are necessary, since discussion can otherwise be sidetracked and mired down in a semantic bog. A state has a two-party system if it satisfies the following conditions:

(1) Not more than two parties at any given time have a genuine chance to gain power.

(2) One of these is able to win the requisite majority and stay in office without help from a third party.

(3) Over a number of decades two parties alternate in power.

Such a statement has the merit of being politically realistic. It recognizes that, even where two giant organizations dominate the political process, some Lilliputian groups may exist alongside of them. Only if one of the latter should succeed in holding the balance between the principal contenders does the two-party system cease, as is the case, for instance, in contemporary Australia. The list of conditions further permits the possibility that a major party may dwindle and decline and eventually be replaced by a newcomer, just as the British Laborites supplanted the Liberals. While this is happening, of course, a three-party system may emerge temporarily (witness Britain in the period from 1918 to 1931). It is also compatible with a two-party system for a major party to suffer a prolonged eclipse and be overshadowed by its rival in a series of elections, as the Whigs overwhelmed the Tories from 1714 to 1760 and the Liberals led the Conservatives between 1846 and 1874, and the Conservatives in their turn prevailed from 1886 to 1905. The presence within the system of minor parties which are unable to affect the control of power; a lengthy ascendancy of one party; even the extinction of a major party and the rise of a new one; these phenomena do not signify the abandonment of the two-party system provided that the previously stated conditions are fulfilled. What really matters is that over the long run government through two parties be clearly revealed as the norm, from which any departure is only temporary and to which the system always returns.[1] Judged by these criteria, Britain may be said to have operated the two-party system for two and a half centuries. Thus the long Whig ascendancy that began in 1714 did not prevent a Tory resurgence in 1760. Domestic conservatism during the Napoleonic period and immediately afterwards did not make impossible the Liberal-sponsored reforms of the 1830's. The Conservatives split in 1846 over the protection of home-grown wheat, but were reassembled by Disraeli so as to triumph in 1874. The Liberals were splintered in 1885–86, but came firmly into power in 1905–6. The Laborites were divided and routed in 1931, yet returned to sweep the country in 1945. A three-party system existed in the latter decades of the nineteenth century because of the Irish question and the talents of Parnell, and again in the 1920's when Laborites were rising and the Liberals were declining. But the two-party system reasserted itself after each of these seeming deviations. . . .

II

Many reasons have been offered for the existence in British politics of two-party government. The various explanations are broadly of two

---

[1] In suggesting that British politics are characterized by a two and a half party system, Carl J. Friedrich overemphasizes the deviations. *Constitutional Government and Democracy* (rev. ed.; Boston, 1950), p. 414.

kinds. Sometimes the system is interpreted as the outcome of specific institutions which supposedly lend themselves to the formation of two major parties and no more than two. Alternatively the roots of the two parties are traced to the foundations of British society and economics. . . .

The notion that the two-party system is a by-product of the cabinet system encounters some fatal objections. There is, for example, the elementary chronological fact that the clustering of political factions into two major groups occurred at an earlier date than the emergence of the cabinet and thus could not have been caused by that institution. Like complex tapestries, the Whig and Tory combinations were woven of many strands, some of which connect directly with the Civil War between Parliamentarians and Royalists, while others may be more deviously and tenuously traced to the religious controversies of the sixteenth century or to earlier feuds among the nobility such as the Wars of the Roses. Certain it is, however, that after the last and most stupid Stuart was compelled to abdicate, the reigns of William and Mary and of Anne did witness the more orderly beginnings of bipolar politics with its essential corollary of alternation in office. For if it was the Whigs who understood Britain's interest in the War of the Spanish Succession, who pitted the nation's strength against the Sun-King, and who discovered the first genius with the surname Churchill, it was the Tories who divined when the time for peace had come and negotiated the Treaty of Utrecht.

The cabinet system, however, postdated these events. Its central principles—that the Crown should select as ministers only those who are supported by a parliamentary majority and that these should be collectively responsible for the acts of one and all—could be applied in practice only because the parties were already there to make them work. Indeed, as G. M. Trevelyan has observed, the party was the vital difference through which cabal was converted into cabinet.[2] Add the fortunate accident of personality that a Walpole's talents were available to exercise among Englishmen the arts of leadership which a German-tongued Hanoverian prince could not, and thus the same party system which produced the ministry endowed it with its prime minister.

Comparative evidence presents another difficulty to adherents of the view that the cabinet produces two-party politics. Such evidence, it is true, must be cautiously employed, since it is impossible to prove by means of imported data that something must have, or could not have, happened in a particular country. Nevertheless, the fact remains that virtually all the countries of continental Europe which have adopted

---

[2] "The party bond introduced a principle of unity among Cabinet Ministers other than that of mere individual obedience to the orders of the King. For that reason, party is the real secret of the step upwards from Cabal to Cabinet. The mutual loyalty of members inside the Cabinet was a reflection of the habit of party loyalty among the same persons in the world outside." *The Two-Party System in English Political History*, Romanes Lecture (Oxford, 1926).

cabinet government also have multi-party systems. This suggests that the cabinet, *per se*, was not the prime cause of the party system in Britain, for, were that the case, it might reasonably be expected that when cabinets were installed elsewhere, they would give rise to the same consequences. Since the cabinet system, however, can be found associated in more cases with multi-party systems than with a two-party system, and since the latter instances occur only within the British Commonwealth, the existence of two parties would appear to be the product of other elements that are peculiar to the British tradition.

One such element, which some political scientists have proffered in argument, is the cabinet's use of the power to dissolve a parliament. How this is supposed to discourage the formation of more than two parties is thus explained by Harold F. Gosnell:

> In Great Britain the two-party system is also perpetuated by the type of parliamentary government which the British have evolved. The Prime Minister can dissolve Parliament and declare new elections. This gives the party in power a firm grip over its members in the House of Commons, and discourages their trying any insurrections or new ventures, since re-election is a troublesome and uncertain matter. In doubtful British constituencies, winning an election is difficult, and the support of a major party is almost a necessity. The party in power keeps its members in the House from straying, and the opposition party is well disciplined because this is the only way that it can hope to come to power.[3]

The case is further buttressed by a reference to France, the classic example of multi-party politics. Because under the Third Republic the power to dissolve the Chamber of Deputies was used only once and then became obsolescent, people often assume that this fact helps to explain why the legislature, dominated by the cabinet in Britain, dominates over it in France. This line of reasoning scarcely supports the pretended conclusion, since it omits a number of considerations that point in another direction. The argument assumes that a ministry is better equipped to enforce party regularity among its followers in the Commons because it alone can take the initiative of deciding when to hold a general election and, if defeated in parliament, may prefer to go to the country rather than tamely resign. But precisely how this flexibility in the timing of elections strengthens the disciplinary control of the cabinet is not proven. Such a control does, of course, exist. But it rests primarily on other foundations: the cost of winning a general election; the centralization of party finances; the dependence of many members on their salaries; the power of the party leadership to endorse local candidates; and the absence of any requirement that a candidate must reside in his district, which makes him depend for his seat more on the leaders and less on his constituents. In the light of such potent considerations, it makes relatively little difference to most backbenchers whether a general election will be called this year, next year, or

---

[3] *Democracy: the Threshold of Freedom* (New York, 1948), p. 242.

two years hence. At some time, as he well knows, the day of reckoning must come. Whenever it does, he depends for renomination on the favor of the leadership, and that dependence would still hold good in Britain even if elections were held there with the clock-work regularity of the American system.[4]

The point is clearly illustrated by the experience of the country whose politics approximate most nearly to the British model. New Zealand has a similar two-party pattern; both parties are well disciplined; and its cabinet, of the familiar British type, dominates the legislature. For six decades after 1889, however, the power of dissolution was never employed. Elections were regularly held every three years, save on three occasions when Parliament extended its own life. Even when the power of dissolution was resuscitated in 1951, the circumstances in no way involved the survival of the ministry, a split in the government party, or a parliamentary stalemate. A system of two tight-knit parties, therefore, does not depend upon a power to dissolve and the practice of having irregularly spaced elections.

Furthermore, if the power to dissolve were actually such a deterrent to party rebels as is believed, how does one explain the cases of defiant party members, and actual splits that have occurred? The ministerial power of dissolution did not deter Disraeli from rising against Peel in 1846, or Chamberlain and the Liberal Unionists from crossing over to the Conservatives in 1886, or Henderson and his cohorts from breaking with MacDonald in 1931. Indeed, there may even be occasions when a group of dissidents, so far from coming to heel, withdraw their support from ministers and deliberately provoke a dissolution in the hope that an election may work to their own advantage, as was clearly Parnell's stratagem when he switched from Gladstone to Salisbury in 1885.

Nor can French politics during the Third Republic be properly adduced as evidence that the absence of a power to dissolve modifies the character of the party system. That reasoning is fallacious because it takes for granted, instead of proving, the point which is really in issue. What has to be explained is why a power that was explicitly written into the Constitutional Law of February 25, 1875, and was employed as early as 1877, was never used again. The answer is, of course, that, owing to the politics of the *Seize Mai* affair, a trick which the monarchists had devised against the republicans recoiled upon the heads of its promoters, for it was the republicans who won the election which their rivals engineered. Henceforth the Right feared to risk a second attempt, so that even

---

[4] It is worth noticing that though the intervals between British elections are irregular, the average length of Parliaments corresponds to the term of the President. Between 1832 and 1952, there were thirty general elections in one hundred and twenty years. Moreover, the change from the Septennial Act of 1715 to the quinquennial term provided under the Parliament Act of 1911 made no difference in this respect. From 1832 through 1910 twenty elections occurred in almost eighty years; from 1911 to 1952, ten were held in four decades.

Doumergue failed to reactivate the power of dissolution in the early 1930's; and the Left were reluctant to invoke it, since they remembered 1877, and in any case they were unlikely to enlist the necessary consent of the conservatively-inclined Senate. But the implications of this truth have often been misunderstood. The truth is that the power to dissolve atropied because the structure of the party system precluded the use of its potentialities. When there are many parties, and every government is a coalition, it is harder to reach agreement about the time to dissolve than when a single party takes the decision. It was the parties, in other words, that determined the use, or rather disuse, of the power to dissolve, and not the latter which determined the character of the parties. . . .

III

The preceding discussion contains a clear implication: namely, that the character of the party system depends on and derives from factors more fundamental than the structure of political institutions. To understand these factors one must turn to the society within which the parties have their roots and grow. A political party is a collection of individuals clustering around an interest whose furtherance they make an issue and whose value they generalize into an ideal. Anything about which men cohere and feel deeply may become the basis for political activity and conflict. Interests may be simple or complex and their adherents more or less numerous. People may group and regroup in several combinations whose membership is not identical. Hence the party structure takes its substance from the interests which men engender in society and its form from the relations that are organized between them. This poses the question: what sort of divisions can be found in British society which provide the basis for partisan opposition? If sectional, cultural, religious, or economic cleavages occur, how have these been represented by the parties?

It is an arguable hypothesis that the two-party system emerged in Britain because the social order of that country was relatively homogeneous and offered little possibility for a multiple splintering of parties. This is to say that in a number of matters which are fundamental to society such a preponderant majority existed on one side of the question that the arena of practicable controversy was much restricted, and conversely the remaining issues on which two sides were opposed in nearly equal strength were few and the divisions between them fairly simple. Thus, if the small territorial expanse of the British Isles precluded the formation of sectional groups, the numerical superiority of Anglo-Saxons and Protestants prevented the rise of a Celtic or Catholic party. Likewise the dominance of agriculture until the end of the eighteenth century, and of urbanism since the middle of the nineteenth, clarified the battle-lines of economic conflict since it was impossible in the earlier period to dedicate a party wholly to the interests of city-folk, or more recently to those of farmers.

These generalizations are true in the main, but they need to be explained and in certain particulars qualified or corrected. Take, for example, the question of sectional influences on British party organization. It is, of course, doubtful whether parties are ever founded anywhere on a purely sectional base. Even in states that cover a huge area a section acquires much of its political relevance from other factors which happen to be reinforced by geographical concentration. Certainly in a country whose total area slightly exceeds that of Oregon, and where even the hillier terrain does not approach the contours of a Switzerland, there is less occasion for that sense of a separate political identity which physical remoteness can at least abet or aggravate. To the extent that sectional forces have obtruded into British politics, they have done so because they largely coincided with the boundaries of cultural and religious diversity and represented a genuine economic antagonism. The one clear instance of a party confined to a single section where it predominated is that of the Irish Nationalists. In nine successive elections from 1885 to 1918 their parliamentary seats showed a small variation between a high of 86 and a low of 80. The decision to form a separate block, instead of working inside one of the major parties, was based on Parnell's calculation that he could hold the balance between the Liberals and the Conservatives and disrupt the United Kingdom by obstructing its parliament. Theirs, however, was a solitary and special case and serves as the exception to point the rule. Stemming from cultural, religious, and economic differences, the ardent nationalism of the Irish was fostered by the existence of a water barrier and by embittered memories of past warfare. But the significance of the religious cleavage in this whole complex can be gauged by the fact that Ireland ceased to be politically solid in the counties of the northeast where Protestantism was strong and the opponents of Home Rule voted Conservative.

The contrast between Ireland, on the one hand, and Scotland and Wales, on the other, is instructive. The two latter communities, though both belonging to the "Celtic fringe" and maintaining their own brands of nationalism, did not develop a separate Welsh or Scottish party. Why was this? One may suggest that a hilly border has produced among Scots and Welshmen less of an isolationist psychology than a sea channel can do; that their economic grievances were less acutely felt than those of the Irish; and that the divisions between Protestant churches were more easily bridged than the gulf between Protestant and Catholic. Instead of creating sectional parties, the Scots and Welsh have preferred to pursue their objectives within the fold of one or other of the two major organizations. The commonly and accepted generalization assigns the Celtic areas to the Liberals at least during the nineteenth century, which was true in the main, though Disraeli was able to make inroads on the Liberal strength at the time of the Conservative victory of 1874. But the generalization does not apply to Scotland in the eighteenth century, and, of course, has little force today. In the first half of the eighteenth century Scotland had a politically split personality. Its Jacobite sympathies endowed it with Tory leanings; while those who were antagonized by the Stuart preference for Catholicism sided with the Whigs. Later in the same century the talents of Dundas and his skillful use of jobbery consolidated the Scottish votes into a solid Tory bloc, which was placed—for a price—at the disposal of Tory ministries. The Liberal decline in the twentieth century has proceeded more slowly in Scotland than in England, and still more slowly in Wales than in Scotland. What little is left of the Liberal organization nowadays might be called the last protest of the Celt against the Anglo-Saxon. Those Celtic constituencies where it formerly dominated have been partitioned between Labor and the Conservatives. To the former have gone the Welsh coal-mining areas and most of the "industrial waist" of Scotland; to the latter, the Scottish counties.

Sectional and cultural differences have had less effect on the general development of the British party system than religious dissension. Not only the origins of the Whig and Tory parties in the years from 1660 to 1700, but their continued rivalry in the following century and the subsequent opposition of Conservative to Liberal, would be inexplicable unless viewed in the light of those religious controversies that have plagued the country since the reign of Henry VIII. But how did this issue contribute to the growth of a two-party system? On this point Carl J. Friedrich has commented: "England escaped the religious division (and the consequent development of a Catholic party) on account of the overwhelmingly Protestant nature of the country, buttressing this religious uniformity by depriving Catholics and other religious dissenters (nonconformists) of political privileges until well into the nineteenth century."[5] That is a curious statement because it both explains too little and implies too much. If being "overwhelmingly Protestant" means having "religious uniformity," why did some Protestants think it necessary to deprive others of "political privileges"? What "political privileges" were these, and, if uniformity was so securely "buttressed," did the relations between churches cease to be relevant to the strife between parties? Finally, by the same logic, why did the overwhelmingly Catholic character of France or Belgium not promote a two-party system in either of those countries?

The fact is that in the seventeenth century the kingdom was split by religion into three segments. In the middle stood the adherents of the Church of England, who were flanked on one side by the large group of Puritans and on the other by the smaller Catholic group. When the monarchy was restored in 1660, the Anglicans turned the tables on the Puritans, who had predominated in the Cromwellian decade, and wrote

[5] *Op. cit.*, p. 413.

their triumph into the Clarendon Code. Though subsequently challenged, the central principles of that Code continued in force and formed the line of demarcation between those Protestants whose church was established and those whose churches were not. The threat of a Catholic revival under James II temporarily solidified the Protestant ranks. But when their victory was assured in 1688, the old cleavage re-emerged. In essentials the politics of the revolutionary settlement amounted to a deal between the two major factions. Parliamentary supremacy was accomplished by the Whigs, Anglican supremacy by the Tories. Neither party was wholly satisfied with this *modus vivendi*. Both, therefore, strove to undo that portion of it which favored their rivals. But the balance of forces was so nearly equal that two generations had to elapse before the agreement could be fundamentally amended. With George III on the throne the Tories assisted in the recrudescence of monarchical power. Owing to the debacle of the monarch's American policy, however, and his later fits of insanity, the principle of parliamentary authority was rammed down their throats.

To secure a Tory acceptance of religious toleration took longer. Throughout the entire eighteenth century and the first two decades of the nineteenth, the Tories were identified with the Church of England and championed its establishment. The Whigs were thus cast in the role of representing the Protestant nonconformists, whose numbers were notably swelled by the impact of the one great spiritual force that appeared in eighteenth century Britain—to wit, John Wesley. The political disabilities of the nonconformists were not total, however, and their influence was far from negligible. The intent of the Test and Corporation Acts was to debar dissenters from holding public office. But by no statute were they disfranchised. Still less were they prevented from giving financial assistance to the Whigs. Even the ban on their taking office was not rigorously enforced, and regularly after 1727 an annual Indemnity Act was passed by Parliament to exempt from legal penalties those office holders who did not swear the necessary oaths. The truth is, therefore, that eighteenth century Britain contained not religious uniformity, but religious dualism; and this was carried over directly into a two-party system. Nobody has expressed this with greater clarity than G. M. Trevelyan in the following passage:

. . . From the Restoration to the latter years of the nineteenth century, the continuity of the two parties in English politics was very largely due to the two-party system in religious observance, popularly known as Church and Chapel. . . . The dualism of the English religious world, and the disabilities imposed on Dissenters, form a large part of the explanation of the peculiarly English phenomenon of two continuous political parties in every shire and town of the land, surviving even when obvious political issues seem asleep or settled, or when the party programmes seem in certain important respects to have changed hands. . . . The dualism in the religious life of the nation reflected itself in a political dualism.[6]

---

[6] *Op. cit.*, pp. 26–27.

Because this political inequality survived on the statute-book for over a century and a quarter, the time-hardened pattern of a Tory affinity for the Anglicans and a Whig alliance with nonconformists continued to exist long after the decade of the 1820's when the disabilities of the latter and of the Catholics were at last removed. Even in modern times, therefore, it has made some sense to generalize about the church-frequenting Conservative and the chapel-going Liberal or Laborite.

How was this split over a religious issue connected with conflicts of economic interest? Or, to put the question another way, what "durable source of factions" was present in the sphere of economics which could give rise to partisan opposition, and especially to a division into two parties and not more?

Until the end of the eighteenth century British society was primarily rural and the farming interest predominated in the economy. The commercial interest, though far from negligible, was secondary. Under such circumstances party opposition admitted only one possibility. The land-owning aristocracy divided into a majority who formed the Tories and a minority who united with the commercial interest to constitute the Whigs. Since the country squires were mostly Anglican, while the leaders of commerce were largely nonconformist, the religious split comple-mented the economic—a fact that contributed materially to a two-party system. Thus founded and fortified, the system had more than a century in which to settle down before encountering its severest test—the impact of rapid technological changes on the economic and social order. The cumulative effect of such changes has been to substitute an overwhelm-ingly urban society for one that was rural and to make farming yield pride of place to industry.[7] How did the parties adapt themselves to so major a transformation? Were the old bottles able to hold the new contents?

The answer is that the system, though subjected to an agony that was acute and prolonged, did in the end survive the strain. But during the course of readjustment, both great parties were respectively the victims of a major shock, whose results crippled one patient for thirty years and killed off the other. The first of these crises occurred when the manufac-turing interest had grown to such proportions that it could challenge the farming interest and assert its predominance by altering to its advantage institutions which formerly favored the owners of land. That was done in the political reform of 1832, amending the franchise and the apportion-ment of seats in the Commons, and in the ensuing economic reform of 1846, which abolished the protective tariff on food. The immediate sufferer was the Conservative party, which cracked under the blow. The Peelites, including Gladstone, separated off and within a few years coalesced with the Liberals. The Conservative residue followed Disraeli. He, having correctly prophesied the permanent decline of British agri-

---

[7] In recent British censuses less than 20% of the population are classified as rural. About 5% of the gainfully-employed are engaged in farming.

culture and knowing that a party devoted to a minority interest could not win majorities, looked around for a new source from which to replenish its strength—a task that occupied three decades.

At the very time that the Conservatives were emerging with renewed vitality, the crisis of the Liberals was beginning; for the same causes that helped the former harmed the latter. The contest between manufacturers and farmers amounted to a vertical division in the British economy wherein industrial wealth was arrayed against landed wealth. But with industrial predominance secured, a horizontal fissure soon opened in urban politics and poverty now challenged riches along class lines. The factory workers, in order to obtain improvements in their living and working conditions, besought the same voting rights that their Liberal employers had gained in 1832. On this issue there occurred in 1866 the first of the splits that were to prove fatal to Liberalism, since many a manufacturer was unwilling to see his employees enfranchised. When the suffrage was extended in 1867, the statute was enacted by a coalition of the minority Conservatives and the progressive wing of the Liberals. To whom would the huge new labor vote be given? For several decades it was actually divided between the two parties, since some working men voted for the Liberals as champions of nonconformists and social progress, while others were attracted to the benevolent paternalism of Disraeli's "Tory democracy" and to the hope of an imperial market for their products. Gradually, however, as the Liberal party weakened after a further split on the Irish question, and as tariff-conscious manufacturers drifted over into the Conservative camp, more Laborites began to whisper: "A plague on both your houses." The birth of a separate Labor organization ushered in temporarily a three-party system which lasted until, and ended with, the depression of the early nineteen-thirties. Even as they broke asunder, however, the Liberals continued to serve their country well, for, by entering the other parties, they made reform more palatable to the Conservatives and the constitution more palatable to Labor.

IV

Throughout this entire process, the timing and the order of events have evidently been crucial to the retention of a two-party system. Its early development, as Friedrich has stressed,[8] gave the system an initial advantage, and it was particularly fortunate that the main outlines of the constitutional system were already settled before the social order was convulsed by industrialism. But there is another important aspect of the timing which has received insufficient emphasis. What distinguishes Britain's political history in the nineteenth century is the gradualism whereby the franchise was extended to successive waves of new voters. The great

---

[8] *Op. cit.*, p. 413.

reform acts were spaced at such intervals— 1832, 1867, 1884—that the two-party system, already established prior to the first reform, was able to guide, absorb and assimilate the additions to the electorate. Each new interest, as its members received the suffrage, was thus mobilized by and embraced within the system. Every extension of voting rights stimulated more intensive organization by the parties in order that the recently enfranchised might be registered and captured, and better organization reacted upon the parties and fortified them. For purposes of contrast the experience of France is illuminating. That country went to the limit and adopted adult male suffrage in 1848—prematurely, as the result showed, since Napoleon III's *coup* shortly followed. The same broad franchise was reintroduced at the birth of the Third Republic, and with it simultaneously appeared the multi-party system which reflected the diversity and conflict of interests in French society. British gradualism in this respect was better adapted to the rise and retention of a two-party system than French universalism.

If this survey of the causes of the two-party system in Britain warrants any general hypothesis, it is that parties appear primarily to be the product of their society and are only secondarily the offshoot of governmental institutions. Though the latter are not without influence upon the party structure, they serve mainly to brace and bolster a system whose foundations are deeply embedded in and shaped by the cultural, religious, and economic components of a nation. Moreover, before wider application can be given to evidence drawn from a single country, allowance must be made for any unique elements in its history, which in the case of Britain are certainly the timing sequence and the rate of political adjustment to socio-economic upheaval. Finally, this last word of caution must be offered to those who would diagnose causation: to have shown what caused a certain party system in a given country is not to demonstrate that these causes, and only these, are necessary to produce it in any and every country.

---

22. PARTY SYSTEMS IN SCANDINAVIA*

Neil Elder

PARLIAMENTARY government in each of the five Scandinavian countries has its own indigenous characteristics and it is not an easy matter to treat the region as a unit in this context without introducing a certain artificiality into the analysis. There is one respect, however, in which all the

* From "Parliamentary Government in Scandinavia," in *Parliamentary Affairs* (Summer, 1960), pp. 363–73. By permission of the Hansard Society for Parliamentary Government.

Scandinavian states are alike: they all have multi-party systems. Thus
Finland at the present time has seven political groupings represented in
her legislature; Norway and Denmark have six apiece (excluding in
the latter case the representatives for Greenland, the Faroe Isles and the
German minority in Slesvig); Sweden has five and Iceland four. Admittedly not all of these groups are politically weighty, but, if the less
significant be left out of the reckoning, the Finns, Norwegians and
Danes can be said to be working a five-party system and the Swedes and
Icelanders each to have four major groups.

One reason for this galaxy of parties is that all five countries use one
form or another of proportional representation in their electoral systems.
This to some extent reflects an adherence to the radical liberal stream of
democratic thought and desire to have all sections of national opinion
represented in the legislature. In Finland especially, where P.R. was
introduced in 1906 while the country was still under Russian rule, the
radical reformers were inspired by nationalist sentiment: there was a wish
to show tenderness to all minorities within the nation by way of reaction
against the insensitivity of Nicholas II's régime to any expression of
Finnish opinion. But to some extent also the adoption of P.R. in Scandinavia was due to tactical political considerations—in Sweden and
Denmark, for example, the Conservatives were anxious to check their
decline during the first two decades of this century in face of the steadily
increasing pressure from the Left. Whatever the reason for its first
appearance, P.R. has had its usual effect of ensuring the representation of
small fringe parties and making more difficult the healing of splits in
existing political groups.

Social conditions almost certainly also play a part in bringing about a
complex party pattern. Even if single-member majority elections were to
be introduced in Scandinavia—the question is an academic one except
possibly, as will be mentioned later, in Sweden—it is doubtful whether a
two-party system on familiar lines would readily emerge. In the first
place, a considerable section of the farming community in each country
has become accustomed to defend its interests by voting for its own
agrarian party. The Finnish Agrarians probably command the steadiest
and proportionately the largest vote of any farmers' party in the five lands
(they have fairly consistently controlled a quarter of the seats in the
Finnish Parliament since the war). The Icelandic Progressive party is
relatively the next strongest, but Sweden (the Centre party) and Norway
(Agrarians) also have sizeable contingents. Denmark is the least clear-
cut case: here the Moderate Liberal (Venstre) party draws almost a half
of its support from the farmers, but there is in addition a Radical Liberal
party which commands the allegiance of many smallholders. Probably
except in Denmark, then, the introduction of single-member majority
elections would not from this viewpoint tend to reduce the number of
parties, for the farming vote is geographically localized and would still be

able to make itself felt as a separate force. Again, other types of voter can be found preponderating in one geographical area though they may be in a minority in the country at large, and these too would tend to be perpetuated—e.g. pockets of Communist voting strength in both Finland and (less importantly) Sweden. It may perhaps be mentioned in passing that both Sweden and Denmark had several parties in existence during the era of single-member majority elections that preceded the adoption of P.R. in 1909 and 1915 respectively. Probably, however, little can be proved from this, for the franchise was then restricted and parties were comparatively rudimentary.

Proliferation of Parties

The difficult question now arises of the effect which the proliferation of parties in Scandinavia has had on the nature of parliamentary government in the region. One would expect the usual rule to hold good—the more numerous the parties, the more unstable the governments (and the stronger the legislatures). One might then perhaps look for signs of dissatisfaction with the system and attempts to revise the constitution so as to strengthen the executive and restore the lost prestige of government. Some of all this there has certainly been in the Scandinavian states, but on the whole surprisingly little. Probably the best way to examine the matter is by first reviewing how matters stand in the individual countries and then looking at the region as a whole.

Iceland, where parties have been fairly evenly balanced in the Althing, has been ruled by a series of coalitions and minority governments (but mostly by coalitions). At present a combination of Social Democrats and Independence party men is in power with a working majority behind it. The electoral system was revised by the Althing in the direction of greater proportionality in 1959. It would appear, therefore, that the country is able to combine efficient government with a multi-party system, but the evidence is regrettably too fragmentary to justify any very secure conclusion.

In Denmark no party emerged with a clear lead over any other at the immediate post-war elections in 1945, and it proved impossible to revive the coalition of Social Democrats and Radical Liberals which had ruled the country with a majority from 1936 till the Nazi occupation. Nor has any party emerged with an absolute majority at any time since 1945. As a result, a succession of minority governments held sway between 1945 and 1957 and the political centre of gravity alternated from left to right between the Social Democrats and the Moderate Liberals. Part of the difficulty seems to have been due to the temporary phenomenon of the powerful Communist vote at the 1945 elections. Certainly the Social Democrats gained ground steadily after this initial setback until at the 1953 elections they came to outnumber single-handed the combined forces of the two right-wing groups (Conservatives and Moderate Liberals). They suffered a slight recession in 1957 but have apparently strongly entrenched themselves in power by entering into a coalition government that same year with the Radical Liberals and the small new Single-Tax Party, thus giving Denmark her first majority government since the war.

The post-war party situation in Norway offers a remarkable contrast to the pre-war scene. During the inter-war years no single party got a majority in the legislature and no government had a majority either. Consequently eleven ministries were formed in all during the period with an average life-span of two years each. Since the war the Norwegian Labour party has completely dominated affairs, and changes of ministry have been no more than domestic internal reshuffles. Labour emerged with an absolute majority in the 1945 elections and has never lost it—despite an electoral reform carried through in 1952 which was designed to meet complaints that under the old system majority parties got bonuses of seats to which they were not entitled. A considerable programme of social welfare legislation has stood the party in good stead, and it draws support from fishermen and from the small farmers of the west as well as from industrial workers.

A similar political phenomenon appeared for some time to be developing in Sweden. The Social Democrats in that country registered a fairly steady advance in the country and in the Riksdag from the turn of the century onwards, and the continuous increase in the numbers of the industrial working class in town and country alike seemed likely to carry the party to a well-nigh impregnable position. The first minority Social Democrat government was formed as early as 1920, and after a period of some uncertainty in the 1920s the party's strength in terms both of votes and seats grew apace at a whole series of elections from 1932 onwards. In 1932 a minority Social Democrat government came to office and very shortly afterwards established itself in a strong parliamentary position by entering into a working agreement with the Centre (Agrarian) party to carry out a programme of public works and aid to primary producers. In 1936 this agreement was consolidated into a formal alliance, and a "Red-Green Coalition" ruled the country with the comfortable majority until the outbreak of the war. In the 1940 elections the Social Democrats proved strong enough to command the legislature on their own for the first time. But these were the years of national coalition government in Sweden (as elsewhere) and the Social Democratic overall majority in the Riksdag faded away at the next elections in 1944. The party has, however, been in office, either in coalition or alone, continuously since 1932, with the exception of a brief interlude in 1936.

The post-war years have been a falling-off in Social Democratic predominance, and, while that party still remain by far the largest single grouping, they seem further than ever from an absolute majority position. From 1945 to 1951 they ruled alone. From 1945 to 1948 their strength in the Lower House was equal to that of all other parties combined, but since 1948 they have declined to a minority position in that Chamber. From 1951 to 1957 they revived the old alliance with the Centre party and could control the ligislature with all the ease of the immediate pre-war years. But in 1957 the Centre party retired from the coalition because it disagreed with a Social Democratic pensions plan, and since then the Social Democrats have been in an increasingly precarious position. In general it can be said that the Social Democrats have been forced to rely mainly on the disunity of their opponents for the passage of their bills during their spells of single-party rule. In respect of financial measures their position has been somewhat stronger, because these are passed by a joint vote of the two Houses and the Social Democrats have been able to dispose of a majority in the Upper House sufficient to carry the day. Now even this resource is failing them, and a situation of near-deadlock has been reached in the Riksdag over the last three years. The proportional representation electoral system is not on the whole well adapted to resolving a political impasse of this kind because landslides in one direction or the other are rare and shifts in party strength tend to occur slowly over a period of time. . . . There is some talk on the Social Democratic side of introducing single-member majority elections if the present state of affairs persists.

The problem of finding a working majority for a government is probably more acute in Finland than in any other Scandinavian country owing to the peculiar political conditions prevailing there. There is in the first place a fairly strong block of Communist deputies which has generally accounted for about a quarter of the seats in the unicameral Finnish Parliament during the post-war years (the Communist party in Finland was outlawed before the war and only re-emerged in 1945). The Agrarian party has similarly maintained itself at or about the level of a quarter of the seats in the legislature, and the same was true of the Social Democrats until they split into two factions in 1957. The rest of the field has been divided between the numerically small but highly influential Swedish People's party representing the Swedish-speaking section of the population (just under 10 per cent of the total); a small post-war grouping, the Finnish People's party, which is predominantly a Liberal party; and a Conservative party which polls strongly enough to give it a fairly constant representation of thirty or so out of a total parliamentary membership of 200.

This intractable and rigid party situation is complicated still further by the vigorous partisanship which marks the Finnish political scene and by the frequent head-on clashes of interest between the Agrarian and Social Democratic groups over questions of wages and prices. It has been made even more awkward at times by the exceptionally heavy inflationary pressures which Finland has experienced in the post-war years. On occasions, indeed, a party government of any description has been found impossible, and caretaker régimes of a non-party character have had to be resorted to in order to tide things over. Thus M. von Fieandt, the President of the Bank of Finland, was Prime Minister of a "business cabinet" in 1957 and M. Kuuskoski, the Director-General of the National Pensions Board, headed a government of officials, businessmen and Trade Unionists in the following year until the general elections fell due. For the rest, the story has been one of complex coalitions and minority régimes. The Communists participated in the government from 1945 to 1948 but went out in the latter year under a cloud after President Paasikivi had publicly proclaimed that they were planning a *coup* by infiltration more or less on Czech lines. Since then they have receded into the wings. Coalitions of Agrarians and Social Democrats, usually with some representation for the Swedish People's party, have been quite common more recently. Much though the two major partners differ from each other, they are united in disliking the Communists more. The coalitions thus work along from day to day until some new crisis arises—it may be caused by Agrarian proposals about the prices of farm produce or by some Social Democratic project that is designed to satisfy labour demands and prevent Communist strength from increasing on the union front.

Can any generalizations be made about the workings of the multi-party system in Scandinavia in view of the differences between the political situations in the different states? First, it is evident from Norwegian, and, to a lesser degree, from Swedish experience that a multiplicity of parties does not necessarily rule out single-party majority rule. But this appears to be an exceptional case, something perhaps in the nature of an historical accident, and it would probably be wise not to make too much of it.

Secondly, and more important, the problem of finding and keeping a majority by means of a coalition has proved on the whole easier in the Scandinavian lands than, for example, in France under the Fourth Republic, and this holds true even of Finland. Even when a minority government has had to be formed, it has usually lasted longer than any government of the Fourth Republic. In Denmark, for example, there have been two coalitions and effectively three spells of minority government in the fifteen years since the war ended. The first coalition lasted three years, the second has lasted a similar length of time to date. The minority governments have lasted slightly over three years apiece, discounting internal reshuffles caused by the deaths of Prime Ministers while in office. In Finland the turnover has certainly been more rapid, but this is largely because the occasional non-party régimes only last a few months. Two Agrarian–Social Democrat coalitions since the withdrawal of the Communists from office in 1948 have lasted two years apiece and at least two minority governments have lasted a year or so. Probably the split in the Social Democrats will alter the balance unfavourably, but on the

whole the record of governmental stability in Finland to date can be said
to be good with some bad patches. . . .

In summary, it may be said that the disadvantages of multi-party
systems and of proportional representation do not appear to have been felt
as acutely in Scandinavia as in many other parts of the world. They have
resulted at times, but by no means universally, in a certain amount of
governmental instability and a consequent increase in the power of
Parliament in relation to the executive. This is a state of affairs which the
peoples of the area are, up to a point at least, prepared to accept with
equanimity and even to relish. Certainly no such gulf has opened up
between the legislature and sentiment in the country at large as that which
contributed to bring about the downfall of the French Fourth Republic.
Political differences may be acute at times, as they have been in Finland,
but the lines of division have not been so numerous and so deep as to
debilitate government for any length of time and the authority of
government has not noticeably suffered any general decline.

Chapter VII. Party Organization and Leadership

Introductory Note

THE READINGS below explore problems of party organization and political representation. In all modern party systems the rank and file is unable to play a decisive role. If a party is decentralized and undisciplined (as is usually the case with most of the parties in France and the two major parties of the United States), no channel or machinery exists to be used by the membership in order to make their control effective. If a party is well organized, elaborate provision is always made for consultation of the rank and file in party congresses and conferences where basic policy resolutions are debated and voted. But the party leadership, when united, can carry a conference with it. Only when party leaders fall out among themselves do the rank and file play an important role—not because they take the initiative but because they are mobilized by rival leaders.

The position of members within parties is analogous then to that of the people within the democratic state. In neither case can the masses directly control the organization that acts in their name. All large groups, including political parties, are run by a band of interested persons united by a common set of beliefs or desire for power or both. Political parties are especially susceptible to oligarchical tendencies. While various techniques have been devised to mitigate these tendencies, mass parties remain under the control of a relatively few key individuals.

The leading discussion of the problem of oligarchy is to be found in the work of Robert Michels, *Political Parties*, which is excerpted below. Other important studies of this problem include: Gaetona Mosca, *The Ruling Class* (New York: McGraw-Hill, 1939); Walter Lippmann, *The Phantom Public* (New York: Macmillan, 1925); James Burnham, *The Managerial Revolution* (1941); Carl J. Friedrich, "Oligarchy," *Encyclopedia of the Social Sciences*; and C. Wright Mills, *The Power Elite* (1957). The critics of Michels generally agree that all parties tend to be oligarchic, but argue that even oligarchy can serve democratic purposes. Democracy is distinguished not by the size of the ruling body, but by the right of other interested persons to dispute the actions of the government and to replace the leadership without recourse to violence. The most effective check on party autocracy would thus be the existence of a well-organized opposition enjoying guaranteed freedom to expose mistakes, indiscretions, or abuses on the part of party leaders. But does it work out this way in practice? The student should compare the organization of power within several different parties, ascertain the extent to which the leadership is responsible to the members, and appraise the party organization as it functions within the total political system.

*

Readings

23. THE IRON LAW OF OLIGARCHY*

Robert Michels

Democracy and Aristocracy

In MODERN party life aristocracy gladly presents itself in democratic guise, whilst the substance of democracy is permeated with aristocratic elements. On the one side we have aristocracy in a democratic form, and on the other democracy with an aristocratic content.

The democratic external form which characterizes the life of political parties may readily veil from superficial observers the tendency towards aristocracy, or rather towards oligarchy, which is inherent in all party organization. If we wish to obtain light upon this tendency, the best field of observation is offered by the intimate structure of the democratic parties, and, among these, of the socialist and revolutionary labour party. In the conservative parties, except during elections, the tendency to oligarchy manifests itself with that spontaneous vigour and clearness which corresponds with the essentially oligarchical character of these parties. But the parties which are subversive in their aims exhibit the like phenomena no less markedly. The study of the oligarchical manifestations in party life is most valuable and most decisive in its results when undertaken in relation to the revolutionary parties, for the reason that these parties, in respect of origin and of programme, represent the negation of any such tendency, and have actually come into existence out of opposition thereto. Thus the appearance of oligarchical phenomena in the very bosom of the revolutionary parties is a conclusive proof of the existence of immanent oligarchical tendencies in every kind of human organization which strives for the attainment of definite ends. . . .

The Need for Organization

Democracy is inconceivable without organization. A few words will suffice to demonstrate this proposition.

---

*From *Political Parties* by Robert Michels, Dover Publications, Inc., New York 14, New York.

A class which unfurls in face of society the banner of certain definite claims, and which aspires to be the realization of a complex of ideal aims deriving from the economic functions which that class fulfils, needs an organization. Be the claims economic or be they political, organization appears the only means for the creation of a collective will. Organization, based as it is upon the principle of least effort, that is to say, upon the greatest possible economy of energy, is the weapon of the weak in their struggle with the strong.

The chances of success in any struggle will depend upon the degree to which this struggle is carried out upon a basis of solidarity between individuals whose interests are identical. In objecting, therefore, to the theories of the individualist anarchists that nothing could please the employers better than the dispersion and disaggregation of the forces of the workers, the socialists, the most fanatical of all the partisans of the idea of organization, enunciate an argument which harmonizes well with the results of scientific study of the nature of parties.

We live in a time in which the idea of coöperation has become so firmly established that even millionaires perceive the necessity of common action. It is easy to understand, then, that organization has become a vital principle in the working class, for in default of it their success is *a priori* impossible. The refusal of the worker to participate in the collective life of his class cannot fail to entail disastrous consequences. In respect of culture and of economic, physical, and physiological conditions, the proletarian is the weakest element of our society. In fact, the isolated member of the working classes is defenceless in the hands of those who are economically stronger. It is only by combination to form a structural aggregate that the proletarians can acquire the faculty of political resistance and attain to a social dignity. The importance and the influence of the working class are directly proportional to its numerical strength. But for the representation of that numerical strength organization and coordination are indispensable. The principle of organization is an absolutely essential condition for the political struggle of the masses.

Yet this politically necessary principle of organization, while it overcomes that disorganization of forces which would be favourable to the adversary, brings other dangers in its train. We escape Scylla only to dash ourselves on Charybdis. Organization is, in fact, the source from which the conservative currents flow over the plain of democracy, occasioning there disastrous floods and rendering the plain unrecognizable. . . .

Is it impossible for a democratic party to practise a democratic policy, for a revolutionary party to pursue a revolutionary policy? Must we say that not *socialism* alone, but even a socialistic *policy*, is utopian?

Within certain narrow limits, the democratic party, even when subjected to oligarchical control, can doubtless act upon the state in the democratic sense. The old political caste of society, and above all the "state" itself, are forced to undertake the revaluation of a considerable number of values—a revaluation both ideal and practical. The importance attributed to the masses increases, even when the leaders are damagogues. The legislature and the executive become accustomed to yield, not only to claims proceeding from above, but also to those proceeding from below. This may give rise, in practice, to great inconveniences, such as we recognize in the recent history of all the states under a parliamentary regime; in theory, however, this new order of things signifies an incalculable progress in respect of public rights, which thus come to conform better with the principles of social justice. This evolution will, however, be arrested from the moment when the governing classes succeed in attracting within the governmental orbit their enemies of the extreme left, in order to convert them into collaborators. Political organization leads to power. But power is always conservative. In any case, the influence exercised upon the governmental machine by an energetic opposition party is necessarily slow, is subject to frequent interruptions, and is always restricted by the nature of oligarchy. . . .

As the organization increases in size, the struggle for great principles becomes impossible. It may be noticed that in the democratic parties of to-day the great conflicts of view are fought out to an ever-diminishing extent in the field of ideas and with the weapons of pure theory, that they therefore degenerate more and more into personal struggles and invectives, to be settled finally upon considerations of a purely superficial character. The efforts made to cover internal dissensions with a pious veil are the inevitable outcome of organization based upon bureaucratic principles, for, since the chief aim of such an organization is to enrol the greatest possible number of members, every struggle on behalf of ideas within the limits of the organization is necessarily regarded as an obstacle to the realization of its ends, an obstacle, therefore, which must be avoided in every possible way. This tendency is reinforced by the parliamentary character of the political party. "Party organization" signifies the aspiration for the greatest number of members. "Parliamentarism" signifies the aspiration for the greatest number of votes. The principal fields of party activity are electoral agitation and direct agitation to secure new members. What, in fact, is the modern political party? It is the methodical organization of the electoral masses. The socialist party, as a political aggregate endeavouring simultaneously to recruit members and to recruit votes, finds here its vital interests, for every decline in membership and every loss in voting strength diminishes its political prestige. Consequently great respect must be paid, not only to new members, but also to possible adherents, to those who in Germany are termed *mitläufer*, in Italy *simpatizzanti*, in Holland *geestverwanten*, and in England *sympathizers*. To avoid alarming these individuals, who are still outside the ideal worlds of socialism or democracy, the pursuit of a policy based on strict principle is shunned, while the consideration is ignored whether the numerical increase of the organization thus effected is not likely to be gained at the expense of its quality. . . .

The Iron Law of Oligarchy

The party, regarded as an entity, as a piece of mechanism, is not necessarily identifiable with the totality of its members, and still less so with the class to which these belong. The party is created as a means to secure an end. Having, however, become an end in itself, endowed with aims and interests of its own, it undergoes detachment, from the teleological point of view, from the class which it represents. In a party, it is far from obvious that the interests of the masses which have combined to form the party will coincide with the interests of the bureaucracy in which the party becomes personified. The interests of the body of employees are always conservative, and in a given political situation these interests may dictate a defensive and even a reactionary policy when the interests of the working class demand a bold and aggressive policy; in other cases, although these are very rare, the rôles may be reversed. By a universally applicable social law, every organ of the collectivity, brought into existence through the need for the division of labour, creates for itself, as soon as it becomes consolidated, interests peculiar to itself. The existence of these special interests involves a necessary conflict with the interests of the collectivity. Nay, more, social strata fulfilling peculiar functions tend to become isolated, to produce organs fitted for the defence of their own peculiar interests. In the long run they tend to undergo transformation into distinct classes.

The sociological phenomena whose general characteristics have been discussed in this chapter and in preceding ones offer numerous vulnerable points to the scientific opponents of democracy. These phenomena would seem to prove beyond dispute that society cannot exist without a "dominant" or "political" class, and that the ruling class, whilst its elements are subject to a frequent partial renewal, nevertheless constitutes the only factor of sufficiently durable efficacy in the history of human development. According to this view, the government, or, if the phrase be preferred, the state, cannot be anything other than the organization of a minority. It is the aim of this minority to impose upon the rest of society a "legal order," which is the outcome of the exigencies of dominion and of the exploitation of the mass of helots effected by the ruling minority, and can never be truly representative of the majority. The majority is thus permanently incapable of self-government. Even when the discontent of the masses culminates in a successful attempt to deprive the bourgeoisie of power, this is after all, so Mosca contends, effected only in appearance; always and necessarily there springs from the masses a new organized minority which raises itself to the rank of a governing class. Thus the majority of human beings, in a condition of eternal tutelage, are pre-destined by tragic necessity to submit to the dominion of a small minority, and must be content to constitute the pedestal of an oligarchy. . . .

Thus the social revolution would not effect any real modification of the internal structure of the mass. The socialists might conquer, but not socialism, which would perish in the moment of its adherents' triumph. We are tempted to speak of this process as a tragicomedy in which the masses are content to devote all their energies to effecting a change of masters. All that is left for the workers is the honour "de participer au recrutement gouvernemental."[1] The result seems a poor one, especially if we take into account the psychological fact that even the purest of idealists who attains to power for a few years is unable to escape the corruption which the exercise of power carries in its train. In France, in work-class circles, the phrase is current, *homme élu, homme foutu.*[2] The social revolution, like the political revolution, is equivalent to an operation by which, as the Italian proverb expresses it: "Si cambia il maestro di cappella, ma la musica è sempre quella."[3] . . .

History seems to teach us that no popular movement, however ener-getic and vigorous, is capable of producing profound and permanent changes in the social organism of the civilized world. The preponderant elements of the movement, the men who lead and nourish it, end by undergoing a gradual detachment from the masses, and are attracted within the orbit of the "political class." They perhaps contribute to this class a certain number of "new ideas," but they also endow it with more creative energy and enhanced practical intelligence, thus providing for the ruling class an ever-renewed youth. The "political class" (continuing to employ Mosca's convenient phrase) has unquestionably an extreme fine sense of its possibilities and its means of defence. It displays a remarkable force of attraction and a vigorous capacity for absorption which rarely fail to exercise an influence even upon the most embittered and uncompro-mising of its adversaries. From the historical point of view, the anti-romanticists are perfectly right when they sum up their scepticism in such caustic phraseology as this: "Qu'est ce qu'une révolution? Des gens qui se tirent des coups de fusil dans une rue: cela casse beaucoup de carreaux; il n'y a guère que les vitriers qui y trouvent du profit. Le vent emporte la fumée. . . ."[4] Or we may say, as the song runs in *Madame Angot*: "Ce n'est pas la peine de changer de gouvernement!" In France, the classic land of social theories and experiments, such pessimism has struck the deepest roots.

---

[1] ["The honor of being recruited in the government."]

[2] ["A man elected is a man lost."]

[3] ["There is a new conductor but the music is the same."]

[4] ["What is a revolution? People who fire on each other in the street; that breaks a lot of windows; only the window makers profit. The wind carries away the smoke."]

Final Considerations

We are led to conclude that the principal cause of oligarchy in the democratic parties is to be found in the technical indispensability of leadership.

The process which has begun in consequence of the differentiation of functions in the party is completed by a complex of qualities which the leaders acquire through their detachment from the mass. At the outset, leaders arise SPONTANEOUSLY; their functions are ACCESSORY and GRATUITOUS. Soon, however, they become PROFESSIONAL leaders, and in this second stage of development they are STABLE and IRREMOVABLE.

It follows that the explanation of the oligarchical phenomenon which thus results is partly PSYCHOLOGICAL; oligarchy derives, that is to say, from the psychical transformations which the leading personalities in the parties undergo in the course of their lives. But also, and still more, oligarchy depends upon what we may term the PSYCHOLOGY OF ORGANIZATION ITSELF, that is to say, upon the tactical and technical necessities which result from the consolidation of every disciplined political aggregate. Reduced to its most concise expression, the fundamental sociological law of political parties (the term "political" being here used in its most comprehensive significance) may be formulated in the following terms: "It is organization which gives birth to the dominion of the elected over the electors, of the mandataries over the mandators, of the delegates over the delegators. Who says organization, says oligarchy."

Every party organization represents an oligarchical power grounded upon a democratic basis. We find everywhere electors and elected. Also we find everywhere that the power of the elected leaders over the electing masses is almost unlimited. The oligarchical structure of the building suffocates the basic democratic principle. That which IS oppresses THAT WHICH OUGHT TO BE. For the masses, this essential difference between the reality and the ideal remains a mystery. Socialists often cherish a sincere belief that a new *élite* of politicians will keep faith better than did the old. The notion of the representation of popular interests, a notion to which the great majority of democrats, and in especial the working-class masses of the German-speaking lands, cleave with so much tenacity and confidence, is an illusion engendered by a false illumination, is an effect of mirage. In one of the most delightful pages of his analysis of Modern Don Quixotism, Alphonse Daudet shows us how the "brav' commandant" Bravida, who has never quitted Tarascon, gradually comes to persuade himself, influenced by the burning southern sun, that he has been to Shanghai and has had all kinds of heroic adventures.[5] Similarly the modern proletariat, enduringly influenced by glib-tongued persons intellectually superior to the mass, ends by believing that by flocking to the poll and

---

[5] Alphonse Daudet, *Tartarin de Tarascon*, Marpon et Flammarion, Paris, 1887, p. 40.

entrusting its social and economic cause to a delegate, its direct participation in power will be assured.

The formation of oligarchies within the various forms of democracy is the outcome of organic necessity, and consequently affects every organization, be it socialist or even anarchist. . . . In every form of social life relationships of dominion and of dependence are created by Nature herself. The supremacy of the leaders in the democratic and revolutionary parties has to be taken into account in every historic situation present and to come, even though only a few and exceptional minds will be fully conscious of its existence. The mass will never rule except *in abstracto*. Consequently the question we have to discuss is not whether ideal democracy is realizable, but rather to what point and in what degree democracy is desirable, possible, and realizable at a given moment. . . .

The objective immaturity of the mass is not a mere transitory phenomenon which will disappear with the progress of democratization *au lendemain du socialisme*. On the contrary, it derives from the very nature of the mass as mass, for this, even when organized, suffers from an incurable incompetence for the solution of the diverse problems which present themselves for solution—because the mass *per se* is amorphous, and therefore needs division of labour, specialization, and guidance. "L'espèce humaine veut être gouvernée; elle le sera. J'ai honte de mon espèce," wrote Proudhon from his prison in 1850.[6] Man as individual is by nature predestined to be guided, and to be guided all the more in proportion as the functions of life undergo division and subdivision. To an enormously greater degree is guidance necessary for the social group. . . .

The writer does not wish to deny that every revolutionary working-class movement, and every movement sincerely inspired by the democratic spirit, may have a certain value as contributing to the enfeeblement of oligarchic tendencies. The peasant in the fable, when on his death-bed, tells his sons that a treasure is buried in the field. After the old man's death the sons dig everywhere in order to discover the treasure. They do not find it. But their indefatigable labour improves the soil and secures for them a comparative well-being. The treasure in the fable may well symbolize democracy. Democracy is a treasure which no one will ever discover by deliberate search. But in continuing our search, in labouring indefatigably to discover the indiscoverable, we shall perform a work which will have fertile results in the democratic sense. We have seen, indeed, that within the bosom of the democratic working-class party are born the very tendencies to counteract which that party came into existence. Thanks to the diversity and to the unequal worth of the elements of the party, these tendencies often give rise to manifestations which border on tyranny. We have seen that the replacement of the traditional legitimism of the powers-that-be by the brutal plebiscitary rule

---

[6] [The human species wants to be governed; it will be. I am ashamed of my species.]

of Bonapartist parvenus does not furnish these tendencies with any moral or aesthetic superiority. Historical evolution mocks all the prophylactic measures that have been adopted for the prevention of oligarchy. If laws are passed to control the dominion of the leaders, it is the laws which gradually weaken, and not the leaders. . . .

In view of the perennial incompetence of the masses, we have to recognize the existence of two regulative principles:—

1. The *ideological* tendency of democracy towards criticism and control;

2. The *effective* counter-tendency of democracy towards the creation of parties ever more complex and ever more differentiated—parties, that is to say, which are increasingly based upon the competence of the few.

To the idealist, the analysis of the forms of contemporary democracy cannot fail to be a source of bitter deceptions and profound discouragement. Those alone, perhaps, are in a position to pass a fair judgment upon democracy who, without lapsing into dilettantist sentimentalism, recognize that all scientific and human ideals have relative values. If we wish to estimate the value of democracy, we must do so in comparison with its converse, pure aristocracy. The defects inherent in democracy are obvious. It is none the less true that as a form of social life we must choose democracy as the least of evils. The ideal government would doubtless be that of an aristocracy of persons at once morally good and technically efficient. But where shall we discover such an aristocracy? We may find it sometimes, though very rarely, as the outcome of deliberate selection; but we shall never find it where the hereditary principle remains in operation. Thus monarchy in its pristine purity must be considered as imperfection incarnate, as the most incurable of ills; from the moral point of view it is inferior even to the most revolting of demagogic dictatorships, for the corrupt organism of the latter at least contains a healthy principle upon whose working we may continue to base hopes of social resanation. It may be said, therefore, that the more humanity comes to recognize the advantages which democracy, however imperfect, presents over aristocracy, even at its best, the less likely is it that a recognition of the defects of democracy will provoke a return to aristocracy. Apart from certain formal differences and from the qualities which can be acquired only by good education and inheritance (qualities in which aristocracy will always have the advantage over democracy—qualities which democracy either neglects altogether, or, attempting to imitate them, falsifies them to the point of caricature), the defects of democracy will be found to inhere in its inability to get rid of its aristocratic scoriæ. On the other hand, nothing but a serene and frank examination of the oligarchical dangers of democracy will enable us to minimize these dangers, even though they can never be entirely avoided.

The democratic currents of history resemble successive waves. They break ever on the same shoal. They are ever renewed. This enduring

spectacle is simultaneously encouraging and depressing. When democracies have gained a certain stage of development, they undergo a gradual
transformation, adopting the aristocratic spirit, and in many cases also the
aristocratic forms, against which at the outset they struggled so fiercely.
Now new accusers arise to denounce the traitors; after an era of glorious
combats and of inglorious power, they end by fusing with the old
dominant class; whereupon once more they are in their turn attacked by
fresh opponents who appeal to the name of democracy. It is probable that
this cruel game will continue without end.

24. POWER IN BRITISH PARTIES*

R. T. McKenzie

MUCH OF the confusion about the distribution of power within the major
British political parties arises from a careless use of terms. The phrases
"Conservative Party" and "Labour Party" are commonly used as if each
referred to a unified political entity consisting of three sections: a
parliamentary party, a voluntary mass organization and a professional staff
or party bureaucracy. It is usually assumed that if either party were truly
"democratic," the leaders of the party in Parliament would hold themselves responsible to the "members of the party," i.e., to those who
belong to the mass organization. But an examination of the history of the
two parties shows that in practice they do not. Therefore many observers find themselves driven to cynical or pessimistic conclusions about
the nature of intra-party democracy. Some conclude with Robert Michels
that an "iron law" inevitably prevents the members of a nominally
democratic political organization from controlling their leaders. Others,
paraphrasing A. L. Lowell, conclude that "Both parties are shams, but
with this difference, that the Conservative organization is a transparent,
and the Labour an opaque, sham."

There are good grounds for cynicism about certain features of the
British party system and there is much to be said for both Michels and
Lowell. But a clarification of terms helps to put the problem into
perspective. In fact two *autonomous* political entities face each other in
Parliament; they are "The Conservative Party" and "The Parliamentary
Labour Party" (PLP). Each is associated with a voluntary mass organi-
zation of its supporters outside Parliament, the former by "The National
Union of Conservative and Unionist Associations," the latter by a body
properly known as "The Labour Party." In addition, the Conservative
Party has at its disposal a professional staff of party workers outside

* From *The British Journal of Sociology*, Vol. VI, No. 2 (June, 1955), pp. 123–32.
By permission.

Parliament, the Conservative Central Office (which is responsible solely to the Leader); and on the Labour side, there is a professional organization, the Labour head office (popularly called "Transport House"), which is responsible to the National Executive of the mass organization (although in practice, the Labour professional staff is just as reliable a servant of the parliamentary leaders as is the Conservative Central Office).

Neither parliamentary party is, in the last analysis, responsible to the mass organization of its supporters outside Parliament; if it were, parliamentary government as it is conceived in this country would prove unworkable. When the party is in office, the chain of responsibility is from Cabinet to Parliament to electorate. It cannot be from Cabinet to parliamentary party to annual party conference to the mass membership of the party organization. The mass organization does have an important influence on the activities and policies of the parliamentary party which it sustains. Its influence tends to be greater when the parliamentary party is out of office; and, whether Labour is in office or opposition, the mass organization of the Labour Party tends to have greater influence on the parliamentarians it supports than does the Conservative National Union. But, as the official Labour Party *Handbook for 1951* properly insisted, "The Parliamentary Labour Party is an autonomous body. . . . Provision is made in the Party Constitution for periodical consultation between the Parliamentary Labour Party and the National Executive Committee (of the Labour Party), but the latter has no authority over the actions in Parliament of Labour Ministers or Labour Members."

It was not until the Labour Party found itself first in office and then in power that official party literature began to stress the autonomy of the PLP. From the earliest years of the party it had been an article of faith that no party could call itself "democratic" unless its parliamentary leaders were responsible to the members of the mass organization outside Parliament. This doctrine the Conservative Leaders never for a moment accepted. It is not surprising that the attitude of the two parties should have been so diametrically different when one contrasts the circumstances of their origin. Until well into the nineteenth century the Conservative Party was no more than a loose grouping of a few hundred Members of Parliament and Peers who were associated together for sustaining (whenever it proved feasible) a Conservative Cabinet. They had neither a professional staff of any size nor a mass organization of voluntary supporters in the country; nor did they need them. They were able to rely for the most part on the allegiance and authority of the squirearchy and the generous financial contributions of a section of the business community to provide the very considerable financial resources which were required to win elections in the days of great political corruption.

Two developments forced the Conservative Party to transform itself. The first was the rapid expansion of the electorate especially in 1867 and afterwards; and the second, the drastic tightening of the electoral law against corruption. As a result of these developments, the Conservative parliamentarians found they must present their case to a vastly larger electorate; and simultaneously, the sums they were permitted to spend for electoral purposes were sharply reduced. In addition, the growth of public education and the increased literacy of the electorate made it imperative that the Conservatives should provide themselves with machinery for preparing and distributing pamphlets and leaflets throughout the country. Even if the Conservatives had not themselves become aware that these developments would force a transformation of the party, the initiative of the Liberals under Joseph Chamberlain would certainly have forced them to do so. In any event, a combination of pressures forced the Conservative Party to devise a mass organization of voluntary supporters to sustain the Conservative cause and to secure votes at elections.

The National Union of Conservative and Unionist Associations (as it later became known) was therefore created in 1867; and alongside this voluntary mass organization, a professional body, the Conservative Central Office, was established "to advise . . . to assist . . . to provide all possible help." It was the firm intention (as one of the founders of the National Union put it) that the mass organization should serve as "a handmaid to the party" (in Parliament); there was to be no question of it attempting "to usurp the functions of party leadership." But it was also recognized, as the same spokesman put it, that "we had now out-lived the time of great family influences and also that period which succeeded the first Reform Bill, which might be called the period of middle class in fluence in boroughs. We were living in a day in which the people were to be applied to in a much more direct, clear and positive manner than was the case under the older forms of the Constitution, and, therefore, any party who wished to retain their hold upon the country must ascertain how far their proceedings were in harmony with the wishes of the people."[1] On the whole the National Union accepted its role as "handmaid" to the party in Parliament with surprising docility. For one nightmarish moment in 1883/4 Lord Randolph Churchill appeared to be attempting to galvanize the National Union into "usurping the functions of party leadership"; but it soon became clear that he was more concerned to "usurp" the role of Party Leader for himself. And when his personal ambitions were partially satisfied he soon lost interest in the National Union. Lord Salisbury, who then emerged as undisputed Leader, had strong views on the need to limit the functions of the mass organization and during his 17 years as Leader he saw to it that he and his parliamentary colleagues retained complete control of the affairs of the party.

As if to ensure that these matters should never again be brought into dispute, official Conservative literature has insisted, ever since Lord Salisbury's day, that the Leader of the Party has sole responsibility for almost

---

[1] Raikes, H. C., Chairman of the Council of the National Union, speaking at its annual conference in 1873.

every feature of party activity. The formal description of his powers would suggest indeed that the Conservative Leader is as powerful as the Leader of any totalitarian party. Once he is elected, the Conservative Leader is not required to submit himself for periodic re-election. Nor is he required to report in any formal way on his work as Leader either to the party in Parliament or to the National Union. When his party is in office he chooses his own ministerial colleagues (as of course does the Leader of any other party when he is Prime Minister); but even when the Conservative Party is in opposition, the Leader chooses his own "Shadow Cabinet" associates who become in effect the ruling oligarchy of the parliamentary party. The Conservative Leader, whether in power or in opposition, has the sole ultimate responsibility for the formulation of the policies and the electoral programme of his party. The resolutions of the annual conference and the other organs of the National Union are "conveyed" to him for his information; however emphatic they may be they are in no way binding upon him. Finally, the party secretariat (the Central Office) is, in effect, the personal machine of the Leader. He appoints all its principal officers (who remain responsible solely to him) and he therefore has effective control over the main instruments of propaganda, research and finance.

It would seem ludicrous that a party which claims to be democratic should grant its Leader virtually dictatorial powers; and in practice, of course, it does not. The formal description of the Leader's powers (which the Conservatives themselves provide) gives a grossly misleading impression of the distribution of power within the party, as a review of the modern history of the party shows. But it is entirely understandable that the emergent Labour Party should have decided, when it came to devise its own constitution at the turn of the century, that the internal arrangements of the Conservative Party were intolerably undemocratic. It was in any case inevitable, in light of its origins, that the Labour Party should have a profoundly different conception of the nature of party organization. The mass organization of the Conservative Party was, as has been shown, the creation, and in a sense the creature, of the parliamentary party. Almost precisely the opposite was the case on the Labour side. A mass organization, the Labour Representation Committee (subsequently renamed the Labour Party), was formed in 1900 by the representatives of some hundreds of thousands of trade unionists and a few thousands of members of three tiny socialist societies; its express purpose was to ensure that ". . . working class opinion (should be) represented in the House of Commons by men sympathetic with the aims and demands of the Labour movement. . . ." Largely as a result of pressure from the mass organization outside Parliament, these "representatives of working class opinion" formed themselves first into a "Labour Group" and then into a parliamentary party. Understandably, the members of this parliamentary party were considered to be "servants of the Movement" and frequent attempts were made to "instruct" them as to what they ought to do. The Labour Party of those days eschewed even the use of the word "Leader." The Labour M.P.s annually elected a "Chairman" (he did not become known as "Chairman and Leader" until 1922); he was considered to be little more than spokesman for his parliamentary colleagues. And they in turn were expected to advocate policies which were determined in the first instance by the mass organization of the party.

Thus, in the early years of this century, a reading of the official literature of the Conservative and Labour parties would suggest that they had totally different forms of organization. The one appeared to concentrate all power and authority in the hands of the Leader; the other appeared to have no "Leader" at all. The Conservatives declared that their mass organization was no more than a "handmaid" to the party in Parliament; Labour insisted that the annual conference of the mass organization exerted ultimate control over the Parliamentary Labour Party as well as the party outside Parliament. Fifty years later each party still presents much the same official description of its internal organization. But each description is highly misleading; in fact the distribution of power within the two great parties is remarkably similar.

The Conservative Leader is nothing like the all-powerful figure that party literature seems to suggest. He exercises great authority so long as he retains the confidence of his followers; but the moment he loses their confidence his authority collapses immediately. This has happened with surprising frequency in the modern history of the party. Of the party's seven Leaders since Disraeli, three (Balfour, Austen Chamberlain and Neville Chamberlain) were, in effect, destroyed by revolts among their followers; and a fourth, Stanley Baldwin, had to fight a bitter battle to retain his authority. When the Conservatives are in office, their Leader (who, of course, normally becomes Prime Minister) has almost exactly the same relationship to his followers both inside and outside Parliament as does a Labour Prime Minister. When the party is in opposition, the Conservative remains, as it were, "Prime Minister of the Conservative Party" and appears to be at once more remote from his followers and a more powerful figure than is the Labour Leader in opposition. But the difference is more apparent than real; both Leaders are either former Prime Ministers or potential Prime Ministers or both. It is this consideration, rather than any of the party's own internal constitutional arrangements, which is the real source of the Leader's influence and authority.

Again, the Conservative parliamentary party is nothing like so passive and submissive in its relationship to the Leader (and his colleagues in the Cabinet or Shadow Cabinet) as is sometimes assumed. Certainly since 1951, the Conservative parliamentary party appears to have had as much influence on the policies of the Conservative Government, as did the Parliamentary Labour Party during the lifetime of the Labour Governments of 1945 and 1950.

The Conservative mass organization has never, since Lord Randolph Churchill's day, seriously threatened the autonomy of the parliamentary party. But this is not to say that it has played a negligible part in the history of the party in the past half-century. It played an important (although by no means decisive) part in the downfall of Austen Chamberlain and the Coalition in 1922. It became the forum for great debates on the future of Ireland (in 1921) and the future of India (in the early 1930's). When the parliamentary leaders found themselves in bitter dispute (particularly on the latter issue) the mass organization meeting in conference, served, in a sense, as arbiter, just as the Labour annual conference did in the dispute over the issue of "sanctions" in 1935. On other issues of importance the National Union brought strong (and, some would add, decisive) pressure to bear on the Leader. They played an important role, for example, in pressing Baldwin, who showed some reluctance, to pass the Trades Disputes Act of 1927.

Admittedly the deliberations of the National Union have usually tended to be less colourful and less influential than those of the Labour party conference. But one vital explanation of this has been too often overlooked: in the 60 years from the accession of Lord Salisbury as Leader until the formation of the first majority Labour Government in 1945, the Conservative Party was in office (either alone or in coalition) for no less than 45 years. It is only when a party is in office that it becomes overwhelmingly clear that the party leaders (who constitute the Cabinet) cannot hold themselves responsible to the "party members" meeting in annual conference. It is only then that it becomes obvious that "intra-party democracy" (as it was originally conceived by the Labour Party) is incompatible with the parliamentary system as it operates in this country. And so, with the Conservative leaders in office for so large a part of the period between 1885 and 1945, it was particularly easy for socialists and Labour spokesmen to mock the National Union for its impotence; the members of the Labour Party did not become fully aware that *no* mass organization can direct the activities of a government composed of its own "leaders" until they discovered their own impotence in the matters of "tied cottages" and "equal pay" during the period 1945–51.

The Labour Party has been transformed in the course of 50 years of parliamentary and, latterly, of governmental experience. The "chairman-spokesman" of 1906 has become party Leader and Prime Minister or potential Prime Minister. The parliamentary party still solemnly holds annual elections for the office of Chairman and Leader (although only when the party is *out* of office). But it is not surprising that there should have been only 3 contested elections in the history of the Parliamentary Labour Party; nor that MacDonald and Attlee, the only two persons who have served as Leader during periods when the party has held more than 10 per cent of the seats in the Commons, never faced a rival candidate after their initial election to the Leadership.

When Labour is in opposition, its leader must work with a "Shadow

Cabinet" (the Parliamentary Committee) elected by the parliamentary party. But when Labour took office in 1924 and 1929, MacDonald formed his Cabinet with as little interference from his parliamentary colleagues or the mass organization as any Conservative Leader ever enjoyed. In its revulsion against MacDonald after 1931, Labour attempted to devise mechanisms which would constrain the authority of the next Labour Prime Minister. But Mr. Attlee did not hesitate to ignore all of these provisions when he constructed his ministries after the elections of 1945 and 1950. Indeed both MacDonald and Attlee were able to exercise all the prerogatives of the office of Prime Minister with no greater restrictions on their authority than any Conservative or Liberal Prime Minister would normally expect.

In particular, their relations with their parliamentary supporters were almost identical with those between a Conservative Prime Minister and his followers. In opposition, the Labour Leader and his Shadow Cabinet, unlike their Conservative opposite numbers, must present and defend their policies at meetings of their parliamentary supporters (the Conservative Leader and his Shadow Cabinet do not normally attend the meetings of the Conservative Private Members Committee, known as "The 1922 Committee," although its views are faithfully "conveyed" to the leaders by the Whips and, on occasion, by the Chairman of the Committee). But it is an open question whether the procedures of the Parliamentary Labour Party in this regard ensure to back bench members much greater influence in the affairs of the parliamentary party.

The mass organization of the Labour Party still plays a somewhat larger role in the affairs of the party than does its Conservative equivalent, the National Union. But Labour has evolved (partly, it would appear, by accident, partly by design) a series of devices which normally all but preclude the possibility that the mass organization should try to force the parliamentary party to move in a direction in which it does not wish to go. When Labour is in office the leaders have no trouble at all; they flatly refuse to accept direction from the annual conference. But, in any case, the conference in all normal circumstances, and except on the rarest occasions, votes as it is advised to do by the party leaders. The affiliated trade unions cast five-sixths of the conference votes and so long as the party leaders retain the confidence of the leaders of a few of the major trade unions, there is little danger that the conference will reject their advice.[2]

---

[2] If the party leaders were to lose that confidence, the Labour party organization in its present form might well become unworkable. If the "block vote" were no longer a reliable instrument in the hands of the party leaders, the conference might frequently pass resolutions favouring policies to which the leaders were opposed. The party leaders would presumably be forced to make it clear to the conference that under the Cabinet and Parliamentary system a party conference can have no more than advisory functions. Otherwise, if the leaders submitted and acted on the direction of the conference, then the latter body would soon become more important than Parliament itself.

The constitution of the Labour Party provides that "no proposal shall be included in the Party Programme unless it has been adopted by the Party Conference by a majority of not less than two-thirds of the votes recorded on a card vote." But there is no evidence in the modern history of the party that this provision has in any serious sense proved a handicap to the parliamentary leaders. In any case, it should be noted that the fact that a proposal has secured a two-thirds conference vote does not ensure its inclusion in the party's election manifesto; the parliamentary leaders have a decisive voice in determining which proposals adopted by previous conferences will be included in the manifesto. Indeed it is now clear that the mass organization plays a very minor role in policy making; the initiative and dominant influence lies with the parliamentary leaders.

The inner life of the Labour mass organization is in many respects different from that of the National Union. The conservative mass organization is much less disputatious; at the constituency level it rarely debates policy questions and in annual conference it is even less likely than the Labour conference to reject the advice of its leaders. Indeed the Conservative conference normally contemplates its leaders in variegated moods of deference and adulation. This is not to say that the Conservative leaders can with impunity ignore the views (in so far as it has any) of this amiable and intellectually slothful giant, the National Union; but they need devote much less of their time and energy than do their Labour opposite numbers to ensuring that their mass organization falls into line on important issues. This labour organization is intellectually more virile, and at every level, from constituency to annual conference, there is greater enthusiasm for the discussion of policy questions. Yet it must not be forgotten that most of this activity takes place within the constituency section of the mass organization. And this section casts only one-sixth of the votes at the party conference. The trade union delegates (who don't take up all the places allotted to them at conference) normally represent only about one-half the conference strength; their speakers take up about fifteen per cent of conference time. Yet they cast five-sixths of the conference votes. This helps to account for the atmosphere of seething frustration which often prevails among the constituency party representatives.

Yet despite these differences between the Conservative and Labour mass organizations, there can be no doubt that their primary purpose is the same: these mass organizations are best understood as voluntary associations of the politically-active section of the population who are prepared to work for the return to office of one or other of the parliamentary parties. Each mass organization represents a vast reservoir of largely voluntary and unpaid labour of the sort which is indispensable in the era of the mass electorate. All other functions of the mass organization are, and must remain, subsidiary to their primary task as vote-getting agencies. The mass organizations can and do exact a certain price for their labour; they expect to be listened to by their leaders. Like Bagehot's constitutional monarch, the annual party conference has the right to be consulted, the right to encourage, and the right to warn. But this is not to say that the members of the mass organization have the right under the British parliamentary system to control or direct the actions of their parliamentary leaders.

When the electorate has made its choice the leaders of the successful team don the garments of authority which are provided under the Cabinet system and they retain this authority so long as they retain the confidence of their followers in Parliament (and, of course, of the electorate). Their followers outside Parliament become little more than a highly organized pressure group with a special channel of communication directly to the Leader, the Cabinet and the parliamentary party. Any disposition to take advantage of this special relationship is normally more than neutralized by feelings of pride and loyalty to their leaders and by an anxiety not to embarrass them in the execution of their duties, or to provide aid and comfort to the rival team, who are eagerly preparing to overthrow them at the forthcoming election. Most governments at one time or another find it advisable to make concessions on some issue of policy to the clearly expressed views of their followers outside Parliament. But they make such concessions much more frequently to their followers *in* Parliament on whose day to day support in the division lobbies the government depends, than they do to their followers in the country whose allegiance is tested normally only at five-yearly intervals. While the parliamentary party is in opposition it tends to listen more readily to the voices of its supporters in the country; but even while in opposition no major parliamentary party in the modern period has allowed itself to be relegated to the role of spokesman or servant of its mass organization.

Seen from the viewpoint of society as a whole, mass political parties of the kind that have emerged in Britain fulfil an invaluable set of functions. By exposing the electorate to a cross-fire of political argument and debate they stimulate public interest in the essential business of "attending to the arrangements of society." The mass parties also fulfil an important integrating function. They are one of the main channels through which interest groups and both organized and unorganized bodies of opinion can bring their views to the attention of parliamentarians. The parliamentary leaders in turn must sift, weigh, analyse and evaluate the views that are conveyed through the party organizations. Inevitably these views are taken into account in the formulation of parliamentary policy. Lord Bryce saw American parties as brokers whose primary business it was to serve various interests and to reconcile them. In the much more homogeneous society of Britain the mass parties are inevitably less preoccupied with this task; they do nevertheless play an important role in integrating the diverse and sometimes conflicting interests and opinions in the community. But this paper has been concerned not with the broad social function of parties but with their internal structure and the distribution of power within each. And no emphasis on the auxiliary functions of the mass organizations outside Parliament can be allowed to obscure the basic proposition that the mass parties are primarily the servants of their respective parliamentary parties; that their principal function is to sustain teams of parliamentary leaders between whom the electorate is periodically invited to choose.

The question "What is a democratic political party?" has provoked much fruitless argument mainly because most observers (including Michels) have started from the proposition that for a party to be "democratic" it must be controlled by the members of its mass organization. Such an approach is valid enough in the case of a trade union. If the union leaders are not responsible to their members, they are probably responsible to no one. But as has been argued throughout this paper, the parliamentary system as it is conceived in this country precludes the possibility of "intra-party democracy."

In answer to the question, "What are the criteria which determine whether or not a party is democratic?", one cannot say much more than this: a democratic political party is one which abides by, and is prepared to continue to abide by, the laws and conventions which govern the operation of the democratic system in the country in which the party operates.[3] (Perhaps this proviso should be added: a party may attempt to change some essential feature of the political system, e.g. the Conservatives might propose to strengthen, or Labour to abolish, the House of Lords; but in so fundamental a matter they should seek the agreement of the opposition or the approval of the electorate.) It is no doubt also preferable that a democratic political party should have a large mass organization outside the legislature because such an organization provides a vast reservoir of largely unpaid labour and thus helps to minimize the dependence of the party on wealthy interest groups. But the absence of such a mass organization (as in the case, for example, of American political parties) does not, in itself, prove a party to be "undemocratic."

A parliamentary party may of course choose to hold itself responsible to its mass organization, as do a number of continental parties. This presents fewer problems in a multi-party system, where the parliamentary party is in no danger of winning a clear majority; if by chance the party were to form a single-party government, then this would raise in sharpest form the question whether that government held itself responsible to the legislature or to the party congress. But as parliamentary government is practised in this country there can be no doubt about the answer to that question: the leaders of a parliamentary party can (and in practice, must) be *responsive* to their mass organization but they cannot be *responsible* to it.

---

[3] If the party operates in a society which is not a democracy, then the party may be considered democratic (whatever its own internal structure) if it seeks as one of its aims to establish a democratic system of government.

25. COMPLEXITIES OF PARTY LEADERSHIP*
Richard Rose

STUDYING party leadership is almost as difficult as exercising it. This is because party leaders have strengths and limitations resulting from a variety of governmental, party, sociological and psychological pressures. Relevant studies of party leadership in Britain have usually emphasized only one dimension of the job. In order fully to understand party leadership, it must be studied in all of these contrasting dimensions. When this is done, it appears that a party leader is less powerful than often claimed; he must also be a good follower. And he must be prepared to be checked by those whose authority rests upon foundations outside the structure of the party.

The One, the Few and Sociology

Robert Michels' study of political parties remains relevant nearly half a century after it was written because he pioneered brilliantly the study of oligarchy in nominally democratic party organizations. Writing at a time when "direct democracy" was a concern of political reformers, he sought to confound their efforts by showing how only oligarchy was possible in theory and practice. The argument is best read; it is unfair to sum up its complex development in a single iron law.

Michels was particularly concerned with the growth of parties with national mass-membership organizations. He argued, "as a result of organization, every party or professional union becomes divided into a minority of directors and a majority of directed." Oligarchy the rule by the Few, is "a matter of technical and practical necessity," "the inevitable product of the very principle of organization." This is true notwithstanding the fact that party organizations, especially those of Socialists, may claim to be democratic. Leaders, whether party bureaucrats or parliamentarians, will inevitably develop vested interests different from rank-and-file members due to their high position in the party organization. Rank-and-file members will, individually and collectively, lack power in the organization; furthermore, psychological feelings of gratitude and deference will tend to make them submissive. . . .

Because of the simple antithesis between "direct democracy" and oligarchy, Michels' conclusions are pessimistic, and he ended his life a supporter of Benito Mussolini. But today, our expectations of democracy are more narrow, and can be satisfied even if one grants that individual

* From *Parliamentary Affairs* (Summer, 1963), pp. 257–73. Article and footnotes abridged by the editors. Reprinted by permission of the Editor of *Parliamentary Affairs*.

parties themselves are controlled by the Few. Schumpeter, for instance, treats democracy as a byproduct of electoral competition between competing party élites. Dahl has argued that inequalities exist, but that they are dispersed among a range of leaders, whose actual ability to exercise leadership varies from situation to situation. Schattschneider has described democracy as existing as long as disunity among party leaders results in appeals to the Mass of party members and electors. Elsewhere, I have argued that the existence of competing factions and tendencies within British parties at all levels, from that of the Front Bench in the Commons to the mass of a party's voters, itself provides important restraints upon the dominance of the One or of a Few. But Michels, with higher expectations of democracy, was disinclined to find satisfaction in scaling down expectations. For instance, he thought that conflict within the leadership stratum tended to produce the repressive discipline of factional conflict and contributed "practically nil" to democracy.[1]

R. T. McKenzie's *British Political Parties* is a modern landmark in British political studies, because he analyzes both the theory and practice of party leadership. Historical in emphasis, the study gains in significance—and in controversiality—because it is also a book with a thesis. Although dealing with the same sort of problems as Michels, it differs in concentrating exclusively upon Britain, in a concern with the impact of constitutional offices upon party leadership, and in the greater attention paid to the One who is official leader. . . .

The subtitle of McKenzie's study is: "the distribution of power within the Conservative and Labour Parties." The book does a good job in stating where power does *not* lie—it does not rest exclusively with the One Leader of the Conservative Party, nor does it rest with the mass membership of the Labour Party. But while this knowledge is necessary, it is not sufficient, if one is to locate power in British parties. Many questions remain unanswered. We are not told why it is democratic for the electorate to be offered a choice between two and only two teams of leaders, and whether a choice between Tweedledum and Tweedledee would deny democracy. The effect of the differences in the social psychology of the parties and, for that matter, in their myths of internal government, are not explored. Nor does the author measure power in relation to making party policy so much as in relation to retention of office. Finally, the relative strength of the One and the Few is left unclear. In one sentence, McKenzie can speak of the Leader, by virtue of being actual or potential Prime Minister, as enjoying "enormous authority over his followers"; the Cabinet is presumably included with the followers. Such remarks may shortly be followed by references to the Prime

---

[1] Cf. J. A. Schumpeter, *Capitalism, Socialism and Democracy* (4th ed., 1952), Chapter 22; Robert Dahl, *Who Governs?* (1961); E. E. Schattschneider, *The Semi-Sovereign People* (1960), Chapters 1, 8.

Minister and his Cabinet jointly sharing enormous powers. Any contemporary discussion of leadership in British parties starts with McKenzie but cannot end with him.

The Social Psychological Dimension

The emphasis of sociologists such as Michels and McKenzie upon the structure of parties and government stands in sharp contrast to the approach of those journalists and academics who focus upon the psychology of party leaders and upon the relationship of a Leader or leaders with followers, i.e., the social psychology of leadership. . . .

Though factors of personality are often stressed in writings about party politics, it is noteworthy that when social psychologists study leadership as a general phenomenon in society, they find them of little importance. The work of social psychologists is worth considering because they have explored the complexities involved in the theory and practice of social leadership to a far greater extent than have students of politics, even though in very different circumstances.

The most striking feature of this literature is the emphasis placed upon the reciprocal flow of influence between the Leader and followers. On balance, most writers emphasize the limited personal influence of leaders, especially of an individual Leader. This is because followers have a set of expectations concerning the behaviour of a Leader. In order to maintain the confidence of followers and their consent to his commands, the Leader must frame his commands so that they are in accord with what his followers expect. In other words, the Leader must conform to the already established expectations of his followers. A Conservative Party Leader, taking office in 1957, could hardly have survived if he had repudiated the Suez intervention, which he was expected to support. In 1963, he would risk his leadership if he suggested, say, nationalizing road transport. In the Labour Party, Hugh Gaitskell demonstrated that a Leader could not get his followers to repudiate the symbolic commitment to Socialism enshrined in Clause IV. The virtual absence of public discussion in the leadership stratum of conscription as an alternative to a British H-bomb suggests that Labour MPs expect such a policy to be a non-starter and do not canvass it, anticipating that they could not gain a following for such a cause. A major difference between the Conservative and Labour parties is this: Conservative followers give overwhelming emphasis to expecting success at elections. A Leader is allowed much leeway on policy if he is electorally successful. In the Labour Party, expectations about policy are quite important to followers, and these expectations are likely to be harder to fulfil. A section of the Labour Party, as the post-1959 election debate demonstrated, has been prepared to reject electoral success as its object, expecting a leader to choose Socialism and defeat rather than Revision and possible electoral victory. To turn Michels upside down, one might say that as long as followers remain united in their expectations, they are always victorious. One of the arts of leading a party is to know when one can conquer due to divisions and when one must bow before clear expectations of united followers.

The expectations of followers influence the behaviour of a party Leader long before he occupies the office, in the years when he is serving his apprenticeship as an auxiliary and a member of the leadership stratum. At this point he will be measured by expectations and standards which pre-date his arrival on the scene. As McKenzie emphasizes, the Leader of a party emerges before he is elected. A man such as Anthony Eden or Hugh Gaitskell emerged because he lived up to the expectations of those who choose the Leader. In a reciprocal fashion, men with years of party service, such as Curzon, Morrison, Bevan (and individuals still in the House) have failed to become Leader because they did not fit the expectations of followers. The intrinsic character of an emerging contender for the Leadership may alter standards to a limited degree, but most important of all seems to be the closeness of the fit between followers' expectations and the perceived characteristics of individuals.

Once in office, especially the office of Prime Minister, a party Leader may begin to shape new expectations among followers, just as the expectations of followers may change due to the impact of external events. In other words, there is a dynamic element in the leader-follower relationship; it is not fixed through an individual's term of office. In America, this can be easily recognized in the 'honeymoon' which a newly elected President may enjoy with Congress; this is followed by a period of conflict as his policy preferences emerge, and subsequently, by a relationship in which the ups and downs of the partners are as frequent as in a turbulent marriage. In England, the virtual certainty of a Leader winning a vote on the floor of the House or a party meeting makes it harder to trace ups and downs because one is dealing in intangible measures of confidence. It seems that Harold Macmillan's influence upon his party has not been constant. When he took office in 1957 many things were unclear. By 1959 he had established a considerable measure of personal authority, but this has waned in the past eighteen months, and in the spring of 1963 one could speculate whether his career would end with his influence high, or nearly bankrupt. Neville Chamberlain provides an example of a Leader who rose to the heights and then abruptly fell. Stanley Baldwin, by contrast, gradually gained increasing influence over his followers, and reached a crest shortly before retirement—only to suffer a severe devaluation retrospectively. On the Labour side, Attlee began as a chairman so weak that he would not risk his influence by seeking to have the party end its opposition to service estimates in 1937. As deputy Prime Minister during the war he gained a firm hold on the office. During most of his time as Prime Minister, however, he still showed some deference to Sir Stafford Cripps and Ernest Bevin. Perhaps the height of his personal authority was reached in 1951 when those two had left office. But by the time of his retirement in 1955 his authority within the party had again declined.

Individual leaders may have their ups and downs in office. Equally important, the office of Leader may itself have its ups and downs, when held by men who have differing conceptions of the job. In America, one may readily observe the dramatically different conception of the office which Dwight D. Eisenhower and John F. Kennedy have had. The contrast was as deliberate as that between many earlier holders of the office, such as Franklin D. Roosevelt and Herbert Hoover, or Woodrow Wilson and Harding. Richard Neustadt has succinctly described the position of President as one in which an individual may be functionally a leader or clerk, though the formal powers of the office are the same in both instances. In Britain, as in America, a party Leader's image of his job will greatly influence the kind of relationship he seeks and attains with followers. At one extreme, Lloyd George stood free from stable ties with followers, building *ad hoc* coalitions of supporters. At the other extreme, J. R. Clynes saw himself as tied by the restrictions which followers placed upon a Labour Leader. Baldwin's approach to the Leadership-Prime Ministership was that of a man who gave high priority to maintaining party (and national) unity, even if this meant that in policy terms he was often a do-nothing. Neville Chamberlain, by contrast, appeared to see the office as one in which a man was judged by what he got done, and he pursued an active interventionist course in domestic and foreign policy. Hugh Gaitskell, in his approach to leadership, appeared not only to believe in policy intervention, but also, to believe in settling intra-party disputes by rational discourse, as well as by steamrollering opponents through the pre-arranged mobilization of trade union votes. (This, it might be noted, is never something a Labour Leader can personally command, but from the early 1930s onwards, a Leader who enjoyed Ernest Bevin's confidence could usually enjoy the benefit of this steamroller.) It remains to be seen whether Harold Wilson will take an active part in attempting to stamp his personal policy preferences upon the party, or whether he will often adjust his views in deference to others.

Because a Party Leader, like a President, stands at the centre of several different political institutions and networks, he will inevitably be involved in conflicts of roles; behaviour appropriate in one role may conflict with that suited to another co-existing leader-follower relationship. Clinton Rossiter, writing of the Presidency, lists possible conflicts between the President's roles as chief of state, chief executive, chief diplomat, commander-in-chief of the armed forces, chief legislator, chief of party, voice of the people, manager of the economy, and leader of the free world coalition. Rossiter notes that the President "is all these things all the time," and "several of these functions are plainly in competition, even in conflict with one another." Neustadt comments on this multiplicity of roles:

"The same conditions that promote his leadership in form preclude a guarantee of leadership in fact."

In Britain, the conventions of unified power through Cabinet government somewhat simplify matters. But conflicts nonetheless exist. A Prime Minister is, by turns and often simultaneously, chief partisan, head of a policy faction within his party, symbol of party unity, head of government and administration, supplicant for votes, bargainer and possible persuader of pressure group leaders, subordinate leader in the North Atlantic alliance, senior Prime Minister in the Commonwealth, ambitious of retaining office, and concerned with safeguarding the 'public interest.' The potential for conflict is considerable. Of particular importance is the tendency for actions as a party Leader appealing to partisans to conflict with actions as a national Leader appealing to those without partisan attachments and those with attachments to party opponents. Macmillan, for instance, may recommend a national incomes policy to the nation in his role as national leader. But in seeking to make it work he must succeed as a persuader of trade unions, although he is also Leader of a party viewed suspiciously by them. At great moments of crisis in British party history, individual Leaders have sometimes resolved role conflicts by abandoning their party: this has been true from the days of Peel through the time of Ramsay MacDonald. Given the varied expectations from different groups of followers (and perhaps, from conflicting allegiances in his own mind) a Leader can only hope to minimize conflict; he cannot eliminate what is inherent in his position.

The analysis of leadership from the vantage point of psychology and social psychology does not provide any simple formula by which to explain leadership or to assess leaders. These disciplines do provide wider and deeper insights into the complexities of party leadership. But no single factor will account for all the influence which a Leader may exercise upon followers, or followers upon a Leader. As Sidney Verba has written, in concluding a wide-ranging summary of the literature: "There is no one 'best' leadership structure. What structure is best must depend upon the group setting, task and membership—in short, upon the total situation."[2]

Leadership and Political Power

In order to assess the power of the party Leader and of the leadership stratum, we must go beyond the concern with retention of office, and focus upon the party as a policy-making body. Policies represent, as it were, the output of government. A Leader who cannot affect this output is no more than a figurehead, or a puppet. A leadership stratum that is severely limited in its influence upon this output is far from the potent oligarchy described by Michels.

It is here that the limitation of McKenzie's approach is most notable. In

---

[2] Sidney Verba, *Small Groups and Political Behavior; A Study of Leadership* (1961), p. 243.

the second sentence of his preface he rules out any concern with "party ideologies or programmes." But it is impossible to study the distribution of power within a political party—especially one controlling the Cabinet—without reference to these programmes. McKenzie's emphasis is upon retaining office as an index of power. The motives of the leadership stratum are taken to revolve around the party gaining office through a general election victory and individuals within the stratum receiving office, or promotion. There is a suggestion that the Conservative Leader may have trouble securing allegiance from the Party "when its members are deeply stirred on an issue of principle." Conflicts on principle and policy within the Labour Party are treated curiously. For McKenzie, the "basic issue" between the ILP and the Labour Party in the 1920s and 1930s concerned the relationship of the party in Parliament with the party outside. This writer would interpret it as primarily a conflict on policy; McKenzie's constitutional dictum would have been irrelevant if one held the views of the ILP. One might also ask whether the most important point at issue within the Labour Party in 1960 was a question about parliamentary and extra-parliamentary relations. One might assert the main conflict was between two conflicting foreign policies, one of which was dangerous and one of which was not.

A Leader who cannot influence policy is little more than Neustadt's "clerk." As Neustadt indicates, the President can so reduce his influence upon policy that the very suggestion that he has a programme is enough to send Congressmen into fits of public laughter.[3] When one focuses upon party (and government) policy-making, perspective abruptly changes. The mass membership is largely ignored—but the Leader loses his pre-eminence. He becomes (as in Saul Rose's analysis of the Labour Party, 1952–55) only one of a number of possible sources of policy decisions. Most theoretical analyses of decision-making in politics emphasize the difficulties of assigning pre-eminent political power to one individual. The question is an empirical one, to be answered empirically by investigating the particular circumstances in which policy decisions are made in Britain. Because Americans believe that they have a right to find out how decisions are made in government before all concerned are dead, it was possible for Richard Neustadt to analyze the President's influence upon policy through case studies. This is not permitted here. Because of official restrictions, any analysis is bound to remain a sketch. But a sketch is preferable to leaving an important area blank.

This sketch will concentrate attention upon the power of the party Leader when he is Prime Minister as well as head of a majority party in the House of Commons. (The latter assumption is one that Asquith, Lloyd George and Ramsay MacDonald could not, of course, make.) This is because the machinery of British government gives supreme influence to

---

[3] The incident cited occurred during President Eisenhower's second term.

the majority party at the expense of the minority, a situation different from America, where the existence of competing leaders in Congress complicates matters. It might be argued that just because a Prime Minister has so many role conflicts he is weaker rather than stronger in terms of personal influence on decisions. But because the decisions in which he is involved are government decisions, and not shadow decisions taken in Opposition, his potential power is the greater.

J. P. Mackintosh's *The British Cabinet* has outlined in some detail the historical and contemporary factors working to place the Prime Minister on a different level from his Cabinet colleagues, in terms of involvement in many areas of decision-making. But the pressures of modern communications, technology and an increased load of business weigh upon the Prime Minister individually as well as the Cabinet collectively. We have eloquent testimony from ministers and civil servants of the strenuous pace of departmental life, where simply keeping up with day to day work is difficult enough. Richard Neustadt has given us a picture of a President in office as a man whose time "remains the prisoner of first-things first. And almost always something else comes first." It is difficult to conceive of a Prime Minister remaining sufficiently abreast of the complexities of foreign affairs, economics, defence, depressed areas, colonial affairs, education, housing, security, etc., to be able to exert personal influence when major decisions are to be made in all these fields. (One may avoid this problem by adopting a tautological criterion of major decision: one made by the Prime Minister.) If, as Professor Finer has shown, the responsibility of a minister in fact is somewhat different from the connotations of the term in some theories, then the responsibility of the Prime Minister for 'his' government is also not meant to be taken as personal involvement in all that is done in his name. A strength of British central government is that it simultaneously provides a dignified concentration of authority in the Cabinet, while dispersing efficient decision-making powers to a wide variety of disparate groups.[4]

It would be misleading, however, to regard the expressed personal preference of a Leader or Prime Minister as necessarily his own independent view. Attlee has neatly put the importance of a Leader anticipating what subordinates will expect:

"He has got to collect the voices of his Cabinet. He's got to reflect the views of his party. He's also got to some extent to reflect the views of the country as a whole. That does not mean he does not lead, but he leads in such a way, if he's wise, that he carries either his party or his country or his colleagues with him."[5] For instance, a decision of the Attlee Govern-

[4] Cf. J. P. Mackintosh, *The British Cabinet* (1962) Part Five; R. Neustadt, *Presidential Power* (1960), p. 155; Lord Strang, *Home and Abroad* (1956), Chapter 10; P. C. Gordon Walker, "On Being a Cabinet Minister," *Encounter*, No. 31 (1956); S. E. Finer, "The Individual Responsibility of Ministers," *Public Administration*, Vol. XXXIV, No. 4 (1956).

[5] Quoted in *The Guardian*, 21 April 1963.

ment to nationalize the coal mines presumably represented the personal wish of the majority of the Cabinet, including the Prime Minister. But here, the leadership stratum was acting as the agent for a section of the party, rather than deciding independently. One might argue that the decision of the Prime Minister since 1957 to rely upon a British H-bomb is a sign of weakness, for it is simply going along with the prevailing sentiment of the party. A strong, McKenzie-type Leader might have shown his strength by abandoning the H-bomb and maintaining conscription. In practice, Macmillan has not sought to test his "enormous authority" by exposing such a personal preference. In some circumstances, decisions might be said to be taken by events. For instance, when Neville Chamberlain announced that Britain was at war with Germany in 1939, he had no alternative—and the decision represented his weakness in the face of external pressures, rather than independent authority over events or over followers.

When one surveys the major areas in which the British government is active—foreign affairs, defence, colonial policy, economics, and social welfare—it readily becomes apparent that there is little to fear from concentration of power in the hands of a Party Leader-Prime Minister or in the hands of one or two cliques in a leadership stratum.

In international affairs and defence, the Prime Minister and his associates must bargain with other sovereign states in order to reach common goals. The failure of Britain, with France's aid, to sustain independent activity at Suez in 1956 dramatically indicated the limits of Britain in this field. The abrupt and unexpected switch of Britain's defences from reliance upon Skybolt to Polaris is a more recent example of the way in which the Prime Minister's policy in defence can be decided in Washington rather than London. The Cuban crisis last autumn demonstrated that this diminution in the independent authority of Her Majesty's Government has not been accompanied by a share in making decisions of greater impact. In colonial affairs, the Prime Minister and Cabinet are again taking decisions in a climate which is determined outside Britain, and continuously facing the consequences of unilateral action taken by independence parties and illegal organizations. It would be misleading to say that Cyprus gained independence through a Cabinet decision. It gained independence, primarily as the result of waging a guerilla war. The British Government could influence the timing of such a decision more than its substance.

Economic policy involves decisions which are dependent in some measure for success upon international economic developments. These market factors are beyond the control of the British government, and to some extent, beyond the control of any national government, or any combination. Some economic arrangements can be concluded by bargaining. But the failure of the Prime Minister to enter the Common Market indicated spectacularly that what may have been the personal decision of one Englishman could be frustrated by the countervailing action of one Frenchman. Within the domestic economy, policy involves bargaining between the Government, business pressure groups and trade unions. The creation of the National Economic Development Council may be regarded as a formal recognition that important decisions about the economy are *de facto* taken outside Cabinet.

In the social welfare field the decisions of the Prime Minister and his colleagues are often binding. The decision to hang, or to reprieve, a convicted murderer is atypical; most welfare decisions involve prolonged bargaining with pressure groups, and changes in society may change the consequences of decisions. This for example, is happening in education, where the failure of the birth rate to conform to official projections has created difficulties in maintaining established policy for primary schools, just as the increasing numbers of qualified candidates for university education is having a major impact upon education (and government decisions) at the university level.

The foregoing sketch indicates that the restrictions upon the power of the party Leader which so concerned McKenzie, and of the leadership stratum, which so concerned Michels, are not located within the party organization but outside it. In a democratic society such as Britain, by contrast to a party-dictatorship along Soviet lines, party leaders must work in conjunction with extra-party institutions and influences if they are to make decisions of consequence for their society.

It thus no longer seems accurate to regard Britain as enjoying the type of *simple* constitution which Bagehot credited it with, one "in which the ultimate power upon all questions is in the hands of the same persons." Rather, the distribution of power is what Bagehot termed *composite*, "in which the supreme power is divided between many bodies and functionaries."[6] The latter type of government he described as characteristic of America. It is still characteristic of America and, because of the relative diminution of the influence of Cabinet in terms of the widened responsibilities today placed upon it, it is increasingly characteristic of Britain. The patterns of party and governmental leadership in the two countries are drawing closer together, not because of the increase in the power of the Prime Minister, but because his power is weakening. The dignified parts of British parties and of party government give the impression of great strength in the hands of leaders or a Leader; the efficient working of the political system contradicts this. The most important competition which confronts the party leadership stratum (Schumpeter's élites) comes not from within a party or from the opposition party, but from leadership based upon power rooted in other sections of British society, or outside it.

[6] *The English Constitution* (World's Classics edition, 1955), p. 201.

Chapter VIII. Electoral Systems

Introductory Note

ONE OF the general problems of democratic systems is that of *representation*. How can the various groups and interests and the people at large have a say in government, while still ensuring the majority enough of a margin to govern? There are two major types of electoral systems: plurality election in single member districts, and proportional representation (the election of several representatives from comparatively large districts and in proportion to the number of votes received by each party). The plurality system is used in Great Britain, the United States, and most dominions. It has also been employed for elections to the Chamber of Deputies in the Third French Republic, and has been revived under the Fifth Republic (in both instances with provision for runoffs in case no candidate receives an absolute majority on the first ballot). Proportional representation has been common throughout the continent of Europe. The Federal Republic of Germany holds elections under a combination of the plurality system and PR [See in James K. Pollock (ed.), *German Democracy at Work*, 1955, his succinct chapter, "How the Voter Decides."]

The effect of the plurality system is to discriminate against small parties and favor the development of a two-party system. PR is designed to eliminate the distortions and injustices of the plurality system. Its operation is relatively simple in the smaller nations of Europe. The case of Switzerland is typical. Each Swiss canton serves as an electoral unit, with one councilor elected to the National Council for every 22,000 inhabitants. Parties present lists of candidates to the voters who cast as many votes as there are offices to fill. Since 1919 no Swiss party has received over 30 per cent of the votes or of the seats in parliament. Approximately eight Swiss parties in recent years have had some representation in the National Council. A similar type of PR is used in Norway, Sweden, Denmark, Belgium, and Holland.

The advantages of PR are set forth in John Stuart Mill, *Representative Government* (1861), Chapter 8; C. G. Hoag and G. H. Hallett, *Proportional Representation* (1926); and Ramsay Muir, *How Britain Is Governed* (4th ed., 1940). The plurality system, Ramsay Muir wrote in despair after World War I, "is in the highest degree unjust, unsatisfactory and dangerous." It virtually eliminates smaller parties—like the Liberal Party

249

in Great Britain—and allows for the concentration of enormous powers in the hands of the leaders of the majority party, who form the Cabinet. The British Liberal Party, for example, received 9 per cent of the popular vote in 1945 but only 2 per cent of the seats in Commons, and 9.1 per cent of the vote in 1950 but an insignificant 1.3 per cent of the seats. Similarly, the American Progressive Party received 1,157,172 votes in the 1948 presidential election but did not have a single vote in the electoral college and managed to elect only one member to Congress.

The critics of PR—notably F. A. Hermens, *Democracy or Anarchy?* (1941)—contend that the purpose of an electoral system is not to reproduce in miniature all the divisions of a society, but to make possible the formation of an effective government with a stable majority and, at the same time, offer opposition forces adequate opportunity to criticize the government. The ability of government to *act* vigorously is as essential to the proper functioning of a democracy as the right of the minority to criticize. When several parties have to co-operate in a coalition, the two aspects of democratic government tend to be confounded and the public business does not go forward. For example, if PR had been used in the British elections of 1945, the Labour Party would have won but 48 per cent of the seats in the House of Commons. The Liberal Party, though representing only 9 per cent of the electorate, would actually have held the balance of power since it would have been the key partner in any coalition. Inasmuch as the strength of the major parties in Britain rarely fluctuates more than a few percentage points, there would never be a stable majority in the Commons and hence no stable government.

The student should try to weigh the advantages, disadvantages, and above all the consequences of electoral systems with reference to the unique needs of particular nations. When large parties on the extreme left and extreme right repudiate parliamentary institutions, electoral systems that discriminate against smaller center parties undermine, rather than strengthen, the democratic state. For example, if Italy were to adopt a plurality system tending to favor the development of only the two large parties (Christian Democrat and Communist), then democracy could continue to exist only so long as the Communist Party were kept in opposition. But electoral machinery alone cannot bring about political stability, though it might help prevent total collapse of parliamentary institutions in a badly divided nation. The problem in France and Italy is to eliminate those conditions that have produced warring social forces; whereas the concern in Britain is that the unity of the nation be able to express itself without unduly depriving minorities of representation. There is a general problem in all polities of preventing the abuse of electoral procedures by parties in power in order to maximize the number of seats they will gain in the next election. In the long run, perhaps, methods of voting are of less importance than the nature and ideologies of the social and political forces engaged in the struggle for power.

Readings

26. ELECTORAL SYSTEMS AND POLITICAL LIFE*

Maurice Duverger

IT IS OBVIOUS that the electoral system must influence political life. The radical changes brought about in the structure of various States by the adoption of universal suffrage or the machinery of managed elections, for instance, sufficiently indicate the importance of this factor.

It is, however, extremely difficult to analyse that influence scientifically. The factors conditioning the political life of a country are very closely inter-related, so that any study of the effects of one of those factors considered in isolation is necessarily artificial. All such a study can ever do is to define tendencies, likely to be influenced by the operation of the other factors. In other words, we cannot say that such and such an electoral system leads inevitably to a particular form of political life, but simply that it favours its establishment, that is, reinforces other factors tending in the same direction or weakens those tending in the opposite direction. As a result, no sociological laws we can formulate in this matter can ever be absolute; they are strictly applicable only in ideal conditions of "temperature and pressure," conditions never actually encountered in practice. These laws are therefore valid only so long as we bear in mind that they are relative. . . .

I. ELECTORAL SYSTEMS AND POLITICAL PARTIES

The electoral system affects the political life of a country mainly through the parties. We might almost make a distinction between direct influence (such and such an electoral system tends to a particular form of party organization) and indirect influence (the organization of the parties, largely due to the electoral system, leads to a particular form of political life); only the first type will be dealt with in this study.

We may take as the starting point of our analysis the three following propositions:

(1) Proportional representation tends toward a system of many rigid, independent parties.

(2) The simple majority with a second ballot tends towards a system of many independent but flexible parties.

* From "The Influence of the Electoral System on Political Life," *The International Social Science Bulletin*, Vol. 3 (Summer, 1951). By permission of the United Nations Educational, Scientific and Cultural Organization.

(3) The simple majority vote with only one ballot tends towards a two-
   party system.

These propositions, however, are still only very rough approximations, as
we shall see when we consider more closely the influence exercised by the
electoral system on the number, structure and inter-relationship of the
parties.

(a) Influence on the Number of Parties

The Simple Majority Vote with One Ballot. At first sight, the tendency
of the simple majority vote with one ballot to lead to a two-party system
seems to be the most clearly established. It is notably illustrated by the
Anglo-Saxon countries, in the opposition to the emergence of a third party
in the United States of America, and in the elimination of the third party
in Great Britain and some of the Dominions.

In this respect, the electoral system seems to work in two different
ways: in the pressure it exerts towards the two-party organization, a
distinction may be made between the mechanical and the psychological
aspects of the problem. The mechanical aspect is the under-representation
of the third (that is, the weakest) party, as the percentage of seats it holds
is lower than its percentage of votes. Admittedly, in a two-party system,
the weaker is always under-represented in relation to the stronger, as we
shall see below; but, assuming the existence of a third party, the latter is
still more seriously under-represented than the minority party among the
other two, as the British instance shows particularly clearly. Up to 1922,
the Labour Party was under-represented in relation to the Liberal Party;
since that date the position has been reversed (except in 1931, when
Labour was going through a serious crisis, and the Conservatives won a
crushing victory). The third party is thus placed mechanically at a
disadvantage by the electoral system. As long as a new party attempting to
compete with the two old-established parties is still weak, the system
operates against its growth and opposes its emergence. If, however, it
draws ahead of one of its predecessors, that party then falls into third
place and the process of elimination is reversed.

The psychological factor operates on similar lines. When there are
three competing under a simple majority system with one ballot, the
electors soon see that their votes are wasted if they go on voting for the
third party, so that their natural tendency is to transfer their votes to the
less objectionable of its opponents in order to keep out the worse. This
phenomenon of "popularization" works against the new party as long as
it is the weakest of the three but, like "under-representation," turns
against the less popular of the old parties as soon as the new one draws
ahead. It should be noted, however, that the reversal of the movement in
these two cases is not always simultaneous, under-representation generally preceding the transfer of votes (for it is only with the passage of

time that the electors realize that one party is declining and transfer their votes to another). This naturally entails a fairly long period of confusion, during which the doubts of electors and changes in the under-represented parties combine to throw the relative strengths of the parties completely out of line; Great Britain experienced such difficulties between 1923 and 1935. The trend of the electoral system towards a two-party representation thus makes its effect felt only over a period.

In many cases, however, the uncertainties experienced in the interim period induce the parties themselves to return to a two-party system by fusion of the central party with one or other of its rivals (generally also involving a schism in that party, as some of its members prefer to join the opposite party). In Australia, for instance, Liberals and Conservatives combined as early as 1909 in the face of Labour pressure. In New Zealand they waited until 1936 before doing so: from 1913 to 1928, the Liberal Party was steadily declining and therefore likely to disappear naturally; in 1928, there was a sudden revival which put it once more on an equal footing with the Conservatives; but by 1931 the decline was again setting in and the Liberals were falling back into third place; faced with the Labour menace, aggravated by the economic crisis, the Party decided to amalgamate with the Conservatives for the 1935 elections. In the Union of South Africa, the secession of the Nationalists in 1913, combined with the growth of the Labour Party, resulted by 1918 in four more or less equal parties; in view of the danger of such a situation in a system organized on a single majority vote, the old Unionist Party was absorbed into General Smuts' South African Party, while General Hertzog's Nationalist Party concluded an electoral agreement with Labour, which proved fatal to the latter; the two-party system was restored by the joint effects of fusion and elimination.

Some exceptions to this general tendency of the single majority vote to lead to a two-party system should, however, be noted. The most striking instances are those of Denmark (before the introduction of proportional representation) and Canada (at the present moment).

The case of Canada is particularly interesting, because it enables us to define the limitations of the two-party trend under the simple majority system. There are today four major parties in that country: the Unionists (68 seats), the Liberals (125 seats), the Labour Party (32 seats) and an agrarian party (14). The two latter, however, are definitely local in their appeal; the agrarian party was established in Alberta in 1925 under the name of the "United Farmers of Alberta" and in 1935 became the Social Credit Party, but retained its narrow territorial associations. The Labour Party draws its strength mainly from Saskatchewan, Manitoba, British Columbia and Ontario. The two-party system, which ceased to exist at the national level in 1921, is thus to be found in practice at the local level; there are four parties in the country but generally only two competing parties in each electoral district. It will be seen that the phenomena described above are encountered only locally: the trend of the electoral system is to have two candidates in each constituency. The establishment of local parties, or a certain localization of the national parties, is thus made possible. In Great Britain itself, there was a remarkably stable Irish party from 1874 to 1918, and there may now be a tendency for the Liberal Party to become mainly a Welsh party. . . .

Proportional Representation. It is commonly thought that proportional representation tends to increase the number of political parties. . . .

It is true . . . however . . . that a consideration of the French parties before 1939 (simple majority, second ballot system) and after 1945 (proportional representation) shows no increase in their number. There was even a decrease to be seen in 1945–1946; since then, however, there have been further splits in the Right, the Radical Party has again become important, and the "Rassemblement du Peuple Français" has come into being, thus more or less restoring the former situation. The Belgian case is perhaps still more striking; in the 50 years that proportional representation has been in operation there, Belgium has had the same three parties as at the outset, and the situation has been scarcely altered at all by the presence of a Communist Party, which is weak. Thus, at first sight, the tendency of proportional representation to lead to a multiplicity of parties is much less definite than the two-party trend of the simple majority system. It is nevertheless a real tendency, but its various aspects need to be carefully distinguished.

The first effect of proportional representation is to preserve existing multiplicity. In this respect, we may compare Belgium and Great Britain. In the nineteenth century both countries had a strict two-party system with a simple majority vote. In both countries, at the beginning of the twentieth century, the emergence of a Socialist Party destroyed the two-party system. Fifty years later, England, having retained its simple majority vote, is back with its two parties, while the three parties existing in Belgium in 1900 have been preserved by the adoption of PR. From this point of view, a study of the Belgian elections between 1890 and 1914 is extremely interesting. In 1890, owing to the limited suffrage, the Socialists were still unable to gain representation in Parliament; the two-party system was still working. In 1894, with the adoption of universal suffrage, the Socialists won 28 seats, while the Liberal Party dropped from 60 to 20 although it had twice as many electors voting for it as the Socialists; under-representation was operating to its disadvantage. In 1898, the Liberal Party suffered a further decline, going down to 12 seats; on this occasion, polarization had combined with under-representation, as many former Liberals voted Catholic. The process of elimination affecting the Liberal Party had already gone a long way; it was reasonable to think that two or three more elections would see its end. In 1900, however, proportional representation was adopted as the Catholics wished to prevent the annihilation of the Liberal Party in order to avoid being left alone with the Socialists; the number of Liberal seats immediately went up to 33. It was to rise to 42 after the elections of 1902–1904, probably as a result of "depolarization"—the former Liberal electors who had left the party in 1894 to join forces with the Catholic Party returning to their old allegiance once they had grasped the way proportional representation worked—and finally become fixed at 44 or 45. . . .

The second effect of proportional representation is to foster splinter movements in existing parties. Splits and divisions are not, of course, uncommon under a simple majority system; the English Liberal Party had many, both before and after the rise of Labour. But under that system, divisions are temporary and limited. The two sections either reunite after some time, or one of them joins a rival party; as for example the Liberal Nationals, who are, for practical purposes, members of the Conservative Party. Under a proportional system, on the other hand, seceding groups generally last, as the method of voting prevents the divergent fractions from being crushed by their rivals. It is thus understandable that the introduction of PR has almost always coincided with schisms in old parties, either open and admitted (one old party splitting into two new halves, each laying claim to its succession) or concealed (an allegedly new party being constituted with some of the leaders and rank and file of an old party which, however, still continues in existence). . . .

This second effect of proportional representation is, however, rather limited. Generally speaking, PR keeps more or less unchanged the party structure in being at the time of its introduction. It never has the disruptive effect that some attribute to it; in most cases, the schisms mentioned took the form of the splitting of a large party into two others, which have maintained their positions through subsequent elections. The tendency towards multiplicity shows less in the division of old parties than in the establishment of new ones; and, even so, this third result of PR applies mainly to the smaller parties, which is quite natural, as the main bodies of opinion still follow the traditional parties. It is because some people have overlooked this distinction that they have been able, with apparent truth, to deny that PR increases the number of parties. Another reason is that most of the systems of proportional representation actually in force have taken precautions to avoid the development of small parties which is the natural result of the system; we know, for instance, that the Hondt method, and that of the highest average, which are used in most of the countries where PR is applied, are definitely detrimental to the small parties and thus tend to cancel the results of proportional representation. The same may be said of the Netherlands system, which excludes all lists not securing at least 75 per cent of the quotient from the distribution of remaining votes. In fact, there is no full system of proportional representation anywhere, not so much because of the technical difficulties in applying it, which are comparatively easy to solve, as because of its political consequences, and particularly its tendency to foster the growth of more or less insignificant and more or less fluctuating groups. . . .

The Second Ballot. Theoretically, it would seem that the second ballot must encourage the proliferation of parties, as the splitting up of similar tendencies does not compromise their total representation, since they always have an opportunity to regroup for the second ballot. The phenomena of "polarization" and "under-representation" described above do not operate in this instance, or operate only at the second ballot, each party standing an equal chance at the first. Practical observation in the countries which have employed the second ballot appears to confirm this theoretical hypothesis. In France, Switzerland, Germany and the Netherlands, the second ballot has reflected the multiplicity of parties in forms which, incidentally, differ quite widely: in Germany and in France, there has been a very distinct tendency towards splintering, particularly on the right, while in Switzerland and the Netherlands, opinion has still generally been divided among a few large parties, although there have been more than two of them. But this might perhaps be regarded as due to the influence of differing national temperaments. . . .

The Internal Structure of the Parties. Sociological phenomena differing widely from one another are in fact described by the generic term "parties." There is a very great difference between the structure of the British parties in the nineteenth century and that of the British parties of the present day, as there is between the contemporary American and French parties and, in France in 1950, between the "Parti Republican de la Liberté," the Radicals, the Socialist Party and the Communist Party. There are many factors—historical, geographical, economic and social—to explain the difference. The electoral factor is one of those which has received least consideration, but it is not one of the least important.

The essential difference here seems to be not so much between the system of proportional representation and the simple majority system, as between the system of voting for a list and the system of voting for one candidate, while the provision for a second ballot is also of considerable importance.

(A) In the first place, it might be said that voting for lists brings about a strengthening, and voting for individuals a weakening, of the party structure. There are, however, many exceptions to this general rule. There is a satisfactory rational explanation for it. When an individual is elected in a relatively small constituency, the candidate's personality is of capital importance; a member may thus build up such a strong position in his own constituency that it becomes a sort of fief from which he cannot be dislodged. As his re-election depends on himself and not on the party to which he owes allegiance (under the Third Republic in France many members of Parliament frequently changed their party and went on being re-elected time and again), it is understandable that the party structure cannot be very strong. Each member may have a well organized local election committee, but as this is entirely under the domination of the member, it will hardly accept directions from a central office. In Parliament, on the other hand, there will be very little discipline among the party groups, as each member is far more concerned about the possible repercussions of his vote in his own constituency than about the instructions issued by the party leaders. In the last resort, the system of voting for individual candidates thus tends to bring about the formation of loosely knit parliamentary groups, with a highly decentralized electoral organization, so that the parties—having a very weak administrative machinery, matched by very loose social ties—end by expressing no more than general tendencies of opinion.

Voting for a list, or "general ticket" (*scrutin de liste*) on the contrary, is essentially a collective operation, pushing personalities into the background in favour of the group to which they belong, that is, the party. The practice of placing certain candidates at the head of the list, of course, always reintroduces an element of individual prestige; but it also presupposes a certain readiness on the part of those at the foot of the list to follow their leader. The fact that the constituency covered by the election is wider acts in the same way: the elector has less direct acquaintance with the candidate, which makes the political label of the list, and hence of the party, a preponderant factor. The logical conclusion is the system of fixed lists, whereby candidates are submitted in an unchangeable order determining their election (in practice, this system is applied only under proportional representation); the dominion of the party over the member then becomes enormous. The member's re-election depends on his being again included on the list in a suitable position and, as this rests with the party to decide, parliamentary discipline is very strict. As the success of the lists is also secured by the general party propaganda far more than by local considerations, centralization proceeds apace. This then leads to a rigid party system; a term often used in France is "monolithic parties." If the splitting up of the individual's vote among different parties is allowed, however—which is a normal practice under the system of election from lists by simple majority, but which is exceptional under proportional representation—there is less rigidity and the personal factor again comes into play. Nevertheless, as experience shows that relatively little use is made of the split vote, the party structure remains strong. . . . The example of Belgium may also be quoted, where the list system led to the establishment of parties with a very strong organization long before proportional representation was adopted.

(B) The existence or non-existence of the second ballot also seems to play a very important part. Under the majority system pure and simple, independent candidates are dangerous, as there is a risk that they may influence the voting to the advantage of the opponents with whom their disagreements are greatest; there will therefore necessarily be fewer of them, either because of the political wisdom of the candidates themselves or because of that of the electors, who will "polarize" their votes.

When the influence of both factors tends in the same direction, it is reasonable to suppose that it will be more marked. This explains the general tendency of proportional representation (with voting for lists and the single ballot) to strengthen the party structure. It also explains the special weakness of party structure in France prior to 1939, by reason of the joint effect of single-member constituencies and the second ballot. It explains the strengthening of the structure between 1919 and 1928 by the combination of the list and the single ballot, although the splitting of votes reduced the effect of both these factors. It might even explain the strength of the Belgian parties before 1900, as the second ballot provided for the law was in fact hardly ever held in practice.

There are, however, quite a number of exceptions. The most typical is that of Great Britain. In spite of the single-member elections, the discipline of the parliamentary parties is strong, and the parties in general are highly centralized. The fact that there is no second ballot probably accounts in part for these features, but that explanation, by itself, is insufficient. Moreover, it may be noted that, generally speaking, within any one country at any given time, there are very great variations in the structure of the parties, although the ballot system is uniform for all; we know, for instance, that the parties of the left are more strongly organized than those of the right. The almost completely identical structure of the Communist parties in all countries, in spite of the variety of electoral systems, should likewise be emphasized. These examples indicated the limitations of the influence exercised by the electoral system; the influence of the ballot seems to be greater with regard to the number of parties than to their internal structure.

The Inter-Relationship of the Parties. The problem of the interrelationship of the parties, and of the alliances they may form among themselves, has so far scarcely been studied systematically. It is, however, of very great importance under a multiparty system, as only by contracting alliances is it generally possible to secure a sufficient majority to form a government. A distinction should be made between two types of party alliances: governmental alliances and electoral alliances. The latter generally tend to continue, being converted into the former; but the contrary is not true. Under proportional representation, in particular, we find alliances for the purposes of government alone, with no corresponding electoral alliance, and these are naturally much more easily broken.

In this sphere, the influence of the ballot system is obviously preponderant. It seems to be sufficiently clearly marked to enable us to sum it up in definite rules. Theoretically, the double ballot majority system tends to lead to the formation of close alliances, while proportional representation tends to complete independence. The consequences of the majority system with a single ballot vary greatly, according to the number of parties involved; under a two-party system it leads to complete independence, but under a multiparty system the trend is towards close and strong alliances. These rules obviously apply only to electoral alliances. Alliances for the purposes of government in the strict sense seem to be associated with the existence of numerous parties; they are therefore likely to be found under proportional representation, where there are many parties but no electoral alliances. These very general tendencies, however, are often much modified in practice. . . .

II. ELECTORAL SYSTEMS AND REPRESENTATION

In the theory of democracy, the person elected is considered to be the representative of the elector, in the legal sense of the term; the effect of the election is to give the former a mandate form the latter to speak and act on his behalf in the ordering of public business. The word "representation" is not, in the present context, taken in this traditional sense; it refers not to a situation in law but to a state of affairs. For our purposes, the elected member represents the elector not in the sense that an agent represents his principal but in the sense that a picture represents a landscape; representation connotes nothing more than the resemblance between the political opinions of the nation and those of the members of Parliament it has chosen.

In this sphere, the electoral system has a tremendous but as yet ill-defined influence. Politicians have long been aware of this fact, and they generally consider the ballot system less from the point of view of its possible effect on the number and structure of the political parties, than from that of its influence on the distribution of the available seats among them, every government majority constantly striving to adopt the combination which is most likely to keep it at the head of affairs. The simplest form this tendency takes is what the Americans call "gerrymandering" (changing the boundaries of electoral districts), but the present variety of electoral systems now offers a very wide range of processes capable of adaptation to suit many situation. . . .

(a) Accuracy of Representation

The Representation of the Parties. At first sight, there seems to be a very simple method of assessing how accurate representation is: to compare the percentage of the seats and the percentage of the votes gained by each party. If the two coincide, it will be taken that the representation is accurate; the first is higher than the second, we shall have "over-representation"; if it is lower, "under-representation." This type of investigation is not really conclusive; we shall show below that the numerical representation of the parties is very different from the real representation of public opinion. If, however, we confine ourselves to the former (as is generally done), it is possible to achieve a fairly exact correlation between the electoral system and the accuracy of representation.

(A) <u>By definition, proportional representation is obviously the system ensuring the greatest accuracy; it is in fact designed for that purpose.</u> The practical changes which have been made in PR in operation, however, often reduce its accuracy. If a perfectly accurate result were to be obtained, it would be necessary either for the whole country to be regarded as one constituency, or for the distribution of the remaining or "unused" votes to be made on a nation-wide basis. Various political reasons generally lead to the rejection of both these in favour of others less conformable with the purity of the system. There is then a disparity between the proportion of seats and the proportion of votes, which varies according to the system adopted for the distribution of "unused" votes, the frame-work of the constituencies, the possibility of splitting votes or making "friendly arrangements," etc. This disparity is quite small in certain countries and quite large in other. . . .

(B) Nevertheless, the disparity is infinitely smaller under proportional representation than when election is by <u>a simple majority with one ballot, which leads to a maximum inaccuracy in the numerical representation.</u> One constant tendency is to be noted in this connexion whenever there are only two parties: <u>the majority party is over-represented and the minority party under-represented.</u> This is not a very serious matter: it simply means that the differences of opinion among the electorate are accentuated, as we shall show below. But if this electoral system is found in conjunction with a number of parties, the representation may be more arbitrary, even though it still more or less follows the same general line: any party which has more votes than its nearest rival is theoretically over-represented in relation to the latter, i.e., either more "over-represented" or less "under-represented" than the other.

If, however, the difference between the numbers of votes is very small, <u>the representation may, in exceptional cases, be completely distorted: the party with the smallest number of votes may secure the most seats,</u> and vice versa. This happened, for instance, in Great Britain in January 1910, when the Liberals won 275 seats with 43.1 per cent of the votes, and the Conservatives 273 seats with 47 per cent. It happened again in 1929, when the Labour Party won 289 seats with 37.5 per cent of the votes and the Conservatives 262 with 37.97 per cent. This situation may arise even under a two-party scheme. The opponents of the simple majority with a single ballot naturally seize upon such cases to show the absurdity of the system, but they generally neglect to stress that they are quite exceptional. . . .

(C) It is practically impossible to specify what are the exact effects of the second ballot on the representation of the parties, owing to the change of opinion in comparison with the first ballot implied on the part of the electors who transfer their votes to the most acceptable rival. It is generally said that <u>the second ballot reduces the differences which result</u>

from the simple majority system with a single ballot. From the purely numerical point of view there is some doubt on this point; if the number of votes secured by the parties at the first ballot is compared with the total number of seats they secure after the second, considerable disparities are found. These are, of course, generally less obvious than the exceptional anomalies sometimes resulting from the simple majority system; but they seem to be comparable with the average anomalies of that system. They may even be considered more serious because of the trend they induce, for the actual size of the difference matters less than its direction. Under a single ballot system with two parties, however great the over-representation of the majority party and the under-representation of the minority party may be, neither usually alters the general picture of the division of opinion. When there is a second ballot, on the other hand, the over-all picture is completely distorted: the number of votes obtained by the respective parties no longer determines the trend of the disparities in their representation, but their political positions and the alliances between them. Generally speaking, the second ballot is favourable to the centre and unfavourable to the extremes—i.e., the former is over-represented and the latter under-represented. The political history of the Third Republic in France is a good illustration of this rule, signs of whose operation can, incidentally, be seen in almost all the systems where there are two ballots: the Netherlands, Norway, and Germany. . . .

Obviously, if the final percentage of the seats is compared with the percentage of votes secured in the second ballot, the disparity disappears completely; that is, of course, the reason for the system. It may then be claimed that it secures a more accurate representation than the single ballot system; but to do so implies a serious error of method. It is in fact only from the first ballot that we may derive a picture of the distribution of votes among the parties comparable with that produced by the single ballot majority system or by proportional representation. The second ballot entails an obligatory regrouping of votes which makes it impossible to distinguish their political colour. It is certainly a distortion of the truth to count as Radical the Communist votes which were transferred to the "Valoisien" or Radical candidates at the second ballot during the 1936 elections in France because they headed the Popular Front. The votes cast at the second ballot are divided according to tendency instead of according to party; but this takes us from the idea of party representation to what we might, for want of a better name, call the representation of opinion.

The Representation of Opinion. . . . It is generally concluded that PR gives a more accurate reflection of opinion, and that the simple majority with a single ballot seriously distorts it. The matter is not quite so simple. It is not certain that the accentuation of differences in opinion resulting from proportional representation, as a consequence of its tendency to the multiplication of parties and of the independence it confers on them, gives a truer picture of the facts than the simplified view obtained under the majority system. It may be wondered whether public opinion does not in fact tend to split into two great rival factions, each, of course, containing a multitude of shades of opinion but each fairly sharply outlined. It is interesting, in this connexion, to find that much the same conclusions have been reached in widely differing studies. Some sociologists suggest that a distinction should be made between two fundamental political temperaments (the "radical" and "conservative"); the Marxists conceive of the dynamics of society as a struggle between two great opposing classes; and the founders of electoral geography in France recognize, behind the apparent multiplicity of political opinions in our country, an enduring fundamental opposition between the Right and the Left, between order and movement.

As a consequence, even admitting that the defect of the majority system is that it tends to eliminate minor divergencies within each "spiritual family," the system has the essential merit of giving an accurate reflection of the general antagonism between them; the proportional system, on the other hand, has a serious defect in that it completely obscures this fundamental cleavage of opinion and unduly exaggerates disagreements over details. On the whole, the latter is probably a far less accurate means of representing opinion than the former, contrary to the belief generally held. From this point of view, the second ballot system has a certain advantage, in that it makes it possible at the same time—as a result of the alliances formed at the second ballot—to reflect the fundamental division into two camps as well as the minor conflicts within each of the major groups of opinion. It should be noted, incidentally, that a two-party system would produce the same result if the structure of each party remained so flexible as to permit the development and co-existence of diverse factions.

Another aspect of the problem relates to the width of the gulf between the opposing currents of opinion; on this point the same confusion as we have already seen between the representation of the parties and the representation of opinion gives rise to similar errors. It is commonly said that proportional representation has the advantage of reducing this gulf, by breaking up the great opposing groups into several fractions, whereas the majority system pure and simple leads to the system of two blocs, i.e., to the sharpest possible opposition. This statement confuses the numerical differences in party representation in parliament with the depth of political divergency. In reality the respective effects of PR and the majority systems are the exact opposite of what is commonly believed. Holcombe, in his article in the *Encyclopaedia of Social Sciences*, has noted that the parties tended to draw closer together under a two-party system (normally resulting from a single ballot election), but does not go into the factors bringing about this growing similarity. They are fairly easy to define. We may take as a specific example the case of Great Britain at the present day, leaving out of account the Liberal Party which is no longer important. Who will decide whether the Conservatives or the Labour Party win at the elections? Not their out-and-out supporters, who will naturally vote for them in any event, if they have no opportunity to vote for another party further to the right or further to the left, but the two or three million moderate Englishmen and women, standing politically in the centre, who sometimes vote Conservative and sometimes Labour. To win these votes, the Conservative Party will be compelled to tone down its Conservatism and the Labour Party its Socialism, both adopting a calm and reassuring tone. Both will have to put forward middle-of-the-road policies, therefore essentially similar to one another; we thus have the paradox that the centre influences the whole parliamentary life of a country, in which the electoral system is such as to prevent the formation of a central party. The result is the manifest diminution of the gulf between political opinions. The myth of the "two blocs," which is so firmly cherished in France, does not square with the facts. We may compare the British case with that of the proportional system in France. In the ordinary way, each party can increase its representation only at the expense of its immediate neighbours: the Communists at the expense of the Socialists, the Popular Republicans at the expense of the Moderate Radicals or the RPF, etc. This means that each will endeavour to stress the difference of detail between itself and its closest rivals instead of drawing attention to their underlying similarity, and the result will be to aggravate political divisions and to add to the number of points on which there is disagreement.

We might attempt to complete this analysis by demonstrating that the second ballot, which works to the advantage of the centre parties as far as numerical representation is concerned, is much less favourable to them with regard to the representation of opinion itself. For most of the elected members of the centre get in at the second ballot, some with the support of the right, some with the support of the left. The centre parties thus tend to be perpetually torn between two opposing poles. They are reduced to framing a policy now of the right and now of the left, in an attempt to restrain both tendencies. The case of the Radical party under the Third Republic would be an excellent illustration of this tendency. But, in the absence of more numerous and definite supporting evidence, these remarks should be considered merely as provisional hypotheses subject to revision. . . .

27. IN SUPPORT OF PROPORTIONAL REPRESENTATION*

A. Dami

I HAVE READ with the greatest interest Professor Duverger's distinguished report on "The Influence of the Electoral System on Political Life." It is an excellent and most absorbing document, especially for those interested in political science and electoral theory.

I would venture, however, as a convinced supporter of proportional representation, to explain briefly why I still hold firmly by the principle of electoral justice based on the rule: number of seats in proportion to the number of votes.

To come straight away to the crux of the matter, I would say that, while I am quite prepared to agree to modifying the system by introducing a minimum vote (of five per cent, seven per cent or ten per cent) and, still more readily, to the exclusion of any list which fails to obtain the *quota*—I am absolutely against the system of fixed party lists in use in France, where it leads, in fact, to a caricature of proportional representation. The elector is quite unable, in principle, to make any change in the list, even in the numerical order of the candidates; in order to change the order, the majority of electors would have to decide on a different order, an event which in practice never occurs, as it is scarcely conceivable that a majority of the electors should be able to reach agreement in advance throughout any one Department. Secondly, and still more important, the elector is not allowed to split his vote. The result is that all the candidates on the list in fact get the same number of votes, and that they are thus elected in the order determined by the party committee. I call this a caricature of proportional representation, since the most wholehearted supporters of the system never intended to deprive the elector of his freedom of choice, not only among different lists but within each individual list, leaving the selection of successful candidates entirely in the hands of the party committees instead of in those of the electors. In Switzerland, we have not only the possiblity of splitting the individual vote among different parties, and what is known as "latoisage" (striking out names), but also the cumulative vote (possibility of casting more than one vote for on candidate). And, whatever objections may be raised to the last mentioned procedure, which is not particularly democratic (especially if there are already "cumulative" candidates on the list), it is nevertheless true that in Switzerland and other countries using the proportional system, the elector is free to cast his vote as he pleases and the candidates on each list which have secured most votes are elected. . . .

---

* From *The International Social Science Bulletin*, Vol. 3 (Summer, 1951). By permission of the United Nations Educational, Scientific and Cultural Organization.

Nor is it true that PR makes it impossible to form a parliamentary majority, or more accurately, it is not PR which is at fault. Either one party, or group of parties, immediately obtains an absolute majority of the votes and therefore of the seats, in which event PR provides that majority at least as well as and perhaps better than the majority system with single or several-member constituencies; or no party or group of parties obtains such a majority, in which event it is quite as likely that it will be impossible to form a parliamentary majority under the simple majority system of election as under proportional representation; in either case it may happen that the results in the different constituencies cancel out and balance. The so-called "majority" system has never made the formation of a parliamentary majority certain; any such mathematical certainty would be possible only under a two-party system and, even then, the English instance shows that whenever the result of the elections has been a divided House consisting of two almost equal groups—in spite of the two-party system and when the third party has been reduced to negligible size—it has been necessary to hold a fresh election the same year or the next. . . . And yet they say that the proportional system reduces differences and prevents the formation of a majority! We thus find the apparently—but only apparently so—paradoxical situation that even the majority system with a single ballot and a relative majority, even under a two-party system, may produce a parliament divided exactly in halves, where there is therefore no majority or an infinitesimal majority. The result is that the election has to begin all over again, and a small difference in the votes in a particular constituency may then either form, or reverse, a working majority. . . .

It should be added that at the present time, in view of the existence of Communism, we have not two but at least three opposing tendencies throughout most of Europe (Communism, Socialism and Middle Class Liberalism in the wide sense of the term) and in fact four if we count the "reactionary" parties proper. . . . In these circumstances, a majority system would completely distort the picture in the different parliaments, by compelling the electors to unite against reaction, or against Communism either at the first ballot (as in England) or at the second. The gravitation towards the centre which worked to the advantage of the Radicals under the Third Republic and which, it seems, should in future work to the advantage of the Socialists, becomes impossible as soon as either of those two parties is too weak to form the nucleus of an absolute majority against the two extreme parties, whether or not in coalition. . . .

I should like to end by replying to our colleague who has reproached us, Mr. Duverger and most of the speakers, for discussing the electoral system as if it were something existing in its own right, operating, as it were, *in vacuo* and quite distinct from political life and, above all, from life itself; everything depends, he said on social conditions, and politics cannot be separated from the rest of the country's life. My reply is that, at least under a proportional system, the elections do in fact reflect all the conditions of a country, including, and most important, its social conditions; for instance, in an agricultural country, the elections will bring to power the peasant party or parties representing agricultural interests; in an industrial country, they will reflect the predominance of working-class interests, and so on.

Chapter IX.   Social and Ideological Trends

Introductory Note

IN MODERN, industrialized nations the major social groups tend to associate themselves with certain politicals parties and ideological orientations. For example, the middle classes tend to support conservative parties and ideologics, while the working class usually supports socialist or communist parties and ideologies. The complex relationship between groups, parties, and ideologies is one of the most important subjects of comparative analysis. As regards the ideologies themselves, all three trends mentioned above—conservatism, socialism, and communism—are undergoing internal crises and transformation. Throughout the Western world there is considerable controversy within the *conservative* movement over the merits of laissez faire and state action. Those in the tradition of Tory Democracy have accepted the general philosophy of John Maynard Keynes, according to which the State creates suitable conditions for economic expansion by means of fiscal and credit controls. Some continental conservatives also hope to transcend the class struggle by "integrating" the workers in the economic and social structure. Thus the Christian Democrats in Germany advocate "co-management" of industry by owners and workers, and the Gaullists in France have proposed a scheme of labor-management associations. Important elements within the conservative movement, however, reject both Keynesian economics and co-determination in favor of free enterprise and competitive capitalism. The necessity of winning electoral majorities has tended to isolate the advocates of laissez faire and has given an advantage to those who wish to make use of the State in stimulating and directing the economy. Successful conservative parties have thus found it increasingly necessary to compromise the beliefs of their most militant supporters.

Similarly, all *socialist* movements are going through a period of ideological reassessment and adjustment. Throughout the nineteenth century socialist parties were split by the conflict between revolutionaries and moderates. The former argue that the interests of the workers can be realized only by eliminating the capitalist system. The moderates disagreed with the Marxist emphasis on revolution, and urged participation by the workers in the institutions of the democratic state. These controversies have continued and have seriously reduced the effectiveness of socialist parties. The French Socialist Party (SFIO), for example, retains many revolutionary symbols, yet co-operates with other democratic parties in both elections and parliament. As a consequence, it has frightened away both middle-class supporters (because of its platform) and working class militants (because of alliances with bourgeois parties).

The dilemmas of contemporary socialism are especially evident in Great Britain—the only major nation in which a socialist party has gained power. A bitter debate within the party has been taking place over program and tactics. The moderates fear that the middle class is being alienated by undue emphasis on nationalization of industry. They urge the party to concentrate on central planning (rather than public ownership) of the economy, along with elimination of class and social inequalities. The Left-wing leaders contend that nationalization should be accelerated, and that the workers be given direct powers of management and control in the publicly owned industries. The vitality of the socialist movement would be restored, they claim, and electoral victory assured.

Communist ideology has also been modified significantly in the past century. It has been found necessary to reinterpret key doctrines in order to explain developments within both capitalist and communist systems. Even orthodox Marxists have admitted that the development of capitalism does not inexorably bring about poverty and degradation, and with it a sharpened class consciousness. The most highly industrialized nations in the world, the United States and Great Britain, do not have proletarian revolutionary movements. It is in the economically retarded nations that the "communist" revolution has triumphed. Lenin tried to explain the shortcomings in Marx's analysis by postulating a further stage in the development of capitalism: imperialism. As a result of imperialist adventures, he contended, capitalists are able to secure "super-profits" enabling them to buy up or "bribe" certain labor leaders and even some segments of the working class. The trade unions become concerned above all with extracting concessions from the capitalists rather than overthrowing the whole capitalist system. Yet Lenin does not expect capitalism to collapse because of the contradictions described by Marx. It becomes necessary, then, to create a revolutionary party that will do the job originally assigned to the revolutionary proletariat.

Marxist "revisionists" argue that Lenin failed to appreciate an important political development in the West. Modern democracies, they point out, accept responsibility for sparing the masses the kind of suffering Marx believed would explode in revoltuion. The involvement of the democratic state with the economy, usually over the determined opposition of capitalist interests, has had the consequence of improving conditions of labor and stimulating production in whose profits workers share. The "class struggle" in a modern democracy, they contend, is not a straight fight between only two classes, but a rivalry of multifarious groups and interests for a greater share of political and economic power.

The End of Ideology?

Many political observers have discerned a trend towards "depoliticization" or the "end of ideology" in modern democracies. The conflict between capitalism and socialism, they argue, is being muted. All modern states are involved in regulating or stimulating the economy. Capitalism or private enterprise is evolving toward the welfare state and the planned economy. Democratic socialist parties are moving away from nationalization as a policy, in favor of the welfare state and the planned economy. Thus the differences between conservatives or liberals and socialists are becoming a matter of political tactics in dealing with concrete problems rather than of clashing ideologies.

The decline in the intensity of ideological controversy may be caused by a transformation of social structure which seems to take place in industrialized societies at a certain stage of their development. Members of the working and middle classes increasingly share a common way of life and experience the same kind of social discipline. Politics becomes a matter of allocating the national revenue; and while this issue may be important and dramatic, it does not involve the fate of the political institutions themselves. The argument is developed by Otto Kirchheimer in the essay reproduced below. Philip Converse and Georges Dupeux present evidence concerning mass attitudes towards political issues which seems to support the thesis of "depoliticization." The reader is also referred to Daniel Bell, *The End of Ideology* (1960), and S. M. Lipset, *Political Man* (1960) and "The Changing Class Structure and Contemporary European Politics," *Daedalus* (Winter, 1963). This thesis has been challenged by Jean Meynaud, *Destin des idéologies* (Lausanne, 1961), and by several contributors to the collective volume edited by Georges Vedel, *La Dépolitisation: mythe ou réalité* (Paris, 1962). H. Stuart Hughes also expresses doubts about the end of ideology in the essay reproduced below.

Whatever the situation in modern democracies, it is apparent that intellectual elites in the developing nations are becoming ideologically oriented. They respond especially to the ideology of communism—not as a scientific critique of capitalism, but as a recipe for a rapid solution to their problems. They view Marxism above all as an affirmation of the ability of rational men to resolve problems. Ideological controversy today is rife mainly in those nations just starting on the way to industrialization and modernization.

On the evolution of modern capitalism, see especially Adolf A. Berle, *The 20th Century Capitalist Revolution* (1954); John K. Galbraith, *American Capitalism: The Concept of Countervailing Power* (1952); and Francis X. Sutton, and others, *The American Business Creed* (1956).

Important recent works on socialism include: Clement Attlee, *As It*

Happened (1954); Leon Blum, *For All Mankind* (1946); E. F. M. Durbin, *The Politics of Democratic Socialism* (1940); Joseph Schumpeter, *Capitalism, Socialism and Democracy* (1950) and C. A. R. Crosland, *The Future of Socialism* (1956). A useful survey of recent trends of contemporary socialism can be found in the *Antioch Review* (Summer, 1960).

There is a vast literature on commuist ideology and practice. The student might begin with R. N. Carew-Hunt, *The Theory and Practice of Communism* (1951); E. H. Carr, *A History of Soviet Russia*, 4 vols. (1951–55); Issac Deutscher, *Stalin: A Political Biography* (1949); Merle Fainsod, *How Russia Is Ruled* (1953); and Bertram D. Wolfe, *Three Who Made a Revolution* (1948). A succinct and useful study is A. G. Meyer, *Communism* (1960).

Readings

28. WORKING CLASS POLITICS IN WESTERN EUROPE*

Val R. Lorwin

How FAR has economic development conditioned working-class politics in Western Europe in the last century and a half? Are there stages of economic development in which protest is always sharp and others in which it is dull? To what extent are the differences in protest among the nations due to differences in economic growth, to what extent to different patterns of general historical development caused by other factors? What types of studies may promote our understanding of these questions? These are questions I propose to raise or to discuss here. . . .

Working-class protest, like economic development, has been a matter of some agitated public concern since the Second World War. But people have been proclaiming it a chief problem of modern times since Carlyle wrote of the "bitter discontent gone fierce and mad, the wrong conditions therefore or the wrong disposition of the Working Classes of England"[1] and Harriet Martineau warned that "this great question of the rights of labor . . . cannot be neglected under a lighter penalty than ruin to all."[2] . . .

Political protest can be measured in some of its more orderly forms:

---

* From "Working Class Politics and Economic Development in Western Europe," *The American Historical Review*, Vol. LXIII, No. 2 (January, 1958), pp. 338–51. By permission.

[1] Thomas Carlyle, "Chartism," *Critical and Miscellaneous Essays*, in *Works* (30 vols., New York, 1900), Vol. XXIX, p. 119.

[2] *A History of the Peace: Being a History of England from 1816 to 1854* (4 vols., Boston, 1866), Vol. IV, p. 622.

party membership, election results, and—for the most recent years, in many nations—whatever it is people tell to those who take public opinion polls. For periods before the working class attained full suffrage, however, the test of votes is only partially applicable, and complete and equal manhood suffrage was not attained until the First World War in most of the advanced European nations. We do not know how workers voted, moreover, or who voted for the parties claiming to represent the working class, except in some one-industry areas like the miners' constituencies. Nor have all Socialist votes or all Communist votes been of equal intensity as protests. Some votes have implied rejection of the social order, others, merely hopes of immediate economic self-interest; still others, vague and diffuse frustrations.

On the eve of the Industrial Revolution, Henry Fielding remarked: "The sufferings of the poor are less observed than their misdeeds. . . . They starve, and freeze, and rot among themselves, but they beg, and steal, and rob among their betters."[3] Soon the laboring poor were able to do more, when they were thrown out of work or their wages were cut, than "beg and steal and rob among their betters." Modern economic development created a new sort of political protest by generating the industrial, essentially urban, wage-earning groups in such numbers and force that they were, for all their medieval and early modern predecessors, in most ways a new class—as yet only "camped in society . . . not established there."[4] This was, said the ex-worker Denis Poulot, "the terrible sphinx which is called the people . . . this great mass of workers which does not know what it is, except that it suffers."[5] Huddled in the wretched new factory towns or in the slums of renowned old cities, oppressed by long hours of work, arbitrary shop rules, and monotony, sorely tried by recurrent unemployment, unlettered, this mass inspired more fear than solicitude. Lord Liverpool, congratulated by Chateau-briand on the solidity of British institutions, pointed to the capital outside his windows and replied: "What can be stable with these enormous cities? One insurrection in London and all is lost."[6]

Hunger will turn political. In the hard year of 1819 the banners of the crowd at Peterloo, before the Yeomen rode them down, typified the mixture of the economic and the political: "A Fair Day's Wage for a Fair Day's Work," "No Corn Laws," and "Equal Representation or Death."[7]

It was not hunger alone. "The poor have hearts as well as stomachs," said Cooke Taylor but deemed it a fact not known to many who passed

---

[3] *A Proposal for Making an Effectual Provision for the Poor, 1753*, in *Works* (16 vols., New York, 1902), Vol. XIII, p. 141.

[4] Michel Chevalier, *De l'industrie manufacturière en France* (Paris, 1841), p. 37.

[5] *Le Sublime* (3d ed.; Paris, 1887; first pub. in 1870), p. 27.

[6] Chateaubriand, *Mémoires d'outre-tombe* (Brussels, 1849), Vol. IV, p. 210.

[7] F. A. Bruton (ed.), *Three Accounts of Peterloo by Eyewitnesses* (Manchester, 1921); William Page (ed.), *Commerce and Industry* (2 vols., London, 1919), Vol. II, p. 47.

for wise men.[8] Carlyle knew it: "It is not what a man outwardly has or wants that constitutes the happiness or misery of him. Nakedness, hunger, distress of all kinds, death itself have been cheerfully suffered, when the heart was right. It is the feeling of injustice that is insupportable to all men. . . . No man can bear it or ought to bear it."[9]

Michel Chevalier looked at manufacturing and said: "Fixed points are totally lacking. There is no bond between superior and inferior, no rapprochement between equals. . . . Nothing holds, nothing lasts."[10] Slowly, "fixed points" were established; the working classes gained in education, self-discipline, and political experience. In the course of industrialization in every Western country, despite crises and wars, workers' levels of living improved vastly. Did this resolve working-class protest?

Continuing economic development would resolve the very protest it brought into being, Marx argued, but only by the inevitable substitution of a new order for the captialist society, which would prove incapable of continuing the triumphant progress of economic growth. Until the coming of the new order, declared the *Communist Manifesto*, "the development of class antagonism keeps even pace with the development of industry," and in *Capital* Marx affirmed that "there is a steady intensification of the wrath of the working class." (I use a few of Marx's significant statements as beginning points for discussion, not attempting an analysis of Marx or Marxism.)

These predictions have been contradicted by the experience (thus far) of all the Western nations except France and Italy—nor do France and Italy actually support the prophecy. Here is one of the ironies of the history of Marxist prediction. Only in the two countries where, among all the great industrial nations of the free world, capitalism has shown the least sustained dynamism has the "wrath of the working class" permitted the Communist party to take and hold a preponderant position among workers.[11] These two countries require a closer look.

In France and Italy, economic growth alone could not resolve the noneconomic problems created by wars, religious tensions, social distance, and the relations between the individual and the state. We cannot go into the noneconomic factors here. But the sense of injustice in these countries also grew, in part, out of the qualities of economic growth: the character of entrepreneurship, the distribution of income, and—even more—the nature of employer authority. The bourgeoisie of France and of Italy were insistent in their demands for protection against labor as well

---

[8] *Notes of a Tour in the Manufacturing Districts of Lancashire* . . . (London, 1842), p. 157.

[9] "Chartism," pp. 144–45.

[10] *Op. cit.*, p. 38.

[11] Nor, clearly, has the experience in the Soviet orbit borne out the Marxian prophecy any better, since revolution won in countries in early stages of industrial capitalism and had to be imposed from without on more advanced countries.

as protection against competition. Niggardly and tardy in concessions to their workers, they flaunted inequalities by their style of living. Their class consciousness helped shape the class consciousness of workers.

Workers, moreover, doubted the ability of their superiors to fulfill their economic functions as an entrepreneurial class. The slowness of economic growth evoked protest, particularly in France. Before the First World War, labor leaders shared with many orthodox economists and publicists the impression that their country was stagnating, although it was progressing in the two decades before the war. The gloomy view arose in part from comparisons with the industrial growth of the United States and with the industrial and military growth of Germany. That view also reflected the state of labor organization, greater in the stagnant old industries such as building and in the thousands of small workshops of Paris than in the newer industries such as the booming steel mills of Lorraine. Later, in the interwar period, the labor movement was strong in the civil administration and public service industries rather than in the new and technically progressive branches of private industry—chemicals, synthetic fibers, automobiles.

French employers groaned constantly about their high costs, especially of labor, and their inability to compete with foreign producers. Labor leaders argued, however, that the employers' difficulties really came from their sterility; "their very slow progress, from their timidity; their uncertainty, from their lack of initiative. We ask the French employers to resemble the American employer class. . . . We want a busy, active, humming country, a veritable beehive always awake. In that way our own force will be increased."[12] But the unions' own force remained weak. Their weakness, along with pessimism about the country's economic growth, gave to French labor that curious combination of low immediate hopes and utopian dreams which has characterized it during most of this century.

Management's own leaders praised smallness of scale and slowness to mechanize. In 1930 the president of the General Confederation of French Manufacturers congratulated his members on "the spirit of prudence in the management of firms, which is the surest guarantee against the dangers of a fearful crisis," and on "the French mentality of counting on regular and steady dividends, rather than on the saw-toothed variation of dividends fashionable in some great industrial nations." The year of this speech marked the beginning of fifteen years of economic decline and stagnation in France.

The dramatic inequalities between the poorer, agricultural areas and the industrialized regions of both Italy and France created further tensions in each nation. Finally, the bourgeoisie showed a fear of the people and a

---

[12] Victor Griffuelhes, "L'Infériorité des capitalistes français," *Mouvement socialiste*, no. 226, Dec., 1910, pp. 329–32.

political bankruptcy at history's critical hours. Workers in Italy and France tended to merge judgments of the political and the economic performance of the powers that were. Their doubts as to the competence and courage of the bourgeoisie deepened their feelings of both the injustice and the fragility of the social and political order. Here let us leave France and Italy to return to the general question.

Some would turn the Marxian assertion upside down and argue that there is a "hump of radicalism" early in a nation's industrial development and that once the economy, by a big "initial push," surmounts its early difficulties, protest inevitably falls off. The history of a number of countries gives support to this analysis. But, despite Marx and many anti-Marxists, in the history of social relationships the several factors never long "keep even pace" with each other. In England the working class has not seriously threatened the political order since Chartist times, to be sure; but the syndicalists of the immediate pre-1914 period and the Socialists of the post-1918 period were far more critical of the social and economic order than the New Model unionists and the "Lib-Labs" of the 1850's, 1860's, and 1870's. France and Italy show a series of humps of radicalism.

Economic development has attenuated early protest by changes in the structure of the working classes. "Within the ranks of the proletariat," announced the *Communist Manifesto*, "the various interests and conditions of life are more and more equalized, in proportion as machinery obliterates all distinction of labor, and nearly everywhere reduces wages to the same low level. . . . The modern laborer, instead of rising with the progress of industry, sinks deeper and deeper below the conditions of existence of his own class." Marx was observing a period of development in which the machine was breaking down old skills, especially in the textile trades. The historian was being unhistorical in assuming that the trend must continue.

By the turn of the century it was already clear to a good observer like Eduard Bernstein (who was aided by residence in England) that economic growth and social reforms were blurring the sharpness of class among wage and salaried workers.[13] This is the now familiar phenomenon of the rise of the "new middle class." (Let us accent the word "new," for we use the old, imprecise words "middle class" for lack of a more descriptive phrase.) George Orwell spoke of the "upward and downward extension of the middle class" and of the growing importance of the people of "indeterminate social class."[14] This is the result of the swelling of the so-called tertiary sector of the economy—of public administration, commerce, services, and, within the industrial sector itself, the expansion of

---

[13] *Evolutionary Socialism: A Criticism and Affirmation*, trans. by E. C. Harvey (London, 1909), esp. pp. 103–6, 206–7, 219. See also Peter Gay, *The Dilemna of Democratic Socialism: Eduard Bernstein's Challenge to Marx* (New York, 1952).

[14] *The Lion and the Unicorn* (London, 1941), pp. 53–54.

professional, technical, and administrative jobs. Even among those in traditional forms of wage employment, middle-class attitudes have flourished, made possible not only by higher real wages and greater leisure but also by enhanced security, housing in socially mixed communities, longer schooling, and an increasingly classless culture wafted on mass communications.

The people of the new middle class have most often sought individual rather than collective solutions. Their political preferences have been divided—although unevenly—among almost all the parties. On the Continent in crisis times, fearful of being dragged down to proletarian status, many have hearkened to authoritarian voices. The new middle class called into question many of the traditional appeals of working-class politics. The parties of labor were obliged to appeal to other classes and to more complex attitudes than, rightly or wrongly, they formerly took for granted among workers.

Another change which came with economic growth was the differentiation between the economic and the political organizations of the working classes. Early forms of action had confused the economic and political. Then there generally came a separation between unions and political parties and, albeit with interlocking directorates and memberships, a cooperative division of function. France, Italy, and Spain, however, did not achieve this division of labor; while England was developing "Sidney Webbicalism,"[15] they developed syndicalism. This was the confounding of politics and economics in the name of "a-political" action. Anarcho-syndicalism, with its refusal to recognize the reality of politics and its disdain for parliamentary democracy, had fateful consequences. It prevented an effective working relationship of the unions with the socialist parties, to the great mischief of both, and helped leave workers poorly prepared later to distinguish between democratic political protest and communist politics.

Politics could not be denied, however much some workers' leaders might plead the sufficiency of economic action. No movement came to be more dependent on political action for economic gains than the "a-political" French unions. Even the robust British workers' consumer cooperatives, founded on the Rochdale principle of political neutrality, formed a Cooperative party (which became a small tail to the Labour party kite). When British labor attempted in the 1926 general strike to solve by industrial action a problem too big for industrial action alone, the result was catastrophe. Even there, moreover, the Trades Union Congress used its economic power in only a halfhearted way for fear of damaging the nation's political foundations.

The once lively anarchist and syndicalist movements practically disappeared under the hammer of economic development. The libertarian

---

[15] The term is *Punch's*, quoted by G. D. H. Cole, *The World of Labour* (4th ed.; London, 1920), p. 3. In Italy syndicalism was important but not the dominant current.

movements could not survive in the climate of assembly line production, modern industrial organization, or the modern welfare state. It was the communists, opposed though they were to the deepest libertarian impulses, who by their militant rejection of bourgeois society claimed most of the anarchists' and syndicalists' following. To the completely power-centered movement fell the heritage of those who had refused to come to any terms with political power.

Among the socialists, the bearded prophets gave way to the smooth-chinned organizers, parliamentarians, and planners. Socialist militancy was a victim of socialist success, itself made possible by economic growth. Economic growth produced a margin of well-being and facilitated the compromises and generosity which reconciled groups to each other in most of the liberal democracies.

Along with socialist militancy, socialist certitudes faded. The motto of "Socialism in our time" was amended, at least *sotto voce,* to "Socialism . . . but not in our time." Socialism became less than ever a doctrine and more a political temper. Despite an addiction to worn-out slogans, it was mellowed and strengthened, particularly after the First World War, by its identification with the noneconomic values of national life against threats from extreme left and extreme right.

Where it was most doctrinal, socialism was least effective—and often least true to its own doctrine. It proved most effective where it was most pragmatic, in the lands where the habits of civic responsibility and political compromise were strong; these were all (except Switzerland) constitutional monarchies. In France and in Italy, however, the Communist party rushed into the gap between socialist reasonableness and workers' old resentments, between socialist uncertainties and workers' pent-up hopes. Spain and Portugal were limiting cases; their hours of democracy were of the briefest, in part because of long economic stagnation.

"Modern industrial labor, modern subjugation to capital, the same in England as in France, in America as in Germany, has stripped [the proletarian] of every trace of national character. . . . National differences, and antagonisms between people, are daily more and more vanishing," said the *Communist Manifesto.* Instead, the working-class movements have all followed different national patterns. For many years it could be said that the only thing the socialists had nationalized was socialism.

Britain developed a labor movement of class solidarity and class organization without class hatred; France and Italy, class hatred but ineffectual class organization. Scandinavia developed on the British pattern, overcoming class conflict and moving on to an even higher degree of class restraint and responsibility than Britain's. The Belgian, Dutch, and Swiss working classes have shown a remarkable degree of responsibility, although their highly developed class organizations have followed the religious and political cleavages in each nation. The Communist Internationals have exercised central controls, but over parties which have differed not only from continent to continent but also from nation to contiguous Western European nation.

"A number of things govern men," said Montesquieu, "climate, religion, laws, maxims of government, the examples of things past, customs, manners; from all this there is formed a general spirit."[16] Economic development was only one of the factors that influenced social structures, cultural patterns, political habits and institutions, and what for short we call national character.

National character is often a bundle of contradictions, however, and it changes in time. The form and temper of working-class action also change. In Norway, for example, the tremendous onrush of industrialization early in this century evoked a radical protest which gave the union movement a syndicalist turn and took the Labor party into the Communist International. But the party soon broke with the Comintern, and party and unions developed into one of the most solid—yet independent and imaginative—labor movements in the world.

In Belgium, about 1891, social conflict seemed so irreconcilable that Paul Vinogradoff thought revolution must break out in this "overcrowded country, where the extremes of socialist and Catholic opinion were at that time most in evidence,"[17] and that such a revolution would touch off a general European war. But before the First World War, Belgian workers had somehow assimilated their conflicts in a structure of compromise and appeared as among the most moderate in Europe.

The study of differences and similarities between the nations, as well as change within the nations, sheds light on our problems. One may, for example, compare France and Belgium, separated by a rather artificial frontier but by many historical differences. The reconciliation of the Belgian working class to the political and social order, divided though the workers are by language and religion and the Flemish-Walloon question, makes a vivid contrast with the experience of France. The differences did not arise from the material fruits of economic growth, for both long were rather low-wage countries, and Belgian wages were the lower. In some ways the two countries had similar economic development. But Belgium's industrialization began earlier; it was more dependent on international commerce, both for markets and for its transit trade; it had a faster growing population; and it became much more urbanized than France. The small new nation, "the cockpit of Europe," could not permit itself social and political conflict to the breaking point. Perhaps France could not either, but it was harder for the bigger nation to realize it.

Comparisons of different groups within nations and among nations are

[16] The year 1956 reminded us again, in hope and tragedy, of the "general spirit" of peoples. Upsurge against Soviet rule came, where if anywhere among the satellites one might have expected it, from the "brave" and "romantic" Poles and Hungarians.

[17] H. A. L. Fisher, "Memoir," in *The Collected Papers of Paul Vinogradoff* (2 vols., Oxford, 1928), Vol. I, p. 19.

of the essence too. Some occupations seem prone to long phases of radicalism. Dangerous trades, unsteady employment, and isolation from the larger community are some of the factors which make for radicalism among dockers, seamen, lumbermen, and miners in many—though not all—countries. Yet radicalism has had successes among the more stable occupations too.

It is not generally those who are in the greatest economic distress who are the leaders in protest. First, one may recognize the element of chance in the occupational selection of leaders of protest (as in all selections of leadership). It is happenstance that the lifelong leader of the French unions, Léon Jouhaux, came out of a match factory and that the great leader of Danish Social Democracy, Thorvald Stauning, came out of the cigar maker's trade. Beyond the chance elements, however, there is a process of selection for leadership of protest from strength rather than misery, by the capacity of the group rather than its economic distress. First those in the skilled artisan trades (notably the printers and building craftsmen), then the metal workers, miners, and railroad men have been in the vanguard in many lands. In relation to economic development, some of the leaders have come from the groups of skilled operatives menaced by technological change, others from skilled or semi-skilled workers in positions of continuing opportunity or in stable, strategic locations in the industrial process. . . .

Apparently similar economic trends may give rise to, or at least be accompanied by, different consequences of protest. British miners' protest mounted bitterly as the coal industry sank into the doldrums of the 1920's. On the other hand, the porcelain workers of Limoges, vigorous socialists at the turn of the century, became torpid as their industry declined into torpor.

If only in passing and by inference, I hope to have recalled some examples of the particular subjects which invite the historian and some of the values of comparative studies. We need to study many more individuals, in biographies, and many more occupations and industries, in their settings of period and place, as, with fond intensity and imaginative erudition, Georges Duveau has studied the workers of the Second Empire,[18] before we can safely generalize. But men will, as men should, generalize long before they can safely generalize.

Here I have thought that modest ground-clearing considerations would be most useful. To assume my share of responsibility, however, I offer a few working hypotheses. For some of them, the nature of the evidence has been hinted at in the preceding pages; for others, not even that. They are not meant to be "laws" or "universal" but merely to sum up a few aspects of the experience of the past 150 years in one area of the world, an

---

[18] *La Vie ouvrière en France sous le Second Empire* (Paris, 1946) and *La Pensée ouvrière sur l'éducation pendant la Seconde République et le Second Empire* (Paris, 1948).

area full of intriguing differences yet with enough homogeneity in culture and industrial development to make generalization valid and comparison significant.

Economic development is process, environment, and goal; it provides a framework, and sets problems, for man's capacities for political and social action.

Rapid growth in the early stages of industrialization generates protest by reason of the bewildering dislocations and (for many) the sacrifices out of current consumption which it imposes. Continued economic growth permits the satisfaction of much of this protest. But some attitudes of protest persist well beyond the economic conditions which aroused them.

Sluggish economic growth may generate the deepest and longest lasting protest by reason of the society's inability to provide well-being and social justice to match social aspirations and by reason of the economic elite's failure to inspire confidence. Slow growth of cities and slow recruitment of the industrial work force facilitate the carry-over of traditions of protest from generation to generation.

The gradual delineation of the separate (but overlapping) spheres and organizations of political and industrial protest makes for reconciliation and absorption of protest in each sphere.

The labor movements most dependent on the state may show the greatest hostility to the state. The working classes best integrated with their national communities are those which have built labor movements that are more or less autonomous centers of power.

The successive phases of a nation's economic development are not inevitably reflected in corresponding attitudes and behavior of labor protest. Moreover, different phases of development exist side by side in the same regions and industries. Different forms of working-class politics also exist side by side.

National differences shape the response of workers and labor movements to economic change. These differences are only in part due to the differences in patterns of economic development. In large part they are due to noneconomic factors—politics and religion, cultural patterns and class structure—and to historical accident and personalities. ("Everything is dependent on everything," however, and most of the noneconomic factors are themselves conditioned by economic change.)

These are a few of the problems on which we need further descriptive findings and further comparative analysis. Comparative studies may remind those of us who wear monographic spectacles to look up to the horizon from time to time and may remind those who strain at the horizon to put on the spectacles occasionally for closer observation.

It is to the more modest forms of comparative historical work that I refer, not to the abused "grand manner" of universal history. Yet even modest comparative studies will help put our problems in their broader settings of the history of man's relation to his work and his fellows, of the history of social organization and political striving, of the endless searches for justice, order, and freedom.

29. THE WANING OF OPPOSITION*

Otto Kirchheimer

POLITICAL OPPOSITION is an eternal paradox. It postulates the principle that impediments to political action may be wholesome and are therefore to be protected. But what is the chance of institutionalizing such limitations? The parliamentary regime, and the favorable climate it created for the rise of the political party as a vehicle for the exercise of both governmental and opposition functions, has been one of the more felicitous inventions in the limited field of political institutions. But contemporary parliamentary institutions, working as they do in the framework of mass democracy, obey different laws and pressures from those governing their predecessors half a century or a century ago.

Reinvestigation of the meaning of opposition under the conditions of the present age may be in order. For the sake of preciseness these remarks will be restricted to European parliamentary regimes, omitting the role of opposition under presidential regimes, which obey somewhat different political and, as the case may be, social considerations.

I should like to put up three models, two of which pertain to the forms of political opposition. First is the "classical opposition" under the parliamentary form of government, developed from the practices of eighteenth-century England. Second is what might be styled "opposition of principle," bent not only on wrenching power from the government of today but on ending once and for all the system on which that government rests. The third is a counter-concept to the other two; it relates to government under various forms of cartel arrangements among political organizations operating within the framework of parliamentary institutions. . . . [ED.—Professor Kirchheimer's discussion of the "classical opposition" and the "opposition of principle" has been omitted.]

[Let us turn to . . .] the elimination of major political opposition through government by party cartel. What I have in mind here are not the national or national-unity governments of war and crisis vintage. By their very definition they are exceptional occurrences. Moreover, two of them, the MacDonald government of 1931 and Doumergue's attempt in 1934, were nothing but transparent endeavors to hide an attempt at political realignment and to cash in on the possible goodwill of the national-unity label. Rather, I have in mind the more than temporary abandonment of the government-opposition relation in contemporary Austria.

* From "The Waning of Opposition in Parliamentary Regimes," *Social Research*, Vol. 24, No. 2 (Summer, 1957). By permission.

Between the end of World War I and the 1934 civil war Austria had a record of bitter and incessant struggle between two major parties, both resting on an amalgamation of social class, political creed, and religious conviction, with a third party too small and inconsequential to play a balancing role. After a relatively short period of coalition between the two major parties immediately subsequent to World War I, the Christian Social Party entrenched itself firmly in the saddle of national government. For over a decade its socialist competitor hovered uneasily between the position of a parliamentary opposition and that of an opposition of principle. After World War II approximately the same party constellation emerged, with the two major parties dividing more than eighty percent of the total vote almost evenly between themselves. In view of the difficult situation of Austria, occupied by both Eastern and Western powers, and the republic's historical record of political frustration and abiding suspicion, the parties decided on a carefully prearranged system of collaboration.

Renewed after the 1956 election, this system has outlasted the occupation. Neither party has been willing to leave the conduct of public affairs in the hands of its competitor or of a civil service working exclusively under its competitor's direction. The two parties proceeded with a detailed parceling out, among their adherents, of all cabinet posts and the majority of the significant administrative positions. This involved explicit understandings on many issues, on appointments, on the filling of regional, local, and semi-governmental jobs, and on the elaboration of legislative programs.

This procedure has led to significant changes in the function of parliamentary institutions in Austria. The inconsequential right-wing and left-wing opposition parties have kept their freedom of parliamentary action. But the members of the two big parties can exercise their normal parliamentary prerogatives—what is now called "acting within the coalition-free area"—only with the permission of the partner party. It would jeopardize the functioning of the cartel agreement to allow party caucuses or individual backbenchers to oppose bills proposed by the government or to introduce motions themselves without previous clearance with the cartel. The area free of the binding rule of the coalition government is predetermined neither by general criteria nor by pre-established subject matter. In each case the parties' possibility of taking back their freedom of action rests on a particular agreement between the coalition partners. Major parliamentary criticism is thus relegated to the status of opposition by joint license.

What have been the consequences of this cartel arrangement? Curiously enough, the restricted exercise of parliamentary opposition has not dried up the competition between the two major parties for the votes of the new voters, of potential switchers from each, and of the declining reservoir of third-party voters.[1] In effecting this competition in face of the stringent rules of the cartel agreement, both partners have been quite ingenious in discovering and profiting from any opportunity for competition. A minister may utilize the key position assigned to him under the coalition pact in order to carry through some controversial policy by administrative fiat, thus trying to create a fait accompli in favor of his own party. On the other hand, if a party has to agree to a compromise particularly distasteful to its clientele, it will be allowed to make enough parliamentary and extraparliamentary noises to convince its clientele of the intensity of its reluctance. This then leads to a new kind of built-in opposition which the Austrians themselves have baptized *Bereichs-opposition,* meaning opposition to what is happening under the agreed-upon jurisdiction of the other party. The Socialists may fight verbal battles against a monetary policy of the Ministry of Finance, controlled by the Christian People's Party. The latter may pay back in vehement extraparliamentary and measured parliamentary criticism of the conduct of the Socialist ministry responsible for transport, electricity, and—until the jurisdictional changes of last summer—nationalized enterprises.

Although Austria has come close to being a two-party state, the election does not decide which party will form the government and which will be relegated to the opposition. Nevertheless, as the 1956 election has convincingly shown, the electoral process retains a clear-cut meaning. The shift of votes decides the conditions of collaboration. Administrative and legislative determination of the issues that are controversial between the parties is heavily influenced by the verdict of the voters. But it takes place by agreement and compromise worked out on the basis of election results rather than by majority fiat.

What about the compatibility of the different social-economic orientations of the partners of a coalition government? How are the views of the proponents of extensive state intervention and of an important planned sector made compatible with the endeavors of those who want a so-called free-market economy? The problem looks more formidable in theory than it is in practice. All governments operate within the limits and necessities of their period, which rarely allow either a consistent interventionist or a consistent free-market pattern. The most arduous adherents of

---

[1] The relevant election results—taken from Hans Müller, "Die Wahlen im Spiegel der Statistik," in *Die Zukunft* (May–June 1956) p. 136—are as follows:

	1945	1949	1953	1956
Registered voters	3,449,000	4,391,000	4,586,000	4,614,000
Election participation in % of reg. voters	95%	96.8%	95.8%	95.9%
Percent of valid vote received by:				
Christian People's Party (OVP)	49.8	44.4	41.26	45.96
Socialist Party (SPO)	44.6	38.7	42.1	43.04
Independents (Freedom Party 1956)	....	11.68	10.59	6.52
Communist Party (KPO)	5.41	5.08	5.28	4.44

a free-market economy have steadfastly followed a policy of protection and interventionism in the agricultural sector, with the Austrian government assuredly no exception to this rule. Everything is therefore a matter of degree and compromise; and these compromises have to be carried out irrespective of whether they are forced on a classic one-party alternation government, by the needs of multifarious political clienteles, or on a coalition government, where the various currents are represented by distinct parties. Changes rarely spring Minerva-like from Zeus's head at the prompting of program builders who got the ear of the public at election time. More often than not it is the imperative requirement of a new societal situation which makes such programs sprout and be adopted by all those who want either to stay or to get a fresh start in the political business. What at first looks like a clear-cut dichotomy is mostly in point of fact a continuum.

A more fundamental objection to the Austrian-type cartel agreement, and one that has been voiced against similar tendencies of some present-day German state governments, rests on the resulting absence of the opposition's control function. Each party may have an interest in covering up the inefficiency, waste, and corruption of its partner. Hence arise all the problems of institutionalized reinsurance practices. Neither public opinion, to the extent that such an animal exists independently of interest groups closely tied in with the major parties, nor the small opposition of principle represented in parliament has enough breadth of action, inside knowledge of the administration, or authority with the public at large to compensate for the absence of a major parliamentary opposition group. Control is mutual control in the matrix of a government acting within the confines of the coalition agreement; the party and parliamentary discussion sets the frame for the compromise effected inside the government. And the contours of this discussion are doubtless more skimpy than those indicated by the classical distinction between opposition and obstruction. In any case the voters, by increasingly concentrating their votes on the two major parties, have decided that from their viewpoint the two parties' right to participate jointly in government and administration is of greater social and political consequence than the traditional opposition function, and has preference over it.[2]

One might argue that the Austrian case constitutes an extreme pro-

[2] The East German bloc system, which forces artificially created parties into collaboration with the State Party, has little similarity with the voluntary cartel described here, or, for that matter, with any of the other forms of coalition government. In order to protect the State Party and the other admitted political organizations from unfair competition, the DDR prevents the rise of any non-participating organization. Its government thus becomes a full-fledged compulsory cartel, dominated by one of its members, the State Party, with the latter allocating tidbits of power to the other participants, strictly according to its own devices. Moreover, any element of competition among the cartel participants themselves is excluded by the device of common electoral lists, with prearranged quotas of seats allocated to each participant. . . .

cedure responding to the particularities of a very difficult local situation in a weak nation. But while the Austrian arrangement may differ considerably from other European coalition governments, they all to a greater or lesser extent depart from the principle of concentrated responsibility and alternative government inherent in the classical formula. The deviation may be small when the main governmental coalition partner, as at present in Sweden or in the Federal Republic of Germany, or the major opposition party, as in Belgium, is so strong that the system in some respects, though by no means in all, operates as if there were a clear-cut government-opposition dichotomy. The deviation is bound to become much more accentuated in France . . . and in Italy, where the existence of a substantial opposition of principle forces the traditional parliamentary parties into a kind of compulsory cartel, irrespective of whether they form part of the government. If the regime is assailed by a substantial bloc of non-cooperators on both the right and the left flanks, or if cooperation can be bought only at unacceptable terms, opposition and opposition of principle may become almost identical.

In France, despite the presence of a substantial opposition of principle, either the working of the election system—especially tailored for that purpose in 1951—or, in the present assembly, the availability of blocs of overseas deputies for a variety of governmental combinations has left a certain margin within which individual political figures may whip varying party combinations into line. But from the viewpoint of the public at large the major difference between parliamentary groups and extraparliamentary mass movements operating within parliament as an opposition of principle tends to blot out more subtle distinctions. The French elections of January 1956 gave evidence that in the voter's mind the major decision lies between the traditional parliamentary groups and the opposition of principle. Transfer of votes to and from the opposition of principle is of greater importance than the internal transfer of votes among the various parliamentary groups. Acting in this fashion, however, the voter largely abdicates the role assigned to him under the classical government-opposition scheme, namely, to participate in the arbitration of conflicting leadership claims among parties operating within the framework of the regime. Thus the vote determines at best the margin that the groups loyal to the regime retain to form and reform their ephemeral alliances, and influences to a lesser degree the process of cabinet forming. This insensitivity of government formation toward popular currents allows the opposition of principle to contest the moral title of the government to represent the country, thus confronting the *pays légal* with the *pays réel*.

There may be neither abiding suspicion, leading to a watertight voluntary cartel, nor crisis of the regime, leading to a compulsory or near-compulsory cartel arrangement: coalition government may be simply a consequence of a well established multiparty system, as in present-day Holland, Weimar Germany, or interwar Czechoslovakia. But whatever the reason for the coalition arrangements, their establishment and practices are all bound to lead to deviations from the classical norm. The major government party may be concerned mainly with dislodging one partner or switching coalition partners. The opposition parties too may fight on various fronts; without the possibility of setting up a government of their own, they may concentrate energy on improving tactical chances of government participation. This purpose may involve subtle modulations of policy in regard to various governmental or other opposition parties. The possible variations and combinations are of great variety. Neither of the constellations is conducive to a sharp differentiation between government and opposition policies. The tortuous ways of the multiparty government and of multi-opposition tactics are the province of the political professional. The public at large looks at the results, while the more loyal party public may judge also by intentions.

Nevertheless, a multiparty coalition government need not be congenitally weak, nor need a divided opposition be impotent. Everything depends on the character of the various participants and their leadership, and on the temper of national political discourse and action. The maxim "where all govern, nobody governs" does not correctly describe all relevant factual situations. Prewar Czech and postwar Dutch governments, though they were difficult to assemble, show a reasonable record of stability and efficiency. On the other hand, multiparty government in the larger countries has more often than not been weak. The difficulty in bringing together various factions, the limited minimum program to which the coalition partners are willing to subscribe, and the concomitant attempts to restrict the mandate given to the parties' representatives in the cabinets inevitably provoke sharp counter-thrusts. Each cabinet minister will try to assert his maximum independence of his group, emphasize the dignity and independence of his office, and make the most of his assertion that he is His Majesty's or the nation's representative. He will therefore fall in most eagerly with the higher ranks of the bureaucracy who might liberate him from the embraces and demands of his party.

Such "liberation tendencies" are not restricted to representatives of multiparty coalition governments. But the fact of having been carried to power by a strong party, whether within the frame of the classic two-party system or as participant of a strong and stable coalition, enhances the chance that a minister will be willing and able to implant his party's value scale and program. Ministers of a weak coalition government are more predisposed to become instruments in the hands of their official advisers. It is in such cases that the always latent nineteenth-century antinomy, with parliament opposing the administration as an intrinsically inimical institution—so well known from the practice of presidential regimes—has a tendency to become universal. But unless the parties want to be relegated to the role of political prayer mills, this can be only a transitional and, from the viewpoint of the parliamentary regime, uncomfortable solution.

Political opposition as a continuing function presupposes the existence of a yardstick for governmental performance. The opposition on principle need not bother to unearth such a yardstick, as the very existence of the government is sufficient proof of its wickedness. In contrast, opposition within the confines of the parliamentary system presupposes some semblance of coherence if at least some vestige of a rational alternative to the government's policy is to be preserved.

This coherence may have its roots in program, ideology, and tradition. To be sure, coherence is always threatened, if for no other reason than the fact that in our day and age both government and opposition are always faced with unforeseen and unforeseeable situations requiring immediate action without their catechism offering satisfactory or, indeed, any answers. Gone are the days when a man could make up a program at the outset of his career to last all his life. But coherence is more likely with a party that has a tradition and some hold over its clientele, and therefore can afford the luxury of convictions, than with a marginal group whose survival, depending on the outcome of the next election, requires that it make its decisions on exclusively tactical grounds. The freedom of movement of the first is principally determined by the objective requirements of the situation it encounters when it comes to power; the latter is subjected to all the additional impediments stemming from its uneasy and always imperiled relations with its more comfortable competitors. To the extent that coalition government and multifarious opposition rest on quickly shifting and purely tactical alignments, they provide only an indistinct focus for the exercise of governmental responsibility and the complementary function of parliamentary opposition.

The question arises whether this desiccation of the opposition function that has here been followed through a number of variations can be attributed to more or less technical factors, and hence could be reversed by technical changes in election procedures or parliamentary rules. Can it be maintained, for example, that the voluntary cartel system of Austria, the erosion of the opposition function under the semi-compulsory cartels of France and Italy, the abuses of some multiparty coalition governments—all detrimental to the exercise of the classic opposition function—could be changed by the introduction of more suitable electoral systems or by different practices governing rules of no-confidence, dissolution, and the setting up of new governments? It seems unlikely. There is no meaningful connection between the form of the electoral system, the practices and malpractices of government formation, and the crisis of the concept of political opposition. It may be more rewarding to look into the incongruities between continental party systems and the social realities of the twentieth century.

Continental European parties are the remnants of intellectual and social movements of the nineteenth century. They have remained glued to the spots where the ebbing energy of such movements deposited them some decades ago. The more violent twentieth-century eruptions, fascism and communism, have surged much further, but in flowing back have petrified rather than envigorated the existing system. Postwar attempts at rationalization have produced some new variations, but have not eliminated the basic heritage of the parties. They were built around combinations of nineteenth-century class, occupational, and religious, or, as the case might be, anti-religious interests. How does this heritage relate to the most important stages of twentieth-century transformation?

From the viewpoint of political dynamics, the most important change is probably the emergence of a substantial new middle class of skilled workers, the middle ranks of white-collar people, and civil servants. All their work is done under instruction from superiors. Similarities of situation, thought processes, and expectations outweigh still existing traditional distinctions. Their consumption expectations, resting on the concept of increasing prosperity, as well as the demands they address to the community at large for sufficient protection against institutional and personal hazards of life, are identical. The cleavage that separates them from the more successful elements of the older independent middle classes—the artisans and peasants of medium-size holdings, both with enough capital equipment to profit from technological progress—is diminishing. The technological revolution is changing the outlook of these tradition-bound and conservative groups at the same time that it reduces their size. Increasingly enmeshed in the fortunes of the national economy, they now raise claims, identical with those of the new middle class, for guaranteed real-income levels and participation in social insurance schemes. To this extent the struggle between the independent old middle class and the employed new middle calss is more a struggle for similar goals than a clash of incompatible programs.

To the extent that all major parliamentary parties are permeated by the opinions and attitudes of these groups, strategic on account of both their size and the compactness of their professional organizations, one may justifiably say that diminished social polarization and diminished political polarization are going hand in hand. As Beatrice Webb expressed this particular phenomenon forty-odd years ago, "the landslide in England towards Social Democracy proceeds steadily, but it is the whole nation which is sliding, not the one class of manual workers."[3] We are faced with a somewhat languishing system of interparty competition which in many cases is even overshadowed by intraparty competition, the attempt of the various interest groups represented in one party to have an official party stand adopted that is maximally favorable to them.[4] The parliamentary

---

[3] Beatrice Webb, *Diaries, 1912–1924* (London 1952) p. 18.

[4] These trends appeared earliest and in the most succinct form in Sweden. See Herbert Tingsten, "Stability and Vitality in Swedish Democracy," in *Political Quarterly*, vol. 26 (1955) pp. 140–51: "As the general standard of values is so commonly accepted, the function of the state becomes so technical as to make politics appear as a kind of applied statistics." See also his statements (p. 148) on the nature of political parties.

party has thus become in a double sense a harmonizing agency. It harmonizes first the conflicting claims within its ranks, and on this basis participates in interparty adjustments on the governmental level.

The same harmonizing tendencies are potently reenforced by the contemporary opinion-forming process. The rise of the nineteenth-century party was inseparably linked with the growth of newspapers as vehicles for the creation and expression of public opinion. The newspapers, being politically oriented, and helping aspirants for political power to obtain recognition and spread their doctrine, were the handmaidens of emerging parliamentary government. Twentieth-century media of communication are not primarily politically oriented. They are business enterprises bent on maximizing profits from huge investments by catering to the inclinations and aspirations of a presumed near totality of readers and listeners, rather than appealing to an educated elite. They interlace the consumption expectations of their readers and listeners with the interests of their backers and advertisers. In order to fulfill this dual mission they preserve a maximum of neutrality, not only between the possibly conflicting interests of the various advertisers but also between the prejudices of the various strata of their readers and listeners. Resting on a presupposed harmony of interests among advertisers, financial backers, readers, and listeners, they are using the Hays-office technique of neutralizing and playing down divisive elements or transferring elements of conflict from the domestic to the international scene. The rise of consumer-oriented public-opinion formation has been one of the most powerful elements in the reduction of the political element to the semi-entertainment level.

Thus objective factors of social development and conscious efforts join in breaking down barriers between some strata of society and in creating what has been rather prematurely styled a unified middle-class society. This theme of a unified middle-class society has been pressed most consistently in postwar Germany; one author has recently gone so far as to approximate present-day conditions with the classless society, alluding in this context to the well known slogan of the transformation of the state into an organ for day-to-day administrative concerns.[5] It is open to question to what extent such utterances both overstress and generalize from some particular aspect of German postwar experiences. At any rate, analogous, if not always so pronounced, social and economic changes in other continental European countries have not been followed to the same degree by tendencies toward privatization which allow, as it were, for the transformation of political problems into administrative and technical routine; the persistence of a large opposition of principle in France and

---

[5] The extreme formulation is that of S. Landshut, "Die Auflösung der Klassengesellschaft," in *Gewerkschaftliche Monatshefte,* vol. 7 (1956) p. 451; in the same direction is H. Schelsky's speech, "Haben Wir heute noch eine Klassengesellschaft?" reprinted in *Das Parlament,* February 29, 1956.

Italy is inevitably leading to an emphasis on the repressive function of the state.

Moreover, the same process that has created a new middle class and lessened the distance between the old and new elements has everywhere uprooted diverse other social strata, and has so far failed to assign them a satisfactory position within the new society. The main victims of this process of transformation have been older people whose income has not kept pace with inflation, small peasant holders, small artisans and retailers without the capital to modernize their shops, and white-collar elements, economically outflanked by many groups of manual workers and unable to acquire a new feeling of "belonging" to compensate for the meagerness of their occupational existence. These changes, too, have indelibly marked the present party system. These strata form a steady source, even in present favorable economic circumstances, for a predominantly but not exclusively right-wing opposition of principle. By the same token, they are an element in the petrification of the traditional parliamentary parties.

To compete with the opposition of principle for this substantial vote, the parliamentary parties find it useful to fall back on their nineteenth-century heritage. This heritage may vary widely· with the socialists it may mean an occasional harking back to the class basis of political structure and its promise of a classless society; with the vaguely Christian catch-all parties, in vogue after the war, it may mean the concept of spiritual brotherhood or a specific religious appeal, transcending the cleavages of the day; and with the liberal or radical socialist parties it may refer to the autonomy claim of the non-collectivized individual, raised against both church and state. What we are here concerned with, however, is not the content of the often interchangeable doctrines but their survival as an element in keeping together or bringing again together the various elements of formerly unified groups, now torn asunder in the process of social transformation, employing here the unity of the working classes or there the image of a self-reliant independent middle class.

To be sure, not all—or even most—members of status-threatened disadvantaged and dissatisfied groups join the ranks of the opposition of principle. But this is probably less significant as indicating the continuing attraction of the parliamentary party than as emphasizing the fact that the primarily consumption-oriented thought process of their more fortunate brethren has become for them a natural habit. They momentarily accept the parliamentary party not because it struggles to uphold a lien on their grandfathers' social vision, but because they grant some advance credit to its promise to give a high priority to their material claims. Mistrustful of the more remote if all-embracing solutions of the opposition of principle, they accept the parliamentary party's arbitration regarding the extent to which their claims can at present be honored without conflicting with other weighty claims. But some claims have to be honored here and now if their loyalty to the parliamentary party is to last.

In the final analysis it is this urgency of group claims which militates against the parliamentary party's breathing for any length of time outside the precincts of government. It has greatly weakened the party's desire to don the robes of parliamentary opposition, as this would lessen its effectiveness in the adjudication of group claims, which in our time has become its raison d'être. If a party chooses voluntarily to go into opposition—which happens under conditions of a multiparty state—it does so for purely tactical reasons, in order to fasten the burden of unpopular policies on some political competitor, or in order to be free to outbid the opposition of principle by espousing some manifestly inflated group claims.

The rise of the consumption-oriented individual of mass society thus sets the stage for the shrinking of the ideologically oriented nineteenth-century party. After the unlimited extension of the party concept, first in the traditional *Weltanschauungs* party and more recently in the totalitarian movement, its recent reduction to a rationally conceived vehicle of interest representation becomes noticeable.[6] By and large, European parliamentary parties are reducing their special ideological and material offerings. Instead, they substitute a demand for a wide variety of ever expanding community services, open on a basis of eqality to whole categories of citizens. Unlike the totalitarian movements they are not equipped to overrun the state machine; at best they aspire to participate in the rewards and premiums it offers. In reminiscence of tradition, or more likely as a planned investment in a public career, individuals may still become party workers. But the tendency for the party to exercise a brokerage function for specific interest groups is present, and is likely to become more accentuated as time goes on. Thus the non-professional in politics is destined to be relegated to a back seat. The interest group, however, as distinct from the individual party member, manifests a loyalty that is limited and contingent. Not only may this loyalty be transferred to more useful political groups, but support may be given simultaneously to groups competing in the political arena. . . .

[The] transition from the ideologically oriented continental party of earlier times to the more limited congeries of interest-oriented groups is one of the elements behind the erosion of the classic opposition. But the demise of the opposition is not tantamount to the complete dismantling of the European party, relegating it to some form of procedural device to be used for every comer to fight particular and eternally changing issues, as

---

[6] Of course, there are exceptions. Israel, with its odd mixture of avant-garde and arrière-garde elements, responds to a conscious transfer of traditional European institutional patterns and the pressing material needs of the moment. Its parties are conceived of both as ideological entities and as vehicles for special party-connected customer services. An intensive party life results. See Benjamin Azkin, "The Role of Parties in Israeli Democracy," in *Journal of Politics*, vol. 17 (1955) p. 507; but note especially his remark on page 519, visualizing the possibility of a receding of direct intervention of parties into social matters in the foreseeable future.

the stereotype of the political party in the United States would have it. Other factors still favor some measure of party cohesion. One is the existence of an opposition of principle, threatening the continuation of present political patterns. Another is the fact that there are fairly constant elements—slurred and overlapping though they may be—determining which type of interest a party may pick up.

Thus the parliamentary party may continue as a relatively stable entity. But the unifying and leveling element of the mass media and a certain lessening of social polarization mark a definite stage in the decline of this delicate part of our political heritage, the classic parliamentary opposition. It is in this sense that the Austrian practice of coalition pacts with built-in opposition devices commands interest. It presents a limited survival and revival of the opposition concept at a time when opposition ideologies either have come to serve as handmaidens of total and revolutionary social and political change or are becoming downgraded to the role of relatively meaningless etiquettes and advertisement slogans within the framework of interest representation.

30. POLITICIZATION IN FRANCE AND THE UNITED STATES*

Philip E. Converse and Georges Dupeux

THE TURBULENCE of French politics has long fascinated observers, particularly when comparisons have been drawn with the stability or, according to one's point of view, the dull complacency of American political life. Profound ideological cleavages in France, the occasional threat of civil war, rather strong voter turnout, the instability of governments and republics, and the rise and fall of "flash" parties like the R.P.F. in 1951, the Poujadists in 1956, and the U.N.R. in 1958 have all contributed to the impression of a peculiar intensity in the tenor of French political life.

It is a sign of progress in the study of political behavior that such symptoms no longer seem to form a self-evident whole. We feel increasingly obliged, for example, to take note of the level in the society at which the symptoms are manifest. Most of our impressions of the French scene reflect only the behavior of French political leadership. Growing familiarity with survey data from broad publics has schooled us not to assume perfect continuity between the decision-making characteristics of a leadership and the predispositions of its rank and file. The extremism of the military elite in Algeria or ideological intransigence in the French

* From "Politicization of the Electorate in France and the United States," *The Public Opinion Quarterly* (Spring, 1962), pp. 1–24. Article and footnotes abridged by the editors. Reprinted by permission of *The Public Opinion Quarterly*.

National Assembly are in themselves poor proof that the shipyard worker in Nantes has political reflexes which differ from those of the shipyard worker in Norfolk.

We feel increasingly obliged, moreover, to discriminate between some of these well-known symptoms of turbulence, for they no longer point in a common direction as clearly as was once assumed. Two signs which unquestionably reflect mass electoral behavior in France provide a case in point. Turnout levels in France are indeed high relative to those in the United States,[1] suggesting that, in the politically indifferent strata of the electorate where nonvoting is considered, political motivations are more intense. On the other hand, we now doubt that the rise and fall of "flash" parties are parallel symptoms of intense involvement. Rather, it seems likely that such episodes represent spasms of political excitement in unusually hard times on the part of citizens whose year-in, year-out involvement in political affairs is abnormally weak.[2] Obviously, for France and the United States, the basic traditions of a two-party or a multiparty system affect the likelihood that the flash party phenomenon will occur. But other things being equal, it seems that such phenomena are hardly signals of long-term public involvement in politics but betray instead a normal weak involvement. The durably involved voter tends toward strong partisan commitments, and his behavior over time stabilizes party fortunes within a nation.

Other less direct indicators add doubt as to the high involvement of the broad French public. Demographically, French society differs from the American in its lesser urbanization and lower mean formal education. Intranational studies have persistently shown higher political involvement among urban residents and, more strongly still, among people of more advanced education. While cross-national extrapolation of such data may be precarious, it does leave further room to question our intuitive impressions.

We intend in this paper to examine comparative data on the French and American publics in an effort to determine more precisely the locus of Franco-American differences in these matters.[3] We shall consider the locus in qualitative terms, covering an extended series of political charactersistics which run from expressions of involvement, acts of participation, and information seeking to orientations whereby the voter links party alterna-

---

[1] They are not, of course, outstanding against the backdrop provided by other Western European nations.

[2] For a fuller discussion, see Angus Campbell, Philip E. Converse, Warren E. Miller, and Donald E. Stokes, *The American Voter* (New York: John Wiley & Sons, Inc., 1960), Chapter 15.

[3] The French data were gathered in three waves of a national cross-section sample in the fall of 1958, during the constitutional referendum launching the Fifth Republic and the ensuing legislative elections. Informal cross-national collaboration prior to the 1958 French study led to a French interview schedule permitting more rigorous comparative analysis than unrelated studies usually offer.

tives to the basic ideological issues in the society. We shall throughout maintain an interest as well in a vertical locus of differences. That is, we shall think of the two electorates as stratified from persistent nonvoters at the bottom, through the large middle mass of average voters, to citizens who engage in some further partisan activity, and thence by extrapolation to the higher leadership whose highly visible behavior is so frequently the source of our cross-national impressions. Such extrapolation is necessary, of course, because it is unlikely that the handful of "activists" whom we can distinguish at the top layer of both national samples include more than one or two persons who have ever had any direct hand in a leadership decision of even a parochial party organization or political interest group.

INVOLVEMENT, PARTICIPATION, AND INFORMATION SEEKING

While a relatively large number of comparisons may be drawn with regard to simple manifestations of political involvement in the two countries, these comparisons vary widely in quality. Broad differences in institutions and political practices in the two societies can serve to channel public interest in different directions. The French political poster, often a full-blown campaign document, is addressed to other goals than the American political billboard, and hence the reading of such posters in the two societies is in no sense comparable activity. Similarly, the national control of the domestic airwaves in France means that two media of communication are given a totally different cast than in the United States. This fact, coupled with reduced access to radio or television sets in France, renders the attention paid by the two publics to such political broadcasts fundamentally incomparable. Or, in a different vein, certain manifestations of involvement are known to vary widely in their frequency within a nation from one type of election to another, or for the same type of election between periods of crisis and troughs of routine politics. While an extended American time series has provided some useful norms, these were more difficult to find for the French data. In general, then, we shall elaborate upon only a few of the most solid comparisons, referring summarily to the flavor conveyed by other, looser comparisons.

Given the broad institutional differences between the two societies, it might seem useful to draw contrasts between self-estimates of psychological involvement between the two nations, however differently institutions might channel the ultimate behavioral expressions of such interest. While the data permit a number of matches between questions on political interest, posed at comparable times with comparable wording and with superfically comparable alternatives, one hesitates at comparisons which depend on crude "amount words" such as "very," "fairly," and the like. Cautiously, however, it may be observed that Americans gauge their interest in their elections at a rather higher level than do the French. Two to five times as many French respondents indicated that they were "not at all" interested in the 1958 elections as is the tendency for Americans with regard to their presidential elections; three to four times as many Americans say that they are "very" interested. Distributions from France in the more normal political year of 1953 show slightly higher levels of expressed interest, but even this distribution fails to approach the most unenthusiastic American distributions collected at the time of off-year congressional elections. For what it is worth, then, it is relatively hard to get French citizens to confess much interest in their elections.

More solid are comparisons of reported acts of political participation selected as involving comparable motivation in the two systems: membership in political organizations, attendance at political rallies, and attempts to influence the political choice of others through informal communication. As Figure 1 suggests, the cross-national similarities on these items are

FIG. 1. Rates of several forms of political participation, France and the United States.

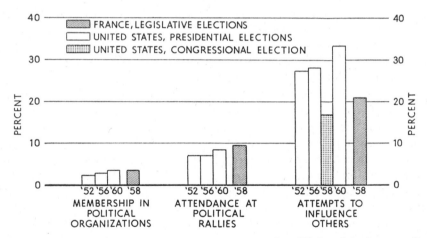

impressive. Furthermore, we can examine such additional points as the number of meetings attended by those French and Americans who do attend political gatherings. Graphs of the frequency of attendance by attender are almost indistinguishable between the two countries. The mean number of meetings attended among those who attend at all is in both cases a slight fraction over two. In sum, it is hard to imagine that any slight divergences in rates of attendance are crucial in any dramatic differences between the two systems.

Data were collected in both countries as well with regard to dependence on the mass media for political information. Here one of the most excellent bases for comparison which the data afford is provided by reports of the regularity with which political news about the elections was followed in daily newspapers. Although the structured alternatives again involve "amount words," there is a more tangible standard for responses

implicit in the rhythm of newspaper production. "Regularly" or
"never," when applied to readership of daily papers, has a common
meaning in any language. Furthermore, we find empirically that responses
to the newspaper questions show much higher stability for individuals
over time than the direct interest questions. It is clear that we are dealing
here with stable habits which are reliably reported.

When we compare distributions from the two countries (Table 1),

TABLE 1

FREQUENCY OF NEWSPAPER READING FOR POLITICAL INFORMATION
(*In per cent*)

	France, 1958		United States, 1960	
	Post-referendum	Post-election	Post-election	
Regulièrement	19	18	44	Regularly
Souvent	12	10	12	Often
De temps en temps	25	29	16	From time to time
Très rarement	19	21	7	Just once in a great while
Jamais	25	22	21	Never
	100	100	100	

there seems little doubt of higher American devotion to newspapers as a
source of political information. Furthermore, the French citizen appears
also to monitor other media for political information less. Thus, for
example, he is less likely to have a television or radio set than his American
counterpart; but even among those French who possess sets, attention to
political broadcasts is markedly less than for comparable Americans. As we
have observed, these latter differences are not in themselves proof of lesser
French motivation, since the choices offered through the airwaves are not
comparable cross-nationally. But such facts, along with further comparisons as to magazine reading, indicate that lower French attention to
political material in the newspapers is not compensated for from other
sources. Since elite political competition in France, even when reduced to
simplest terms, is considerably more complex than two-party competition
in the United States, it is ironic that the French voter exposes himself less
faithfully to the flow of current political information. . . .

By way of summary, then, comparisons up to this point create a general
sense of Franco-American similarity, with occasional mild divergences
suggesting stronger American political involvement. . . . In a rough way,
we may observe that the American data seem to show somewhat higher
motivation in the middle ranges, with cross-national differences narrowing
near the very top, and perhaps even showing a slight French advantage.

Interestingly enough, this pattern would describe as well the cumulative frequency distributions expressing differences in years of formal education in the two countries. This identity is, of course, no proof that education accounts for the involvement divergences. But it does remind us that these patterns, if they differ cross-nationally at all, may partake of the sharper discontinuities in France between a tiny elite and the remainder of the population that one suspects for a variety of characteristics, and can readily demonstrate for education.[4]

PARTISAN ORIENTATIONS

The gross similarities between the two publics in apparent political interest do not, to be sure, remove the possibility that the Frenchman in his interested moments may respond to politics in much different terms than his American counterpart. Actually, when we consider the character of partisan ties felt by citizens in the two countries, we strike upon some contrasts of great magnitude.

If Americans are asked to locate themselves relative to the American party system, 75 per cent classify themselves without further probing as psychological members of one of the two major parties, or of some minor party. In France, somewhat before the elections, less than 45 per cent of those who did not refuse to answer the question were able to classify themselves in one of the parties or splinter groups, while another 10 to 15 per cent associated themselves with a more or less recognizable broad *tendance* ("left," "right," a labor union, etc.). The cross-national differences of 20 to 30 per cent are sufficiently large here to contribute to fundamental differences in the flavor of partisan processes in the two electorates. For a long time, we wrote off these differences as products of incomparable circumstances or of reticence on the part of the French concerning partisanship, most of which was being expressed not as refusal to answer the question, but as some other evasion. As we grew more familiar with the data, however, these differences took on vital new interest.

The hypothesis of concealed partisanship was very largely dispelled by a close reading of the actual interviews. It is undeniable that nearly 10 per cent of the French sample explicitly refused to answer the question, as compared with a tiny fraction in the United States. However, we have

---

[4] We shall not treat Franco-American differences in vote turnout, save to observe that they are probably more institutional than motivational. American registration requirements in many states are such that an American is persistently confronted by an institutional barrier which is rarely erected in France. It can be argued most strongly that the act of getting somewhere to register demands higher political motivation than getting to the polls on Election Day. Indeed, over half the Americans who fail to vote in major elections blame such registration barriers as change in residence, failure to renew on time, etc. If such reports are credited, the registration toll in the United States would easily make up the apparent Franco-American differences.

already subtracted this group from the accounting. Beyond the explicit refusals, the remarks and explanations which often accompanied statements classified as "no party," or as "don't know which party," had a very genuine air about them which made them hard to read as hasty evasions. No few of these respondents were obviously embarrassed at their lack of a party; some confessed that they just hadn't been able to keep track of which party was which. The phrase "je n'y ai jamais pensé" was extremely common. Others indicated that they found it too hard to choose between so many parties; some indicated preferences for a specific political leader but admitted that they did not know which party he belonged to or, more often, had no interest in the identify of his party, whatever it might be. Others, forming a tiny minority of the nonparty people, rejected the notion of parties with some hostility.

It became clear, too, that people reporting no party attachments were distinct on other grounds from those who willingly classified themselves as close to a party. On our vertical involvement dimension, for example, they tended to fall in the bottom stratum of the least involved, just as the paper-thin stratum unable to choose a party in the United States consists heavily of the least involved. Demographically, these nonparty people were disproportionately housewives, poorly educated, young, and the other familiar statuses which tend to be uninformed and uninvolved.

Among actual party identifiers in France there was further interesting variation in the character of the party objects to which reference was made. A very few linked themselves with small new ideological splinter groups which had developed during the political crises of 1958. For these people, it was not enough to indicate that they felt closest to the Radical-Socialists, for example: they had to specify that they were Mendesists or anti-Mendesists, Valoisiens, and the like. Most identifiers suffered no difficulty in seeing themselves as "Radical-Socialists," completely shattered though the party was. Others, perceiving the system even more grossly, linked themselves only with a broad *tendance*. On involvement measures these groupings showed the expected differences: the grosser the discrimination, the lower the involvement.

In other ways as well it was clear that the extreme ideological fractionation of parties in France has few roots in the mass population, members of which simply pay too little attention to politics to follow the nicer discriminations involved. When asked whether the number of parties in France was too great, about right, or too few, 97 per cent of those responding said there were too many parties, and less than 1 per cent said there were too few. In response to an ensuing question as to the desirable number of parties, the mean of the number seen as optimal was 3.5 for the handful of adherents of the new ideological splinters, 3.0 for the partisans of the traditional mass parties, and less than 2.8 among those who had formed no party attachments. Perhaps the most apt expression of the problem of partisan fractionation and discrimination came from the naïve respondent who opined that France should have two or three parties, "enough to express the differences in opinion."

The fact that large proportions of the French public have failed to form any very strong attachments to one of the political parties should not be taken to mean that these people are totally disoriented in the French party system. In particular, a sensitivity to the gulf separating the Communist Party from the remainder of French parties does pervade the mass public. There seems to be less confusion as to the identity of the Communist Party than for any of the other parties; and for the bulk of non-Communists, the Communist Party is a pariah. There are some nonidentifiers who appear to shift from Communist to non-Communist votes with abandon, and were all of these votes to fall to the Communists in the same election, the Party would undoubtedly exceed its previous high-water mark in its proportion of the French popular vote. At the same time, however, one cannot help but be impressed by the number of respondents who, while indicating they were not really sure what they were in partisan terms, indicated as well at one point or another in the interview that they were not only non-Communist but anti-Communist. In other words, were the descriptions of party adherents to proceed simply in terms of a Communist, non-Communist division, the proportion of ready self-classification would advance considerably toward the American figure, and would probably exceed that which could be attained by any other two-class division in France.

Nevertheless, the limited party attachments outside the Communist camp in France retain strong theoretical interest, as they seem so obviously linked to a symptom of turbulence which is clearly not an elite phenomenon alone—the flash party. With a very large proportion of the electorate feeling no anchoring loyalty, it is not surprising that a new party can attract a large vote "overnight," or that this base can be so rapidly dissolved. Furthermore, there is a problem here that is peculiarly French, in that the low proportion of expressed attachments cannot simply be seen as a necessary consequence of a multiparty system per se. Fairly comparable data from Norway, where six parties are prominent, show party attachments as widespread as those in the two-party United States.[5]

The French sample was asked further to recall the party or *tendance* which the respondent's father had supported at the polls. Here the departure from comparable American data became even more extreme. . . . Of those Americans in 1958 having had a known father who had resided in the United States as an American citizen, thereby participating in American political life, 86 per cent could characterize his partisanship, and another 5 per cent knew enough of his political behavior to describe him as apolitical or independent. Among comparable French respondents, only 26 per cent could link fathers with any party or with the vaguest of

---

[5] Angus Campbell and Henry Valen, "Party Identification in Norway and the United States," *Public Opinion Quarterly*, Vol. 25, 1961, pp. 505–25.

tendances (including such responses as "il a toujours voté pour la patrie"), and another 3 per cent could describe the father's disposition as variable or apolitical. In other words, among those eligible to respond to the question, 91 per cent of Americans could characterize their father's political behavior, as opposed to 29 per cent of the French.

It goes without saying that differences of this magnitude rarely emerge from individual data in social research. And they occur at a point of prime theoretical interest. We have long been impressed in the United States by the degree to which partisan orientations appear to be passed hereditarily, from generation to generation, through families. It has seemed likely that such transmission is crucial in the stability of American partisan voting patterns. Therefore, we find it startling to encounter a situation in which huge discontinuities seem to appear in this transmission.

What do the French responses concerning paternal partisanship really mean? As best we can determine, they mean what they appear to mean: the French father is uncommunicative about his political behavior before his children, just as he is more reserved in the interviewing situation than Americans or Norwegians. It seems highly unlikely, for example, that Franco-American differences in recall represent French concealment: large numbers of the French willing to speak of their own party preference are unable to give the father's preference of a generation before, and explicit refusals to answer, while attaining 10 per cent or more where own partisanship is at stake, are almost nonexistent for paternal partisanship.

Furthermore, we have come to reject the possibility that the bulk of the Franco-American difference is some simple consequence of the more fluid and complex French party system. Responses to a similar question in the Norwegian multiparty system look like our American results, and not like the French. Nor is there reason to believe that the Frenchman has trouble finding comparable modern terms for the party groupings of a generation ago. As we have observed, the respondent was invited to give a rough equivalent of his father's position in terms of *tendance*. Moreover, where there are any elaborations of "I don't know" captured in the interview, the consistent theme seemed to be that the respondent did not feel he had ever known his father's position ("je n'ai jamais su"; "je ne lui ai jamais demandé"; "il ne disait rien à ses enfants"; "il n'en parlait jamais"). Finally, if special problems were occasioned on the French side by the changing party landscape over time, we should certainly expect that older French respondents would have greater difficulty locating their fathers politically than would younger respondents. They do not: the tabulation by age in France shows only the slightest of variations attributable to age, and these lend no support to the hypothesis (e.g., slightly less knowledge of father's position for children under thirty) and are variations which may be found in the comparable American table as well.

If we accept the proposition, then, that there are basic discontinuities in

the familial transmission of party orientations in France, all of our theory
would argue that weaker party attachments should result in the current
generation. The data do indeed show a remarkable association between
the two phenomena, once again involving differences of 30 per cent or
more. Both French and Americans who recall their father's partisanship are
much more likely themselves to have developed party loyalties than are
people who were not aware of their father's position. Of still greater
importance are the more absolute Franco-American similarities. Setting
aside those people whose fathers were noncitizens, dead, apolitical, or
floaters, or who refused to answer the question, we can focus on the core
of the comparison (in per cent):

	Know Father's Party		Do Not Know Father's Party	
	France	U.S.	France	U.S.
Proportion having some partisan self-location (party or vague *tendance*)	79.4	81.6	47.7	50.7
Proportion that these are of total electorate	24	75	63	8

Where the socialization processes have been the same in the two
societies, the results in current behavior appear to be the same, in rates of
formation of identification. The strong cross-national differences lie in the
socialization processes. In other words, we have come full circle again: we
have encountered large national differences but have once again succeeded
in moving them to the marginals of the table. This is our best assurance
that our measurements are tapping comparable phenomena.

Partisan attachments appear therefore to be very weakly developed
within the less politically involved half of the French electorate. While
undoubtedly a large variety of factors, including the notoriety which the
French parties had acquired in the later stages of the Fourth Republic,
have helped to inhibit their development, more basic discontinuities of
political socialization in the French family appear to be making some
persisting contribution as well. Of course, similar lack of party attachment
does occur among people indifferent to politics in the American and
Norwegian systems as well; but the strata of unidentified people are
thinner in these systems and do not extend greatly above that layer of
persistent nonvoters which is present in any system.

The link between an electorate heavily populated with voters feeling
no continuing party attachments and a susceptibility to "flash" parties is
an obvious one. It must be recognized at the outset, of course, that such
phenomena arise only under the pressure of social, political, or economic
dislocations occuring in some segment of the population, thereby generating an elite which wishes to organize a movement and a public which is

restive. This means that even a system highly susceptible to such phenomena is not likely to experience them when it is functioning smoothly:
their prevalence in postwar France cannot be divorced from the severe
dislocations the society has been undergoing. Once misfortunes breed
discontent, however, the proportions of partisans in an electorate is a
datum of fundamental significance. One cannot fail to be impressed by the
agility with which the strong partisan can blame the opposing party for
almost any misfortune or deny the political relevance of the misfortune if
some opposing party cannot conceivably be blamed. Hence, where partisans are concerned, misfortunes do relatively little to shift voting patterns.
Independents, however, have no stake in such reinforcements and defenses
and move more massively in response to grievances. In France, the
institutions which conduce to a multiparty system make the organization
of new party movements more feasible from an elite point of view than it
is likely to be under two-party traditions. At the same time, the presence of
a large number of French voters who have developed no continuing
attachments to a particular party provides an "available" mass base for
such movements. This available base is no necessary concomitant of a
multiparty system, but is rather a peculiarity of the current French
scene.

PARTIES AND POLICY CONTROVERSY

Whatever differences exist in partisan orientations, no assessment of
politicization would be complete without consideration of the manner in
which ideological conflict is worked out through the party system. If
parties are recognized at all in the classical view of democratic process,
they are relegated to a distinctly secondary position: they are means to
policy ends, and should be judged by the citizen accordingly. In this light,
the number of Americans with strong party loyalty and a poor sense of
what either party stands for in policy terms represents a distinct perversion
of the democratic process. In this light, too, weaker partisan orientations
in the French populace might simply mean a relegation of party to second
rank, with a primary focus on policy goals.

At an elite level, of course, there are distinct Franco-American differences in the phrasing of the means-end relation between party and policy,
and these contrasts weigh heavily in our impressions of differences in
quality of political process between the two systems. That is, while
French political elites are not insensitive to party formations as instruments toward policy goals, the fact remains that parties are split and reshaped with relative freedom in order that the party may be the purest
possible expression, not only of the politician's position on a single basic
issue dimension, but of the total configuration of positions adopted on
cross-cutting issue dimensions. On the American side, remarkable policy
accommodations are made to preserve the semblance of party unity, and

party competition for votes "in the middle" leads to a considerable blurring of interparty differences on policy. The crucial role of basic political institutions in stimulating either multipartite or bipartite trends has often been discussed, and whether French elite activities would survive long under American ground rules is a moot point. We may consider, however, whether the ideological clarity or intransigence associated with French political elites and the policy compromise or confusion which characterizes the American party system reflect properties of their mass publics.

Data have been collected in both countries concerning reactions to a variety of issues confronting the two systems. While both sets of items must be regarded as only the crudest samplings of hypothetical issue universes, selection on both sides was performed in an attempt to tap some of the most basic controversies of the period. In France, three items were devoted to the classic socio-economic left and right, with one concerning the role of labor and the other two the relative roles of government and private enterprise in housing; two more involved the clerical question; a sixth item had to do with military expenditures and national prestige; a seventh concerned the freedom of the press to criticize the government. Of eight American questions, two dealt with social-welfare legislation and a third with the relative role of government and private enterprise in housing and utilities, covering the classic right and left; two more dealt with the government's role in racial matters (FEPC and school desegregation); and three others were concerned with the internationalist or isolationist posture of the government in foreign affairs. All questions were in Likert scale form.

We shall focus upon three properties of these issues which we can more or less crudely measure in the two countries: (1) the degree to which public opinion is sharply crystallized on each issue; (2) the degree to which opinion within the two publics is polarized on each; and (3) for each issue, the degree to which individual opinion is associated with partisan preference. Assuming the items do give fair coverage to most primary issue dimensions in the two nations, we are interested to see if opinion in France at a mass level appears more sharply crystallized or polarized, and to assess the manner in which policy concerns are linked with party preference. As before, we shall distinguish layers of both populations in terms of partisan involvement. At the top, we isolate as political "actives" those people who were either party members or reported attending two or more political rallies in the respective election campaigns, a group which amounts to 5 to 7 per cent within each population and hence is sufficiently large for analysis. We also continue to distinguish between party identifiers (three-quarters of the American population, but half of the French) and nonidentifiers. . . .

It is interesting to compare the stability over time of reactions to parties with the stability of responses to these "basic" controversies. . . . This assessment is rather difficult on the French side in view of the frequent indeterminacy of party locations, however, it seems that, in a comparable period of time, affective reactions to the parties are more stable than issue reactions even in France. In the United States, we know that partisan reactions show dramatically greater stability than the issue responses. Most important, perhaps, is the failure of data . . . to support an image of the mass French public as remaining aloof from party sentiments while hewing dogmatically to ideological goals. Beyond the political actives, stability of issue opinion seems unimpressive, and, for the majority of French voters without party attachments, the articulation of party choice with any of the issue dimensions covered here is slight indeed. . . .

While the instability of opinion in both nations is of primary interest . . . , several further comparisons may be summarized. The major cross-national contrast comes in the party-relatedness column, where French actives and partisans show much higher coefficients than their American counterparts. The most obvious American phenomenon which blunts interparty policy differences is the disparity between the Southern and non-Southern wings of the Democratic Party. While setting aside the Southern Democratic rank and file does not remove the perceptual problem posed for Northern Democrats who may find the top leaders of their party at odds on many issues, . . . even for actives, this regional limitation does not begin to bring the American coefficients up to the French level. While the higher French coefficients are no statistical necessity, it is likely that, in practice, closer party-relatedness is inevitable in the multiparty system. The interparty differences in opinion among French *partisans* appear to lie in about the same range as those found in Norway. However, as we have seen, party attachments are more prevalent in Norway than in France; when the unidentified enter the French electorate in an actual vote, it is likely that individual issue opinions receive less clear expression across the electorate as a whole than is the case in Norway.

Beyond this primary contrast, [there are] . . . impressive . . . cross-national similarities. Actives in both countries show more highly crystallized opinions, and usually more polarized opinions as well, although American actives differ less sharply and consistently from their mass public than do French actives. In neither country do identifiers differ reliably from nonidentifiers with regard to crystallization or polarization of opinion. In both countries, however, there are quite reliable differences in party-relatedness, not only between actives and the remaining 95 per cent of the population, but between identifiers and nonidentified. In other words, while the partisan manner of relating to the political process makes little difference in basic opinion formation save for the extremely active, the translation of these attitudes to some kind of party choice seems increasingly haphazard as party attachments become weaker.

Throughout these comparisons, however, we may remain struck by the fact that the "slope" is steeper on the French side: the differences between actives and mass are large relative to those in the United States. From the upper end of this steep slope, one might wish to extrapolate to the sharp and rigid cleavages on policy matters for which French elites are noted; for our purposes, it is sufficient to observe that these cleavages blur rapidly and lose their tone in the mass of the French electorate.

Finally, it should be observed that the issues seem to sort themselves into two rough categories in both nations: (1) emotional-symbol issues involving some of the more gross group conflicts within the two societies (racial in the United States, religious in France, along with items which touch in a direct way upon labor as an interest group), which show relatively high crystallization and polarization; and (2) more complex questions of relations between the state and private enterprise which, along with all foreign policy issues, tend to be less crystallized.

These differences in crystallization are scarcely surprising, as the objects and means involved in the second group of issues are clearly more remote from the common experience of the man-in-the-street. Yet the pattern is ironic, for the issues which show a stronger resonance in both mass publics tend to be those which both elites make some attempt to soft-pedal, in favor of direct debate over such more "ideological" matters as arrangements between state and private enterprise. The more resonant issues are not dead, of course, and are used for tactical advantage by elites in both countries. Calculations of vote gain are made in the United States on the basis of the religion of the nominee, and the clerical question in France has been resuscitated repeatedly as a handy crowbar to split apart government coalitions. At the same time, however, there is genuine elite effort to keep such cleavage issues in the background: the American public is told that religion is not a proper criterion for candidate choice, and the battleground for elite debate on the racial issue is usually displaced quite notably from race itself in the modern period. Similarly, much sophisticated French opinion has for some time argued that even the secondary role which the clerical question has been playing in elite debate exaggerates its importance.

Given this common background, the different manner in which the two types of controversy weave into partisan choices in the two countries is fascinating. In France, there is fair coincidence between the ordering of issues in terms of party-relatedness and the ordering on the other two properties. The clerical questions, for example, are highly crystallized and polarized, and show high levels of party-relatedness as well. The structure of party competition is such that, elite values notwithstanding, these emotional cleavages achieve prominent partisan expression. Such is not the case in the United States: there is little coincidence between the party-relatedness of issues and the other two properties. Indeed, the racial issue finds little clear party expression, while the "elite" issue concerning government and private enterprise, one of the least crystallized issues, is at the same time one of the most party-related across the full electorate.

Where mass or elite control of issue controversy is concerned, then, the two systems have rather paradoxical outcomes. By conception, the French party system is geared to elites, encouraging them to a multifaceted ideological expression which is too complex for most of the public to encompass. At the same time, the multidimensional clarity of party positions serves to return a measure of control to part of the public, for the more involved citizens can single out certain dimensions to reduce the system to manageable simplicity. These reductions are naturally made in terms of issues which are more resonant in the public, even if these are not the dimensions which the elites might wish to stress. The American system is less elite in conception; it is sufficiently simple in its gross characteristics that it is easier for the common citizen to follow it with only limited attention. But this simplification requires great blurring of party differences across most of the universe of possible issues, and the differences which are maintained are those which the competing elites select as battlegrounds. Hence, control of controversy which can be given partisan expression is, paradoxically, more nearly in elite hands.

CONCLUSIONS

We have attempted to sort through a number of those characteristics of French politics which add up to vague impressions of intense French politicization, in order to identify more precise loci for Franco-American differences. It appears likely that the more notable of these differences stem from the actions of elites and require study and explanation primarily at this level, rather than at the level of the mass electorate. While certain peculiarities reminiscent of French political elites are visible in the most politically active twentieth of the French population, these peculiarities fade out rapidly as one approaches the more "representative" portions of the broad French public.

It is unlikely that the common French citizen devotes any greater portion of his attention to politics than does his American counterpart, and he may well give less. His behavior is constrained within a much different set of political institutions, and these differences have important consequences for the character of his political behavior, including the opportunity of closer articulation between any crystallized opinions he may hold and an appropriate party instrument. However, the data give no striking reason to believe that the French citizen, either through the vagaries of national character, institutions, or history, is predisposed to form political opinions which are more sharply crystallized or which embrace a more comprehensive range of political issues than do comparable Americans. On both sides, opinion formation declines as objects and arrangements become more remote from the observer; and much of politics, for both French and Americans, is remote. Hence the proliferation of choices offered by the multiparty system is itself a mixed blessing: it is capitalized upon only by the more politically interested segments of the electorate, and appears to represent "too much" choice to be managed comfortably by citizens whose political involvement is average or less.

Over the range of characteristics surveyed, only one striking difference at the level of the mass public was encountered which seemed more uniquely French than the multiparty system itself. There is evidence of a widespread absence of party loyalties, a phenomenon which can be empirically associated with peculiarities in the French socialization process. This characteristic has obvious links with the major symptom of French political turbulence, which is based on the behavior of the mass population rather than that of elites—the current availability of a mass base for flash party movements under circumstances of distress.

31. THE SOCIALIST DILEMMA IN EUROPE*
H. Stuart Hughes

FOR A FULL decade now—for a span of years that is gradually coming into focus as a historical epoch in its own right—the major countries of Western Europe have been living under conservative rule. This situation has created new and unanticipated problems in the functioning of democratic institutions. More particularly, it has raised an agonizing dilemma for the chief forces of loyal, constitutional opposition—the Social Democratic and Labor parties.

The turn toward conservatism came first in Italy. By his crushing electoral victory over the Communist-Socialist bloc in April 1948, Prime Minister Alcide de Gasperi inaugurated a period of Christian Democratic rule that has persisted ever since. A year and a half later, the new state of Western Germany was launched under similar auspices; here also government by Christian Democrats has proved unshakable. In June 1951, the French electorate for the first time since the war sent a conservative majority to the National Assembly. The following autumn, the British did the same thing. In the British case the reversal proved decisive: the narrow Conservative majority of 1951 was steadily enlarged in succeeding elections. In France the trend to the right appeared to be temporarily checked by fifteen months of Socialist rule in 1956 and 1957. But this government in fact existed on conservative sufferance, and on the crucial issues of colonial policy—Suez and Algeria—it followed a nationalist and imperial course. The coming to power of De Gaulle in 1958 reaffirmed a drift toward conservative solutions that had already been apparent for seven years.

* From *Dissent* (Autumn, 1961), pp. 432–40. Reprinted by permission of *Dissent*.

The result of this succession of conservative triumphs has been a "one and a half" party system. On the surface it tends toward the two-party norm which Anglo-Saxons have traditionally considered ideal. And in all fairness one must grant that it marks a simplification of the multiparty competition which vexed European democracy in the inter-war period and was at least partially responsible for the turn to fascist solutions in the 1930s. But the real point about the evolution of the 1950s and 1960s has not been its gradual elimination of minor parties as serious contenders. It has rather been the creation of a two-party system with a crucial difference—a hybrid state of affairs in which one of the parties seems to stand almost no chance of electoral victory.

The outlines of this paradoxical situation first appeared in Germany. As Chancellor Adenauer's Christian Democrats raised their electoral margin every four years—as the Social Democrats lost in 1949, 1953, and 1957 . . . [and 1961] . . . —it began to appear that the steady squeezing out of lesser contenders was not having the expected effect of equalizing the two major parties. The near-disappearance of the Communists and the Refugees, the German Party and even the Free Democrats, as important electoral formations simply strengthened Adenauer's existing lead. Two years later a similar tendency became evident in Britain. By 1959, after three successive electoral defeats—and four elections in which the Labor party had lost seats—Hugh Gaitskell began to lament that something "almost unprecedented in British political history" seemed to be occur-ring.

In France and Italy the electoral evolution of the 1950s did not follow so neat a pattern. For one thing, the existence of strong Communist parties, which remained quarantined from participation in government while still commanding more than one-fifth the popular vote, kept a large segment of the electorate from effective political influence. In Italy this situation of "frozen" leftist votes was reinforced by the fellow-traveling attitude of the main body of the Socialists. From 1948 to 1956 Italy languished in a condition approaching one-party rule in which no effective opposition was possible. It was not until the Soviet suppression of the Hungarian revolution shocked the Italian Socialists out of their alliance with Communism that Italian politics began to approach the "one and a half party" norm. Since then, with each succeeding Socialist party congress, the evidence has been mounting of a slow but irreversible sepa-ration of Italian Socialism from Communist entanglement. In the past two years, it has begun to function as a constitutional "half party" opposition to Christian Democracy's dominance of public life.

In France the advent of De Gaulle brutally upset the whole complicated chequer-board of party relationships. Traditional alignments and cleavages seemed lost in a monotonous uniformity of Gaullist allegiance. More recently the outlines of a constitutional opposition have begun to appear. And once again, as in the other major countries of Western Europe, the chief elements of this opposition have been Socialist—whether it be the cautious and qualified anti-Gaullist stand of Guy Mollet's official Socialism, or the far weaker but more militant "autonomous" Socialism of André Philip and Mendès-France. In either case the evolution toward a one and a half party situation has begun.

•

(How are we to explain a state of affairs in which conservative parties and movements have not only held on to power but enhanced that power for a decade and more? This would not be so surprising if the social situation in the countries in question had been stable or only gradually altering. In fact, however, the past decade has seen very rapid economic and social changes. The great paradox of Western European society and politics is that the parties which apparently resist change are doing well while the parties with a vested ideological interest in change are doing badly.

Very briefly, what has been happening in Western Europe during the past few years has been a vast speed-up in a long-term shift toward a mobile, undifferentiated, and consumer-oriented society resembling that of the United States. The conservative parties have learned how to adjust to this change. Coming to power just as the great shift was beginning, they soon discovered how to exploit the new social trends. They have accepted the welfare state; they have fostered the tendencies toward conformity that a mobile society brings with it; they have systematically encouraged the corresponding turn from ideological and political involvement—the apathy, the "privatization" of life, the blurring of ideological distinctions, the mounting suspicion that political debate is not very important, and the tendency to keep the larger public issues from general discussion. Above all, the conservatives have known how to identify themselves with the undeniable fact of economic prosperity.

In contrast, European Socialists have seemed disoriented and bewildered. Their political footwork has been slower than that of the conservatives—indeed, it is frequently the Socialists themselves whose instinctive responses have appeared the more conservative of the two. And it is true that the Socialist parties in general have a longer and more continuous institutional history than the various conservative formations. On the Continent the abrupt changes of regime during the past half century, more particularly the experience of fascism and the Second World War, broke up or demoralized the parties of the Right; in Britain alone there was no break in Conservative continuity. The Socialists, however—even when they were operating underground or in exile—never completely lost the sense of a functioning political machine. In this respect, their parties are the oldest and most routine-minded in Europe. *As machines*, they are conservative by definition.

And yet to pile on a counter-paradox, the Socialists alone seem able to muster a significant opposition following. They may be functioning as only half a party, but no other democratic opposition has been able to win more than an insignificant fraction of the electorate. Socialism may be old and unexciting, but it offers the alternative that the politically disaffected naturally turn to when they want a change from conservative rule. All efforts to build progressive parties on a non-Socialist basis have failed, from Mendès-France's attempt in the mid 1950s to modernize the French Radical party to the constantly disappointed predictions that British Liberalism is about to make an electoral comeback. Mendès' eventual decision—after the advent of De Gaulle—to unite his shrunken forces with those of the Autonomous Socialists, was an act of simple political realism. The opposition to conservative rule had to be Socialist if it was to exist at all.

•

In trying to take account of this puzzling situation of semiperma-nent exclusion from power together with an unchallenged role as *the* con-stitutional opposition, the Socialist parties of Western Europe have pro-posed two widely contrasting solutions. They have agreed on the factual analysis of their plight. Nearly all discerning Socialists have recognized that the central practical problem for their parties is to break out of the confined circle of almost hereditary Socialist allegiance which on the Continent has restricted them to between 35 and 15 per cent of the vote.

This problem goes back as far as the 1890s, when a few far-seeing Socialists of strongly democratic loyalties like Eduard Bernstein realized that the Marxian prediction of the proletariat increasing to become the majority of mankind would never be realized; in advanced industrial societies the percentage of factory hands would remain stable or actually fall—it was the white-collared and clerical, rather, whose numbers were rising. Hence a new type of appeal to reassure the peasantry and the small middle class was required. The succeeding decades brought no clear solution for this difficulty. Indeed, they intensified the earlier problems. The secession of the Communists after 1917 meant an irreplaceable loss from an already inadequate following. Postwar conditions pushed Socialist parties into power prematurely and without the parliamentary majority that was essential if they were actually to put their program into effect; government by Socialists in Germany in 1918 and 1928, in Britain in 1924 and 1929, and, most crucially, in France with the Popular Front govern-ment of 1936, brought disillusion rather than a sense of accomplishment—a loss rather than a reinforcement of popular following. But a full-scale re-examination of Socialist assumptions was never undertaken. It was not until the apparently far more favorable circumstances of the second postwar era had once again ended in disappointment that European Socialism began the examination of conscience that had been on its agenda for more than half a century.

The first (and more widely accepted) of the currently proposed solutions has been that of British Labor and the German Social Democrats. These have traditionally been the largest, the most influential, and the most conservative of European Socialist parties. In the autumn of 1959 both of them at last made explicit the departure from the hallowed Socialist goals that had long underlain their day-to-day political activity. They virtually scrapped the standard central plank of all Socialist programs; they demoted the collectivization of the basic means of production—the nationalization of industry—from its position at the pinnacle of Socialist goals to a merely auxiliary (and unessential) status among a number of possible devices for economic control. They all but eliminated the idea of class struggle from their public pronouncements, and they aligned themselves unequivocally with the foreign policy of their national governments, pledging support for an alliance with the United States based on the protection of thermonuclear weapons.

In the two countries the ideological change differed markedly in tone and content. In Britain the meeting at Blackpool was held in the shadow of the third of Labor's successive electoral defeats, and the mood was one of somber reflection on past errors. Moreover, the party was not fully united behind its official leaders, and Gaitskell and his allies did not obtain a clear-cut victory. Although at Blackpool Gaitskell staked his party leadership—and won—on his insistence that Labor repeal the clause in its party constitution pledging the eventual nationalization of all means of production, distribution, and exchange, he was subsequently obliged to accept a compromise formulation. And on foreign policy, the disaffection of the party's left wing counselled a similar caution; the storm was already brewing that in the following year seemed about to sweep Gaitskell himself from authority.

In the autumn of 1959 the German Social Democrats, midway between elections, were recovering confidence after their defeat two years earlier, and they were trying to put themselves in a good position for the election of 1961. Hence there was a bounce and aggressiveness about them which British Labor understandably lacked. Moreover, the Germans were troubled neither by a vociferous left wing nor by the memory of a period in power which had to be rationalized and defended. This was particularly important in the matter of nationalization. The German Social Democrats had never held national office since the Second World War; they had not passed through British Labor's experience of actually carrying out a collectivist policy in the half-decade immediately following the war; they did not need to grapple with the British problem of whether to renationalize those branches of the economy—notably steel and road transport—which the Tories had subsequently returned to private ownership. The German rejection of nationalization, then, was less equivocal than the British. In its recognition of the virtues of free enterprise, the new Social Democratic program voted at Bad Godesberg rose to almost lyric heights.

"Competition as much as possible— planning only as much as necessary" was a slogan calculated to dismay the party faithful. To the uncommitted, on the other hand, the program suggested moderation and class reconciliation. It pledged a "new political style of honesty, of objectivity, of cooperation, of synthesis." And the following year, by its decision to pass over the older party leaders and to present the young and "dynamic" Willy Brandt as Social Democracy's candidate for the chancellorship, the party once again recognized the value of electoral sex appeal. It proposed to take advantage of Brandt's position as mayor of West Berlin in offering the public a Social Democratic image of patriotism and orthodoxy in the Cold War.

In France Guy Mollet is apparently trying to lead the larger wing of French Socialism along the same path on which Gaitskell and Brandt have been moving in Britain and in Germany. He agrees with them that nationalization and class warfare should no longer be emphasized, and that the new respectability of European Socialism can be most profitably expressed through giving bi-partisan support to the Atlantic Pact. He seems to believe as Brandt and Gaitskell do that the way to adjust to the present European evolution toward an American-type society is to convert European Socialism into a catch-all welfare-state movement, with fluid ideological boundaries, rather like the Democratic party in the United States.

The alternative solution for resolving the Socialists' current difficulties is both less clear-cut and less influential than that proposed by Gaitskell, Brandt and Mollet. Its chief proponents are the left wing of British Labor, the militantly oppositionist fraction of French Socialism that calls itself "autonomous" or "unified," and the majority organization of the Italian Socialist party. In Italy alone—for special reasons of history and temperament—this second body of opinion within European Socialism holds a predominant position.

The most arresting distinction between the Socialist Left and the most powerful moderate current is on foreign and military policy. As opposed to the nearly unqualified support that the official leaders of British and German Socialism give to the foreign policy of Macmillan and Adenaur, the Socialist Left is worried and disaffected. But it is far from clear about the substitute it would offer. While the majority of left Socialists argue for retention of the Atlantic alliance in modified form, some of the French are frank neutralists. The Italians for the most part restrict themselves to opposing the stationing of American nuclear weapons on their country's soil. The British—drawing on the popular enthusiasm mobilized by the Campaign for Nuclear Disarmament—advocate Britain's unilateral renunciation of thermonuclear weapons and the closing down of American bases in Europe. In the autumn of 1960 they actually succeeded in winning a majority in the party congress—until their position was re-

versed by the votes of Labor members of Parliament who remained loyal
to Gaitskell. Yet for all its militancy, British Labor's left wing does not
explicitly spurn the "defense umbrella" of nuclear retaliation launched
from the United States. Obviously this is a question that it has not completely mastered. Throughout Western Europe, the logic of the left Socialist position is either a neutrality sympathetic to America or a new type
of Atlantic Pact pledged to defend Europe by conventional weapons
alone. But most of the adherents of Socialism's left wing have not reached
that far in their thinking. While they argue that their countries' present
foreign policy is dangerous and mistaken, they have not yet found an
unambiguous substitute for it.

On the domestic front, the lack of full-scale rethinking is at least as
apparent. Most left Socialists are unwilling to discard the old battle cries
of nationalization and class warfare. But they have difficulty explaining
why they feel this way. They suspect that men like Gaitskell and Brandt
are engaging in a "sell-out" of traditional Socialism. At the same time the
better economic heads among them have absorbed enough of Keynes to
have lost their faith in the panacea of nationalization, and any honest left
Socialist must recognize that class lines are far less sharp in Europe today
than they were a generation ago. Very often the rhetoric of left Socialism
boils down to little more than an appeal for a return to first principles and
a restoration of political militancy.

The Italian Socialist party epitomizes the confusion. For a half century
the Italians have ranked as the farthest left of the major European Socialist
parties. In its insistence on class struggle—in its adherence to a "maximum"
program—in its reluctance to make a clean break with Communism, the
Italian party has reflected the peculiar social conditions of the slowest-
to-develop and the least prosperous of the great nations of the West. In
Italy, human misery of the nineteenth-century type is still a sharp reality.
Quite understandably, its Socialists have reflected this condition by
clinging to a nineteenth-century faith in proletarian solidarity and to a
romantic vision of a new world of human brotherhood.

The Italian Socialist party carries around with it an enormous burden
of past errors. It was the only great party that in the first postwar era tried
to straddle the issue of affiliation with the Third International—the only
branch of European Socialism whose majority failed to see the necessity
of making a clear choice for or against the Bolshevik road to the future.
After the Second World War, the Italian Socialists were equally blind to
reality. Their decade and more of fellow-traveling grievously eroded
their moral capital, breeding a distrust among liberal-minded Italians
which it will take at least another decade to efface. Yet for all this there is
something amazingly innocent about Italian Socialism. It has a quality of
popular spontaneity that in other countries has quite disappeared from
contemporary politics. Its faith in the future is of almost childlike
intensity; it made its catastrophic mistakes in good faith. The new-

old freshness of the Italian party offers a puzzling and still unexploited asset in European Socialism's current struggle for self definition.

●

At first glance it would seem that the British or the German solution —the path of Gaitskell and of Brandt—has everything in its favor. In the short run, this is certainly true. It is undeniable that the European Socialist parties will not begin to win elections until they have convinced the middle-class electorate that they offer no real threat to private property or the prosecution of the Cold War. They will not be within striking distance of power until they have converted themselves into welfare-state parties only marginally different from their conservative opponents. The evidence is overwhelming—at least in Britain—that a turn to the left would mean an almost automatic loss of Socialist votes.

But is the current winning of elections the whole, or even the central, question? Even if Labor were to gain a parliamentary majority in Britain, or the Social Democrats should come to power in Germany, would they truly have solved their problem? History is full of examples of parties that have reached authority and then have lost power very rapidly, because they have not known how to behave once they were there. The defining characteristic of the Gaitskell-Brandt policy is what in this country used to be called "me-tooism." And the great weaknesses of "me-tooism" are its lack of political coherence and the fact that it is so easy a game for two to play. So long as European Socialists pursue this course, they can always be outflanked by an ideologically more supple conservative party.

It is only half true to say, as I did earlier, that nationalization of the basic means of production has traditionally been the major tenet of European Socialism. This is true only in an instrumental sense; nationalization has been the means, not the ultimate goal, of Socialist policy. Indeed this goal has not really been economic at all. It has been envisioned as a moral change—a transformation in the *quality* of life from an absorption with private economic satisfactions to a concern for human personality and the well-being of the community as a whole.   *N. B.*

This is the central point at issue between the dominant Right and the uneasy Left within the European Socialist parties. Here lie the true grounds for that suspicion of a sell-out on the part of men like Gaitskell and Brandt that the Left has spotted so accurately but has seldom expressed with clarity. The official leadership of British and German Socialism is currently ready to settle for something way short of what European Socialists have always dreamed of. This is the real charge against the Right—far more than its faltering on a merely technical question like nationalization. The truly damning indictment that the Left hurls at the Right is its willingness to accept a society dedicated to private consumption, a politically and ideologically apathetic society in which public goals are almost forgotten in the scramble for individual satisfactions. This we Americans know to be true of our own country. American society is democratic by almost any definition one might choose to propose—far more democratic than the societies of Britain and France and Germany and Italy have ever been. But it is also a smug and consumer-oriented society, in which private affluence is cancelled out by public penury, and most of whose citizens lack a living faith in their own values.

Hence the European Socialists of the Left are convinced that their own countries' transition to an American type of democracy is far from being a total blessing. Nearly all of them recognize that contemporary capitalism has vastly reduced the harshness and egoism of its nineteenth-century predecessor. At the same time, they argue that the new capitalism of the twentieth century, along with an unanticipated levelling of classes, has brought with it equally unanticipated evils of its own. This is what Aneurin Bevan, in one of his last major utterances as the eloquent spokesman of British Labor's left wing, meant when he declared that capitalism had *not* succeeded, that it had produced an ugly society in which values had "gone all wrong."

The Socialist Left, then, is trying both to restore an old tradition of ideological affirmation and to adjust its goals to contemporary conditions, when it argues that in place of or alongside the conventional cure-all of nationalization, something more imaginative is required than mere adjustment to welfare-state capitalism. As opposed to the short-term "realism" of Socialism's right wing, it proposes such long-range measures as nationwide economic planning, a coherent public investment policy, and a vastly expanded program for raising the cultural level of the whole population. Such planning emphasizes "social priorities" for the entire community; the corresponding cultural policy stresses adult participation and development at least as much as formal schooling. It is characteristic of the "New Left," not only in Britain but on the Continent also, to criticize the present situation "in terms of moral and esthetic, rather than economic, criteria." Its "concern is above all with the impoverished quality of life . . . , the lack of a common culture, the decline of community, the dehumanizing effects to the mass media." In this sense its manifestoes resemble such American works of social criticism as Paul Goodman's *Growing Up Absurd*. And the moral impetus behind them comes from a revulsion against the threat of thermonuclear destruction that is leading through a steady logical progression to neutralism or even the preaching of non-violence in the Gandhian tradition.

But where does this leave the middle class? What do these noble aims have to do with the overriding practical question of breaking out of a half generation of conservative dominance and winning over a new segment of the electorate? The answer is that the Socialist Left is taking a long gamble on the future. It is convinced that the policy of the Gaitskells and the Brandts is myopic and, in the end, self-defeating. Ultimately, it believes, a mere consumers' paradise will prove disappointing. A thirst for Utopia will reawaken everywhere. Finally this longing will reach the middle class itself. Or rather—since the familiar class lines will have broken down so profoundly—dissatisfaction with the consumer society will become diffused throughout the population. Then the old moral message of European Socialism will come to have a new relevance. And those parties and groups which have maintained through countless checks and errors their Utopian aspirations undimmed, will find themselves no longer marginal half parties in a sterile and electorally hopeless political debate, but leaders and mentors of a great ideological reawakening.

Part Three–Political Institutions

INTRODUCTORY ESSAY

•

INTERESTS and interest groups are the raw material of politics. Through the political parties, or through other larger groupings, they press their claims upon the governmental structures and the decision-making organs of the political system. Policy is often the result of such claims. The farmers wish protection; the workers ask for wage increases; the military for special appropriations; the church for subsidies; the business community for lower taxes. To the uninitiated the striving for satisfaction by various interest groups, the multiplicity and the intensity of conflict, the incompatibility of the interests involved, often make a political community seem something like a jungle where the survival of the fittest or the strongest appears to be the only rule.

Yet over and above interest and interest conflict there is something that we may call the basic consensus or the fundamental rules of the game, that is, the acceptance of certain rules according to which conflict will be waged, interests articulated, and conflict resolved. All political systems are characterized by the existence of these rules—what A. D. Lindsay in his book *The Modern Democratic State* calls "operative ideals." That is, in every political society there is an organ which makes decisions according to certain procedures, and these decisions are accepted and obeyed. The state has authority and prestige, not only force.

Constitutions

The general organization and structure of authority is in essence a "constitution." Whether written or unwritten a constitution expresses the "fundamental agreement" of the political society on how it will be governed. It usually defines the scope of governmental authority, the way in which decisions are made, and the manner in which decision makers are selected and held accountable. It both creates and limits power. The legacy of the Middle Ages was to define, what we call today, rights that limit arbitrary power and narrow the scope of the State's authority. With the beginning of the nineteenth century most political systems began to establish responsibility of the governors to the governed through representative assemblies and periodic elections.

A system in which a constitution is widely accepted may be referred to as *consensual*, that is, the people in it agree on how they will resolve their differences. They do not "bicker about fundamentals." Political systems may well be defined, therefore, in terms of this criterion. In some systems the agreement on fundamentals is not widely shared or intensely felt—they have a *low degree of consensus or legitimacy*. In others, there is no such agreement—they are *highly divided or transitional systems*. In still others, the agreement is overtly manufactured through the control of the media of communication by a small group of political leaders—this is the case in totalitarian systems. But totalitarianism is not in itself evidence of low consensus, for in some cases leadership may bring about a high degree of unity and perhaps popular support.

Great Britain is often cited as an example of a highly consensual system. The monarch symbolizes national unity, while the Parliament and the Cabinet are universally accepted organs of decision making. The basic principle of the British Constitution is the unlimited, unfettered, supremacy of Parliament. As Blackstone explained in his *Commentaries*, Parliament ". . . can, in short, do everything that is not naturally impossible. . . . Thus the phrase, the omnipotence of Parliament. True it is, that what the Parliament doth, no authority upon earth can undo." Blackstone's dictum was pungently illustrated by later commentators, who held that Parliament can do everything "except make a man a woman and a woman a man" (since this is "naturally impossible"). Whenever Parliament really wishes to perform a certain action, there is no *legal* obstacle.[1]

Parliament, for example, determines when and whether general elections are to be held. Although its term of office is limited by the Parliament Act of 1911 to five years, Parliament has twice (during both world wars) extended its own life by resolution and with the agreement of all political parties. If it were so minded, Parliament might abrogate the Bill of Rights, Act of Settlement, and the Reform Acts, since these statutes, in spite of their historic importance, do not constitute a "higher law."

Parliament, then, is without any legal restrictions. But what is "Parliament"? Under modern conditions it consists of at least two well-organized and highly disciplined groups of members whose primary function is to support or criticize the ministry. The Cabinet tends to control deliberations of the House of Commons because its supporters constitute a majority in the chamber and therefore carry the day for the government so long as the majority remains solid. Juridically, Parliament can do anything; actually, Parliament enacts into law the program of the Cabinet.

Perhaps the most vital part of the British Constitution involves relationships of Parliament, Cabinet, and the people as they operate through *the party system*. These relationships, almost wholly ignored by Parliament as a lawmaking body, are governed by "conventions" (well-understood practices) of the Constitution. The most important constitutional conven-

---

[1] See Sir Ivor Jennings, *The Law and the Constitution* (London, 1952), pp. 153–54.

tions relate to the position of the minority party in the Commons and the country. The minority party in the House of Commons is recognized by the government as a "Loyal Opposition." It is consulted by majority leaders, afforded an opportunity to criticize the government's proposals to Parliament, and not hindered in its legal efforts to overthrow the government majority at the next election. Other important conventions of the Constitution include the following propositions: the king must follow the advice of his responsible ministers; the prime minister, in our times, is usually selected from the House of Commons; and the Cabinet, if defeated on an important vote in the House of Commons, must either resign or call a new election.

Constitutional conventions are generally the product of long-developing custom. As late as 1912, during the controversy over Home Rule for Ireland, King George V was advised by Mr. Bonar Law, the Leader of the Opposition, and Sir William Anson, perhaps the most eminent constitutional lawyer of the era, that he (the king) possessed the power to refuse his assent to a bill if he believed it did not reflect the will of the electorate. Fortunately the matter did not come to a head at that time; it is now generally accepted that the monarch has no right to refuse assent.[2] It was not until 1923 that the appointment of Mr. Stanley Baldwin, rather than Lord Curzon, as prime minister, established the practice of choosing the chief minister from the Commons. In 1963 this convention was modified when Lord Home succeeded Mr. Harold Macmillan as prime minister, he thereupon resigned his peerage and was elected to the House of Commons in a by-election.

Constitutional conventions are maintained primarily because they correspond to the political expectations of the British nation at any given time. Flouting a convention would therefore lead to extraordinary difficulties. If a member of the House of Lords were prime minister, the chief spokesman of the Cabinet would not be able to defend its policies in the politically dominant House of Commons, thereby giving the advantage in debate to the Opposition. If the monarch did not take the advice of his ministers, he would find himself without a government—since no responsible politician would accept office under such conditions. If the Opposition were not recognized in debate, it would resort to obstructionist tactics, thus paralyzing the parliamentary process.

In short, an omnipotent Parliament has been adapted to the requirements of modern democracy by the gradual development of responsible political practices. The British Constitution has proved to be a supple, living organism.

A consensual political system has been functioning in Britain for a longer period of time than in any other country—its foundations having been laid in the thirteenth century. It was reshaped by the end of the

[2] See Harold Nicholson, *King George the Fifth* (London, 1952), pp. 118–19, 200–202.

eighteenth century so that new interests and classes created by the Industrial Revolution found a ready-made instrument for a resolution of their conflicts. Slowly the system absorbed, or rather integrated the new social groups, notably the workers. At times the system was subjected to great strain, particularly during bitter controversies over the workers' demands for a Charter (mid-nineteenth century), and Home Rule for Ireland. Eventually the political institutions were used to work out satisfactory compromises. Government came to be looked upon as a problem-solving mechanism.

In France, and other countries of the continent, a radically different situation prevailed. Parliaments in these countries knew an uneasy and eventful life, becoming the source of unresolved opposition to the powers of the king or the nobility. The French representative assemblies were not allowed to meet for over a century and a half. When finally they met in 1789, they set aside the powers of the king and ushered in a period of turmoil. A democratic constitution was accepted only by a part of the population. The nineteenth century was a period of conflict and struggle in which sometimes democracy and sometimes monarchy or personal government (Bonapartism) triumphed. The working classes found it impossible to accommodate themselves with one or the other form and developed a utopian or revolutionary outlook. Thus by the end of the nineteenth century there was no widespread agreement in France about any constitution; sizable fractions of the population had not been integrated into the system; and people remained divided not only about interests and aspirations but also on how they should resolve their conflicts. The French found it difficult to "agree on how they were to disagree."

The constitutional system of the French Third Republic (1875–1940) consisted of a fairly even balance between a powerful civil service led by a precariously poised cabinet on the one hand, and a theoretically omnipotent Parliament responsible to the electorate on the other. Under the Third Republic the control of Parliament over the Cabinet was asserted in numerous ways: cabinets were brought down frequently by interpellation and votes of no confidence (there were over one hundred cabinets in sixty-five years); the various standing committees of the two chambers encroached upon the executive functions of the Cabinet; and the Senate acquired more and more power. In Britain during the same period the Cabinet was solidifying its position, the committees of the House of Commons were rudimentary and incapable of rivaling the Cabinet, and the influence of the House of Lords was diminishing.

The French Constitution was a negative agreement among many contradictory political and ideological forces. It reflected a deep desire on the part of the French nation that the government should never be powerful enough to override the many conflicting interests of the society. "What France needs," said one French statesman of the Third Republic, "is a weak government." That is, French society was so divided that only an inactive government could keep peace among the discordant elements; only a majority opposed to action could secure lasting support in the Parliament—with occasional exceptions during periods of danger to the nation, when the parliamentary machinery and the republican regime broke down. The Third Republic in a sense institutionalized the principle of negativism, tempered by a highly centralized bureaucracy which carried on the tasks of government.

On October 21, 1945, the French people were presented, at a nation-wide referendum, with the choice of reverting to the Third Republic (in which case the deputies to be chosen at the same time would reconstitute the Chamber of Deputies), or to elect a Constituent Assembly charged with the task of drafting a new basic law for France. The electorate decided overwhelmingly that the representatives they voted for should make up a Constituent Assembly, draft a constitution for a Fourth Republic, and then submit their work to a referendum for approval. The French nation was thus offered a precious opportunity to refashion its political institutions.

The Constitution of the Fourth Republic repudiated both presidential government and assembly government, with their associations of personal rule and revolution. It went back to the basic principle of the Third Republic: that of a balance between the executive (consisting of a chief of state, a ministry, and the civil service) and the legislature (composed of a National Assembly and a Council of the Republic, corresponding to the former Chamber of Deputies and Senate). As the rapporteur of the Constitution declared in making his final report: "The presidential regime being condemned, Assembly government being discarded, we are forced to return to the parliamentary system."

However, the new regime was unable to work out dynamic policies or to secure the support of the masses—especially among the workers, many of the farmers, the lower middle classes on the Left, and a number of groups on the Right, such as the army and veterans. An uprising by the French settlers in Algeria in May, 1958, was supported by the army, and the leaders of the Republic were compelled to call upon General de Gaulle to return to power. A new constitution, inspired mainly by De Gaulle's desire to introduce a measure of presidential government, was approved by the voters in September, 1958.

Throughout the nineteenth and early twentieth centuries, constitutional instability was also the rule in most other European countries where sharp incompatibilities and ideological divisions were very much in evidence. The threat of revolutionary uprising by the underprivileged groups that had never been fully integrated into the system was ever present. The Bolshevik Revolution of 1917 gave sharpness and meaning to their demands. The Nazi system in Germany and, to a lesser degree, the Fascist system in Italy, gave hope to the wealthier groups, to the military, some of the conservative elements of the Church, and to the many lower middle-class groups that a "strong" government, based on one-party rule, could provide stability and unity. Both the Bolshevik and Fascist movements imperiled democratic constitutionalism and provided their followers with an armed vision that undermined the tolerance and agreement on which democracy rests.

Constitutions are sometimes only empty forms, masking the real structure of power. In the Communist countries the disparity between written texts and reality is almost complete. In Latin America and the "new nations" solemn constitutional declarations and texts often conceal the real power which remains in the hands of a small group of leaders. Ceylon, Indonesia, the former British colonies in Africa and elsewhere, the new "Republics" of formerly French Africa and Madagascar, have written constitutions tailored after the British and French pattern, with some evidence of American influence. But in all these cases the "constitution" has not as yet gained acceptance, has no "legitimacy," and as a result remains precarious. Large segments of the population still live in their tribes. The masses are illiterate. Their living conditions afford them no possibility to think about politics intelligently or to organize and speak for themselves. They remain unintegrated in the political system. Yet the creation of a constitutional democracy will require the political integration of the masses. This in turn will be a gradual process based upon growing literacy, economic opportunities and well-being, the development of skills, the acquisition of property by a greater number of persons, and the free expression of interests and aspirations. Constitutional democracy faces, therefore, a severe challenge in the "new" States. There is a decided tendency on the part of the newly emancipated native leadership to follow the authoritarian model. They seem to prefer rapid activation and integration of the masses into a one-party system, along with rigorous discipline for the achievement of national objectives—particularly industrialization.

Governmental Institutions

The decision-making functions of all political societies have been distinguished traditionally into three separate types: the executive, the legislative, and the judicial. However, this threefold division is not a realistic guide to the exercise of political power. In some systems the legislature assumed the totality of decision-making power with the executive simply executing the will of the lawmakers and the judiciary applying and interpreting the law in case of litigation. In other instances, a precarious balance between the executive and the legislature was established with the executive slowly assuming increased powers and independence of action. In other systems—notably those with a federal organization of power—the judiciary emerged as a genuinely independent organ with wide latitude to interpret the constitution and in so doing to limit the powers of the legislature and the executive.

The nineteenth century was the period of legislative supremacy in most of the Western constitutional democracies. Walter Bagehot writing in the latter part of the century pointed out that the Parliament nominated the members of the executive, passed laws, prepared and voted the budget, supervised the Cabinet and finally aired grievances and ventilated issues, thus helping to mould and shape public opinion. It was primarily a body of men who represented the upper and middle classes of the community, fundamentally in agreement about the policies to be pursued, unharried, embodying the complacency and stability of the Victorian period. They usually debated broad political problems—educational reform, extension of the franchise, the rights of associations and individuals, and international treaties. Controversy was resolved in compromise legislation that could be spelled out in general parliamentary enactments. This was also the case in some other systems where parliamentary democracy developed—Sweden, Holland, Norway, and Denmark. In the United States the pendulum swung between "presidential" government, especially in times of crisis, and "congressional" government.

On the continent representative assemblies were often regarded as the instruments of popular rule against the privileged groups. They claimed on behalf of the people the totality of political power, and relegated the executive to the role of an agent. This was notably the case of France where the legislative assemblies reduced the Cabinet to a subservient role.

Outside of western Europe, North America, and the British Dominions, representative government in the nineteenth century was virtually unknown. In the Balkans and Latin America, constitutions and parliamentary institutions were provided on paper but the practice belied the constitutional forms. Most of these systems were oligarchies where political power, irrespective of the forms, was in the hands of the landowners, the military, or the Church. Others were traditional societies, in which political rule was hereditary. They had not experienced the conflicts and modernization, associated with the French Revolution and industrialization, that led to progressive political emancipation of the masses in Europe. Their political systems were encrusted in tradition and immemorial custom.

With the beginning of the twentieth century, an important change in the organization and functioning of democratic institutions can be discerned. The internal balance of power between the three organs—executive, legislative, and judicial—began to shift in favor of the executive. This trend reflects profound modifications in the social and political structures of modern societies.

Representative institutions operated well when the pressure upon them to make decisions was light. The free-market system provided an automatic mechanism of decision making. Matters of wages, hours of work, employment, social security, education, technological improvement, investment and economic development were to remain outside of the province of the State. The increasing complexity of the industrial society called, however, for regulation of economic activity. The need for State intervention grew, and demanded special knowledge and skill. The legislature proved singularly unfit to perform these tasks. The legislature was cumbersome; its members had neither technical knowledge, nor expertise, nor time. Slowly the burden of decision making shifted to the political executive and the civil service.

Political reasons also accounted for this shift. Most significant were the extension of suffrage and the growth of large national parties. The two phenomena are historically associated. Elections became increasingly confrontations between two or more parties appealing to a mass electorate on specific issues or on a general program for action. Thus the legislature was slowly bypassed since victory at the polls meant that the leadership of the majority party would form a government to carry out its pledges. Wherever party discipline was strong, therefore, popular elections were equivalent to the selection of the "government," i.e., the executive.

Political and technical trends reinforced each other and during the interwar years the executive assumed more and more powers. Representative assemblies have lost virtually all of the functions attributed to them by Walter Bagehot in the nineteenth century. The vast majority of legislative projects emanate from the executive; the preparation of the budget has become an executive function in which the Cabinet, in association with the top civil service or independent executive bodies, drafts the specifications involving public expenditures and revenue. Parliament has even virtually lost the power to nominate the cabinet. Finally, the very scope of lawmaking has changed. Special laws or regulations are needed which can best be made by those in touch with the problems of developed industrial societies—that is to say, by the executive departments and the civil service. Thus the legislature has fallen into the habit of drafting general laws in which regulatory powers are generously delegated to the executive. For all practical purposes such delegation is so broad as to invest the executive and civil service with virtual lawmaking powers.

In almost all contemporary political systems leadership has shifted to the executive with the legislature acting mainly as a forum for the airing of grievances. The executive has taken the initiative as regards general lawmaking, and foreign and defense policy. Finally, the extension of State control over the economy, and the establishment of nationalized industries have called for extensive financial and physical planning by the executive. Assumption of these new responsibilities and the increasing concentration of these functions in the executive branch have led to a proliferation of new agencies and bureaus. The executive has become "bureaucratized." It initiates policy, co-ordinates policy decisions, and is responsible for their implementation and execution. Institutions have developed within the executive corresponding to these three phases of the policy-making process.

In both presidential and parliamentary systems, a small group of political leaders are in charge of over-all policy initiation and formulation. They are the president, or the prime minister, and their immediate advisers. In France there has been a noticeable trend under the Fifth Republic toward a presidential system: matters of defense and foreign policy are decided upon by the president of the republic with the advice of a small group, which includes the prime minister. To assist the top leaders in the formulation of policy there are a number of "adjunct" administrative staff organizations. They draft policy papers on economic planning, foreign policy, defense, and the budget. In the United States, the Bureau of the Budget, the National Security Council, and the Council of Economic Advisers perform important deliberative and policy-initiation functions. In Britain and France, cabinet committees are responsible for similar activities. Thus deliberation is institutionalized at the executive level.

Policy proposals put forward by various executive agencies must then be co-ordinated. Suggestions and counter-suggestions are thrashed out in the cabinet, or in small ministerial committees made up of top civil servants, the chiefs of staff, and the personal advisers to the president or prime minister. Reconciliation of conflicting proposals may require the ultimate intervention of the president or prime minister himself. The interdependence of military, economic and foreign policy has called increasingly for such interdepartmental co-ordination.

Finally, it is necessary to execute decisions. This is the task of the vast majority of civil servants—to inspect, repair, perform, and check. They do what the employees of any large corporation do—they perform on the basis of orders and regulations decided by their superiors.

The Civil Service

It is one of the characteristics of industrialized societies, irrespective of their form of government, to develop a civil service recruited on the basis of specific technical requirements. "Bureaucratic administration means fundamentally the exercise of control on the basis of knowledge," observed Max Weber. It is above all a rational organization characterized by: *a*) a clearly defined sphere of competence subject to impersonal rules; *b*) a hierarchy which determines in an orderly fashion relations of superiors and subordinates; *c*) a regular system of appointments and promotions on the basis of free contract; *d*) recruitment on the basis of skills, knowledge, or technical training; and *e*) fixed salaries.

The Prussian civil service was an early example of a professional service with clear-cut demarcation of spheres of competence, rigid rules of recruitment, and allocation of posts on the basis of skills. It reflected the high degree of military organization and centralization of that country. After the unification of Germany the same standards were made applicable to the whole German bureaucracy.

In Great Britain professionalization was introduced officially in 1853 by the Northcote–Trevelyan Report on the "Organization of the Permanent Civil Service," which opened the civil service to talent on the basis of competitive examinations. Until then civil service appointments were made on the basis of political considerations and were, by and large, restricted to the nobility. The Report recommended examinations for which certain types of education were a prerequisite. It also divided the civil service into three "classes," each corresponding to a distinct function: 1) the Administrative Class, which is the highest policy-making group within the departments; 2) the Executive Class, whose main task is the execution of policies; and 3) the Clerical or Manipulative Class, whose work is primarily clerical and manual.

The educational requirements for entrance into the Administrative Class were unique. Until the end of the nineteenth century, applicants were supposed to have a thorough training in the humanities—Greek, Latin, philosophy, and mathematics. The advantage was thus given to the well-educated university man, as the term was interpreted during the Victorian age, rather than the specialist. Since this kind of education was provided only in the exclusive and expensive "public schools" (which despite their name were privately endowed) potential civil service applicants came either from the nobility or the wealthy middle classes. It was only after World War I that it became possible to offer specialized subjects in satisfying the entrance requirements. Expansion of scholarships and the growth of provincial universities also gave an opportunity to the lower middle classes, and even the working class, to receive the kind of education that prepared them for the examinations and admission. Nonetheless, the bias in the British recruitment system is still in favor of the "humanist" rather than the "specialist," the upper middle classes rather than the lower.

In France it was only after the Liberation in 1944 that drastic reforms—inspired in large measure by the organization of the civil service in Britain—were made. First, a general entrance examination has been established for all candidates. Previously each department did its own recruiting. The examination stresses law, political science, economics and social sciences in general. Secondly, the civil service was broadly divided into two classes: *a*) civil administrators (approximating the British administrative class) and *b*) "secretaries of administration"—corresponding to the "executive class." Thirdly, the *Ecole Nationale d'Administration* has been founded to serve as the training school for all prospective civil administrators. Students are considered public officials from the moment they enter, receive a stipend, and after successful completion of their studies and the passing of the final examinations, are assigned to an executive department. Throughout their training, which is jointly offered by civil servants and academicians, an effort is made to depart from the formalistic and legalistic approach so typical of the past and to create a self-reliant and imaginative civil servant.

The American civil service has also been "professionalized," beginning with the Pendleton Act of 1883. Recruitment is on the basis of competitive examinations, but the emphasis tends to be on specialized knowledge rather than a broad, liberal education. There is no clear-cut division between an administrative and executive class, in terms of rigidly separate educational requirements and examinations, though of course those who occupy the highest "general classes" within the hierarchy in effect perform the policy-making function. The American civil service thus is not as homogeneous as its European counterparts. American top-level administrators are graduates of universities all over the nation and are drawn from a wider range of social classes. There is also considerable movement of individuals between the civil service and private life (business, universities, and law practice, for example)—which is rare in Europe. The undoubted advantage of the European system is to create a corps of administrators who have demonstrated brilliance in academic studies during their youth, and who have shared common experiences. The result is a remarkable *esprit de corps*. In the United States, on the other hand, it is easier to invigorate the administrative establishment by providing new recruits from private life, and also to make use of talented individuals who may not have distinguished themselves as college undergraduates.

Enforcement of Responsibility

The executive has become in all contemporary industrialized societies a huge bureaucracy in which millions of people work, performing thousands of interrelated tasks. A small group of persons are ultimately responsible for the policies made and the manner in which they are implemented. They alone have to confront the public in periodic elections and give an account of their activities. They have to answer questions raised in the representative assemblies and reply to criticism. They have the burden of political responsibility—and this applies to totalitarian and democratic systems alike, though the forms of enforcement may differ.

But political responsibility, even where enforced through periodic elections and accountability to legislative assemblies, is not enough. The magnitude and the complexity of modern government is so great that no legislature (not even through its committees) can take full cognizance of them. Legislative control has often proven inadequate for effective supervision of the operations of nationalized industries, the performance of regulatory actions, and many other technical decisions.

The crucial problem facing all democratic systems today is to devise other forms and techniques of executive accountability. One possibility is the development of a sense of "internal responsibility" within the civil service itself. This can be inculcated by education and the development of strict rules of performance and rules of accountability of subordinate to superior. Another technique often suggested is the creation of specialized legislative committees to deal with specific areas of executive activity—nationalized industries, delegated legislation, defense, and the budget. A third one is the establishment of advisory bodies in which the major interests affected by policy decisions may participate. Recently there has been considerable discussion concerning the parliamentary Ombudsman (or Grievance Man) in Scandinavia, and the possibility of transplanting this office in other parts of the world. None of these techniques, however, appear to be fully successful and the truth of the matter is that they cannot be. The twentieth century notion of "political responsibility" appears to be increasingly anachronistic in an era of massive technological development. The leaders of any modern society—democratic or totalitarian—confront the challenge of implementing common aspirations. Success or failure depends mainly upon the technical competence and skill of the political leadership.

The growth of the executive and its assumption of policy-making functions, the tremendous expansion of public services coupled with the ineffectiveness of political controls over the bureaucracy, pose serious threats to individual freedom. A highly complex bureaucratized apparatus geared to performance is potentially an ever-present danger to the individual, even when it claims to serve his interests. To the old "reason of state" may be added a new, perhaps even more dangerous, "reason of service." Managerialism or *technocratie,* as the French call it, may finish by exalting efficiency, skill and organization over criticism, freedom, and individualism. It may encourage conformity rather than eccentricity, unity rather than pluralism, action rather than thought, discipline rather than freedom. An astute author writing some twenty years ago predicted that managerialism would be the political form of the future in all contemporary industrialized societies—democratic or not.[3]

The rise of the large bureaucratized state as well as the example of totalitarianism have aroused widespread concern for the protection of individual rights and freedoms. In some post-World War II constitutions, higher courts were given power to scrutinize legislative acts and see to it that the legislative and executive branches remained strictly within the confines of the constitution. In Western Germany, Italy, Austria, and recently in France, constitutional courts were established for this purpose. Both in England and in the United States administrative courts have been created to try cases involving litigation between the State and individuals. "Administrative law," long misunderstood by American and British observers of the French scene, has developed slowly as a guarantee of the rights of individuals in their dealings with the administrative and regulatory agencies of the State.

Other safeguards have also been sought. Federalism, for instance, has as a major purpose internal limitation upon the omnicompetence of the State. Even in unitary states, like Britain and France, efforts have been made to revitalize local governments in order to stimulate experimentation and avert uniformity and rigidity of centralized control.

[3] J. Burnham, *The Managerial Revolution,* 1941.

However, the techniques of judicial review, administrative courts and federalism have not proved capable of bringing central bureaucracies under effective political or legal control. Ordinary courts are even less qualified than legislative committees to evaluate the work of bureaucratic agencies In the English speaking countries, the common law bias of the courts disposes them to favor property rights, which seriously interferes with the government's efforts to solve pressing social and national problems. The American Supreme Court's antipathy to social welfare legislation—up to about 1938—is a striking illustration of this tendency. Administrative courts are of limited utility. Federalism has been evolving, even in the United States, into a unitary system for all practical purposes. The problems of modern society are so complex and far ranging that local governments are simply incapable of meeting them. Only the central government has the financial resources, the administrative expertise, and the power to work out an effective solution. Administrative decentralization can reduce the burden somewhat, but is more than counterbalanced by the continual increase in the responsibilities of the central government. The difficulty of protecting the governed by enforcing responsibility of the governors remains a central political problem.

Chapter X. Constitutions

Introductory Note

A CONSTITUTION is a written document or a set of traditions, customs and understandings incorporating the general agreement of a community as to the manner in which it is to be governed. Most countries have written constitutions in which both rules and goals are formally specified. The most notable exception is Great Britain, where the constitution is an ever-evolving network of customs (or "conventions") buttressed by some fundamental parliamentary enactments, such as the Bill of Rights of 1689, the Reform Bill of 1832, and the Parliament Act of 1911.

Students of constitutions have dealt primarily with their formal characteristics—their length or brevity, their rigidity or flexibility (referring to the manner in which a constitution is amended), their supralegality. A good discussion of constitutions in such terms may be found in James Bryce, *Modern Democracies* (1921) and his *Studies in History and Jurisprudence* (1901) and in Woodrow Wilson's *The State* (1903).

Of greater importance are the procedures established by a constitution. Does it provide for the political responsibility of the governors to the governed? Does it limit governmental authority? Does it specify an area of individual rights? An answer to these questions in the affirmative or the negative will indicate whether a political system with a constitution—written or unwritten—is also dedicated to the principles of *constitutionalism:* responsible government and individual rights. The student will find an excellent discussion of the meaning of constitutionalism in C. J. Friedrich, *Constitutional Government and Democracy* (1950) and *Man and His Government* (1963). Another interesting view is presented by Giovanni Sartori, "Constitutionalism: A Preliminary Discussion," *American Political Science Review* (December, 1962). For background material see A. D. Lindsay, *The Modern Democratic State* (1947); and Charles McIlwain, *Constitutionalism and the Changing World* (1939).

The effectiveness of a constitution depends upon the manner in which it is accepted and implemented, that is, upon its "legitimacy." In some systems the constitution as a written document is so much at variance with political reality and the actual location of political power that it may be considered little more than a literary curiosity. In other political systems the constitution undergoes violent changes primarily because it is not widely accepted by the community. This has been notably the case in

France, which in the course of the last generation has had four different constitutional arrangements.

The student interested in modern constitutions should consult H. L. McBain and L. Rogers, *The New Constitutions of Europe* (1922), Arnold Zurcher (ed.), *Constitutions and Constitutional Trends since World War II* (1955), and K. C. Wheare, *Modern Constitutions* (1960). J. L. Mecham, "Latin American Constitutions: Nominal and Real," *Journal of Politics* (May, 1959) analyzes the disparity between constitutional forms and practices in Latin America. On individual constitutions, see for Britain: W. I. Jennings, *The British Constitution* (1941), Harold Laski, *Reflections on the Constitution* (1951), and L. S. Amery, *Thoughts on the Constitution* (1953). On France: S. Hoffmann, "The French Constitution of 1958," *American Political Science Review* (June, 1959), Henry Ehrmann, "Direct Democracy in France," *ibid.* (December, 1963), and R. C. Macridis and B. E. Brown, *The De Gaulle Republic* (1960) and *Supplement to the De Gaulle Republic* (1963). On Germany: C. J. Friedrich, "Rebuilding the German Constitution," *American Political Science Review* (1949), E. H. Litchfield (ed.), *Governing Postwar Germany* (1953), and Arnold J. Heidenheimer, *The Governments of Germany* (1961). On the Soviet Union: Julian Towster, *Political Power in the USSR* (1948), John Hazard, *The Soviet System of Government* (rev. ed., 1963), and Merle Fainsod, *How Russia Is Ruled* (rev. ed., 1963).

Readings

32. THE POLITICAL THEORY OF THE NEW DEMOCRATIC CONSTITUTIONS*

Carl J. Friedrich

ANY ATTEMPT to assess the political theory of the new constitutions is confronted with the problem whether to treat the constitutional documents as prima-facie evidence or to search for underlying trends that these documents may or may not express. When Charles A. Beard threw out his challenge concerning "the economic interpretation" of the American Constitution—a challenge which in later years he sought to soften considerably—he implied, if he did not state explicitly, that the words the constitution-makers at Philadelphia used were modeled upon their economic interests and the views which stemmed from them. In an interesting detailed application of this general thought, Walton Hamilton and Douglass Adair in their *The Power to Govern* argued that the word "com-

* From *Constitutions and Constitutional Trends since World War II*, edited by Arnold J. Zurcher (New York University Press, 1951). By permission.

merce" must be interpreted in accordance with what "commerce" meant to the fathers: that a broad, mercantilist notion was what the constitution-makers "intended" to have understood in the commerce clause. An examination of the political thought of the new constitutions in such exacting and refined terms would be a Herculean task, little short of an intellectual and social history of Continental Europe during the last two generations. All that is being attempted here is to indicate the broad framework of general ideas on politics into which these constitutions are set.[1]

The very phrase "political theory" is intended to provide a limiting concept. The new constitutions deal with a great many matters, not strictly "political" in the sense in which that term has come to be specialized for purposes of modern political science. Everything today is "political," of course. But "political" in the stricter sense is confined to the organizational pattern of government, the control relationships, if you please, its functioning processes, and the like. In this sense, the new constitutions represent restorations, rather than revolutions, although they are stases or overturns in the Aristotelian sense. And, yet, closer inspection reveals a revolutionary change of unintended proportions, which I am proposing to designate by the term "negative revolutions."

The revolutions of 1640 and 1789 were carried forward with a positive enthusiasm for freedom. The drama and the failure of both revolutions were dominated by this fact; both revolutions provided the stage for long drawn out struggles to write a constitution. Each produced a crop of such constitutions, and eventually a dictator emerged to carry on by force and authority what could not be arranged by cooperation. But the lesson of the struggle for constitutional freedom was not lost; the idea of the rights of man was not dead. In the United States, a group of small, seemingly inconsequential, colonies got together and merged the ideas of both revolutions, forged them into a lasting charter: the Constitution of the United States. In England and in France the same impulse produced constitutional systems in the course of the next generation, and these systems remained.

The same cannot be said for the revolution of 1917. In impulse and in effect it was anticonstitutional. The dictatorship of the proletariat was, in the revolutionary vision, not linked to a constitutional democracy but to a direct democracy of the Rousseauistic model; yet no corresponding realistic appreciation of the limits, as far as size and spirit are concerned, characterized the vision. Both the revolutionaries themselves and the Fascist reaction they brought on stressed total authority and accepted coercion and violence thinly disguised by alleged necessities and dangers.

---

[1] The constitutions to be considered here include the French Constitution of 1946, the Italian Constitution of 1947, and the German Basic Law of 1949. . . . Attention is also given to the emergent Constitution of Europe. . . .

But now a strange turn has occurred. Out of the battle of revolutionaries, counterrevolutionaries, reactionaries, and innocent bystanders, a third force has emerged. And this third force is spreading. It is recapturing the impetus of the revolutions of 1640 and 1789. In France, in Italy, even in Germany, constitutions have been written by men who are certainly far from the "mad inspiration of history" which Trotsky called a revolution. These constitutions are not the result of any positive enthusiasm for the wonderful future; they flow rather from the negative distaste for a dismal past. What these odd revolutionists are saying primarily is: "No." They do not want Fascism and dictatorship. They do not want Communism and dictatorship. They do not want liberalism and the anarchy of the "free market" and its enterprises growing into gigantic monopolies. What, then, *do* they want? The answer seems to be: "We want peace. We want a chance to live and *if* possible to live well. We want something better than either free enterprise or the planning economy. We insist that there must be an order beyond Communism and Fascism, and we want to try to work it out." That is why I propose to call these revolutions "negative."

France affirms the rights of man of 1789, Italy affirms the rights and duties of Mazzini's good citizen, Germany affirms the dignity of man and abolishes the death sentence and compulsory military service. Are these not positive beliefs? Certainly they once were. In 1789, the Declaration of the Rights of Man was expected, however, to usher in the millennium. Did the makers of the French Constitution of 1946, reaffirming these rights, share such expectations? Hardly. They only knew that such a program would be less bad than what they rejected: the weakness and confusion of the Third Republic, the glum serfdom of the Vichy dictatorship, the terror of the Communist comrades. Similar observations apply to the other two democratic constitutions. When read with the cynicism of the twenties, or the ideological spectacles of Marxist orthodoxy, these constitutions have, in fact, a hollow ring. There does not pulse in them that passion, based upon the weird mixture of romanticism and scientism, which animated constitution-makers from 1789 to Weimar.

Are the negative revolutions a species of restoration? Do they seek to rebuild what was once there? Admittedly, neither Charles II nor Louis XVII ever restored the past either; they just tried. But their policies and programs did express the exhaustion of a generation that was tired of enthusiasm, tired of ideas, tired of change. It might seem as if the same exhaustion were sweeping Europe today. Yet, there is a sign that this analogy does hold, and this sign provides a possible key to the situation. Genuine enthusiasm is felt in many quarters of Europe for the possibility of effective unification. Underlying the strictly practical and pragmatic grounds there exists an undercurrent: a vivid sense of cultural unity and community. It found striking expression in the French Assembly debate that settled Germany's admission to the European Union. This sense of unity, this idea of European culture, unlike the shadowy and somewhat disturbing concept of world culture (behind which lurks the Soviet Russian slogan of world revolution), corresponds to vividly felt realities in spite of the bitter conflicts, and to some extent even because of them. . . .

The political theory of the new constitutions that are democratic in the traditional Western sense (the "people's democracies" are here excluded, because their constitutions are façades to a much greater extent than constitutions necessarily are) revolves, then, around four major focal points which distinguish them from their predecessors: (1) reaffirmation of human rights; *but* (2) efforts to restrict these rights in such a way as to make them unavailable to the enemies of constitutional democracy; (3) stress upon social goals and their implementation through socialization; *but* (4) efforts to circumscribe these goals and their implementation in such a way as to prevent the re-emergence of totalitarian methods and dictatorship. With reference to all four aspects, a comparison reveals that, generally speaking, they are most explicit in the German Basic Law, and least so in the French Constitution of 1946, the Italian Constitution occupying a middle ground. This fact is in keeping with the relative depth of the totalitarian impact, comparatively, in the three countries, as well as with the time sequence of the three constitutions: 1946, 1947, 1948. This sequence deserves attention, because it suggests that we are here face to face with an emergent trend still in the process of crystallization.

At this point the question may well be asked: What right have we to consider the French, the Italian, and the German Constitutions together? . . . One common ground of these three constitutions is the Rousseauistic tradition regarding democracy that the three countries share to a large degree. What I mean by this tradition is not necessarily something to be found in Rousseau himself, but something associated with his work and thought since the French Revolution: radical majoritarianism. It is the view that the majority, as such, provides an implicit and indubitable "legitimacy" in the determination of public policy and general laws. Reinforced by Jacobinism in France, by Mazzini in Italy, and by Kant and the Kantians in Germany, this view inclines to reify the concept of the general will in terms of actual votes taken in elections, referendums, and the like. That is to say, with a general skepticism about the capacity of man to free himself of such prejudice-creating frameworks as his class and economic interest goes the conviction that the general decisions in the body politic result from an act of will, rather than rational deliberation. Also involved is a tendency to disregard (a) the degree of reversibility of decisions, and (b) natural limits to any decision, resulting from the inherent conditions with which the decision is concerned. But politically decisive is the disregard for the minority, including the individual. There is little understanding in this tradition of the delicate balance between the majority's and minority's "rights" in a free society and the persistent difficulties inherent in any scheme which sets out to achieve this balance in such a way that neither of two undesirable results arises: (a) that the minority is tyrannized over by the majority, (b) that the majority is prevented from acting by the recalcitrant minority. Much of the best thought of constitutional theorizing in English-speaking countries has, as everyone knows, gone into the exploration of these issues: Harrington and Locke, the *Federalist* and John Stuart Mill, and a host of others have tried to resolve the numerous problems posited by what I once called "one majority against another: *populus semper virens.*" This problem is, of course, at the heart of constitutional liberty, as Kant well knew and made explicit in spelling out the implications of Rousseau's concept of the general will. But Continental European democrats, in the tradition of the Jacobins, have tended to neglect these problems, with the result that constitutionalism has been a weak ingredient in their democratic ideology.

It is not possible to consider constitutional provisions in detail, let alone the debates in terms of which their meaning becomes clear. It must suffice to indicate some broad lines of analysis. . . . Relatively small is the influence of British and American constitutional experience upon these new constitutions, in spite of the manifest "success" of these models in mastering the political tasks with which men, working with and through them, have had to deal. Vague excuses, such as "America is different" and "Britain's parliamentary system is inimitable," served to insulate native thought habits from undue disturbance by these Anglo-American traditions. In Germany, this propensity to stick to local habits was, of course, reinforced by the brutal fact of occupation, which made it unattractive for a politician seeking popular approval to appear to copy the occupants' ideas on democracy in detail; it was bad enough to have to "democratize" under instructions. For the Social Democrats, the unscrupulous propaganda of the Communist party exploiting this weakness was a prime factor in making them move with the greatest circumspection in all matters of this kind. Whatever the reasons, the influence of British and American constitutional thought was certainly quite limited.

There is, however, one important feature of American constitutionalism that has taken hold of Continental European theorists to an unprecedented extent, and that is the idea of making the courts, or at least a judicial body, the guardian of the constitution, rather than the legislative and/or executive authorities. . . . This recognition of judicial protection for constitutional charters is of fundamental significance for the political theory of the new constitutions: not only does it relate clearly to the broader and deeper appreciation of the importance of civil rights, but it also clearly signalizes a recognition of the constitution as a fundamental law in a manner not customary in Continental Europe before. It represents a departure from the older, radically majoritarian, position noted earlier. . . .

Before concluding this general sketch of the political theory of the new European constitutions of a Western democratic type, it seems important to note one rather striking divergence from the American, if not from the British, climate of opinion. Nowhere on the Continent is there to be found any genuine "belief in the common man," as that belief is taken for granted in the United States. In fact, the very term is nonexistent and hence untranslatable. This extraordinary personification of American democratic traditions is, throughout Continental Europe, confused with the mass man. Attacks upon the mass man, such as Ortega y Gasset's, have achieved very wide currency among Europeans of presumably democratic convictions. Not only Europe's deep attachment to culture, but the Marxist insistence upon the class-conscious elite (in the socialist sector), and the corresponding elite notions in the catholic tradition, have combined to prevent the rise of any such confidence in the common man's ability to deal with common concerns of the community as is generally accepted in America, even by people with sophisticated ideas about the workings of democracy. Somehow, this lacuna in European democratic thought seems related to the exaggeration of the majority's views on one side and to the role of the state on the other. In both cases, we must recognize in European democratic theory a stronger emphasis upon the collective aspects of society and government and a corresponding weakness, when it comes to the individual. Characteristically, European parliaments make quite inadequate provisions for the contact between the citizen and his representative. European party leaders tend to become authoritarian, as soon as they have achieved a measure of status and leadership. The resulting reaction of the people at large is one of indifference, cynicism, and even antidemocratic (though not necessarily protototalitarian) sentiments. Whether a belief in the common man could be generated to remedy these defects seems doubtful. As the gentleman was the embodiment of England's ideal of man in an aristocratic age, so the common man seems America's personal "mirror of man." Some of the more thoughtful European theorists appreciate the weakness resulting from the absence of such a personal projection of democratic ideals, especially in the face of an aggressive totalitarian challenge. But is that enough?

In sum, the negative revolutions that have occurred in Western Europe as a result of the victory of British and American arms over Fascism are animated by a spirit of reconstruction. The political theory associated with these revolutions and with the resulting constitutions is one of moderation and compromise. It seeks to transcend the totalitarian challenge, not by a blind appeal to the past, but by a patient effort to recapture the essentials of human freedom and dignity. The political thought of the negative revolutions is motivated by the social and economic ills of an aging industrial society, rent by violent revolutionary claims for radical improvement. Yet, on the whole, it is still true that Continental Europeans stress abstract principles, rather than specific procedures and concrete solutions. Quite a few years ago, John Stuart Mill wrote:

> The common-places of politics, in France, are large and sweeping practical maxims, from which as ultimate premises men reason downwards to particular applications, and this they call being logical and consistent. For instance, they are perpetually arguing that such and such a measure ought to be adopted, because it is the consequence of the principle on which the form of government is founded: of the principle of legitimacy or the principle of the sovereignty of the people.[2]

It is a curious but undeniable fact that these observations still hold true to a remarkable degree, not only of France, but of Italy and Germany as well. If Mill thought that "it would be often a much stronger recommendation of some practical arrangement, that it does not follow from what is called the general principle of the government, than that it does," I believe that this thought is as "weird" and "incomprehensible" to Europeans today as it was nearly a hundred years ago. From which it follows that the political *theory* of these constitutions is probably a good deal more important than an Englishman or American is likely to assume. This reflection may serve as a humble excuse for seeking to elucidate the theorizing of those who have developed these new constitutions: rejecting the totalitarian dictatorship, they are groping for workable principles of social order with genuine theoretical concern.

33. THE DE GAULLE CONSTITUTION*
Roy C. Macridis and Bernard E. Brown

THE LEGAL FRAMEWORK

THE LANDSCAPE of the Constitution of the French Fifth Republic is a familiar one. The executive power is shared by the President of the Republic and the prime minister with his Council of Ministers. The legislative power is vested in the National Assembly and Senate. The government is responsible before Parliament. The Economic Council, an advisory body representing the various professional organizations, becomes the Economic and Social Council. The High Council of Justice and the High Court of Justice are reconstituted. The old Constitutional Committee is replaced by the Constitutional Council with somewhat broader powers of constitutional review. Some new features are: a habeas

---

[2] John Stuart Mill, *Logic* (1st ed.; London, 1843), Vol. II, p. 618.

* Condensed from Chapter X, *The De Gaulle Republic: Quest for Unity* (Homewood, Ill.: The Dorsey Press, Inc., 1960) and *Supplement to the De Gaulle Republic* (The Dorsey Press, 1963), Chapter II.

corpus clause, a provision requiring political parties to adhere to the democratic principles of the constitution, and a revised amending clause. The major innovations of the constitution lie in the manner in which the institutions are to function.

The Executive: The President of the Republic and the Government. The presidency of the Fifth Republic is a reaction against the development of the office since 1875. The framers wished to give to the president the prestige and prerogatives that would enable him to provide for the continuity of the State, to cement the bonds of the Community, and to supervise the functioning of the constitution. In the words of Michel Debré, he is to be the "keystone of the arch" of the new Republic—both the symbol and the instrument of reinforced executive authority. To accomplish this the framers modified the manner in which he is elected and strengthened his powers. The president was originally elected by an enlarged electoral college which, in addition to the members of the Parliament, included the municipal councilors, the general councilors, and the members of the assemblies and the municipalities of the overseas territories and Republics.

The Constitution of the Fifth Republic maintains the "irresponsibility" of the president but at the same time gives him personal powers that he can exercise solely at his discretion. It gives him also the power to make decisions concerning all matters related to the Community and allows for a virtual veto power over a large, even if ill-defined, area of policy making.

The president designates the prime minister. Though it is presumed that such a designation will be made with an eye to the existing party configuration in the National Assembly, it is a personal political act. The president virtually chooses the prime minister when we take into consideration his other powers, and particularly his power of dissolution of the National Assembly. Under the practice of the Fourth Republic, dissolution of the Assembly could take place only under very stringent conditions upon the request of the prime minister. The role of the President of the Republic was simply to sign the dissolution decree presented to him by the prime minister, if and when the conditions for dissolution were met. In the new constitution, dissolution is a discretionary act of the president. He can dissolve at any time, on any issue, and for any reason. There is only one limitation—he cannot dissolve twice within the same year—and one formality—he must "consult" with the prime minister and the presidents of the two legislative assemblies.

When the institutions of the Republic, the independence of the nation, the integrity of its territory, or the execution of international engagements are menaced in a grave and immediate manner and the regular functioning of the public powers is interrupted, the president may take measures necessitated by the circumstances (Article 16). Again this is a personal and discretionary act. The president is required only to inform the nation by a message and to "consult" the Constitutional Council. The National Assembly, however, reconvenes automatically and cannot be dissolved during the emergency period.

The constitution also vests explicitly in the president other powers that he can exercise at his discretion. He has the nominating power for all civil and military posts and, unless it is otherwise provided by an organic law, he signs all decrees and ordinances prepared by the Council of Ministers. He can raise the question of unconstitutionality on a bill or on a law before the Constitutional Council. The president also enjoys all the prerogatives that were vested in the office in the past. He presides over the meetings of the Council of Ministers, receives ambassadors, and sends messages to Parliament. He may ask for the re-examination of a bill or some of its articles, which cannot be refused; promulgates laws within fifteen days after their enactment; negotiates and ratifies treaties, and is kept informed of all negotiations leading to the conclusion of international agreements; and he is commander in chief and presides over the Committee of National Defense.

Finally, the president can bring certain issues before the people in a referendum:

> The President of the Republic on the proposal of the government . . . or on joint resolution by the two legislative assemblies . . . *may* submit to a referendum any bill dealing with the organization of the public powers, the approval of an agreement of the Community or the authorization to ratify a treaty, that without being contrary to the Constitution would affect the functioning of existing institutions [Article 11].

The calling of a referendum is however a personal act of the President of the Republic. He may elicit or refuse it depending on the circumstances.

The constitution explicitly consecrates the large influence of the president over the functioning of the institutions and policy making:

> The President of the Republic shall see that the Constitution is respected. He shall ensure, by his arbitration, the regular functioning of the governmental authorities, as well as the continuance of the State.
> He shall be the guarantor of national independence, of the integrity of the territory, and of respect for Community agreements and treaties [Article 5].

Mediation is a personal act involving the exercise of judgment. As a result, the president is given implicitly a veto power on almost every conceivable aspect of policy. He may refuse to sign a decree or to make a nomination; he may dissolve or threaten to dissolve the National Assembly and call for a referendum. His position in the Community gives him a direct influence over decisions in all other matters. He becomes an integral part of policy making and policy execution despite the fact that he is politically irresponsible.

The list of presidential prerogatives is thus an impressive one. The framers, while rejecting presidential government, wished nonetheless to establish a president who can act on his own. In matters of war, foreign policy, the preservation of internal peace, and the functioning of the institutions, his powers are overriding and he can bring them to bear upon every type of policy and decision. His acts thus have a political content. He can no longer remain an "irresponsible head of the State" like the British Crown.

The Government. The government, composed of the prime minister and his ministers, "determines and conducts the policy of the nation" and is "responsible before the Parliament." Special recognition is accorded to the prime minister. He "directs" the action of the government and is "responsible" for the national defense. He "assures the execution of the laws and exercises the rule-making power"—but on condition that all decrees and ordinances are signed by the President of the Republic (Articles 20 and 21). He determines the composition of his cabinet, presides over its meetings, and directs the administrative services. He defends his policy before the Parliament, answers questions addressed to him by the members of Parliament, states the over-all program of the government in special programmatic declarations, and puts the question of confidence.

Many of these powers lend themselves to future expansion. The prime minister may find it tempting to seek the support of Parliament in order to oppose the President of the Republic. He may invoke his political responsibility to cope with the impressive array of weapons that the constitution gives to the President of the Republic. Thus, a conflict between a "responsible" prime minister and an "irresponsible" president is likely to occur under certain conditions.

The Legislature. The Parliament of the Fifth Republic is, as in the past, bicameral. It consists of a National Assembly and a Senate. The first is elected for five years by universal suffrage. The Senate is elected indirectly by the municipal councilors, the departmental councilors, and the members of the National Assembly. One third of its membership is renewed every three years. The two chambers have equal powers except in two respects—the traditional prerogative of the lower chambers to examine the budget first is maintained, and the Senate cannot introduce a motion of censure and bring about on its own initiative the fall of the cabinet. The government, however, if it so desires, may invoke its responsibility before the Senate, presumably with all the consequences that it entails. The new Senate was designed primarily to limit the powers of the National Assembly. It can block the decisions of the lower house and under certain circumstances exercises an absolute veto.

The new constitution establishes a "rationalized Parliament" in a number of ways. Only two sessions of the two assemblies are allowed—two months and a half from October to December and about three months and a half from the last Tuesday of April to the end of July. The first session is to be devoted to the budget and the second to major legislative texts. Extraordinary sessions may take place at the request of the prime minister or of a majority of the members of the National Assembly "on a specific agenda." They are convened and closed by a decree of the President of the Republic. The lawmaking functions of the Parliament are restricted to matters limitatively defined in the constitution. The government can legislate on all other matters by simple decree. The legislative agenda is no longer the outcome of interminable debates between the president of the National Assembly, the presidents of the parliamentary groups, and a government delegate. The government now fixes the order of business. The vote of the deputies is personal. Only under specific conditions can there be a vote by proxy, and it is stated that "no deputy can receive more than one proxy." Attendance at the debates is obligatory, and unauthorized absence entails sanctions. The president of the National Assembly is elected for the whole legislative term, thus avoiding annual elections that in the past placed him at the mercy of the various parliamentary groups. The Senate elects its president every three years.

The Parliament can no longer establish its own standing orders. They must be approved by the Constitutional Council before they become effective. The number of parliamentary committees is reduced and their functions carefully circumscribed. Only six committees are allowed by the constitution. It is further stated that the government text of a bill and not the committees' amendments and counterproposals, as under the Fourth Republic, come before the floor. The government has the right to reject all amendments and to demand a vote on its own text.

All these provisions are directed against "Assembly government." By putting rules into the constitution that are essentially of a procedural character, it was hoped to limit Parliament to the performance of its proper functions of deliberation and to protect the executive from legislative encroachments. The new rules reflect a genuine desire to correct some of the more flagrant abuses of the past and are consistent with the strengthening of the executives in modern democracies. Some of the rules, however, are designed to weaken Parliament, for instance, the limitative enumeration of matters on which Parliament can legislate, and the manner in which the relations between the government and Parliament are established.

Relations between Parliament and Government. Four major provisions of a general character determine the nature of the relations between Parliament and the government: (1) the incompatibility between the parliamentary mandate and a cabinet post, (2) the manner in which the responsibility of the cabinet before the Parliament comes into play, (3) the distinction between "legislation" and "rule making," and (4) the introduction of the "executive budget."

THE RULE OF INCOMPATIBILITY. Article 23 of the constitution is explicit: "The 'office' of member of government is incompatible with the exercise of any parliamentary mandate." Thus, a member of Parliament who joins the cabinet must resign his mandate for the balance of the legislative term. He is replaced in Parliament by the person whose name appeared together with his on the ballot—the *suppléant*. Nonparliamentarians may become cabinet members, which was the rare exception in the Third and Fourth Republics. Despite the rule of incompatibility, cabinet members sit in Parliament and participate freely in the debates.

The purpose of the rule was to introduce a genuine separation of powers and to discourage parliamentarians from trying to become ministers, which was one of the major causes for the high rate of cabinet turnovers. It was also the avowed intention of the framers to establish a government that would be better able to resist pressures emanating from parliamentary groups and thus be in a position to give its undivided attention to its duties.

RESPONSIBILITY OF THE CABINET BEFORE THE LEGISLATURE. The responsibility of the cabinet to the legislature comes into play in a number of ways. After the prime minister has been nominated by the President of the Republic, he presents his program before the National Assembly and, through a minister, before the Senate. This programmatic statement calls for a vote in favor or against. In the first case, the cabinet, to use the terminology of the Fourth Republic, is "invested," while in the second case, the prime minister must submit his resignation to the President of the Republic. A vote by simple majority against the prime minister and his program is all that is required to dismiss the government at this stage. In the course of the year the prime minister may, at his discretion, make before the National Assembly "declarations of general policy," which may or may not, at his discretion, give rise to a vote.

After the cabinet has been invested, its responsibility to Parliament can be engaged in the following manner: The National Assembly (but not the Senate) has the right to introduce a motion of censure, which must be signed by one tenth of the members of the National Assembly. The vote on the motion takes place forty-eight hours after it has been introduced. The motion is lost unless it receives an absolute majority of the members composing the National Assembly. Blank ballots and abstentions count for the government. If the motion is carried, the government must resign; if the motion is lost, then its signatories cannot move another one in the course of the same legislative session.

The prime minister may, after consultation with the cabinet, stake the life of his government on any general issue of policy or on any given legislative text. Although the constitution does not use the term, this is equivalent to putting the "question of confidence." In the first case, the declaration of a general policy is presumed to be accepted unless there is a motion of censure voted under the conditions mentioned previously. In the second case, the bill becomes law unless a motion of censure is introduced and voted according to the same conditions, but with one difference: The same signatories may introduce a motion of censure as many times as the prime minister stakes his government's responsibility.

Thus, if the motion is carried by an absolute majority, the bill does not become law and the government resigns. If, however, the motion is lost, and it is lost even if carried by a relative majority, then the text becomes law and the government stays in office.

"LAW" AND "RULE MAKING." The constitution provides, in accordance with the canons of parliamentary government, that "law is voted by Parliament." Members of Parliament and of the government can introduce bills and amendments. The scope of law making, however, is defined in the constitution (Article 34) to include:

> . . . the *regulations* concerning:
> civil rights and the fundamental guarantees granted to the citizens for the exercise of their public liberties; . . .
> nationality, status and legal capacity of persons, marriage contracts, inheritance and gifts;
> determination of crimes and misdemeanors as well as the penalties imposed therefor; criminal procedure; . . .
> the basis, the rate and the methods of collecting taxes of all types; the issuance of currency; . . .
> the electoral system of the Parliamentary assemblies and the local assemblies; . . .
> the nationalization of enterprises and the transfer of the property of enterprises from the public to the private sector; . . .
> [and the] fundamental *principles* of:
> the general organization of national defense;
> the free administration of local communities, the extent of their jurisdiction and their resources;
> education;
> property rights, civil and commercial obligations;
> legislation pertaining to employment, unions and social security.

This enumeration of legislative power is limitative and cannot be enlarged except by an organic law. Article 37 makes this point clear. "*All other matters,*" it states, "*than those which are in the domain of law fall within the rule-making sphere.*" It goes even further, "Legislative texts pertaining to such matters may be modified by decree." Thus, past laws dealing with matters that are now declared by the constitution to be beyond the powers of the legislature can be modified by simple decree. They are "delegalized." The same article and other provisions of the constitution ensure the distinction between legislation and rule making for the future by a series of safety devices.

The constitution provides expressly that all lawmaking power enjoyed by Parliament may be delegated to the executive. The system of *décrets-lois* of the Third Republic and analogous practices of the Fourth are thus enshrined in the constitution. "The government may for the execution of its program ask Parliament to authorize it to take by ordinances, within a limited period of time, measures which are normally reserved to the domain of law [Article 38]." Such ordinances come into force as soon as they are promulgated, but they are null and void if a bill for their ratification is not submitted by the government before Parliament within a prescribed time, or if the ratification of the bill is rejected.

THE BUDGET. The constitution introduces the "executive budget." The budget is submitted by the government to Parliament. Proposals stemming from members of Parliament "are not receivable if their adoption entails either a diminution of public resources or an increase in public expenditures [Article 47]." No bill entailing diminution of resources or additional expenditures is receivable at any time.

Safeguards buttressing the executive character of the budget have been written into the constitution. If forty days have elapsed after the budget has been submitted and the National Assembly still has not "decided" on the bill on a first reading, then the government may take the budget before the Senate, which is to make a decision within fifteen days. If it does, then the bill is returned to the National Assembly. In case of disaccord between the Senate and the National Assembly a conference committee between the two chambers may be set up at the discretion of the government. But "if Parliament has not decided within seventy days" after the introduction of the budget, then "the budget bill can be promulgated and put into effect by simple ordinance." [Article 47, par. 2 and 3].

The most striking innovation is a Constitutional Council composed of nine members who serve for a period of nine years. A variety of powers has been devolved upon the Constitutional Council. It supervises the presidential elections and the referendums and proclaims the results; it is the judge of the validity of all contested legislative elections, thus avoiding bitter and long controversies in the legislative assemblies. It is the ultimate court of appeal on the interpretation of the constitution on a limited number of matters. Thus, all bills, including treaties, may be referred to it, before their promulgation, by the President of the Republic, the prime minister, or one of the presidents of the two assemblies. A declaration of unconstitutionality suspends the promulgation of the bill or the application of the treaty. It is the judge of the constitutionality of all standing orders and organic laws, which go before it automatically. It is, finally, the guardian of legislative-executive relations in all matters concerning the respective legislative competence of the two branches.

EVOLUTION OF THE GAULLIST CONSTITUTION

General de Gaulle's view of the presidency underwent a change in the first five years of the Fifth Republic. In 1958, when the constitution was being drafted, De Gaulle rejected presidential government; he insisted rather on the "responsibility of the prime minister and his cabinet before the National Assembly," which is the hallmark of a parliamentary system. In 1961, however, he declared: "Let us say that our regime is both parliamentary and presidential in terms of what both the requirements of balance and the traits of our character demand."[1] De Gaulle summed up his view of the presidential office:

. . . and there is also a Chief of State. . . . You know the nature of the functions of the President of the Republic has undergone a profound modification. . . . It is for me to assure, no matter what happens, the continuity of the State and the regular functioning of the public powers. It is for me to be, whatever may happen, the guarantor of the independence and the integrity of France and of the execution of the treaties signed, in other words of the honor of France; if the ordinary operation of the public powers is not adequate it is for me to appeal directly to the people by referendums. It is for me, when the Republic is menaced to take the measures needed by the circumstances. . . .[2]

As a consequence of the President's role as "custodian" and guardian of the Constitution, his policy-making power has been expanded. In a remarkable exchange in the National Assembly with the socialist leader Guy Mollet, Prime Minister Michel Debré spoke as follows:

I must add that the Constitution makes of the Chief of State an arbiter. Arbitrage—may be envisaged in two ways. Either the Chief of State arbitrates among political formations in order to assure the functioning of the constitutional mechanisms or he arbitrates among all the interests of national importance in order to discover and express national interest.[3]

Many instruments were available to the President in performing this exalted role: the threat of dissolution, emergency powers, and a Cabinet that was in effect a creature of the President. In all matters pertaining to the reserved presidential sector—especially with regard to matters of defense, Algeria, and foreign policy—a number of *ad hoc* committees were created, composed of ministers and De Gaulle's personal advisers. The great decisions on negotiations with the Algerian rebels, the status of Sahara, the independence of the members of the French Community, an atomic striking force, the refusal to participate in the Geneva disarmament conference, the Common Market, the Franco-German treaty of cooperation, and the exclusion of England from the Common Market, were all made by De Gaulle. The weekly meetings of the Council of Ministers were limited to a confrontation of views and opinions. There was no deliberation from which decisions flowed.

The President of the Republic decided also upon the composition of the Cabinet. He dismissed Antoine Pinay, the Minister of Finance, in January, 1960. Later Jacques Soustelle was expelled from the Cabinet without the knowledge of the Prime Minister. De Gaulle was personally responsible for the appointment of Louis Joxe as Minister of Algerian Affairs. The Prime Minister, Michel Debré, resigned in April, 1962, because of a decision by the President, not the Parliament. The new Prime

---

[1] Press conference of April 11, 1961.

[2] Speech of November 4, 1960, in *Année Politique*, 1960, p. 662.

[3] André Passeron, *De Gaulle Parle* (Paris, 1962), p. 20.

Minister, Georges Pompidou, was De Gaulle's personal choice. Thus not only is there a Presidential Cabinet overshadowing the regularly constituted one, but the composition and the work of the latter depend upon the wishes of the President of the Republic. Article 20 of the Constitution of the Fifth Republic, which states in the most unequivocal terms that the "government shall determine and direct the policy of the nation," is virtually a dead letter.

At the very outset General de Gaulle warned the legislature not to display the factionalism and divisions of the Fourth Republic. Its task was to use the limited powers given to it by the Constitution, to make "good" laws and cooperate with the government. If the legislature failed to do so, there was the ever-present threat of dissolution or referendum. With the passage of time De Gaulle became increasingly impatient with the national "intermediaries."

In his speech of April 6, 1962, De Gaulle outlined a new conception of the role of the referendum:

Already, in four years, we have accomplished, by means of the referendum, three major changes, which it had been impossible to bring about until then in spite of countless trials and endless debates. It was by this very method —the method of referendum—that we gave ourselves such institutions that stability, authority and the continuity of the state have replaced a system of crises, impotence and confusion. It was by this same method that we transformed into cooperative relations with twelve African republics and the Malagasy Republic the colonial relations that we formerly pursued on their territories—cooperative relations which have brought about in this vast complex a state of peace, progress and truly exemplary understanding, which forms a striking contrast to the agitation, the conflicts and the rivalries which are stirring so many African, Asiatic and American regions. It was by this same method that, at the proper time, we recognized Algeria's right to selfdetermination and, at the same time, brought an appeasement of feelings, prevailed upon the leaders of the rebellion to agree to negotiations, saw to it that all attempts to force the will of the country in the opposite direction could not be, and are not, anything but adventures that are both futile and criminal. . . .

Provided by the Constitution, the referendum enters into our habits, adding something essential to the legislative role of Parliament. From now on every citizen will be able, as is the case now, to express himself directly on a vital issue, to judge and to assume his part of the responsibility. Without doubt the character and the functioning of the institutions will be profoundly influenced.

The scope of the referendum has been broadened to include the process of constitutional amendment. Nowhere does the Constitution state that an amendment can be submitted to the people without prior approval of the Parliament. Article 11 states limitatively the matters that can be submitted directly to the people in a referendum. The referendum has also become an instrument of direct delegation of legislative powers to the President. The second part of the text submitted to the people on April of 1962, reads as follows:

Until the institutions of the new political organization that will ultimately emerge from the self-determination of the Algerian populations, the President of the Republic may enact, by ordinance, or as the case may be, by decrees passed by the Council of Ministers, all legislative regulatory measures concerning the application of the government declaration of March 19 [the Evian Accord].

Popular endorsement, in other words, established a *régime d'exception* in which the power derived by the President from the referendum overshadowed all others. Finally De Gaulle used the referendum on all occasions to secure a popular vote of confidence in his own person and his own leadership. On January 6, 1960, De Gaulle stated in urging the voters to vote in favor of the policy of Algerian self-determination: "Your answer will be given for me." He concluded his address as follows: "Yes, I need to know what is in your minds and hearts. This is why I turn to you above all intermediaries. To be frank—and who does not know it?—the matter is between you all, men and women, and myself." Speaking on the eve of the referendum of April, 1962, he declared:

Finally, I can and I must, say that to give an affirmative and massive answer—as I ask—to the question that I am presenting to the French people, is for them to answer me personally, that in my capacity as Head of State, they are giving me their adherence; that they are conferring upon me the right to perform, despite any obstacles, what is necessary in order to attain the goal; in short, that in the very trying task that is incumbent upon me and of which *the Algerian affair is one part among others, I have their confidence with me for today and tomorrow.*

For the referendum of October, 1962, the appeal was even more blatant. "For me," he exclaimed in his televised address of October 4, "each vote *given to me* by each one of you—women and men—will be . . . the direct proof of his or her confidence and encouragement." In the midst of the Cuban crisis he implied that if the majority in favor of his proposal was "weak or uncertain" he might resign from office. What was originally conceived as a popular consultation on specific issues became an instrument for constitutional reform and delegation of lawmaking power and a periodic vote of confidence in the President for "today and tomorrow." The issues involved became a secondary consideration. The referendum was transformed into a plebiscite.

The expansion of presidential power was accompanied by a modification with regard to the election of the president. On October 4, 1962, in a special message to Parliament, De Gaulle unveiled his plans for a new reform. The "presidential college" was to be abolished. The president was to be elected by direct popular vote. In the event that no candidate received an absolute majority, a second ballot would be held two weeks later in which only the two leading candidates or, in case of withdrawals, two of the "most favored" candidates would run. No modification was suggested in the powers of the president. No checks were introduced against the exercise of his prerogatives notably dissolution, referendums, and emergency powers. No re-examination was undertaken of the relations between president, prime minister, and the National Assembly. The new mode of election simply reinforces the power of the president.

The extraordinarily broad powers of the president, whoever he may be, pose a continuing threat to the democratic system. A constant temptation will be dangled before any man of lesser stature than De Gaulle. If the National Assembly attempts to interfere in the exercise of his powers and if the prime minister sides with the Assembly a clash between the president and the Parliament will be unavoidable. Or it may take the form of prolonged and paralyzing frictions to which neither a referendum nor a dissolution with elections may provide a satisfactory solution. A president who resorts to emergency powers may have his way but not without endangering democratic freedoms and leaving a backlog of resentment and illwill. The constitutional reform suggested by General de Gaulle and endorsed in the referendum has left the institutional problem intact. In case of international tension or domestic crisis the system may invite a presidential dictatorship, or the emergence of a strong man supported by the president. The ghost of the Weimar Republic may yet stalk modern France.

After five years of Gaullist rule the formidable constitutional powers given to the president have been expanded even further. The regime operates today on the basis of a number of premises (one cannot speak of rules or norms as yet) that underline its personal character. The president, it is now understood, interprets the constitution whenever the Constitutional Council is not competent. Since the powers of the latter are limitatively defined, the president is given great discretion over a host of matters. The president can dismiss both the prime minister and individual ministers. The president participates actively and intervenes personally in the formation of the cabinet and the appointment of cabinet ministers. It is now held that virtually all policy matters, including even labor disputes, come under the jurisdiction of the president and his staff. The president no longer merely presides over discussions in the meetings of the Council of Ministers—he makes the decisions. The president, after declaring a state of emergency, remains the sole judge of its duration. Finally, calling a referendum is a personal act and the subject matter on which the people are to render their sovereign verdict can also include a delegation of power to the president—a delegation providing a source of legal authority that transcends law and even the Constitution itself.

Thus the French system is not parliamentary. The lawmaking functions of Parliament, its ability to question and scrutinize and hold the prime minister responsible are narrowly circumscribed. Above all, in contrast to the British, German, and all other parliamentary systems, it is not the responsible prime minister who makes policy, but the president. But neither is the regime presidential. In the United States the president does not enjoy many of the powers the French president has today. He cannot dissolve, he cannot hold a referendum over a policy question, and he cannot legislate, except within limits narrowly defined by Congress. Nor is he a final judge of the meaning of the constitution. The political system in France is neither "parliamentary" nor "presidential." It is personal rule.

Chapter XI. Representative Government

Introductory Note

THE MOST characteristic trend in virtually all contemporary systems, as we noted in the introductory essay to this section, is the concentration of deliberative and decision-making power in the hands of the executive branch of the government. The "decline" of the British Parliament was perceived early by John Stuart Mill and James Bryce. In the United States, Woodrow Wilson's sharp criticism of congressional interference with the executive prerogatives has often been repeated in a series of books such as W. Y. Elliott's *The Need for Constitutional Reform* (1935); Henry Hazlitt's *A New Constitution Now* (1942); Thomas K Finletter's *Can Representative Government Do the Job?* (1945), and many others. Richard Neustadt's recent, *Presidential Power: The Politics of Leadership* (1960) and Clinton Rossiter's, *The American Presidency* (1958) demonstrate that initiative and policy formulation is increasingly lodged in the president's office. Thus, "presidential government" has become a reality in the United States.

Deliberation means confrontation of various points of view, and debate, in order to reach a decision. The process requires accurate information and expert knowledge. Intelligence must be "institutionalized" so that decisions will be based upon relevant data. The provision of intelligence, expertise, and information has become the province of specialized executive agencies. The vast majority of persons working in these agencies hold no political and representative office. They are civil servants or technicians, hierarchically responsible to the president or the prime minister.

With the growth of the executive a number of parallel developments can be noted. Interest groups have been increasingly attempting to gain access to the executive and its agencies. Frequently, functional committees or advisory bodies have been created, enabling interest groups to express their views within the executive. This tendency has been commented on in Kenneth Wheare, *Government by Committee* (1955); Roland V. Vernon, *Advisory Bodies: A Study of Their Uses in Relation to Central Government* (1940); and Jean Meynaud, *Groupes de Pression en France* (1959). The same is true for the United States as indicated in the studies by R. Cushman, *The Independent Regulatory Commissions* (1941); W. Gellhorn, *Federal Administrative Proceedings* (1941); and Avery Leiserson, *Administrative Regulation* (1942).

351

There has been a shift in all parliamentary systems from "democracy by delegation" to "democracy by consent." That is, the nineteenth century idea according to which public opinion through voluntary associations and political parties delegated to the government power to carry out specific policies has been gradually abandoned. Democratic government now acts on the basis of over-all consent, rather than a clearly defined popular mandate. Initiation and policy making is increasingly in the hands of an elite composed of political leaders, civil servants, top military personnel, and industrial managers.

The threat of manipulation of the public by this elite is ever present. Perhaps the major function of the legislature and the political parties is to present different points of view, to mobilize the public in favor of alternative schemes and policies, thus providing safeguards against the possibility that consent will be manufactured, as in totalitarian systems. In the "new nations" the trend is distinctly in favor of a government by manipulation in which public opinion is created and directed by a small core of political leaders.

Readings

34. THE PROPER FUNCTIONS OF REPRESENTATIVE BODIES*

John Stuart Mill

THE MEANING of representative government is, that the whole people, or some numerous portion of them, exercise through deputies periodically elected by themselves the ultimate controlling power, which, in every constitution, must reside somewhere. This ultimate power they must possess in all its completeness. They must be masters, whenever they please, of all the operations of government. . . .

But while it is essential to representative government that the practical supremacy in the state should reside in the representatives of the people, it is an open question what actual functions, what precise part in the machinery of government, shall be directly and personally discharged by the representative body. Great varieties in this respect are compatible with the essence of representative government, provided the functions are such as secure to the representative body the control of everything in the last resort.

There is a radical distinction between controlling the business of government and actually doing it. The same person or body may be able

* From *Representative Government* (1861), Chapter V.

to control everything, but cannot possibly do everything; and in many cases its control over everything will be more perfect the less it personally attempts to do. The commander of an army could not direct its movements effectually if he himself fought in the ranks, or led an assault. It is the same with bodies of men. Some things cannot be done except by bodies, other things cannot be well done by them. It is one question, therefore, what a popular assembly should control, another what it should itself do. It should, as we have already seen, control all the operations of government. But in order to determine through what channel this general control may most expediently be exercised, and what portion of the business of government the representative assembly should hold in its own hands, it is necessary to consider what kinds of business a numerous body is competent to perform properly. That alone which it can do well it ought to take personally upon itself. With regard to the rest, its proper province is not to do it, but to take means for having it well done by others.

For example, the duty which is considered as belonging more peculiarly than any other to an assembly representative of the people, is that of voting the taxes. Nevertheless, in no country does the representative body undertake, by itself or its delegated officers, to prepare the estimates. Though the supplies can only be voted by the House of Commons, and though the sanction of the House is also required for the appropriation of the revenues to the different items of the public expenditure, it is the maxim and the uniform practice of the Constitution that money can be granted only on the proposition of the Crown. It has, no doubt, been felt, that moderation as to the amount, and care and judgment in the detail of its application, can only be expected when the executive government, through whose hands it is to pass, is made responsible for the plans and calculations on which the disbursements are grounded. Parliament, accordingly, is not expected, nor even permitted, to originate directly either taxation or expenditure. All it is asked for is its consent, and the sole power it possesses is that of refusal.

The principles which are involved and recognized in this constitutional doctrine, if followed as far as they will go, are a guide to the limitation and definition of the general functions of representative assemblies. In the first place, it is admitted in all countries in which the representative system is practically understood, that numerous representative bodies ought not to administer. The maxim is grounded not only on the most essential principles of good government, but on those of the successful conduct of business of any description. No body of men, unless organised and under command, is fit for action, in the proper sense. Even a select board, composed of few members, and these specially conversant with the business to be done, is always an inferior instrument to some one individual who could be found among them, and would be improved in character if that one person were made the chief, and all the others reduced to subordinates. What can be done better by a body than by any individual is deliberation. When it is necessary or important to secure hearing and consideration to many conflicting opinions, a deliberative body is indispensable. Those bodies, therefore, are frequently useful, even for administrative business, but in general only as advisers, such business being, as a rule, better conducted under the responsibility of one. Even a joint-stock company has always in practice, if not in theory, a managing director; its good or bad management depends essentially on some one person's qualifications, and the remaining directors, when of any use, are so by their suggestions to him, or by the power they possess of watching him, and restraining or removing him in case of misconduct. That they are ostensibly equal sharers with him in the management is no advantage, but a considerable set-off against any good which they are capable of doing: it weakens greatly the sense in his own mind, and in those of other people, of that individual responsibility in which he should stand forth personally and undividedly.

But a popular assembly is still less fitted to administer, or to dictate in detail to those who have the charge of administration. Even when honestly meant, the interference is almost always injurious. Every branch of public administration is a skilled business, which has its own peculiar principles and traditional rules, many of them not even known, in any effectual way, except to those who have at some time had a hand in carrying on the business, and none of them likely to be duly appreciated by persons not practically acquainted with the department. I do not mean that the transaction of public business has esoteric mysteries, only to be understood by the initiated. Its principles are all intelligible to any person of good sense, who has in his mind a true picture of the circumstances and conditions to be dealt with: but to have this he must know those circumstances and conditions; and the knowledge does not come by intuition. There are many rules of the greatest importance in every branch of public business (as there are in every private occupation), of which a person fresh to the subject neither knows the reason or even suspects the existence, because they are intended to meet dangers or provide against inconveniences which never entered into his thoughts. I have known public men, ministers, of more than ordinary natural capacity, who on their first introduction to a department of business new to them, have excited the mirth of their inferiors by the air with which they announced as a truth hitherto set at nought, and brought to light by themselves, something which was probably the first thought of everybody who ever looked at the subject, given up as soon as he had got on to a second. It is true that a great statesman is he who knows when to depart from traditions as well as when to adhere to them. But it is a great mistake to suppose that he will do this better for being ignorant of the traditions. No one who does not thoroughly know the modes of action which common experience has sanctioned is capable of judging of the circumstances which require a departure from those ordinary modes of action. The interests dependent on the acts done by a public department, the consequences liable to follow from any particular mode of conducting it, require for weighing and estimating them a kind of knowledge, and of specially exercised judgment, almost as rarely found in those not bred to it, as the capacity to reform the law in those who have not professionally studied it. All these difficulties are sure to be ignored by a representative assembly which attempts to decide on special acts of administration. At its best, it is inexperience sitting in judgment on experience, ignorance on knowledge: ignorance which never suspecting the existence of what it does not know, is equally careless and supercilious, making light of, if not resenting, all pretensions to have a judgment better worth attending to than its own. Thus it is when no interested motives intervene; but when they do, the result is jobbery more unblushing and audacious than the worst corruption which can well take place in a public office under a government of publicity. It is not necessary that the interested bias should extend to the majority of the assembly. In any particular case it is often enough that it affects two or three of their number. Those two or three will have a greater interest in misleading the body, than any other of its members are likely to have in putting it right. The bulk of the assembly may keep their hands clean, but they cannot keep their minds vigilant or their judgments discerning in matters they know nothing about; and an indolent majority, like an indolent individual, belongs to the person who takes most pains with it. The bad measures or bad appointments of a minister may be checked by Parliament; and the interest of ministers in defending, and of rival partisans in attacking, secures a tolerably equal discussion: but *quis custodiet custodes?* who shall check the Parliament? A minister, a head of an office, feels himself under some responsibility. An assembly in such cases feels under no responsibility at all: for when did any member of Parliament lose his seat for the vote he gave on any detail of administration? To a minister, or the head of an office, it is of more importance what will be thought of his proceedings some time hence than what is thought of them at the instant: but an assembly, if the cry of the moment goes with it, however hastily raised or artificially stirred up, thinks itself and is thought by everybody to be completely exculpated however disastrous may be the consequences. Besides, an assembly never personally experiences the inconveniences of its bad measures until they have reached the dimensions of national evils. Ministers and administrators see them approaching, and have to bear all the annoyance and trouble of attempting to ward them off.

The proper duty of a representative assembly in regard to matters of administration is not to decide them by its own vote, but to take care that the persons who have to decide them shall by the proper persons. Even this they cannot advantageously do by nominating the individuals. There is no act which more imperatively requires to be performed under a strong sense of individual responsibility than the nomination to employments. The experience of every person conversant with public affairs bears out the assertion, that there is scarcely any act respecting which the conscience of an average man is less sensitive; scarcely any case in which less consideration is paid to qualifications, partly because men do not know, and partly because they do not care for, the difference in qualifications between one person and another. When a minister makes what is meant to be an honest appointment, that is when he does not actually job it for his personal connections or his party, an ignorant person might suppose that he would try to give it to the person best qualified. No such thing. An ordinary minister thinks himself a miracle of virtue if he gives it to a person of merit, or who has a claim on the public on any account, though the claim or the merit may be of the most opposite description to that required. . . . Besides, the qualifications which fit special individuals for special duties can only be recognised by those who know the individuals, or who make it their business to examine and judge of persons from what they have done, or from the evidence of those who are in a position to judge. When these conscientious obligations are so little regarded by great public officers who can be made responsible for their appointments, how must it be with assemblies who cannot? Even now, the worst appointments are those which are made for the sake of gaining support or disarming opposition in the representative body: what might we expect if they were made by the body itself? Numerous bodies never regard special qualifications at all. Unless a man is fit for the gallows, he is thought to be about as fit as other people for almost anything for which he can offer himself as a candidate. When appointments made by a public body are not decided, as they almost always are, by party connection or private jobbing, a man is appointed either because he has a reputation, often quite undeserved, for *general* ability, or frequently for no better reason than that he is personally popular.

It has never been thought desirable that Parliament should itself nominate even the members of a Cabinet. It is enough that it virtually decides who shall be prime minister, or who shall be the two or three individuals from whom the prime minister shall be chosen. In doing this it merely recognises the fact that a certain person is the candidate of the party whose general policy commands its support. In reality, the only thing which Parliament decides is, which of two, or at most three, parties or bodies of men, shall furnish the executive government: the opinion of the party itself decides which of its members is fittest to be placed at the head. According to the existing practice of the British Constitution, these things seem to be on as good a footing as they can be. Parliament does not nominate any minister, but the Crown appoints the head of the administration in conformity to the general wishes and inclinations manifested by Parliament, and the other ministers on the recommendation of the chief; while every minister has the undivided moral responsibility of appointing fit persons to the other offices of administration which are not permanent. In a republic, some other arrangement would be necessary: but the nearer it approached in practice to that which has long existed in England, the more likely it would be to work well. Either, as in the American republic, the head of the Executive must be elected by some agency entirely independent of the representative body; or the body must content itself with naming the prime minister, and making him responsible for the choice of his associates and subordinates. To all these considerations, at least theoretically, I fully anticipate a general assent: though, practically, the tendency is strong in representative bodies to interfere more and more in the details of administration, by virtue of the general law, that whoever has the strongest power is more and more tempted to make an excessive use of it; and this is one of the practical dangers to which the futurity of representative governments will be exposed.

But it is equally true, though only of late and slowly beginning to be acknowledged, that a numerous assembly is as little fitted for the direct business of legislation as for that of administration. There is hardly any kind of intellectual work which so much needs to be done, not only by experienced and exercised minds, but by minds trained to the task through long and laborious study, as the business of making laws. This is a sufficient reason, were there no other, why they can never be well made but by a committee of very few persons. A reason no less conclusive is, that every provision of a law requires to be framed with the most accurate and long-sighted perception of its effect on all the other provisions; and the law when made should be capable of fitting into a consistent whole with the previously existing laws. It is impossible that these conditions should be in any degree fulfilled when laws are voted clause by clause in a miscellaneous assembly. The incongruity of such a mode of legislating would strike all minds, were it not that our laws are already, as to form and construction, such a chaos, that the confusion and contradiction seem incapable of being made greater by any addition to the mass. Yet even now, the utter unfitness of our legislative machinery for its purpose is making itself practically felt every year more and more. The mere time necessarily occupied in getting through Bills renders Parliament more and more incapable or passing any, except on detached and narrow points. If a Bill is prepared which even attempts to deal with the whole of any subject (and it is impossible to legislate properly on any part without having the whole present to the mind), it hangs over from session to session through sheer impossibility of finding time to dispose of it. It matters not though the Bill may have been deliberately drawn up by the authority deemed the best qualified, with all appliances and means to boot; or by a select commission, chosen for their conversancy with the subject, and having employed years in considering and digesting the particular measure; it cannot be passed, because the House of Commons will not forego the precious privilege of tinkering it with their clumsy hands. . . . It is one of the evils of the present mode of managing these things that the explaining and defending of a Bill, and of its various provisions, is scarcely ever performed by the person from whose mind they emanated, who probably has not a seat in the House. Their defense rests upon some minister or member of Parliament who did not frame them, who is dependent on cramming for all his arguments but those which are perfectly obvious, who does not know the full strength of his case, nor the best reasons by which to support it, and is wholly incapable of meeting unforeseen objections. This evil, as far as Government bills are concerned, admits of remedy, and has been remedied in some representative constitutions, by allowing the Government to be represented in either House by persons in its confidence, having a right to speak, though not to vote. . . .

Instead of the function of governing, for which it is radically unfit, the proper office of a representative assembly is to watch and control the government: to throw the light of publicity on its acts: to compel a full exposition and justification of all of them which any one considers questionable; to censure them if found condemnable, and, if the men who compose the government abuse their trust, or fulfil it in a manner which conflicts with the deliberate sense of the nation, to expel them from office, and either expressly or virtually appoint their successors. This is surely ample power, and security enough for the liberty of the nation. In addition to this, the Parliament has an office, not inferior even to this in importance; to be at once the nation's Committee of Grievances, and its Congress of Opinions; an arena in which not only the general opinion of the nation, but that of every section of it, and as far as possible of every eminent individual whom it contains, can produce itself in full light and challenge discussion; where every person in the country may count upon finding somebody who speaks his mind, as well or better than he could speak it himself—not to friends and partisans exclusively, but in the face of opponents, to be tested by adverse controversy; where those whose opinion is overruled, feel satisfied that it is heard, and set aside not by a mere act of will, but for what are thought superior reasons, and commend themselves as such to the representatives of the majority of the nation; where every party or opinion in the country can muster its strength, and be cured of any illusion concerning the number or power of its adherents; where the opinion which prevails in the nation makes itself manifest as prevailing, and marshals its hosts in the presence of the government, which is thus enabled and compelled to give way to it on the mere manifestation, without the actual employment, of its strength; where statesmen can assure themselves, far more certainly than by any other signs, what elements of opinion and power are growing, and what declining, and are enabled to shape their measures with some regard not solely to present exigencies, but to tendencies in progress. Representative assemblies are often taunted by their enemies with being places of mere talk and *bavardage*. There has seldom been more misplaced derision. I know not how a representative assembly can more usefully employ itself than in talk, when the subject of talk is the great public interests of the country, and every sentence of it represents the opinion either of some important body of persons in the nation, or of an individual in whom some such body have reposed their confidence. A place where every interest and shade of opinion in the country can have its cause even passionately pleaded, in the face of the government and of all other interests and opinions, can compel them to listen, and either comply, or state clearly why they do not, is in itself, if it answered no other purpose, one of the most important political institutions that can exist anywhere, and one of the foremost benefits of free government. Such "talking" would never be looked upon with disparagement if it were not allowed to stop "doing"; which it never would, if assemblies knew and acknowledged that talking and discussion are their proper business, while *doing*, as the result of discussion, is the task not of a miscellaneous body, but of individuals specially trained to it; that the fit office of an assembly is to see that those individuals are honestly and intelligently chosen, and to interfere no further with them, except by unlimited latitude of suggestion and criticism, and by applying or withholding the final seal of national assent. It is for want of this judicious reserve that popular assemblies attempt to do what they cannot do well—to govern and legislate—and provide no machinery but their own for much of it, when of course every hour spent in talk is an hour withdrawn from actual business. But the very fact which most unfits such bodies for a Council of Legislation qualifies them the more for their other office—namely, that they are not a selection of the greatest political minds in the country, from whose opinions little could with certainty be inferred concerning those of the nation, but are, when properly constituted, a fair sample of every grade of intellect among the people which is at all entitled to a voice in public affairs. Their part is to indicate wants, to be an organ for popular demands, and a place of adverse discussion for all opinions relating to public matters, both great and small; and, along with this, to check by criticism, and eventually by withdrawing their support, those high public officers who really conduct the public business, or who appoint those by whom it is conducted. Nothing but the restriction of the function of representative bodies within these rational limits will enable the benefits of popular control to be enjoyed in conjunction with the no less important requisites (growing ever more important as human affairs increase in scale and in complexity) of skilled legislation and administration. There are no means of combining these benefits except by separating the functions which guarantee the one from those which essentially require the other; by disjoining the office of control and criticism from the actual conduct of affairs, and devolving the former on the representatives of the Many, while securing for the latter, under strict responsibility to the nation, the acquired knowledge and practised intelligence of a specially trained and experienced Few.

35. THE CRISIS OF MODERN PARLIAMENTS*

Karl Dietrich Bracher

THE DILEMMA

THE PHRASE "crisis of parliamentarism" is nearly as old as the phenomenon of modern parliamentary democracy. It is closely bound up with the deeply rooted social and intellectual transformations in which the process of emancipation—first with a liberal, then with a socialistic stamp—broke the framework of constitutional government based on privileged estates, and in which the principle of full representation and participation of all citizens in a parliament chosen in a general and equal election was carried out. This development reached its critical peak after World War I. For the concept of parliamentary democracy the moment of apparently complete victory over the autocracies of old Europe signified at the same time the beginning of a structural crisis which particularly affected the newly created parliamentary democracies of Europe and which aided the strongly antiparliamentary dictatorial movements toward a quick rise.

With the exception of Czechoslovakia and Finland this crisis quickly displaced and destroyed all new parliamentary democracies: in Russia and the Baltic states; in Poland, Hungary and the Balkan countries; in Italy, Germany and Austria; in Spain and Portugal. Everywhere in this area the parliamentary system seemed to prove itself unworkable; almost nowhere did it seem capable of absorbing the political and social tensions of the "age of the masses" in a democratic order that was both stable and flexible. The transition from the old liberal parliamentarianism of well-to-do individuals (*Honoratiorenstaat*) to egalitarian party-state parliamentarianism led to serious functional disturbances even in the tradition-bound older democracies of Europe. In England, to be sure, it was possible to absorb the effects of these disturbances by thorough-going changes in the system of parliamentary rule; in France the Third Republic was able to sustain itself, but only with difficulty. Even in the Scandinavian countries, spared by the World War and apparently sheltered against the European crises, minority governments were often only provisionally able

---

* From "Problems of Parliamentary Democracy in Europe," *Daedalus* (Winter, 1964), pp. 179–98. Reprinted by permission of the American Academy of Arts and Sciences, the Editor of *Daedalus*, and the author.

to contain the tensions; even they scarcely provided a proof of the workability of the parliamentary system.

The second postwar epoch of the European parliamentary democracies is of course significantly different from this first crisis period, which ended in the catastrophe of another world war. On the one hand it was still confronted with those basic problems of democratic structural change which the nineteenth century had laid in the cradle of European parliamentarianism. But on the other hand conditions had deeply changed, giving a new profile to the attempts at reconstruction or new construction of parliamentarianism in western Europe after 1945. On three levels these new perspectives were opened.

1. *Constitutional:* The experience of the twenties and thirties directed attention to possible precautionary measures and modifications in the parliamentary system for the protection of its substance and its efficiency. The West German "chancellor democracy" and even more the half-parliamentary presidential regime of the Fifth Republic in France are examples of this attempt at a limitation of parliamentarianism.

2. *Sociological:* At the same time the process of realignment and leveling of society—the product of the radical changes of the war and postwar period, a tendency away from ideologizing and toward pragmatizing of the parties—fostered the concentration of parties and finally the approach to a two- or three-party system, which was strengthened and hastened by constitutional and technical electoral provisions. West Germany was the most strongly affected by this process, in the course of the immigration and absorption of well over ten million displaced persons. But the tendency characterized much too simply as "Americanization" of party and parliamentary life was strong in the rest of Europe as well. This development seemed to simplify the formation of an administration and an opposition, to clarify political alternatives and to allow the parliamentary process to become less hindered by the formation of ideological fronts.

3. *Foreign Affairs:* The decisive phase of European political change at the end of the forties was marked by an increasingly firm opposition to the dynamics of Soviet Russia's European politics. The American politics of restraint, the Marshall Plan, the establishment of NATO placed western Europe within the framework of a broader international cooperation. It opened aspects of a supranational integration which could have an incomparably more lasting effect on the internal politics and structure of the European states than the League of Nations had once had. The idea and the weight of a European and Atlantic community formed, first of all, a kind of protection for the new parliamentary democracies; insofar as they were still limited by powerful groups hostile to democracy—as in the case of France and Italy with their strong Communist parties—the growing interdependence meant a supplementary support.

The starting conditions for the "new Europe" thus seemed more favorable than in 1918. The attempt at a self-limitation of sovereignties had taken the place of a confusion of national ambitions, which at that time had made the rise and triumph of nationalistic dictatorial movements possible. The East-West conflict seemed to outweigh the internal explosive forces of national parliamentarianism. In the foreground stood the overlapping problems of political cooperation, economic and military networks, and the overcoming of the colonial age. In the face of such problems intrastate tensions tended to diminish in sharpness and importance or at least to recede to a deeper level of confrontations more specific and more suited to compromise. Such a prognosis seemed especially plausible from the German point of view. Had not Germany immediately after the occupation joined, as the Federal Republic, the European and Atlantic politics of alliance, within whose frame the West German parliament system could develop and stabilize itself almost without hindrance? Indeed, the experience of a parliamentary democracy operating with political and economic success was something entirely new in the history of German political thought, which had learned from the catastrophes of 1848, 1918 and 1933 to identify parliamentary politics with crisis and collapse.

But these positive perspectives reflect only the external, superficial image of the reconstruction period. They say nothing about the real stability and functional capability of the reconstituted parliamentary democracies of western Europe. Upon closer inspection it has quickly become apparent not only that the old problems of parliamentary politics continued to exist unsolved under the double protection mentioned, but also that the new conditions of the postwar period, with their revolutionizing consequences in the economic, social and intellectual areas, necessarily led to new crises of adjustment in the political system. It became a question whether and how, in the light of the changes cited, the individual parliaments would be able to carry out their role—which was still conceived in the classical sense of control and "decision-making"—in the actual practice of national politics. The increasingly complicated network of the modern industrial state confronted them with a dismaying array of new problems for which political common sense and the old parliamentary practice no longer seemed adequate. These problems threatened to undermine the competence and decision-making ability of the individual member of parliament, to strengthen at the cost of parliament the power of committees, experts and the bureaucracy of the executives and to lead toward an undermining of the parliamentary system of government from within.

As a result a series of surprisingly similar basic questions came to the fore in all of the western democracies. Is a parliament as such still capable, under such circumstances, of exercising an effective control of politics, not even to mention active participation in the formulation of political desires? Further, is it possible any longer to defend the submission of complicated economic, social and military decisions, which demand precise planning, to the tedious discussion procedure of technically incompetent large assemblies, considering that the deliberations of a small circle of committee experts are simply repeated in these sessions? And under these circumstances is it at all possible to continue upholding the classical basic principle of parliamentarianism—to combine democratic representation and the correct decision of all questions—or does not the parliamentary process become reduced to a formality in the face of the incompetence of the mass of the representatives?

A further consideration derives from the fact that precisely the supra- and international network of those technical decisions transcends the capacities of the national parliaments and at the same time must impose sensitive limitations upon them. The development of European institutions has demonstrated in recent years what a great effect this consideration has had in shifting politics from the parliamentary level to that of administration and bureaucracy. A European bureaucracy of a new character has gained a decisive advance upon the parliamentary organs in those institutions; the supranational formation of politics has been shifted extensively to an extra- or superparliamentary area of competence handled by experts and governments; in the face of this power the merely advisory function of the European "parliaments," which moreover have possessed only a derivative legitimation, not a direct one through direct European elections, has had little effect.

In view of these problems our diagnosis of parliamentarianism in western Europe will consider the following elements. We shall inquire about the model, the reality and the structural transformation of "classical" parliamentarianism, which has also been the point of departure for the parliamentary democracies of postwar Europe. We shall analyze the most important factors and arguments that form the basis of this structural change. What are their consequences: the transformation or the decline of parliamentary politics? Last, we shall endeavor to ascertain what efforts toward reform, substitute forms and future perspectives can be recognized within the national and supranational framework. Although the examination will proceed from Germany to the particular conditions of the various countries, attention will be devoted principally to the typical instances of those problems which today more than ever bear a general European character, both in positive and in negative regards.

STRUCTURAL TRANSFORMATION OF DEMOCRACY

The "crisis of parliamentarianism" figured, immediately following World War I, as the central theme of countless conferences of the Interparliamentary Union—in Washington, Ottawa, Geneva, Paris, Prague and Berlin. The discussion probed deeply into essentials. It dealt with the actual and necessary adjustment to the new European situation; it vacillated between a modernization or a limitation of parliamentarianism. At the same time it became increasingly clear that parliamentarianism had undergone an actual structural transformation which also needed to be put into effect constitutionally and institutionally.

Indeed the language of the constitutions and of their interpreters—insofar as it referred to the original model of the "classical" parliamentarianism, developed according to the idealistically elevated English pattern—was so far from reality that it appeared to be more and more fictitious. Whereas constitutional theory held to the concept of the independent member of parliament, responsible only to his conscience, in reality the representative found himself to be working within a network of social and political ties, a network which had become increasingly dense with the complication of modern industrial society and with the organizational consolidation and increase in importance of parties and organized interest groups. The result was that the member of parliament, contrary to the postulates of the constitutions, was subjected increasingly, whether consciously or unconsciously, to an "imperative mandate" by party interests and other joint interests. His role as representative of the people as a whole had thereby become unreal. The classical-liberal form of representative parliamentarianism gave way to a parliamentary democracy determined by plebiscite and party politics, a democracy which also brought about far-reaching changes in the process of forming political opinion and the function of the parliament as an organ for decision and control.

The interrelationship of this "structural transformation of democracy" (Leibholz) with modern party history has meanwhile been thoroughly analyzed. After World War II some of the European constitutions tried to give the new reality its due—though only in a makeshift way and rather incidentally—by dedicating a few articles to the role of the parties and their structure. Probably the most prominent instance of this was in the Basic Law of the Federal Republic of Germany, the West German constitution of 1949, in which (contrary to the Weimar Constitution) not only is the participation of the parties in determination of political policy emphasized, but their democratic structure and their agreement with the ordinances of the constitution are also specifically required. To be sure the old postulate of representative democracy was also preserved. The deputies are considered the "representatives of the people as a whole, not bound to specific commissions and directions, and subject only to their consciences" (Art. 38); thus they are supposed to be free of the "imperative mandate" to which they are in fact so thoroughly bound by the manner of nomination of candidates, electoral modes, parliamentary practice and party coercion.

The whole tension between theory and practice continues in these introverse stipulations. In other European countries the situation appears to be scarcely any different. In the merely laconic, usually meaningless reference to the parties there still prevails that "conspiracy of silence"

(Loewenstein) with which the constitutions hold to the fiction of party-less parliamentarianism and the superparty parliament member. This is true of the Italian constitution (Art. 49) as well as of the French constitutions of the Fourth and Fifth Republics, even though the beginnings of a transformation are visible and in the practice of constitutional interpretation there is a growing attempt to give the political reality of party democracy its due. It is expected that this reality will be taken into account still more thoroughly by the new Swedish constitution, which has been in preparation for years with the authoritative participation of political science.

There is, however, a further aspect of that structural change which, although so far it has enjoyed less attention, has a more fundamental, comprehensive significance than the constitutional-political reform of the relationship between party, parliament and government. This is the expansion of the organized interest groups on the one hand and of public administration on the other hand. The consequence of both is that "unpolitical" experts and superparty planning confront the parliament's claim to power of decision and control with an increasing claim to primacy, attempting to undermine or even displace the parliament. The reasons for this development are as various as they are obvious. They lie in the need for continually improved, rational organization and planning in a complex, highly differentiated, sensitive society which can no more afford mere improvisation and dilettantism than can modern economics and industry.

But at the end of this development, which opposes to the political process of parliamentary democracy the greater effectiveness of the "unpolitical" experts, the objectively planning and rationally functioning, specialized bureaucracy in state and society, there appears the frightful image of a mere technocracy, a rule by the managers and functionaries, which would evade control and the entire realm of democratic-parliamentary decision-making. Thereby the balance of power would be seriously disturbed and a new form of dictatorship would be coldly brought into being. It is this opposition between highly specialized expertise and the principle of democratic participation that appears as the central structural problem of all western parliamentary democracies. To be sure this dilemma is also by no means new, however sharply it confronts us today on all sides.

Bureaucratization and specialization, no less than liberal and social emancipation movements, accompanied the development of parliamentary democracy at an early stage and continue to do so to an increasing degree. They have governed its forms and at the same time complicated them. The development of the apparatus of government has meant more than an expansion of its political functions. It has fostered the rise of the modern professional bureaucracy, which especially in nineteenth-century Germany was most closely tied to the continuation of absolutistic and authoritarian-official (*obrïgkeitsstaatliche*) elements in the structure of state and society. This became especially apparent after the establishment of the Weimar Republic, which tried, with the army and the state bureaucracy, to incorporate the great, allegedly indispensable supports of political continuity into the new order of parliamentary democracy—an attempt which is known to have been a huge failure. The collapse of the first German democracy was to a considerable degree a result of the unsolved tension between parliamentary and bureaucratic-authoritarian elements of structure; this tension was already prepared for in the dualism of the Weimar Constitution; it finally ended with the victory of a bureaucratic presidial dictatorship and its pseudo-democratic manipulation and subjugation by Hitler.

To be sure, the cause for this was not simply a faulty construction of the constitution. Rather, the problems of the first German republic showed how unavoidable was a clarification of the relation between the conflicting elements. Max Weber had already recognized at the end of World War I the tendency toward bureaucratization and expertise in the leadership of the state as a dominating sign of the age; according to him there remained only the choice between bureaucratization and dilettantizing. Later Karl Mannheim saw our "period of social change" to be essentially determined by the fact that great "strains" arose "out of the contiguity of the principle of competition and the principle of regulation and planning," strains which could be solved only by a system of "planning for freedom."

This problem certainly did not apply exclusively to the democracies. The authoritarian and totalitarian regimes were also unable to solve the strain, even after eliminating the parliaments; it continued to exist almost undiminished in the dualism of state and party, especially visible in the "Third Reich." And finally it became apparent in postwar France and Germany how great an importance is possessed by the continuity and the growing weight of the elite of experts in organized interest groups or unions and in state bureaucracy as opposed to the politically-parliamentary dynamics. Only recently it was once more pointed out, by Maurice Duverger, that the bureaucracy of experts in France plays a stabilizing role that alone makes government possible. The Fifth Republic deduces from this fact the consequence—albeit a disputed one—of a restriction of parliament, which ultimately aims at a *gouvernement de legislature* in which the parliamentary and the presidial systems would be merged. This, however, could be the end of real parliamentarianism and the victory of rule by executive mandate with a plebiscitary façade.

In West Germany, which with controversial arguments held to the continuity of the political apparatus beyond the period 1933–1945, the development proceeded somewhat differently. Here the "chancellor democracy" commanded a continually growing governing and steering apparatus whose complication and indispensability in the modern bureaucratic state works against a change of government. Now that it has outlasted several parliamentary periods this apparatus is far superior in technical knowledge to the parliamentary agencies of power, which in the Bonn system are curtailed anyway. In addition there is the fourteen-year duration of the political constellation, which is modified only by the federalistic structure. Here the danger of instability of the government is averted at the cost of disempowering the parliament, whose capability for control becomes inferior to the claim to expert knowledge and the stability of the political apparatus. The head of the government himself was able, thanks to his constitutionally assured position and to the special authority of Adenauer as Chancellor and party head, to extend the executive power far into the parliament, which then converts his will into laws prepared for him by the government bureaucracy.

In both cases, even though by different courses, the consequence of the unsolved strain is a tendency toward authoritative remodeling of parliamentary democracy. Of course in both cases the concrete form owes much to a personal element. It may not outlast de Gaulle and Adenauer. But the development itself would scarcely be thinkable without the factual and structural problems which lie at the basis of the crisis of parliamentarianism in the industrial and mass state of the twentieth century.

BETWEEN CRISIS AND REFORM

In the following survey we shall try therefore to summarize the most important points of view and arguments which characterize the critical discussion of parliamentarianism in Europe.

In the representative system the direct contact with the will of the people is lost, since in the large modern state the parties of rank have become mass parties, and elections based on personality have become impersonal, machine elections. One consequence is the stronger demand for plebiscitary arrangements, which correspond to a more general tendency toward "supraparty" ties. Just recently de Gaulle, who set the Fifth Republic on this course, criticized the lack of such arrangements in the Bonn democracy. All the recent experiences indicate, however, that they are feasible only in the smaller framework of a direct democracy (such as Switzerland still is), if the danger of uninformed demagogy or even of a new autocracy is to be avoided.

The prestige of the members of parliament has fallen precipitously since they no longer have to resist an autocratic principality and are enjoying a career that is almost without risks. To the public they seem to be dispensable: a constitutional state and a functioning government are already insured by good organization and efficient development of the political apparatus.

The organization of parliamentarianism, originally created for political problems, is not suited to deal with the penetration of economic and social problems into the concerns of government. Lawmaking has extended its boundaries considerably. It embraces almost all areas of social existence and it makes too great demands on the abilities of the members of parliament, both technically and temporally. The results are extended periods of session and necessary specialization. The participating citizen is replaced by the professional politician, who himself becomes a bureaucrat, a functionary, without having the experience and the specialized training of the state official.

Thus the continual broadening of functions of the state threatens traditional parliamentarianism, which is thereby alienated from its real function and fragmented in its effectiveness. On the other hand, a limitation of the extent of parliamentary control, especially in the economic area, has proved fatal, the more complicated the economic and social organism of the modern state has become and the more it has called for coordination and planning. But one is confronted with the facts that the state is seldom a capable entrepreneur and that the parliament is not a good organ of control for economic undertakings, especially since in this case it will transfer its prerogatives to a great extent back to the political bureaucracy. A system of decentralization scarcely offers the satisfying solution either. Federalism can of course unburden parliamentarianism, given the appropriate historical premises (as in Germany or Switzerland) by disseminating responsibility and control more broadly. But thereby coordination and planning become more difficult and complicated.

As the expansion of the state places too great demands on the abilities of the members of parliament, it at the same time lowers their position and the importance of their activity. An elected representative cannot, by the nature of the thing, be equal to the many-sided detailed problems with which society and bureaucracy confront him. The fact that he has to make pronouncements and decisions and exercise control in these matters, as if he were an expert, contributes to the lessening of the prestige of parliamentarianism in the eyes of the public and makes the member of parliament himself vulnerable, insecure and resigned in the face of the real or alleged specialists inside and outside of the political institutions. It also does not help to make his activity more attractive to the really suitable persons. At the same time that technical and political competence is concentrated in a minority within the parliamentary parties, the representative becomes dependent on an apparatus of reporters and specialists, and parliamentary debate is reduced to a mock struggle in the foreground behind which work those anonymous and nonresponsible apparatuses upon which the member of parliament is dependent to a great extent in technical matters.

The consequence is not only a weakening of the parliamentary debates but also that loss of substance and interest which has become characteristic for the greater part of parliamentary activity, with the exception of the few debates over matters of principle; this is also especially true of that domain particularly proper to parliament, which has become so complicated—household politics. The attendance in the parliament chamber is often meager; the parties function as mere voting machines; their activity seems to the critical public to be an expensive waste and complication; derogatory remarks against the conduct of parliament, whether they come from the government and the bureaucracy or from the interest groups, fall upon fruitful ground; finally, the institution itself is no longer taken seriously and it is overridden wherever possible and led into error. Overtaxed in its assignments, the parliament limits itself to topics that have an effect on the elections and abandons important decisions in practice to the planning and formulating bureaucracy. Thus their roles are often exactly reversed. Lawgiving is transferred to the apparatus of administration and parliament loses its authority to a quasidictatorship of the executives. Finally the will of the experts triumphs over the parliamentary art of submitting technical decisions to political decision and control; the decisions have already been made.

The structural transformation into the party state has sharpened these problems still more. The advance determination of decisions in the party committees so extensively binds the parliamentary member, whose parliamentary existence rests upon the party's favor, that even without express party coercion his parliamentary flexibility is extremely limited. Discussion, the basic element of democracy, no longer takes place chiefly on the parliamentary level but in the preparliamentary area of party politics, and largely to the exclusion of the public. Parliamentary decisions are prefabricated there and become a mere matter of form, since the voices are previously counted; the minority, that is usually the opposition, is left with mere resignation—until the next election—or with increasing anger, which can become intensified to enmity toward the regime itself, to a revolutionary mood. Old and new attempts to put an end to this development—for instance by prohibiting the "imperative mandate"—are of course condemned to failure. But the consequences can be lessened, above all under two conditions: by the loosening effect of decentralization and federalism and by a greater flexibility and elasticity of the parties themselves if they are no longer strictly bound to certain classes and programs and if there is a continuation of the process of leveling and pragmatization, which is so characteristic for the postwar development, especially that of Germany. On the other hand, here as in Italy and other countries the phenomenon of the "Christian party" has been thwarting this process and has added a new chapter to the European history of the (ideological) "Weltanschauung" parties.

The selection and education of the members of parliament is not holding pace with the complication of political tasks. Even the process of selecting the candidates seems inadequate from this point of view. The central dilemma of modern parliamentarianism becomes apparent here. A strong influence of the central party leadership is the only guarantee for the nomination of objectively suited, specialized candidates for parliamentary and party work; but this method endangers precisely that immediate contact with the constituency which seems to be possible only by way of local electoral committees, through a decentralized party organization. The technical question of the electoral system is secondary to this. The point of view of the continental backers of the majority election, in so passionately supporting the reform of parliamentarianism by a "personality election," is still oriented to the older model of parliamentarianism. However, empirical observations in England have confirmed that with the change from prestige democracy to party democracy, the elections have also changed from personality elections to party elections regardless of the electoral system.

It is felt especially urgent, therefore, that the representatives to parliament be better informed and equipped. An advance technical examination of the candidates, such as has been called for again and again, can be neither politically justified nor technically realized; it seems impossible to set up suitable standards. On the other hand, an expansion of the apparatus for information and assistance is under way everywhere. Assistants, experts, forces of aid of all sorts are to see to it that the balance of power between the government apparatus and the parliament, which is supposed to control the government apparatus, does not become too unequal in the conduct of affairs. But precisely this may give rise to another problem. A second big apparatus is created which is scarcely less subject to the tendencies of bureaucratization than is the government apparatus. Such a bureaucratization of parliamentarianism once more calls up, only on a different level, the old danger that the member of parliament is overridden by or becomes dependent upon extraparliamentary, nonresponsible experts. The collaboration of government officials, experts and members of parliament in committees of experts does increase the possibilities for objective information and controls, but it also considerably complicates the course of government and committee activity and in addition confuses the executive and legislative competences. One way out is the formation of commissions of experts in the government, as they are used in England with some success; thereby the technical knowledge of the organized interest groups is drawn especially into economic and social planning. But that does not essentially foster either a solution of the control problem or the reactivation of parliamentarianism as a whole; it only shifts, and probably sharpens, the tendencies to "expertocracy."

In all of this it is the ponderousness of the parliamentary system that is especially exposed to criticism. The first principle of modern government and economy, the principle of rationality and effectiveness, is apparently contradicted by the existence and practice of the parliaments so strikingly that the critics question not only their ability to function but also their justification for existence. Important decisions—as in Germany a new penal law, the social reform or the party law expressly required in the constitution—and also a plethora of detailed tasks are often postponed over several periods of sessions or remain entirely unsettled. For the greater part of the representatives the sessions mean up to 90 per cent idle time; for the public they mean a waste of valuable working power. This too scares many a qualified person away from the parliamentary career. Therefore recommendations have been put forward again and again for the technical rationalization of parliamentary procedure, which is still in the state it was in the eighteenth and nineteenth centuries. For example, time-wasting sessions might well be curtailed by the exchange of opinion and voting in writing or by telephone, extensive use of electric brains and other methods. But there are still narrow limits set to the simplification and shortening of the procedure. It is precisely the nature of the parliamentary system, as distinct from and contrary to bureaucratic procedure, to achieve a more comprehensive basis and sharper control of political decision through more extensive proceedings.

The idea of a second chamber of experts to bridge the gap between expert knowledge and political power has been playing a significant role right up to the present. Made up on the basis of technical suitability and professional grouping from the various provinces of economic and social life, such a "parliament of experts" could contribute as an auxiliary organ of the parliament and government to the objectification of the political process. To be sure, it has proved an insolvable difficulty to decide in what way and according to what key such an institution could be recruited. All previous attempts have also either run aground in useless technical discussions, as in the economic council of the Weimar Republic, or have been misused for the purpose of deposing the parliamentary system by authoritarian regimes, as in Mussolini's stato corporativo and similar institutions in Greece, Poland, Austria and Portugal in the thirties. In France since 1945 and especially in the Fifth Republic the idea of an economic council has been institutionalized; but this coincides again with a threat to parliamentary democracy.

Theoretically the auxiliary function of such an agency, which makes it possible to incorporate technical-economic expertise into the political process, should be hailed as a support of parliamentarianism. But the practical realization of it appears to be incomparably more difficult than the formation of commissions and councils, which according to the English example of the royal commissions and committees would have to bridge expert knowledge and politics and simultaneously curb and channel the pressure of interest groups. A chamber of professionals and experts seems to be not only historically discredited but also a danger in the present. The interest groups' influence on politics, which is already almost too strong, would have in such a chamber an additional vehicle and instrument. Therefore as a guarantor of objectivity it would be scarcely better qualified—indeed, its members would be still more subjectively tied to particular interests than the members of parliament, who have to represent various interests at once and therefore are more predestined for a comprehensive manner of making decisions. The primacy of politics is also indispensable in all matters of technical decision.

An especially weighty argument of the critics is finally the lack of stability of parliamentary governments. This was especially true of the unbridled parliamentarianism of the period between the wars. The twenty-one administrations in the fourteen years of the Weimar Republic were a frightening example. Even after World War II the French Fourth Republic exhausted twenty-five administrations in the space of thirteen years. It is true that the rapid change of cabinets was mitigated by the fact that often there were only minor shifts in the personnel component. But without a doubt, not only the total triumph of Hitler (and the assent of broad circles in Germany) but also the more moderate victory of de Gaulle over parliamentary democracy are to be ascribed in no small way to discontent about the discontinuity of parliamentary state politics. This discontinuity has been particularly consequential in periods of economic and political crises, which have needed the more far-sighted objective planning and persistent execution of a course of consolidation to a greater extent. Parliamentarianism appears to be not only a particularly cumbersome but also an unreliable form of government which, because it is entirely bound up with the transitory present, is incapable of demanding unpopular sacrifices for more far-reaching politics from a short-sighted "will of the people."

Thus the tendency of European democracy is toward a modification of the parliamentary system of government. Its particular goal is to lengthen the duration of periods of government and to render more difficult the overthrow of cabinets and the dissolution of parliaments. This of course has always implied the danger of lessening or even blocking political dynamics, the flexibility and capability for decision of the political forces. The rigidifying chancellor democracy of Adenauer and the pseudo-presidential regime of de Gaulle are examples of this problem, which can result in the undermining and displacement of a lively parliamentarianism rather than in reform. There are various forms of this modification. The Fifth Republic has established a dualistic system, which runs on two tracks by placing representative and plebiscitary execution of the popular will in a parallel position and thus producing a peculiar system of balance in which finally the presidial-plebiscitary element dominates. From the German point of view this recalls all too vividly the faulty construction of the Weimar Republic; a decision for genuine presidential democracy or for the restitution of parliamentary democracy will not be avoidable when the present special form is no longer protected by the peculiar phenomenon of de Gaulle.

But the forms of modification in the Bonn democracy are also disputed. Undoubtedly an astonishing stability of the political constellation has been brought about by the elimination of splinter parties by the 5-per-cent clause, by the officially privileged position of the parliament parties by state financing, by hindrances put in the way of the overthrow of government by the "constructive vote of lack of confidence"; at the same time the dissolution of parliament is impeded, owing to a weakened position of the federal president. But the other weaknesses of parliamentarianism enumerated above have appeared all the more prominently. And more particularly the government, the bureaucracy and the interest groups, protected by the stable parliamentary conditions, have achieved such a great weight that many clear-sighted critics characterize the Bonn democracy as an actual government by bureaucracy and interest associations. This parliamentary democracy also will not have to stand its test until the moment of a change of administration; the end of the Adenauer era leaves many questions open, even though it seems to be less dramatic than the transition to the post-de Gaulle era.

This summary of the critical points in European parliamentarianism, as incomplete as it is, nevertheless indicates the central significance of the inquiry into the relation between politics and technical knowledge with regard to the future of European parliamentary democracy. This problem should now be pursued first in the national, then in the supranational, contexts.

PERSPECTIVES TOWARD A SOLUTION

Three main directions are taken in the attempts to solve—without a loss of democratic substance—the sharpened conflict between parliamentary politics and technical planning in the expanding industrial state of present-day Europe. The first direction is pursued especially in England and in the Scandinavian countries. It is the attempt to democratize the growing phenomenon of specialists and experts by making it useful and at the same time bringing it under control within the framework of, or in association with, the apparatus of government. This attempt proceeds from the insight that the activity of the interest groups cannot be separated from the political process and abandoned or consigned to a fictitious neutrality of the experts. In England the development of the royal commissions and similar institutions is significant in this line and at the same time poses a counterbalance to the rule of an isolated state bureaucracy. To be sure, new problems are created by the expansion of such commissions, which advise the government and administration in economic, social and cultural-political questions with technical competence, but also with their own interests prevailing. The importance of the experts has been fostered, the "anonymous empire" (S. Finer) of interest groups becomes institutionalized, but the parliaments' loss in substance has progressed further while the cabinet system, which is founded on parties and the administrations, has grown stronger.

A second course proceeds by way of the attempt *to submit parliamentarianism itself to the tendencies toward technology and rationalization* which have led to the advance of the expertise-and-planning system. This course has been pursued most decisively in France by means of the unburdening of the parliament (which of course also means its loss of importance), and by means of the institutionalizing of the system of expertise in large planning commissions. Another variation of this "rationalization" of parliamentarianism is the progressive shifting of technical decisions from the plenum to the commissions of the parliament, as is especially characteristic of the German development. The plenum retains little more than the sanctioning of the decisions that the members of the commissions bring before it. Therefore the selection and incorporation of the experts into the parliamentary party groups becomes the principle content of parliamentary activity. Here too the "rationalization" results in a loss of substance and significance of the actual parliamentary discussion. The system of *hearings*, which could steer this development, is lacking in the European parliamentary democracies with the exception of the Swiss democracy, which has a different form. Substitutes such as the interrogation hour of the Bonn system, in which the ministers must answer critical questions before parliament, are hardly sufficient, although in some cases (as the Spiegel affair) it proved quite important. But the basic principle remains in danger—the principle that decision is the prerogative of the politically responsible, elected officials of the parliament and of the government, and that it is not to be relegated to the bureaucracy or to the experts, with or without an interest-group slant.

All the more important are the efforts toward a new delimitation of the altered functions of parliament, government, administration and the organized interest groups which are undertaken in view of this dilemma. Their premise is that in view of the general tendency to bureaucratization the future of democracy depends upon whether objectivity and expertise can also be exercised outside of bureaucratic areas of organization. A clear separation of political decision (parliament) and technical planning (bureaucracy) is not possible; it would finally lead to the hypertrophy of the administrative state, to the victory of the hierarchy of officials over open democracy. To equate bureaucracy with expertocracy could appear as the tempting solution to the problems. But it contains serious dangers; it implies an evasion of democratic control and creates a new gap between the state and the citizens; it sharpens their dependence and helplessness in the face of the political-social process and degrades them to subjects facing a highly specialized, uncontrollable network of rule without comprehension. The result could be indifference and resignation; the political answer could become an erroneous reaction such as that of 1933 in Germany, if in place of a political solution to the problems a bureaucratic one were to prevail.

It is indisputable that the number of the actual decision-bearers in the modern state is becoming steadily smaller and the tendency toward rule by experts is becoming steadily harder to control. Thus the future of democracy depends all the more on whether it becomes possible to open up new ways for the citizens to participate in political and social affairs and thus to rise above the role of mere observers. Parties, organized interest groups and self-rule offer possibilities to create a counterweight against the threatening depolitization; an improved political education seems to be its precondition. This is true at the same time for the expert in the planning and steering committee. His "democratization" and control is most likely to become feasible if every kind of monopoly and hierarchy of the agencies of competence is avoided and if room is made for the principle of free competition in the sense of competition for achievement.

The basis for all attempts at solving the problem is therefore the insight that there must be no necessary opposition between expert knowledge and politics, between expertise and democracy. The primacy of politics must be maintained. The question is only what place parliamentarianism is to retain here, in what form it is to be brought into accord with the changed conditions of modern state, social, economic and military politics. The parliament and the parties which support it still have the double function of first working for contact and conjunction between the various areas of expertise, interests and politics, thereby guaranteeing the openness, readiness for compromise and competition; and second of control of technical counseling and technical planning, re-examining them in the discussions between administration and opposition and relating them to concrete political reality.

For both tasks—the uniting of political determination and technical planning on the one hand; the critical examination of the interest associations and also those of the experts on the other hand—the European democracies now as before need parliamentary institutions that are capable of functioning. We have indicated what possible modifications are being discussed and also to some extent realized to reduce the disadvantages and crises of parliamentarianism and to consider the structural changes of society and state. These modifications are resulting everywhere—not only in France—in a limitation of the "classical" parliamentary rule. But at the same time they aim at an intensification and rationalization of parliamentarianism in its indispensable functions. Improvement of the channels of information, expansion of the system of commissions, more conscious policy in the selection of their own experts on the part of the parliamentary parties and incorporation of the specialists into the work of the parliament are the means of this rationalization. Its goal continues to be to work as a clearing house and counterweight to the technical claims of the bureaucracy of government as well as of interest groups, and to provide the comprehensive impetus for the primacy of political decision.

This is particularly applicable to the new problems that have been brought forward by the international network and the creation of *supra-*

national institutions. Today an isolated view of intrastate parliamentarianism is no longer possible. It is superseded by the comprehensive question as to how the separation of politics and planning, of democracy and expertocracy can be bridged in the sphere of the European network, and partly also in the Atlantic network. Here too only an inadequate political control by the governments confronts the forward-moving, expanding bureaucracy of administrators and specialists. Commissions and ministerial councils of the European economic community incorporate this tendency as do the other European administrative offices. And here too the parliamentary institutions have remained far behind. As qualified as some of their members are and as favorable as the supranational exchange of thought is, European parliamentary institutions have little actual weight as long as they lack legitimation through direct European elections and as long as they carry out only insignificant advisory functions. Here too it must be recognized that technical planning needs political planning and control if it is to be both effective and democratic.

The danger of self-satisfied expertocracy is heightened still more by the economic and technical successes of cooperation on the level of bureaucracy. The collapse of negotiations between the Common Market and England fits into this complex. If England can be counted as a model of a parliamentary democracy that has succeeded in adjusting to the changed conditions without a breach of the basic principles, then England's inclusion would without doubt shift the politics of European unification from the bureaucratic level to the parliamentary level. Therein—and not only in a French claim to leadership—lies one of the reasons for the resistance of de Gaulle, who may fear the disturbing effect of such tendencies on the economic-technical development of the European cooperation. But therein also lies the reason for the all too long hesitation of England, which regards with mistrust the reciprocal effect on the tested institutions of its own political system.

Not only in Italy and the Benelux countries but also in Germany these political aspects of the problem—along with the economic and military ones—have in the meanwhile come into such prominent awareness that the French standpoint appears considerably isolated. The Fifth Republic is considered a special case, not a model for the solution of the problems of European parliamentarianism. Precisely at a moment in which a Europe of reduced sovereignties is considering its strengthened role in the world, a retreat into national, or even regional, small-European isolation has become unthinkable. This is not only a question of economic and military potential. It is still more a political question. The danger that threatens the European democracies externally because of their geographical position, and internally still more because of the multifariously broken tradition of their parliamentarianism, also has not been averted by their rapid reconstruction. In the search for security and necessary reform the European states need not only close association among themselves but also with the

Anglo-Saxon democracies, which command the strongest traditions and experiences in the art of the adjustment of a firmly established parliamentarianism to the new conditions of the industrial world.

CONCLUSION

While there are striking parallels and similarities in the appearance and problems of parliamentarianism in present-day Europe, the differences between the national forms of its realization still seem very great. In Germany, the experience of the Weimar Republic and the causes of its fall form the exit-point for all discussions about the relation of parliament, government and bureaucracy. The pseudo-presidential experiments of 1930–1933, which led to the dictatorship of Hitler, seem to justify the widespread mistrust against all attempts to minimize the position and function of parliament in favor of bureaucracy. In France, under the impact of the failure of classical parliamentarianism in the Fourth Republic, the experiences influencing public opinion and discussion support a very different view, almost contrary to the German version of a parliamentary party state. While in both of these cases, however, the main tendency goes toward a modification of parliamentary democracy, in Italy the older type of a multi-party system still prevails, confronted with the classical problems of a parliament which is split up in many political groups hardly able to form stable coalitions.

Such profound differences in the domestic scene of the European states must be considered if the prospects of coordination and integration of the national systems into a "new Europe" are examined. Besides strong remnants of the past—including very different experiences—it is a question of how to combine strong government and executive authority with effective control, which has led to individual solutions of the problems of parliamentarianism; decentralization and federalism—as traditional in Germany—are further elements of difference. The quest for European integration may as well complicate these problems as it tends to neglect them. It is also for such reasons that the position of a European parliament as a legislative body seems still very uncertain.

If the relation between parliament, government and bureaucracy demands new answers on the national as on the supranational level, this applies even more to the role of parties, interest groups and expert commissions within the institutional framework of parliamentary democracy. Beyond all national differences, two main tendencies are discernible: the growing importance of pressure groups, tending even to a *Verbände-Staat;* at the same time, the decline of ideological parties. This process, to be sure, is modified by the existence of strong Christian parties which may work as integration factors in a biconfessional society, as in Germany; but it may simultaneously block the tendency to open two-party systems, as does the unbroken strength of Communist parties in Italy and France.

In summing up, the development of democracy in western Europe, showing so many different traits and tendencies, has posed many new questions. On the level of domestic politics, there are as yet no common answers in terms of a "new Europe." This will be the future task of interstate compromises which may result in the creation of a European parliament. In spite of the experiments of the French Fifth Republic, however, the substantial form of European governments has remained that of parliamentary democracy, though modified: a fundamental change in the direction of a presidential system seems outside of all possibilites. On this point, the difference between Europe and the United States, whose peculiar political system seems not fit for export, remains a reality which in its importance for European and Atlantic politics should not be overlooked.

36. THE EXECUTIVE IN THE MODERN STATE*

Jean Meynaud

IN SPITE of the diversity of experience in different countries, a comparative analysis of the actual situation of the executive reveals certain obvious resemblances—its wide field of competence, its extensive prerogatives and responsibilities, and the efforts being made to improve the institutional structure of this branch of the government and render it equal to its tasks. It is by no means certain that these attempts at reorganization have achieved their aim or that they correspond to actual requirements; as a result, the executive is not always entirely fitted to its task, and this can be a serious handicap to the political system.

Extent of Tasks and Responsibilities

All government bodies have found their duties increasing in many respects. These duties however, do not seem to have been evenly distributed. It has become a commonplace to remark that parliamentary assemblies are ill-suited to the new responsibilities assumed by twentieth-century governments, and that the larger share of these responsibilities has devolved upon the executive branch. The expansion of the field of activity of the State thus seems to have done much to destroy the balance between the various organs of the governmental system.

This trend is particularly marked in economic and social policy. The

---

* From *The International Social Science Bulletin*, Vol. X, No. 2 (1958). By permission of the United Nations Educational, Scientific and Cultural Organization. [Note: Professor Meynaud makes reference in this article to "national studies." These are studies of the role of the executive in various nations, carried out under the auspices of Unesco, and reprinted in the same issue of the *International Social Science Bulletin*.]

regulation of economic affairs by the public authorities, though it varies
from one country to another, is common to all of them; and it would
appear to be exercised chiefly by the executive, whose authority reaches
its culminating point whenever planning techniques or measures to speed
up industrialization (with the resultant emphasis on the relationship
between investment and consumption) are introduced. The introduction
of the welfare state and the improvement and diversification of social
services lead to similar results.

To adopt the phraseology of functional analysis, the most striking
feature is the important role assumed by the executive in decision-making
and the initiation of operations. Perhaps, . . . this is a matter of selecting
from among the projects drawn up by the different sectors concerned,
rather than a really independent choice. Nevertheless, in many cases—the
majority, perhaps—the executive is beginning to appear as the motive
power, though the problem of what elements are capable of stimulating or
impeding that power remains unsolved. The importance in the United
States of the 'presidential program' provides an excellent example of this
tendency.

It is less surprising to note the preponderant role of this branch of
government in the implementation of decisions. Here we must bear in
mind the further decline in authority suffered by parliament owing to the
practice, under various names and with varying intensity, of delegated
legislation. The executive even has a share in control (by which we mean
the stimulation of the political responsibility of the governing group) by
the adoption of methods which vary according to the system under
consideration ('dissolution of parliament, presidential veto, etc.).

It is not certain whether this general consideration, conducted on
traditional lines and based on a clearly defined set of tasks, gives a
complete view of the situation. It is not even certain that it penetrates to
the roots of the executive's responsibility in the modern State. Here we
should like to introduce certain aspects of the problem which are usually
ignored or underestimated in current investigations, since the great scarcity of available studies makes it necessary to be satisfied for the time
being with impressionistic formulae.

Stress is often and justifiably laid on the fact that in present-day
political structures the executive seems to be expected to provide the
impetus. It should not, however, be forgotten that the management of
public business consists largely in achieving compromises between rival
interests or conflicting claims. At the result of a spontaneous and powerful
movement, the executive has come to be regarded as the governmental
body called upon to settle disputes—even the most acute of them—and to
bear responsibility for any delay in seeking and applying a solution.
Strikes are an excellent example: in a modern industrial country a collective refusal to work may, in certain circumstances, disrupt the whole
social organization. If the parties cannot reach agreement on their own,

the executive is inevitably called upon to take steps to settle the matter. Many instances of this responsibility might be quoted; one of its most important aspects is the allocation of public funds for the various possible uses (that is, in the last resort, among the various social categories, the various regions or the various economic sectors). There is at present a marked tendency to reduce (and in some cases almost to abolish) in budget debates the initiative of members of parliament with regard to expenditure—which amounts to leaving the process of selection with the executive, a step whose importance will be appreciated if we remember that the budget figure may easily amount nowadays to a quarter, or sometimes even to a third of the national product.

This function of arbitrator requires an ability to compromise which, whatever may be said to the contrary, is among the qualities essential to a politician. It also entails reference to a certain criterion of appreciation, to a set of standards of judgement. This introduces the concept of the 'general interest'; few ideas are more pressed into service frequently not to say done to death in political discussions, and few are more vague. To examine this concept in detail would lie outside the scope of this article. Two points should, however, be emphasized. A clearly defined conception of the general interest is indispensable to a firmly-knit community; the notion that the general interest is nothing more than the sum of all the particular interests of the society leads straight to anarchy. The general or public interest is, precisely, that deliberative factor which makes it possible to arbitrate between the various demands, moderate them and bring them into line with possibilities. But it is not a concept which has objective reality, which can be noted, like the level of the temperature. The theorists of the welfare school have made tremendous efforts of ingenuity in the attempt to arrive at a scientific definition of the conditions most favourable to governmental action; but they have never got beyond the stage of commonplaces or subjective judgements. The definition of 'general interest' is a purely conventional one, based on a series of options the arbitrary nature of which cannot be seriously questioned.

Yet, judging by the way things are in contemporary political communities, one would think that it was the task of the executive to define the criteria of the general interest and put them into practical effect. It would be by no means unreasonable to attempt a classification of political systems either according to the sources to which the executive refers in establishing these criteria (i.e. enforcement of a system of pre-established standards or an effort to interpret the wishes of the community), or according to the means employed to ensure their adoption (i.e. in particular, the importance given to methods of education and persuasion, the significance of which differs fundamentally from one system to another). From the philosophical point of view, there are those who consider that political parties should play a leading role in clarifying the vague and fugitive concept of public interest; but an empirical approach leads one to the conclusion that the electoral system, with its inevitable competition, renders this task difficult and that the parties very frequently take little or no interest in the matter. The burden of responsibility upon the executive in this respect thus becomes an increasingly heavy one.

The task of the executive is complex, more especially in communities which are not unanimous as to the direction in which their destiny lies. There is a danger that in such communities the general interest may be used as a weapon by whatever class is permanently or temporarily in command. The difficulties caused by such attitudes affect not merely the executive, but the whole mechanism of the State. Nor can the fact be ignored that even where such obstacles are not present, the executive is by no means firm or consistent in its behaviour in this respect.

A further feature characteristic of the position of the executive in the modern world is the vague but undeniable tendency of the social body to assume that it is called upon to deal, immediately and on its own initiative, with the profound and often violent upheavals by which the life of the nation is disturbed. This tendency is a consequence at least in part, of the speed with which decisions must be made; the desire for effective action all too frequently runs counter to respect for traditional parliamentary procedures.

Economic fluctuations, for instance, can only be mitigated by the surprise effect of the action taken against them. This need for rapid, not to say instantaneous, adjustment is particularly evident in international relations. Even in peace-time it is essential to keep pace with the adversary's initiatives and reactions and if possible to forestall him so as not to be forestalled: if he scores some striking success, the immediate reaction of public opinion—and of parliament as well—in the countries concerned, will be to place the blame upon the executive. Moreover, in the event of acute international tension between the great powers, the nature of present-day weapons and the fact that the first hours (if not the first minutes) of any conflict would be decisive, would have the effect of laying a really tragic burden of responsibility on the executive alone.

A final point should be mentioned: in the present diplomatic situation where a large proportion of the countries of the world are ranged in different camps, certain States are placed *de facto* in positions of domination; the behaviour of their respective executives is thus liable to influence the fate of many nations, such nations are therefore no longer entirely free to decide their own destiny, except at the moment of the initial choice. This 'internationalization' of responsibilities has perhaps never before been carried to such lengths.

Two observations will help us to gain a more concise idea of the significance of the movement in question:

1. These tasks—and especially these world responsibilities—none of which are written into the text of any constitution, are of overwhelming

gravity. And there are various contingent factors which make them even more weighty—the rapidity with which many decisions have to be made and the empirical attitude that the effort of adaptation to a constantly changing world demand, the seriousness of the repercussions of any action taken either by the whole or by part of the community; and the consequent intensity of the various pressures brought to bear upon the authorities.

2. It seems to be the unavoidable duty of the executive to meet these obligations. Parliaments seldom appear able to carry them successfully. The administration may to a certain extent compensate for the inadequacy of the executive: but there is a sharp difference—clearly evident in a number of countries—between capable administration and the exercise of political leadership. Moreover, if the politician abdicates unconditionally in favour of the expert, the system will tend to change gradually into a technocracy, and this is not generally desired.

It may thus be said that if the executive is incapable of fulfilling the functions which present political trends tend to impose upon it, or is prevented from doing so by opposing forces, there can be no alternative solution, but only certain palliatives. In such cases the only logical solution would be to reduce the functions carried out by the State to a level not exceeding the capacities of the institutional system in general and of the executive branch in particular: needless to say, however, this suggestion is completely utopian, and it is surprising to find it mooted by certain well-informed writers. The extension of the functions of the State is not so much the result of a deliberate choice as a result of the general trend of social life, the accumulated pressure of which eventually becomes irresistible. Hence the importance of the efforts directed towards making the executive an instrument capable of fulfilling its allotted functions.

Adaptation of Structures and Working Methods

While the institution of such efforts is widespread, the speed and the nature of the measures adopted are conditioned by governmental structures and political customs and it is difficult, if not impossible, to express them in cut-and-dried formulae. Furthermore, very few comparative studies as yet exist. We shall therefore confine ourselves to a general description of the chief directions in which the executive, as an institution, appears to be developing at the present period.

The first tendency is to attempt to unify the executive, or rather to set up a sort of leadership within its ranks, in cases where such a centre of gravity is not automatically created by the political system (as in the so-called monocratic executive, of which the presidential type is one variety; cf. Article II, section 1 of the American constitution, which states that 'The executive power shall be vested in a President of the United States of America'). France provides a good example of this tendency. Under the

Third Republic, the position of the prime minister *vis-à-vis* the other ministers was merely that of *primus inter pares;* he was responsible for a particular ministry (not always the same one) and could seldom take real command except by exerting his personal authority. The Fourth Republic has striven, with only partial success, to raise the status of the prime minister, making him the motivating influence and the natural arbiter in the executive. This is no isolated instance. In the political system of the Federal Republic of Germany the chancellor is the real head of the executive. According to Article 65 of the Basic Law it is he and he alone who has authority to lay down the main lines of the policy to be pursued, and the cabinet's discussions conform to these principles: the strong personality of the present chancellor (who is sometimes accused of treating his ministers as no more than technical assistants) has merely breathed life into a constitutional principle. Similarly, Article 95 of the Italian Constitution declares that 'the President of the Council of Ministers shall direct the general policy of the government and bear the responsibility for it. He shall maintain unity in political and administrative action by promoting and co-ordinating the activities of the ministers.'

At first sight this tendency seems incompatible with the system of the dual executive, often adopted in modern States (the parliamentary type of constitution). But it is true that the head of the State finds his time taken up, more often than not, with official appearances and the exercise of personal influence (which may, of course, yield quite appreciable results). It may even be wondered whether any attempt to endow him with real political authority might not inevitably lead to confusion.

One may compare this tendency with the efforts made to achieve closer concordance between the different sections of the executive. This question has received special attention in the United Kingdom where the co-ordination of public business is assumed to be a matter for the cabinet. . . . This example has been followed in many countries, where committees differing considerably in structure and powers, have been set up to prevent waste of effort and the pursuit of conflicting policies; these experiments do not, on the whole, appear to have been entirely successful. It is, of course, difficult to co-ordinate functions which are actually in the process of expansion.

A second tendency is to provide the nucleus thus established with an administrative structure of its own, giving it the human and material resources it needs in order to assert its views. This is sometimes described, especially in the United States, as the 'institutionalization' of the executive. Offices set up during the last twenty or thirty years around the person of the President help him carry out his manifold and extremely exacting duties; as matters stand at present it would not be entirely true to say that the executive consists of one man alone (helped when necessary by a few personal assistants). Realistically speaking, it consists of the combined forces of a President and of a civil service which is supposed to be entirely under his authority. In other words, in addition to his recognized functions, the head of the American executive is expected to carry out the complex task of co-ordinating the work of the bodies placed at his immediate service.

A movement impelled by similar notions may be discerned in those parliamentary-type systems where there is a tendency to consolidate the position of the prime minister or the head of the cabinet. For instance, the Chancellor of the Federal Republic of Germany has at his disposal an administration—the Chancellery—which works exclusively for him. This institution is generally recognized as playing a very important political and administrative role—it co-ordinates matters within the executive, prepares the chancellor's speeches during meetings, and makes his views and official attitudes to certain questions known to the public. Some people go so far as to say that it has a considerable (though occult) influence on appointments to the highest civil service posts. In France owing to a development which can probably be traced back to certain decrees promulgated in 1934 and 1935, the office of the prime minister has become an important part of the whole machinery of government. In Canada a similar movement has led to the creation of a body somewhat different in scope—the cabinet secretariat concerning the role of which the Canadian article is quite explicit.

At first sight, this attempt at 'institutionalization' of the executive, which was without doubt rendered inevitable by the multiplicity and complexity of the problems to be dealt with, seems worthy of approval. For without adequate administrative machinery the responsible head of the executive would hardly be in a position to impose his own policy. There is, however, a darker side to the picture. It is possible that—even, for example, under the influence of a particularly dynamic president— these new services, introduced at the apex of the State structure, might clash with the traditional civil service departments, which naturally cling to their independence; and this may lead to tension, not to mention the risk of duplication. Such offices should not, therefore, be set up without careful administrative planning. Furthermore, the creation of these offices might tend to encourage the transfer of the real responsibility from the political to the administrative sector—one aspect of a process of encroachment the total extent of which will become apparent in the next part of this study. The ultimate danger is that this attempt at rationalization may create an impression that political leadership has lost some of its importance and that should the executive prove to be inadequate or incapable —for whatever reason—the essentials will be preserved by the smooth working of a competent and well-tried administrative mechanism.

This is a mistaken view and a very dangerous one, especially in regimes of the presidential type. The administration can, it is true, deal with matters of daily routine, and often does so with remarkable efficiency; but it is ill-prepared to make the great decisions and the important choices which in normal circumstances devolve upon the executive. With or without 'institutionalization,' political leadership retains its supremacy; no administrative apparatus can compensate for its deficiencies.

This leads us to the possibilities of action conferred by 'charisma' upon those leaders who are fortunate enough to possess it. The credit of such leaders is enhanced and, other things being equal, their freedom of action is increased both within the governmental system and outside it. This situation, in a sense, affects the functioning of the whole system. This is the case with the constitution of India, originally modelled on the British constitution; owing to the personal prestige of Mr. Nehru its mode of operation has now acquired certain quite individual characteristics.

A third tendency (signs of which are to be observed throughout the whole governmental system) is to modernize the executive machinery from the point of view of the organization of administrative activity and information services. This latter point is important. Few things would be more valuable, in investigating the manner in which political decisions are arrived at, than an examination of the data on which those concerned rely to make and defend their preferences. What is the range of vision of the leaders, how and through what channels are they informed? Can we feel certain that the mechanical improvement of sources of information, the technical perfection of means of communication, have really led to a substantial improvement in the leaders' understanding of the problems that confront them? One of the characteristics of information at the present day is its abundance. Who selects and in some cases 'screens' it, and according to what criteria? These are questions to which only somewhat sketchy answers can yet be given. . . .

To sum up, efforts have been made to fit the structures and working methods of the executive to the far-reaching responsibilities which now devolve upon it. One has the impression that adaptation is slow, sporadic and insufficiently co-ordinated with the other sections of the governmental system, and that its methods are sometimes suspect. These defects and failings may lessen the ability of the executive to deal with the practical issues that confront it. This first deficiency, however, is not the only one. To it must be added those that result from the reactions of the other forces involved in political life. . . .

The Executive and the Governmental System

All the characteristics of a governmental structure may have repercussions on the functioning of the executive. This is particularly to be observed when a State is organized on federal lines.

The present trend of development of the federal States is marked by an extension of the *de facto* and *de jure* powers of the central authority (though this need not necessarily lead to the systematic deterioration of the individual units of the federation). The fact alone is sufficient to lay an increasingly heavy burden upon the federal executive; but the separate units may further complicate the task of the executive by showing resistance—which is perfectly legitimate in a federal structure—to schemes or policies contemplated or desired by the central authority. By way of example one may mention the difficulties encountered in Switzerland (where the problem is complicated still more by the fact that the various interested parties may also have recourse to the institution of the referendum) in such matters as the reform of the federal finance system or the construction of a unified network of highways. The administrative autonomy of the local communities may also constitute a similar, though much less influential, factor.

A comprehensive study of the question is rendered impossible by the diversity of the institutional systems in the different countries. We shall therefore confine ourselves to a consideration of the two most important sectors, which are of universal significance—the parliamentary assemblies and the administration.

The Executive and the Parliamentary Assemblies. Here we have the old problem of relations between executive and legislature—which, though not the sole or even the principle aspect of this subject, is still one of its most important parts. This can be dealt with fairly briefly, as it has already been analysed in a number of works, the findings of which are well known.

As we have already pointed out, parliaments have failed to adapt themselves satisfactorily to the new functions of the modern State. The reasons for this failure have been frequently described—the fact that work has increased to an extent out of all proportions to the time that the parliamentarians can devote to it; the complexity and technical character of the subjects to be dealt with, which are difficult for the non-expert to handle; the unwieldy nature of traditional legislative procedure, etc. To this may be added the fact that many questions are seriously complicated by the method of public debate—a method which can hardly be contemplated in the case of such decisions, for example, as the date and extent of a currency devaluation. There are many problems which can be settled only by a compromise involving sacrifices on both sides; public statement of the positions of the different parties, however, has the effect of crystallizing these positions and rendering it more difficult for the parties concerned to make the necessary concessions freely and without embarrassment. In cases such as social disputes or international tension, to take two particularly obvious examples, discussion in parliamentary assemblies seems hardly the best method of bringing the parties to agree upon terms acceptable to both sides.

These reasons are too numerous for the comparative eclipse of the assemblies to be regarded as a temporary phenomenon due to fortuitous circumstances. The position of parliament, it is true, varies considerably from one country to another, but it seems possible to state without fear of contradiction that the general trend is towards a decline of the real power of the assemblies in political life. Efforts have been made to increase the efficiency of parliamentary activities by revising working methods and amending legislative procedures; but these seem unlikely to arrest the course of events.

The practically universal adoption of the delegation of legislative powers is one of the symptoms of this situation. It is a tacit recognition by the assemblies of their inability to rise to certain occasions. But, at least in certain countries, it is also the result of a readiness on the part of the parliamentarians to leave it to the executive to introduce such measures as are both unavoidable and unpopular.

The danger is that the assemblies may try to offset this weakness—which some consider tantamount to an abdication of power—by continually interfering in the work of the executive by every possible means and more especially in systems of the parliamentary type, by challenging the political responsibility of the cabinet. We thus have the disconcerting spectacle of a parliament incapable of dealing effectively with the business on hand and at the same time preventing the executive from doing so: ministerial instability is the natural consequence of such an attitude, and of this France offers a particularly striking example.

Such a situation is avoided in systems where the assemblies are not responsible for appointing the executive (though the former are still in a position to hamper the government seriously in its work). Neither does it arise in countries where the party structure is such that every general election produces an absolute majority, lasting throughout the life of the parliament thus elected. The two-party system (in which the leader of the victorious party becomes prime minister) gives the best guarantees of permanence, though it diminishes the role of parliament as such. This stability is also secured in certain States—such as the Scandinavian countries—which have a number of parties, one of which dominates to an extent that ensures it an absolute or practically absolute majority. These elementary considerations illustrate the well-known fact that a connexion exists between party structure on the one hand and the role of the parliaments and the stability of the executive on the other.

This decline of the influence of the assemblies is a matter of widespread concern. At its forty-sixth conference (London, September 1957), the Inter-Parliamentary Union, in its turn, considered the problem. It adopted a resolution recommending that within the framework of the different political and constitutional systems, serious efforts should be made to confirm the supremacy of parliament which should, to this end, represent the genuine expression of the will of the people. In the preamble to this resolution the wish is expressed that parliament should have full latitude to intervene and give its views on matters of domestic and foreign policy. What are the implications of this attitude, and what are its chances of success?[1] Speaking during the conference, the Soviet delegate declared that greater parliamentary control of governments was a practical necessity, adding that peace and better living conditions for the people depended to a great extent on the progress made to this end. However, . . . the problem presents itself in a quite exceptional form in the U.S.S.R., owing to the fact that the control of the State machinery by the Communist Party is a 'fundamental principle' in that country. One result of this is that within the governmental system as a whole there is a climate favourable to unification which is quite unknown in the multi-party systems; for the latter, therefore, the resolution adopted by the Inter-Parliamentary Union raises problems of crucial importance.

At the present stage of political development it is very doubtful whether parliament is in a position to exercise the general function of motivation, or even of arbitration, indispensable to the operation of any governmental system; in this respect its action is likely to be spasmodic and fragmentary. The smaller the political units constituting the parliament, the truer this supposition is likely to prove. What hope can there be of securing even the tacit recognition of some standard conception of the general interest if the assembly is composed of a number of small units, always at loggerheads and driven by the inexorable logic of the situation to assess every measure in terms of electoral influence?

One might be tempted to regard this as a subjective observation; yet it is based first and foremost on the actual behaviour of the parliaments of many countries over the last twenty or thirty years. It should not, however, be allowed to disguise the fact that an active contribution by the parliamentary assemblies to the work of the government is useful, and even essential. It seems indispensable for the assemblies to supervise the general functioning of the executive and to maintain a legislative activity in conformity with the needs and wishes of the country. Any further weakening of parliament would have unfortunate political results, if only by denying the opposition any possibility of making its voice heard to practical effect; in this connexion one should point out that parliament, in a multi-party system normally provides an invaluable platform for the expression of public opinion. The problem is to ensure that this function is exercised in a manner and by methods which leave the executive sufficient scope for the accomplishment of its tasks.

The organization of relations between the executive and the legislature should not be envisaged in doctrinal terms: it is a practical problem in the art of politics, and its solution must be expected to vary as traditions vary from one country to another. Here again we should beware of arbitrary comparisons and transpositions: a verbal question does not have the same connotations in certain continental parliaments as it does in the House of Commons; and except in countries of British tradition the dissolution of

---

[1] An account of the proceedings of this conference is given in the *Inter-Parliamentary Bulletin*, 1957, 4th quarter, pp. 126–41.

the assembly inevitably tends to be regarded as a dangerous expedient. In other words each country should strive to solve this problem in a manner suited to its own individual genius and cultural structures.

Executive and Administration. This problem, though less familiar, and also less frequently analysed than the one we have just considered, is no less important; in the long run, indeed, it may prove to be of prime importance to the functioning of political systems.

It originates in the considerable and continuous expansion of the administrative machinery. This widened scope is the natural and inevitable consequence of the extension of the functions of the State. The latter, as the services it provides for the public becomes more and more numerous, is naturally forced to increase the number of its employees. But it soon became apparent that in addition to this quantitative development a more subtle qualitative change had also taken place, reinforcing the influence of the administration itself and altering the balance between political circles and the administrative sector.

According to the traditional view, civil servants are at the service of the political authorities and more especially the executive, their particular task being to carry out the latter's decisions and to put its chosen policies into effect. This leads to a distinction between those who shape policy and those who carry it out. In the management of public business the latter have a part to play which, though important, is subordinate. This view is correct as regards a considerable number of civil servants (especially the junior members of the service, who are the most numerous). But it does not take into account the individual influence exerted by certain sectors of the administration.

Two factors have helped to consolidate this influence—the multiplicity of the questions dealt with, and the technical character of those questions. In the majority of political systems, the men in positions of responsibility in the individual ministries have only an amateur knowledge of the problems with which they are required to deal; even if they were specialists they could not hope to be familiar with all the business they must undertake. Thus, in different ways and by different stages, it has become more and more an established custom to associate the officials of the State—and particularly the senior civil servants—with the process of determining policies to be adopted and making decisions. Legal appearances are kept up in many cases,[2] but from the point of view of real influence there can be no doubt about the important part played by the

---

[2] In this respect, the case of Finland calls for separate consideration. In that country, from time to time, when it is found impossible to form a ministry on a political basis, a cabinet of senior civil servants is appointed. At the time of writing, for instance (January 1958), Finland has a cabinet headed by the President of the National Bank. It is hoped that he will be able to enforce the strict economic and financial policy that the situation of the country demands (in any case, the politicians would have been reluctant to make themselves responsible for such a policy in view of the approaching general election).

administration in the process of decision-making. This point has frequently given rise to somewhat exaggerated interpretations. In France, for instance, there was at one time talk of a 'fourth power,' and in more recent years, there has been some anxiety as to whether the country might not be falling into the hands of a politically irresponsible 'technocracy.' . . . The strength of the civil services is much more the consequence of the weakness of the ministers than the result of a conspiracy. However, even when it is reduced to its true proportions, this tendency deserves very serious attention. It has led several writers to assert that any realistic enumeration of the component parts of the executive should in future include a certain number of senior civil servants who are closely associated with the preparation of decisions and capable of exerting a decisive influence on choices which appear to be made on the responsibility of the politicians themselves.

This action on the part of the administration may take either of two forms. It may serve to provide impetus—since civil servants are exceptionally well placed to suggest measures and urge the implementation of projects which are in line with their own opinions. There are occasions on which the ministers seem to be merely the sponsors, on the political level, of programmes planned entirely in their departments—or, to put it differently, instruments used by dynamic directors, with clear and firm views on the subject of stability, to obtain the necessary funds to carry out their projects. But bureaucracy may also act as a curb; the employees of the State have their own methods of 'torpedoing' any decision they regard as undesirable. It must even be admitted that on some occasions they may go so far as to delay the execution of measures already decided upon. One factor serves, however, to limit this influence—the existence of rivalries between the various offices. The civil service, like the other governmental organs, is not a monolithic block, but is composed of branches, part of whose activity consists in striving to neutralize one another's efforts.

The course of development thus described appears to be irreversible; it is linked with a particular set of social structures and relationships which renders utopian any attempt to restore the traditional division (regarded, in certain quarters, as somewhat fictitious) between administration and politics. There are some who regard this trend as being intrinsically a favourable one; they claim that in many cases the civil service has become the staunchest defender of the general interest and provides a welcome counterbalance to the partisan decisions of politicians. Others, however, stress the susceptibility of the administration to the pressure of private interests. The argument cannot be finally settled on the strength of the information available, especially as the alternative put forward is not a completely relevant statement of the problem. The important point is that the political sector cannot discard its responsibilities without fundamentally altering the nature of the system and depriving the community of the machinery by means of which it is (or at least should be) possible to make choices of major importance in matters that lie outside the orbit of daily routine.

The question which then arises is that of instituting control of the administration by the executive so as to bring the activity of the civil service departments—which it would be futile and even dangerous to attempt to reduce—into line with the concepts and programmes of the political leaders. It is almost impossible to lay down general rules for such control, the nature and methods of which are strongly influenced by the special features present in every system. We may mention two of the main factors on which it depends:

1. The statutory position of civil servants and, in particular, the degree of stability of employment guaranteed to them. Though it is steadily losing ground, the system of recruitment by patronage (of which the 'spoils system' is the most marked form) still survives over a fairly wide area. Moreover, no statutes, however precisely worded, can give absolute protection to civil servants from the interference of politicians; though, under several regimes, various provisions (combined, it is true, with a certain moral atmosphere) assure them reasonable security, thus favouring an independent attitude on occasion. This state of affairs is even more evident in countries where ministerial instability is particularly marked, and where the permanence of the State employee contrasts with the brief term of office of the cabinet minister.
2. The legal relationship between executive and administration. It is a curious fact that in some States—for instance Sweden—a deliberate effort has been made to institute a complete separation between the ministries and the government offices responsible for current business. Experience shows that this severance by no means prevents the ministries from exerting influence on the offices, and vice versa. . . .

In countries where the parliamentary system is traditional, another method is usually adopted: here each minister acts as the administrative head of the ministerial department for which he is responsible. In practice, the problem is to determine the point at which the political and administrative mechanisms interlock. In France, recent studies have emphasized the role played in this respect by the cabinet; the instability of ministries and the somewhat indeterminate situation of the cabinet frequently make cooperation difficult. The Federal Republic of Germany has no institution corresponding to the cabinet; the point of junction would appear to be the Secretary of State, who is the senior official in a ministry. As he cannot be appointed from among the members of parliament he is in the position of a political official, i.e. to all intents and purposes a permanent fixture.

. . . In the United Kingdom, it may be wondered whether the traditional theory that 'the ministers govern' is always in conformity with the facts. The matter is now being considered by a committee appointed by the prime minister. None of the solutions contemplated (including, in particular, the division of the larger ministries into several departments of more manageable size) seems entirely satisfactory. But the parliamentary system at least provides a theoretical control, even if its influence is incomplete and, in many cases, purely formal. The presidential system, on the other hand, would seem to make it easier for civil servants to attempt to gain a hold over the executive.

Summarizing the observations made in the course of this study of the governmental system, we find that under the pressure of several influences, a twofold movement is becoming perceptible as regards spheres of competence and effective power—from the legislature to the executive and from the executive to the administration. Carried to extreme lengths, this movement would result in government by civil servants (which some people consider to have been already achieved in part even if only in view of the share taken by civil servants, sometimes of junior rank, in the drafting of the budget and the appropriation of funds). It rests with the executive—whose central position is thus again demonstrated—to check this tendency by keeping control over the administration. The extent to which the executive succeeds in meeting its responsibilities, whether written or unwritten, depends largely on its ability to assert its leadership of the administration—always provided that this is not undermined by the assemblies, the influence of which is frequently negative. Despite their essential importance, however, these factors constitute only one aspect of the problem, its other aspect being the effect on the executive of the interplay of social forces.

Executive and Social Forces

This brings us to the sources from which decisions emanate. Like any other part of the governmental system, the executive functions in a social setting for whose cohesion, protection and development it is, in the long run, responsible. The extension of the functions and responsibilities of the executive inevitably increases its contacts with the various categories of citizens (a similar phenomenon is to be noted at the administrative level).

These relationships are of a complex character. The executive is stimulated and supported by society, but it is also criticized and restrained by it. This is not, however, a one-way process; by adopting measures that meet with popular approval and by instituting some form of popular education or even of propaganda, the executive can exercise a direct or indirect action upon the milieu in which it operates. In addition to the long-established methods of exerting influence (by the use of secret funds, for instance) there are now new methods, resulting from the development of information techniques (press conferences, television programmes), the uses of which have not always been above criticism.

A two-way current of energy (either motivating or restraining) is set up between the executive and society. The hesitancy observable in scientific explanations of this is due to the fact that it is extremely difficult to detect this exchange and quite impossible to estimate its intensity. It is, however, clear that both the everyday operation of the executive and its ability to deal with its individual responsibilities are dependent upon this process. . . .

We may perhaps pause a moment to sum up the principal conclusions to be drawn from the preceding observations.

1. The real composition of the executive differs somewhat from the conventional definition of it. In systems with a dual executive, the Chief of State plays a very small part—sometimes, in fact, a purely symbolical one—in decision-making, the role of the administration being preponderant. According to some writers, executive and bureaucracy can be classed together in the same category. Others take a more qualified view, pointing out that there is no hard-and-fast line of demarcation between the two institutions, but that an intermediate zone exists: thus the senior ranks of the civil service may be said to form part of the executive since they take an active share in the shaping of policy. This second view seems preferable, inasmuch as the greater part of the bureaucracy continues to be occupied with practical tasks, involving no encroachment upon the responsibilities of political circles.

2. During the last twenty years or so the tasks of the executive have steadily increased, to the detriment of the parliamentary assemblies, whose influence (especially as a source of stimulus) seems on the whole to be declining. Moreover, this trend of development has the effect of vesting in the executive certain serious (unwritten) responsibilities. This is offset by a tendency to transfer powers to the administration, which may be interpreted as a tendency on the part of political circles to surrender certain of their functions to the civil service. It seems as though the executive, having undertaken more tasks than it is capable of carrying out, finds itself obliged to pass them on, sometimes by tacit consent, to civil servants (not necessarily of senior rank): these anonymous officials, though they take no share in decision-making, nevertheless occupy a position of importance, since their executive work may sometimes escape political supervision.

    These remarks are by no means intended to minimize the importance of the administrative machinery. No present-day State could carry out its functions without an efficient (that is to say, a competent, honest and stable) bureaucracy; it is well known that in countries with a weak executive the administration may constitute the last buttress of the regime. But this situation has its less agreeable aspects, and in any case the shifting of responsibility is contrary to the spirit of the representative regime.

3. Efforts have recently been made to strengthen the structure of the executive with a view to making it more homogeneous and improving

its working methods. The aim is to increase its efficiency as a mechanism of command and co-ordination. But amendment of the institutions and methods inherited from the liberal age is proving to be a delicate matter; this is one source of the difficulties encountered by the executive in its attempts to deal with its tasks and responsibilities.

4. Furthermore, the activity of the executive is conditioned by its relationship to the other organs of government—more especially to parliament and to the social forces so expressed, principally, through the political parties and the pressure groups. The terms of the problem vary considerably from one country to another, but its substance remains the same: it turns upon the degree of independence, the freedom of action, on which the executive can count to enable it to fulfil its mission and to promote the general interest rather than that of individual groups. Another problem to be considered—and one directly connected with the structure of the political parties—is that of the stability of the executive (for which the permanence of the civil service can only be a partial substitute).

5. Quite apart from institutions and mechanisms, the personality of the men who are to lead and compose the executive remains a factor of fundamental importance. However perfect the administration, it cannot possibly compensate for inadequacy or feebleness on the part of the political leaders.

In the light of these observations we may now consider the problem usually described as 'reform of the executive.' A brief glance at the experiments now proceeding and the schemes under consideration reveals two tendencies—one, comparatively insignificant, leading to a weakening of the relative position of the executive (or, to put it differently, to a tightening of the control to which it is subjected); the other, far more marked, directed towards reinforcing it. The apparent contradiction between these two attitudes can be easily dispelled if we bring in the ideal concept of a point of balance between the executive on the one hand and the other governmental organs, together with the social forces, on the other. These two attitudes are then seen to express an awareness that this balance has been destroyed, either to the advantage or to the detriment of the executive; by analysing a few concrete examples we shall be able to determine their significance.

Attempts to Control the Executive

The Yugoslav Study serves as an excellent starting point for a study of this attitude: it describes a systematic attempt to reduce the relative importance of an executive which was tending to exert a rigid, unilateral authority over all the forces in the country and to become the only source of impetus.

The writer, who argues along Marxist lines, declares that a powerful executive of undisputed authority is indispensable in certain historical circumstances—it alone, by bringing the revolution to birth, is capable of winning freedom for the masses. Afterwards, however, 'it tends gradually to throw off the shackles of its allegiance to society and to become the master of those very masses.' This trend is intensified when the means of production are handed over to the State, for 'the social class—consisting chiefly of the official executive authorities—which controls the means of production becomes, in the course of time, all-powerful and independent of the process of social determinism.'[3] The report gives a very clear and vigorous description of the various methods employed to weaken the central executive and organize the regime on the basis of 'the theory of the commune.' It should, however, be remembered that these efforts are being pursued within an ideologically unified system, Yugoslavia having refused to allow the establishment of a second party, and in particular of that demanded by Djilas. . . .

In pluralist communities, the increase in the powers of the executive (and consequently of the administration) has raised the question of the protection of the individual citizen. It is characteristic to note in the British report that during recent years in the United Kingdom there has been a revival of interest in organizations of the type of the French Conseil d'Etat, as affording protection against arbitrary conduct or excessive zeal on the part of the administration. This is no isolated example. In Norway various circles, and particularly the Liberal Party, have declared that the public must be more satisfactorily protected against the bureaucrats: they have suggested recourse to a method instituted in Sweden nearly 150 years ago—the appointment of a procurator-general, whose duty is to help private individuals to obtain redress for injustices. It would be going too far to say that this is an attempt to weaken the executive, but the tendency, in so far as it is designed to institute a check on the basic means of action of that branch of the government, cannot be overlooked.

It is true that in many other countries there is a feeling that the executive should, on the contrary, be strengthened.

Efforts to Strengthen the Executive

Walter Lippmann has written a book[4] to show that the weakness of the executive in the democracies is a historical catastrophe and constitutes one of the principal causes of the 'decline of the West.' This view . . . has

---

[3] Readers will compare this statement with the views set forth by Milovan Djilas in his book, *The New Class*, New York, 1957. The difference is that according to Professor Djordjevic, Yugoslavia has deliberately set to work to break up this domination and introduce a democratic form of Socialism, whereas according to Djilas nothing has been done (or, in fact, can be done) to alter the situation—the only solution being to abolish the monopoly at present enjoyed by the Communist ideology.

[4] W. Lippmann, *Essays in the Public Philosophy*, Boston, 1955.

not met with unanimous agreement. For instance, a German authority, Dr. Gilbert Ziebura, considers Mr. Lippmann's fears regarding the executive to be unfounded so far as the Federal Republic is concerned; in his view the executive in that country draws its strength from its almost complete identification with the views of a powerful political party and a very large neo-bourgeois class, which receives the greatest share of the national income and regards the executive as its qualified representative, its most genuine creation. There are probably not many States organized on a pluralist basis whose experts would be inclined to echo this statement; the situation varies, of course, from one country to another, but in most of them the question of the more satisfactory adaptation of the executive to its present tasks and responsibilities is one that frequently arises. The problem becomes particularly acute in cases of marked ministerial instability. The discussion devoted to this subject, though considerable, cannot be said to have been really enlightening or convincing. Without going into details we may mention its chief points; reference to various plans for analysis will serve as a useful guide in this connexion.

The most usual approach to the problem is by way of the legal institutions. This is an optimistic approach, since it assumes that the position can be improved by merely altering the framework and, more particularly, by simply obliging all the forces concerned to conform to the new rules of the game. Some people may regard this as a superficial procedure, and the case of France will supply them with excellent arguments in support of their contention. A case in point is the restricted character of the provisions included in the constitution of 1946 with a view to limiting ministerial instability; the result is that only a few ministries have fallen in accordance with the procedures laid down in the constitution, the remainder having resigned without being legally obliged to do so. As this article is being written, discussions are proceeding in France with a view to strengthening the executive (for instance, by the adoption of procedures which would make it more difficult to effect the overthrow of the cabinet—so often the result of heterogeneous and makeshift coalitions—and to facilitate the dissolution of the National Assembly); what kind of reception the parliament will give to these projects is still a matter of conjecture. The suggested measures obviously affect only the most superficial aspects of the problem. If adopted they might perhaps lengthen the life of a ministry, but it is doubtful whether they would in themselves suffice to increase the power and efficiency of the executive as an instrument of command.

The view that the legal reforms are of slight importance is not altogether unrealistic, but it cannot be accepted without some reservations. It is, according to circumstances, either vain or dangerous to transplant into a country institutions which conflict with its traditions (such as the presidential executive in France or the parliamentary cabinet in the United States); but reforms planned with an eye to local conditions may do much to improve the efficiency of an institution, even if on paper they appear very slight. In France, mere procedural reforms (affecting, for example, the excessive prerogatives of the permanent commissions) might have an effect greater than would result from a reform of the constitutional machinery itself.

A second approach to the problem, of a less superficial nature, is to attack the political structures, especially the parties. This does not mean embarking upon a fruitless and in many ways dangerous criticism of the parties as such; it means suggesting amendments to their structure and functioning, which would improve the operation of the governmental system and more especially that of the executive. Studies of this kind have been written, and have sometimes reached a high level of scientific debate.[5] One of the weaknesses of this approach is that it attempts to act, sometimes in isolation, on the historical product of a whole series of social factors and cultural features (for instance, the connexion between the multiplicity of parties and the diversity of ideological conflicts). It may also encounter strong hostility from those affected by it—witness the difficulties met with in certain countries when an attempt has been made to induce parliament to legislate for the control of political parties, and the storms to which 'electoral reform' has been known to give rise (in those countries where the actual electoral system is not an intangible convention and tends to be regarded as a political weapon). Such methods may, it is true, have their effects, but it would be unwise to expect any really decisive results, unless we admit the possibility of an upheaval so far-reaching that social conditions, and not only political structures, would in reality be transformed by it.

This leads us to the third way of envisaging the problem, i.e. from the angle of social relationships. This is a constructive approach, since it does not separate the problem of the executive from the general position of the State in society. What some authorities have represented as a crisis affecting merely the executive is shown to be a crisis involving the State as a whole; the executive cannot be expected to be more efficient or to obtain a wider hearing than the governmental system in its entirety.

Our generation, which is fond of giving new names to familiar phenomena, is inclined to adopt the term 'consensus' instead of the 'collective will to live' regarding which Renan wrote some memorable pages. Once that will ceases to be unanimous (because, for example, of the presence of ethnical minorities or social classes which for various reasons feel themselves 'alienated' from the community), the State begins to develop an organic weakness which inevitably has repercussions on the situation of the executive. The attitude of the latter will then depend on the weight of

---

[5] One of the best examples of this is a study, published by a committee of the American Political Science Association, entitled *Toward a More Responsible Party System;* this originally appeared as a supplement to the September 1950 number of the *American Political Science Review.*

public support it can command, and inversely on the weight of opposition of those sectors which refuse to recognize it. The natural tendency, with all the hazards that it implies, is to replace the 'consensus' by resorting to the use of force, if not of open violence, either against the entire community or merely against whichever section is regarded as rebellious (assuming that such procedure can be restricted to certain categories). This disturbs the balance to the advantage of the executive, which amounts to an attempt to solve the problem by denying its existence.

A particularly complex case is that of those democratic countries where ideological differences are very marked. There are certain problems which arouse opposite and apparently irreconcilable currents of opinion (e.g. the religious question in France—and also, perhaps to an even greater extent, in Belgium); any attempt to impose a solution of such problems may lead to an outburst, or at least to a permanent desire for revenge. In other words the adoption of an evasive attitude may in some circumstances be a political virtue; or, to put it differently, in certain climates of opinion the potential strength of the executive varies according to the problem under consideration. The situation is even more difficult in countries where the range of ideas is so wide that groups form and break up afresh each time an important question comes up for consideration.

To sum up, the legitimate authority (as Ferrero puts it) vested by the community in the State fixes limits within which it is possible to establish an executive which need not be strong in order to avoid being weak. In other words, it determines the limits within which a reform of legal and political structures seems likely to yield results, or at any rate not to be foredoomed to failure.

There remains the case where the aim is to alter the social structures themselves by deliberate action (the speeding up of industrialization, the reorganization of the agricultural system, etc.). A programme such as this frequently excludes the possibility of securing a consensus of opinion in fairly large sections of the community. The next and almost inevitable step is then to create, or plan the creation of, a powerful State machine acting through a strong executive, capable of bending the will of the individual to those aspects of the general interest involved. The degree of pressure required, or rather the indispensable measure of coercion, depends upon the scope of the programme in question. If the government does not acquire sufficient power the programme will have small chance of being carried out. The system cannot be relaxed unless the public is prepared to accept the objectives laid down (in which case methods of persuasion will be sufficient, at least to some extent) or unless the scope of the activity undertaken is subsequently restricted. Various factors may help to restore the 'consensus,' one of the most effective being the sense—whether real or artificially induced—of national danger.

In conclusion we can only emphasize the fact that the balance previously referred to is difficult to define, to achieve and to preserve. Since no system can boast of having reached a condition of complete stability, especially during the present phase of profound technological changes, such balance can be maintained only by a constant process of adaptation. The best that can be hoped for, then, is that actual conditions will not depart too radically, either in one direction or the other, from the central point of balance. Sceptics will no doubt regard this statement as utopian, and in the light of present experience it would be difficult to contradict them with absolute conviction.

37. A DEBATE ON THE PARLIAMENTARY AND PRESIDENTIAL SYSTEMS

Don K. Price and Harold J. Laski

THE PARLIAMENTARY AND PRESIDENTIAL SYSTEMS* BY DON K. PRICE

To KEEP the administration of government under the control of the people, to invigorate it for effective action in their behalf, and to adjust national policy and its administration to the needs of various regions and institutions—these are urgent problems in this time of crisis.

While in Great Britain as well as in the United States new political and administrative institutions are being worked out to meet the needs of the hour, it is curious that much of the academic and journalistic criticism of government in America is based on a desire to imitate the classic parliamentary system of government. This is all the more curious since the British long ago abandoned the classic parliamentary system as definitely as they abandoned the classic theories of political economy.

Perhaps only a psychoanalyst could explain America's peculiar nostalgia for the obsolescent political institutions of the mother country, but the persistence of her obsession with the parliamentary system makes it not only an interesting theoretical problem but a practical political and administrative issue.

It is easy to understand why Woodrow Wilson started the fashion. When he wrote *Congressional Government* as a graduate student (even before he ever set foot in the United States Capitol), the memory of Johnson's impeachment and the scandals of Grant's administration were fresh in his mind, in sharp contrast to the leadership of Gladstone and Disraeli over the House of Commons that they dominated and the electorate that they were creating. And he had undoubtedly read Walter Bagehot's monumental study, *The English Constitution* which gave the classic description of the parliamentary system.

---

* Reprinted from *Public Administration Review*, III, No. 4 (Autumn, 1943), by permission of the American Society of Public Administration.

Bagehot pointed out in 1867 that the term "Her Majesty's government" had become only a polite fiction, although a very useful one. Under the parliamentary system, which he preferred to call Cabinet government, the executive and legislature were not independent of each other as in the American presidential system; the House of Commons virtually elected the Cabinet and could force it to resign whenever it lost confidence in its policies or its efficiency. Thus the executive was always responsible to the legislature, and through it to the people. On the other hand, the executive was assured of enough power to discharge its responsibility because, if the House refused to vote funds and enact laws as it recommended, it could dissolve the House and call for a new election. "It" meant the Cabinet, the Government of the Day, the committee of legislators who individually served as ministers of departments and collectively were dismissed if the action of any one of them was not supported by the House. Thus the parliamentary system provided immediate political responsibility and at the same time gave the executive enough power to make all special interests balance into a coherent national policy.

Wilson found this system far preferable to the presidential system, which seemed to encourage continual squabbles between the executive and the Congress. Senator Pendleton, the author of the civil service reform act had proposed several years before that the President's department heads be given seats in Congress, in order to defend their administration before the legislators. The idea of adopting an outright parliamentary system by constitutional amendment or of giving Congress or its committees some sort of control over the appointments of department heads has persisted.

"If we had a parliamentary form of government," says Mr. David Lawrence, ". . . we would be able to hold to accountability all the various bureaucrats who nowadays do as they please under presidential appointment." Mr. Lawrence is one of many who have followed the lead of Mr. Henry Hazlitt, who wants us to adopt a parliamentary system by constitutional amendment. Others are for limited action. Mr. Walter Lippmann has suggested that "when the voters turn against an administration in midterm, the cabinet officers responsible in the field where the issue was drawn will as a matter of course resign," since a department head "has lost his usefulness when he no longer has the confidence of the people's representatives."

Supported by this assumption that members of Congress are representatives of the people while the President is not, that Congress should govern while the President should be restrained as a threat to our liberties, some members of Congress have undertaken to pinch off bits of the executive function. . . .

This tendency is not supported as a whole by anybody in particular, or opposed by anybody in particular. It simply goes on because we use terms and ideas, in thinking about the President's relations with Congress, that we have borrowed from the British. Congressmen are supposed to represent the people, while the President is not, because the British House of Commons is elected while the British King is not. Department heads are not supposed to be responsible unless a legislature can discharge them. We, the people, could hold ministers responsible through a legislature, but we, the people, look on a President's appointees as bureaucrats—especially if we do not happen to like the policies they carry out with money voted them year after year by Congress.

But perhaps the facts on which Bagehot based his logic are no longer so. Perhaps the classic parliamentary system, even though it were ideal for Great Britain, might not fit the United States. Perhaps the United States should consider its system of legislative-executive relations in the light of the world as it is today and may be tomorrow. To do so it will have to ask some critical questions about the classic theory of parliamentary government.

The Legislative Function

Much of the sentiment for the parliamentary system in the United States springs from a dislike of executive influence over legislative proceedings. For this reason it is pleasant to recall that in Great Britain "must" legislation is always enacted and very few other statutes are while the "purges" of party members who refuse to follow their leaders are almost always successful.

In the British system the nice balance between the Cabinet and the Commons has long since been upset. A half-century ago it was not too unreasonable to argue that the power of the House to dismiss the Cabinet, balanced against the power of the Cabinet to dissolve the House, would always result in a perfect balance of democratic control and executive authority. Within limits, the system worked that way; the Cabinet could never outrage public opinion for fear of losing the support of the House, the members of which went home every week end to get the opinion of the County families if not of the people; the House would never yield to minority interests, for the Cabinet would have the House dissolved if defeated on a policy question, and the members, not wishing to risk their seats in a general election, would not vote against the Cabinet. The equation balanced until a new factor—the electorate—became continuously instead of only potentially effective.

The British in effect did to the House of Commons what the Americans did much earlier to their Electoral College: they made it an automatic machine for registering the vote of the people, as organized into parties for a Prime Minister. Once the Prime Minister is in office, with the Cabinet that he selects, the House remains in session to enact the bills proposed by the Cabinet, to vote the funds requested by the Cabinet, and to serve as the place where Cabinet ministers make speeches for the newspapers to report to the public but rarely remain to listen to the speeches of other members.

In theory, the House has the power to turn the Cabinet out of office or to refuse to enact the laws it proposes. But that consititutional power seems to be going the way of the King's power to appoint ministers and to veto legislation. Theoretically it exists, but politically it is rarely exercised. Since 1895 only two Cabinets have been refused a vote of Confidence and turned out of office by the House, and neither of them had majority support to begin with. A political machine does not elect men to vote against its boss, and the Prime Minister is leader of the party and boss of the machine.

By invading and taking over the executive power the House of Commons destroyed its own independence. The very privilege of holding the Cabinet responsible makes it impossible for the House to think independently. No members of the House will accept office and serve in the Cabinet if the House will not support them. After taking office they will not accept defeat by the House without dissolving the House, calling for a new election, and appealing to the voters to return members who will support them. Because this is constitutionally possible, the members of the House who select and support a Cabinet put the desire to keep their men in office ahead of all minor considerations. The party machinery therefore controls the members fairly rigidly; if the Cabinet wants a measure passed, it will be passed, according to the schedule of debate which the Cabinet considers expedient. As soon as the House of Commons took away the power of the House of Lords by the Parliament Act of 1911 it had to surrender its independence to its leaders; in the cautious words of Sir William Anson, on that date "legislative sovereignty may be said to have passed to the Cabinet."

The day of the independent landed gentry, holding seats in the Commons as a matter of family privilege, is gone, and the discipline of parties, especially of the Labour Party, over their members goes far beyond American practice. There is no tradition that a legislator should live in his own district in Great Britain; it is a matter of course to elect a candidate who never visited the district before in his life. The party leaders could therefore defeat nearly any of their members in his own constituency by withdrawing their support, or even by sending in a strong national leader to oppose him. The "purge" of members who do not support the national organization is taken for granted, but members are generally cooperative enough to make it unnecessary.

This control by party machines over the political fortunes of members is a corollary of the similar control by the Cabinet over the legislative procedure. The Cabinet takes for its legislative program just as much of the time of the House as it needs, and during the 1920's and 1930's that was about seven-eighths of the total. The remainder went to consideration of measures proposed by private members (private members are all those except the seventy-odd members who are a part of the "Government" as ministers or assistants to ministers), who drew lots for the privilege of getting their bills considered by the House. No private member's bill could be passed if the Cabinet opposed it, and in practice private members who drew the right to introduce a bill would often ask the Cabinet (or its Whips) for a bill to introduce. . . .

The House of Commons has no committees, in the sense that Congress understands that term. At one stage a bill is referred to a committee—one of several large committees which do not deal with any specialized subject matter, which do not have any fixed membership, and which have no initiative or influence whatever of their own, being little more than devices to permit interested parties to testify. Funds are appropriated and statutes enacted without any independent review, and as the Cabinet requests.

The House votes the funds requested by the Cabinet; it does not have the constitutional power to vote more money for any purpose than the Cabinet asks for, and it has never during this century voted any less. In theory the private member may offer amendments to legislation proposed by the Cabinet, but in practice, as Mr. W. Ivor Jennings puts it, "Members appeal to the minister to accept amendments; they do not compel."

In short, through the party machinery the Cabinet controls the House of Commons on every question that is important enough to be called policy, and it *must* control the House as long as it is "responsible" to the House. The British short-cut the House of Commons to elect their executive as effectively as American voters short cut the Electoral College. But between elections, since they have reduced their legislature to a voting machine under the control of the Cabinet, they have to rely on the executive to take complete charge of legislation, restrained and guided effectively only by public opinion as it is expressed through the press and through a multitude of private organizations as well as in the House. This is what Mr. Lloyd George meant when he told a Select Committee on Procedure on Public Business in 1931 that "Parliament has really no control over the Executive; it is a pure fiction."

Now "control" has at least two meanings. One is to restrain or check, and the House of Commons, by acting as a sort of barometer of public opinion (though not the only one, and perhaps not even the most important one) certainly exercises an effective though impalpable restraint on the Cabinet. The other meaning is to direct, and in this sense of "control" Mr. Lloyd George was right in saying that the House does not control the Cabinet. For the essence of the cabinet system is that the Cabinet must be supported on every issue not only by a majority but by the *same* majority. If the Conservatives are in power, the Conservative member dares not vote against the Cabinet on any issue even if he disagrees, because if he and others like him do so they might make up a majority against the Cabinet and force it to resign. Likewise, the Labour

Party member cannot afford to vote with a Conservative Cabinet even if he approves of one of its actions, because that issue might be his own party's chance of getting into power. This line of reasoning and the type of party discipline that it brings about makes independent voting extremely rare. . . .

The merit of this arrangement is that it makes impossible a national policy that seems inconsistent to the Cabinet or the Prime Minister. If two groups of members of the House, even two majority groups, want the Cabinet to follow policies that the Cabinet considers inconsistent, they cannot have their way. To take a hypothetical example, if a majority of the House wished to protect a system of private enterprise, but also wished to build a public power project in a certain depressed area, it would not be able to do so if the Cabinet considered the two purposes inconsistent.

From one point of view, this system brings about an admirable coherence of policy; if a Cabinet is engaged in carrying out a certain program, it has a right to insist that its responsibility not be hampered by the enactment of measures that are inconsistent with it. But, from another point of view, the issue whether certain policies are consistent with each other is the most important issue to be decided, and the most important issue ought to be decided by the supreme authority. And if a Cabinet should tell the House that it could not be held responsible for (for example) the encouragement of private enterprise if the House should insist on building a public power project, it would be putting its view of administrative practicality ahead of the legislature's view of public policy. The system that lets it do so puts the Cabinet over the House for most practical purposes, no matter which body elects the other. . . .

Thus the House cannot itself make decisions on the several major issues of policy that exist at any one time; constitutionally it can only choose which Cabinet to entrust those decisions to, and as a matter of practical politics it can only keep in office the men it is elected to keep in office.

What is true of policy is even more true of administration. The outlines of departmental organization are fixed by Cabinet action, without legislation, and so are the principal procedures of management, such as budgeting, planning, and personnel. The Cabinet itself now operates through a hierarchy of committees and subcommittees which have no hard-and-fast membership and no formalized existence; any decision on which agreement cannot be reached by common consent is passed on up the line to the Cabinet, to be settled in the last analysis by the Prime Minister. The freedom of the Cabinet to handle administrative questions with this degree of independence undoubtedly makes for a high degree of coordination.

It is no wonder that even Mr. Stanley Baldwin admitted to the Select Committee in 1931 that (in Mr. Hore-Belisha's words) members of the House of Commons felt that they had "nothing much to do of a responsible nature." This lack of function was reflected in practical arrangements. The House had enough seats for only about half its members. Most of the members carried on their other occupations by day, and to let them do so the more important sessions of the House were held in the late afternoon and evening. As Sir Austen Chamberlain complained, the leading Cabinet members, who in the nineteenth century would have spoken at the climax of debate at 11 o'clock and then waited to hear their opponents, had taken to reading their speeches (usually prepared for them by others) early in the evenings in time to be reported by the morning papers and then leaving the House immediately, so that debate, "the essence of Parliamentary government," had become a lost art. Members could not make up for the decline in debating by detailed work as members of committees, for the committees had no independent function. As individual members they were not expected to make any great contribution, or even to work full time. . . . The only private accommodation each member had was a locker in the corridor. On this point, one member of the 1931 Select Committee remarked in what must have been a wistful tone of voice, "I think that in the American Congress every Member has a small room."

In this contrast, the accommodations that the Congressman enjoy are significant of their function. Congress, since it has not taken over control of administration, has not had to feel responsible as an organization for getting the work of government accomplished. For that reason it has not had to organize itself into a tightly disciplined body, controlled by a single small committee that can act in a businesslike way. If it should do so, the individual members would have to surrender to their organization the individual freedom of action and decision that now enables them to criticize and restrain at their discretion even an administration that they generally propose to support.

During the Napoleonic war, according to Lord Mountararat in *Iolanthe*,

> The House of Lords throughout the war
> Did nothing in particular
> And did it very well

The House of Commons has succeeded to the role which Mr. W. S. Gilbert described with his usual precision of language. The House of Commons has influence, it does an important job, and it does it very well. But it does not control things "in particular." Its control has become so general, it is exercised through so rarefied a medium, that the Commons seem to be following the Lords into the status of one of the "theatrical elements" of the British constitution.

The Executive Function

. . . A democratic country has two problems in controlling its public service: how to get it to do what the people want, and how to keep it from doing what the people do not want. One is the problem of avoiding red tape and lethargy; the other, of preventing oppression. . . .

The United States has a constitutional series of Four Year Plans, during each of which the President can assure his subordinates of a chance to make a record for themselves. Since the President is to be in office for four years and has control over the tenure of his subordinates, he can call to the government service men from private business, universities, or state and local governments. This process keeps the federal service from becoming a closed corporation; it always includes men with a wide variety of prejudices and it has never developed a guild spirit. . . .

The popular control of the executive is a double control: the people elect the President and the President holds his appointees responsible, retaining the power to discharge them at his discretion; and the people elect the Congress, which controls the executive by statutes, by appropriations, and by investigations. For failing to comply with congressional legislation, a public official is subject to legal penalties; for being so zealously opposed to administration policy that his administrative usefulness is ended, he is subject to removal by his administrative superiors. But since the advocacy of policy by the administrative official does not threaten the tenure of Congressmen, it does not need to be prohibited. Unlike the House of Commons, the Congress retains the power to regulate and control the executive in detail, without putting at stake on any issue the tenure of office of its own members or the President or (generally speaking) subordinate executives. For this reason, it largely divorces questions of policy from questions of party politics in its own proceedings, and executive officials are therefore free to participate in discussions of policy as much as they like—if they are willing to risk their jobs by making themselves no longer useful to the President or his successor. In public discussions of policy they are no more bound as a matter of democratic principle by the restrictions that apply to the British civil service than the President is bound by the restrictions that apply to the King—and for exactly the same reason.

Democratic control over a public official is most effective if it is backed up by the sanction of dismissal and if that sanction is a practical, not merely a theoretical, weapon. In the Middle Ages the English barons, when mortally offended at some act of the King's, felt obliged to protest their loyalty to his person, to blame his acts on bad advice, and to punish the advisers. History does not lead us to believe that this system had much effect on the character of kings as long as kings had real power. The parliamentary system operates on the same theory with respect to the civil service; you must not fire leading civil servants, for the minister is "responsible" if they are wrong. And the political ascendancy of the Cabinet over the House of Commons has made it nearly impossible to fire the minister on the mere judgment of the members of the House—it takes a considerable revulsion of popular feeling.

In enforcing the responsibility of public officials, the parliamentary system has another practical disadvantage in addition to the difficulty of dismissal. That disadvantage, like several others, springs from the Cabinet's inevitable jealousy of any rivals within the legislature: it is that the minister must be the sole channel of communication between the House and the department. What the minister cannot tell Parliament or the country, after proper coaching, about the policies of the department must remain untold. Sir Austen Chamberlain pointed out to the 1931 Select Committee that a specialized parliamentary committee would have difficulty in learning the details of government policy, since naturally no minister could permit his civil servants to testify before a committee on any question in which policy was involved. The "question hour" lets the members of the House of Commons put the minister on the spot, but the questioning is emasculated by a procedural etiquette which no committee of Congress would tolerate for a moment. The parliamentary system draws clear lines between the House and the Cabinet, between the minister and the administrator, between the administrator and the technician, and these lines are barriers to the transmission of information and the operation of democratic control over the details of policy.

The presidential system, although it unifies responsibility for the execution of a program, does not unify responsibility for the preparation and enactment of a legislative program, as does the parliamentary system. Thus the voters are less able to hold a party clearly responsible for its administration of the program as a whole. On the other hand, the voters have a double check on their government administratively through the President, their only national representative, and legislatively through the Congress. And they know that, however poorly the President and the Congress are carrying out their responsibilities, they are not kept from exercising their controls by a system of mutual deference that results from the fear of disturbing each other's tenure of office.

. . . A federal constitutional republic needs a separation of powers to keep its federalism adjusted to the wishes of the people. If a single national representative body is omnipotent, it is likely to disregard subordinate loyalties in carrying out its program. Much of the friction that arises between the President and Congress grows out of the conflict between the national program as planned by the executive branch and the impulse of the legislators who modify it in the interests of their constituencies. Since the American executive is not a part of Congress, members of Congress have no institutional incentive to nationalize our system and to ignore the rights and interests of state and local governments. Their lack of individual responsibility for the administration of any federal program enables them to protect local interests and often to overemphasize them. . . .

But in the meantime, the flexibility of the presidential system has its advantages. We can make progress piecemeal, without waiting for a whole program to get approval in principle. The chief executive can get a majority from these groups on one issue, from those groups on another. The party discipline can be relatively loose; groups that oppose the administration on one issue for local or special reasons need not oppose it on the next. A parliamentary cabinet, by tending to command the same majority on all issues (since that majority wants to keep its administration in office) also tends to keep the opposition always against it. If that minority is concentrated in national or regional or social groups that appeal strongly enough to the loyalty of their members, such opposition is apt to become uncompromising and irreconcilable.

The neat logic of the parliamentary system requires the legislature to hold the executive responsible for a little issue in the same way as for a big one, for a technical detail or a subordinate's error in judgment in the same way as for a major policy decision. This was tolerable enough when government had very little to do with the daily lives of people. But now the dividing line between governmental and other institutions has become very shadowy, all sorts of hybrid agencies and corporations exist, and many private corporations and institutions carry on functions for governmental agencies. In such a situation, if a legislature is to keep the whole organism working in the public interest, it cannot depend mainly on a power to hire and fire the head of it, but it must approve one action and condemn another, encourage here and reprove there, expand this agency and restrict that one.

Under the parliamentary system the legislature must always hold a sword over the head of the executive and cannot stoop to slap his hand. To keep a discussion of the British Broadcasting Corporation from bringing up a vote along party lines on which the Cabinet might be ousted, the Cabinet had to set it up by a statute that makes it generally impossible for the House to control its detailed operations or even to ask questions about them. If an executive and a legislature have a degree of mutual independence, the legislature may review the budget of a government corporation and force it to change its policy without conflicting with the chief executive at all.

In their system of legislative control over the executive the British have let the Americans outdo them in refusing to conform to an abstract theory. The omnipotence of the House of Commons, the absolute responsibility of the ministers to Parliament—these ideas are so mystical that they can be explained only in terms of nostalgia for the nineteenth century. They are corollaries to other absolutes of the nineteenth century that we now see melting away—the idea of the absolute sovereignty of each nation, the idea of the complete freedom of private business from governmental interference. In the years that lie ahead, we shall probably work out a great many compromise adjustments between the world program and the interests of nations and their component parts; between governmental policy and the freedom of private corporations and institutions. If a legislative body is going to play an active role in such developments, it will need to be able to make up its collective mind coherently and responsibly, as the parliamentary system has been supposed to require it to do. But it will also need freedom to be inconsistent, to restrain the executive even when it wishes to support him, and to keep people and institutions from being fitted to the Procrustean bed of unified policy. Every step toward unification with the executive is a step toward the loss of that freedom.

The Sanctification of a Subterfuge

. . . In appraising their systems of legislative-executive relations, the British and the Americans are both inclined to make the classic theory of parliamentary government their touchstone. Neither nation can really make it work under twentieth-century conditions, but both are curiously fascinated by it and judge the systems as they actually exist in terms of patterns that are now dead. But the effects of this spell on the two nations are different in one respect. In Great Britain, the innovators are fairly free of it; it is the traditionalists who are eager to go back to the middle of the nineteenth century. The innovators, at least, are in a position to propose something practical, as did Mr. Ramsay Muir in 1931 when he argued for a hierarchy of Cabinet committees much like the one which now exists under the Cabinet. But in the United States the traditionalists and the innovators, among our academic and journalistic critics, argue for what will amount to the same thing. Our traditionalists want to go back to the American practice of the days of Buchanan and Grant and Harding—a weak executive and government by congressional committees—while our innovators, who always seem to turn to the classic theory of parliamentary government for their arguments, want to go back to the House of Commons of the middle of the nineteenth century. . . .

The British have been pretty enterprising since World War II began in discarding the dogmas of the parliamentary system. In their peculiar informal way, they seem to be putting into effect something more like the presidential system. . . .

It is odd enough to find Americans who seek to increase legislative control over the executive arguing for the system that in Britain has given the executive control over the legislature, or Americans who seek to remove unpopular department heads arguing for a system that in Britain keeps the administrative heads from being known, much less responsible, to the people. But it is even more peculiar, at a time when people are thinking about the creation of international federal institutions, to find Americans proposing to discard the presidential system that has been associated with constitutional federalism, in favor of a system that has never proved its ability to accommodate the interests of diverse areas and populations in a federal republic.

America is a federation that is becoming a nation; the institutional system that has helped her do so will be of interest to the whole world as it moves toward greater unity. She gets her job of government done by popular control over two cooperating branches—an executive that provides unity and enterprise, a legislature that furnishes independent supervision and the restraining influence of local interests. Members of her public service are as varied in their origins and experience as the mixture of public and private institutions in her society itself; the leading members of that service come from private life and return to it freely, looking on the government as the people's agency open to their participation.

The assumptions that the legislature alone represents the people and that the administrative officials and departments are responsible to the people only through the legislature served the cause of democratic government well when the executive departments were under a hereditary monarch. They are the classical assumptions of the parliamentary system. Under the presidential system they can only set up an impossible relationship as the ideal to be attained and handicap the legislative and executive branches alike in their efforts to work together to meet the demands of a new age.

THE PARLIAMENTARY AND PRESIDENTIAL SYSTEMS*
BY HAROLD J. LASKI

ON THE issue of whether the parliamentary or the presidential system is more suited to the circumstances confronted by the United States at the present time, it is clearly a matter for Americans only to pronounce; and I have therefore no concern with the debate between Mr. Don K. Price and those with whom, like Mr. Henry Hazlitt, he differs. My purpose is the very different one of attempting to annotate some of his conclusions, both on the British system and on the American—for, as it seems to me, his account of the first is hardly aware of the changing social order of which it is the expression; and his account of the second, if a foreigner may judge, suffers somewhat seriously from those sins of omission in description which it is the natural temptation of a patriot to exhibit as virtues. And the whole argument, if I may say so, is built upon a series of unexplored and unstated assumptions which have an importance far beyond anything that Mr. Price is ready to recognize. I am, therefore, in no way seeking to eulogize the parliamentary system at the expense of the presidential or vice versa; each seems to me to have its own special merits, and neither is likely to be capable of transference to another environment, where alien traditions are deep-rooted, without becoming something very different from what it was in the country of its origin. . . .

The function of a parliamentary system is not to legislate; it is naive to

---

* Reprinted from *Public Administration Review*, IV, No. 4 (Autumn, 1944), by permission of the American Society for Public Administration.

expect that 615 men and women can hope to arrive at a coherent body of policy unless they are organized for this purpose. Its function is essentially three-fold in our time. It must ventilate grievance and thereby scrutinize the executive's policy as a process of administration; it must so discuss the principles upon which the government of the day proposes to proceed that the virtues and defects are fully known to the electorate of the time; and it must exercise that selective function which, in its ultimate form, may mean the withdrawal of its confidence from ministers and, as a result, a general election. And it must so perform each of these functions that it shows awareness and responsiveness to public opinion outside, that intricate amalgamation of parties and interests to which it owes its authority and by whose will it is able to maintain itself as a going concern.

I do not think that Mr. Price could seriously analyze the parliamentary history of Britain in the last generation and conclude that the system has failed in any of these regards. . . . Even the secrecy which necessarily enshrouds the operations of war has not prevented question time in the House of Commons from remaining a vital check on the habits of the executive, and no one knows better than the prime minister that his colleague who cannot survive the ordeal of "supplementaries" with undimmed reputation is not likely to survive at all. So far as the making of policy is concerned, nothing is easier, and nothing is more false, than to believe that cabinet initiative is imposed upon an army of faithful slaves. . . . And, in my judgment, there is no aspect in which the House of Commons appears to better advantage than in its performance of the selective function. It will always listen with respect to some member who has something to say; its benches will always empty when a member, even if he be a minister of the crown, is talking, not of the real business in hand, but either to his constituents, or, as the member thinks, in a few cases of outstanding vanity, to History. It is not easy for a prime minister, however autocratic, to keep a colleague whom the House refuses to respect; and it is not easy for him to maintain his authority if he tempts the House to that temper where a minister is looked upon with dislike or with distrust. . . .

Mr. Price is distressed by the fact that the House cannot make policy but is restricted to the choice of men to whom the making of policy is entrusted. Upon this view, there are certain observations to be made. In the first place, the Cabinet (emergency apart) does not produce a policy as a conjurer produces a rabbit from his hat. It produces the policy that, at least in its large outlines, is likely to satisfy the established expectations of the majority by which it is supported. A cabinet does not come into office without a pretty clear notion in the public mind of the line it is likely to follow. Mr. Price admits that the system produces "an admirable coherence of policy." It is difficult to think of a legislative object that is more important in a modern community. For coherence, after all means, first, that the direction in which it is moving is clearly defined; and it means, second, that the source of responsibility for action is beyond mistake. It is difficult to think of anything more important in a democratic society than the achievement of clear responsibility; for nothing else does so much to enable the electorate to make up its mind. Compared to this, the independence of the private member is a matter of lesser import. As Burke said, nearly two hundred years ago, if a member of Parliament cannot, after election, find a body of members with whom he wishes to work, he must be either a beast or a god. . . .

I must not be taken from all this to be arguing for a moment that the parliamentary system, both on its legislative and on its executive side, is not in need of drastic reform. I think it is in such need; but I think the grounds for that need arise out of quite different considerations from any Mr. Price puts forward. For the most part, I suggest, he is arguing not from life but from literature. The real problem the British system confronts is born of the fact that its institutions presuppose, both in the legislature and in the executive, government by the gentlemen in the age of the positive state. . . . I do not think it is a rash prophecy to suggest that there will be a large-scale institutional adaptation in the parliamentary system to meet the demands of a new world undreamed of in 1931 or, indeed, in 1939, by the "gentlemen of England" who have ruled Great Britain, with barely an interval, since 1688. At any rate, it is relatively obvious that either the adaptations must be made, or the foundations of the system itself will be in jeopardy. . . .

The "unity and enterprise" of which Mr. Price speaks is operative in the American system only when there is genuine presidential leadership, and when Congress is prepared to cooperate in its acceptance. What Mr. Price calls "independent supervision" seems to me only too often an attempt on the part of Congress to destroy the effectiveness of that leadership. . . . Indeed, I think a strong case could be made out for the view that when cooperation between the president and Congress is lacking there is, behind either the one or the other, a "sinister interest," in Bentham's sense of the term, which deprives the people of the United States of the legislation to which it is entitled. The "parochialism" to which Mr. Price refers seems to an outsider like myself to have many and more evil results than he notes. It can arrest the development of great projects, as when the hostility of Senator McKellar to Mr. Lilienthal held up the progress of the TVA. It maintains the evil practice of "senatorial courtesy," which only too often has been no more than a polite name for enabling a particular senator to insist that the power of patronage be used to protect his hold upon the party machine in his own state. It results in a considerable wastage of public funds in the fulfilment of works projects which are not seldom indefensible in conception and inadequate in execution, and when the "independent supervision" of the executive by Congress results in investigating committees like that [on Un-American Activities], the abyss between the purpose Mr. Price attributes to the system and the consequences actually achieved seems to me far wider than he seems to admit.

It is easy to say lightly that the United States is "a federation that is becoming a nation"; that seems to pass over not only the degree in which American federalism is obsolete but, also, the degree in which the presidential system intensifies that obsolescence. That emerges, I suggest, in the vastly different standards of education, factory conditions, public health, to take three examples only, in the different parts of the Union. . . . Mr. Price emphasizes the urgency of keeping "the administration of government under the control of the people, to invigorate it for executive action in their behalf," especially in this time of crisis. But he does not inquire whether there is in fact that popular control, nor whether the presidential system is a method of invigorating the administration. . . .

These annotations have, I hope, established the thesis that the problems involved in any comparison between the parliamentary and the presidential systems are far more complicated than Mr. Price is willing to concede. I should not for one moment claim that one system is better than the other, still less that the parliamentary system is more suited to the genius of the American people than the presidential. A system of government is very like a pair of shoes; it grows to the use of the feet to which it is fitted. But it is well to remember of governments what is true, also, of footwear—that the shoes must be suited to the journey it is proposed to take. . . .

Chapter XII.   Administration

Introductory Note

IN ALL complex industrialized societies the scope of state activity has broadened. Government in democratic and nondemocratic nations alike has assumed ever larger responsibility for transportation, full employment, research, higher education, atomic energy, urban redevelopment, health, medical care, and social security. In England and France railroads, aviation, the banking system, the production of coal, gas and electricity—amounting to over 20 per cent of the economy—have come under the direct control of the State. The State also directs, in large part, capital investment for technological progress and modernization. In the United States and Western Germany, regulation and indirect controls rather than direct ownership and administration are the rule. In the Communist countries, almost every type of economic activity has been nationalized. Among the nations that have recently emerged from colonial rule, State ownership is widespread. The immense task of running nationalized industries and regulating the economy in all cases has been taken on by the executive.

The result has been the emergence of a huge apparatus—the bureaucracy—consisting of millions of men and women, often accounting for more than 10 per cent of the total working force. In order to perform its manifold duties the bureaucracy, or civil service, must be well organized, competent and efficient. Within its internal structure there must be a clear distinction between superiors and subordinates, and between staff and line (or operational) personnel. The recruitment of competent and motivated men and women raises a host of problems. Should an advantage be given to university graduates? Should emphasis be placed on general education, or on training for a specific job? Above all, should candidates be drawn from all segments of the population, or from one major social group? These questions are all related to a larger issue: whether the civil service can or should be a neutral instrument of policy made by others. The very bulk of the civil service makes it a formidable political force. Yet, civil servants are as likely as any other group to display varied political attitudes and aspirations. Students of administration have therefore been increasingly concerned with the values and orientations of civil servants and their actual role in the formulation of policy.

On the theoretical problems of bureaucracy and organization, see:

414

Robert K. Merton (ed.), *Reader in Bureaucracy* (1952) and Herbert Simon, *Administrative Behavior* (1945). On the changing patterns of administrative organization: H. R. Greaves, *The Civil Service in a Changing World* (1947); Roger Gregoire, *La Fonction Publique* (1954); and F. Morstein Marx, *The Administrative State* (1957). Bureaucracy in the developing nations is dealt with in W. J. Siffin (ed.), *Toward the Comparative Study of Public Administration* (1957) and J. LaPalombara (ed.), *Bureaucracy and Political Development* (1963).

Readings

38. BUREAUCRACY: THE "IDEAL TYPE"*

Max Weber

THE EFFECTIVENESS of legal authority rests on the acceptance of the validity of the following mutually inter-dependent ideas.

1. That any given legal norm may be established by agreement or by imposition, on grounds of expediency or rational values or both, with a claim to obedience at least on the part of the members of the corporate group. This is, however, usually extended to include all persons within the sphere of authority or of power in question which in the case of territorial bodies is the territorial area—who stand in certain social relationships or carry out forms of social action which in the order governing the corporate group have been declared to be relevant.

2. That every body of law consists essentially in a consistent system of abstract rules which have normally been intentionally established. Furthermore, administration of law is held to consist in the application of these rules to particular cases; the administrative process is the rational pursuit of the interests which are specified in the order governing the corporate group within the limits laid down by legal precepts and following principles which are capable of generalized formulation and are approved in the order governing the group, or at least not disapproved in it.

3. That thus the typical person in authority occupies an 'office.' In the action associated with his status, including the commands he issues to others, he is subject to an impersonal order to which his actions are oriented. This is true not only for persons exercising legal authority who are in the usual sense 'officials,' but, for instance, for the elected president of a state.

---

*Reprinted from *The Theory of Social and Economic Organization* (trans. A. M. Henderson and Talcott Parsons, ed. Talcott Parsons), pp. 329–40. By permission of Talcott Parsons and The Free Press.

4. That the person who obeys authority does so, as it is usually stated, only in his capacity as a 'member' of the corporate group and what he obeys is only 'the law.' He may in this connexion be the member of an association, of a territorial commune, of a church, or a citizen of a state.

5. In conformity with point 3, it is held that the members of the corporate group, in so far as they obey a person in authority, do not owe this obedience to him as an individual, but to the impersonal order. Hence, it follows that there is an obligation to obedience only within the sphere of the rationally delimited authority which, in terms of the order, has been conferred upon him.

The following may thus be said to be the fundamental categories of rational legal authority:—

(1) A continuous organization of official functions bound by rules:

(2) A specified sphere of competence. This involves (a) a sphere of obligations to perform functions which has been marked off as part of a systematic division of labour. (b) The provision of the incumbent with the necessary authority to carry out these functions. (c) That the necessary means of compulsion are clearly defined and their use is subject to definite conditions. A unit exercising authority which is organized in this way will be called an 'administrative organ.'

There are administrative organs in this sense in large-scale private organizations, in parties and armies, as well as in the state and the church. An elected president, a cabinet of ministers, or a body of elected representatives also in this sense constitute administrative organs. This is not, however, the place to discuss these concepts. Not every administrative organ is provided with compulsory powers. But this distinction is not important for present purposes.

(3) The organization of offices follows the principle of hierarchy; that is, each lower office is under the conrol and supervision of a higher one. There is a right of appeal and of statement of grievances from the lower to the higher. Hierarchies differ in respect to whether and in what cases complaints can lead to a ruling from an authority at various points higher in the scale, and as to whether changes are imposed from higher up or the responsibility for such changes is left to the lower office, the conduct of which was the subject of complaint.

(4) The rules which regulate the conduct of an office may be technical rules or norms.[1] In both cases, if their application is to be fully rational, specialized training is necessary. It is thus normally true that only a person who has demonstrated an adequate technical training is qualified to be a

---

[1] Weber does not explain this distinction. By a 'technical rule' he probably means a prescribed course of action which is dictated primarily on grounds touching efficiency of the performance of the immediate functions, while by 'norms' he probably means rules which limit conduct on grounds other than those of efficiency. Of course, in one sense all rules are norms in that they are prescriptions for conduct, conformity with which is problematical.—ED. [Parsons.]

member of the administrative staff of such an organized group, and hence only such persons are eligible for appointment to official positions. The administrative staff of a rational corporate group thus typically consists of 'officials,' whether the organization be devoted to political, religious, economic—in particular, capitalistic—or other ends.

(5) In the rational type it is a matter of principle that the members of the administrative staff should be completely separated from ownership of the means of production or administration. Officials, employees, and workers attached to the administrative staff do not themselves own the non-human means of production and administration. These are rather provided for their use in kind or in money, and the official is obligated to render an accounting of their use. There exists, furthermore, in principle complete separation of the property belonging to the organization, which is controlled within the sphere of office, and the personal property of the official, which is available for his own private uses. There is a corresponding separation of the place in which official functions are carried out, the 'office' in the sense of premises, from living quarters.

(6) In the rational type case, there is also a complete absence of appropriation of his official position by the incumbent. Where 'rights' to an office exist, as in the case of judges, and recently of an increasing proportion of officials and even of workers, they do not normally serve the purpose of appropriation by the official, but of securing the purely objective and independent character of the conduct of the office so that it is oriented only to the relevant norms.

(7) Administrative acts, decisions, and rules are formulated and recorded in writing, even in cases where oral discussion is the rule or is even mandatory. This applies at least to preliminary discussions and proposals, to final decisions, and to all sorts of orders and rules. The combination of written documents and a continuous organization of official functions constitutes the 'office'[2] which is the central focus of all types of modern corporate action.

(8) Legal authority can be exercised in a wide variety of different forms which will be distinguished and discussed later. The following analysis will be deliberately confined for the most part to the aspect of imperative co-ordination in the structure of the administrative staff. It will consist in an analysis in terms of ideal types of officialdom or 'bureaucracy.'

---

[2] *Bureau.* It has seemed necessary to use the English word 'office' in three different meanings, which are distinguished in Weber's discussion by at least two terms. The first in *Amt*, which means 'office' in the sense of the institutionally defined status of a person. The second is the 'work premises' as in the expression 'he spent the afternoon in his office.' For this Weber uses *Bureau* as also for the third meaning which he has just defined, the 'organized work process of a group.' In this last sense an office is a particular type of 'organization,' or *Betrieb* in Weber's sense. This use is established in English in such expressions as 'the District Attorney's Office has such and such functions.' Which of the three meanings is involved in a given case will generally be clear from the context—ED. [Parsons.]

In the above outline no mention has been made of the kind of supreme head appropriate to a system of legal authority. This is a consequence of certain considerations which can only be made entirely understandable at a later stage in the analysis. There are very important types of rational imperative co-ordination which, with respect to the ultimate source of authority, belong to other categories. This is true of the hereditary charismatic type, as illustrated by hereditary monarchy and of the pure charismatic type of a president chosen by plebiscite. Other cases involve rational elements at important points, but are made up of a combination of bureaucratic and charismatic components, as is true of the cabinet form of government. Still others are subject to the authority of the chief of other corporate groups, whether this character be charismatic or bureaucratic; thus the formal head of a government department under a parliamentary regime may be a minister who occupies his position because of his authority in a party. The type of rational, legal administrative staff is capable of application in all kinds of situations and contexts. It is the most important mechanism for the administration of everyday profane affairs. For in that sphere, the exercise of authority and, more broadly, imperative co-ordination, consists precisely in administration.

The purest type of exercise of legal authority is that which employs a bureaucratic administrative staff. Only the supreme chief of the organization occupies his position of authority by virtue of appropriation, of election, or of having been designated for the succession. But even *his* authority consists in a sphere of legal 'competence.' The whole administrative staff under the supreme authority then consists, in the purest type, of individual officials who are appointed and function according to the following criteria:[3]

(1) They are personally free and subject to authority only with respect to their impersonal official obligations.

(2) They are organized in a clearly defined hierarchy of offices.

(3) Each office has a clearly defined sphere of competence in the legal sense.

(4) The office is filled by a free contractual relationship. Thus, in principle, there is free selection.

(5) Candidates are selected on the basis of technical qualifications. In the most rational case, this is tested by examination or guaranteed by diplomas certifying technical training, or both. They are *appointed*, not elected.

(6) They are remunerated by fixed salaries in money, for the most part with a right to pensions. Only under certain circumstances does the employing authority, especially in private organizations, have a right to terminate the appointment, but the official is always free to resign. The

---

[3] This characterization applies to the 'monocratic' as opposed to the 'collegial' type, which will be discussed below.

salary scale is primarily graded according to rank in the hierarchy; but in addition to this criterion, the responsibility of the position and the requirements of the incumbent's social status may be taken into account.

(7) The office is treated as the sole, or at least the primary, occupation of the incumbent.

(8) It constitutes a career. There is a system of 'promotion' according to seniority or to achievement, or both. Promotion is dependent on the judgment of superiors.

(9) The official works entirely separated from ownership of the means of administration and without appropriation of his position.

(10) He is subject to strict and systematic discipline and control in the conduct of the office.

This type of organization is in principle applicable with equal facility to a wide variety of different fields. It may be applied in profit-making business or in charitable organizations, or in any number of other types of private enterprises serving ideal or material ends. It is equally applicable to political and to religious organizations. With varying degrees of approximation to a pure type, its historical existence can be demonstrated in all these fields.

1. For example, this type of bureaucracy is found in private clinics, as well as in endowed hospitals or the hospitals maintained by religious orders. Bureaucratic organization has played a major role in the Catholic Church. It is well illustrated by the administrative role of the priesthood in the modern church, which has expropriated almost all of the old church benefices, which were in former days to a large extent subject to private appropriation. It is also illustrated by the conception of the universal Episcopate, which is thought of as formally constituting a universal legal competence in religious matters. Similarly, the doctrine of Papal infallibility is thought of as in fact involving a universal competence, but only one which functions 'ex cathedra' in the sphere of the office, thus implying the typical distinction between the sphere of office and that of the private affairs of the incumbent. The same phenomena are found in the large-scale capitalistic enterprise; and the larger it is, the greater their role. And this is not less true of political parties, which will be discussed separately. Finally, the modern army is essentially a bureaucratic organization administered by that peculiar type of military functionary, the 'officer.'

2. Bureaucratic authority is carried out in its purest form where it is most clearly dominated by the principle of appointment. There is no such thing as a hierarchy of elected officials in the same sense as there is a hierarchical organization of appointed officials. In the first place, election makes it impossible to attain a stringency of discipline even approaching that in the appointed type. For it is open to a subordinate official to compete for elective honours on the same terms as his superiors, and his prospects are not dependent on the superior's judgment.

3. Appointment by free contract, which makes free selection possible, is essential to modern bureaucracy. Where there is a hierarchical organization with impersonal spheres of competence, but occupied by unfree officials—like slaves or dependents, who, however, function in a formally bureaucratic manner—the term 'patrimonial bureaucracy' will be used.

4. The role of technical qualifications in bureaucratic organizations is continually increasing. Even an official in a party or a trade-union organization is in need of specialized knowledge, though it is usually of an empirical character, developed by experience, rather than by formal training. In the modern state, the only 'offices' for which no technical qualifications are required are those of ministers and presidents. This only goes to prove that they are 'officials' only in a formal sense, and not substantively, as is true of the managing director or president of a large business corporation. There is no question but that the 'position' of the capitalistic entrepreneur is as definitely appropriated as is that of a monarch. Thus at the top of a bureaucratic organization, there is necessarily an element which is at least not purely bureaucratic. The category of bureaucracy is one applying only to the exercise of control by means of a particular kind of administrative staff.

5. The bureaucratic official normally receives a fixed salary. By contrast, sources of income which are privately appropriated will be called 'benefices.' Bureaucratic salaries are also normally paid in money. Though this is not essential to the concept of bureaucracy, it is the arrangement which best fits the pure type. Payments in kind are apt to have the character of benefices, and the receipt of a benefice normally implies the appropriation of opportunities for earnings and of positions. There are, however, gradual transitions in this field with many intermediate types. Appropriation by virtue of leasing or sale of offices or the pledge of income from office are phenomena foreign to the pure type of bureaucracy.

6. 'Offices' which do not constitute the incumbent's principal occupation, in particular 'honorary' offices, belong in other categories. . . . The typical 'bureaucratic' official occupies the office as his principal occupation.

7. With respect to the separation of the official from ownership of the means of administration, the situation is essentially the same in the field of public administration and in private bureaucratic organizations, such as the large-scale capitalistic enterprise.

8. At present [collegial bodies] are rapidly decreasing in importance in favour of types of organization which are in fact, and for the most part formally as well, subject to the authority of a single head. For instance, the collegial 'governments' in Prussia have long since given way to the monocratic 'district president.' The decisive factor in this development has been the need for rapid, clear decisions, free of the necessity of

compromise between different opinions and also free of shifting majorities.

9. The modern army officer is a type of appointed official who is clearly marked off by certain class distinctions. . . . In this respect such officers differ radically from elected military leaders, from charismatic condottieri, from the type of officers who recruit and lead mercenary armies as a capitalistic enterprise, and, finally, from the incumbents of commissions which have been purchased. There may be gradual transitions between these types. The patrimonial 'retainer,' who is separated from the means of carrying out his function, and the proprietor of a mercenary army for capitalistic purposes have, along with the private capitalistic entrepreneur, been pioneers in the organization of the modern type of bureaucracy. . . .

THE MONOCRATIC TYPE OF BUREAUCRATIC ADMINISTRATION

Experience tends universally to show that the purely bureaucratic type of administrative organization—that is, the monocratic variety of bureaucracy—is, from a purely technical point of view, capable of attaining the highest degree of efficiency and is in this sense formally the most rational known means of carrying out imperative control over human beings. It is superior to any other form in precision, in stability, in the stringency of its discipline, and in its reliability. It thus makes possible a particularly high degree of calculability of results for the heads of the organization and for those acting in relation to it. It is finally superior both in intensive efficiency and in the scope of its operations, and is formally capable of application to all kinds of administrative tasks.

The development of the modern form of the organization of corporate groups in all fields is nothing less than identical with the development and continual spread of bureaucratic administration. This is true of church and state, of armies, political parties, economic enterprise, organizations to promote all kinds of causes, private associations, clubs, and many others. Its development is, to take the most striking case, the most crucial phenomenon of the modern Western state. However many forms there may be which do not appear to fit this pattern, such as collegial representative bodies, parliamentary committees, soviets, honorary officers, lay judges, and what not, and however much people may complain about the 'evils of bureaucracy,' it would be sheer illusion to think for a moment that continuous administrative work can be carried out in any field except by means of officials working in offices. The whole pattern of everyday life is cut to fit this framework. For bureaucratic administration is, other things being equal, always, from a formal, technical point of view, the most rational type. For the needs of mass administration to-day, it is completely indispensable. The choice is only that between bureaucracy and dilletantism in the field of administration.

The primary source of the superiority of bureaucratic administration lies in the role of technical knowledge which, through the development of modern technology and business methods in the production of goods, has become completely indispensable. In this respect, it makes no difference whether the economic system is organized on a capitalistic or a socialistic basis. Indeed, if in the latter case a comparable level of technical efficiency were to be achieved, it would mean a tremendous increase in the importance of specialized bureaucracy.

When those subject to bureaucratic control seek to escape the influence of the existing bureaucratic apparatus, this is normally possible only by creating an organization of their own which is equally subject to the process of bureaucratization. Similarly the existing bureaucratic apparatus is driven to continue functioning by the most powerful interests which are material and objective, but also ideal in character. Without it, a society like our own—with a separation of officials, employees, and workers from ownership of the means of administration, dependent on discipline and on technical training—could no longer function. The only exception would be those groups, such as the peasantry, who are still in possession of their own means of subsistence. Even in case of revolution by force or of occupation by an enemy, the bureaucratic machinery will normally continue to function just as it has for the previous legal government.

The question is always who controls the existing bureaucratic machinery. And such control is possible only in a very limited degree to persons who are not technical specialists. Generally speaking, the trained permanent official is more likely to get his way in the long run than his nominal superior, the Cabinet minister, who is not a specialist.

N.B.

Though by no means alone, the capitalistic system has undeniably played a major role in the development of bureaucracy. Indeed, without it capitalistic production could not continue and any rational type of socialism would have simply to take it over and increase its importance. Its development, largely under capitalistic auspices, has created an urgent need for stable, strict, intensive, and calculable administration. It is this need which gives bureaucracy a crucial role in our society as the central element in any kind of large-scale administration. Only by reversion in every field—political, religious, economic, etc.—to small-scale organization would it be possible to any considerable extent to escape its influence. On the one hand, capitalism in its modern stages of development strongly tends to foster the development of bureaucracy, though both capitalism and bureaucracy have arisen from many different historical sources. Conversely, capitalism is the most rational economic basis for bureaucratic administration and enables it to develop in the most rational form, especially because, from a fiscal point of view, it supplies the necessary money resources.

Along with these fiscal conditions of efficient bureaucratic administration, there are certain extremely important conditions in the fields of communication and transportation. The precision of its functioning requires the services of the railway, the telegraph, and the telephone, and becomes increasingly dependent on them. A socialistic form of organization would not alter this fact. It would be a question whether in a socialistic system it would be possible to provide conditions for carrying out as stringent bureaucratic organization as has been possible in a capitalistic order. For socialism would, in fact, require a still higher degree of formal bureaucratization than capitalism. If this should prove not to be possible, it would demonstrate the existence of another of those fundamental elements of irrationality in social systems—a conflict between formal and substantive rationality of the sort which sociology so often encounters.

Bureaucratic administration means fundamentally the exercise of control on the basis of knowledge. This is the feature of it which makes it specifically rational. This consists on the one hand in technical knowledge which, by itself, is sufficient to ensure it a position of extraordinary power. But in addition to this, bureaucratic organizations, or the holders of power who make use of them, have the tendency to increase their power still further by the knowledge growing out of experience in the service. For they acquire through the conduct of office a special knowledge of facts and have available a store of documentary material peculiar to themselves. While not peculiar to bureaucratic organizations, the concept of 'official secrets' is certainly typical of them. It stands in relation to technical knowledge in somewhat the same position as commercial secrets do to technological training. It is a product of the striving for power.

Bureaucracy is superior in knowledge, including both technical knowledge and knowledge of the concrete fact within its own sphere of interest, which is usually confined to the interests of a private business—a capitalistic enterprise. The capitalistic entrepreneur is, in our society, the only type who has been able to maintain at least relative immunity from subjection to the control of rational bureaucratic knowledge. All the rest of the population have tended to be organized in large-scale corporate groups which are inevitably subject to bureaucratic control. This is as inevitable as the dominance of precision machinery in the mass production of goods.

The following are the principal more general social consequences of bureaucratic control:—

(1) The tendency to 'levelling' in the interest of the broadest possible basis of recruitment in terms of technical competence.

(2) The tendency to plutocracy growing out of the interest in the greatest possible length of technical training. To-day this often lasts up to the age of thirty.

(3) The dominance of a spirit of formalistic impersonality, '*Sine ira et studio*,' without hatred or passion, and hence without affection or enthusiasm. The dominant norms are concepts of straightforward duty without regard to personal considerations. Everyone is subject to formal equality of treatment; that is, everyone in the same empirical situation. This is the spirit in which the ideal official conducts his office.

39. THE CIVIL SERVICE OF PAKISTAN*

Ralph Braibanti

[I]

A DOMINANT professional value of the highest ranking executives of the Pakistan public service has been that of classical generalism or guardianship similar conceptually to Confucian and Platonic canons. Max Weber's characterization of the Chinese mandarinate as literati is probably pertinent in new states with strong administrative but weak political traditions and is certainly pertinent in modern Pakistan. Indeed there is evidence that the classical generalism of the British Civil Service, and of the Indian Civil Service from which the Pakistani system is derived, were conceptually influenced by the ancient Chinese system which attracted Weber's attention. The emphasis of these systems has been on the recruitment of young men of presumably tested intellectual attainment in humane letters, aloof from politics, devoting their lives to the interests of the state. . . . The sources of this tradition as it is manifest in Pakistan are deeply rooted in the historical development of the Indian Civil Service. Reluctance within Pakistan government to depart from the system as it presently exists can be explained in large measure by the long pragmatic process by which it evolved, a process attended by minds of considerable distinction. It is not every civil service system which can claim the combined genius of a Wellesley, a Macaulay, and a Malthus among its mentors. . . .

Thomas Babington Macaulay, both during his career in India from 1834 to 1838 and in England later, greatly influenced the training of civil servants in the middle of the nineteenth century. His renowned minute of February 2, 1835, now sometimes cited by those Pakistani who regret the Anglo-orientation of Pakistan's education, placed principal reliance on the gradual permeation of Indian culture by western ideas.

We must at present do our best [said Macaulay] to form a class who may be interpreters between us and the millions whom we govern; a class of persons,

---

* From "The Civil Service of Pakistan: A Theoretical Analysis," *The South Atlantic Quarterly*, Vol. LVIII, No. 2 (Spring, 1959). By permission.

Indian in blood and colour, but English in taste, in opinions, in morals, and in intellect. To that class we may leave it to refine the vernacular dialects of the country, to enrich those dialects with terms of science borrowed from the western nomenclature, and to render them by degrees fit vehicles for conveying knowledge to the great mass of the population.

. . . To this minute may be traced the practice of English usage in modern India and Pakistan, curse or blessing that it may be.

Lord Macaulay defended with considerable vigor the proposition that the civil servant of the East India Company required the same education as the professional man who remained in England. European literature and science were to dominate this education, though Sanskrit and Arabic, which he deemed to be classical languages, need not necessarily be excluded. He proposed a curriculum which would include English language and literature, Greek, Latin, French, German, Italian, mathematics, natural sciences, moral sciences, Sanskrit, and Arabic. Yet Macaulay seemed less particular about the subjects studied than he was about the rigor and intellectual discipline of English education. Indeed, his earlier brilliant defense of English as being superior to the Indian vernaculars seems to be contradicted by his assertion that

whatever be the languages, whatever be the sciences, which it is in any age or country, the fashion to teach, the persons who become the greatest proficients in those languages and those sciences will generally be the flower of the youth; the most acute, the most industrious, the most ambitious of honourable distinctions. . . . If instead of learning Greek, we learned the Cherokee, the man who understood the Cherokee best, who made the most correct and melodious Cherokee verses, who comprehended most accurately the effect of the Cherokee particles, would generally be a superior man to him who was destitute of these accomplishments.

. . . The competitive examinations required for entrance into the Indian service assured the continuation of a generalist, humanistic education. This educational system provided the executives for what became probably the most distinguished civil service in the world.

It was inevitable in the traumatic circumstances of the 1947 partition of India that Pakistan continue the traditions and structure of the Indian Civil Service. That the traditions had deep roots in a different culture and different era; indeed, that the Muslims had themselves resisted those traditions; that the structure was designed for rule of the conqueror over the vanquished—these factors could ill be considered at a time when a nation had to be formed quickly from two patches of land on the subcontinent. The Pakistan public service system was in the grip of history to which time adds only tightness and strength and from which release seems possible only by a violent wrench. . . .

[II]

It is quite clear that the scope of duties required of the civil servant of executive rank in prepartition India and Pakistan required precisely the kind of education which evolved. The question now is whether this pattern of education and the accompanying predispositions it assumes have changed.

The available documentary evidence indicates that applicants for appointment in the Central Superior Services regard their own competence as being overwhelmingly classical and literary. Recruitment as well as the entire examining and grading processes for the Central Superior Services are carried on by the Federal Public Service Commission, whose functions are constitutionally defined. Recruitment for all Central Superior Services, except for the Engineering Service and Survey of Pakistan Services, is by competitive examination consisting of a written part and an interview. Candidates must be between the ages of twenty-one and twenty-four years and must also be graduates of British, India, Burmese, or Pakistani universities approved by the government.[1] The highest total score possible in the examination is 1400. Of this total, 300 points is the maximum value of the interview and the remaining 1100 points are divided among thirty-three possible subjects in which the candidate may be examined. Three subjects, English essay, English, and general knowledge, counting for a total of 500 points, are compulsory. The remaining 600 points may be taken from among thirty subjects, ten of which are valued at 100 points and the remaining twenty at 200 points each. Applicants rarely offer more than four optional subjects.

The score attained by the successful applicant in the examination is a crucial determinant in his entire career. His standing in the competition is one of the factors in determining the service to which he will be assigned. The services by tradition are ranked *inter se*, the Civil Service and the Audit and Accounts Service having, in that order, greatest prestige. Of the available vacancies, 20 per cent are filled in order of merit as determined by standing in the examination. The remaining 80 per cent are shared by areas and provinces, but the candidate's position on his respective area or provincial list is determined by his standing in the examination. Moreover, young executives appointed in any given year rank in seniority according to the score on this examination, the grade given while a probationer at the Civil Service Academy, and the score attained in a final Passing Out Examination given at the end of a probationary period of about one year in the field. This then becomes a permanent rank which is one of the criteria used in assigning or promoting him for the remainder of his service in government. The "confidential report" or efficiency report

---

[1] Approved universities are listed in an appendix to "Rules Relating to the Examination" published in some issues of the *Report on the Central Superior Services Examination*. See, for example, Appendix I, *ibid.*, January–February, 1953 [PPSC-8(R)6], pp. 23–24. The list found there continued in force through 1958. Although it is uncommon at present for an applicant to have a bachelor's degree from a university in the United States or Canada, there is a provision that a degree or diploma from universities other than those listed "will be considered on its merits and may be accepted or rejected as the Commission sees fit" (*Ibid.*, p. 24).

prepared by his superior is also an important determinant in his career. Transfer from one service to another is almost never made, although theoretically it can be authorized by the Establishment Division of the Cabinet Secretariat. These circumstances thereby create a situation in which there is unusual reliance on evaluating a civil servant at the beginning of his career without allowing for the potential of growth and experience. . . .

. . . For the years under review the candidates appointed to the Central Superior Services in the Public Service of Pakistan were examined principally in the humanities rather than in the social sciences, pure sciences, or in mathematics. It is significant to note that the Federal Public Service Commission itself has directed attention to this condition in its reports and has suggested the application of remedies for it.

It is pertinent to inquire whether the inclination toward classical generalism is modified by subsequent training. Successful candidates who are appointed to the Civil Service of Pakistan or the Audit and Accounts Service are then posted to an appropriate academy for nearly a year of study in residence. The Civil Service Academy at Lahore is for CSP officers; its counterpart is the Finance Services Academy in Walton about six miles distance from Lahore. The Civil Service Academy, created in 1948, seeks to continue the finest traditions of the Indian Civil Service: the development of character, a sense of dedication and service to the state, and impartial, efficient administration. The physical surroundings are reminiscent of life of the civil servants before partition. The academy is housed in a large handsome structure, formerly an official residence, surrounded by beautiful lawns and gardens. Here the probationers live and study under the guidance of a director, one of the few former English members of the Indian Civil Service still remaining in the service of the government of Pakistan. Classes, conducted both by the director and a teaching staff of four officials, are given in land revenue, criminal and civil law, constitutional development, and *Islamiat*. Much attention is necessarily given to the land revenue systems of both West Pakistan and East Pakistan. There is a field exercise in land settlement and assessment which is undoubtedly extremely valuable in grounding the probationers in the basic economic structure upon which the ultimate success of Pakistan government rests. Certainly the instruction and field exercises in land revenue can be said to be empirically oriented, since they seek to establish by minute examination of historical records the validity of claims to land ownership.

This practical work is woven into a context of character-building in which there are developed standards of conduct and an ethos of the service. This ethos results in part from the fact of twenty-five probationers living together, and from the inculcation of the spirit of the Indian Civil Service by the personality and character of the director himself. Once a week the probationers wear evening dress at dinner and invite guests from among other government officials and military officers. There is a required course in equitation each morning, a training the utility of which has been questioned by some Pakistani, who assert that most districts are now accessible by jeep or, in East Pakistan, by boat. They point out further that even in districts of difficult terrain horses are no longer regularly maintained at district headquarters, and that, in any case, physical conditioning can be accomplished by other means. The validity of such criticism is open to question, but it is likely, however, that equestrianism continues because of a feeling that it perpetuates the ethos of guardianship which characterized British rule through the Indian Civil Service. Certainly the academy succeeds in stamping each of the probationers with its mark. Its aim is to inculcate a concept of guardianship sufficiently strong to resist the corrosive influences of political pressures to which post-partition bureaucracy seems subject. Its reliance on Anglicization to accomplish this purpose widens the hiatus which already exists between the Islamic-oriented public mass, whose servant the bureaucrat is presumed to be, and the ruling elite. But this should be regarded as an observation rather than a negative criticism. If, indeed, the wellsprings of governmental efficiency and morality lie in the ethical system of the British tradition, then an effort to recapture and preserve that tradition appears justifiable.

Three months of the year's assignment at the Civil Service Academy are spent in supervised service in Bengal, and then the probationers are posted for one full academic year to either Oxford or Cambridge universities where they pursue a regular academic course. This period in England, while it doubtless has a broadening effect on the outlook of the Pakistani probationer, serves also to alienate him from the Islamic masses he is to serve. It is ironic that the Hindus of India, who quickly accepted British education before partition, ceased sending their probationers to England after independence had been won but the Muslims of Pakistan, despite their history of resistance to British education, continue to rely on it for the civil service. During the entire period of two years, the probationers remain under the disciplinary control of the director of the Academy, who makes a confidential evaluation of each one. . . .

The academies reflect the exaggerated independence of the parts of the public services. Although located only a few miles apart, the academies conduct no joint classes in subjects taught at both institutions, and there is little social contact between the two groups of probationers or the faculties. It is probable that both succeed in transmitting a *mystique* of the ICS tradition and in creating a sense of *esprit*, however elitist in attitude it may be. If the civil service (and I would add the finance services) has indeed been the "steel frame" of government, the academies are trying to keep the metal from corroding, though what may be needed is a different quality of steel and a different construction of the frame to support a vastly different governmental superstructure.

[III]

The intellectual problem of the roles of the specialist and generalist in government has provoked disputation for decades and it would serve no purpose here to review or to analyze the substance of this issue. Our immediate concern is the absence in Pakistan of significant deviation from the Confucian and Platonic formularies of guardianship even though the problems faced by bureaucracy demand an empirical frame of reference and the ethical core of that guardianship has been eroded by consequences of the partition of the subcontinent.[2]

It is assumed that when the preponderating value of the bureaucratic ethos is that of nonempirical generalism there is a denigration of the attitudes and skills of the technically competent. The prime example of classical generalism is the Chinese mandarin whose long fingernails were public evidence that as a philosopher-poet he was above the tasks of record-keeping and other trivia. The consequent devolution of important administrative work on the office of underclerk resulted in corruption in local administration despite a value system remarkable for its pious regard for justice and integrity.

The public services of Pakistan are not unlike the Chinese mandarinate in their attitude toward empirical tasks. It is not here being argued that there should be no hierarchic distinctions of functions based on degree of responsibility and other factors; such distinctions are essential to any administrative order. What is important is that the functions have been isolated from each other to an exaggerated degree. The relative statuses of the classical-generalist functionary of the CSP and the technically oriented official are rigidified further in Pakistan by a social system already divided into castes on the basis of occupation. Nor is it being argued that the technically trained should have as much to do with making policies as the generalist executive, for there is now fairly common agreement that the policy-making positions of bureaucracy are best filled by those with ability to manage complexity, and that the expert should be "on tap but not on top." The Civil Service of Pakistan enjoys unusual esteem, and even official nomenclature refers to it as the "premier service," "*corps d'élite*," and "superior service," while the other services are called "inferior" and "subordinate." The pay scales continue to reflect this order of prestige. Under the present system a probationer with a bachelor's degree appointed to the CSP starts with a salary of Rs. 350 a month whereas an agriculturalist with a bachelor's degree starts at Rs. 200. The differentials of salary and status are great enough to make it difficult to attract those with technical skills and to create serious frustrations and tensions among

---

[2] The disintegration of ethical values in Pakistani government and politics was given as the principal reason for the assumption of personal control by Iskander Mirza and later by General Mohammad Ayub Khan. . . .

those technical experts that are ultimately recruited. The animosity felt by technical personnel toward members of the CSP is intense, especially among engineers and others trained abroad, where they have experienced adulation of the scientist and technocrat.

An excessively generalist orientation in the Pakistan bureaucracy and the accompanying rigid compartmentalization of the services has several serious disadvantages. The wisdom of placing generalists in policy-making positions is conceded, yet it seems uneconomic to label a career civil servant a generalist or a technical expert at twenty-two years of age and force him to remain in one or the other category for the whole of his career. The sources to be tapped for the executive who can manage complexity are many, and neither the means of identifying such capacity nor the character of education to develop it has been clearly determined even in governmental systems which have long applied themselves systematically to the task. Some executives trained as generalists cannot qualify for executive positions beyond a certain level of complexity and responsibility; some technically trained officials manifest the qualities required in the highest levels of management. The present system in Pakistan which limits the source of executives to those whose talents were "discovered" between the ages of twenty-one and twenty-four does not adequately take account of the unscientific and imprecise nature of identifying executive talent.

An attitude or philosophy of a bureaucracy that leads it to depreciate if not reject an empirical point of view is of more crucial significance than the status of personnel, for it is the attitude which determines how much use will be made of an empirical methodology. Even in Western political thought, preoccupied as much of it is by concern for submergence of the human spirit under the lava of scientism and technique, it is easy to forget the abject dependence of a constitutional system on technical efficiency. The equitable assessment and collection of taxes, the maintenance of records, control of disbursement, auditing of expenditures, evaluation of civil service personnel, preparation and conduct of elections and counting of ballots—these are technical requirements which undergird a successful constitutional system. When a nation evolves its constitutional forms slowly, the emergence of such skills may accompany its political growth at nearly the same rate. Or, as was the case in the United States, technical, administrative, and fiscal skills developed first in private competitive enterprise were gradually absorbed into the governmental sector. But Pakistan, in company with other new states, finds that the demands of modern government exceed the pace of attitudinal adjustment necessary for empirically oriented technical management. There can be no borrowing of skills from private enterprise, for the latter has not developed sufficiently. The supply of bureaucratic leadership capable of creating an empirical attitude is severely limited. Yet all the problems confronted by older nations over decades, if not centuries, have now been compressed into a few years. The requirements of a foreign policy astute enough both to represent the national aspirations and to assure continued existence of the state and of the maintenance of military power adequate to sustain such foreign policy are foremost among such problems. Finally there is the urgent need of planned economic development sufficient to cope with the phenomenon of rising expectations—or else the political finesse to deal with the consequences of the inability to meet them.

The problem of economic development is aggravated by at least three factors. The first is the developing awareness among the masses of disparity in living standards between highly industrialized nations and underdeveloped areas. Thus either the tradition-oriented villager demands a standard of living he formerly knew little about or could do nothing about under foreign colonial rule, or, more importantly, a western-oriented elite, fired with a passion for progress and improvement, spearheads such demands in the name of patriotism and the welfare of the masses. Political independence has placed the responsibility for development on indigenous governments responsive to the popular mandate, and the buffer of resignation and apathy which colonial rule provided between people and government is gone. Independent nations which learned to expect little under foreign rule, now expect everything under their own rulers and expect it at once. This vexing combination of problems—preserving the state, developing a viable constitutional system, and uplifting the economy, can best be dealt with by governors whose minds are of an empirical and rational bent. Yet the leadership of Pakistan must ultimately—whether under constitutional forms or the martial law of Ayub Khan—answer to the public masses, whose disposition is essentially intuitive and non-rational, who elevate feeling as a primary means of arriving at truth, and who minimize rationality accordingly. To meet the problems of governing, the rulers must rely on a bureaucracy torn between the two traditions, a bureaucracy which espouses the empiricism of the west but gives it expression in the western brand of classical generalism. The chasm thereby created between the nature of the problems faced and the philosophical apparatus a nation can muster to face them is at the root of difficulties of many Asian nations which have turned in desperation to military dictatorship. Of all sectors of the public bureaucracy the military, by virtue of its mission, has more quickly discarded both the intuitive disposition of the masses and the related literary-generalist tradition of the civil bureaucracy. It is, of course, preoccupied with the requirements of order and stability, but its concern for precision in situation-analysis disposes it favorably toward empiricism. Indeed, if military rule manifests sufficient patience with the complexities of long-range planning, it is possible that it can create an environment more favorable for economic development than a civil government can. This does not diminish in the slightest the hazards of authoritarian military rule, which are great and cannot ultimately be overcome, but these hazards lie in the realm of developing political viability and popular responsibility rather than in the realm of establishing economic order.

It is understandable that Pakistan bureaucracy, nurtured in the Wellesley–Macaulay traditions, has been repelled by its contact with some of the extreme, mechanistic views of administrative science as known in Europe and the United States. The structural engineering principles of V. A. Graicunas or the scientific management movement of F. W. Taylor are regarded as examples of dangerous subordination of the humane to the technocratic. That administrative science has moved away from Taylorism to the more fruitful conceptualization of Barnard and others has not been appreciated. But even appreciation of this fact would not divest the newly emergent sovereign state of the necessity of elevating empiricism and related technical skills to a new position of esteem. An administration that has practiced and absorbed technics over a long period may ridicule the mechanistics of Fayol, Graicunas, or Taylor but such ridicule is not becoming in a bureaucracy that has never developed technical interests and skills. Domination of the bureaucracy by the predisposition of the classical generalist is likely to be detrimental to the attainment of administrative efficiency and integrity and to the aim of accelerating economic growth. It can be assumed that a bureaucracy so dominated will be suspicious of rational planning and forecasting and inclined to minimize the utility of an empirical methodology. Yet administrative and economic order depend on the accurate reproduction of reality, the isolation of predictable factors, and the assessment of their impact on existing reality, all with a view to modifying reality to approximate a set of value aspirations. . . .

[IV]

It is assumed that in Pakistan for the foreseeable future the bureaucracy will be the principal factor in determining, interpreting, and safeguarding the polity of the state. This responsibility will diminish only in proportion to the rise in effectiveness and prestige of the national legislative process. As that process matures, and is a more effective reflection of the public will, the hiatus between the Anglo-oriented "secularly Islamic" higher public service and the illiterate, devoutly Islamic masses will change. They will move closer to each other, and the bureaucracy will probably move faster in the direction of the masses than the masses in the direction of bureaucracy. This is assumed because the bureaucracy has the literate skills requisite to ease such a change and because the sheer weight of tradition, combined with the growing power of the public masses, will induce a shift in that direction. Already, for example, Urdu has been introduced as the medium of instruction in the schools of West Pakistan and there has been a consequent rapid decline in the effective use of English. In the interim, strong regional differences will continue to exist and effective local government capable of responding adequately to a central government's program of economic development and political advancement will be slow in emerging. This augurs that the civil servant will continue to exercise broad powers in local areas as agent of the central government.

The literary and humanistic qualities implicit in Platonic guardianship and now dominant in the Pakistani bureaucracy are vital. To him who is entrusted with decisions involving values, there must be given a knowledge of the inner philosophy of his society, the historical conditions controlling it, and the human nature within it. This insight he cannot have so long as he is a stranger to the literary, scientific, and artistic heritage which constitutes that civilization. This is the significance of the dictum that cultured men are needed in statecraft. As government, or any segment of its activity, grows in importance there is danger of that government or that segment mistaking itself for the social totality. One way, though not a certain way, of impeding this dominance is the resistance of a bureaucracy sufficiently aware of its own culture to be able to judge without passion its own role and limits in a larger society.

The role of empirical methodology, of technique, must be admitted to a level of esteem equalling the literary role. Yet a combination of humanistic and technical elites failing to appreciate the popular base of a constitutional democracy is ultimately as dangerous as either humanistic or technical dominance. Nor is the solution to the problem necessarily made easier by the declaration of martial law, for while control by the military enhances the possibility of a more empirical government, the ultimate problem will be the degree to which the military elite can identify itself with the Islamic-oriented public masses. Pakistan approaches its problems of the public service with the long influence of a British literary tradition and the newer but more aggressive influence of an American technical bias. From these may be achieved a synthesis of modern guardianship rivaling that of the ancients, but we have yet to see if a viable synthesis will be effected.

Chapter XIII. Responsibility and Control

Introductory Note

IN ALL democracies the expansion of the State domain has resulted in increasing use of *delegated legislation,* that is, rules, regulations, and orders having the force of law issued by the executive under express authorization of the legislature. The executive in effect is invited to legislate on many matters: to fix prices and rates; regulate production; reorganize the executive branch and the civil service; increase or decrease taxes; modify the tariff; supervise and control the manufacture of drugs, the transportation of goods, the administration of hospitals; allocate funds voted by the legislature; establish the conditions under which persons will be drafted into the armed forces or be exempted from service, and so on.

This reflects a profound transformation of the character of law. Diversification of groups and conditions in an industrialized society is so great that the only way to provide for equal opportunities and equal rights is to legislate not according to general rules, but with full realization that conditions call for differential treatment and regulation. Legislative assemblies may attempt to control, to criticize, and to engage the over-all political responsibility of the executive, but they cannot cope with the technical problems that legislation involves. They are forced to delegate virtual lawmaking power to the executive.

A widely used device for implementing State control over the economy in democratic nations is the *public corporation.* These are administrative agencies enjoying autonomous status. They are generally free to develop their own personnel policies, and are exempt from the normal budgetary and auditory controls to which the regular departments of government are subject. Within certain limits they are allowed to conduct their operations in the manner considered most expeditious and efficient by the directors. Too much control entails the intervention of the minister or the legislature in technical matters of a managerial nature; too little allows the members of a board to refer only to considerations of managerial efficiency in making decisions—it would leave the nationalized industries in the hands of "technocrats." Too much control would involve too much politics. Too little control would eliminate all political considerations. The problem is dealt with at greater length in the article by E. L. Johnson, reproduced below.

Thus, one of the pressing problems of modern democracies, and of nondemocratic systems as well, is to render the civil service responsible without undermining its efficiency. The readings reproduced below are addressed to this problem. How can the bureaucracy be brought under political control? What kind of internal controls may be devised? How can autonomous power to act on the basis of expert and specialized knowledge be reconciled with control by a political superior who does not possess this knowledge? Problems of responsibility are examined in Carl J. Friedrich (ed.), *Responsibility* (1960). With reference to dele gated legislation and the problems it poses, see: the relevant chapters of Lord Campion (ed.), *Parliament: A Survey* (1955); William A. Robson, *Justice and Administrative Law* (3d ed., 1951); and C. K. Allen, *Law and Orders* (1945). See also, Clinton Rossiter, *Constitutional Dictatorship: Crisis of Government in the Modern Democracies* (1948).

Administrative law is a generalized expression of the administrative state and the existence of administrative, as distinct from ordinary, courts reflects the need of new rules and procedures in order to safeguard individual rights and interests. For a critical view of administrative law and delegated legislation: A. V. Dicey, *The Law and the Constitution* (1885); Lord Hewart, *The New Despotism* (1929); and Friedrich Hayek, *The Road to Serfdom* (1945). A balanced treatment may be found in Brian Chapman, *The Profession of Government* (1959); Charles E. Freedeman, *The Conseil d'Etat in Modern France* (1961); Bernard Schwartz, *French Administrative Law and the Common Law World* (1954); and Arthur W. Macmahon, *Delegation and Autonomy* (1961).

Regular courts may also be used as instrumentalities for the control and review of administrative and even legislative acts. The leading example of judicial review in the name of the supremacy of the constitution is, of course, the United States. A classic statement is E. S. Corwin, *The Doctrine of Judicial Review* (1914). For a more recent assessment, see Robert G. McCloskey, *The American Supreme Court* (1960).

The American practice has not been widely copied. In Britain the supremacy of Parliament cannot be contested by any court of law. In France this was also the case until 1958. Under the Weimar Republic, a special court was empowered to scrutinize legislation and set it aside, but only under very restrictive conditions. Since World War II, on the other hand, there has been a revival of judicial review in Europe, mainly as a reaction to the disregard of individual rights in Nazi Germany, as is indicated in the essay by Taylor Cole, reproduced below. In France, under the Constitution of the Fifth Republic, a special Constitutional Court has been set up whose power, however, is limited to jurisdictional conflicts between the executive and the legislature, the standing orders of the Parliament, and the validity of electoral returns. For a survey of some recent trends, see G. Dietze, "America and Europe—Decline and Emergence of Judicial Review," *Virginia Law Review* (December, 1958).

Readings

40. COMPLEXITY AND CONTROL*

C. B. Macpherson

RECENT TECHNICAL change has made it easier to measure and compute many things, but not to measure or compute the political consequences of technical change. Nevertheless, the spectacular successes of technology, and the effects they are having on all ways of life and thought, impose an obligation on political scientists to attempt some assessment of the political effects of technical change.

The importance of such an inquiry is as obvious as are the difficulties. The apparently boundless possibilities of industrial advance through electronic computation and automation have caught the imagination of writers both popular and scientific, to a degree surpassed only by the possible future of atomic energy. Technical advances in the production of foodstuffs, and in the extraction and processing of materials for clothing and shelter, are somewhat less striking, but here too the possible rate of advance is seen as enabling a vast improvement in world standards of living in spite of the expected population increases. The transformation and control of nature which is, in the largest view, the productive process, has clearly reached a new stage. The productive, or physical, consequences of technical advance are direct and clear: so long as technical advance does not destroy civilization, it can scarcely be prevented from enhancing at least its physical basis.

The rate of actual advance in man's control over nature now depends, to an unprecedented extent, on political decisions. It is national and international political decisions about nuclear armaments that will determine whether, or for how long, there is to be any civilization at all. Given that these decisions do permit the continuance of civilization, it is again political decisions which will determine the rate of advance. For although it may be admitted that science and technology have their own momentum, it is evident that in both socialist and non-socialist countries political decisions as to the rate and direction of economic growth and as to the support to be given to technical and scientific education and research will be fundamental to the rate of technical advance.

* From "Technical Change and Political Decision," *International Social Science Journal*, No. 3, 1960, pp. 357–68. Reprinted by permission of the United Nations Educational, Scientific and Cultural Organization.

Thus the central importance of political decision is clear. The question, then, is whether technical change itself is doing or can do anything to make political decisions more efficient—efficient in the ultimate democratic sense which would be accepted in both the Western and the communist concepts of democracy—or whether technical change is making democratic decision less easy or less possible. These questions cannot be answered with any precision. Indeed, even the data for answering them cannot be assembled with any precision. Technical change, of which, as we have said, one of the most striking features is the new ability to measure and assemble data and so to facilitate decision-making, may well have created more political problems than it can help to solve; but it has certainly not made it possible to say whether this is so or not. Much will depend on political man's adaptability and inventiveness, and we do not know any way to quantify the present level or predict the possible future level of these human qualities.

Another difficulty presents itself at the outset of any such inquiry. Technical change cannot easily be analytically separated from the economic and social changes which accompany it: each is to some extent both cause and effect of the others, and abstract debate about the primacy of one or the other is not very helpful here. Any inquiry into the political effects of technical change alone would be fruitless. One must take into account, along with specific technical changes, significant changes in social relations and ways of thinking and living, for these are limiting, directing, and propulsive forces acting on technical change, whether or not they are themselves thought to be resultants of technical change. An inquiry as broad as this constantly faces the difficulty of becoming an unmanageable inquiry into the political consequences of everything. We can, at most, hope to disentangle some threads of the whole complex question.

The Democratic Quality of Decisions

An inquiry into the political effects of technical change must have as one of its central concerns the effects of technical change on the democratic quality of political decisions. By the democratic quality of decisions we mean not simply the degree to which they express the day-to-day and year-to-year demands of the citizens; we mean, rather, the degree to which the decisions do successfully compound those demands with that knowledge, both administrative and expert, which the decision-makers are supposed to possess or to have at their command.

If an inquiry into the effects of technical change on the democratic quality of political decisions is to have more than a very limited reference, it must take into account the existence of very different systems and concepts of democracy in the world today. Democracy, in any sense of the term, requires that the wills of the people shall enter into the making of political decisions in some effective way. This in turn requires more than the formal stipulation, which is found in every democratic state, that those who are authorized to make the political decisions shall directly or indirectly be chosen by the electorate. What further arrangements are supposed to be required varies with different concepts of democracy. In the liberal or Western concept of democracy the essential means of making the wills of the people prevail are (a) competition between political parties, such that an existing set of decision-makers can be periodically replaced by another set and so can be held accountable by the electorate, and (b) some mechanism, usually both formal and informal, by which the public, or more frequently particular publics, are sounded out or specifically consulted before decisions are made. In this view of democracy, while both accountability and consultation are held to be important, accountability is the more so; in the last analysis it is because the decision-makers are accountable that they must, as a matter of prudence, consult those on whose approval their continued authority will depend.

In the communist concept of democracy the order of importance of accountability and consultation may be said to be reversed. There is no competition between political parties to render the top decision-makers accountable to the electorate, and while administrative accountability at lower levels is provided for, it is as much accountability to those above as to those below. The reason why accountability is given relatively little weight in the communist concept of democracy is well understood. In the communist concept, democracy is more a social goal, a form of social relations to be attained by a transformation of society, than a method of current decision-making. The transformation of society is held to require strong direction from the top for an uncertain period of time; hence, during that time, the idea of accountability can be given little weight. But since, in the communist concept, the move towards full communism (and full democracy) requires the active participation of the largest possible number of citizens (in their capacity as producers and in other capacities), the importance of what we have called consultation is very considerable. Consultation must be continuous and widespread, at least at the level of implementing and modifying the general economic plans, and since in the soviet type of government there is no sharp line between legislation and administration, such consultation can be an effective means by which the wills of the governed enter into the decisions of the governors.

We need not, in an introductory essay, pursue these distinctions any further. In any full comparative study of the effects of technical change on democratic political decisions, it would be necessary to examine the specific differences between systems which have such different emphases on accountability and consultation. Here we may content ourselves with considering the effects of technical change both on accountability and on consultation.

A Pattern of Inquiry

Two leading questions suggest themselves at once, arising out of two of the most obvious implications of technical change. We may ask, first, whether the speed with which political decisions must be taken as a result of technical change has led to, or tends to lead to, a decline in the democratic quality of political decisions, that is, a decrease in accountability or in effective consultation. And secondly, does the complexity of the political decisions which now have to be made, or the amount of knowledge required to make those decisions intelligently, lead to a decline in the democratic quality of decision-making?

When we address ourselves to these questions, we soon find that it is convenient to make a further distinction: between decisions of the first order of importance, and those of the second and subsequent orders of importance. No one will dispute that decisions about war or peace now outrank in importance all other political decisions. The elevation of those decisions to first rank is itself the result of the outstanding technical change of our age. Decisions as to whether to continue the manufacture and export of nuclear armaments, decisions as to the circumstances in which they are or are not to be used, and decisions of foreign or international policy which may affect the possibility of their use or the demand for their use, are clearly in a class by themselves.

In the second order of importance we may put national economic policies, that is, the main decisions as to the rate of investment, the redistribution of income through taxation or pricing policies, and so on. These decisions must now be made by national governments of every kind, socialist and non-socialist. They have a profound effect on the pace and direction of a country's development and on the daily lives of the citizens. In the third order of importance—not to complicate our classification unnecessarily—we may put all other kinds of governmental decisions, including the many legislative decisions and the thousands of administrative decisions that must be made in working out the decisions of the second order of importance.

This crude classification is indeed somewhat arbitrary. It might well be argued that certain decisions, here relegated to the third order of importance, should have been put in the second order. But the contents of the orders could be varied to some extent without significantly affecting the analysis that would follow from the suggested classification. Hence this over-simple classification will serve. . . .

Speed, Accountability and Consultation

Let us look first at the question of the speed with which political decisions must now be made. It will be granted that if there is a significant increase in the speed with which any classes of political decision must be made as a result of technical change, the increase in speed will operate to decrease the degree of effective consultation between those authorized to make the decisions and those affected by them. The quicker the decision, the fewer (even of those within the government) can be consulted. To this, one proviso must be made: if, before the increase in speed, the degree of consultation in any class of decisions was close to zero, the change in the degree of consultation will be insignificant.

The effect of increased speed of decision-making on the accountability of the decision-makers is less obvious, but one would expect it also to be negative. For there is no reason to suppose that an increase in the speed of making decisions will be matched by an increase in the speed with which the reasons for the decisions can be explained to and judged by the people. Yet the people cannot effectively hold the decision-makers to account, consistently with any rational concept of democracy, except in the measure that they know enough to do so. The same proviso must be made here as in the case of the degree of consultation: if, before the increase in speed, the degree of accountability in any class of decisions was close to zero, the change in the degree of accountability will be insignificant.

Bearing in mind these general propositions, we must now ask whether the speed with which political decisions must now be made has been significantly increased as a result of technical change, in any of the classes of decisions we have distinguished. In decisions of the first order of importance, one such increase in required speed does indeed haunt us: the decision to push the button which would send nuclear ballistic missiles towards a supposed enemy country must be made within a few minutes of the moment of the appearance of supposedly hostile objects on radar screens. The human consequences of the decision, together with the chances of error and accident, are appalling. The decision must be made by very few people, and in the nature of the case they cannot be held accountable. We seem to have here a clear case of technical change having resulted directly in a diminution (indeed, a disappearance) of democratic consultation and accountability in a decision of the first order of importance. However, the decision whether or not to push the button in such circumstances is not a political but a technical decision. The political decision was, and is, whether or not to have the push-button.

This decision is a continuing one, both in the countries which have nuclear armament and those which have not, and with it, of course, a whole range of foreign policy decision is inextricably involved. Is the speed with which these decisions must be made, in country after country, any greater now than in the pre-nuclear age? In principle, yes. For it is admitted on all sides, including the governments which maintain nuclear armaments, that nuclear disarmament is necessary for the survival of civilization. And, although this is not so widely admitted, the time available for making the political decisions that are necessary to put this into practice grows steadily less, because the statistical probability of the totally destructive mechanism being set in motion through accident or error increases more rapidly the longer those decisions are delayed.

But how, if at all, does the logical necessity for greater speed in those decisions work out in practice? The necessary decisions have not yet been made. But governments now show a greater readiness than ever before to move more steadily towards the agreements that are needed for those decisions. International conferences are more frequent, more protracted, and more readily resumed in some other form, than in the pre-nuclear era. To what extent this limited change has been due to the pressure of public opinion, and to what extent to the decision-makers' understanding of the new logic of the situation and their new vulnerability, we do not know. Nor can we be sure to what extent the future course of decisions will be a response to public opinion and thus an evidence of the effectiveness of public opinion in the new circumstances. For the technical change in armament has set in motion two opposite tendencies in the democratic process. On the one hand, the immensity of the consequences of nuclear decisions seems to have produced in some parts of the public a fatalistic apathy. On the other hand, there is in some quarters a new sense of the urgency and importance of organizing new pressures on the decision makers.

We can perhaps say that just because the nuclear revolution has made the political issues more stark, and in that sense simpler to understand, the pressure of public opinion should be capable of making itself felt more rapidly on these decisions in the future than in the past. It is possible, then, but not demonstrable, that the speed with which democratic pressure is formed and brought to bear on decisions of the first order of importance will increase in the same measure as, or in greater measure than, the required increase in the speed with which the decisions must be made; if so, there need be no diminution, and there may even be an increase, in the democratic quality of the decision-making. And when, finally, we bring into the calculation an estimate of the earlier degree of democratic control of decisions of foreign policy, any diminution of their democratic quality as a result of the technical change in question seems unlikely. For in every nation, however democratic its system of government, foreign policy decisions and especially the decisions for war or peace have usually been the least democratically made. The degree of accountability and of consultation that characterized those decisions before the nuclear era was close enough to zero that no significant decrease in their democratic quality can be charted.

Turn now to decisions of the second and third orders of importance, in which there has normally been an appreciable amount of accountability and consultation. Has technical change brought any increase in the speed with which these decisions are made, and if so has it tended to reduce accountability and consultation? We may pass very briefly over these questions, for there is little reason to think that technical change has brought any change in the speed of these decisions; the effects of technical change here are to be sought rather in the effects of increased complexity than of increased speed. It might of course be argued that in, for instance, decisions of national economic policy, changes in the techniques of economic and statistical analysis (notably with the development of electronic computation) have increased the speed with which material can be organized in usable form, and hence the speed with which decisions can be made, without there being any increase in the speed with which they must be made. If the speed with which decisions must be made does not increase, while the speed with which the material for decisions can be assembled does increase, the time available for democratic consultation appears to be greater. But this does not necessarily follow. Consultation on decisions of central economic policy is normally between the government and officers of the large organizations representing various economic interests. Anyone who has observed such consultations will have noticed that the more quickly statistics can be produced on both sides of the table, the more time is consumed in arguing about their validity and their interpretation. It cannot be concluded that the degree of effective consultation is increased.

Complexity, Accountability and Consultation

It is apparent that the question of speed of decision-making merges into the question of complexity, and we may turn at once to the latter. In considering the effects of increased complexity of political decisions on the democratic quality of decision-making, we shall confine ourselves largely to decisions of the second and third orders of importance. Decisions of the first order can be neglected here for two reasons, both suggested earlier. First the degree of accountability and consultation in decisions for war and peace and in foreign policy decisions generally has always been sufficiently close to zero that no increase in their complexity would significantly reduce their democratic quality. Secondly, while in one sense these decisions share the growing complexity of political decisions generally, in another sense the possible finality of such decisions in the nuclear age simplifies them in the popular understanding; they cannot therefore be assumed to be automatically increasing in complexity.

Going on, then, to decisions of the second and third orders of importance, we have to consider whether technical change has increased their complexity, and whether any such change has reduced (a) the extent to which the decision-makers can be held accountable, and (b) the extent to which democratic consultation enters into the decisions. It is tempting to answer all these questions immediately in the affirmative. It is amply apparent that the number of decisions made by governments and governmental agencies is much greater now than it was 50 or even 20 years ago. All such decisions must, to some extent, be made in relation to each other, for each has some bearing on others at various levels, notably at the level of the national budget or national economic plan. Thus every increase in the number of decisions may be said to increase the complexity of each decision. And one would assume that the greater the complexity, the greater the distance between the decision-makers and the non-decision-makers, and so the less the accountability and the effective consultation.

But while it is tempting to argue that technical change thus leads to decline in the democratic quality of decisions, it is not valid to do so. For the increase in the number and complexity of governmental decisions is hardly at all due to technical change. It is the combined result of the rise of the socialist state and the rise of the welfare state. And however one may explain their rise, whether as the outcome of changes in the fundamental nature of society, changed relations of production, or changes in the degree of class or national consciousness, one can hardly explain it as the outcome of technical change, except in the remote sense that improvements in the techniques of production have been a necessary condition of the emergence of the socialist and the welfare state. In short, it is for reasons having little directly to do with technical change that the number and complexity of governmental decisions has increased.

This being so, we must restate our question. Acknowledging the increase in complexity (from causes other than technical change), and assuming that any increase in complexity tends by itself to reduce the degree of democratic accountability and consultation, we must ask whether technical changes have done or can do anything to counteract the tendency to reduced democratic accountability and consultation. The question so stated is still somewhat too simple. For while the main increase in complexity of decisions is not due to technical change, it is true that the number of governmental decisions into which technical expertise must enter has increased. And it may also be found that the amount of expertise that must enter into the average decision is steadily increasing. The special skills of the town-planner, the economist, the specialist in nutrition or in mental health, the civil aviation expert, the agronomist, and so on, must increasingly enter into political decisions. And as each of these skills becomes more refined, it becomes more difficult to convey the results of expert thinking to the politicians and the public in terms which they can understand.

Every increase in the special knowledge required to make political decisions may be considered an increase in the complexity of those decisions. Hence there is, after all, some increase in complexity of decisions as a result of technical change. Our question, then, should be restated again. We should ask whether technical changes have done or can do more to counteract the tendency to reduced accountability and consultation than to reinforce it.

The problem when stated in this way can be seen to be a problem of communication in the broadest sense of that term. The heart of the problem is whether the public, and particular publics, can know enough to hold the decision-makers responsible or to enter into effective consultation with them. With every increase in the complexity of political decisions and the special knowledge that is required to make them, the ability of the public, and of particular publics, to understand the factors in the decision must increase if the democratic quality of the decisions is not to diminish.

We have referred to the public and particular publics. Political scientists are no longer satisfied with the simple model of democracy in which detached, informed, citizens make their wishes felt through their elected representatives, and periodically choose rationally between two or more sets of policies by voting for one party or another in general elections. It is true that in democracies which operate by a system of competing parties, the periodic choosing of governing parties by the whole electorate remains of central importance; so therefore does the ability of the whole electorate (the public) to comprehend the issues. But the electorate as a whole can at best give only a very general verdict at elections. The democratic quality of decision-making in between elections has come to depend increasingly on the degree to which particular publics can make their demands enter into the decisions. It is easier for governments to deal with organized groups than with an amorphous general public. These organized groups may themselves be political parties, or they may be interest groups (*groupes de pression*) which seek to influence governments at either the administrative or political levels or both. Such interest or pressure groups can, in the theoretical model now widely favoured, do much to make up for the obvious deficiencies of democratic control by the general electorate.

In this view, it is the ability both of the general public and of these particular publics to keep pace with the increasing complexity of governmental decisions that will determine the democratic quality of the decisions. Their ability to keep pace is largely a function of communication. Between whom must communication be adequate in order to maintain the democratic quality of decisions? First, between the politicians and the public, in both directions. Secondly, between the politicians and particular publics, again in both directions. And thirdly, since many decisions, especially among those of the third order of importance, are now made not by ministers or parliaments but by administrative officials, between the officials and the publics. And one might add, fourthly, between the politicians and the administrative officials.

What must be communicated, in order to maintain the democratic quality of decisions? The decision-makers must be able to communicate to the publics an understanding of the numerous factors that must or should enter into a decision that is to be made or that has been made; this involves an understanding of the relations between the factors and of the consequences of attaching different weights to them. The publics must also be able to register their views and to make them felt. But more than this is required. For we should not assume that the initiative should always come from the government. Members of the public, or of particular publics, should be able to take the initiative and to make the government aware of new problems and new possibilities. If the democratic quality of decisions is not to be reduced, communication of all these kinds must keep pace with the increasing complexity of the decisions.

This is a formidable list of requirements. The tasks it sets for technical change are not easy. Have technical changes in communication, in the broadest sense, done anything, or can they do anything, to offset the growing complexity of what must be communicated? It will be convenient to include here, under the heading of technical changes in communication, modern developments in electronic computation and even in automation, so far as the latter may be found relevant. Although they could equally well be treated in their own right, they can be considered to be aspects of communication: electronic computation is a means by which information can be sorted and transmitted in usable form to decision-makers; automation is an extension of that process to include the automatic making and execution of decisions according to a pre-arranged pattern.

Is the electronic revolution at all relevant to our problem of the democratic quality of decision-making? Electronic computation devices enormously increase the amount of information that can be assembled and put into usable form for decision-makers within the time in which decisions must be made. Indeed, if all the criteria that are thought to be relevant, and the weights to be attached to them, can be decided beforehand, the machine can make the decision. In automation the decisions are not only made but automatically carried out. In both computation and automation, the decisions as to what factors are relevant and what weights are to be given to them must be made in advance. Now it is evident that a great many administrative and political decisions are made today on the basis of less than the desirable amount of up-to-date information. Any technical changes which could increase the amount of information gathered and sorted, and the speed with which this could be done, would be a welcome contribution to the efficiency of the decisions. There is no reason why electronic devices cannot be beneficially introduced into public administration as well as into commercial and military administration. But the possible extent of their usefulness in political decision-making is far more limited than in commercial or military decision-making.

No electronic devices can be expected to reach as far as the democratic element in decision-making. This can readily be seen when the essential characteristics of the different types of decision are compared. In commercial and military operations the criteria are simpler, in that they can more nearly be stated in terms of a single objective and a single measurement of gains and costs. In commercial operations, while there are problems of long-run versus short-run net advantages, profit is the single criterion and all the factors affecting it can be reduced to the same monetary unit of calculation. In military operations the object is equally a single one, to impose one's will on the enemy. And while military commanders will normally try to do this at the least cost in lives (that is, of the lives on their side), the final weighting of human losses against strategic gains is not a military but a political decision.

In short, political decisions differ from commercial and military ones precisely in the one respect that we are here concerned with. In political decisions, if they are to have any democratic quality, the objectives themselves are not given (as they are in the other kinds of operations). More accurately, in democratic political decisions the weights to be given to different possible gains and different possible costs cannot be reduced to a single measurable standard nor determined by a single universally acceptable criterion. For this reason the use of electronic devices by the authorized political decision-makers cannot be expected to improve the democratic quality of political decisions.

So far we have been considering electronic computation as a communications device in a rather special sense: we have been looking at the way it communicates information from the environment so to speak, to the decision-makers. What of its possible role in communication in the more usual sense? Might it improve the quality of communication between the decision-makers and at least the particular publics that we call interest groups, by enabling the data for consultations between them to be assembled more fully and accurately? It might be argued that in such a way electronic computation could offset the growing complexity of the material which must now enter into effective discussion, and so improve the democratic quality of the consultation. Some improvement in the effective relation between governmental agencies and interest groups might thus be possible. But we must not overlook one effect which any increased use of such devices would have within the interest group itself: it would tend to give more real power of decision to the officials and experts within the interest groups at the expense of their membership. Anything which renders the internal structure of the interest groups less democratic is unlikely to improve the democratic quality of consultation between them and the government.

We cannot leave the subject of electronic developments without noticing one indirect but pervasive political effect that may be attributed in part to automation. In many countries political apathy is becoming a serious threat to effective democracy. Individuals, especially the younger generation of the electorate, have lost confidence in the democratic process or have no confidence in themselves as elements in the democratic process. This is attributable in part at least to technical changes in industry, changes of which automation is merely the most recent instal-

ment. Technical change in industry and commerce increases the size of
the average unit, increases the degree of expertise required for control and
decision-making, and brings more and more of the work under an
automatic discipline which calls for little judgement and skill and is best
done by apathetic workers, perhaps soothed and moderately diverted by
piped-in music. The disinterest and sense of personal insignificance so
engendered in men in their working time affects their whole personality,
and easily spills over into their political life, the more so to the extent that
they see the same sort of people in directing and managerial positions in
politics as in industry.

The net effect, then, of the technical changes we have considered so far
appears to be to diminish the democratic quality of political decisions. It
need not be so. A realization of the new possibilities for human freedom
and initiative that are being released by technical changes in the productive process could, if widespread enough, bring an upsurge of democratic
feeling counteracting the trend towards withdrawal and apathy. We do
not know at present which tendency will prevail.

We may also consider briefly one other technical development which
can have a direct bearing on the democratic process, namely, television.
We need only pass in review some of the more evident possible effects of
its spread. The most direct political effect is to be expected from the fact
that political leaders can now be seen and heard by the whole electorate at
once. Here, surely, is a technical change of very great importance, an
enormous improvement in the means of communication between politicians and the public.

But this is communication in one direction only. The public can sit
back but cannot talk back; their part is a wholly passive one. The same
could of course be said about the role of the public in relation to the other
mass media of communication: the general public has never been able to
use the radio or the press to talk back. But we must consider also the
ability of particular publics (the political parties and pressure groups) to
answer back in the same medium. Here we do find some difference
between television and the other media. The access which particular
publics have to television is likely to be somewhat less than their access to
the older media. Access to television broadcasting tends to be more limited
to the orthodox within and among parties and pressure groups, because
television, even more than the other media, is subject to monopoly or
oligopoly control. Yet unless minority movements both within and among
parties and pressure groups can effectively present new views, new ways
of seeing problems, and new ways to their solution, a necessary part of the
democratic process is impaired. Competition between the orthodox is no
doubt more democratic than no competition at all, but in the measure that
competition is confined to the orthodox the democratic quality of political
communication is diminished. Thus, to the extent that television supplants

other media of communication, the effect of its oligopolistic control is to reduce the democratic quality of the political process.

Much else could be said, and has been said by many observers, about the apparent political effects of television. It enhances the role of personality in politics, to the detriment of democratic responsibility. It turns elections into plebiscites or into single combats between leaders. Its general impact on the public contributes powerfully to that trivialization of culture and pulverization of the mind which were already well advanced from other causes. All these charges would bear analysis; if true, the net effect of televison on the democratic process would be disastrous. But even without extensive analysis one may suspect that while the effects are as stated, they are not effects of television but of the prevailing economic and social relations of our time.

Prospects

We return thus to the point made in the beginning. The effects of technical change on the democratic process cannot readily be isolated from the effects of changes in economic relations, in class structures, in nationalist aspirations and other fundamental social changes, none of which can themselves be attributed (except very indirectly) to technical change. The technical changes which have, or can have, a direct part in democratic decision-making may hinder or hasten tendencies which existed independently of those changes. But the impact of technical changes seems in every case to be of slight force compared with the other changes. The increased complexity of the decisions that must be made by governmental agencies is due in much larger part to the increase in the tasks they must perform in the socialist and the welfare state, than to the greater degree of special knowledge required for the performance of these tasks. Technical changes in the processing and communication of data, while they may improve the efficiency of the decision-makers, seem unlikely to touch the democratic quality of the decisions. And technical changes in the media of public communication appear, so far, to be of little consequence beside the changes in attitude and behaviour of the electorate which must be ascribed to other causes.

But if the force of technical change is less than the force of other changes, the two may still combine to produce results more striking than simple addition would yield. The effect of technical change on the democratic process cannot be detached from the larger question of the effect of technical change on the chances of maintaining civilization. The critical point is whether a democratic decision (or rather, the necessary series of democratic decisions) between the disastrous and the beneficial effects of technical change can be made in time to permit the continuance of civilization, and with it a further unfolding of democracy. The same qualities of imagination and social inventiveness that are needed to make those decisions should be quite sufficient to deal with the continuing problems of democratic decision-making.

41. THE ACCOUNTABILITY OF THE BRITISH NATIONALIZED INDUSTRIES*

Eldon L. Johnson

GREAT BRITAIN's giant nationalized industries pose unprecedented problems for a free nation. Are the old governmental forms appropriate? Can the new forms be held accountable to the public? Can public accountability and business efficiency be reconciled? The five key industries, formed out of thousands of former enterprises, employ almost two million workers—almost three times the number of civil servants. Even the strictly "business" problems are unprecedented. In personnel, the transport industry is double the size of American Telephone and Telegraph. Coal is three times the size of General Motors. Admitting that the final answers on accountability had not been found, Herbert Morrison, then Lord President of the Council, well stated the prevailing British attitude: "We are in the early years of novel constitutional and social experiments of great long-term significance, and we can be certain that as experience grows the methods which are in use at present will need to be modified and additional methods will be evolved."

The problem of public accountability, already challenging because of the new subject matter, commercial enterprise, is greatly accentuated by the organizational form chosen for nationalization: the public corporation. The "public corporation," a combination of the governmental adjective and the business noun, spins restlessly between the worlds of government and business. It evolved from a fear of governmental power on the one hand and business irresponsibility on the other; or, conversely, from the attraction of the independent initiative of private business and the dependent accountability of public government. It understandably became the common denominator, the point of compromise, between the contending political forces which molded the nationalization of Britain's basic industries. The mere removal of the profit motive, some people thought, would enable an equilibrium of accountability to be established short of the full-fledged departmental type of organization.

While the public corporation was going into eclipse in the United States, it was emerging in Great Britain to shine with unprecedented

* From *The American Political Science Review*, Vol. XLVIII, No. 2 (June, 1954). By permission.

brightness on socialism's brave new world. What the skeptical Congress was trussing up, comparatively speaking, in the Government Corporation Control Act of 1945, the optimistic Parliament was unshackling for unparalleled extensions of the public's business. It is true that the new British public corporations are held accountable in ways unknown in the prewar prototypes and that, therefore, both the United States and Great Britain have moved toward *more* control. It is significant, however, that the "more" is much less in Great Britain, where the new pattern is still the "pure" and "authentic" type of public corporation. The board form of government is used exclusively; the function is invariably business; and independence is great, with self-sufficiency the goal. It is paradoxical that the private business form which built Western capitalism has become the public form which is making socialist Britain—and making it when America, at least, seems to be less and less certain of the merits of the new mutation. In contrast, Professor William A. Robson of the London School of Economics and Political Science confidently predicts that this "most important constitutional innovation which has been worked out in Great Britain during the past 50 years" will "play as important a part in the field of nationalized industry in the twentieth century as the privately owned corporation played in the realm of capitalist organization in the nineteenth century."[1]

No thoughtful Englishman assumed that public ownership automatically guaranteed public accountability. It was taken for granted that something else, something special, needed to be done under socialism to assure sufficient accountability for a democracy so greatly changed in its responsibilities, yet the corporate form of the enterprises interposed special obstacles. Something special, in fact several things special, were done by the Labour government and Parliament—whether successfully or not is, of course, a matter of debate. Parliament is still deeply involved in the search for improvement. Some old controls were unchanged, some readapted; some new controls were added. Electoral and judicial controls remain unchanged. Relations with ministers and Parliament were recast into a new balance. Consumers' councils, joint consultation, and systematic annual reporting were introduced as new devices. These taken together constitute the public accountability mechanism for the new titans of public industry, accorded the freedom of businesses but checked by the control of government—molded neither in the cast of the autonomous government corporation, such as the British Broadcasting Corporation, nor in the cast of the regular government department, such as the Post Office. The BBC plan was too independent in the controversial phase of nationalization and the Post Office plan was too rigid, too subject to day-to-day interference both by minister and by Parliament, for creative business enterprise. Therefore, the nationalized industries were placed in a

---

[1] *Problems of Nationalized Industry,* ed. William A. Robson (London, 1952), p. 53.

new in-between relationship with Parliament. Each was made flexible by being created a semi-independent corporation and each was made accountable by being placed under the general surveillance of a minister who could issue directions on general policy without answering to Parliament for day-to-day operations. This, as so often in politics, strikes a necessary but precarious balance, with a constant interplay of forces consciously or unconsciously threatening the equilibrium. The results of the experiment are worthy of the attention of partisans of democracy the world round.

I. MINISTERIAL CONTROL

Proper responsibility to Parliament is the ultimate key to public accountability itself. But the relation to Parliament, as evolved, was through the minister, who, in addition to his appointive power over the industry boards, alone was given the power to make decisions binding on the industries. He in a real sense picked up the equity interest which passed from the shareholder to the general public. Ministerial control, therefore, calls for attention first.

The great nationalized industries, in comparison with the prewar public corporations, are of the "public corporations, strong minister type," with less financial independence and more ministerial influence. They are less free, more controlled. When public ownership was enormously extended, the bonds of accountability were tightened up. In his relations with the industry board, the minister was given several significant powers: appointment of members; issuance of general directions on matters appearing to him to affect the national interest, with its corollary of informal consultation on policy; veto or approval power over specific matters, especially involving finance and development; and solicitation of information. The purpose is clearly to make the minister statutorily responsible for the general policy of the corporations but to leave the boards responsible for day-to-day administration.

The minister's control over the composition of the directing boards is great, almost complete if he cares to exercise it. He sets the tenure and conditions of appointment, either by private instrument of appointment or by a regulation laid before Parliament. Even the latter, public method ordinarily provides for appointments to be "for such term not exceeding five years as may be determined by the Minister before appointment of such member or, with his consent, *at any time*." In other words, the ministers may find, and have found, means of removing board members at will, even without stating reasons, although the statutes clearly contemplate removal for specific reasons, such as ill health, misconduct, or absence from meetings. In practice, however, removals for political or other capricious reasons are rare. The Conservative government made no effort to change boards upon entering office in 1951. . . .

The crux of ministerial control, at least in its potentialities, is the power of giving directions of a general character on the performance of the corporations in matters appearing to the minister to affect the national interest. It should be noted that the variables—the generality of the directions and the involvement of the national interest—greatly enhance ministerial discretion. This is a far cry from the clear line of demarcation which the Conservatives originally wanted drawn between the boards and the minister, as indeed the Labour members themselves advocated for the prewar corporations. The Labour government chose for its nationalizing instrument devices which would, in its words, keep the public monopolies from exercising power inimical to the public interest. The minister was given the power—and a most important power it is—to see that national and social policy transcend commercial policy if necessary.

Despite Conservative cries of dictatorial powers, this new weapon has been, chiefly, a stick behind the door. The ministers have the instruments of accountability at hand, but they have exercised them so cautiously that the critics have turned from cries of tyranny to complaints that the ministers are too timid. For the first six years no general directions were given the industries at all. Only one has been issued to date. In actual practice, the ministers deal with the boards on what Herbert Morrison once called the "old boy" basis: through informal relationships, telephone conversations, and unrecorded meetings. They consult and influence; they almost never order. They have repeatedly resisted Parliamentary pressure to intervene and have avoided the use of general directions, preferring informal influence, even when the minister himself wanted specific action taken. The Labour Minister of Fuel and Power *asked* the Area Electricity Boards to put into effect the highly controversial Clow Committee plan for seasonal variations in rates, but he did not *direct* them. Indicative of the efficacy of this informal influence, the boards complied with the ministerial preference, against their own judgment, rather than be formally directed. Ministers have often made clear that they are "in constant touch" with corporation officials, that they meet with the board chairmen when necessary, and that correspondence and conversations are strictly confidential. The Conservative government, in the recent railway fares controversy, asked patience for "working out an arrangement harmoniously" with the British Transport Commission to "obviate the necessity of further direction." This illustrates the informal means to avoid a distasteful end.

As a result of these practices, accountability procedures are gradually being driven underground in a manner not foreseen when the statutes were passed. . . .

Another important ministerial power is that of the veto, or approval power, over a variety of specific board actions: the framing of programs of reorganization and development calling for large capital outlay; schemes for training, education, and research; form of accounts; and, with Treasury approval, the issuance of new stock. With Treasury approval, the minister may also give directions on the creation and management of reserve funds, redemption of stock, and disposal of surplus revenue. Other special powers are conferred by statutes for particular industries; for example, he may direct the British Transport Commission to discontinue any of its activities or dispose of any part of its business. In these ways the minister may determine the broad lines along which the boards are to proceed in vital matters of internal administration. These powers, for example, enabled the Minister of Supply, pending denationalization, to direct the Iron and Steel Corporation not to alter its financial structure or management. Specific directions on financial matters, unlike general directions, have been issued by ministers on many occasions. In other words, the minister does have a great deal of financial control, although it is chiefly of an approval rather than initiatory character.

To implement his other powers, the minister may also require information from the corporations. This may, in general, be designed to serve the minister's own official purposes, to aid Parliament, or to prescribe the form of the annual reports.

II. PARLIAMENTARY CONTROL

The ministers are in turn responsible to Parliament, and it is Parliament to which we must look for ultimate control, next to the people themselves. Yet every political scientist has been saying for decades that Parliament has neither the time for more duties nor the expertness for different duties. Nevertheless, the nationalized industries inevitably load on Parliament more duties and different duties. Inevitably also, Parliament tries laboriously to meet these new obligations with the old techniques of control: with questions directed to ministers under whom the industries operate; with debates; and with inquiries and reports of select committees—yet with full recognition that it must, by its own self-denying ordinance, control with a loose rein and in a different spirit.

Questions. The technique most discussed, most jealously guarded by Parliament, and probably most effective to date, is the question time. This time-honored practice has undergone some change to accommodate the new status of the public corporations. Ministers answer questions, of course, only on matters for which they are responsible. They are not responsible for day-to-day administration of the corporations. Therefore, questions on the nationalized industries are more restricted than those on the regular government departments. Questions asked concerning the Post Office, for example, always number more than those for any of the corporations.

The overriding consideration is again the balance between the minister's general control and the board's day-to-day management. The question is often asked: How can the House of Commons exercise control over the administration of these industries when the admissible questions extend

only to the minister's responsibility, which excludes day-to-day administration? Such a question refuses to acknowledge the philosophy behind
the nationalization statutes. The corporations are deliberately removed
from meticulous control. But, even so, the extent of restriction on
Parliament depends on what constitutes an acceptable question for ministerial answer. Acceptability is clouded by several factors: uncertainty as to
what is a matter of day-to-day administration; uncertainty as to the
Speaker's standard of "public importance" in accepting questions; uncertainty as to what the minister can and cannot do, as well as whether he
is doing it directly or through influence on others; and, finally, uncertainty
as to whether the minister will answer the question put to him, even if
eligible on all counts. . . .

What ministers have actually answered and refused to answer is almost
as diverse as the opinions expressed by members in the House of Commons.
One minister answered many questions on dirty coal; another refused on
grounds this was a management problem. A question on cheap fares on the
railways was refused at one time but the issue of railway fares later led to
the greatest of all controversies about ministerial and Parliamentary control. Questions on industrial disputes are usually refused. Likewise, even
matters of information, such as on staffs and salaries, have been refused
despite the minister's clear legal power to demand such information.

Petty though these arguments and decisions may seem, they penetrate
to the core of the accountability problem because they raise the question of
the distribution of power among corporation, minister, and Parliament.
The minister's acceptance of a question which calls for his intervention,
where no intervention was countenanced before, actually changes the
autonomy of the nationalized industry. His acceptance of a question of
information calls for more staff, more paper work, and more centralization. The real difficulty has been that time is too short and that most of
the questions do not relate to policies determining the success or failure of
the industry. Questions on details, on abuses, and on constituents' complaints are most popular. . . .

Debates. Accountability through debate extends to broader coverage
than Parliamentary questions but efficacy is severely hampered by the
shortage of Parliamentary time, the lack of technical competence, and the
dominance of the political party in making final decisions. Debate need
not be restricted to general policy; it may relate to questions of day-
to-day management and local problems, subject to the Speaker's, rather
than the minister's, opinion of propriety for discussion. An exhaustive
study published by the Acton Society Trust showed that never had more
than 31 hours a year been given debate on any nationalized industry; that
12 to 15 hours was more common; and that "it is very unlikely that
Parliament could debate all major nationalized industries once a year."

The two most important occasions for debate are the Supply Vote of the minister supervising the nationalized industry and the motions taking note of the annual reports of the industries. For the five-year period ending October, 1950, eleven supply debates, usually lasting about six hours each, were held on the nationalized industries: six on civil aviation, two on coal, one on the fuel and power industries, and two on transport However, other debates on supply days tend to crowd out the nationalized industries because the opposition has to choose among twenty-five departments and a host of grant-in-aid agencies. Debate on the annual reports is an encouraging accountability trend. Parliament has important information before it, but the discussion is fragmentary, discursive, and long after the event. It is common for the debates to occur a year or more after the closing date covered by the reports.

Other opportunities for general debate can be made by the government in laying down a substantive motion or by the opposition in attempting to amend the Queen's speech. Occasions for shorter debate are found on the motion for adjournment, granting from a half hour to three hours for discussion of some action taken or failed to be taken; on a motion to approve or annul an order of a minister supervising an industry; on proposed modifications of nationalization laws; and on private bills submitted by the corporations.

The whole debate technique as an instrument of control would be greatly improved if it could be kept above party controversy, a vain hope at the present stage of socialization. Illustrative of the partisan approach, when the Labour minister in 1949 made a motion worded as innocuously as possible, "That this House take note of the First Annual Report, etc." of the Transport Commission for 1948, merely as a peg on which to hang the debate, the opposition moved at once to amend by adding, "but regrets the loss sustained in 1948, the further marked deterioration disclosed in 1949, the mounting cost and the increase in fares and rates so detrimental to the public." It is not hard to imagine the enlightenment which followed. Nationalization will have to gain the respectability of age before accountability in the public interest can replace control in the partisan interest.

Parliamentary Committees. Parliament provides control also through the scrutiny of its existing committees and its power to appoint others to investigate and report. For the nationalized industries, this has been, until the present session of Parliament, more potentiality than reality. The new industries, like the old departments, are placed under the scrutiny of the Committee on Public Accounts. That committee, however, is deprived of expert aid for its new task. It cannot use the Comptroller and Auditor General and his staff because the socialized industries have special commercial auditors named by the minister. Already harnessed with an impossible task and deprived of expert assistance, the Committee on Public Accounts is virtually helpless. The Committee on Estimates is even more ineffectual. It has no opportunity for control unless a subsidy is involved, as in the case only of the three airways corporations. There is no means of control if the same public stake is created in some other way: by a price increase or by a government loan to the industry.

Despite the debates, the questions, and the committees, the accountability of the nationalized industries to Parliament is not thoroughly pleasing to anyone. Techniques differ from those of long-standing use for government departments only in that they are more restricted in application. They are less extensive, therefore less commonly employed, and less susceptible to Parliamentary use of expert assistance. It is not surprising, therefore, that some new remedies have been sought. . . .

If Parliamentary control was somewhat weakened when extended to the nationalized industries, it was at least supplemented in an effort to make adequate the *total* pattern of public controls. The supplementation came in three ways: special representation for consumers, consultation for employees, and special informational sources for everyone involved in public control.

III. CONSUMERS' COUNCILS

As the nationalized industries are great state monopolies, replacing the so-called sovereignty of the consumer, some special check on the new Titans of Government seemed to be in order. Parliament, therefore, created a consumers' council or system of councils in each of the nationalized industries, ranging from the simplicity of a single national council, as originally provided in iron and steel, to the complexity of 15 area consumer councils, with from 70 to 80 local councils, in electricity. The members come from all walks of life, appointed by the minister for each industry on the basis of representation of the chief consumer interests involved, with from five to thirty persons on each council. Although strictly advisory, the councils have the task of serving as watchdogs of the consumers' interests in all matters of charges and services, with power to make recommendations to the minister. They may act at the urging of a consumer, on their own initiative, or at the request of the minister. Remedial action lies with the minister, who may, as we have seen, give directions to the industry. The councils, therefore, are empowered to raise the right questions, questions of the broadest scope, but their advisory function leaves the finding of the right answers to the amenability of the boards, or to the minister in the final analysis.

Despite some spottily distributed successes in consumer representation and in the settlement of grievances, the consumers' councils do not inspire much confidence among consumers. They have two serious defects: they are not sufficiently independent of the government and they are too little known and used.

They need to be independent of the industry if they are to give the consumer a vigorous voice; but, on the contrary, they are appointed by the minister, occupy offices furnished by him or the industry, use staff similarly supplied, have nationalized industry representatives as members, stand at the mercy of the government for information, and sometimes find themselves being used by the government to give testimonials for some unpopular policy. Worse yet, they have no research or investigating staffs; they cannot employ their own experts for independent study. It is not surprising that many critics have charged that the councils are merely "stooges," securely "in the pocket" of the boards; and that they have taken a strange posture deferring to the industry rather than to the consumer. In the few instances in which the minister has been forced to arbitrate a showdown between a consumers' council and a nationalized industry, he has always taken his stand with the industry. This is itself a commentary on the weight and independence of the councils.

No one is pleased with the use to which the councils are put by consumers, by ministers, or by the nationalized industries. Despite increasing publicity efforts by the councils, members of Parliament still complain that they get too many letters which should be going to the councils. When Lord Hurcomb, Chairman of the British Transport Commission, answered 1800 Parliamentary inquiries in one year, he surely answered some which should have gone first to the consumers' council for transport. Other deterrents to council use are the absence of any satisfactory organization of general consumer interests and, also, plain consumer indifference. To make matters considerably worse, all the councils have placed restrictions on their communication with the press and the public.

One has to say, in summary, that the consumers' council device has enjoyed only modest success. If, however, one stops trying to make the councils a David against Goliath, which they cannot be, he must conclude that they may supply an alternative test of the public interest, provide suggestions and cautions for policy-making, and capitalize on consumer interests as they become organized. Much of each council's strength lies in the quite undramatic business of keeping the consumers' interest in the forefront of the attention of the nationalized industry or its supervising minister, and in serving as a symbol and a constant reminder of a goal always to be sought.

IV. JOINT CONSULTATION

Internal as well as external control becomes a major type of public accountability in a socialized society, because an increasing number of citizens are state employees. Industrial democracy is a primary goal.

Following this philosophy, the authors of nationalization in Great Britain wrote into their statutes the guarantee of joint machinery, between management and labor, not only for collective bargaining but also for consultation on safety, health, welfare, training, efficiency, and other matters of mutual interest. This is, however, a far cry from worker control; instead, it is merely worker participation in control. How far short this falls of management abdication is shown by the fact that the board of the nationalized industry is left with the initiative in the establishment of a consultation agreement, it is the sole judge of which employee organizations are to be dealt with, and it, not the workers, assumes full executive responsibility. . . .

Despite these difficulties, joint consultation as established in the nationalized industries does provide a wide-open door of opportunity for worker participation, and internal accountability. The real problem is one of utilizing the opportunity afforded. Neither management nor labor is making the most of its possibilities. This weapon of control is still clumsy and crude, but it is taking shape, with a consciously held purpose in mind. It recognizes the creativity of employees.

V. ANNUAL REPORTS

Still another means of assuring public accountability in the nationalized industries is the common requirement of annual reports, made to the minister and referred to both houses of Parliament. Accountability cannot exist without information. The annual reports for each industry are intended to provide much of that information. Each report supplies a veritable storehouse of facts and figures which would have been quite unobtainable in the days of scattered, private ownership. Nevertheless, two careful British studies of the reports conclude that they still leave much to be desired. While informative, with an impressive quantity, they lack quality at many key points, one of the studies concludes. Despite the statistics, accounts, graphs, and descriptive coverage, the reports do not sufficiently deal with the factors which make for success or failure, or with trends and improvements in efficiency. They can hardly be said to be strictly objective. It is not surprising that they put the industry's best foot forward, avoiding failures and deficiencies. . . .

The release of the annual reports is the occasion for news and editorial comment and for Parliamentary debate on policies and shortcomings. In at least one case the complete and somewhat formidable report has been digested and reproduced for wide citizen appeal. These are the raw materials of accountability. At least, such is the intention—an intention which needs, and can easily have, further implementation. Perhaps, as has been implied, the boards are still too much impressed by their business character and too little aware of their public obligations.

CONCLUSIONS

After seven years of experience, all sections of British political opinion are still committed to the public corporation, genuinely removed from meticulous governmental control, as the chosen instrument for operating the giant industries taken over by the public. Confidence that the right general path is being followed is as strong as the conviction that the desired balance has not yet been attained. The British have been hammering out a significant kind of accountability: power to control decisively when need be, but little use of it; power to act at the broad, vital spots rather than on the minutiae; power of accountability made effective by its presence rather than by its exercise. The unused power to block an artery may be more effective than the daily use of pinpricks on the capillaries. This is the theory of ministerial and Parliamentary control: the power to issue general directions and the power to investigate and legislate.

Yet several questions remain. Since the big weapons are rarely used, does accountability, in practice, give control over minor rather than major matters and, therefore, produce the worst of both worlds, instead of the best so confidently expected by the corporation advocates? Or does this indicate major satisfactions and minor irritations, with the general policy merely having no practical meaning except in its specific manifestations? Can business independence and the interjection of social or welfare considerations be reconciled? Yet without such interjection, what is the point to public ownership? If such considerations, irrelevant for commercial purposes, are introduced, isn't the corporation's policy *political* and, therefore, properly subject to careful Parliamentary scrutiny? Can the development of the confidential relationship between minister and board, with surreptitious ministerial intervention, be permitted without close Parliamentary control? Does the public corporation really force a choice between accountability and efficiency? These difficulties all stem from an attempted merger of the benefits of that which is private and that which is public. To what end is accountability exercised? If exercised to achieve what the public wants, the standard of success is likely to be tentative, shifting, and sometimes contradictory, less simple than the old measure of profit in the private sector. The merger merely recasts the familiar struggle: in this case, for balance between liberty to achieve one desired purpose, business initiative and efficiency, and authority to achieve another, responsibility to the public and conformity to its policies. . . .

Insistent pressure for fuller accountability is likely to continue to beat upon Parliament. The temptation to move toward more and more control will be great. Even Herbert Morrison recently confessed: "I agree right off, in the case of electricity, there is a strong case to argue that it could be run by a Government Department." It also remains to be seen whether the Labour party, in its zeal to nationalize, chose an instrument sufficiently amenable to the policy integration required for national planning. But while British confidence in the public corporation idea remains, the major problem is not machinery for control, but balanced use of it. A great deal of machinery now exists, far more than is effectively utilized.

42. THREE CONSTITUTIONAL COURTS*

Taylor Cole

I

CONSTITUTIONAL COURTS have been established in . . . [Western Germany, Italy and Austria] in accordance with the provisions of their respective Constitutions, as implemented by the necessary legislation. These Constitutions are the Austrian one of 1920 (as amended in 1925 and 1929) which was reinstituted during the uncertain postwar period in 1945, the Italian Constitution of 1948, and the West German Basic Law of 1949. Though the Austrian Constitution presents a special case, all three may be classed as of post–World War II vintage. The Constitution of West Germany and Italy were the product of negative revolutions, reflecting a deep distaste for the "dismal past." As characterized by [Professor Friedrich] "the political theory of the new Constitutions which are democratic in the traditional Western sense . . . revolves . . . around four major focal points which distinguish them from their predecessors: (1) reaffirmation of human rights, *but* (2) efforts to restrict these rights in such a way as to make them unavailable to the enemies of constitutional democracy, (3) stress upon social goals and their implementation through socialization, *but* (4) efforts to circumscribe the goals and their implementation in such a way as to prevent the reëmergence of totalitarian methods and dictatorship."[1] To achieve these goals, the specially provided Constitutional Courts were to play an important part.

In seeking the explanations for the adoption of these special Courts, we are reminded that judicial review in continental Europe, as in the United States, had its roots in the higher law background and conceptions of ancient and medieval times. The precedents for special courts to protect the fundamentality of the Constitution can be traced at least as far back as the 18th century, when written constitutions came into being, with the proposals of Abbé Siéyès in the 1790s for the creation of a constitutional jury. The work of a succession of distinguished advocates of judicial review, who refused to accept some of the implications and influences stemming from the French Revolution, followed at later periods.

That this heritage and this special advocacy were alone inadequate to account for the later creation of Constitutional Courts is evident from a

---

* From "Three Constitutional Courts: A Comparison," *The American Political Science Review*, Vol. LIII, No. 4 (December, 1959). By permission.

[1] C. J. Friedrich, "The Political Theory of the New Democratic Constitutions." [Reproduced above, Reading 32.]

glance at the history of Western Europe. It was not until postmortems on World War I that the Austrian Constitutional Court came into being. And there were particular considerations after World War II which gave an impetus to the establishment of special courts in West Germany and Italy.

The most obvious influence was that of national precedent. In the case of West Germany, there were precedents which could be traced from the constitutional proposals of the National Assembly of 1848 down to the history of the National Supreme Court (*Reichsgericht*), and of the High Court (*Staatsgerichtshof*) of the Weimar period. The High Court had jurisdiction over the settlement of disputes between states (*Länder*) and between states and the *Reich*, as well as over impeachment cases. The Supreme Court passed upon the compatibility of state laws with federal laws, and it reviewed the constitutional validity not only of state, but also in several instances of federal legislation. But there were various limitations which operated to restrict the scope and effectiveness of the activities of these Courts. In Austria, traces of the Austrian Constitutional Court can be found in constitutional developments of the period between 1848–1851, and especially in the establishment in 1867 of the Court of the Empire (*Reichsgericht*). As time went on, this Court exercised jurisdiction over the claims of the provinces (*Länder*) against the Empire and *vice versa;* it dealt with conflicts of competence between judicial and administrative authorities at both the provincial and national level, and with complaints of citizens over the violation of constitutionally guaranteed political rights after other remedies had been exhausted. As for Italy, though there were certain pre-1922 procedures and institutions which pointed toward judicial review, these were of limited significance. The first noteworthy Italian precedent was provided by the Sicilian High Court, created by the Regional Statute of May 15, 1946.

Foreign example can also be stressed. Certain of the practices and procedures in Switzerland, particularly the use of the constitutional complaint, were given serious attention during the drafting of the Bonn Basic Law. The exercise of judicial review by the United States Supreme Court has received continued attention in European countries. As one Italian professor has observed, the "impact of *Marbury* vs. *Madison* was felt in Italy almost a century and a half after the decision." To these considerations may be added indirect pressures which were brought to bear by the occupying powers after 1945, especially by the United States in Germany. However, evidence that direct Allied pressure was responsible for the final action taken is lacking in all three instances.

But it was definitely the reaction to excesses of the Fascist and Nazi regimes which was the most important factor in the decisions finally taken in Austria to restore her Constitution of 1920, as amended in 1925 and 1929, with its provision for a Constitutional Court; and in Italy and Germany, to establish new Courts. There was remarkable unanimity among most of the democratic parties in all three countries to grant the power of judicial review to some type of court. This same reaction helps explain the incorporation of elaborate bills of rights, to protect the individual, and of federalistic arrangements which, while borrowing from the past, were directed against the centralization of the Fascist period. Judicial review, in some hands, was widely accepted as necessary to safeguard these guaranteed liberties and arrangements. Disagreements existed over the type of court, its organization and composition, and over the method of selecting the judges. The answers were provided by the special Constitutional Courts. In short, external influences and pressures combined with domestic concerns to explain the final decisions which were taken. . . .

The jurisdiction of the West German Constitutional Court is the most extensive and that of the Italian Court the most limited of the three Courts. With variations as to scope and application, the Courts in all three countries have the power to review the constitutionality of federal and state, or provincial and regional, legislation. They pass upon disputes involving "conflicts of competence" between the central governments and the states, provinces, or regions, as well as between these latter political units. They also can decide jurisdictional disputes between "organs" of government at the national level in West Germany and Italy, and between the courts, or courts and administrative authorities, in Austria. They can try impeachments or accusations against certain officials at the national level in West Germany and Italy, or against federal and provincial officials in Austria. Both the Austrian and West German Courts have some jurisdiction in cases involving disputed elections and international law. In addition, each Court possesses some special competences which are unique to it. For example, the West German Court may pass upon the constitutionality of political parties and the forfeiture of basic rights. Advisory opinions were authorized by legislation in Germany until the repeal of the empowering provisions in 1956.

But a mere mention of the competences of the Courts will tell little, without a recognition that their functioning depends heavily upon the nature of the social structures within which they operate. These societies have been referred to as fragmented ones in which there is sharp competition between political cultures. The extent of political involvement by the citizen and the development of institutional pluralism vary in the three countries; the degree of consensus, on procedural if not substantive matters, is lower in all instances than that to be found, for example, in Britain. The legal backgrounds of the three countries, with their differing ingredients of Roman and Germanic law, affect the position of the judges. And there are many other considerations which have a bearing on the role of the Courts. The federalism of West Germany and Austria, and the "attenuated federalism" of Italy, merit particular attention. The nature of the party system (with the trend toward the two-party system in West Germany, government by party cartel "with built-in opposition" in

Austria, and shifting coalitions based upon a mass party in the center in Italy) affects the legislative product of the parliaments which is subject to review by the Courts. We must of necessity leave these matters with only passing mention, though with a full appreciation of their significance in appraising the work of the Constitutional Courts.

II

In examining the work of the Courts, some attention may be directed to selected decisions dealing with (1) equality before the law, (2) federalism, (3) delegation of legislative powers, and (4) legislation and public service relationships dating from the Fascist and National Socialist periods.

The Constitutions of each of the three countries contain an almost identical guarantee that "all persons shall be equal before the law." In addition, they include certain other clauses which are to make more specific the general guarantees. The differences among these reflect the varied historical circumstances under which these constitutional provisions had their origins. . . .

It has been particularly in cases involving equality before the law that the West German Federal Constitutional Court has given some evidence of its recognition of a higher law above the positive law, that is, of a superior and unwritten constitutional law. Though there were earlier statements by the Court to which natural law adherents might point, the Court perhaps gave its clearest expression of the acceptance of a "hierarchy of norms within the Basic Law" and of certain natural law "guidelines" in a decision of December 18, 1953, involving the equality of the rights of men and women. There the Court did acknowledge the possibility in "extreme cases" of conflicts between the positive law of the Basic Law and of the higher law.[2] The Court was here reflecting something of the natural law revival in post–World War II Germany, which had resulted in part from a reaction against the earlier positivist justifications for the Nazi regime. Since 1953, it appears that the Court has been deliberately more careful in its references. It has tended more to stress the "basic principles" of the Constitution as expressed in the specific provisions of the Basic Law, and it is being cautious in providing continuing opportunity to reopen the debates on "unconstitutional constitutional norms."

Of the three Courts, the Italian Court has been the most careful to confine its reasoning narrowly to the provisions of the Constitution and to avoid overt reference to value judgments based on natural law in its decisions. Certainly, the Italian Court has insisted that its jurisdiction is limited to examination of the compatibility of laws and of acts having the

---

[2] Such words and phrases as "supra-positive basic norms," "natural justice," "fundamental postulates of justice," "norms of objective ethics," etc., have been used in cases. . . .

force of law with the Constitution, and that it is not competent to pass upon the constitutionality of constitutional norms. The position of the Austrian Court appears to be different from the other two: it has not rejected completely the review of constitutional norms, as has the Italian Court, nor has it claimed the right to subject constitutional provisions to review in the light of higher or natural law precepts. In its much discussed decision on provincial citizenship on December 12, 1952, the Court recognized that it could not review the substance of constitutional provisions in the light of higher or supra-positive ideas "since, in general, any standards for such an examination is missing." It has, however, insisted upon its power to decide whether a proposed amendment involves a "total revision of the Constitution" and hence is subject to a popular referendum. In this instance, the Court must go beyond the formal requirements of enactment to a consideration of those basic constitutional principles whose alteration would involve "total revision." Thus, in all three countries, the quest of the judges for foundations on which to base some of their decisions regarding individual rights and, specifically, the application of the equality before the law provisions of the Constitutions, continues.

The restraints which are imposed by a federalistic system and by federalistic arrangements upon the exercise of arbitrary power at the center were recognized by many of the framers of the Bonn Basic Law and the Italian Constitution. They also helped influence the sequence of events in Austria in 1919–20 and, again, during 1945–46. Since only four of the regions in Italy have as yet been created, the relationships in that state can be called only pseudo-federalistic. Nevertheless, the regions which have been established are guaranteed a significant degree of autonomy which can be altered only by constitutional amendment.

It is easy to overstress the centralizing trends in West Germany, unless there is adequate appreciation of the functioning of the *Bundesrat* and of the Federal Constitutional Court. Two of the most significant decisions of the Federal Constitutional Court, in particular, have evidenced its efforts to draw the lines between the competences of the Federal and the state governments. In the highly controversial Concordat case, decided on March 26, 1957, while the Court recognized that the Concordat of 1933 was still a binding treaty, it did sustain the school legislation of Lower Saxony as falling under its reserved powers.

Several events in the spring and early summer of 1958 provided the setting for the much publicized atomic rearmament referenda cases involving the states of Hamburg, Bremen, and Hesse and decided on July 30, 1958. In the play of party politics, the Social Democratic Party had sought and failed to secure the passage by the *Bundestag* of an act to provide for a national referendum on atomic rearmament. It resorted to other tactics to secure what it termed "consultative plebiscites." The states of Hamburg and Bremen, both with legislative bodies containing

Social Democratic majorities, passed legislation for holding referenda at the state level. At the request of the Federal Minister of Interior, the Federal Constitutional Court issued on May 27, 1958, restraining orders to prevent the implementation of state laws pending a final decision by the Court as to their constitutionality. The Court, in following certain selected arguments of the Federal government in its joint decision, found the acts of Hamburg and Bremen to be unconstitutional. They represented attempts to provide for the participation of the citizens "in an area within the exclusive jurisdiction of the Federal Government." In addition, "instructions" through referenda from the people of the state to "representatives" were violative of the Basic Law. The Court, in its brief decision, was particularly parsimonious in its discussion of Article 28 of the Basic Law, which recognizes the right of the states to deal with their own constitutional organization as long as they meet "republican, democratic, and social rule of law" requirements. But, recognizing the restricted grounds on which it based its decisions, the Court did give evidence that it would impose limits on the efforts of the states to explore at the behest of a political party uncharted jurisdictional areas under the federal system. These, and other recent decisions, indicate some of the efforts of the Federal Constitutional Court to draw the lines between the competences of the federal and state governments.

The Constitutional Court in Austria has been faced with equally complex problems. After World War II, this Court has taken again as a basis for some of its decisions the theory of freezing of the distribution of competences (*Versteinerungstheorie*) at a given time in the constitutional development during the First Republic. The date chosen was that of the effectiveness of the first constitutional amendment on October 1, 1925. Nevertheless, certain general trends in the decisions of the Court may be noted. During the first years after 1946, the Court's decisions were seemingly directed toward the protection of the modest sphere of reserved powers of the provinces. However, in later years, the Court has more frequently decided in favor of the Federation. Thus, by a decision in 1951, the Constitutional Court upheld the second Nationalization Law of March 26, 1947, which recognized the power of the Federation to nationalize electricity and power plants. Again in 1952, the Court sustained the law of 1949 providing for the equalization of economic burdens as falling within federal jurisdiction. In a suit brought in 1953, while several provisions of the law establishing the Federal Chamber of Commerce were invalidated, the essential contentions of the plaintiff government of Vienna were rejected. In 1954, the Court recognized that the control of radio fell entirely within the jurisdiction of the Federation, in 1956, the first Nationalization Law of 1946 was sustained. These decisions must, of course, be compared with those which have favored the provinces. But they must also be read in the light of the realities of the coalition government and of the changing international status of Austria, which have served to encourage federal legislation tending to narrow progressively the area of provincial autonomy.

Though the constitutional provisions have been only partially implemented, regionalism in Italy has provided more than its share of legal controversy. Indeed, more than half of the 381 cases "disposed of" by the Italian Constitutional Court prior to March 31, 1957 involved disputes between the central government and the regions. The most controversial questions have involved the relations between the Sicilian High Court, which was created in accordance with Articles 24–30 of the Special Statute for Sicily on May 15, 1946, and was authorized to pass upon the constitutionality of laws enacted by the Sicilian legislature and the compatibility of national laws with the Regional Statute. After the Italian Constitutional Court began to function in 1956, the problem of the relationship of the two Courts arose. In a decision of February 27, 1957 the Constitutional Court refused to recognize the possibility of a co-existing and competing jurisdiction with the High Court, at least over subjects within the competence of the Constitutional Court. But there are still unsettled questions involving the relationships between the two, as recent decisions of the Constitutional Court bear witness. Indeed, the Italian Constitutional Court has evidenced a cautious approach in its efforts to demarcate the autonomous sphere of the sensitive regions.

Thus, the West German Court is looked upon more as a protector of the reserved powers of the states than is the Austrian Court. The decisions of the Federal Constitutional Court appear to be of the greater significance in the total political picture, but its competences are broader. Its decisions have commanded more attention, but it is the newer creation. There has been less concern generated by the decisions of the Austrian Court, possibly because there is little evidence that its decisions have threatened major parts of the legislative program of the coalition government. The jurisdictional controversies between the central government and the regions in Italy, while occupying much of the Court's attention, necessarily have limited application.

The concern over the dangers of unlimited delegation of legislative powers was reflected in the attempts of the Constitution makers to place constitutional restraints upon such delegation, as, for example, in Article 80 of the Basic Law in West Germany. This Article, empowering legislative bodies to authorize the Federal Government, a minister, or a state government to issue decrees implementing legislation, requires that the "content, purpose, and scope" of the statutory basis be specific. In 1956, and again in 1958, the Court has found provisions of legislation to be lacking in clarity as to "content, purpose, and scope" insofar as they authorized certain implementing decrees. But, said the Court in 1958, in a case involving designated paragraphs of the Price Law of 1948, it is not necessary that "content, purpose, and scope" be expressly stated in the statutory basis; it suffices if they can be deduced from the whole statute, its styling, its meaning in context, its history. "This can be done in the present case."

In Italy, Article 76 of the Constitution provides that "the exercise of the legislative function cannot be delegated to the Government unless directive principles and criteria have been determined and only for a limited time and for definite purposes." There the Court has recognized that the determination of cases involving the unconstitutional delegation of legislative powers is one of its most important tasks. The Court has invalidated, as being in effect "unconfined and vagrant," a law which left to the administrative authorities the determination of contributions (and of the persons required to contribute) to the tourist offices. While it did not do so, the Court might well have borrowed from the language used by Justice Cardozo in 1935 in dissenting in the *Panama Refining Co.* and in concurring in the *Schecter* cases.

The complicated history of restraints on legislative delegation, and of the legality of "law-amending ordinances" in Austria, defies brief summarization. But, according to numerous decisions of the Court, Article 18 of the Constitution permits the legislature to authorize the issuance only of implementing and not of "law-amending" ordinances; in order to justify the implementation, the statutory basis must prescribe the essential limits within which the intended regulations will be confined and the purposes toward which they will be directed. The Court has not hesitated to strike down statutory provisions which have violated these requirements. In short, in differing ways but with rather similar results, the Constitutional Courts of the three countries have been concerned with the application of constitutional provisions designed to prevent the legislature from leaving ill-defined and broad discretion in the hands of the administrator. . . .

If we have dwelt at some length on certain selected decisions of these Courts, it has been to indicate the ways in which the Constitutions are being interpreted by the judges of the Constitutional Courts. They have clearly pointed out some of the effective constitutional limits beyond which the legislator and the administrator cannot go in their actions affecting individual rights.

III

Any conclusion regarding the role of the Constitutional Courts must be highly tentative and subject to much more critical examination. The record of the West German Constitutional Court has occasioned more comment than that of either Italy or Austria, possibly because of the breadth of its jurisdiction, its daring during the formative years, and the controversial character of some of its decisions.

In the relation of the Constitutional Courts to other governmental organs at the national level, there have been crisis periods in each of the countries. The German crisis occurred during 1952–53, when the consideration of the European Defence Community Treaties eventuated in what one critic called a "period of judicial frustration."[3] However, despite the critical position taken at that time in certain official quarters, the Adenauer Government has looked with increasing sympathy upon the Court in recent years. The *Bundesrat* has furnished more friendly support for the Court than has the governmental coalition in the *Bundestag*. The Social Democratic Party, as the opposition party, and the governments of certain of the states, as the weaker elements in the federal system, have viewed the Court as the protector of the rights of minorities. Although there have been various proposals coming from several circles for the reform of the Court, such minor changes in composition, organization, and jurisdiction as were made by legislation in 1956 and 1959, have emanated from the Court itself.

The crises in the brief history of the Italian Court were those which took place during the long period of delay after 1948, before implementing legislation could be enacted, and after 1953, before the judges were finally appointed. The assortment of internal and external problems faced by the Court, culminating in the final resignation of its first President, De Nicola, in 1957, were brought sharply to public and parliamentary attention. However, the reticence of the Court to go behind a legislative finding of facts in Italy and the limited exercise of the power to invalidate statutes enacted since 1948 have kept parliamentary criticism at a minimum.

In Italy, dissatisfied groups and organizations have on occasion attacked decisions of the Court. For example, the Communists have objected to certain ones respecting land reform legislation; the Church, to others involving the application of constitutional provisions regarding freedom of worship. Some opposition to the Court has also come from the lower bureaucracy. But the really violent opposition has emanated from the regions, especially from Sicily. These reactions, when coupled with the lethargy of the Italian populace toward the Constitution, have combined to create a negative image of the Court which is gradually being erased.

In Austria, neither of the major political parties nor any important pressure groups have made the Constitutional Court a target for continuing criticism. There have been past occasions, as in 1956–57, when partisan differences almost involved the Court, but these were exceptional instances. The relationship between the Constitutional Court and the other highest courts has provoked some controversy, and there has been continuing academic discussion of the right of access to and the jurisdiction of the Court. Those who favor an expansion of its jurisdiction sometimes look toward West Germany; those who favor a more restricted

---

[3] Karl Löwenstein, "The Bonn Constitution and the European Defense Community Treaties, A Study in Judicial Frustration," *Yale Law Journal*, Vol. 64, pp. 805–39 (1955).

status, may point toward Italy. But the recent constitutional law and legislation of 1958 dealing with the Court have resulted in only slight changes in its jurisdiction and organization. In Austria, as in West Germany and Italy, there has been general acceptance of the Court, though without either generous enthusiasm or violent criticism.

There have been problems of implementation of decisions. Some have been considered in West Germany, in connection with the atomic rearmament referenda cases, and others with decisions requiring parliamentary action. The failures on the part of the parliament and the bureaucracy in Italy, to accept his strictures as to implementation, help explain De Nicola's threatened resignation in 1956 as President of the Court. But the record does not show any situation comparable to the effective nullification of a Court's decision, as occurred in the United States during President Jackson's administration following the Cherokee Indian cases. There have been more warnings to the Federal Constitutional Court of Germany to exercise "intellectual humility," and "self restraint" in not pushing its jurisdictional bounds beyond the limits of the feasible and the practicable, than there have been in Italy and Austria, where the more limited jurisdiction of the Courts and the greater hesitancy to question legislative enactments have been evidenced. Its record indicates that the West German Court is seeking to follow this advice, and is sensitive to the charges of "judicial legislation," but it apparently has been unable to extricate itself from involvement with what the United States Supreme Court would call political questions.

The Constitutional Courts in Europe are in part the products of reaction against a gloomy past, as previously mentioned. Some of their activities have been devoted to a liquidation of this heritage and to a prevention of its repetition. But, today, the Courts are increasingly faced with the new issues which have developed during the post–World War II period. These new issues, as well as the old ones, have continued to involve the application of the pertinent constitutional provisions regarding equality before the law, federalism, and the delegation of legislative powers.

The idea that courts, or some judicial body, should serve as the final guardian of the constitution had its roots and origins in Europe. It has seen its widest acceptance and expansion in the United States. In turn, American application and judicial experience have helped undergird the European precedents and theoretical support for the formation of special judicial bodies to guarantee the fundamentality of their constitutions.

Today, there are those who believe that the significance of judicial review in the United States is diminishing and that our Supreme Court can no longer serve as an effective protector of individual liberties and minority rights against legislative majorities and executive discretion. Is it possible, asked one thoughtful observer, that we may borrow in the future from the experience of these European Constitutional Courts rather than contribute to it—that there will be another period in the "give-and-take between the new and the old worlds?"[4]

However, it is still too early in their history to speculate about the future of these Constitutional Courts. During the past decade, they have not faced that type of crisis which economic adversity, the messianic leader, or foreign military experiment might provide. Until such a time there will be uncertainty as to the degree to which constitutional democracy today reflects an active faith, and the extent to which it is the formal expression resulting from Allied political pressure, a prosperous economy, and anti-totalitarian resentment. Only then will we know how deeply rooted are the constitutions for which these Courts serve today as interpreters and guarantors.

43. THE PARLIAMENTARY OMBUDSMAN*
Donald C. Rowat

EACH OF the Scandinavian countries—Sweden, Finland, Denmark and Norway—now has an officer of parliament commonly known as the Ombudsman, whose job is to investigate complaints from citizens about the way they have been treated by government officials and, when he finds it necessary, to recommend remedial action. Recently, this Ombudsman scheme has gained widespread attention in other countries, particularly in the English-speaking world, and much discussion has taken place about whether it should be adopted elsewhere. In this article, then, we consider the history and nature of the scheme, the reasons why it is thought to be desirable in the modern democratic state, and arguments that have been raised against its transplantation to other countries.

I

The office of Ombudsman was first created by the Swedish Constitution Act of 1809, over 150 years ago. It has an even earlier prototype, however, the King's Chancellor of Justice, which extends far back into Swedish history. The Chancellor of Justice was empowered by the King to supervise the application of the law by judges and other officials. With the rise of parliamentary democracy in Sweden it became clear that the Chancellor's status as part of the executive made him too dependent upon

---

[4] Gottfried Dietze, "America and Europe—Decline and Emergence of Judicial Review," *Virginia Law Review*, Vol. 44, p. 1272 (1958).

* From "The Parliamentary Ombudsman: Should the Scandinavian Scheme Be Transplanted?", *International Review of the Administrative Sciences* (No. 4, 1962), pp. 399–405. Reprinted by permission of the Institut International des Sciences Administratives, Brussels. Footnotes abridged by the editors.

executive authority. As a result, Parliament wrested the office from the executive by gaining power over the appointment of the incumbent. But Parliament lost its control over the executive after a short period, in 1772. When it regained control, in 1809, it decided to appoint an additional officer, the Ombudsman, as its own defender of the law. Just as the British Parliament's struggle for financial control over the executive laid the groundwork for the appointment of an Auditor General, the Swedish Parliament's struggle for political control laid the basis for the appoint ment of an Ombudsman.

Finland, too, has long had a Chancellor of Justice with powers of supervising the courts and the administration. Unlike Sweden, however, Finland, under its 1919 Constitution, made the Chancellor partially in dependent of the executive. In addition it created a parallel office of parliamentary Ombudsman. Thus Finland, like Sweden, has two public defenders, each with the power to receive and investigate complaints. But because of the historic prestige and independence of the Finnish Chan cellor, he is much more powerful than his Swedish counterpart, and is perhaps even more important than the Finnish Ombudsman as a defender of the law.

Impressed with the obvious advantages of the schemes in Sweden and Finland, Denmark decided to adopt the institution under its new Con stitution of 1953, and its first Ombudsman was appointed in 1955. Although the Norwegian Committee on Administrative Procedure, headed by the Chief Justice, had recommended a civilian Ombudsman for Norway in 1958, it was not until 1961 that the Norwegian Government introduced a bill on the subject, and the Parliament did not actually adopt the institution until the summer of 1962. The new Norwegian scheme is patterned mainly upon its Danish counterpart.

As one might expect, there are some significant differences among the Nordic countries in the Ombudsman's powers and procedures. The jurisdiction of the Swedish and Finnish officers is more extensive than that of their Danish and Norwegian counterparts. In Sweden and Finland the Ombudsman supervises not only the administration but also the courts, and has the direct power to prosecute officials before the courts for illegal acts. In Denmark he may only order that a prosecution be initiated, while in Norway he may only recommend this. Finland used to be the only country in which the Ombudsman supervised local government officials, but Sweden extended his jurisdiction to include them in 1957, Denmark did likewise in 1961, and it is expected that Norway will do so too. In Sweden and Norway the Ombudsman's jurisdiction does not extend to the armed services, because these countries have a special Military Ombuds man, dating in Sweden from 1915 and in Norway from 1952.

Another significant difference is that in cases where administrative authorities have been given discretionary power, in Sweden the Ombuds man has no specific right to criticize the wisdom of a decision and rarely does so, while in Denmark he has been given the right to do so if he considers the decision to be unreasonable. The Norwegian Committee proposed a similar power for the Ombudsman. The Norwegian Government at first refused this recommendation, but then accepted the wording "clearly unreasonable." The importance of these differences should not be exaggerated, however, because the Danish Ombudsman has used this power sparingly, while the Swedish Ombudsman has usually managed to intervene on grounds of illegality where a decision was patently unreasonable. He may conclude, for example, that a decision not based on the facts should be considered illegal. Moreover, the Nordic countries provide opportunities for appealing discretionary decisions that are wider than in the common-law countries. Both Finland and Sweden have a system of administrative appeal courts, which in Sweden may deal specifically with the reasonableness of decisions, and the courts in all four countries may hear appeals on grounds of both law and fact.

In other respects the competence and practices of the Nordic Ombudsman are much the same. All of them can receive and investigate any written complaint, which can be submitted in a sealed envelope without reference to any superior authority. All can initiate investigations and make inspections, without first having received a specific complaint. All can call upon government agencies to give reports and all have the power to demand departmental records. All are appointed by Parliament, are entirely independent of the executive, and report annually to a special committee of the House. All can comment critically on official actions in their annual reports, and all can make a report on an urgent matter at any time. In the Commonwealth countries, the position of the Auditor General as an officer of Parliament is a close parallel, except of course that the Auditor General checks financial transactions rather than administrative decisions.

When the Ombudsmen find that a complaint is justified, in the less serious cases they make critical comments directly to the officers of the department or agency concerned. Many cases involve no more than explaining fully to the bewildered citizen the reasons for the decision of which he has complained, and warning the government office in question that in future it should give adequate reasons for its decisions. But the Ombudsmen's conclusions on important cases are given wide publicity and exert a profound influence on future administrative practice. Moreover, on questions of principle arising from cases investigated, the Ombudsmen can propose amendments in the regulations or the law.

The matters they investigate range all the way from official misbehaviour and outright illegality to less serious complaints of tardiness, inefficiency, or negligence. It is in the latter type of case that the Ombudsman comes into his own, for it is here that the biggest gap occurs in our systems of administrative control. Examples range from complaints about getting no answer to an application, leisureliness in replying to mail, tardiness or bias in making decisions, to giving insufficient information on a decision or right of appeal. Nevertheless, some of the Ombudsmen's most valuable work has been done on serious cases of illegality involving the liberty of the subject. Here are some recent examples from Sweden and Denmark: a mental patient complained that a male nurse had assaulted him; inadequate consent was given for mental patients to undergo shock treatment and brain operations; police unjustifiably recorded telephone conversations; a prison warden barred a magazine from his prison simply because one issue had criticized prison authorities; handcuffs were used unjustifiably; and the police refused to remove an acquitted person's photograph and fingerprints from police files. Nearly all of these are cases in which redress might have been given had they been taken to the courts, but in most of them the citizen could not be expected to know his rights, would not know what to do about it if he did, and very likely could not afford expensive aid. In several such cases the Ombudsmen have secured court action and free legal aid for the complaint. In others, they have simply demanded direct redress for the action and assurance that similar actions will not occur again. Where the authority refuses this redress, the Ombudsmen will of course report critically on the case to Parliament.

Some idea of the nature and extent of the Ombudsmen's work may be gained by considering the number and disposition of the cases with which they deal. Each handles about 1,000 cases per year (not counting about 1,000 handled by the Military Ombudsman and the Chancellor of Justice in Sweden, and 1,500 by the Chancellor in Finland). Most of them arise out of complaints from the public, but cases initiated by the Ombudsman himself, as a result of inspections or reports in the press, account for a large proportion of the criticisms and prosecutions. In Finland and Denmark only 10 to 15 per cent of all cases require criticism, recommendations, disciplinary action or prosecution, but in Sweden the proportion is above 20 per cent. Probably the reason for the higher percentage in Sweden is the greater number of cases that arise from inspections, nearly all of which require criticism or remedial action. Another reason may be the long experience with the institution in Sweden and the public's better knowledge of which actions are likely to be condemned by the Ombudsman.

The total number of cases per year requiring criticism or remedial action is about 70 in Denmark, and in Finland is nearly 100 (not counting about 200 handled by the Chancellor of Justice). In Sweden, a country of about eight million, the total was close to 300 in 1960 (not counting about 200 handled by the Military Ombudsman and a few by the Chancellor). This will give the reader some idea of the number of cases of maladministration and injustice that may be going unnoticed in other countries each year. The number may even be proportionately greater in the common-law countries, because of the weaker role played by the courts and administrative appeal bodies, and also because the mere existence of the

Ombudsman scheme is a powerful preventive influence. Yet a democracy should be ashamed of even one substantial case of unremedied injustice per year.

II

The success of the new Ombudsman scheme in Denmark, and the discussion and recent adoption of it in Norway have caused other countries to become interested in the idea. In 1957, Western Germany adopted the institution of the Military Ombudsman, patterned to some extent on the systems in Sweden and Norway, and it is reported to be working successfully there. Partly as a result of the Danish Ombudsman's willingness to write and lecture in English about his new office, the United Kingdom and New Zealand took up the idea. Widespread discussion has ensued in the United Kingdom, and in 1961 the British Section of the International Commission of Jurists, *Justice,* issued a report, the so-called Whyatt Report, recommending the scheme.[1] So far, however, the British Government has made no favourable pronouncement on the matter. The New Zealand Government, on the other hand, has pursued the idea enthusiastically, and in 1961 introduced a bill on the subject. This bill was re-introduced and passed in the summer of 1962, and Sir Guy Powles, former High Commissioner to India, has been appointed as Ombudsman. In Canada, too, the scheme is now being discussed widely, and in the United States several articles have appeared favouring its adoption, with suitable adjustments, at least by the state and local governments.[2] In 1961, a Committee appointed by the Mayor of Philadelphia and chaired by the Dean of Law at the University of Pennsylvania recommended the system for Philadelphia, and the Administrative Conference of the United States, is now considering the idea for the national government. In the summer of 1962 the United Nations held a European seminar in Stockholm on protections against the abuse of administrative authority, at which the scheme was fully discussed. Several Western European countries are now becoming more interested. In the Netherlands, for example, a semi-official committee under the chairmanship of A. D. Belinfante, Professor of Constitutional Law at the University of Amsterdam, is considering the scheme. Since the war, other countries of the world, such as Indonesia and the Philippines, have set up related schemes with similar functions. In the Philippines, for example, President Magsaysay appointed a complaints committee to receive and investigate complaints about official action.

---

[1] *The Citizen and the Administration* (London, 1961); Director of Research, Sir John Whyatt.

[2] See, for example, H. J. Abraham, "People's Watchdog against Abuse of Power," *Public Administration Review,* Vol. XX, No. 3 (Summer, 1960), pp. 152–157, and K. C. Davis, "Ombudsmen in America," *Public Law* (Spring, 1962), pp. 34–42.

The reason for this widespread interest in the Ombudsman type of institution is not far to seek: there is need for additional protection against administrative arbitrariness in the modern democratic state. All democratic countries in the twentieth century have experienced a shift from the laissez-faire to the positive state. The accompanying tremendous growth in the range and complexity of government activities has brought with it the need to grant increasing powers of discretion to the executive side of government. As one of Britain's great constitutional lawyers, A. V. Dicey, has warned, "Wherever there is discretion, there is room for arbitrariness." In other words, it is quite possible nowadays for a citizen's rights to be accidentally crushed by the vast juggernaut of the government's administrative machine. In this age of the welfare state, thousands of administrative decisions are made each year, many of them by minor officials, which affect the lives of every citizen. If some of these decisions are arbitrary or unjustified, there is no easy way for the ordinary citizen to gain redress. In the preface to the recent Whyatt Report, Lord Shawcross expressed the situation in these words (p. xiii):

The general standards of administration in this country are high, probably indeed higher than in any other. But with the existence of a great bureaucracy there are inevitably occasions, not insignificant in number, when through error or indifference, injustice is done—or appears to be done. The man of substance can deal with these situations. He is near to the establishment; he enjoys the status or possesses the influence which will ensure him the ear of those in authority. He can afford to pursue such legal remedies as may be available. He knows his way around. But too often the little man, the ordinary humble citizen, is incapable of asserting himself. . . The little man has become too used to being pushed around: it rarely occurs to him that there is any appeal from what "they" have decided. And as this Report shows, too often in fact there is not.

In the past the courts were the bulwark of individual rights. But the ordinary courts have lost their flexibility and are no longer an effective instrument for remedying the wrongs of modern administrative action. The courts are too costly, cumbersome and slow, and in the English-speaking world the extent of their power of review is not at all clear, though certainly severely limited. Generally, they will review a decision only on a question of legality and refuse to review its content, wisdom, or even reasonableness. For these reasons, in most common-law countries special administrative appeal bodies have been created, to which an aggrieved citizen may take his case. But these bodies cover only a small portion of the total field of administrative action, and the vast majority of administrative decisions carry no formal right of appeal. The situation is better, of course, in those European countries that have developed a comprehensive system of administrative courts, where appeal is easy and cheap. But even administrative courts can be imperfect. Many of them are cumbersome and slow, so that the delay in deciding cases results in a denial of justice. It is significant that though Sweden and Finland have administrative courts, in recent years their Ombudsmen have found it increasingly necessary to extend their supervision over administrative agencies.

The right to complain to one's Member of Parliament does not meet the problem. Citizens often do not know of this avenue of appeal, and it is usually unsuitable anyway. In countries with a parliamentary system of government, especially where there are only two major parties, the executive tends to dominate the legislature and to maintain a tradition of secrecy. Hence it is difficult to bring cases of maladministration to light. The Member's usual method of dealing with a complaint is to send an inquiry to the department concerned. Naturally the department is likely to put the best light on its own case, and the Member has no impartial source of information. If he is dissatisfied with the department's reply, about all he can do is ask a question of the Minister in the House. Even though the Minister may have had nothing to do with the original decision, he will naturally consider himself a party to the decision and will defend it as his own. About the only further recourse is for the Member, still with inadequate information, to debate the complaint in the House—in which case it will turn into a political battle with the dice loaded in favour of the Minister. The opposition party can of course demand a formal inquiry, but an inquiry is costly and cumbersome, and is accepted by a government only after enough public outcry has been raised. Clearly it is not an adequate device for remedying the average administrative wrong done to the little man. Even in countries where there is a multi-party situation and the executive is not quite so dominant, there is usually no adequate parliamentary procedure for handling complaints, sifting evidence or making recommendations.

In view of the shortcomings of all of these traditional protections against administrative arbitrariness, we may conclude that the office of Ombudsman has a number of desirable characteristics which argue for its adoption. In the words of the Whyatt Report (p. 52):

First, there is the principle of impartial investigation. If a citizen makes a complaint against the conduct of a civil servant, the matter is investigated and reported upon by the Ombudsman, who is an impartial authority entirely independent of the Administration. Secondly, the impartial authority acts on behalf of Parliament although he is also protecting the interests of the individual complainant. Thirdly, the investigation is conducted openly . . . Fourthly, the method of submitting complaints and the investigation of complaints is very informal.

And one might add that, fifthly, since the great weapon of the Ombudsman is criticism, he does not interfere with day-to-day administration. Unlike appeal bodies, he does not substitute his judgment for that of the official, nor does he, like the courts, quash decisions.

III

Let us now consider some of the arguments that have been raised against transplanting the Ombudsman scheme. One reason the English-speaking world took so little interest in the institution before it was adopted in Denmark is that nothing was known of the Finnish plan, and of the Swedish scheme it was argued that the systems of government and law in Sweden were too different for the scheme to be applicable. Sweden has administrative appeal courts, a different system of court review, and a unique tradition of publicity whereby the press and the citizens may have access to departmental files at any time. More important, Sweden has an administrative system radically different from most others; Swedish departments resemble public corporations in their independence, and are not subject to detailed day-to-day control by the Ministers responsible to Parliament. Because of these differences, it was said that the scheme would not work elsewhere. However, its successful adoption in Denmark and its proposal for Norway exploded these claims. For the systems of law and cabinet government in these countries resemble those of the Commonwealth much more closely; neither country has a system of administrative courts, neither has a strong tradition of administrative publicity, and both have the system of ministerial responsibility for administration characteristic of parliamentary government elsewhere.

Too much has been made of the dangers of administrative publicity, in any case. Even in Sweden there are laws against revealing state secrets or information that would be injurious to private persons or commercial firms. The names of complainants and officials involved in cases are not ordinarily revealed, and the amount of publicity given to cases is partly at the discretion of the Ombudsman and is voluntarily controlled by the press. In the nature of things no publicity is given to minor cases of no news interest, and of course important cases *should* be discussed publicly.

A closely related argument against transplanting the office is that, in view of the revelations of the Ombudsmen, the need for a check on officialdom must be greater in the Nordic countries than elsewhere. The Nordic countries, however, are among the best-governed democracies in the world. The standards of their public services are extremely high, and their provisions for appeal of administrative decisions are certainly more ample than in the English-speaking countries. In adopting the Ombudsman system, Denmark and Norway have simply recognized that in the age of the welfare state, traditional controls are not good enough. . . .

Curiously, the opposite argument has also been raised—that the need is greater in the English-speaking countries, and is in fact so great that an Ombudsman would be overwhelmed with complaints. *The Times* warned (January 13, 1960) that in a large country like Britain the office might burgeon into something like the Chinese Control Yuan during the Han dynasty (206 B.C.–A.D. 220), which became a parallel branch of government constantly looking over the shoulder of the harried official. Instead of a public watchdog over the official's acts, the Ombudsman might become a bloodhound sniffing after his every decision. But as the *Economist* replied (January 31, 1960), this argument is to stand logic on its head. It is tantamount to saying that because the demand would be overwhelming the need should not be met at all. In any case, the fear is false. The Ombudsman performs his task in the Nordic countries with only five or six legal officers and a few office assistants, and he is certainly no super-administrator with power to substitute his judgment for that of other officials. In fact, he rarely comments on the content of a discretionary decision but rather on the *way* in which the decision has been made, to ensure its legality and fairness. That the bloodhound theory arises from a false fear is shown by the reversal in the attitude of civil servants in Denmark. Before the scheme was introduced they opposed it, but after its adoption they soon realized that the office was an aid rather than a hindrance. For in nine cases out of ten the Ombudsman vindicated their decisions and hence increased public confidence in the civil service. The scheme also shifted much of the task of handling the public's complaints from the civil service to the Ombudsman. Furthermore, minor officials soon found that the Ombudsman was an ally in their own dealings with arbitrary superiors. It is true, of course, that in the absence of a comprehensive system of administrative appeals, the work of an Ombudsman would be greater, but this problem must be attacked at its source.

It is frequently argued that to be the little man's defender the Ombudsman's office must be a highly personal one, while in large countries the size of the office would cause it to lose this personal touch. This argument has also been inverted: it is said that the office is *too* personal, too dependent upon one man's integrity, understanding and daily time; and that the nature of the office demands for its success a virtual impossibility—finding exactly the right man for the job, in particular one who combines a profound knowledge of the law with wide experience in various types of administration. These arguments, too, can be easily challenged. In the first place, there has been a lot of sentimental twaddle about the Ombudsman's personal touch. The principle of impartiality is far more important than the personal touch. Certainly citizens need to know that there is an independent authority to which they can turn for an impartial investigation, but this objective can be achieved without the paternalism inherent in a personalized office. Moreover, there are good grounds for the view that important and complex cases of a judicial nature should *not* be decided by a single person. (In fact, they are not so decided under the Ombudsman scheme. Although the Ombudsman deals with all important cases personally, naturally he and his expert staff discuss all such cases before he reaches a final conclusion, so that in effect they work as a group.) The old adage applied to the higher courts that two heads are better than one also applies here. For this reason I would recommend for populous countries a commission of three members, which might be called the Parliamentary or Administrative Complaints Commission. Commissioners would decide important cases together, but could decide minor cases individually. Each could specialize in a particular area or type of administration. The commission could include a judge and an experienced administrator (and perhaps also a representative of the public). In this way the proposal by-passes the argument that it is virtually impossible to find in a single man the qualities demanded by the office.

Having seen that most of the arguments that have been raised against transplanting the Ombudsman scheme may be effectively demolished, we should at the same time keep in mind that it cannot be a panacea. A number of people in Britain seem to regard "Ombudsman" as a kind of magic word that will cure all their administrative ills. But the age-old problem of the relation between the state and the individual is far too complex to be solved by one simple scheme. We need a whole variety of controls over administrative action, and the Ombudsman scheme must be accompanied by a number of other reforms that are needed to plug the gaps in our systems of control. Otherwise, the scheme may fail because we are trying to make it do too much. We must remember that in the Nordic countries the scheme only supplements a battery of other effective controls, and that New Zealand is adding this scheme to an already well-developed parliamentary grievance system.

On the other hand, the danger in setting up a network of controls is that if the administration is surrounded with too many controls it will be unable to move. This is the danger in extending court review too far or in judicializing the administrative process too much. The United States has already gone too far in this direction, and recent British changes and proposals seem to point to the same danger. What we need is a fence along the administrative road, not a gate across it. The great virtue of the Ombudsman scheme is that its weapons are publicity and persuasion rather than cumbersome controls; it is in the category of the fence rather than the gate.

Part Four – Political Change

INTRODUCTORY ESSAY

IN ALL POLITICAL systems there must be institutions that translate claims and demands into decisions which inevitably modify existing conditions. Change is inherent in the political process. New groups assume a position of power and influence while others lose their prerogatives; new rights are proclaimed and new services provided. Throughout the nineteenth century, for example, there was a continuing struggle for the attainment of political rights on the part of the social groups brought into being by the industrial revolution. The twentieth century is witnessing a similar struggle for political emancipation in the rest of the world and assumption of collective responsibility for economic development and social welfare.

The nature of change, the rate at which change takes place and the specific correlates of change are not yet fully understood. Nor is it easy to tell in advance the direction change is likely to take. According to the Marxists, societies evolve through clearly defined stages, from feudalism through capitalism to socialism, as a result of economic pressures. Under certain conditions change is wrought by violence and revolution since the groups and classes that wield power are unwilling or unable to adapt to new conditions. Innovation may also bring about sweeping changes in social and political institutions. All societies which have undergone the technological and scientific revolutions of the past two centuries have been transformed, regardless of their particular cultures and political systems. At the present time economic, social, and political change is taking place at an accelerated rate throughout the world, not simply in the advanced nations. Political leaders almost everywhere are now committed to a drastic overhaul of their societies. They are attempting to popularize new values and norms, and create new attitudes in order to achieve industrialization, prosperity, and equality. There is an unparalleled urgency in this movement, which is taking place in a variety of ways and through a number of political forms. A major challenge before students of comparative politics is the development of analytic categories in terms of which the component elements of change can be understood and societies undergoing rapid change fruitfully compared.

Traditional and Modern Societies

It will be useful for analytic purposes to distinguish between two "ideal-types" or "models" of societies: the *traditional* and the *modern*.

481

These terms do not imply any value judgment. A traditional society may include a large number of highly educated persons whose level of culture and social grace is higher than that of the mass of inhabitants of any modern society. Futhermore, these terms refer only to abstract "constructs"; they do not describe any existing societies. For example, the United States is a predominantly modern society, but one with many traditionally oriented groups in its population.

The distinction here suggested is a familiar one in the literature of the social sciences. Similar classificatory schemes have been suggested by such eminent theoreticians as Sir Henry Maine, Ferdinand Tönnies, and especially Max Weber.[1] The Weberian categories of *traditional, charismatic*, and *legal authority* can be viewed not only as analytic general categories but also as developmental stages. Political development for Weber implies a transition from traditional and charismatic to legal systems in which a rational (goal-oriented) type of motivation predominates. It is, therefore, identical with a trend toward individualism, the articulation of interests through multiple associations and groups, each of which operates and acts in the context of known and accepted institutions. In a legal system power is legitimized and general rules emerge through which conflict is resolved and policy formulated.

In both traditional and modern societies the individual participates in the political process through groups or associations, but there are fundamental differences as regards their nature and importance. Traditional societies are characterized by the predominance of the family and family-type groups (that is, "primary organizations") in which the members are in a "face-to-face" relationship. An individual's status in the society is determined by his family's status. He is nurtured, cared for, educated, and protected by the family, which tends to be a self-sufficient economic as well as social unit. The dominant economic activity is agriculture, which requires the participation of the family as a cohesive group. Virtually the entire population (and not one in ten, as in modern societies) is engaged in agriculture, the hunt, or fishing in order to provide their sustenance. There is little knowledge of science or technology, no opportunity to accumulate reserves of food, no leisure class able to devote itself to the arts and culture. The people live close to nature, even as part of nature. They are almost completely at the mercy of the seasons, storms, droughts, and

---

[1] A rigorous theoretical analysis is presented in *The Politics of Developing Areas*, edited by Gabriel A. Almond and James S. Coleman (Princeton, N.J.: Princeton University Press, 1961), particularly in Professor Almond's introductory chapter. Other significant theoretical studies on which we have drawn include: Fred Riggs, "Agraria and Industria—Toward a Typology of Comparative Administration," in W. J. Siffin (ed.), *Toward a Comparative Study of Public Administration* (Bloomington: University of Indiana Press, 1957), pp. 23–116; Daniel Lerner, *The Passing of Traditional Society: Modernizing the Middle East* (Glencoe, Ill.: The Free Press, 1958); Everett E. Hagen, *On the Theory of Social Change* (Homewood, Ill.: Richard D. Irwin, Inc., 1962); and Wilbert E. Moore, *Social Change* (Englewood Cliffs, N.J.: Prentice-Hall, Inc., 1963).

rains. Superstition and magic permeate the society. Men seek to relate events in their own lives with external occurrences, the stars, or the seasons.

Family values—personal loyalty, authority, reverence—pervade the whole social structure. The State tends to resemble the family, with the king or chief of State in the role of father, whose paternal authority derives from a superhuman source. The various families gathered together in clans or tribes are his children, bound to obey for the same reason that each elder in the tribe is obeyed by the younger leaders. Insofar as a bureaucracy comes into existence to administer the will of the chief, it is like a huge household—with nepotism an expected practice.

"Politics" is a continual striving of families and clans for economic and military superiority. The contenders for power characteristically resort to armed force in order to establish undisputed hegemony and thus profit from the labor of their rivals. Government in such societies is usually a mechanism for tax collection and exploitation. The conquered groups attempt to conceal their wealth, resist the appropriation of their produce in the form of taxes, and by and large view the government as an appendage of the ruling families or tribes.

Examples of traditional societies at the present time may be found throughout Africa. Anthropologists have distinguished two main types of social organization in Africa, based primarily on economic activities. *Pastoral societies* predominate in east, central, and southern Africa, and *agricultural societies* in west Africa.[2] In pastoral societies, status and wealth are measured in terms of animals (generally cattle). The tribes live entirely off the produce and meat of these animals. As a consequence of their self-sufficiency there is little exchange of produce among tribes, and there are no cities. Social organization is based on age grades, with rites marking passage of the male from one grade to another. An example is the Masai, a people numbering about 200,000, who live mainly in the high planes of Kenya. They own over two million head of cattle and an equal number of sheep and goats. The Masai literally live on the meat, milk, and blood of their herd. Wives are purchased with, and honor defined by the appearance of, cattle.

The agricultural societies of west Africa are characterized by a settled population, producing enough for subsistence and frequently a surplus. Market places and towns have come into being, and there is some specialization of labor and class divisions. Large kingdoms and empires have even emerged and maintained themselves for long periods. The Ashanti, of Ghana, are a typical agricultural people. Cultivation and

---

[2] See James S. Coleman, "The Politics of Sub-Saharan Africa," in Almond and Coleman, *The Politics of the Developing Areas, op. cit.,* pp. 247–368; David Apter, *The Gold Coast in Transition* (Princeton University Press, 1957); and Melville J. Herskovits, "Peoples and Cultures of Sub-Saharan Africa," *The Annals* (March, 1955), pp. 15–19.

ownership of land is the fundamental value of Ashanti culture. A complicated system of matrimonial bonds is the basis of property rights and political rule. Reverence for ancestors pervades the whole culture and serves to surround the land and the chiefs with an aura of mystery. The chiefs are named by a "Queen Mother," but the choice is actually determined beforehand by the tribal elders. All chiefs occupy a stool or throne, in which resides the spirit of the ancestors. The chiefs are supposed only to interpret this spirit and do not rule in their own name.

There have been, historically, a wide range of types *within* the general category of "traditional societies," from the subsistence agriculture and pastoral societies of primitive tribes in Africa, to the military structure of Egypt, the land empires of Asia Minor and China, the island civilization of the Aegean, Ancient Greece and Rome, and the feudal age. All of these societies, however, preceded the technological and industrial breakthrough of the eighteenth century.

Technical and scientific progress brought in their wake far-reaching change in social and political organization. The old agricultural subsistence economy was replaced by an industrial market-place economy. In the "model" modern society, an individual gains his livelihood not within the family but in a factory, commercial enterprise, or office. Population concentrates in the great urban centers, creating a host of administrative problems (sanitation, transportation, education, etc.). Modern societies are characterized by the predominance of *secondary organizations,* that is, large specialized and impersonal associations like labor unions, corporations, farm co-operatives, veterans' groups, political parties, universities, and churches. Unlike the family, the secondary organizations have large numbers of members who need not be in a face-to-face relationship, are joined by a voluntary action of the prospective members, and carry on highly specialized activities. Most of the former functions of the family are assumed by the new associations (education by the schools, charity by the State, religious instruction by the Church, and exchange of produce by the banks and market place. The State itself tends to take on the character of these secondary organizations. It becomes large, complex, impersonal, and increasingly rational. Old ideas of divine right fall into disrepute, and more rational themes of legitimacy (for example, popular sovereignty) come into vogue. The family itself is grievously weakened and is based more and more on consent and mutual interest.

After a period of evolution, the State expands to meet the needs of an industrialized economy. The civil service, for example, cannot fulfill its obligations as the closed preserve of a single family or clan, but must recruit able men from all layers of society. As Max Weber has pointed out, a modern bureaucracy is "rational," that is, recruits universally, boasts a system of tenure, grade classifications, and fixed salaries. Political conflict resembles the market place itself: each specialized group puts forth its offers and demands, with the State acting as a broker.

Individuals express their interests primarily through the secondary organizations to which they belong.

These analytic categories—traditional and modern—can be used for a study of the likely stages that the new nations will follow and for the exploration of contemporary trends in most of these nations. There is a clear tendency for these societies to move from the traditional category into a *transitional period* during which they acquire many of the characteristics of modern society while retaining some traditional features. But it is impossible to foretell the exact development of any of these societies. For example, the so-called "uncommitted" nations are doubtless on the way to modernization. But there are two chief prototypes of advanced industrial states in the world: the Western countries (especially the United States) and the Communist nations (notably the Soviet Union). After which model of modernity will the developing societies pattern themselves? Though we cannot predict the exact form of change, we may assume that it will be determined by a limited number of factors operating within only a limited range of possibilities. Prediction can only indicate the *possible* or likely direction of change.

Elites in the Developing Nations

Comparative study could usefully be focussed on the decision-making or political elite: their social origin, position with respect to the masses, technical or educational qualifications for governing, and relationship with the important social groups within the nation (for example, landowners, army, Church, civil service, and intellectuals), and their characteristic ideologies. At least four different leadership "types" can be distinguished in the developing nations: traditional, liberal, authoritarian, and radical.

The *traditional* leaders derive their authority from historical status and prestige, and from one predominant form of property—land. They constitute a self-perpetuating group in that recruitment comes from a small circle (either royalty, or landowning nobility) by virtue of birth. Their values vary from one system to another, but generally reflect a family structure—the emphasis is on kinship, loyalty, devotion, duty, and courage. They are averse to changes which will endanger their economic and social position. They are apt to react unfavorably to any economic or technological innovations which might weaken the political system. They insist upon the preservation of prevailing modes of political recruitment and hence are hostile to popular participation in politics. They are opposed to industrialization and to its political and social implications.

The *liberal* leaders are in favor of "reforming out of existence" the traditionalist-oriented economy, society, and political system. They are in favor of industrialization and mass participation in political affairs. They accept both the goals *and the methods* of the Western constitutional democracies. Thus, the liberals desire political reforms, establishment of a constitutional order with guarantees of individual rights, the articulation of interests within an accepted legal order, and the gradual displacement of the traditionalist groups from positions of power. They wish to create the proper conditions within which meaningful political choices can be made by the whole people. Recruitment of the liberal elite is usually from the professional and middle classes, particularly among those who have attended European and American universities. The traditionalists and liberals tend to be allied in their respect for property rights but split over the question of democratic reforms and modernization.

What we call *"authoritarian"* leaders, like the liberals, tend to accept democracy as an ideal or goal. But they do not believe it can be achieved by indiscriminate adoption of all features of Western systems. They distinguish between "formal" or "procedural" democracy (elections, parliaments, organized opposition, etc.) and "real" or "substantive" democracy (equal opportunity, economic development, moral regeneration). An active opposition only obstructs the efforts of the government to bring about "real" democracy, and hence must be suppressed. The emphasis is therefore on "guided democracy," or "personalism"—that is, on national unity, and the direction of the efforts of the masses by an educated, informed, morally responsible elite. Frequently the hope is held out that the people, one day in the future, after rapid economic progress has been accomplished, will be ready for representative government of the Western type. Authoritarian leaders, like the liberals, come mainly from the professional and middle classes, and occasionally from the landed aristocracy.

The fourth "type" of leadership is *radical*. Inspired by a revolutionary ideology, the radicals are committed to drastic and rapid change of the economic and social structure. They organize their followers in a manner that will enable them to take the system by assault. The classic pattern is the single mass party led by professional revolutionaries, along lines laid down by Lenin. Radical leadership comes from the "alienated" groups, particularly the intelligentsia, and it appeals to the disaffected elements of the population—the peasants, the students, and the city workers. They are in favor of industrialization, but at the expense of the liberal values— individual rights, political freedoms, and private property. Above all they impose collective goals upon the total society, and discipline the masses in order to achieve those goals. The main differences between the authoritarians and radicals are of degree and social origin: the latter want more change more rapidly, with greater social control and discipline, and tend to be drawn from less favored social classes. The radicals are also much more suspicious of the Western powers, and tend to seek aid as well as ideological inspiration from the Communist camp.

The Politics of Modernization

The "benefits" of modernization have been felt throughout the world in the form of manufactured goods, moving pictures, radio broadcasts, and so on. All native populations have had their expectations aroused or modified as a consequence. The economic structure of traditional systems has been undermined. Landownership is no longer a secure base for a political elite. New economic activities have created new social groups and stimulated others who now view the traditional elite as a stumbling block on the road to further economic development. They seek the removal of this hindrance.

Industrialization, however, is viewed only as a means for the attainment of new economic goals and the satisfaction of wants. Its prerequisites—the development of skills, the training of the masses, the establishment of an orderly pattern of social intercourse, and particularly discipline and regular work in the factory—are understood only by a small group of political leaders. Industrialization is often equated with a vision of plenty in the foreseeable future and as such it becomes a potent political force. The discipline required for industrialization, however, is appreciated by very few, and perhaps only by the "radical" leaders.

As the conflict develops between the traditional leaders and the new groups which demand industrialization, the political position of the ruling elite becomes precarious. Their legitimacy is brought into question. There follows a period of instability, overt defiance of authority, and sporadic uprisings. The new political leaders—liberal, authoritarian, and radical—vie for control. A limited number of alternatives for future political development present themselves.

One alternative is the maintenance of traditional social organization and leadership. This alternative, though always possible, is becoming anachronistic. Most of the traditional forces are fighting a losing battle for survival. The independence movement is associated with an ideology calling for social and economic reforms which are inconsistent with the interests of the traditional forces. Mobilization of the masses in the struggle for independence brings with it profound modifications in the economic and social structure. Change may be held off by a temporary alliance between the traditional and new leaderships and groups for the realization of independence, by the inability of one particular group to impose its ideology, or by foreign intervention. But the will for change in a society generally indicates that the emerging political elites will use every means available to eliminate the traditional leaders who are still desperately clinging to the last vestiges of their rule.

At a certain stage, the liberal elements come into sharp conflict with the authoritarian and radical elements. The liberals advocate a relatively slow pace of structural modifications and industrialization, technological improvements, a rising standard of living, the gradual training of managerial and labor groups, progressive land reforms, and involvement of the masses in politics through the extension of literacy and education. But these demands are made with little urgency and the envisaged manner of their implementation is permissive rather than coercive. Liberal elites attempt to create the conditions within which the individual can become capable of choice—always considered in the best tradition of liberalism as an individual act. The system should provide opportunities for the individual and only "hinder the hindrances."

The authoritarians and radicals, on the other hand, urge coercive and authoritarian practices in order to bring about quickly the same over-all goals. Suspicious of the continuing strength of the traditionalist elements (particularly among the peasants), they insist on rapid mobilization of the masses in a manner that will wrench them from their former way of life. Distrustful of the colonial powers, they seek to industrialize rapidly by using their own human resources and by accepting aid from the Communist countries. This political leadership, therefore, uses force and not persuasion, seeks the outright organization of the masses rather than a gradual process of political education, stresses social discipline rather than general legal rules, norms, and individual guaranties.

In the contest for power, the "liberal" leaders are at a severe dis-advantage. In relatively backward economies, the application of liberal economic doctrine does not result in rapid industrialization or structural change. Development of a market economy favors consumers goods production and the merchant class, and fails to satisfy the pent-up demand of large social groups. Subordination of social goals to individual choice only increases the feeling of social injustice on the part of the masses. All too often, it leads to "private wealth and public poverty." Politically, liberalism has no slogan which can activate and mobilize the masses. Most important, liberalism as a social force fails to inculcate new social in-centives for the purpose of industrialization. In brief, liberal elites are generally unable to reach the people, to capture their imagination, and to lead them into the modern era. On the other hand, the great advantage enjoyed by the authoritarian and especially the radical leaders is that they create a system of controls under which industrialization may take place.

Of course, it is impossible to predict the exact evolution of events in the developing nations. New forces may come to the fore, perhaps slowing down the tempo of modernization and permitting the traditional elite to rally. Industrialization may follow the Western historical experience and lead to the establishment of a legal order within which individual freedoms are guaranteed. The technician and the manager may win out over the party boss and the commissar—perhaps even in existing totalitarian sys-tems! Indications are, however, that the new nations are departing from the norms and institutions of Western democracies. Liberal elites are finding it exceptionally difficult to attract mass support. The Soviet revolutionary and historical experience seems to be the model for the most dynamic leadership groups in the new nations, even though they may follow "their own path."

Comparative study of change, revolution, and modernization obviously calls our attention to the dynamics of the political process. Are there any similarities in conditions which precede revolutions? Are the new nations in a "revolutionary" situation like that of France before 1789 or Russia before 1917? Comparative study may focus on specific social groups—the intellectuals, the working class, the peasantry—to see how they react to the traditional elite, and to what extent they are influenced by revolutionary ideas. Comparison should also be made of political evolution in the developing nations. Liberal elites are more successful in gaining mass support in such nations as the Philippines and Nigeria than in Indonesia and Ghana. What factors account for these similarities and differences? Analysis of political and social change in the "non-Western" world is perhaps the most serious and challenging task of contempory political science.

Chapter XIV. Patterns of Legitimacy

Introductory Note

As HAS BEEN pointed out in Part Two, every political system provides for the making of decisions which are widely obeyed. In order to inculcate obedience—which is essential to the maintenance of the State—authority is reinforced by a whole network of symbols, beliefs, and ideologies. In primitive societies the myth of supernatural right to rule is propagated by the priests, medicine men, and other interpreters of tribal customs. Modern systems universally make use of symbols which evoke a favorable emotional response—flags, seals of office, uniforms, anthems, and so on. They also disseminate beliefs, through the schools and other institutions, which unify the society. Fundamentally, these beliefs *justify* the existing power structure. They legitimize the system.

One of the best-known attempts to classify types of legitimacy was made by Max Weber. He suggested that claims to legitimacy may be based on:

1 Rational grounds—resting on a belief in the "legality" of patterns of normative rules and the right of those elevated to authority under such rules to issue commands (legal authority).

2. Traditional grounds—resting on an established belief in the sanctity of immemorial traditions and the legitimacy of the status of those exercising authority under them (traditional authority); or finally,

3. Charismatic grounds—resting on devotion to the specific and exceptional sanctity, heroism or exemplary character of an individual person, and of the normative patterns or order revealed or ordained by him (charismatic authority).[1]

One implication which may be drawn from Weber's scheme is that the three types correspond to historical development from simple to more complex societies. In the former, obedience is to the person of the chief, and the values of the family permeate the whole social system. A society breaks out of this stage usually under the leadership of a charismatic chief, who is obeyed because of his personal or heroic qualities. In modern societies obedience is to the legal order. It is associated with the office more than with the person who occupies it. Legitimacy is a prerequisite of all political systems. Yet the belief patterns which predominate in a given society are continually undergoing challenge and change.

---

[1] Max Weber, *The Theory of Social and Economic Organization* (New York: Oxford University Press, 1947), p. 328.

Weber's category of "rational" authority would apply to all complex, industrialized societies—democratic and totalitarian alike. Although the exact "meaning" of democracy has always been a matter of controversy, there is a large area of agreement among such modern commentators as Max Weber, A. D. Lindsay, Robert M. MacIver, Joseph Schumpeter, and Walter Lippmann. The distinctiveness of democracy is that the people can choose and change their government. The role of the public is to intervene from time to time in order to decide which set of leaders shall be vested with the State power. Democracy cannot exist unless it establishes basic civil liberties (freedom of speech, freedom of the press, freedom of criticism) through which the people are able to express their views for or against policies and leaders. The right to criticize, if it is to be effective, must include the right to *organize* opposition.

The dominant Western view of democracy is thus *procedural*. It is characterized by free elections, free expression, and free parties. The existence of these procedures serves to legitimize the actions of the State in the eyes of the citizenry. But this emphasis on procedure is rejected by Fascists and Communists alike as irrelevant. Legitimacy for the anti-democratic critics derives from some other source—the nation or class or race. It can never be the product of argument and opinions of groups and individuals.

Communist theories have always distinguished between "bourgeois parliamentarism" and "Soviet democracy." Parliamentarism, Marx contended, means that the people have only the right to decide which members of the ruling class are to exploit them for the next few years. Parliamentary "prattle" is designed mainly to delude the masses into believing that they have some political importance, whereas in reality power is firmly in the hands of the capitalists, operating through the bureaucracy. In Communist regimes, legitimacy comes mainly through manipulation and control but ultimately, if the government is to survive, from achievement and performance.

Fascism secures the obedience of the people, mainly by exploiting nationalist sentiment. Adolf Hitler strove to liberate Germany from the restrictions imposed by the Treaty of Versailles, mobilize popular support in the name of the uniqueness of the German race and destiny, and then to bring about the unification of Europe by conquest. It can hardly be denied that the great majority of the German people considered these aims proper, and that the Nazi State and Party were thereby "legitimized."

In all modern states the masses are drawn into the political process. Activation and mobilization of the people is perhaps the central characteristic of modernization—whether it be in the tradition of parliamentary democracy, fascism, or communism. In developing nations the participation of the people in the political system, indeed their awareness of the existence of a political system, is in itself a revolutionary event. Through the ideology of nationalism the people identify themselves with the political system, which thus acquires legitimacy.

Comparative study and analysis of legitimacy would be both useful and revealing. What are the basic types of legitimate authority? Do they correspond to any set of economic or social conditions? Above all, under what conditions do belief systems become modified or transformed? Examination of these problems leads naturally into the study of change and revolution.

Among the best modern works on democratic theory are: A. D. Lindsay, *The Modern Democratic State* (1943); Robert M. MacIver, *The Web of Government* (1947); Joseph A. Schumpeter, *Capitalism, Socialism and Democracy* (1947); and Walter Lippmann, *The Public Philosophy* (1955). On modern dictatorship the student may consult: C. J. Friedrich (ed.), *Totalitarianism* (1954); C. J. Friedrich and Z. Brzezinski, *Totalitarian Dictatorship and Autocracy* (1956); Hannah Arendt, *The Origins of Totalitarianism* (1958); and Franz L. Neumann, *Behemoth* (2d ed., 1944). Recent books on nationalism include: Karl Deutsch, *Nationalism and Social Communication* (1953); Rupert Emerson, *From Empire to Nation* (1960); and K. H. Silvert (ed.), *Expectant Peoples* (1963). The nature of legitimacy is treated in MacIver, cited above; Charles E. Merriam, *Systematic Politics* (1945); and Karl Loewenstein, *Political Power and the Governmental Process* (1957).

Readings

A. Democracy

44. THE WORLD REVOLUTION OF OUR TIME*

Harold D. Lasswell

The Developmental Construct

As A MEANS of improving judgments of the future such special tools as the "developmental construct" have been invented. A developmental construct characterizes a possible sequence of events running from a selected cross-section of the past to a cross-section of the future.[1] Taken critically, all interpretations of our epoch are developmental constructs (such as the

---

* Reprinted from Harold D. Lasswell's *The World Revolution of Our Time*, with the permission of the publishers, Stanford University Press (copyright 1951 by the Board of Trustees of the Leland Stanford Junior University). Article and footnotes abridged by the Editors.

[1] This tool was proposed in Lasswell, *World Politics and Personal Insecurity* (New York: McGraw-Hill, 1935), Chapter 1. The volume is reprinted in *A Study of Power* by Lasswell, C. E. Merriam and T. V. Smith (Glencoe, Ill.: The Free Press, 1950).

alleged passage from "nineteenth-century capitalism" to "twentieth-century socialism"). However, these constructs are often put forward as though they were "scientific" and "inevitable." If we strip such self-serving declarations from a theory of history and lay bare the developmental picture, what remains is the statement of hypotheses which may prove to be helpful guides to judging the period.

By emphasizing that developmental constructs are not scientific propositions, it is not implied that available scientific knowledge is irrelevant. On the contrary, a disciplined use of developmental constructs calls for the study of both trends and conditions. Strictly, we might demonstrate that a given construct can be derived from accepted scientific generalizations. For expository purposes the alleged passage from "capitalism" to "socialism," for example, may be connected with many propositions which are basic to psychology and social science. But the complexity of such a demonstration would do away with one of the chief advantages of the construct, which is the succinct, stimulating contribution that it makes to an inquiring mind. The construct is a tool for sketching the plains, plateaus, and mountain chains of the continent of events comprising past, present, and future. The developmental pattern throws the time axis—the "from what, toward what"—into relief.

The task of thinking responsibly and critically about the future has ramifications which have been insufficiently explored even in this method-conscious era. The burden is especially heavy since some of the most reliable guides are able to make only limited contributions to the undertaking. For example, we cannot depend upon the future to conform to the ordinary postulates of probability theory, such as that a series of uniform events is in prospect (as in the tossing of the same penny to show "heads" or "tails"). In estimating the future, part of the problem is the likelihood that future events will be uniform; or, in other words, it is necessary to appraise the degree to which the more familiar probability postulates will apply.[2]

Because technical issues have been little discussed, it is not inappropriate to consider at greater length the postulation of goal values, the choice of time period, and the weighing of conditioning factors.

The Starting Point: Goal Values

How do we go about inventing and evaluating hypothetical constructs about our epoch? Our reply: select according to goal values.

The grounds of this advice are the characteristics of rational thought.

---

[2] The mathematical analysis of choice has been sharpened by the work of John von Neumann and Oskar Morgenstern in the *Theory of Games and Economic Behavior* (Princeton: Princeton University Press, 1947); N. Rashevsky, *Mathematical Biophysics* (Chicago: University of Chicago Press, 1948); Norbert Wiener, *Cybernetics* (New York: Wiley, 1948). See the discussion of the use of mathematical models in the social sciences by Kenneth Arrow in Lerner and Lasswell (eds.), *The Policy Sciences* (Stanford: Stanford University Press, 1951).

Rational thinking takes the consequences of its own exercise into account. Among the factors moulding the future are interpretations of the future. Since expectations have an impact, however modest, upon policy, we proceed rationally when we operate with a clear conception of our possible effect upon the shape of things to come. Since the function of policy is to achieve goal values, our initial step is the clarification of these values.

Without introducing an extensive treatment of our values at this point, we submit the following anticipatory comment: we are concerned with the dignity of man. We want to participate in the realization of human dignity on the grandest possible scale. Hence we are opposed to the prevalence of caste in human society and in favor of mobile societies in which the rule is individual merit rather than family privilege. This is equivalent to saying that we are in favor of shaping and sharing values on a wide rather than a narrow basis. Without pretending that the following list of values is exhaustive, we use eight terms: power (a voice in the making of decisions); wealth (economic goods and services); well-being (physical and psychic health); skill (opportunity to acquire and exercise latent talent); enlightenment (access to information and comment on which rational choices depend); affection (congenial human relations); rectitude (common standards of responsibility in theory and fact); respect (absence of discrimination on grounds other than merit). This list of values is not intended to be exhaustive of all possible values, although it can be used without serious distortion to classify all values, if desired. The order of mention does not constitute a rank order, but a random sequence. The relative significance of values for persons and groups is to be discovered by inquiry and not settled by definition.[3]

By taking human dignity as our central focus, we are in step with ideal values of the American tradition, and with the progressive ideologies of our epoch. Liberalism and socialism are united in affirming the free man's commonwealth as a goal of human society. That man's dignity is not to be realized in this world is the principal forecast of whoever takes a dim view of human perfectibility.

Alternate Constructs

Until recently it was not fantastic to imagine that the next few decades would mark the triumph of free societies throughout the globe. Today it

---

[3] See the programmatic statement, "Legal Education and Public Policy: Professional Training in the Public Interest," *Yale Law Journal*, LII (1943), 203–95 (reprinted in somewhat condensed form in Lasswell, *The Analysis of Political Behaviour: An Empirical Approach* [New York: Oxford University Press, 1947]). See further, McDougal, "The Role of Law in World Politics," *University of Mississippi Law Journal*, XX (1949); and McDougal and Gertrude C. K. Leighton, "The Rights of Man in the World Community: Constitutional Illusions versus Rational Action," *Yale Law Journal*, LIX (1949). The eight value terms are developed in Lasswell and Abraham Kaplan, *Power and Society: A Framework for Political Inquiry* (New Haven: Yale University Press, 1950).

must be conceded that anti-progressive tendencies may win out. In a crisis of such serious proportions, we may be disposed to cramp our interpretations into a single mould. As a precaution against the warping effect of these factors, we use more than one construct, and continually weigh these alternatives against one another.

Alternative One: The historic trend away from caste societies will continue until the free man's commonwealth is achieved on a global stage. A commonwealth is free to the extent that values are widely rather than narrowly shared: power, respect, rectitude, affection, wealth, well-being, skill, enlightenment.

Alternative Two: The direction of history is reversing itself, and moves toward the restoring of caste. More specifically: Assuming that the world crisis of insecurity continues, power and other values will be further concentrated in a few hands in the name of providing for the common defense. As the world is bipolarized between the United States and the Soviet Union, perpetual crisis favors the loss of freedom, and the eventual consolidation of garrison-police states. As power and influence concentrate in the hands of the soldier and political policeman, other groups decline in weight, perhaps disappearing entirely (such as the businessman and the free professional man in the Soviet Union). In the end, if the process is carried to the logical (thinkable) conclusion, the leaders of the garrison-police state will constitute the top layer of the new caste system. . . .

The Critique of Values

We now consider in further detail the specific framework of values which are postulated in the present inquiry. We associate ourselves with the dignity of man, the ideal aim of American policy. Our list of eight values can be directly related to the "life, liberty, and pursuit of happiness" of the Declaration of Independence. For life we read "well-being." Liberty includes the ideal of shared "power," and "enlightenment"; and since liberty is not license, it includes shared "rectitude" in the sense of a responsible attitude toward the fundamental goals of a free society. The pursuit of happiness is the pursuit of property ("wealth") and "respect" and of opportunity for the acquisition and exercise of "skill." It is also congenial intimate relations, and devotion to the larger group ("affection").

The choice of eight categories for the classification of values is the result of several considerations, one of which is the simple need of brevity in characterizing a fundamental phase of the social process. We think of the social process as man pursuing *values* through *institutions* on *resources*. In describing values we need a short list which can be used from culture to culture for the purpose of classifying the inexhaustible detail of "institutions." We expect to find "power" or "respect" in all cultures, but the "institutional practices" specialized to the shaping and sharing of power or any other value will be enormously diversified.

The categories are influenced by the division of academic labor in the United States and in Western Europe. Each of our value-institution relations is the subject of specialized research and teaching in the social and psychological sciences. Power and government are studied by political scientists, lawyers, and specialists on international politics; wealth and economic institutions come within the province of economists; respect and social class institutions are the concern of sociologists and anthropologists who are specialized on the study of social structure; well-being comes within the scope of social medicine; enlightenment is the subject matter of specialists on mass media and public instruction; affection and the institutions of family, friendship, and large-group loyalty fall mainly within the field of sociology, social psychology, and anthropology; rectitude and the institutions of morality concern students of comparative religious and moral standards; skill and the institutions of skill are the field of specialists upon professions and vocations (and include aesthetic creation and criticism).

We do not assume that the values are embedded in genes and chromosomes; rather, it is to be discovered by empirical study whether any clear line of development connects the genetic predispositions of original nature with the ultimate choice of roles in any given society.

Although we do not assume that the eight values are definitive, we have found no difficulty in classifying the institutional detail from societies of widely contrasting culture. (Perhaps it is worth repeating that the rank enjoyed by one value in relation to another is to be ascertained by empirical investigation, whether we are considering the personality as a whole or as a culture.)

No amount of empirical research can be expected to alter our basic preference for human dignity, rather than the indignity of man. If other cultures, or if parts of our own culture, do not share our fundamental standard of judgment, we want to know it, partly as a matter of scientific curiosity, and partly for the purpose of discovering the courses of action by which destructive discrepancies between goals and acts can be overcome (at least sacrifice of values).

To say that we do not intend to change our basic values in the light of more facts does not mean that we are determined to be unaffected by the facts revealed by research. Although our attachment to human dignity is an absolute of intention, we do not know how to recognize all the institutional means by which human dignity can be made explicit in all conceivable circumstances. Perhaps the principal function of a comprehensive program of global and historical inquiry is that of assisting in the discovery of which institutional patterns exemplify our goal values in various contexts, and which condition the realization of these goals in concrete circumstances.

In recent years it has become increasingly apparent how complex is the conception of human dignity. It is not within the scope of the present discussion to celebrate or to justify the dignity of man, rewarding as such an enterprise may be. The special problem at hand is that of amplifying our brief definitions of human dignity in more specific ("operational") terms. The moment anyone tries to pass from the "ambiguous" to the "operational," empirical questions arise. For example: how many members of the adult population, participating how often in the election of official personnel, enable us to classify a given institution as "democratic" (power-sharing)?

Fortunately, it is seldom useful to draw lines separating the "either" from the "or." For comparative purposes it is more fruitful to describe the full pattern of an election (in its community context) than to evolve and apply super-precise definitions in a pedantic and routine way. We shall therefore seldom classify specific details as "X" or "not X" ("democratic," "non-democratic," for instance). By describing the practices which are relevant to the making of an ultimate judgment of the context, we defer the classification of concrete patterns until the whole has been described.

In this way we soften the difficulties that arise in cross-cultural or cross-period research. The experts on any period, or culture, know the connection between each detail and the whole. Although our value categories facilitate the ultimate comparison of one total context with another, we do not begin by making these comparisons. On the contrary, we encourage the specialist to use his customary habits of work, and to start by assuming the frame of mind of the participants in the culture or period under consideration. Then he is able to decide whether the participants recognize a cluster of patterns called "governmental" or "economic" as constituting an identifiable entity. (And so on through the value-institution list.) "Functional" classifications are made when "conventional" data are available for the entire context. . . .

Democracy (Shared Power)

The first value mentioned in our list is power, and the first goal value specifies our preference for the wide sharing of power in the community, hence ultimately in the world community. The short definition of power is "decision making," a definition which is intended to distinguish decisions from other acts of choice, such as buying or selling in a competitive market. The distinction is made by stipulating the nature of the perspectives that must be realized in the concrete situation. We specify that a decision is the culminating point of a situation in which the participants entertain certain "expectations" and "demands." The expectation is that the choice to be made will be defended against any challenger (present or prospective) by inflicting extreme deprivations upon him. The demand is for a share in making the choice. We can therefore speak of the passing of a statute by a legislature as constituting a decision if it is assumed by the legislators that the statute will be enforced against any challenger, and if the members of the legislature demand a voice in passing the statute. In many situations it is obvious that the demand to participate is restricted to a few, even though the expectation is widely entertained that the choice is enforceable. Even where the demand to participate is widely shared, there may be denial in fact.

When severe deprivation is taken as a defining characteristic of a decision, we do not limit the deprivation to the well-being value, such as the imposition of capital punishment. Any value may be at stake, as when a business is confiscated (wealth deprivation), or reputations are ruined (respect deprivation).

We assess power according to the degree of influence exerted over decisions, which is a matter of position in the final outcome (vote or military victory, for instance), and also of impact upon pre-outcome activities.

In the empirical study of power it is a matter of research convenience to begin with indexes of "conventionally" defined institutions of "government." We then consider whatever institutions are locally assumed to specialize upon the "influencing" of government, such as "political parties" and "pressure groups." Before the final inventory of power relations, functionally defined, the entire network of community institutions must be surveyed (since it may be true that severe deprivations are in fact not limited to the "conventional" institutions of government).

"*Government.*" When we begin with what is locally known as "government," the first step is to describe the prevailing myth. We therefore look for the doctrines pertaining to power which embody the "high-level abstractions" on the subject, and endorse or condemn power sharing. We examine the formulations made in fundamental documents, or in declarations by prominent figures. (The Declaration of Independence; Lincoln's Gettysburg Address.)

Since doctrinal statements are not necessarily binding, they may not be part of the formula, which are the authoritative prescriptions of the community. The "law" of a given body politic prescribes "who" is authorized to decide "what." If the authority to change the constitution is vested in the people as a whole, acting directly by referendum or indirectly through elected officials, the state is democratically organized (to this extent). The same criteria apply to decisions which are less comprehensive in scope than constitutional questions. In a democratic formula, referenda or elections must be prescribed at frequent intervals, and the freedom of choice on the part of voters must be safeguarded.

The miranda of a body politic are democratic when the popular version of history and destiny assume that decisions are properly in the hands of the people. In a full democracy the songs, poetry, anecdotes, and dramas portray and reinforce the democratic ideal.

After describing the myth of a given body politic, we turn to the myth in action (the technique of power). We look first at the outcomes of decision-making situations. Even though the constitutional document calls for regular and popular elections, we may learn that no elections are actually held, or that, if held, they are participated in by a minute fraction of the people. Unless elections are frequent and participation is general, we cannot regard power as shared.

Even when elections are frequent and non-voting is rare, we cannot be sure that democracy prevails unless coercion is at a minimum. In the absence of further information, the absence of a minority (opposition) vote is a suspicious sign (in large industrial states). In a large state, when minorities are constantly crossing from the victory to the loss column, and back again, power is shared. The presence of a chronic minority (composed of the same members) does not necessarily contradict the requirements of a democratic polity, since nothing in democratic theory says that every individual must want what the majority wants when the majority wants it. This is true, even when it is admitted that deeply entrenched differences may compromise the unity and security of the commonwealth. (But this refers to a conditioning and not a defining factor.)

Another partial index of democracy is the turnover of elected officials, which indicates something of the responsiveness of leadership. If there is little change in personnel, common sense tells us that this may be because the leaders know how to entrench themselves against shifting sentiments among the rank and file. This presumption can be refuted under special circumstances, as in Britain, where Parliament dispenses with general elections during war, and resumes the practice once fighting stops.

It is also true that rapid official turnover is not invariably a sign of effective control by the rank and file. The French Chamber can overturn the Cabinet without running the risk of a general election, which puts a premium on personal and factional maneuvers to reorganize the Cabinet. The no-confidence vote is not used for the purpose of forging a general working agreement on policy.

A partial index of sharing is afforded by the affiliation of decision makers with the social structure. Few would doubt that people are likely to be more powerful when they are represented among decision makers than when they are not. The simple fact of representation does not make sure that the viewpoint of a person or a group will be considered, much less that it will prevail; but to say the least, representation is rarely a handicap. We take the weight of representation as indicating something of the existing distribution of power.

While diversity of affiliation with all parts of the community is a plausible index of representation, such an index may be falsified by such practices as separation from the home and neighborhood, as in the civil service of Byzantium.

The preceding indexes have referred to the line-up at the terminal phase of decision making. It is important to consider the earlier phases of the process. Investigation may show that terror is used to shape the final consensus, or that bribery and favoritism may be decisive. We know that every conceivable gradation exists between power as physical intimidation and as persuasion techniques. When we are examining the values by means of which decisions are affected, we are studying the "base" values by which "scope" values are affected. Power may be a base for protecting and expanding power—as indeed may every value.

Any systematic study of base values calls for the surveying of routes along which policies are whipped into shape. No completely systematic research of this kind has been published, although case studies give ample indication of the routes prevailing now or in the past in the U.S., for example. Initiative often lies with the executive departments and agencies, rather than with the Congress; also, legislative and administrative ideas often germinate in the minds of individuals connected with the numerous pressure organizations.

The analyst of politics must go further than the simple recording of routes along which specific decisions are formulated. Part of his problem is the study of *potential* as well as actual power. What *might* happen under various conditions of changes in the environment or in the internal equilibrium of a specific body politic? Since many thinkable contingencies have been but partially approximated in any known historical situation, analytic work is essential to the setting up of hypotheses which may be verified only under future circumstances.

When we analyze the past as a guide to the future, it is important to keep two "yardsticks" distinct from one another. A decision may be classified according to a standard which is satisfactory to a historian or political scientist. But the decision may also be described from the point of view of the decision maker. To some observers, a big frog in a small pool is nevertheless a very little frog. But the little frog may think that he "does all right." The present question refers to whether little frogs are satisfied to croak where they are, or whether they want to move along. And it is obvious that with unrealized aspirations, tension may continue to be stirred up despite apparent success.

As a means of estimating political conduct, it is useful to re-classify the decisions made during a given period according to the intensity of the conflict involved. The assumption is that a gauge of intensity is the degree to which a participant is willing to sacrifice or to imperil his value position.

It is often possible to discover which values are close to the core of the value system of an individual or group. This particularly is important in the study of international politics, for instance, since a major question is under what circumstances will a nation believe that it is in serious danger. The people of the U.S. were far from united in perceiving the magnitude of the threat represented by certain countries in 1914 and 1939. The technical question may be stated in these terms: what communications or overt events will be interpreted as threatening when brought to the focus of attention? Manifestly, such responses will depend upon the predispositions of the official or unofficial persons who are exposed to the reports or incidents. In estimating potential acts in the arena of politics it is necessary to make an inventory of probable environing changes, and of probable levels of predisposition.

"Political Parties and Pressure Groups." From the study of "government" a comprehensive inquiry will turn to the examination of associations which are conventionally assumed to affect official acts.

For many purposes it is enough to define a political party as an organization specialized to the presenting of candidates and of issues under its own name in elections. (Elections are defined so that any significant use of coercion is excluded.) So conceived, the term "party" does not apply to the so-called "single parties" of the totalitarian regimes, since no true elections occur. We speak of Communist, Nazi, and Fascist organizations as "political orders" rather than true parties (when it is useful to be precise).

Often it is convenient to restrict the definition of a political party in another direction. If a "party" sticks to one issue, and refrains from offering a comprehensive program, it is a different kind of organization from the party with a comprehensive program. Single-issue parties have more in common with pressure groups than the true party. The following definitions exclude Prohibition pressure groups as "parties": Political parties are organizations which put forward candidates and comprehensive programs under their own names in elections; pressure groups are specialized to the bringing of the influence of the electorate to bear upon governments and political parties, without organizing as a party.

In a comprehensive study of any party or pressure group, the same categories apply as in describing the decision making process in "government," including myth and technique . . .

Fraternity

The next step is to consider the values connected with "fraternity": to wit, the sharing of respect, rectitude, affection, and enlightenment. We deal first with respect, enlarging first upon the functional definition of the term.

Shared Respect. What are the "outcomes" of a situation relatively specialized to respect? We speak of "prestige," the giving and receiving of affirmations or denials of one's worth as a human being, and of one's individual merit. An elementary example of giving and receiving prestige is a testimonial dinner, or the conferring of a decoration. More complex examples are the inclusion or exclusion of persons from access to any value on grounds irrelevant to merit. We speak of respect as shared in a community where the prevailing myth declares that individuals are worthy of respect because they are human, and also because of personal merit. "Careers open to talent" sloganizes one of the great doctrines of respect; and when this is a rule laid down by public or private associations, the slogan is also part of the formula. If the slogan is disseminated in the folklore, it is also part of the miranda.

The most direct method of ascertaining the relation between myth and technique is to examine the operative facts at first hand. In communities where the myth does not provide for a rigid class and rank system (and indeed may expressly repudiate such a structure), research may demonstrate that respect groups do in fact exist, though perhaps not strictly "hereditary." In the U.S.A. studies have been made during recent decades of the class pattern of several cities and towns. One procedure is to induce everyone to classify everyone else. Such testimony is the most advantageous index of prestige distinctions. (Other indexes may be used, but they are most satisfactory when they can be calibrated with direct testimony.) Community members are continually classifying one another according to social class, a category which can be defined as the largest group demanding and obtaining the same distinctions.

The prestige pattern of any community can be most successfully described by qualified persons who participate intimately in local life. In an inquiry into the working of caste and class in a southern town, three field workers spent eighteen months on the spot. The observers entered the situation as "adopted" classmates of individuals occupying high positions in the Negro and White caste strata. While they were learning how to act toward the other castes, they were also being inducted into the stratification internal to each caste.[4]

Since respect is only shared when it is given and received on the basis of personal merit, it is necessary to go beyond the static distribution of respect, and to discover how these distributions are related to merit. Although the individual may be a reliable source of knowledge on how he classifies other persons, he is not a reliable source for the bases of prestige, or for estimating the degree to which the values affecting prestige are accessible. Comparative knowledge of culture is indispensable to the making of such appraisals.

It is possible to obtain a rough guide to the facts in a given community by constructing an index of aggregate mobility among prestige positions. If there is little shift from one generation to another, so that families neither rise nor fall, it is reasonable to infer that a *de facto* set of castes exists, and that respect standards are violated.

Even where the aggregate index of mobility from one prestige position to another shows that there has been active interchange, the results cannot be taken without further study as a satisfactory index of shared respect since comparable access to the values on the basis of which individuals rose or fell may not have been provided.

---

[4] A. Davis, B. B. Gardner and M. R. Gardner, *Deep South: A Social Anthropological Study of Caste and Class* (Chicago: University of Chicago Press, 1941).

Light can be thrown upon the openness of access to base values by case studies of rising and falling persons and families.

Since respect outcomes are often unorganized (though not unstructured) scholars have less experience in gathering indices of respect than of power.

Shared Rectitude. We speak of a "rectitude outcome" when the participants are making evaluations of goodness or badness. More generally, a rectitude evaluation is in terms of responsibility or irresponsibility. Such judgments are prevailingly serious, sober, insistent. Indeed, a typical response to violation of a positive standard is moral indignation.

In a civilized society, there is little difficulty in finding doctrinal statements about power. Doctrines relating to rectitude, however, are likely to be less comprehensive. In Western culture, however, general rules of ethics do exist: "Do unto others as ye would they do unto you," "Honor thy father and thy mother," and so on.

Apparently some cultures have few if any general propositions about ethics. It is reported that the "good-bad" dichotomy is entirely absent from some cultures. Rules for the guidance of conduct may be found in profusion, but phrased as imperatives. In terms of content, such rules are commands sanctioned by threat of deprivations said to emanate from natural or supernatural forces. The conception of "ought" as a value (distinguished from a "must" supported by fear of annihilation by supernatural powers) is what we define as rectitude. It is not a question of terror-stricken conformity, but of perspectives in which the "self" demands that the "self" adhere to norms in harmony with, and contributory to, interpersonal relations.

Our doctrinal postulate is that each person ought to feel, think, and act responsibly for the purpose of perfecting the good society (defined as the maximum sharing of all values). We have in mind personalities who demand (of themselves and others) the bringing of conduct into harmony with the goal values of a free society. A responsible person chides himself for any failure to live up to the norm, and tries to do better next time. The point can be phrased by saying that we want a sense of impulsion to act for the common good; and we want this sense free of compulsiveness. ("Compulsiveness" is an imperious impulse not open to insight; that is, to self-knowledge). We are speaking of seriousness without solemnity, earnestness without morbidity, persistence without flagellation. The sense of responsibility, as we understand it, is serenity of mind, not a neurotic symptom of disassociation or of obsession. We are recommending that human beings respect one another. We are also saying that it is right for human beings to do so; and that it is right to share power, wealth, and other values.

In estimating the degree to which common standards of rectitude prevail in a given society, it is illuminating to go beyond doctrine to the formula, and to study the criminal codes. Criminal codes are not necessarily phrased in the language of rectitude. Statements which unambiguously express an ethical demand use terms like "ought." Strictly speaking, the statement, "If you hurt him, we'll hurt you," is no assertion of rectitude. "You ought not hurt him; if you do, we'll hurt you" includes one rectitude statement. It is more complete when amplified: "You ought not hurt him; but if you do, I ought to hurt you, and I will." In practice, statements found in social formulas are often condensed and elliptical. (Obviously, words like "criminal, immoral, vicious, and unethical" are synonymous in English for "ought not" in describing a pattern of conduct.)

Besides the criminal codes of the state, there are disciplinary provisions in most organizations, regardless of the value or values to which they are specialized. In our civilization the church is conventionally regarded as specialized to rectitude; and systems of canon law are worked out in detail.

In our civilization, as in others, a vast miranda exists for the moral guidance of young and old.

It is desirable to use field research in attempting to connect the rectitude myth of a given society with the facts of overt conduct. In probing into respect, we noted the usefulness of having the members of a community classify one another. In studying rectitude, such a procedure is less helpful, since in complex societies only extremes of "good" or "bad" are clearly recognized. In studying rectitude-in-action it is expedient to begin with organized, and then to investigate unorganized activity.[5]

If we start with churches, we look for the occasions when evaluations of rectitude are made. When we analyze the rules invoked in condemning unruly members, it may appear that some rules are never, or almost never invoked, which points to a probable discrepancy between standard and conduct. (Final judgment will depend upon studying circumstances in which it would be appropriate for the rule, taken textually, to be invoked.) By comparing the record of one church with all the churches in the society we learn something of the degree of consensus in interpreting rectitude.

Besides noting which rules are invoked for the purpose of stigmatizing offenders, we see in what terms favorable judgments are expressed. If there are numerous citations for morality in the name of a standard which is actively invoked at the same time in disciplinary cases, there is evidence of conflict over the standard, either because it is questioned, or because inducements to violations are great.

Shared Affection. Turning briefly to indexes of affection, we note that in some societies doctrine emphasizes the significance of affection in human nature, and glorifies the ideal of congenial human relations (the family circle, and ever-enlarging circles until the world community is itself included). On the other hand, doctrines may portray man as a

---

[5] The contextual view of a "rule" is described with characteristic clarity and vigor in Bronislaw Malinowski, *Crime and Custom in Savage Society* (New York: Harcourt, Brace, 1926).

predatory rather than a loving animal. Between these extremes lie doctrines which teach that human nature is partly lovable, partly unlovable. . . .

In order to study the distribution of affection special techniques have been invented by social scientists and psychologists. As in the assessment of respect, the statements made by the giver of affection provide the most satisfactory data about the fact of a relationship. (Other indexes can be appraised in terms of the results of such direct testimony taken under appropriate conditions.) One method is to ask every member of a group to make a confidential ranking of all other members according to congeniality. The question can be posed in reference to some concrete possibility, such as working or living together.

Rough estimates of congeniality can often be made on the basis of such relatively crude indexes as conspicuous failures of congeniality (divorce, for instance).

Shared Enlightenment. When we study the shaping and sharing of enlightenment, we are reminded of the high importance attributed to enlightenment in the doctrinal tradition of the Western world. In many communities, however, we find that doctrine and formula are united in opposition to the idea that there should be wide access to available knowledge on matters of important public policy. Measures hostile to enlightenment may be negative (censorship) or positive (as when propaganda is deceptive or distractive). In the West the miranda typically include the demand to give currency to the doings of public officials, at least.

The giving and receiving of knowledge is the culminating relationship in an enlightenment situation. A direct index of sharing is the state of public information on significant questions of policy. It is also possible to describe the contents of the media of communication in order to discover their degree of conformity to such standards of sharing as the following:

Everyone has access to media of communication in which news of current developments is reported; the media provide interpretations of the news which place them in relationship to a comprehensive context in which goals, alternatives, trends, factors, and projections are included; members of the community have access to media for the dissemination of facts and interpretations; the sources of statements are disclosed on which policy judgments depend; there is a presumption against lying; there is a presumption against non-rational statement (the irrelevant, for example); there is a presumption in favor of statements from a competent source; there is a presumption against advocacy or neutrality, and in favor of inquiry.

Security

By the term security we mean the sharing of the values of well-being, wealth, and skill.

Shared Well-Being. The culminating moment in well-being, positively conceived, is an interpersonal relationship in which the psychic and somatic potentials of the participants are at their highest. Without going into detail, we think of well-being as shared under these conditions:

The myth emphasizes the importance of somatic and psychic well-being and interprets the ideal in a scientifically acceptable manner; there is adequate treatment of the diseased, injured, and handicapped; there are deliberate and successful efforts to prevent disease, injury, and handicap; progress is being made toward optimum psychic and somatic activity throughout life; the motives and circumstances leading to suicide, murder, war, and civil violence are reduced or eliminated; progress is made toward the lengthening of life.

Because of our great concern for ultimate freedom from deprivations of well-being imposed in the name of social groups (like belligerent nations) indexes of the following type are of particular interest to us (in addition to general information about the incidence of mortality and morbidity):

Number of casualties by years in war
Casualties by years in revolutions, revolts and rebellions
Casualties in other group conflicts (labor-management, ethnic, religious, etc.)
Proportion of civilian and military casualties in war
Proportion of women and children casualties in war
Position in the social structure of war casualties (affiliations in terms of power, wealth, etc.)
(Maps) Where casualties occurred in wars; revolutions, revolts, and rebellions; other group conflicts; in relation to origin of the victim (e.g., U.S. casualties in World War II inside and outside continental U.S.)
Changes of government by violence
War scares among the powers (periods of intense expectation relating to war)
Scares concerning other forms of group violence (revolution, revolt, rebellion, other group conflicts)
Peace demands (intense activity demanding an end to specific wars or to wars in general; demands for civic concord)
Conflict demands (support of war in general or specific wars; other forms of violent clash)
Proportion of national income spent on armament, police, and informal violence (or violence preparation)
Number under arms by years in various branches
Length of military experience among citizens of a power
(Map) Most important permanent military installations
Policemen in government service
Policemen in private and quasi-private military formations[6]

Shared Wealth. We speak of wealth as shared under the following broad conditions:

---

[6] A convenient beginning is in Quincy Wright, *A Study of War* (2 vols.; Chicago: University of Chicago Press, 1942).

The myth emphasizes the importance of expanding production in order to have the possibility of expanding the standard of living; the myth stresses the importance of a balanced (graduated) distribution rather than a division of the community into "rich" and "poor"; a progressively larger aggregate income is available for distribution; the pattern of income distribution is in fact balanced (graduated) rather than dichotomous; security of basic income is guaranteed in theory and fact; opportunities are open to every capable person to earn more than the basic income; opportunities are provided to develop potential capacities as producers and consumers.

Because of the great importance of economic changes in modern times it is possible to present a rather comprehensive picture of the economic relations called for in the previous paragraph.

Shared Skill. We speak of skill as a distinct value and take as the culminating moment in a skill situation the "performance," since a performance provides both the exerciser of the skill with an outlet and the audience with an occasion for the exercise of taste. Many doctrines endorse skill. But skill may also be de-emphasized, not only when there is neglect, but through the endorsement of attitudes that minimize incentives for skill. Indolence and casualness, for example, may be "aristocratic," and "luck" may lead to the disregarding of skill. Skills are intimately interwoven with all values, since the processes of creation are usually capable of being thought about separately and made the subject of deliberate efforts at the improvement of performance. Thus in some societies the base value for power, prosperity, health, and holiness (rectitude) may be the skillful conduct of rituals and ceremonies.

The formula in a given culture may prescribe tournaments of skill. In industrial societies the requirement of full employment is often justified as a means of preventing the skill deterioration of the working and managerial force. Provision is usually made for discovering and developing talent, notably by the system of instruction. Among prescribed arrangements designed to encourage skill, may be cited the laws of patent and copyright.

Folklore, of course, is saturated with references to skill. Some legends appear to work against the cultivation of skill by stressing the degree to which it is a matter of inborn "genius."

When we look into the actual practices of a society, we discover that the level of performance is constantly being appraised as high, mediocre, or low; and that performers are classified accordingly. The degree of skill mastery can be approximately ascertained from the systems of examination and certification in vogue in some societies. Sometimes a register of professional and non-professional skills exists.

We speak of a community as exhibiting a high level of shared skill when the following conditions occur:

The myth attaches importance to the maturing of latent talent into socially acceptable skills and encourages excellence of performance; opportunities are provided for the full exercise of skills (full employment); opportunities are made available for the discovery of latent capacity and for its development; the base values upon which the acquisition and exercise of skill depend are accessible according to merit.

This emphasis upon skill as a value comes in part from the psychological study of individuals, which underlines the fact that among the deepest sources of human gratification are the maturing of latent capacities, including the tastes. Every form of expression develops perceptions of style which characterize the arrangement of the elements of which the entire performance is composed. These criteria are "intrinsic" and have no necessary reference to the "extrinsic" ends for which the operation may be carried out.[7]

Interrelated Values and Indexes

We have been discussing goal values up to the present point as though they were capable of being segregated into separate compartments for which distinct indexes can be obtained. For purposes of analysis this is a convenient introduction. But once certain differentiations have been made, it is important to underline the extent to which any sequence of human activity involves all values in varying degree. Consider what goes on in a legislative session: from the standpoint of power, we may identify certain power culminations, like the final vote on a controversial bill. We also identify respect culminations, since the legislators may make laudatory or contemptuous remarks about one another (and others). It is possible to detect enlightenment culminations, as when pertinent information is presented for the consideration of the group. Affection culminations are involved, as when friendly jokes and allusions are made. Rectitude culminations take the form of denunciations. Skill may be exemplified in the adroitness of the presiding officer. Wealth may be transferred as a reward for successful manipulation of the legislature and the public. The stress and strain of the session may take its toll in the health of members. To some extent these culminations occupy a "base-scope" relationship.

Each index presupposes a procedure by the use of which the scientific observer relates himself to the context which he is to describe. It has been implied, though not made explicit, that the procedures vary in the intensiveness of the orientation required of the scientific observer toward the situation. Intensiveness is partly a question of time, since the participant-observer who spends several weeks with a legislature may be expected to arrive at a more penetrating characterization of the situation than a more cursory observer. Intensiveness is partly a question of the use of special or laymanlike methods. Among the special methods may be the

---

[7] The importance of allowing latent talent to mature into socially useful skill is a major theme in the psychology of education and of industrial employment, in particular.

use of tests (such as projective tests) or psychiatric interviews. Systematic content analyses may be applied to the speeches on the floor and the conversations in the anteroom.

45. SOME SOCIAL REQUISITES OF DEMOCRACY*

Seymour M. Lipset

THE CONDITIONS associated with the existence and stability of democratic society have been a leading concern of political philosophy. In this paper the problem is attacked from a sociological and behavioral standpoint, by presenting a number of hypotheses concerning some social requisites for democracy, and by discussing some of the data available to test these hypotheses. In its concern with conditions—values, social institutions, historical events—external to the political system itself which sustain different general types of political systems, the paper moves outside the generally recognized province of political sociology. This growing field has dealt largely with the internal analysis of organizations with political goals, or with the determinants of action *within* various political institutions, such as parties, government agencies, or the electoral process. It has in the main left to the political philosopher the larger concern with the relations of the total political system to society as a whole.

INTRODUCTION

A sociological analysis of any pattern of behavior, whether referring to a small or a large social system, must result in specific hypotheses, empirically testable statements. Thus, in dealing with democracy, one must be able to point to a set of conditions that have actually existed in a number of countries, and say: democracy has emerged out of these conditions, and has become stabilized because of certain supporting institutions and values, as well as because of its own internal self-maintaining processes. The conditions listed must be ones which differentiate most democratic states from most others. . . .

Clearly in order to discuss democracy, or any other phenomenon, it is first necessary to define it. For the purposes of this paper, democracy (in a complex society) is defined as a political system which supplies regular constitutional opportunities for changing the governing officials. It is a social mechanism for the resolution of the problem of societal decision-making among conflicting interest groups which permits the largest

* From "Some Social Requisites of Democracy: Economic Development and Political Legitimacy," *The American Political Science Review*, Vol. LIII, No. 1 (March, 1959). By permission.

possible part of the population to influence these decisions through their ability to choose among alternative contenders for political office. In large measure abstracted from the work of Joseph Schumpeter and Max Weber,[1] this definition implies a number of specific conditions: (a) a "political formula," a system of beliefs, legitimizing the democratic system and specifying the institutions—parties, a free press, and so forth—which are legitimized, *i.e.*, accepted as proper by all; (b) one set of political leaders in office; and (c) one or more sets of leaders, out of office, who act as a legitimate opposition attempting to gain office.

The need for these conditions is clear. *First*, if a political system is not characterized by a value system allowing the peaceful "play" of power—the adherence by the "outs" to decisions made by "ins" and the recognition by "ins" of the rights of the "outs"—there can be no stable democracy. This has been the problem faced by many Latin American states. *Second*, if the outcome of the political game is not the periodic awarding of effective authority to one group, a party or stable coalition, then unstable and irresponsible government rather than democracy will result. This state of affairs existed in pre-Fascist Italy, and for much, though not all of the history of the Third and Fourth French Republics, which were characterized by weak coalition governments, often formed among parties which had major interest and value conflicts with each other. *Third*, if the conditions facilitating the perpetuation of an effective opposition do not exist, then the authority of officials will be maximized, and popular influence on policy will be at a minimum. This is the situation in all one party states, and by general agreement, at least in the West, these are dictatorships. . . .

No detailed examination of the political history of individual countries will be undertaken in accordance with the generic definition, since the relative degree or social content of democracy in different countries is not the real problem of this paper. Certain problems of method in the handling of relationships between complex characteristics of total societies do merit brief discussion, however.

An extremely high correlation between aspects of social structure, such as income, education, religion, on the one hand, and democracy, on the other, is not to be anticipated even on theoretical grounds, because to the extent that the political sub-system of the society operates autonomously, a particular political form may persist under conditions normally adverse to the *emergence* of that form. Or, a political form may develop because of a syndrome of fairly unique historical factors, even though major social characteristics favor another form. Germany is an example of a nation in which the structural changes—growing industralization, urbanization, wealth, and education—all favored the establishment of a democratic

---

[1] Joseph Schumpeter, *Capitalism, Socialism and Democracy* (New York: Harper and Bros., 1947), pp. 232–302, esp. 269; Max Weber, *Essays in Sociology* (New York: Oxford University Press, 1946), p. 226.

system, but in which a series of adverse historical events prevented democracy from securing legitimacy in the eyes of many important segments of society, and thus weakened German democracy's ability to withstand crisis.

The high correlations which appear in the data to be presented between democracy and other institutional characteristics of societies must not be overly stressed, since unique events may account for *either* the persistence *or* the failure of democracy in any particular society. Max Weber argued strongly that differences in national patterns often reflect key historical events which set one process in motion in one country, and a second process in another. To illustrate his point, he used the analogy of a dice game in which each time the dice came up with a certain number they were increasingly loaded in the direction of coming up with that number again.[2] To Weber, an event predisposing a country toward democracy sets a process in motion which increases the likelihood that at the next critical point in the country's history democracy will win out again. This process can only have meaning if we assume that once established, a democratic political system gathers some momentum, and creates some social supports (institutions) to ensure its continued existence. Thus a "premature" democracy which survives will do so by (among other things) facilitating the growth of other conditions conducive to democracy, such as universal literacy, or autonomous private associations. This paper is primarily concerned with explicating the social conditions which serve to *support* a democratic political system, such as education or legitimacy; it will not deal in detail with the kinds of internal mechanisms which serve to *maintain* democratic systems such as the specific rules of the political game.

Comparative generalizations dealing with complex social systems must necessarily deal rather summarily with particular historical features of any one society within the scope of the investigation. In order to test these generalizations bearing on the differences between countries which rank high or low in possession of the attributes associated with democracy, it is necessary to establish some empirical measures of the type of political system. Individual deviations from a particular aspect of democracy are not too important, as long as the definitions unambiguously cover the great majority of nations which are located as democratic or undemocratic. The precise dividing line between "more democratic" and "less democratic" is also not a basic problem, since presumably democracy is *not* a quality of a social system which either does or does not exist, but is rather a complex of characteristics which may be ranked in many different ways. For this reason it was decided to divide the countries under consideration into two groups, rather than to attempt to rank them from highest to lowest. Ranking *individual* countries from the most to the

---

[2] Max Weber, *The Methodology of the Social Sciences* (Glencoe, Ill.: The Free Press, 1949), pp. 182–185; see also S. M. Lipset, "A Sociologist Looks at History," *Pacific Sociological Review,* Vol. 1 (Spring, 1958), pp. 13–17.

least democratic is much more difficult than splitting the countries into two classes, "more" or "less" democratic, although even here borderline cases such as Mexico pose problems.

Efforts to classify all countries raise a number of problems. Most countries which lack an enduring tradition of political democracy lie in the traditionally underdeveloped sections of the world. It is possible that Max Weber was right when he suggested that modern democracy in its clearest forms can only occur under the unique conditions of capitalist industrialization. Some of the complications introduced by the sharp variations in political practices in different parts of the earth can be reduced by dealing with differences among countries within political culture areas. The two best areas for such internal comparison are Latin America as one, and Europe and the English-speaking countries as the other. More limited comparisons may be made among the Asian states, and among the Arab countries.

The main criteria used in this paper to locate European democracies are the uninterrupted continuation of political democracy since World War I, *and* the absence over the past 25 years of a major political movement opposed to the democratic "rules of the game."[3] The somewhat less stringent criterion employed for Latin America is whether a given country has had a history of more or less free elections for most of the post-World War I period. Where in Europe we look for stable democracies, in South America we look for countries which have not had fairly constant dictatorial rule (See Table I). No detailed analysis of the political history

TABLE I

CLASSIFICATION OF EUROPEAN, ENGLISH-SPEAKING AND LATIN AMERICAN NATIONS BY DEGREE OF STABLE DEMOCRACY

European and English-speaking Nations		*Latin American Nations*	
Stable Democracies	Unstable Democracies and Dictatorships	Democracies and Unstable Dictatorships	Stable Dictatorships
Australia	Austria	Argentina	Bolivia
Belgium	Bulgaria	Brazil	Cuba
Canada	Czechoslovakia	Chile	Dominican Republic
Denmark	Finland	Colombia	Ecuador
Ireland	France	Costa Rica	El Salvador
Luxemburg	Germany (West)	Mexico	Guatemala
Netherlands	Greece	Uruguay	Haiti
New Zealand	Hungary		Honduras
Norway	Iceland		Nicaragua
Sweden	Italy		Panama
Switzerland	Poland		Paraguay
United Kingdom	Portugal		Peru
United States	Rumania		Venezuela
	Spain		
	Yugoslavia		

[3] The latter requirement means that no totalitarian movement, either Fascist or Communist, received 20 per cent of the vote during this time. Actually all the European nations falling on the democratic side of the continuum had totalitarian movements which secured less than seven per cent of the vote.

of either Europe or Latin America has been made with an eye toward more specific criteria of differentiation; at this point in the examination of the requisites of democracy, election results are sufficient to locate the European countries, and the judgments of experts and impressionistic assessments based on fairly well-known facts of political history will suffice for Latin America. . . .[4]

[ED.—Professor Lipset's discussion of economic development and democracy is omitted.]

It is obvious that democracy and the conditions related to stable democracy are essentially located in the countries of northwest Europe and their English-speaking offspring in America and Australasia. It has been argued by Max Weber among others that the factors making for democracy in this area are a historically unique concatenation of elements, part of the complex which also produced capitalism in this area. The basic argument runs that capitalist economic development (facilitated and most developed in Protestant areas) created the burgher class whose existence was both a catalyst and a necessary condition for democracy. The emphasis within Protestantism on individual responsibility furthered the emergence of democratic values. The greater initial strength of the middle classes in these countries resulted in an alignment between burghers and throne, an alignment which preserved the monarchy, and thus facilitated the legitimation of democracy among the conservative strata. Thus we have an interrelated cluster of economic development, Protestantism, monarchy, gradual political change, legitimacy and democracy. Men may argue as to whether any aspect of this cluster is primary, but the cluster of factors and forces hangs together.

LEGITIMACY AND DEMOCRACY

In this section I turn to an examination of some of the requisites of democracy which are derived from specifically historical elements in this complex, particularly those which relate to the need of a democratic political system for legitimacy, and for mechanisms which reduce the intensity of political cleavage. These requisites are correlated with economic development, but are also distinct from it since they are elements in the political system itself.

---

[4] The historian Arthur P. Whitaker, for example, has summarized the judgments of experts on Latin America to be that "the countries which have approximated most closely to the democratic ideal have been . . . Argentina, Brazil, Chile, Colombia, Costa Rica, and Uruguay." See "The Pathology of Democracy in Latin America: A Historian's Point of View," *Am. Pol. Sci. R.,* Vol. 44 (1950), pp. 101–118. To this group I have added Mexico. Mexico has allowed freedom of the press, of assembly and of organization, to opposition parties, although there is good evidence that it does not allow them the opportunity to win elections, since ballots are counted by the incumbents. The existence of opposition groups, contested elections, and adjustments among the various factions of the governing *Partido Revolucionario Institucional* does introduce a considerable element of popular influence in the system. . . .

Legitimacy and Effectiveness. In the modern world . . . economic development involving industrialization, urbanization, high educational standards, and a steady increase in the overall wealth of the society, is a basic condition sustaining democracy; it is a mark of the efficiency of the total system.

But the stability of a given democratic system depends not only on the system's efficiency in modernization, but also upon the *effectiveness* and *legitimacy* of the political system. By effectiveness is meant the actual performance of a political system, the extent to which it satisfies the basic functions of government as defined by the expectations of most members of a society, and the expectations of powerful groups within it which might threaten the system, such as the armed forces. The effectiveness of a democratic political system, marked by an efficient bureaucracy and decision-making system, which is able to resolve political problems, can be distinguished from the efficiency of the total system, although breakdown in the functioning of the society as a whole will, of course, affect the political sub-system. Legitimacy involves the capacity of a political system to engender and maintain the belief that existing political institutions are the most appropriate or proper ones for the society. The extent to which contemporary democratic political systems are legitimate depends in large measure upon the ways in which the key issues which have historically divided the society have been resolved. It is the task of these sections of the paper to show *first*, how the degree of legitimacy of a democratic system may affect its capacity to survive the crises of effectiveness, such as depressions or lost wars and *second*, to indicate the ways in which the different resolutions of basic historical cleavages—which determine the legitimacy of various systems—also strengthen or weaken democracy through their effect on contemporary party struggles.

While effectiveness is primarily an instrumental dimension, legitimacy is more affective and evaluative. Groups will regard a political system as legitimate or illegitimate according to the way in which its values fit in with their primary values. Important segments of the Germany army, civil service, and aristocratic classes rejected the Weimar Republic not because it was ineffective, but because its symbolism and basic values negated their own. Legitimacy, in and of itself, may be associated with many forms of political organization, including oppressive ones. Feudal societies, before the advent of industrialism, undoubtedly enjoyed the basic loyalty of most of their members. Crises of legitimacy are primarily a recent historical phenomenon, following the rise of sharp cleavages among groups which have been able, because of mass communication resources, to organize around different values than those previously considered to be the only legitimate ones for the total society.

A crisis of legitimacy is a crisis of change, and therefore its roots, as a factor affecting the stability of democratic systems, must be sought in the character of change in modern society. It may be hypothesized that crises of legitimacy occur during a transition to a new social structure, if (a) all major groups do not secure access to the political system early in the transitional period, or at least as soon as they develop political demands; or, if (b) the *status* of major conservative institutions is threatened during the period of structural change. After a new social structure is established, if the new system is unable to sustain the expectations of major groups (on the grounds of "effectiveness") for a long enough period to develop legitimacy upon the new basis, a new crisis may develop.

Tocqueville gave a graphic description of the first general type of loss of legitimacy, referring mainly to countries which had moved from aristocratic monarchies to democratic republics: ". . . epochs sometimes occur in the life of a nation when the old customs of a people are changed, public morality is destroyed, religious belief shaken, and the spell of tradition broken. . . ." The citizens then have "neither the instinctive patriotism of a monarchy nor the reflecting patriotism of a republic; . . . they have stopped between the two in the midst of confusion and distress."

If, however, the status of major conservative groups and symbols is not threatened during this transitional period even though they lose most of their power, democracy seems to be much more secure. Striking evidence of the link between the preserved legitimacy of conservative institutions and democracy is the relationship between monarchy and democracy. Given the role of the American and French republican revolutions as the initiators of modern democratic political movements, the fact that ten out of 12 of the stable European and English-speaking democracies are monarchies seems a rather ludicrous correlation. Great Britain, Sweden, Norway, Denmark, the Netherlands, Belgium, Luxemburg, Australia, Canada, and New Zealand are kingdoms; while the only republics which meet the twin conditions, of stable democratic procedures since democracy was instituted, and the absence of a major totalitarian movement in the past 25 years, are the United States, Switzerland and Uruguay. Nations which have moved from absolutism and oligarchy (linked to a state church) to a democratic welfare state, while retaining the forms of monarchy, more frequently seem able to make changes while sustaining a continuous thread of legitimacy for their political institutions.[5]

The preservation of the monarchy has apparently retained for the system the loyalty of the aristocratic, traditionalist, and clerical sectors of the population which resented increased democratization and equalitarianism. And, by more graciously accepting the lower strata, by not resisting to the

---

[5] Walter Lippmann, referring to the seemingly greater capacity of the constitutional monarchies than the republics of Europe to "preserve order with freedom," suggests that this may be because "in a republic the governing power, being wholly secularized, loses much of its prestige; it is stripped, if one prefers, of all the illusions of intrinsic majesty." See his *The Public Philosophy* (New York: Mentor Books, 1956), p. 50.

point that revolution might be necessary, the conservative orders won or retained the loyalty of the new "citizens." Where monarchy was overthrown by revolution, and orderly succession was broken, those forces aligned with monarchy have sometimes continued to refuse legitimacy to republican successors down to the fifth generation or more.

The one constitutional monarchy which became a Fascist dictatorship, Italy, was, like the French Republic, relatively new and still illegitimate for major groups in the society. The House of Savoy alienated the Catholics by destroying the temporal power of the Popes, and was also not a legitimate successor in the old Kingdom of the Two Sicilies. Catholics, in fact, were forbidden by the church to participate in Italian politics until close to World War I, and the church rescinded its original ban only because of its fear of the Socialists. A similar attitude was taken by French Catholics to the Third Republic during the same period. Both Italian and French democracy have had to operate for much of their histories without loyal support from important groups in their society, both on the left and on the right. Thus, one main source of legitimacy lies in the continuity of primary conservative and integrative institutions during a transitional period in which new social institutions are emerging.

The second general type of loss of legitimacy is, as indicated above, related to the way in which societies handle the "entry into politics" problem. The determination of when new social groups shall obtain access to the political process affects the legitimacy of the political system, either for conservative or for emerging groups. In the 19th century these new groups were primarily industrial workers; the "entry into politics" crisis of the 20th century typically involves colonial elites, and peasant peoples. Whenever new groups become politically active (*e.g.*, when the workers first seek access to economic and political power through economic organization and the suffrage, when the bourgeoisie demanded access to and participation in government, when colonial elites demand control over their own system), comparatively easy access to the *legitimate* political institutions tends to win the loyalty of the new groups to the system, and they in turn can permit the old dominating strata to maintain their own status integrity. In nations such as Germany, where access was denied for prolonged periods, first to the bourgeoisie and later to the workers, and where force was used to restrict access, the lower strata were alienated from the system, and were led to adopt extremist ideologies which, in turn, alienated the more established groups from an acceptance of the workers' political movement as a legitimate alternative.

Political systems which denied new strata access to power except through revolutionary means also inhibited the growth of legitimacy by introducing millenial hopes into the political arena. Groups which feel obliged to push their way into the body politic through forceful means tend to overexaggerate the possibilities which political participation afford. Their hopes are for far more than the inherent limitations of political stability permit. Consequently, democratic regimes born under such stress will not only face the difficulty of being regarded as illegitimate by those groups loyal to the *ancien regime*, but may be also rejected by those whose millenial hopes were not fulfilled by the change. France seems to offer an example of such a phenomenon. Right-wing clericalists have viewed the Republic as illegitimate, while sections of the lower strata still impatiently await millenial fulfillment. Many of the newly independent nations of Asia and Africa face the problem of winning the loyalties of the masses to democratic states which can do little to fulfill the utopian objectives set by nationalist movements during the period of colonialism, and the transitional struggle to independence.

We have discussed several conditions bearing upon the maintenance, or the initial securing of legitimacy by a political system. Assuming reasonable effectiveness, if the status of major conservative groups is threatened, or if access to the political system is denied at crucial periods, the legitimacy of the system will remain in question. Even in legitimate systems, a breakdown of effectiveness, repeatedly or for a long period, will endanger its stability.

A major test of legitimacy is the extent to which given nations have developed a common "secular political culture," national rituals and holidays which serve to maintain the legitimacy of various democratic practices.[6] The United States has developed a common homogeneous secular political culture as reflected in the veneration and consensus surrounding the Founding Fathers, Jefferson, Lincoln, Theodore Roosevelt and their principles. These common elements to which all American politicians appeal are not present in all democratic societies. In some European countries, the Left and the Right have a different set of symbols, and different historical political heroes. France offers the clearest example of a nation which has not developed such a common heritage. Thus many of the battles involving use of different symbols between the left and the right from 1789 down through much of the 19th century are "still in progress, and the issue is still open; everyone of these dates [of major political controversy] still divides left and right, clerical and anti-clerical, progressive and reactionary, in all their historically determined constellations."[7]

As we have seen, nations may vary in the extent to which their political institutions are viewed as legitimate by different strata. And knowledge concerning the relative degree of legitimacy of a nation's political institutions is of key importance in any effort to analyze the stability of these institutions when faced with a crisis of effectiveness. The relationship

---

[6] See Gabriel Almond, "Comparative Political Systems," *Journal of Politics* (1956) [reproduced above, Chapter II, Reading 6].

[7] Herbert Luethy, *The State of France* (London: Secker and Warburg, 1955), p. 29.

between different degrees of legitimacy and effectiveness in specific political systems may be more graphically presented in the form of a four-fold table, with examples of countries characterized by the various possible combinations.

Societies which fall in box A, those which are high on the scales of both legitimacy and effectiveness, will clearly have stable political systems. Nations like the United States, Sweden, and Britain satisfy the basic political needs of their citizens, have efficient bureaucracies and political decision-making systems, possess traditional legitimacy through long-term continuity of the key symbols of sovereignty, the monarchy or constitution, and do not contain any important minorities whose basic values run counter to those of the system.[8] Ineffective and illegitimate regimes, those which would be found in box D, must, of course, by definition be unstable and break down, unless they are dictatorships maintaining themselves by force such as the governments of Hungary and eastern Germany today. The political experiences of different countries in the early 1930's illustrate the effect of varying combinations of legitimacy and effectiveness. In the late 1920's, neither the German nor the Austrian republics were held legitimate by large and powerful segments of their populations, but nevertheless remained reasonably effective. In the four-fold table, they fell in box C.

EFFECTIVENESS

	+	−
LEGITIMACY +	A	B
−	C	D

When the effectiveness of the governments of the various countries broke down in the 1930's, those societies which were high on the scale of legitimacy remained democratic, while countries which were low such as Germany, Austria, and Spain, lost their freedom, and France narrowly escaped a similar fate. Or to put the changes in terms of location in the four-fold table, countries which shifted from A to B remained democratic, while the political systems of those which shifted from C to D broke down. It remained for the military defeat in 1940 to prove conclusively the low position of French democracy on the scale of legitimacy. It was

---

[8] The race problem in the American South does constitute one basic challenge to the legitimacy of the system, and at one time did cause a breakdown of the national order. The conflict reduces the commitment of many white Southerners to the democratic rules down to the present. Great Britain had a comparable problem as long as Catholic Ireland remained part of the United Kingdom. Effective government could not satisfy Ireland. Political practices by both sides in Northern Ireland, Ulster, also illustrate the problem of a regime which is not legitimate to a large segment of its population.

the sole defeated democracy which furnished large-scale support for a Quisling regime.[9]

Situations such as those discussed above in which either legitimacy or effectiveness is high while the other is low demonstrate the utility of this type of analysis. From a short-range point of view, a highly effective but illegitimate system, such as a well governed colony, is more unstable than regimes which are relatively low in effectiveness and high in legitimacy. The social stability of a nation such as Thailand—even with its occasional *coups d'états*—stands out in sharp contrast to the situation in the neighboring former colonial nations of Southeast Asia. The link between the analysis of legitimacy and the earlier discussion of the contribution of economic development to democracy is evident in the processes through which regimes low in legitimacy may gain it, and conversely in those which are related to the collapse of a legitimate system. Prolonged effectiveness which lasts over a number of generations may give legitimacy to a political system; in the modern world, such effectiveness mainly means constant economic development. Thus those nations which adapted most successfully to the requirements of an industrial system had the fewest internal political strains, and either preserved their traditional legitimacy, the monarchy, or developed new strong symbols of legitimacy.

The social and economic structure which Latin America inherited from the Iberian peninsula prevented it from following the lead of the former English colonies, and its republics never developed the symbols and aura of legitimacy. In large measure, the survival of the new political democracies of Asia and Africa is related to their ability to sustain a prolonged period of effectiveness, of being able to meet the defined instrumental needs of their populations.

Legitimacy and Cleavage. Prolonged effectiveness of the system as a whole may, as in the cases of the United States and Switzerland, eventually legitimate the democratic political system. Inherent, however, in all democratic systems is the constant threat that the conflicts among different groups which are the life-blood of the system may crystallize to the point where societal disintegration is threatened. Hence, conditions which serve to moderate the intensity of partisan battle, in addition to effectiveness, are among the key requisites for a democratic political system.

---

[9] The French legitimacy problem is well described by Katherine Munro: "The Right wing parties never quite forgot the possibility of a counter revolution while the Left wing parties revived the Revolution militant in their Marxism or Communism; each side suspected the other of using the Republic to achieve its own ends and of being loyal only so far as it suited it. This suspicion threatened time and time again to make the Republic unworkable, since it led to obstruction in both the political and the economic sphere, and difficulties of government in turn undermined confidence in the regime and its rulers." Quoted in Charles A. Micaud, "French Political Parties: Ideological Myths and Social Realities," in Sigmund Neumann (ed.), *Modern Political Parties* (Chicago: University of Chicago Press, 1956), p. 108.

Since the existence of a moderate state of conflict is an inherent aspect of a legitimate democratic system, and is in fact another way of defining it, we should not be surprised that the principal factors determining such an optimum state are closely linked to those which produce legitimacy viewed in terms of continuities of symbols and status. Essentially the character and content of the major cleavages affecting the political stability of a society are largely determined by historical factors which have affected the way in which major issues dividing society have been solved or left unresolved over time.

In modern times, three major issues have emerged in western states. The first was the religious issue: the place of the church and or various religions within the nation. The second has been the problem of the admission of the lower strata, particularly the workers, to "citizenship," the establishment of access to power through universal suffrage, and the legitimate right to bargain collectively in the economic sphere. The third has been the continual struggle over the distribution of the national income.

The significant general question here is this: were these major issues dealt with one by one, and each one more or less solved before the next arose, or did the problems accumulate, so that historical issues and sources of cleavage mixed with newer ones? Resolving tensions one at a time contributes toward a stable political system; carrying over issues from one historical period to another makes for a political atmosphere characterized by bitterness and frustration rather than by tolerance and compromise. Men and parties come to differ with each other, not simply on ways of settling current problems, but rather by fundamental and opposed *weltanschauungen*. They come to see the political victory of their opponents as a major moral threat; and the total system, as a result, lacks effective value-integration.

The religious issue, the place of the church in the society, was fought through and solved in most of the Protestant nations in the 18th and 19th centuries, and ceased to be a matter for serious political controversy. In some states, such as the United States, the church was disestablished and it accepted this result. In others, such as Britain, Scandinavia, and Switzerland, religion remains state-supported, but the state churches, like constitutional monarchs, have only nominal sway and have ceased to be major sources of controversy. It remains for the Catholic countries of Europe to provide us with examples of situations in which the historic controversy between clerical and anti-clerical forces, sparked by the French Revolution, has continued to divide men politically down to the present day. Thus in countries such as France, Italy, Spain, and Austria, being Catholic has meant being allied with rightist or conservative groups in politics; while being anti-clerical (or a member of a minority religion) has most often meant alliance with the left. In a number of these countries, newer issues, when they emerged, became superimposed on the religious question; and for conservative Catholics, the fight against Socialists was not simply an economic struggle, or a controversy over social institutions, but a deep-rooted conflict between God and Satan, between good and evil.[10] For many secular intellectuals in contemporary Italy, opposition to the church legitimates alliance with the Communists. As long as religious ties reinforce secular political alignments, the chances for democratic give-and-take, and compromise, are weak.

The "citizenship" or "political equality" issue has also been resolved in various ways. Thus the United States and Britain gave citizenship to the workers in the early or mid-nineteenth century. Sweden and a number of European nations resisted through the beginning of the 20th century, and the struggle for citizenship became combined in these countries with socialism as a *political* movement, thereby producing a revolutionary socialism. Or to put this in other terms, where the workers were denied economic and political citizenship rights, their struggle for redistribution of income and status was superimposed on a revolutionary ideology. Where the economic and status struggle developed outside this context, the ideology with which it was linked tended to be that of gradualist reformism. In Hohenzollern Germany, for example, the workers were denied a free and equal suffrage in Prussia until the revolution of 1918. This denial of "citizenship" facilitated the retention of revolutionary Marxism in those parts of Germany where equal suffrage did not exist. In Southern Germany, where full citizenship rights were granted in the late 19th century, reformist, democratic, and nonrevolutionary socialism was dominant. The perpetuation of revolutionary dogmas in much of the Social Democratic party served to give ultra-leftists a voice in party leadership, enabled the Communists to win strength after the military defeat, and perhaps even more important historically, served to frighten large sections of the German middle classes. The latter feared that a socialist victory would really mean an end to all their privileges and status.

---

[10] The linkage between democratic instability and Catholicism may also be accounted for by elements inherent in Catholicism as a religious system. Democracy requires a universalistic political belief system in the sense that it legitimates different ideologies. And it might be assumed that religious value systems which are more universalistic in the sense of placing less stress on being the only true church will be more compatible with democracy than those which assume that they have the only truth. The latter belief, held much more strongly by the Catholic than by most other Christian churches, makes it difficult for the religious value system to help legitimate a political system which requires, as part of its basic value system, the belief that "good" is served best through conflict among opposing beliefs.

Kingsley Davis has argued that a Catholic state church tends to be irreconcilable with democracy since "Catholicism attempts to control so many aspects of life, to encourage so much fixity of status and submission to authority, and to remain so independent of secular authority that it invariably clashes with the liberalism, individualism, freedom, mobility and sovereignty of the democratic nation." See his "Political Ambivalence in Latin America," *Journal of Legal and Political Sociology*, Vol. 1 (1943), reprinted in Christensen, *The Evolution of Latin American Government* (New York, 1951), p. 240.

In France, the workers won the suffrage but were refused basic economic rights until after World War II. Major groups of French employers denied legitimacy to the French trade-unions, and sought to weaken or destroy them following every trade-union victory. The instability of the French unions, their constant need to preserve worker militancy to survive, gave access to the workers to the more revolutionary and extremist political groups. Communist domination of the French labor movement can in large part be traced to the tactics of the French business classes.

The examples presented above do not explain why different countries varied in the way they handled basic national cleavages. They should suffice, however, to illustrate the worth of a hypothesis relating the conditions for stable democratic government to the bases of diversity. Where a number of historic cleavages intermix and create the basis for *weltanschauung* politics, the democracy will be unstable and weak, for by definition such political views do not include the concept of tolerance. . . .

The intense forms of cleavage developed by that cumulation of unresolved issues which creates *weltanschauung* politics is sustained by the systematic segregation of different strata of the population in organized political or religious enclaves. Conversely, however, it should be noted that wherever the social structure operates so as naturally to "isolate" individuals or groups with the same political disposition characteristics from contact with differing views, those so isolated tend to back political extremists.

It has been repeatedly remarked, for example, that workers in so-called "isolated" industries, miners, sailors, fishermen, lumbermen, sheep-tenders, and longshoremen, tend to give overwhelming support to the more left-wing tendencies. Such districts tend to vote Communist or Socialist by large majorities, sometimes to the point of having what is essentially a "one-party" system in the areas concerned. Isolation is created by the fact that the requirements of the job make workers in these industries live in communities which are predominately inhabited by others in the same occupation. And this very isolation seems to reduce the pressures on such workers to be tolerant of other points of view, to contain among themselves diverse strains of thought; and makes them receptive to extremist versions of the doctrine generally held by other less isolated members of their class. One should expect that the least "cosmopolitan" (the most isolated) of every political predisposition, or stratum, will be the ones most likely to accept extremism. The political intolerance of farm-based groups in times of crisis may be another illustration of this pattern, since farmers, like workers in isolated industries, tend to have a more homogeneous political environment than do those employed in most urban occupations. . . .

A stable democracy requires relatively moderate tension among the contending political forces. And political moderation is facilitated by the capacity of a system to resolve key dividing issues before new ones arise. To the extent that the cleavages of religion, citizenship, and "collective bargaining" have been allowed to cumulate and reinforce each other as stimulants of partisan hostility, the system is weakened. The more reinforced and correlated the sources of cleavage, the less the likelihood for political tolerance. Similarly, on the level of group and individual behavior, the greater the isolation from heterogeneous political stimuli, the more that background factors "pile up" in one direction, the greater the chances that the group or individual will have an extremist perspective. These two relationships, one on the level of partisan issues, the other on the nature of party support, are linked together by the fact that parties reflecting accumulated unresolved issues will seek to isolate their followers from conflicting stimuli, to prevent exposure to "error," while isolated individuals and groups will strengthen the intolerant tendencies in the political party system. The conditions maximizing political cosmopolitanism among the electorate are the growth of urbanization, education, communications media, and increased wealth. Most of the obvious isolated occupations, mining, lumbering, agriculture, belong to the category of "primary" occupations, occupations whose relative share of the labor force declines sharply with economic development.

Thus, we see again how the factors involved in modernization or economic development are linked closely to those involved in the historic institutionalization of the values of legitimacy and tolerance. But it should always be noted that correlations are only statements concerning relative degrees of congruence, and that another condition for political action is that the correlation never be so clear-cut that men cannot feel that they can change the direction of affairs by their actions. And this fact of low correlation means also that it is important for analytic purposes to keep variables distinct even if they intercorrelate. For example, the analysis of cleavage presented here suggests specific propositions concerning the ways in which different electoral and constitutional arrangements may affect the chances for democracy. These generalizations are presented in the following section.

SYSTEMS OF GOVERNMENT AND DEMOCRACY

From the hypothesis that cross-cutting bases of cleavage are better for the vitality of democracy, it follows that two-party systems are better than multiparty systems, that electoral systems involving the election of officials on a territorial basis are preferable to systems of proportional representation, and that federalism is superior to a unitary state. In evaluating these propositions, it is important to note again that they are made with the assumption of all other factors being held constant. Clearly, stable democracies are compatible with multi-party systems, with proportional representation, and with a unitary state. And in fact, I would argue that such variations in systems of government, while significant, are much less important than those derived from basic differences in social structure of the sort discussed in the previous sections.

The argument for the two-party system rests on the assumptions that in a complex society, such parties must necessarily be broad coalitions; that they cannot seek to serve only the interests of one major group; that they cannot be parties of integration; and that in building electoral coalitions, they necessarily antagonize support among those most committed to them, and conversely must seek to win support among groups which are preponderantly allied to the opposition party. Thus, the British Conservative or American Republican parties must not so act as to antagonize basically the manual workers, since a large part of the vote must come from them. The Democratic and Labor parties are faced with a similar problem *vis-à-vis* the middle strata. Parties which are never oriented toward gaining a majority seek to maximize their electoral support from a limited base. Thus a peasant-oriented party will accentuate peasant group interest consciousness, and a party appealing primarily to small businessmen will do the same for its group. Elections, instead of being occasions on which parties seek to find the broadest possible base of support, and so to bring divergent groups to see their common interests, become events in which parties stress the cleavages separating their principal supporters from other groupings.

The proposition that proportional representation weakens rather than strengthens democracy rests on the analysis of the differences between multi-party and majority party situations. If it is true, as is suggested above, that "multi-partyness" serves to sharpen differences and reduce consensus, then any electoral system which increases the chance for more rather than fewer parties serves democracy badly.

Further, . . . the system of electing members of parliament to represent territorial constituencies, as contrasted with systems which encourage direct group representation (such as proportional representation), is preferable, since territorial representation helps to stabilize the political systems by forcing interest groups to secure their ends only within an electoral framework that involves some concern with many interests and the need for compromise.

Federalism serves to strengthen democracy by increasing the opportunity for multiple sources of cleavage. It adds regional interests and values to the others such as class, religion and ethnicity which cross-cut the social structure.

A major exception to this generalization occurs when federalism divides the country according to lines of basic cleavage, *e.g.*, between different ethnic, religious, or linguistic areas. In such cases, as in India or in Canada, federalism may then serve to accentuate and reinforce cleavages. Cleavage is desirable within linguistic or religious groups, not between them. But where such divisions do not exist, then federalism seems to serve democracy well. Besides creating a further source of cross-cutting cleavage, it also serves various functions which Tocqueville noted it shared with strong voluntary associations. Among these, it is the source of resistance to centralization of power and a source of training of new political leaders; and it gives the "out" party a stake in the system as a whole, since national "out" parties usually continue to control some units of the system.

Let me repeat that I do not suggest that these aspects of the political structure as such are key conditions for democratic systems. If the underlying social conditions are such as to facilitate democracy, as seems true for Sweden, then the combination of multi-partyness, proportional representation, and a unitary state, do not seriously weaken it. At most they serve to permit irresponsible minorities to gain a foothold in parliament. On the other hand, where a low level of effectiveness and of legitimacy has operated to weaken the foundations of democracy as occurred in Weimar Germany, or in France, then constitutional factors encouraging multi-partyness serve to reduce the chances that the system will survive.

PROBLEMS OF CONTEMPORARY DEMOCRACY

The characteristic pattern of the stable western democracies in the mid-20th century is that of a "post-politics" phase—there is relatively little difference between the democratic left and right, the socialists are moderates, and the conservatives accept the welfare state. In large measure this reflects the fact that in these countries the workers have won their fight for citizenship and for political access, *i.e.*, the right to take part in all decisions of the body politic on an equal level with others.[11]

The struggle for citizenship had two aspects, political (access to power through the suffrage) and economic (institutionalization of trade union rights to share in the decisions affecting work rewards and conditions). The representatives of the lower strata are now part of the governing classes, members of the club. Political controversy has declined in the wealthier stable democracies because the basic political issue of the industrial revolution, the incorporation of the workers into the legitimate body politic, has been settled. The only key domestic issue today is collective bargaining over differences in the division of the total product

---

[11] T. H. Marshall has analyzed the gradual process of incorporation of the working class into the body politic in the 19th century, and has seen that process as the achievement of a "basic human equality, associated with full community membership, which is not inconsistent with a superstructure of economic inequality." See his brief but brilliant book, *Citizenship and Social Class* (Cambridge University Press, 1950), p. 77. Even though universal citizenship opens the way for the challenging of remaining social inequalities, it also provides a basis for believing that the process of social change toward equality will remain within the boundaries of allowable conflict in a democratic system.

within the framework of a Keynesian welfare state; and such issues do not require or precipitate extremism on either side.

In most of Latin and Eastern Europe, the struggle for working-class integration into the body politic was not settled before the Communists appeared on the scene to take over leadership of the workers. This fact drastically changed the political game, since inherently the Communists could not be absorbed within the system in the way that the Socialists have been. Communist workers, their parties and trade unions, cannot possibly be accorded the right of access by a democratic society. The Communists' self-image and more particularly their ties to the Soviet Union lead them to accept a self-confirming hypothesis. Their self-definition prevents them from being allowed access and this in turn reinforces the sense of alienation from the system (of not being accepted by the other strata) which workers in nations with large Communist parties have. And the more conservative strata are reinforced in their belief that giving increased rights to the workers or their representatives threatens all that is good in life. Thus, the presence of Communists precludes an easy prediction that economic development will stablize democracy in these European countries.

In the newly independent nations of Asia, the situation is somewhat different. In Europe at the beginning of modern politics, the workers were faced with the problem of winning citizenship, the right to take part in the political game, from the dominant aristocratic and business strata who controlled politics. In Asia the long-term presence of colonial rulers has identified conservatism as an ideology and the more well-to-do classes with subservience to colonialism; while leftist ideologies, usually of a Marxist variety, have been dominant, being identified with nationalism. The trade unions and the workers' parties of Asia have been part of the political process from the beginning of the democratic system. Conceivably such a situation could mean a stable democracy, except for the fact that these lower-strata rights pre-date the development of a stable economy with a large middle class and an industrial society.

The whole system stands on its head. The left in the European stable democracies grew gradually in a fight for more democracy, and gave expression to the discontents involved in early industrialization, while the right retained the support of traditionalist elements in the society, until eventually the system came into an easy balance between a modified left and right. In Asia, the left is in power during the period of population explosion and early industrialization, and must accept responsibility for all the consequent miseries. As in the poorer areas of Europe, the Communists exist to capitalize on all these discontents in completely irresponsible fashion, and currently are a major party, usually the second largest in most Asian states.

Given the existence of poverty-stricken masses, low levels of education, an elongated pyramid class structure, and the "premature" triumph of the democratic left, the prognosis for the perpetuation of political democracy in Asia and Africa is bleak. The nations which have the best prospects, Israel, Japan, Lebanon, the Philippines and Turkey, tend to resemble Europe in one or more major factors, high educational level (all except Turkey), substantial and growing middle class, and the retention of political legitimacy by non-leftist groups. The other emerging national states in Asia and Africa are committed more deeply to a certain tempo and pattern of economic development and to national independence, under whatever political form, than they are to the pattern of party politics and free elections which exemplify our model of democracy. It seems likely that in countries which avoid Communist or military dictatorship political developments will follow the pattern developing in countries such as Ghana, Tunisia or Mexico, where an educated minority uses a mass movement expressing leftist slogans to exercise effective control, and holds elections as a gesture toward ultimate democratic objectives, and as a means of estimating public opinion, not as effective instruments for legitimate turnover in office of governing parties. Given the pressure for rapid industrialization and for the immediate solution of chronic problems of poverty and famine through political agencies, it is unlikely that many of the new governments of Asia and Africa will be characterized by an open party system representing basically different class positions and values.

Latin America, underdeveloped economically like Asia, is, however, politically more like Europe in the early 19th century than like Asia today. Most Latin American countries became independent states before the rise of industrialism and Marxist ideologies, and contain strongholds of traditional conservatism. The countryside is often apolitical or traditional, and the leftist movements secure support primarily from the industrial proletariat. Latin American communists, for example, have chosen the European Marxist path of organizing urban workers, rather than the "Yenan way" of Mao, seeking a peasant base. If Latin America is allowed to develop on its own, and is able to increase its productivity and middle classes, there is a good chance that many Latin American countries will follow in the European direction. Recent developments, including the overthrowal of a number of dictatorships, in large measure reflect the effects of an increased middle class, growing wealth, and increased education. There is, however, also the possibility that these countries may yet follow in the French and Italian direction rather than that of northern Europe, that the communists will seize the leadership of the workers, and that the middle class will be alienated from democracy.

The analysis of the social requisites for democracy contained in this paper has sought to identify some, though obviously far from all, of the structural conditions which are linked to this political system. It has been possible in a very limited fashion to attempt some tests of the hypotheses suggested. These preliminary efforts to apply the method of science to comparative political systems can still be considered only as illustrative since we can say so little about actual variations in national social structures. Considerably more research must be done specifying the boundaries of various societies along many dimensions before reliable comparative analysis of the sort attempted here can be carried out. Although the task obviously presents tremendous difficulties, it is only through such methods that we can move beyond the conventional semi-literary methods of giving illustrative examples to support plausible interpretations.

The data available are, however, of a sufficiently consistent character to support strongly the conclusion that a more systematic and up-to-date version of Aristotle's hypothesis concerning the relationship of political forms to social structure is valid. Unfortunately, as has been indicated above, this conclusion does not justify the optimistic liberal's hope that an increase in wealth, in the size of the middle class, in education, and other related factors will necessarily mean the spread of democracy or the stabilizing of democracy. As Max Weber, in discussing the chances for democracy in Russia in the early 20th century pointed out: "The spread of Western cultural and capitalist economy did not, *ipso facto*, guarantee that Russia would also acquire the liberties which had accompanied their emergence in European history. . . . European liberty had been born in unique, perhaps unrepeatable, circumstances at a time when the intel-lectual and material conditions for it were exceptionally propitious."[12]

These suggestions that the peculiar concatenation of factors which gave rise to western democracy in the nineteenth century may be unique are not meant to be unduly pessimistic. Political democracy exists and has existed in a variety of circumstances, even if it is most commonly sustained by a limited cluster of conditions. To understand more fully the various conditions under which it has existed may make possible the development of democracy elsewhere. Democracy is not achieved by acts of will alone; but men's wills, through action, can shape institutions and events in directions that reduce or increase the chance for the development and survival of democracy. To aid men's actions in furthering democracy was in some measure Tocqueville's purpose in studying the operation of American democracy, and it remains perhaps the most important substan-tive intellectual task which students of politics can still set before them-selves.

---

[12] Richard Pipes, "Max Weber and Russia," *World Politics*, Vol. 7 (1955), p. 383.

B. Dictatorship

46. NOTES ON THE THEORY OF DICTATORSHIP*

Franz L. Neumann

DEFINITION OF DICTATORSHIP

STRANGE though it may seem, we do not possess any systematic study of dictatorship. The historical information is abundant, and there are many analyses of individual dictators in various countries. But there is no analysis that seeks to generalize not only from the political experience of the twentieth century, but from the political systems of the more distant past. The present paper attempts to outline the theoretical problems encountered in the analysis of dictatorship and to indicate whatever answers now can be supplied.

By dictatorship we understand the rule of a person or a group of persons who arrogate to themselves and monopolize power in the state, exercising it without restraint.

The first question raised by this definition is whether the Roman dictatorship and the absolute monarchy should be included in its scope.

It seems more appropriate to classify the Roman dictatorship (prior to Sulla) not as a dictatorship properly speaking, but as a form of Crisis Government. This may seem arbitrary, for the very word "dictator" derives from Roman constitutional law. Nevertheless, the Roman dictatorship was a magistracy, clearly defined in authorization, scope and duration, and it ought not to be confused with a political system in which power is arrogated by an individual or a group, and which does not circumscribe either the scope or the duration of dictatorial power. The Roman dictator was appointed by one of the consuls for a period not to exceed six months, to defend the country against an external enemy or to cope with internal dissension. He was duty-bound to appoint at once a Master of the Horse for the command of the cavalry; he had no authority to change the constitution, to declare war, to intervene in civil law suits, or to impose new fiscal obligations upon Roman citizens. Within these limits, the sovereign power of the Roman people was concentrated in his hands. The consuls became his subordinates; the tribunician power of intercession did not apply against his acts; nor could a citizen condemned in a criminal trial invoke the normal right of appeal (*provocatio*) against him.

The Romans resorted to dictatorship because the collegiate nature of

---

* Reprinted with permission of the publisher from *The Democratic and Authoritarian State* by Franz L. Neumann. Copyright 1957 by The Free Press, a corporation.

the magistracy, including the consulate, and the one-year restriction on its term, made the conduct of war extremely difficult. But the dictatorship itself was to prove unsuitable for wars of long duration. By the end of the fourth century it was already in decline, reappearing in irregular forms during the Punic Wars and disappearing at the end of the Second Punic War (201 B.C.). From then on, the Roman dictatorship (e.g., Sulla's and Caesar's) changes its character radically.

The second problem that our definition raises is the relation between monarchy and dictatorship. The title of the absolute ruler—whether he is designated King, Emperor, Leader or Duce—is not decisive here. This was already recognized by Aristotle, who held the rule of kings among non-civilized (non-Hellenic) peoples to be "similar to that of tyranny" and who defined his fifth type of kingship, the case "where a single power is sovereign on every issue, with the same sort of power that a tribe or a polis exercises over its public concerns," as a *Pambasileia*, an all-kingship or super-kingship.

Actually, from the standpoint of the exercise of power the absolute monarch is a dictator, but from the standpoint of the legitimacy of power, he is not. We may speak of legitimate monarchical rule whenever accession to power is constitutionally regulated by heredity or by election and monarchical rule is generally accepted as the normal form of government. These criteria are rather vague—but so is the actual situation. In the history of political and constitutional thought, the ruler who comes to power through a *coup d'état* (*absque titulo*) is held to be an usurping tyrant, but he may rid himself of this stigma if he succeeds in formally establishing his rule and that of his line, which then becomes "legitimate." On the other hand it was also generally held that a monarch who acceded to the throne legitimately could degenerate into a tyrant through his acts (*quoad exercitio*). Thus, while one may distinguish in principle between monarchy and dictatorship, one must realize that the principle suffers many exceptions and that, consequently, certain forms of the absolute monarchy must also be treated as forms of dictatorship.

Our definition, furthermore, envisages dictatorship only in the state, and in no other social organization. There may be situations in which absolute power of a party boss or of the pater familias may help us understand the mechanisms leading to a dictatorship or serving to maintain its power. But there is as yet no convincing evidence that the dictatorial structure of social organizations necessarily leads to or facilitates political dictatorship. An example is the ambiguity of the social and psychological role of the so-called "authoritarian family."[1] The authoritarian (quasi-dictatorial) family may lead, as some maintain, to a more ready acceptance of political dictatorship,[2] but dictatorship may also be promoted (and more

---

[1] Which, however, need not necessarily be a dictatorial family, because the power of the *pater familias* may well be founded in reason: "rational authority."

[2] T. W. Adorno *et al.; The Authoritarian Personality* (New York, 1950).

frequently, perhaps) by the decay of traditional authority, by the very undermining of the authority of the father. The relation between political and social forms of authoritarianism must, therefore, be taken as a special problem, and not as an automatic correlation.

Moreover, we deliberately do not distinguish among a dictator, a tyrant, and a despot. Tyranny and depotism have no precise meaning. One usually associates despotism with oriental dictatorships, whereas tyranny is often used to designate any system of government that either in its origin or in its practice is tainted by unconstitutional practices or characterized by lack of restraints. Both words are emotionally charged and exhibit in varying degrees rejection and resentment of these systems of government.

Rejection of the terms "tyranny" and "despotism" does not mean, however, that within the general definition of dictatorship there are no subtypes. A number of distinctions are significant.

The first pertains to the scope of the political power monopolized by the dictator. The dictator may exercise his power through absolute control of the traditional means of coercion only, i.e., the army, police, bureaucracy and judiciary. We may call this type a *simple dictatorship*.

In some situations, the dictator may feel compelled to build up popular support, to secure a mass base, either for his rise to power or for the exercise of it, or for both. We may call this type a *caesaristic dictatorship*, which, as the name indicates, is always personal in form.

Even this combination of monopolized coercion and popular backing may be insufficient as a guarantee of power. It may be necessary to control education, the means of communication and economic institutions and thus to gear the whole of society and the private life of the citizen to the system of political domination. The term for this type is totalitarian dictatorship. It may be either collective or personal, that is, it may or may not have a caesaristic element.

It need hardly be mentioned that these classifications are ideal types which will only approximate historical realities. They will help us, however, to understand the structure of the various cases of dictatorship.

CAESARISTIC DICTATORSHIP

The simple dictatorship—whether it be military or bureaucratic, the rule of a junta, a caudillo, or even an absolute monarch—is exercised primarily through the control of what one may call the classical instruments of rule: army, police, bureaucracy, judiciary. This limitation is due less to self-imposed restraints than to the absence of any need for more extensive controls. Simple dictatorship usually occurs in countries where the masses of the people lack political awareness, where politics is the affair of small cliques who compete for favors and hope to gain prestige and wealth by association with the dictator. The mass of the people pay taxes and may have to serve in the army, but otherwise have little to do with political life. The only social controls which may be needed are bribery and corruption of a few influential individuals in order to tie them closely to the system.

In the *caesaristic dictatorship* a new element enters: the need for popular support. The term "caesarism" was apparently coined by Romieu in his little book *L'Ère des Césars* (1850) and its climate most adequately described by Guizot, Louis Philippe's Prime Minister after the revolution of 1830.

"Chaos," says Guizot, "is now hiding under one word—democracy. This is now the ultimate and universal word all seek to appropriate as a talisman. The Monarchists say: Our Monarchy is a Democratic Monarchy; it differs essentially from the ancient monarchy and is adapted to modern conditions of society. The Republicans say: The Republic is Democracy governing itself. This is the only form of government in harmony with democratic society, its principles, its sentiments, and its interests.

"Socialists, Communists, Montagnards wish that the Republic should be pure and absolute democracy. This is for them the condition of its legitimacy.

"Such is the power of the word democracy that no government or party dares to exist or believes it can exist without inscribing that word upon its banner."[3]

Caesarism becomes a necessity when the masses tend to become politically articulate. . . . Much . . . is to be learned from Julius Caesar whose name came to designate this type of dictatorship.

The gradual disintegration of the Roman constitution between the Second Punic War and the murder of Caesar is familiar in its major outlines and need not be elaborated in detail. Personal dictatorship was foreshadowed as early as the close of the Second Punic War by the political pre-eminence of Scipio Africanus. And the first clear-cut rejection of the Roman constitution was Sulla's dictatorship about a century later, for although it traded on the name of the classical emergency magistrate, it was a dictatorship for life and its purpose was to change the constitution by undoing such semi-democratic reforms as the new powers of the tribunate and by restoring the sway of the senatorial oligarchy (*optimates*). But Sulla's system could not achieve this restoration. Less than ten years after his departure from the political scene, his system collapsed and the Republic was in full decline. "Non mos, non ius" said Tacitus, describing the collapse of morality and law. "You see that there is no Republic, no Senate, no dignity in any of us"—thus wrote Cicero in a letter to his brother Quintus.

Julius Caesar's rise to power is due to a number of factors: the

---

[3] Guizot, *La Démocratic en France*, (Leipzig, 1849), p. 2.

disintegration of the constitution; his personal control of a dedicated army; the support of the so-called party of the *populares;* the rise of the equestrian order to economic power; the discontents of the non-Roman Italian population; and the expansion of the Empire. His position, by the time of his death, could not conceivably be reconciled with the constitutional structure of the Republic. He was an absolute monarch in fact. But it is important to note that, much as Caesar would have liked it, he could not, in view of public opinion, take on the title of King. Brutus' deed shows the strength of republican feelings in Rome which are important for the understanding of Augustus' constitutional arrangements.

Modern historians do not tire of arguing that there really was no "democratic" party or movement in Rome, that the populares were in reality a city mob manipulated and bribed by aristocratic cliques held together by the institution of *amicitia* (friendship) and organized into *factiones* or *partes*. This is undoubtedly true. Yet it would be dangerous to construe Roman politics simply as a fight of the "ins" against the "outs" and thus to overlook the political impact of major social problems: the equestrian order's rise to economic power—without corresponding political recognition; the control of political power by a landed oligarchy that no longer monopolized economic power; the deterioration of the position of the small peasants (the Gracchi had already attempted to create an absolute, caesaristic monarchy with their support); the existence of a city plebs—legally defined as those without income or occupation but, through its assemblies and tribunes, exceedingly powerful politically; and finally, the problems of an ever growing empire—the need for defense and communications, and the struggles for participation in the spoils. Seen against this background, caesarism was more than the attempt of a powerful person to make himself supreme; it was in fact the means for reorganizing Rome, Italy, and the Empire. And even if we do not accept Mommsen's image of Caesar as the genius who from the very beginning had set out to do precisely this, the fact remains that these problems brought him into power and that he coped with them, often quite successfully.

Augustus' triumph serves to underline the fact that these social and economic changes had made monarchy inevitable. As Dion Cassius put it: "at this time [after the defeat of Antonius at Actium in 31] the government assumed a better and more salutary form, for it was quite impossible for the Romans to save themselves with the Republican constitution."[4] But what kind of monarchy? The resurrection of the old Roman kingship (the *Rex*) proved impossible. Caesar's death was a warning not to attempt it. The Hellenistic (oriental) monarchy with the deification of the monarch, the proskynesis, and the complete identification of monarch and state was not only an alien tradition, but was associated with Antonius and

---

[4] For details see Leon Homo, *Roman Political Institutions from City to State* (New York, 1947), p. 202.

Cleopatra and ruled out by their defeat. Dictatorship for life, voted by the people, had become almost equally disreputable. Augustus, with his unusual political shrewdness, realized that his personal power must be made to fit the constitution. Prior to 27 B.C., all positions he held—admission to the Senate at the age of 19, consular rank, etc.—were irregular but, so he says, "All Italy took the oath to me spontaneously and demanded me as leader in the war in which I won the battle of Actium. . . ." After 27 B.C., in what Homo calls the organic period, Augustus' Principate was established in what he alleged to be a completely constitutional form. "The Dictatorship was conferred upon me, in my absence and in my presence, by the People and Senate . . . and I did not accept it (22 B.C.). The Consulship for the year and for life was given me at the same date, and I did not accept it . . . I accepted no function contrary to the usages of our fathers. . . . When the people offered me the position of Pontifex Maximus (which my father had held) . . . I refused it." And he continues: ". . . When I had put an end to the civil wars . . . , I transferred the government of the State from my hands to those of the Senate and the Roman people. In return for this service, I was given the title of Augustus. . . . Since that time I have been above all in authority [*auctoritate*] but have had no more power [*potestas*] than those who have been my colleagues in magistracies."

This touching modesty came cheap enough, for Augustus had already proscribed the bulk of his opponents and now, invoking his *auctoritas*, he saw to it that his own men occupied all the positions of influence and power. The patronage system was thus refined and skillfully employed. The Senate was purged, mainly to eliminate adherents of the late Antonius; wealthy plebeians friendly to Augustus rose easily into the equestrian order, and equestrian bankers and traders were elevated to the rank of *optimates*. Moreover, propaganda and the supression of oppositional and critical literature were used to consolidate support, and in his later years Augustus assumed the religious dignity of the Pontifex Maximus in order to further his prestige. But the political victory was consolidated, above all, by changes in the social hierarchy: the doom of the *nobiles* and the rise of *homines novi* in society and politics.

After 27 B.C. Augustus depended for his constitutional powers primarily on two positions: the *imperium proconsulare maius* and the *potestas tribunicia*—both of which he held for life. The former gave him command of the armies in Rome and in the provinces; the latter—granted to him with extended powers—sacrosanctity, the right of intercession, and above all, the democratic legitimation.

This last point is especially important, because the *potestas tribunicia* is the source of the *lex regia* which, in the formula attributed to Ulpian, was the principle that "the will of the *Princeps* has the force of law for, in virtue of the *lex regia* . . . the people . . . transfers to him all its *imperium* and all its *potestas*." And again in the Code of Justinian: "In virtue of the ancient law which was called *lex regia,* all the right and all the *potestas* of the Roman people have been transferred to the Imperial *potestas*." We now know that some such formula was actually enacted, although of course popular sovereignty after Claudius became a mere fiction. And the Roman people (*populus Romanus*) remained sovereign in law and the source of all political authority, even though the later emperors, influenced by Hellenistic conceptions, added a divine legitimation to the pseudo-democratic *lex regia.* . . .

TOTALITARIAN DICTATORSHIP

Totalitarian dictatorship, to which our attention now will be directed, ought not to be confused with caesarism. Up to the nineteenth century at least, caesaristic dictatorship does not necessarily lead to a totalitarian system, nor is the totalitarian state necessarily the result of a genuine caesaristic movement. Totalitarianism is thus a separate problem. For the purpose of a brief discussion the modern totalitarian dictatorship may be reduced to five essential factors.

The first of these is the transition from a state based upon the rule of law (the German *Rechtsstaat*) to a police state. The rule of law is a presumption in favor of the right of the citizen and against the coercive power of the state. In the totalitarian state this presumption is reversed. Details need not concern us here, since the power of executive agencies in totalitarian states to interfere at discretion with life, liberty and property may be taken as the best-known feature of this kind of dictatorship.

The second factor is the transition from the diffusion of power in liberal states to the concentration of power in the totalitarian regime. This concentration may vary in degree as well as form. But there is no role in any totalitarian state for the various liberal devices of diffusing power, such as separation of powers, federalism, a functioning multiparty system, bicameralism, etc.

These first two elements, however, are to be found in the absolute monarchy as well as in the totalitarian dictatorship. What distinguishes totalitarianism politically is the third element, namely, the existence of a monopolistic state party. Such a party is required because the traditional instruments of coercion do not suffice to control an industrial society, and all the less so since bureaucracies and armies may not always be reliable. The monopolistic party is a flexible instrument which provides the force to control the state machine and society and to perform the gigantic task of cementing the authoritarian elements within society together.

Moreover, the monopolistic party involves a socio-psychological aspect pertaining to what is commonly called a "mass" society. Since modern totalitarian dictatorships arise, almost without exception, within and against democracies (weak though the democratic structures may have been), the totalitarian clique has to assume the shape of a democratic movement and to retain this façade even after it has come to power. In other words, it is forced to practice the ritual of democracy even though the substance is totally denied.

The role of the monopolistic party involves the fourth element of the totalitarian dictatorship: the transition from pluralist to totalitarian social controls. Society ceases to be distinguished from the state; it is totally permeated by political power. The control of society, now as important as the control of the state, is achieved by the following techniques:

1. The leadership principle—to enforce guidance from the top and responsibility to the top.

2. The "synchronization" of all social organizations—not only to control them, but to make them serviceable to the state.

3. The creation of graded elites—so as to enable the rulers to control the masses from within and to disguise manipulation from without, i.e., to supplement bureaucracies in the narrow meaning of the term with private leadership groups within the various strata of the population.

4. The atomization and isolation of the individual, which involves negatively the destruction or at least weakening of social units based on biology (family), tradition, religion, or co-operation in work or leisure; and positively the imposition of huge and undifferentiated mass organizations which leave the individual isolated and more easily manipulable.

5. The transformation of culture into propaganda—of cultural values into saleable commodities.

The final factor in totalitarianism is the reliance upon terror, i.e., the use of non-calculable violence as a permanent threat against the individual. Care must be taken, however, not to define a totalitarian dictatorship simply as the rule of violence. Without it, it is true, such regimes could not survive. But they could not endure for any length of time without considerable identification by the oppressed people with its rulers.

These, in brief outline, are the features of the most repressive of political systems. What distinguishes it from absolutism is not primarily the caesaristic element, for this was also characteristic of the absolute monarchy in certain periods of its history, but rather the destruction of the line between state and society and the total politicization of society by the device of the monopolistic party. This is not merely a question of more or less political power. The difference is one of quality, not quantity. Where, as in the absolute monarchy, power is primarily exercised through the traditional bureaucratic instruments of coercion, its operation is governed by abstract, calculable rules, although their execution often may be arbitrary. Absolutism, therefore, already contains the major institutional principles of modern liberalism. Totalitarian dictatorship, on the other hand, is the absolute negation of these principles because the main repressive agencies are not courts and administrative bodies, but the secret police and the party.

A fully developed totalitarian dictatorship is the form an industrial society may adopt if it should become necessary to maximize its repressive elements and eliminate its liberal ones. But totalitarian dictatorship is not the child of modern industrialism alone. Sparta . . . may be briefly discussed as an illuminating earlier experiment.

Those who call Sparta a democracy perniciously forget that the Perioici and, more importantly, the Helots (state serfs) were decisive for its institutions. The case is perhaps otherwise with Athens, where, as Westermann and Jones[5] have shown, slavery was relatively insignificant. But the ratio of Spartans to Helots was about 1:20, and the perpetual danger from the Helots required a system of total repression. Plutarch saw the problem when he described the horrors of the infamous Crypteia, the missions of young Spartans armed with daggers, which the Ephors sent our secretly "from time to time" to terrorize and assassinate Helots. Thucydides also refers to the appalling slaughter of 2,000 Helots in 424 B.C. Service in this dreadful secret police was part of the training of the Spartan youth, for terror, rather than criminal sanction, constituted the backbone of the Spartan system.

The cohesion of the ruling stratum was achieved by the total control of society and of private life through such well-known institutions as the transfer of the children at the age of six to barracks, and the rigid system of state education emphasizing cunning and violence. It is most illuminating to compare Plutarch's description of the Spartans' "liberal" education with Himmler's recipe for the education of Russians under German occupation. Plutarch says, "They learned to read and write for purely practical reasons, but all other forms of education they barred from the country, books and treatises being included in this as much as men." And Himmler: "All they may learn is to count till 12 and to write their names. Beyond this, education is dangerous and not to be countenanced."

We must remember that this totalitarian dictatorship was without a caesaristic element. None was needed due to the completely static character of Sparta's economy and society. Wealth had only two sources: agriculture and robbery (through war). Corruption was enough to make the system function so long as its static character (the pattern of landholding) was maintained. It was the gradual concentration of wealth in the hands of a few which produced Cleomenes' unsuccessful effort to revitalize Sparta through a caesaristic dictatorship. In the end, the Spartan government degenerated into the personal rule of Nabis who, with the cruelty of an oriental despot, seems to have restored the agrarian system and much of the discipline. . . .

DEMOCRACY AND DICTATORSHIP

If we review the various types of dictatorships outlined above, we are forced to conclude that the usual confrontation of liberal democracy vs.

---

[5] W. L. Westermann, "Athenaeum and the Slaves of Athens," in *Athenian Studies presented to W. S. Ferguson* (London, 1940); A. H. M. Jones, "The Economic Basis of Athenian Democracy," in *Past and Present*, No. 1 (February, 1952), pp. 13–31.

dictatorship as an antithesis of good and evil, cannot be maintained from a historical point of view. Moralizing about political systems makes it difficult to understand their functions. The relationship between democracy and dictatorship is not as simple as is sometimes stated.

1. Dictatorships may be an implementation of democracy. But this refers to emergency dictatorships with functions similar to the classical Roman type, which we prefer to classify as a kind of magistracy.

2. Dictatorships may be the preparation for democracy. We may then speak of an educational dictatorship.

3. Dictatorships may be the very negation of democracy and thus be a totally regressive system.

Pisistratus' rule is probably a classical example of an educational dictatorship. As Werner Jaeger puts it: "The masses were still politically inexperienced, so that democracy was far away: it could not come until the aristocracy had been brought low by the Pisistratic tyrants." We may add that the great function of the Pisistratidae was the creation of an Athenian national (or collective) spirit. This was done by facilitating the emergence of a "middle class," which Aristotle believed to be the social prerequisite of democracy. Hence, without the work of Pisistratus the regimes of Cleisthenes and Pericles would hardly be conceivable.

It is well to remember that the Marxist-Leninist conception of a dictatorship of the proletariat was democratic precisely in this sense of a preparatory dictatorship. The concentration of power in the hands of the proletariat was to be used to abolish class rule altogether and to herald a new epoch of freedom in a classless society. That it was not this expectation but the very opposite which materialized cannot be discussed in detail here. However, we may cite the basic reasons why, under modern conditions, every dictatorship tends to be a totalitarian dictatorship and to involve the negation of democracy.

The democratic ideology has become so universal that Guizot's statement seems even truer today than it did in 1848. All modern dictatorships arose from democratic conditions. This is true of Italy, Germany, Spain, Argentina, and perhaps even of the U.S.S.R., although to a lesser degree.

The dictator is therefore compelled to seek mass support and, having obtained it, to practice the ritual of democracy even if its substance is withheld. As Engels already saw, a *coup d'état* seems hopeless against a modern army; the dictator can come to power only with the help or toleration of the army, but to sustain his power, he depends on a mass base.

There is, however, an important distinction between the Fascist-Nazi type and the Bolshevik. In the former, the dictator could rely upon substantial sectors of the traditional ruling groups (industry, finance, agrarians, army, bureaucracy, judiciary) which were committed to a minimum of formal legality since overt rebellion would have jeopardized their own status and security. Consequently, the dictatorship in its rise to power had to play the democratic game (compare Hitler's strategy before his Beer Hall Putsch of 1923 and afterwards). And once it had attained this goal, the requirements of competition with the outside world and the need to secure the active or passive cooperation of industrial labor, led the Nazi-Fascist type of dictatorship to present itself as a higher and nobler form of democracy.

For the Bolsheviks the need for mass support is of a different nature. The original theory of the dictatorship of the proletariat as the dictatorship of the majority over a minority was compatible at least with one version of democracy. But the Russian proletariat was a small minority in 1917, and with the Bolshevik rejection of Trotsky's theory of a permanent revolution, the democratic mass base had to be secured from among the peasants. When this was not voluntarily forthcoming the Bolshevik regime evolved into a full-blown totalitarian dictatorship.

But even in agrarian, colonial, and semi-colonial countries, where democracy did not exist or was inadequately practiced, modern dictatorship tends to become totalitarian. Today every nation experiences democracy vicariously. Due to the world-wide scope of communications, even the most backward peoples have become aware of democracy and want it, awakening mass consciousness usually taking the form of a demand for national emancipation. Consequently, here too a dictator must attempt to be a Caesar by acting out the democratic ritual even if he is compelled to go on towards a totalitarian regime.

THE SOCIAL FUNCTION OF DICTATORSHIP

Neither the attraction of a democratic ideology nor the scope of the dictatorship can fully explain the phenomena of caesarism and totalitarianism. An understanding of the social function of dictatorship would require a comprehensive analysis based upon the following elements:

a) The economic system;
b) The class relationship;
c) The personality structure.

In each historical situation these factors—economic, social, and psychological—must be treated as a unity, not as isolated, independent causes. An index of changes in these elements will frequently—I would even say invariably—be found in the intellectual and artistic trends of a given period, i.e., in philosophy, literature, and the arts. I should like to indicate certain principles that may help in the search for the causes and functions of the various types of dictatorships.

In terms of *class relationships*, the function of dictatorship may be related to three basic and recurring situations:

1. Disenfranchised and insurgent social classes demand recognition of

their interests which the political power-holders refuse to grant. There are two alternatives, depending upon the political maturity of the ascending classes:

If they are politically mature—as the bourgeoisie in England in the seventeenth or in France in the eighteenth century—caesarism will be merely a transitory phenomenon (Cromwell and Robespierre). The new classes, in power and commanding a majority, will for various reasons demand a liberal political system.

But if they are not mature, or too weak, the caesaristic movement will become a dictatorship as in the case of Pisistratus, Cola di Rienzo, or Lenin.

2. The second case is the attempt of a social class threatened with decline and striving to preserve its status and power. Dictatorship may then arise as an attempt to preserve the *status quo*. The most striking examples are Sparta, to a lesser extent the half-hearted efforts of Napoleon I, and probably the regimes of Franco and Perón.

3. The third possibility is the attempt of what one might call doomed classes to change radically the socio-economic situation, to reverse it, and to install a political system that would restore them to their old pre-eminence. This is the kernel of the German and Italian Fascist movements.

These class relationships must be studied in the light of changing economic systems. Totalitarianism, although not a new phenomenon, is determined in its modern form by the features of an industrial society. Modern industrialism is politically ambivalent because it contains and intensifies two diametrically opposed trends in modern society: the trend toward freedom and the trend toward repression. Sociologists usually define this as the problem of "moral lag," holding that the growing potentialities of modern technology outstrip the progress of "morality." This may or may not be true, but it is not, in my opinion, the decisive factor.

It is easy to say that technology is neutral politically and socially, so that any desired result can be attained depending upon the persons who use it and upon their aims. Technological optimists (like Georges Sorel and Thorstein Veblen) hold that only the full development of technological resources and their efficient utilization (e.g., exclusion of "conspicuous consumption"), can bring mankind to its highest perfection. We do not challenge this statement, but should like to explore some of its implications.

Large-scale technology on the one hand may imply the total dependence of the industrial population upon a complex, integrated mechanism, which can be operated only in a highly organized, stratified, and hierarchic system. This system must instill the virtues of discipline, obedience and subordination—no matter who owns the means of production. Thus, modern industrialism preaches the very virtues which every authoritarian political system seeks to cultivate. These virtues are repressive because they are opposed to man's self-determination.

On the other hand, the very opposite virtues may also be strengthened by technology: self-reliance, awareness of one's power and, most particularly, the feeling of solidarity—that is, a spirit of co-operation as opposed to authoritarianism.

THE PSYCHOLOGICAL PROCESSES OF DICTATORSHIP

These two antagonistic trends of industrialism are, in my opinion, essential for the understanding of modern dictatorship. The authoritarian element facilitates the rise of a dictatorship. But the co-operative aspect forces the dictatorship to find some way of replacing solidarity based on a rational interest (such as class interest) with some other identification that does not undermine but rather strengthens the dictatorship. Mussolini tried corporatism; Hitler, the doctrine of the folk community; Stalin, that of the classless socialist state. But in varying degrees all these identifications were a fake. That they nonetheless "succeeded" leads us to our final problem: the psychological processes connected with dictatorship. The basic problem is anxiety and fear and their function in political life.

Freud has defined anxiety as an "increase in tensions arising from non-gratification of [the individual's] need."[6] Anxiety is thus always present—at least potentially—as a situation or a state of indefiniteness. Fear, in turn, is the recognition of a specific danger.

Therefore, external dangers, arising in specific situations and from specific objects, are experienced in the light of internal anxiety, which then becomes externalized and activated.

But this externalization of anxiety through fear is by no means always dangerous to the personality. One may distinguish three functions of fear:

Fear as a warning;
Fear as protection; and
Fear as destruction.

Thus, an external danger may well have a kind of monitoring function: it may warn the individual that something terrible may happen to him. And the reaction to the threat may then perform a protective or even cathartic function. It may not only remove the concrete danger, but allay the anxiety as well and thus make the individual more free. On the other hand, fear may activate anxiety (particularly neurotic anxiety) to the point of making it destructive. (Indeed there are psychoanalysts who derive anxiety from destructive impulses.) Hence, in some individuals, fear becoming operative or latent anxiety may either paralyze the personality and make it incapable of defense (depressive anxiety) or heighten its aggressive instincts (persecutory anxiety).

This bare (and rather thin) analysis of certain terms of individual

---

[6] *The Problem of Anxiety*, trans. by H. A. Bunker (New York, 1936), p. 76.

psychology may now be put to use in understanding the rise of totalitarian movements and the operation of the totalitarian state.

As an illustration let me again take the Spartan state. Plutarch says, ". . . [T]he Spartans dealt with them [the Helots] very hardly: for it was a common thing to force them to drink to excess, and to lead them in that condition into their public halls, that the children might see what a sight a drunken man is, they made them to dance low dances, and sing ridiculous songs . . ." Then they assassinated them. There is little difference between the Spartan aristocracy's behavior toward the Helots and the Nazis' treatment of the Jews. The ancients were well aware of the fact that the passive element in the Spartan character was fear, that this fear was systematically cultivated and that the Spartans' famous courage in battle was nothing but fear of being stigmatized if they failed in their military duty. The actual or feigned fear of the Helots is the integrating principle of the Spartan ruling class, their anxieties being activated into aggressiveness and destruction. The totally repressive character of Sparta (as compared to Athens) rests precisely in this fact.

In totalitarian movements (as contrasted with totalitarian states), there appears a similar element. A distinction should be made between the Nazi-Fascist movement and Lenin's party prior to 1917. The Bolshevik party at that time was not a totalitarian movement, nor may Lenin (in contrast to post-1928 Stalin) be considered a totalitarian leader. The Bolshevik party then did not manipulate fear; this is a later development which began with the defeat of the revolutionary movements in Western Europe.

In contrast, the Nazi-Fascist movement activated the anxieties of the middle classes and turned them into channels of destruction which were made legitimate by means of the masses' identification with a leader, the hero. The nature of such identification has already been discussed by Freud.[7] This phenomenon appears in all caesaristic and totalitarian movements, in various degrees, of course, and with varying historical functions. . . .

47. A COMPARATIVE POLITICS OF MOVEMENT-REGIMES*

Robert C. Tucker

THOSE WHO SPECIALIZE in the study of Soviet government and politics are beginning to feel and acknowledge the need for a more effective theo-

[7] Sigmund Freud, *Group Psychology and the Analysis of the Ego*, trans. S. J. Strachey (New York, 1949).

* From "Towards a Comparative Politics of Movement-Regimes," *American Political Science Review* (June, 1961), 281–89. Article and footnotes abridged by the Editors. Reprinted by permission of The American Political Science Association and the author.

retical apparatus. The post-war years of expanded research in this field have been fruitful in empirical studies of Soviet political history and institutions, but the theoretical development has not kept pace; and now the lag is beginning to inhibit the further fruitful progress of empirical research itself. Instead of a gradually developing body of theory, we still have a mélange of "ten theories in search of reality," as Daniel Bell has summed it up in the title of a recent article.[1]

The purpose of the present paper is not to propound an eleventh theory. It is only an exploratory effort, a consideration of a somewhat different approach to the problem than has been customary in the field of Soviet studies. In presenting it, I shall try to shed the blinkers of a Russian specialist and take a look at the whole political galaxy in which Russia is only the biggest star and probably no longer the brightest one.

I

The best way out of the theoretical difficulty may lie in making the study of Soviet government and politics more comparative than it has generally been so far, thus bringing it into much closer working relations with political science as a whole and particularly with the slowly growing body of theory in comparative politics. As this statement implies, our work on Soviet government and politics has been characterized by a certain theoretical isolationism. The underlying assumption of a great deal of it is that Soviet politics constitutes a unique subject-matter, a political world apart that can only be understood in terms of its own queer if not inimitable laws or motivations. Among the ten approaches surveyed by Bell we encounter, for example, "diaperology," or the view that Soviet politics is what it is largely because the leading participants may have been swaddled in babyhood. . . .

It would not be accurate, however, to say that no one has studied the Soviet political system in a comparative political way. Indeed, much of the work done on this subject in the past fifteen years or so has been built around a kind of comparative concept—"totalitarianism." This term, it may be noted, was not originated by political scientists, but by totalitarians. It appears to have been put into currency by Mussolini or members of his circle.[2] Beginning in the late 1930s, however, Western students of dictatorship began to make use of it. The phenomenon of the

---

[1] "Ten Theories in Search of Reality: The Prediction of Soviet Behavior in the Social Sciences," *World Politics* (April 1958). The article is reprinted in A. Dallin, ed., *Soviet Conduct in World Affairs.*

[2] Mussolini wrote the following in his article on the doctrine of fascism in the *Enciclopedia Italiana* in 1932: "The Fascist conception of the State is all-embracing; outside of it no human or spiritual values may exist, much less have any value. Thus understood, Fascism is totalitarian and the Fascist State, as a synthesis and a unit which includes all values, interprets, develops and lends additional power to the whole life of a people."

totalitarian or all-embracing state was conceived as a distinctively new, twentieth-century development in the theory and practice of despotism. The Soviet Russian state, as reshaped under Stalin in the 1930s, was coupled with the nazi-fascist type of system under the general heading of "totalitarianism." They represented respectively the totalitarianism of the "left" and the totalitarianism of the "right"—two different species of one and the same new political genus. Though the political symbolisms differed, in all essentials the two types of system were identical. They shared the *Fuehrerprinzip,* the mass party brooking no opposition and extending its tentacles into all other organizations, the aggressive ideology and dynamism of external expansion, the use of the mass communications media to keep the controlled population always keyed up, the development of terror by concentration camp into a system of power, the penetration of the total state into every pore of the "atomized" society, and so on.[3]

There was an obvious basis for this trend of thought. The fact is that Stalinism was essentially identical with Hitlerism and the other expressions of fascism. Unfortunately, however, the concept of the twin totalitarianisms of the left and the right did not clearly fix and delimit this fact. The theory of totalitarianism has tended to equate not Stalinism and fascism but communism and fascism, and this is a mistake. The two phenomena have a great deal in common, but they also differ significantly. The difference is visible and traceable within the political history of the Soviet Union itself. That is, communism differs from fascism as Leninism (or Bolshevism) differs from Stalinism. And a clear recognition of this is an essential prerequisite for the advancement of theory in comparative politics as it affects Russia and numerous other countries.

It must be said, too, that the theorists of totalitarianism are conscious of this difference. They show it by suggesting in various ways that Soviet totalitarianism is preeminently a phenomenon of the Stalin era. According to Wolfe, "the Soviet government had been established for more than a decade before Stalin, late in the twenties and into the early thirties, began to impose totalitarian controls upon it." Arendt writes in the same general vein that: "To change Lenin's revolutionary dictatorship into full totalitarian rules, Stalin had first to create artificially that atomized society which had been prepared for the Nazis in Germany by historical circumstances." Friedrich and Brzezinski observe, for their part, that the emergence of totalitarian government in the Soviet Union "is marked by

---

[3] The outstanding and most influential book written from this point of view is Hannah Arendt's *The Origins of Totalitarianism* (1951). A notable attempt to develop the approach systematically has been made by Carl J. Friedrich and Zbigniew K. Brzezinski in *Totalitarian Dictatorship and Autocracy* (1956). Another effective proponent of the view is Bertram D. Wolfe, who calls totalitarianism "a total-power system" under which the state "strives to be *co-extensive* with society." "The Durability of Soviet Despotism," *Commentary,* August, 1957, reprinted in A. Dallin, *op. cit.*

Stalin's liquidation of his erstwhile colleagues in the USSR's leadership and more particularly by his epochal struggle with Trotsky."

The implication of these statements is that something in the nature of a change of political configuration, a transformation of regime, occurred in Soviet Russia between Lenin's time and Stalin's, and this is quite true. Lenin's system—a "revolutionary dictatorship"—was revolutionized by Stalin in a process that involved, among other things, the repression of Lenin's Bolshevik Party, and was supplanted by a Stalinist totalitarian autocracy. This process of transformation is accurately describable as a political revolution, although Stalin, for psychological and political reasons of his own, never admitted that fact. He never permitted his own new political order to be officially described as "Stalinism," and maintained to the end the myth of complete continuity between the regime created in the October Revolution and the new regime created in and through his own political revolution from above.

The theorists of totalitarianism, as has been indicated, recognize that a virtual change of regime occurred, but their theory does not. In effect, it says that the communist political system, established by Lenin and the Bolshevik Party, *is what it became* after Stalin revolutionized it and transformed it into a Stalinist political system. This is a questionable procedure from an analytical point of view. That Lenin's revolutionary dictatorship of the Bolshevik Party paved the way for Stalinism, and that the later system had much in common with the one it supplanted, is true. But if, on this account, we ignore the significant differences between them and view Stalinism as the effective reality of communism, we deprive ourselves of the theoretical basis for a comparative politics of the Soviet Union over time as well as a comparative politics of communism and fascism as two significantly different species of one genus.

A good comparative concept should perform a dual discriminating function: it should direct attention to the ways in which similar phenomena differ, and simultaneously to the ways in which differing phenomena resemble each other. I have suggested that the concept of totalitarianism is deficient in the former respect since it fails to direct attention to significant differences between the closely resembling political phenomena of communism and fascism. I must now extend the argument by suggesting that it also fails to direct attention to significant resemblances between *both* these phenomena and a further class of phenomena belonging to the same genus: single-party systems of the nationalist species.[4]

This century has seen the rise of a large and still growing number of

---

[4] It must be said to the credit of Arendt that she stresses the relationship between the nineteenth-century "pan-movements" of nationalism and the totalitarian movements of the present century. Unfortunately, however, she considers the nationalist movements as simply historical forerunners of totalitarianism, and non-European nationalisms are more or less left out of the picture.

revolutionary nationalist regimes under single-party auspices. Turkey under Kemal-Ataturk, Nationalist China under Sun Yat-sen and Chiang Kai-shek, Tunisia under Bourguiba, Egypt under Nasser and Ghana under Nkrumah are some among the many examples that might be cited. If we disregard all considerations of international relations and look at these regimes simply as regimes, we see a political phenomenon that calls for comparison with communist and fascist regimes. We see the need for a comparative-political framework within which communist, fascist and nationalist single-party regimes may be analyzed in terms of their significant similarities as well as their significant differences, or as three species of a single political genus.

The definition of the political genus presents obvious difficulties. Ideally this definition should fix upon (1) that which is common to all phenomena of the class and specific to no one of the three postulated sub-classes, and (2) that which differentiates this whole class of phenomena from others that may be more or less closely related to it. As a rough attempt I would propose the following formula: *the revolutionary mass-movement regime under single-party auspices.* For brevity I shall refer to it as the "movement-regime."

In advocating this category as a tool of comparative analysis, it is not my object to suggest that the notion of totalitarianism is useless or ought to be discarded from political science. The frequency with which we employ it in political discourse strongly indicates that it answers to a genuine need of intellectual communication. My thesis is simply that the concept of totalitarianism has not adequately stimulated the progress of research in the comparative study of the novel forms of authoritarianism that have arisen in profusion in this century, and that it will have its scientific uses *within* a comparative politics of movement-regimes. Otherwise expressing it, the totalitarian dictatorship as such is not the novel political phenomenon of the present century, but at most one of the forms that this phenomenon takes. The distinctively new type of political formation that needs to be studied as a general form and in its specific varieties is the revolutionary mass-movement regime under single-party auspices.

II

The first element of the formula—"revolutionary"—establishes that we are dealing with regimes born in revolutionary struggle and that once in being they strive to maintain revolutionary momentum. The movement to displace the preexisting system of order then becomes a revolutionary movement for national renovation, or a movement to carry the revolution beyond the national borders, or both. In the case of the nationalist movement-regimes, especially in more recent times, the original revolutionary struggle is typically directed against a foreign colonial regime or regime of foreign dependency. With communist and fascist regimes, the typical—though not necessary or invariable—pattern is one of revolutionary struggle against an indigenous order that is treated *as though* it were foreign. So Lenin in 1902 conceived the Russian revolutionary movement as a nation-wide resistance movement against an essentially alien Tsarist monarchy and its supporters, and for Hitler the Weimar Republic was an un-German phenomenon. Stalin's was a marginal case in which the revolution against the pre-existing (Bolshevik) system of order was conducted from above. It is notable, however, that the purged old Bolshevik leadership was condemned as a treasonable, anti-national element.

The reader may have wondered why "ideology" was not included as an independent element of the formula. It might have been, but for simplicity's sake it seems preferable to consider this extremely important factor under the "revolutionary" heading. The ideology is, in its core, a philosophy of the revolution and program of the revolutionary struggle. As such it not only provides political orientation but serves as a powerful organizing instrument in the hands of the leadership. As Lenin said, "Without a revolutionary theory there can be no revolutionary movement."[5] Every movement-regime is associated with an ideology. As will be suggested later in this paper, comparative analysis of the ideologies may be useful in differentiating communist, fascist and nationalist forms of the movement-regime.

Revolutionary regimes are not at all new in history, but the revolutionary *mass-movement* regime is a relatively novel phenomenon. The idea is traceable at least as far back as Mazzini, and earlier intimations of it are to be found in eighteenth-century France.[6] Thus, Mazzini's contemplated revolution of national liberation and unification of Italy was to bring into being a third and greater Rome, "the Rome of the People," which in turn would provide leadership for all of Europe in creating a Europe of the people. The revolution was to be accomplished, moreover, with the active participation of masses of the people under the guidance and energetic leadership of an elite organization, Young Italy.

The history of politics in the twentieth century could be written in terms of the realization of the dreams of the nineteenth—and the discrepancy between dream and reality. The contemporary world contains a multitude of regimes, born in revolution, that rest upon and represent—or claim to—mass movements of a national or trans-national scope. In the typical case the mass movement is organized during the revolutionary struggle for power and as a means of waging this struggle. Once the regime is in being, the mass movement is enlarged and given new tasks of various kinds in the continuing revolution of national renewal. In some

[5] *What Is To Be Done?*, in *Selected Works* (Moscow, 1946), Vol. I, p. 165.

[6] J. A. Talmond discusses the eighteenth-century background in his *Origins of Totalitarian Democracy* (1952).

instances (present-day Egypt, for example) the development of the mass movement occurs after the conquest of power. In some instances too, it remains largely a political artifact or pretence of a mass movement. Some of the Soviet satellite regimes might be cases in point.

The third common element is the militant centralized revolutionary party, or "vanguard" party as we may call it, which takes power in the name of the movement and the nation and then assumes the new function of governing the country single-handedly. Mazzini's phrase "party of action" foreshadowed the nature of this new type of party. Its character is largely determined by the circumstances of its origin. Since it arises outside of, and in opposition to, an existing system of law and order, electioneering is not its *métier*. Though it may take part in a given election for tactical purposes, it exists to overthrow a political order rather than to come to power within it. In the typical case it develops as a disciplined elite connected with a mass following through party "cells" in the enemy-order, and usually has a single dominating personality as its top leader and organizer. It is in essence a political warfare organization, and as such tends toward conspiratorial habits and a quasi-military, authoritarian concept of its internal organization and relation to the mass following. Since its revolutionary ends transcend the destruction of the old order, the latter event is simply a new beginning. The party becomes the staff headquarters of the new revolutionary movement-regime, the territorial committees and cells become units of rule, and the single-party state is born.

The concept of the revolutionary vanguard party, with its "cellular structure" penetrating the pores of the old society, was rather well developed already in the nineteenth century, particularly among the Russian Populists. But it found its most influential exponent early in the twentieth century in Lenin. Unlike Marx, who tended to think that history itself would make the revolution, Lenin based all his thinking on the premise that revolutions have to be organized. His theory and practice of revolutionary "party construction" not only shaped the organization of communist movements everywhere; it also radiated far and wide into nationalist and fascist movements. A well known instance of this diffusion occurred in the early 1920s, when Sun Yat-sen decided to remodel the Chinese national revolutionary party (Kuomintang) in accordance with the Leninist concept, and the Russian Bolshevik Mikhail Borodin was sent to supervise the overhauling. A little later Chiang Kai-shek gave the Russians a lesson in what might be called "anti-Communist communism" by turning the assimilated Bolshevik-type organizational forms against the Chinese Bolsheviks and their Muscovite mentors. The lesson was not lost on Stalin, who in the 1930s made use of Bolshevik organizational forms in destroying the *Russian* Bolsheviks, save for those whom he permitted to survive as Stalinists.

An instructive present-day example of a nationalist movement-regime with a ruling party shaped in the Leninist image may be found in Tunisia. President Bourguiba's Liberal Constitutional (Neo-Destour) party "has covered the whole country with a network of a thousand cells" which "replace the 'infrastructure' of the modern state." "The party members who are organized in cells form the party Congress, which elects an executive, the Political Bureau. The Political Bureau is the main instrument of government. . . . The Political Bureau exercises tight control over the party machine, in which it has established a kind of 'democratic centralism.' . . . The Liberal Constitutional party has established a large network of organizations which embrace practically the whole population."[7] The exquisite irony of the situation is that the Communist Party of Tunisia is the sole opponent of President Bourguiba's regime.

One further generalization may be offered regarding the movement-regimes as a class. Since the militant centralized revolutionary party becomes the new foundation of political authority, and its cellular structure the "infrastructure" of the new state, the movement-regime takes on the authoritarian character of the founding organization. In certain instances (about which more later) it subsequently grows much more authoritarian, and the adjective "totalitarian" may become applicable. However, the leadership of the authoritarian movement-regime insists that it is also democratic in a "new way" (*i.e.*, not the liberal Western way). This mode of thought, in which the dichotomy of "dictatorship—democracy" is rejected, is an outgrowth of the original concept of the revolutionary struggle as a mass movement for national or supra-national objectives under guidance of a disciplined political elite organization. The result is one or another version of the doctrine of "guided democracy," of which, again, Lenin was the preeminent exponent.

The notion should not be dismissed as simple hypocrisy, although it may be that in any given instance. If "democracy" here loses the connotation of effective popular control over the regime (which is, by self-definition, the group that knows best what is in the interests of the people), it simultaneously acquires the connotation of mass popular participation in the continuing revolution of national renewal. In practice this means the enlisting of masses of people in the activities of trade unions, youth, professional and other organizations that are formally non-party in character but are operated under party guidance and supervision via directorates from top to bottom in which disciplined party members predominate (the so-called "transmission belts" of Leninist theory). A large proportion of the population is thus drawn into the whirlpool of guided public life, and many may derive an experience of political participation that was denied them under the old regime. In Russia the foremost non-party organs of controlled participation are the soviets or local councils, which arose before the October Revolution and

---

[7] Hans E. Tutsch, "Bourguiba's Tunisia—I," *The New Leader*, February 29, 1960, p. 7.

independently of communism but were later reshaped into components of the Bolshevik movement-regime. Today they form a pyramidal network of thousands of party-guided bodies at village, town, district and province level, with deliberative and administrative functions in which several millions of deputies and sub-committee members take part. Very many of these people have no direct Communist party affiliation.

This brings us again to the principle of transferability of organizational forms among movement-regimes of different types. Recently, for example, a pyramidal system of "councils," quite comparable in concept if not in all details to the one just described, has been introduced under the auspices of President Nasser's National Union regime in Egypt, and President Mohammed Ayub Khan's new regime in Pakistan is now introducing a similar setup there under the heading of "basic democracy." A close associate of President Nasser's has explained to a Western journalist that the purpose of the Egyptian councils is to enlist mass participation at the village level in the revolution of national renewal: "The real revolution must come in the villages. . . . Every village has elected a council, replacing the old appointed Mayor. The council constitutes itself a cooperative and works with the Government's agricultural experts." The journalist reports that Nasser aides are not insulted if this system is described as "guided democracy," and he quotes the close associate further as saying: "We have a concept of democracy, it differs from yours. . . . We need something more dynamic, more realistic. . . . If we use your system the Communists will succeed, because they can speak to the masses." Thus, there can be anti-Soviet sovietism in the field of "guided democracy," as well as the previously mentioned phenomenon of anti-Communist communism in the field of party organization.

A final observation about the movement-regime is that it has no restricted habitat in the world. A comparative politics of movement-regimes is not a regional affair, and defies the classifications of political systems according to geographic zone. There is a rough correlation between antecedent colonialism and the rise of nationalist movement-regimes, or alternatively of communist movement-regimes that ride to power on a wave of nationalist revolution. There is a related and still rougher correlation between the movement-regime and the conditions of economic and cultural backwardness, feudalism, stagnation, etc., that lend a special cogency to the revolutionary call for renovation of the nation. All this might suggest the thought that the specific habitat of the movement-regime is the "East" or, more broadly, the "under-developed areas." Yet such regimes, in one form or another, have appeared not only in Russia, Asia, the Middle East, Africa, Latin America and Eastern Europe, but also in parts of Western Europe (Germany, Italy, Spain, Portugal); and Hitler's Germany was hardly an under-developed area. Moreover, movements bearing within themselves the germs of potential movement-regimes have arisen in many other countries, including Great Britain and the United

States. The movement-regime is a political phenomenon to which no nation and no part of the world is completely immune.

III

The differentiation of the species of movement-regime presents a much more difficult and complex problem than the definition of the genus. There are many avenues of approach to it, variously emphasizing social, economic, historical, religious and psychological factors, etc. The most that can be attempted here is to present a few notes on the problem.

First, it must be said that we are dealing with classes of phenomena that may be distinguishable but are not fully distinct. Thus, elements of nationalism are to be found in both communist and fascist movement-regimes, and any formulae for the latter that excluded this fact would be useless. It therefore appears inadvisable to segregate the species under conceptually pure "ideal types." Allowance must be made for complexity of character and even for the possibility of genuine hybrids. In short, nationalist, fascist and communist movement-regimes are best differentiated according to their characteristic *prevailing tendencies*.

What has been said above about the transferability of organizational forms among movement-regimes of different types argues against any attempt to differentiate the types primarily in organizational terms. A more promising basis of differentiation, it seems to me, lies in the motivation of revolutionary politics, or what is often called the "revolutionary dynamism." All the movement-regimes originally have a revolutionary dynamism. They come into being by the revolutionary displacement of a pre-existing order, and seek to maintain revolutionary momentum after they come to power. They may, of course, fail to do so. They may lose revolutionary momentum eventually. When this happens they become what I shall call "extinct" movement-regimes. Like a star that has ceased to give off light, an extinct movement-regime may go on existing for a long while without a revolutionary *raison d'être*. We may say of such a regime what Herzen in 1853 said of the contemporary Russian monarchy, that it "exercises power in order to exercise power."

The revolutionary dynamism of the nationalist movement-regime is relatively restricted in scope and easy to define. Here the goal of the revolutionary movement is, first, national independence, the creation of a sovereign nation-state. Second, the revolutionary movement is aimed at the modernization of the newly independent state, and this typically involves many elements of an internal social revolution. Old class relations in society, old patterns of land tenure, old customs, old traditions of thought and generally old ways of conducting the business of life are assailed in an internal revolution of national renewal. However, purely nationalist revolutionary movement-regimes show a definite tendency to spend their revolutionary force rather early. In some cases this happens soon after the achievement of the original revolutionary goals and prior to the completion of the revolutionizing of the old society. In other words, the nationalist movement-regime is peculiarly the prey of the phenomenon of "extinction."

In the best of cases, of which the Kemalist movement in Turkey might be an example, the revolution of national renewal is carried through far enough under the auspices of the movement-regime to make possible an orderly further development in a new and more democratic direction. More typical, however, may be the case of the Chinese Kuomintang, where the early subsiding of revolutionary dynamism paved the way for the displacement of the nationalist movement-regime by a communist movement-regime that came to power under the slogan of carrying through the "betrayed" revolution of national renewal. In general, communist movement-regimes, where not installed by direct action of a foreign power (as in most of Eastern Europe, North Korea, etc., after World War II), tend to arise as the penalty for either the absence of an effective national revolutionary movement where conditions call for it, or the inability of nationalist movement-regimes, once in being, to maintain their initial revolutionary momentum.

The relatively low revolutionary dynamism of the nationalist movement-regime is correlated with a relatively restricted revolutionary "constituency." The ideology of the national revolution is itself national. The sovereign independence and renovation of the nation are the objectives. Once installed in power, the nationalist movement-regime may develop an active foreign policy within what is likely to be a neutralist orientation in world affairs. But this will not be a policy of active export of the revolution to other lands. Such revolutionary expansionism is, on the other hand, a distinctive characteristic of *both* communist and fascist movement-regimes. Here the sphere of outlet for revolutionary energy is not confined to the national homeland. The politics of revolution embrace not only the revolutionary capture of power and subsequent internal revolution, but also, in varying manner and degree, the turning of the revolutionary dynamism out upon the world. Thus when a new movement-regime embarks upon a course of active export of the revolution to other countries, this may be taken as a fairly strong indication that it belongs not to the nationalist species but to one of the other two. The Castro regime in Cuba would be a case in point.

Communism and fascism are often contrasted on the ground that the one has an international "class appeal" while the other has a "national appeal" and is nationalist in essence. There is something in this idea, but it is also quite misleading. The dichotomy of communist internationalism *versus* fascist nationalism overlooks the fact that national and international elements commingle in both phenomena. On the one hand, the communist movement-regime is committed to a form of the national revolution as well as to the goal of world communism. It appropriates not only the appeals of the revolution of national renewal but also the task of carrying it through (in its own special way) when the movement comes to power.

On the other hand, the fascist revolutionary dynamism shares with the communist a supra-national scope. Both give ideological expression to this by proclaiming a supra-national revolutionary constituency and also an international *enemy* of the revolution. In the classic Bolshevik conception, the revolutionary constituency begins with the working classes of the revolutionary homeland and embraces the working classes of all countries, and the international bourgeoisie (or "international imperialism") is the enemy. Fascist regimes differ in their ideologies, but these regularly show a dualism that is comparable in kind if less comprehensive in scope. They take the *nation* as the nucleus of a larger whole, a supra-national revolutionary constituency or sphere of revolution. Thus, for Hitler the German *Volk* was the nucleus of the "Nordic race," and international Jewry or international imperialism was the enemy of the national-socialist revolution. For Mussolini "Romanism" was the key word, and the larger sphere of revolution was reflected in the slogan: "Italy today, tomorrow the Roman Empire!" Examples could be multiplied. The dual symbolism of President Nasser's movement-regime, which views Egypt or the U.A.R. as the nucleus of a vast "Arab nation" embracing all the separate Arabic nations and Arabs wherever they are, belongs to the pattern in question. Taken in conjunction with Nasserist activity in the export of the revolution to neighboring countries, this suggests that it would be a mistake to construe Nasserism as nationalist in essence although it does display various features of a nationalist revolutionary movement.

In certain instances, typically occurring in smaller countries, we see the phenomenon of "national communism" or, alternatively, "national fascism" (of which present-day Francoist Spain might be a good example). This development may be, and in the latter case no doubt is, indicative of a general loss of revolutionary momentum and the tendency to grow "extinct." On the other hand, it may, as in the case of Titoist Yugoslavia, be accompanied by something in the nature of an internal political "reformation" in which the movement develops with new vigor but in different directions.

One further consideration should be noted in connection with the fascist form of movement-regime. Although its sphere of revolution is not confined to the national homeland, it does typically indulge in strident national self-glorification. It proclaims its nation to be supreme in all the recognized national virtues, and declares that the good of the nation is the highest goal of the regime. This has led some scholars to see in fascism "an inflammation of nationalism."[8] It seems, however, that this inflamed

---

[8] Hans Kohn, *Nationalism: Its Meaning and History* (1955), p. 79.

nationalism is essentially a pseudo-nationalism, and that fascists must be distinguished from authentic nationalists as being, at best, the pharisees of nationalism. Thus, when Hitler saw that all was lost, he desired the destruction of the German nation as punishment for its unworthiness. Germany had not been worthy of its *Fuehrer*. Obviously, the supreme value was not the German nation but the Hitlerite self, and the official glorification of the nation had been a cover and vehicle of the leader's self-glorification.

I take this to be indicative of a critically important general fact about the fascist type of movement-regime, viz., that here the psychology or more accurately the psychopathology of the leader becomes the driving force of the political mechanism. The regime is shaped into a highly complicated instrumentality for acting out the needs of the paranoid leader-personality, whose psychodynamics are politicized, *i.e.*, expressed in political action. Thus, the Nazi regime started the second World War in 1939 at a time when it was militarily not yet prepared and to the chagrin of many of its highest officials, military and civilian. It was propelled into this action not by a cold calculation of relative forces and risks, but by the compulsive need of Hitler for revenge against his enemies. When his advisers warned him against it on the ground of the enemies' strength, he replied: "Then I will build U-boats! U-boats! U-boats! . . . I will build airplanes! airplanes! airplanes! *and I will exterminate my enemies.*" Comparable in character (though not in consequence) was the statement reportedly made by Stalin on the eve of his public assault on Tito in 1948: "I will shake my little finger—and there will be no more Tito. He will fall."

In order to shape the regime into a means of expression of his personal needs, the leader must reduce the ruling party to the role of an important cog in the apparatus of the state. It was pointed out earlier that movement-regimes tend to be headed by a dominating individual personality. This, however, does not imply that they are absolute autocracies. In fact, the broad tendency is oligarchical rule by the top leadership of the ruling party under the overall direction of the dominant personality. The fascist movement-regimes deviate from this pattern and show a pronounced tendency to absolute autocracy, which involves the subordination of the party to the state as embodied in the leader. He emancipates himself from the control of the party oligarchy, and relies heavily upon the secret police and permanent pervasive terror through this organization to ensure unquestioning compliance with his least wishes on the part of everyone from the lowliest man in the street to the highest dignitaries of the regime. Consequently, fascist regimes tend to become highly *statist* in orientation, and the state as personified in the leader displaces the party as the supreme symbol and object of official adoration. For these reasons the most accurate general term for the various fascist movement-regimes would be "fuehrerism," and the most accurate title in each individual instance would be the one formed from the leader's name (*e.g.*, "Hitlerism" rather than "Nazism").

It was said above that movement-regimes may undergo "extinction" when the revolutionary dynamism subsides. Another possible process is "metamorphosis" as a result of the *alteration* of the dynamism. A movement-regime of one species turns into one of another species as a consequence of a qualitative change in the motivation of revolutionary politics. Such a change is determined in its turn by a change or changes in the leadership situation within the regime. For various reasons it may not be possible for the leadership of the metamorphosed movement-regime to admit (even to itself) that the metamorphosis has occurred. The evidence of it must therefore be sought not in the regime's official self-definition but rather in changes in the observable complex of ideological and behavioral patterns.

In conclusion I suggest that the political history of Soviet Russia probably offers the best laboratory for the study of the phenomenon of metamorphosis of movement-regimes. From the standpoint of a comparative politics of movement-regimes, this history is one of different *movements* and of different Soviet *regimes* within a framework of continuity of certain (transferable) organizational forms and official nomenclature. The rise of Stalinism between 1928 and 1938 involved a process of change far more deep and pervasive than is generally realized. It was the metamorphosis of the original communist or Bolshevik movement-regime into a new movement-regime of the fuehrerist type. As indicated at the outset of this paper, the metamorphosis was not accompanied by any change in the regime's official self-definition (although it is significant that Stalin in 1952 banned the word "Bolshevik" from the name of the party and from all Soviet official usage). It was, however, reflected in a whole system of changes in the political process, the ideological pattern, the organization of supreme power, and official patterns of behavior. Partly because of the inadequacy of our theoretical apparatus, and partly too because of the unduly large influence of the Soviet regime's self-image upon our conceptions, Western thinking has not, on the whole, assessed the full significance of the change from the Bolshevik to the Stalinist political system. A basic continuity of the Bolshevik movement-regime has been postulated, as is implicit, for example, in the following statement by Bertram Wolfe: "When Stalin died in 1953, Bolshevism was fifty years old."[9]

Very real and important issues affecting the understanding and interpretation of the political changes in Russia since Stalin's death are involved in what may seem to be a problem of merely historical interest. On the postulate of continuity of the Bolshevik movement-regime from 1917 to 1953, "significant change" will logically mean change *away* from

---

[9] *Soviet Conduct in World Affairs*, p. 268.

Bolshevism or communism. This assumption results in a tendency to deprecate the significance of the post-Stalinist changes in Soviet political processes and policies. If, on the other hand, we operate on the premise that Stalin's political revolution from above transformed the original Bolshevik movement-regime into a new one that was fuehrerist in its inner dynamism and political tendency, we shall reason that when Stalin died in 1953 Bolshevism had been moribund in Russia for fifteen years, and that the main issue was whether it would revive and if so to what extent. This opens the way to a recognition that a whole complex of quite significant political changes have occurred in post-Stalinist Russia within the broad framework of a conscious movement under the aegis of Khrushchev to reconstitute the political system of Bolshevism.

48. CINCINNATUS AND THE APPARATCHIK*
Zbigniew Brzezinski and Samuel P. Huntington

POLITICAL LEADERSHIP IN MODERN SOCIETY

"Кто кого?" asked Lenin. "Who governs?" echoes a contemporary American political scientist. The question is of perennial interest. The "who's" have the capacity to influence the behavior of others. They include *political leaders*, who customarily exercise power through public or governmental bodies, and *non-political leaders*, who may exercise power through the command of other values, such as wealth, income, expertise. Political leaders and non-political leaders together constitute the *elite;* they lead the masses, who, needless to say, greatly outnumber the elite.

Political leadership in modern industrialized societies differs significantly from that in pre-modern agrarian societies. In the latter, typically, the functions of political leadership and non-political leadership are exercised by the same people. The primary distinction is between the elite, or ruling class or aristocracy, on the one hand, and the mass of the people, on the other. The political leaders of society are also its military, economic, cultural, and religious leaders. Certain individuals, of course, may spend more of their lives in politics, or in the church, but they are all recruited from the same relatively limited social class and in many cases the same individuals are leaders in more than one field of endeavor. The gap between elite and mass is vast. Few members of the lower class climb into the elite; the division between the two is usually fixed by heredity. The numerous lower class possesses neither wealth, education, culture,

* From "Cincinnatus and the Apparatchik," *World Politics* (October, 1963), 52–78. Article and footnotes abridged by the editors. Reprinted by permission of the authors.

authority, power, status, nor, in many cases, liberty. The elite possesses all of these. The system is, in Professor Dahl's term, one of "cumulative inequalities."[1]

In varying forms this pattern of organization appears in agrarian societies where landownership is concentrated in a few hands. It was the prevailing pattern in Western Europe until the nineteenth century. It was the prevailing pattern in Russia until 1917. It is the prevailing pattern in many parts of Latin America and the Middle East today. It was also, in less rigid form, the pattern in the United States until about 1820. The principal political impact of industrialization is to diversify the premodern agrarian ruling class. It replaces the system of "cumulative inequalities" with one of "dispersed inequalities." It gives rise to new forms of wealth and power, and it eventually produces a complex society characterized by a multiplicity of functions and a highly developed division of labor. The functions and institutions of military leadership, educational leadership, economic leadership, religious leadership, and political leadership become more specialized. Mass armies develop, commanded by professional officer corps. Specialized economic institutions—corporations or trusts—are created by government or private entrepreneurs and, in due course, themselves give birth to a new class of industrial managers. Scientific and technical knowledge multiplies, giving rise to a variety of experts. The ability of any one individual to be a Renaissance (or Enlightenment) man diminishes, and the ability of any one social class to monopolize the positions of leadership within society also is weakened.

A simple society does not need elaborate or highly differentiated leadership institutions. A complex organization, however, contains within itself many specialists, subgroups, and functional types. Hence, it requires yet another type to coordinate and integrate their activities. This is the role of the political leader; to perform this role he requires some degree of power over others in society. Hence, unlike other individuals who may exercise power, the political leader is formally invested by society with authority to exercise power. He is the general manager of the modern state. His function is comparable to that of the line officer in an army, the broad-gauged executive in a corporation, or the dean in a university. Because he is a specialist in the general direction of society, the political leader faces problems in ordering his relationship with the specialists in other areas of activity. In pre-modern agrarian society, political leaders and non-political leaders were identical. In the complex modern society, the relations between political leaders and non-political leaders equal in importance those between the leaders and the masses.

In modern societies, political leadership is the product of achievement. The problem is: What type of achievement? Who are the political leaders and where do they come from? To a large extent they are recruited from

[1] See Robert A. Dahl, *Who Governs? Democracy and Power in an American City* (New Haven, 1961), 1–8, 84–85.

the class of professional politicians—i.e., individuals who attempt to make a career of political leadership. The expansion and differentiation of society give rise to specialized political institutions and specialized political practitioners. The state bureaucracy expands and is rationalized; cabinets and legislatures develop and acquire more distinctive roles; and, most important, the political party emerges as the key institution for the representation and integration of competing interests and the recruitment and selection of political leaders. Political parties in the sense of divisions or factions are as old as history; political parties in the sense of organized institutions, however, date from the late eighteenth century. Only in the nineteenth century did Western societies evolve a distinct class of professional politicians. Only in the nineteenth century did politics, in Weber's phrase, become a vocation. The professional politician operates the party system and operates through the party system to achieve positions of political leadership in the state.

The history, ideology, and culture of a society shape the character of its political leadership and, particularly, the extent to which that leadership is composed of professional politicians or individuals drawn from other sources, usually the non-political leaders of society. In the modern state all professional politicians are not necessarily political leaders, and all political leaders are not necessarily professional politicians. The pattern in each society is different. In addition, while each modern society has an identifiable class of professional politicians, the characteristics and skills of that class vary from one society to another. They too are a function of the overall character of the society. The professional politician is thus a less universal figure than most of the other specialists in the modern world. Technical skills are universal; social skills are peculiar to particular societies. The skills of a nuclear physicist are the same in the Soviet Union and in the United States; presumably a physicist from Moscow or Leningrad University could easily make himself at home in the laboratories at Harvard or Columbia. A surgeon transferring from a Moscow hospital to a New York hospital also would have little trouble in adjusting to his new institutional environment and job. The manager of a machine tool factory, on the other hand, might have a more difficult time of it: the technical skills would be similar but the social context would be very different. He would have to learn how to negotiate with autonomous labor unions and labor leaders. The professional politician, however, would probably have the most difficult time of all. The specialized knowledge of the politician is almost entirely social in character; it is, in part, knowledge of the universal characteristics of human behavior, but it is, even more, knowledge of the distinctive patterns and characteristics of behavior in a particular society. The professional politician is concerned with the manipulation and control of people. The means and skills for accomplishing these ends may differ greatly from one society to another, and, indeed, in any one society they change over time as the underlying social and political character of the society changes. The leader of a small group in one context and with respect to one set of problems may well be a follower in another context and when the group is confronted with a different set of problems.

LEADERS, POLITICIANS, AND BUREAUCRATS

Professional Politicians

In the United States, the old colonial-Federalist ruling class declined during the nineteenth century and was replaced by a more diversified social-economic elite including new frontier wealth, new merchants, and new industrialists. The decline was also marked by the development of the party system, the extension of the suffrage, the multiplication of elective offices, and the emergence of the American-style professional politician. Confronted with an almost infinite variety of elective offices in local, state, and national governments, the American politician's career consisted of campaigns for elected offices with successively bigger constituencies and broader responsibilities. The key decisions in such a career were frequently ones of selection and timing: which office to run for in which year. The American electoral politician thus differed significantly from his British counterpart, whose election interests were simply to get into the Commons and to stay there. The American professional is an electoral politician, the British professional a parliamentary politician. In America, the term "professional politician" still conjures up the image of a person who is running for elective office, a person who is in elective office, or a person (party chairman or campaign manager) whose job is to get other people into elective office.

In Russia, the ruling class first declined and then was overthrown by an organization of professional revolutionaries. The resulting vacuum in political leadership was filled by the rapid expansion of the party apparatus and the transformation of Lenin's organization of professional revolutionaries into Stalin's organization of professional rulers. In the United States, the professional politician is the product of the democratization of the government. In the Soviet Union, he is the product of the bureaucratization of the party. As professional politicians the Soviet apparatchik and the American electoral politician have some similarities. To some degree each may develop expertise in a particular set of policy problems important to his oblast or constituency. But the distinctive character of each is that he is a generalist, an expert in dealing simultaneously with a variety of issues and pressures, balancing one off against another, attempting to resolve problems at the least cost to the greatest number of interests involved. In addition, the politician in both systems must be flexible in viewpoint, adaptable in outlook, and contingent in loyalties. He must reward his friends and punish his enemies, but he must also be aware that today's friends may be tomorrow's enemies and vice versa. He must be able to adapt to a variety of different circumstances and responsibilities. He must be a mobile individual, committed wholeheartedly to the position or institution he is in at the moment but also able to move quickly on to a different position in a different institutional context. The higher party authorities shift the promising apparatchik every few years from one oblast to another and one type of responsibility to another. The vagaries of the voters and the variety of the opportunities of the American political system require a comparable degree of mobility on the part of the American electoral politician.

Apart from these generic characteristics, the apparatchik and the electoral politician are rather different political animals with different habits and habitats. They differ especially in their degree of political professionalization and their commitment to politics as a career. The typical American politician is really only a semi-pro: he usually combines his public career with the simultaneous pursuit of a private career in law, business, education, or journalism. If circumstances or the voters retire him from his public career, he can still pursue his private one with little loss and perhaps with considerable benefit. His commitment to politics is thus nowhere near as profound as that of his Soviet counterpart. Even for the professional, politics in America is still in many respects an avocation rather than a vocation. Only five of 513 top political leaders in the United States from 1789 to 1953 had no career other than politics.[2] Indeed, the professional politician may well make a public career out of politics with the thought that the primary benefits of this career will be in other fields, that the political ladder may be used to scale non-political heights in business and society. For his Soviet counterpart, on the other hand, a political career is normally a more-than-fulltime commitment for life. The Russian enters upon it as an American might enter the priesthood or the army. He becomes engulfed in the life of the apparatus. Lacking a private career upon which to fall back, he would find escape difficult even if it were conceivable. His life is more focused, his loyalties more exclusive, his commitment more intense than those of the American politician.

Not only is the apparatchik's career commitment exclusive but the career itself is highly professionalized. The apparatus is a sort of cross between the Hague machine and the United States Army. The apparatchik's career in many ways resembles that of the military officer. Although practice has varied, certain minimum educational attainments are usually required. As for the officer, entry is normally at the bottom of the ladder. Like the successful officer, the successful apparatchik moves up the hierarchy to posts of broader and broader responsibility: raion to oblast or krai to Union Republic or to major party organizations such as those of Moscow and Leningrad and eventually to the Central Committee Secretariat. The apparatchik can also move upward in the type of responsi-

---

[2] C. Wright Mills, *The Power Elite* (New York, 1956), 402.

bility at each level: from a position as second secretary in one oblast to a post as first secretary in another. At various points in his career he will be "seconded" to positions in the state or industrial bureaucracy. He will be expected to improve his education regularly through correspondence courses. Like the army officer who goes to a staff school or war college, he may also be sent for a four-year course at the Party School in his Union Republic or to the Higher Party School of the Central Committee in Moscow. The schools were founded in 1946 and during the first decade of their activity some fifty-five thousand individuals were trained in the local Party Schools and nine thousand by the Higher Party School. Party officials under the age of thirty-five and with a good record in party work are nominated for the four-year course at the Inter-Oblast Schools; more senior officials under the age of forty may be assigned for two years to the Higher Party School, which also offers courses by correspondence. (In 1956, two hundred officials were in attendance at the Higher Party School and three thousand more were studying by correspondence.) Several of the younger top party leaders, such as Polyansky, Mazurov, Furtseva, have already received their training there.

The party official assigned to such advanced party studies will receive intensive training designed to improve his political and ideological knowledge, as well as his adeptness at handling economic and technical-managerial issues. Of the 3,200 hours prescribed in 1957 in a typical curriculum of a four-year Inter-Oblast Communist Party School, 41.5 per cent were assigned to strictly political subjects, such as "diamat" and history of the CPSU; 15 per cent to economics, economic organization, and planning; and 43.5 per cent to such varied specialties as industrial technology, agriculture, regional planning, and statistics. The training is obviously designed to develop *professional political leaders of society*, capable of providing expert social-economic direction within the framework of the ideological goals and political vested interests of the ruling party. After "graduation" the rising party official keeps in touch with the latest organizational guidelines and techniques by receiving the regular party journals and through various "handbooks," issued by the Central Committee, containing detailed instructions on how to act in various contingencies.

"Alternation of intensive training with practical experience," one scholar has observed, "is a basic principle of the process of moulding the apparatus official."[3] While he may hold some jobs longer, his normal tour of duty, like that in the United States Army, is three or four years. If he develops a reputation as a trouble shooter in industrial production, agricultural problems, or construction projects, he may well be shifted from one trouble spot to a similar but worse one. Even so, if he demonstrates his ability he will eventually take on jobs with more varied

---

[3] John A. Armstrong, *The Soviet Bureaucratic Elite: A Case Study of the Ukrainian Apparatus* (New York, 1959), p. 37.

responsibilities. He may also serve on the political staff supervising the military. IIis success depends upon his political and administrative abilities and his affiliations with more powerful patrons who can speed his way up the apparatus hierarchy. If he does not succeed at the oblast level, he will be shunted off to a low level secondary post. . . .

The Soviet professional politician functions exclusively in a bureaucratic environment. Since the party apparatus is the most important bureaucracy in Soviet society, the power of the apparatchik depends upon his position in the party bureaucratic structure. Organizational positions are to him what votes are to the American politician. The immediate environment of the latter is, indeed, one of the least bureaucratized segments of American society. The United States has industrial, administrative, military, educational bureaucracies, but it does not have a political one. Hence, the skills which are required of the Soviet politician differ considerably from those of the American politician. The apparatchik requires executive traits: the hard-driving, promoting, bulldozing abilities of the old-style American entrepreneur, plus the flexibility in trimming his sails and blending with his environment of the organization man. He must also be adept at bureaucratic in-fighting, anticipating changes in the party line and party priorities, identifying the rising apparatus stars and the falling ones, and choosing the right side of the critical issue while maneuvering his opponents onto the wrong side. Crucial to his success is not so much the support of large numbers of people as the backing of the right man at the right time.

The American politician, on the other hand, needs to sense the trend of public opinion rather than Presidium opinion, to articulate common symbols which have wide appeal, to avoid commitment on issues where his constituency is divided, and to negotiate satisfying compromises among the interests making demands upon him. He must be expert in the strategy of the forum, the apparatchik expert in the strategy of the closet. In campaigns and in legislatures the American politician functions in an egalitarian environment in which the ability to help and harm operates in both directions. The Soviet apparatchik, however, works in a more asymmetrical bureaucratic environment. While power never flows exclusively in one direction, he is nonetheless largely at the mercy of his superiors while at the same time he exercises extensive controls over his subordinates. The American politician must persuade equals; the apparatchik must please superiors and prod subordinates. When confronted with another politician, the American asks himself, "What's he got to offer?" while the Soviet thinks, "Who is to be master?"

Politicians and Leaders

The differences in the character of the professional politician in the Soviet Union and the United States are matched by the differences in their roles in the system of political leadership. Most of the political leaders in the Soviet Union are apparatchiki. Only a relatively small number of the political leaders in the United States are professional politicians. In the Soviet Union the apparatchiki furnish the Leader for the system, form a majority in the Presidium and the Central Committee, often fill the top posts in the state bureaucracies, and monopolize the Central Committee Secretariat and the party apparatus. In the United States, the electoral politician shares the positions of political leadership with many other types. The professional occupies many posts in state and local government and he usually dominates legislatures at all levels of government. He may also fill the Presidency. With that exception, however, he is rarely found elsewhere in the Administration or in the governmental bureaucracies or in the private bureaucracies of the Establishment. The governmental and private bureaucracies are usually headed by their own products, and Administration leaders are in large part recruited from these products. In addition, of course, even the professional electoral politician usually combines a public and a private career. The model political leader in the Soviet Union, in short, is the apparatchik who has devoted his life to the party. The model political leader in the United States is the Cincinnatus-like distinguished citizen who lays aside other responsibilities to devote himself temporarily to the public service.

On the national level, professional politicians always occupy the top political position in the Soviet Union and they usually occupy it in the United States. Lenin was a professional revolutionary; Stalin and Khrushchev, both apparatchiki. Of their four principal rivals for power, Trotsky, Kirov, Malenkov, and Molotov, the first was a professional revolutionary and the other three apparatchiki. Of the eight American Presidents since 1917, five had almost exclusively political careers; one moved from education into electoral politics; one moved from business into Administration position; and one spent most of his life in the army.

At the next level the difference in the roles of the professional politicians becomes more apparent. Forty-four men and one woman have been on the Politburo or Presidium between 1919 and 1961. At the time of their appointments, five had served most of their careers as underground professional revolutionaries; seven combined revolutionary experience with work in the party apparatus; five combined revolutionary experience with work in the state bureaucracy; one combined revolutionary experience with work in the military establishment; 19 had worked primarily within the party apparatus; six had worked primarily as officials in the state bureaucracy; one was primarily an economist; and one was a military officer. Similarly, of the 175 members of the Central Committee elected in 1961, 66 had spent their careers almost exclusively in party positions, 42 combined experience in party and government, 33 were in industry or commerce, and 34 were specialists in other branches of governmental or technical work.

Unfortunately for the social scientist, the United States has no Central

Committee. One social scientist, however, attempted to identify one by asking knowledgeable people to name the "top leaders in the development of policies affecting the nation."[4] The soundness of this method is not beyond dispute; the result is an arbitrary sample of national leaders; but it is probably as reliable a sample as any other means would produce. In 1958 these 100 leaders were strewn across the commanding peaks of politics, government, business, and the professions. Forty-three were in the national government and two others were ex-Presidents. The only state governor (Harriman) had previously occupied important positions in the national government. Thirty-nine were in business, the majority (26) of them in industry. The remainder included five editors and publishers, two lawyers, four educators, three labor leaders, and one cardinal. . . .

These two leadership samples dramatically suggest the expertise required to run a modern society. With a few minor variations, the same skills and experiences are present in each elite. Approximately one-fifth of each elite consists of individuals with primary careers outside politics, civil government, commerce, and industry. The representation of some of these careers is remarkably similar. Professional military officers, for instance, constitute about 7 to 8 per cent of each elite; each group also includes three trade unionists, and one (SU) or a few (US) persons who have followed exclusively legal careers.

The great difference in the composition of the two samples concerns the balance between politics and government, on the one hand, and commerce and industry, on the other. Thirty-eight per cent of the Soviet leaders were professional party politicians, compared with 19 per cent for American leaders whose careers had been primarily in electoral politics. An additional 8 per cent of the American sample combined careers in electoral politics with private careers in business (4%), education (2%), and law (2%). Twenty-four per cent of the Soviet leaders combined careers in the party and governmental bureaucracies, while only 10 per cent of the American leaders had filled extensive government appointments as well as engaging in business (7%), law (2%), and electoral politics (1%). Thus, the careers of almost two-thirds of the Soviet leaders were primarily political and governmental, compared with somewhat more than one-third (37%) for American leaders whose careers included extensive governmental and political service. Only one-fifth (20%) of the American leaders had careers devoted primarily to politics or civil government. Of these 20 individuals in 1958, 15 were in Congress, three in the executive branch, one on the Supreme Court, and one (Harry Truman) was an elder statesman. Forty per cent of the American leaders, on the other hand, had primary careers in commerce and business and 11 per cent more combined a career in business with one in either politics or government. In

---

[4] Floyd Hunter, *Top Leadership USA* (Chapel Hill, N.C., 1959), 195 ff.

contrast, only 19 per cent of the Soviet leaders had careers primarily in industry. . . .

During the forty-five years after 1917 the role of the apparatchiki in the Soviet political system tended to increase in importance. In terms of sheer size, the growth of the apparatus kept pace with the growth of party membership. In 1922 there were 15,325 responsible officials in the party, approximately 4 per cent of the party membership. In 1962 the professional paid party workers numbered about 150–200,000—or less than 4 per cent of the total membership. The total number of apparatchiki was much larger, however, since many held temporary assignments in the government and specialized bureaucracies. Much more significant than simple numerical growth was the movement of the apparatchiki into most of the key positions of leadership in the Soviet political system. During Stalin's struggle for power in the 1920's, the idealistic revolutionaries and intellectuals were gradually eliminated from the leading party bodies and replaced by Stalin's adherents from the apparatus. Of the 14 new members of the Politburo between 1925 and 1940, 12 were full-fledged apparatchiki, while two (Voroshilov, Kalinin) combined careers in both the party and other bureaucracies. Since then the apparatchiki only declined in importance when the apparatus itself was subordinated during the last years of Stalin's dictatorship and the first years of the succession struggle. Between 1947 and 1953, five new members were appointed to the Politburo or Presidium, no one of whom was primarily a party worker: Voznesensky was an economist; Bulganin was an industrial and then military administrator; Kosygin, Saburov, and Pervukhin were industrial administrators. The victory of Khrushchev, like that of Stalin, brought a new flood of apparatchiki into the Presidium.

While the role of the apparatchiki in the Soviet political system has increased in importance, the role of the electoral politician in the American system has tended to decline. In 1888 Bryce could argue that a distinctive aspect of American politics was the large class of professional politicians who constituted the real governing class of the country. His observations, however, applied primarily to the state and local level. The emergence of the professional politicians was accompanied by a decline in the political experience of leaders at the national level. Prior to the Civil War, the top leaders of the national government (President, Vice-President, cabinet member, Speaker of the House, Supreme Court Justice) spent more of their careers in politics than in other pursuits, the peak being the generation of 1801–1825, which devoted 65 per cent of its working life to politics. Since the Civil War the top members of the national government have usually spent more of their working life in non-political occupations. Between 1901 and 1921 only 28 per cent of the careers of these national political leaders was devoted to politics. A similar decline has taken place in the proportion of top national leaders who have risen primarily or in part through elective office, the percentage who have held state or local office, and the percentage who have served in state legislatures.[5] As the apparatchik rises to dominate the Soviet political system, the electoral politician slowly fades from the American scene.

The same factors responsible for the rise of the apparatchik were also responsible for the decline of the traditional American electoral politician. The fundamental cause was the bureaucratization of modern society. The electoral politician is at home in the state legislature or Congress but he is sadly out of place in an administrative, industrial, or military bureaucracy. The skills of the bureaucrat are not those of the electoral politician. Few men in recent American politics have been able to perform successfully in both worlds. Averell Harriman, for instance, demonstrated a sustained ability in a variety of national government posts: NRA administrator, presidential adviser, ambassador, cabinet member, foreign aid director, Assistant Secretary of State. But he conspicuously failed to achieve the same level of success as governor of New York. Those who follow electoral careers must identify themselves with a single constituency or state. Those identified with national institutions find it difficult to sink the local roots necessary for an electoral career. In many cases they see little reason to do so. "Although they were policy makers," Hunter remarks of the businessmen among his 100 top national leaders, "with rare exceptions they did not wish to run for public office, and they held themselves superior to the men who seek office."[6] The decline of the electoral politician is thus both directly and indirectly the result of the growth of large national institutional bureaucracies. The leaders of these bureaucracies are necessarily political leaders of the nation. The electoral politician, however, is excluded from these new centers of power. In addition, the leaders of the new bureaucracies have moved in on the executive branch of the national government and dislodged the electoral politician from positions which he once normally occupied. Relegated to Congress and to state and local government, the electoral politician operates primarily at the middle reaches of power. Given the American system of government this development was a natural one. It is not, however, an inevitable feature of twentieth-century democratic government. In Great Britain, for instance, the parliamentary politician maintains his preeminence in the cabinet and ministry. The road to the top positions in the British government is still the traditional career of the professional politician.

In most political systems an individual achieves the top office by winning the support of the key political figures with whom he will work

---

[5] These figures are all from Mills, *Power Elite*, 228–31.

[6] Hunter, *Top Leadership*, 208. For other discussions of the gap between congressional-electoral politicians and other elements of the national elite, see Andrew Hacker, "The Elected and the Anointed," *American Political Science Review*, LV (September, 1961), 539–49; James N. Rosenau, *National Leadership and Foreign Policy* (Princeton, 1963), 345–60.

when he is in office. To win out in a succession struggle, a Stalin or Khrushchev gains majorities in the Presidium and Central Committee made up of the people who will be his principal colleagues and subordinates in governing the country. Similarly, in Great Britain, an M.P. normally becomes Prime Minister by first being chosen Party Leader by the members of his party in Parliament. The top party figures both in and out of the Commons whose support he requires to become Party Leader will fill his cabinet when he becomes Prime Minister. In the United States, however, the gap between electoral politics and Administration politics produces a gap between the individuals whom a presidential candidate depends upon to win office and those whom the President depends upon to discharge his office. The first group includes the political leaders and bosses in key states and cities: governors, mayors, state and county chairmen, and perhaps U.S. Senators. They are professional electoral politicians whose national functions are limited to, first, the nomination of the presidential candidate (they appear in full glory at the nominating conventions), and, second, electing him to office. They are the Daley, the Lawrence, the Crotty: local satraps who emerge for a few months every four years to shape the course of the nation. Once the candidate is elected, however, they can be of little help or hindrance to him. To capture the Presidency, the only resources needed are those which can be directly translated into votes. To govern the country, much else is required. The success of the President depends, in part, on the leaders of Congress, who (with some exceptions, like Harry Byrd), because they are leaders in Congress, are usually not the dominant political figures in their parties at home. The President's success also depends, however, on the cooperation of the leaders of the Establishment and his ability to mobilize political and technical expertise in a wide variety of policy fields. This need leads him to segments of American life which he may never have penetrated in his electoral career. Even someone as well-connected as John F. Kennedy, it was reliably reported, "suddenly discovered he didn't know 'the right people.' During his campaigning he had, of course, met practically every politician in the country. But as far as picking a cabinet was concerned, his large circle of acquaintances seemed inadequate. The truth of these remarks, made matter-of-factly and with no suggestion of regret, was subsequently borne out when Mr. Kennedy appointed men not previously known to him to several key posts in his administration."[7] "Nine strangers and a brother" did not quite accurately describe Kennedy's cabinet, but it did acutely suggest the problem which faces an incoming President.

Whatever inner feuds may rack it, the Soviet Presidium, in terms of shared experience, is in a real sense a team. Although its average membership has vacillated from 10 to 15 members, only 45 individuals have served on it between 1919 and 1961, for an average tenure of approximately a

[7] Douglass Cater, "A New Style, A New Tempo," *The Reporter*, xxiv (March 16, 1961), 28.

decade. The situation of the British cabinet is somewhat similar. When a party comes to power, the choices which its leaders can make in forming the cabinet are relatively limited. With a few exceptions, its members are in the Commons; rarely have they been there for less than a decade; and most of them have functioned together for several years as a "shadow cabinet." The Prime Minister can shuffle the chairs among them and decide who will have the more important and who the less important offices, but the nature of his government is in general clear to the electors before he is returned to power. In contrast to the Soviet Presidium and the British Ministry, the American Administration is a completely *ad hoc* body. As a group, its members share no common previous experience. A President must honor his political debts and achieve some balance of interests in his Administration. But within these limits he can appoint almost any individual whom he can persuade to accept office. Soviet political leaders come up through the common channel of the party apparatus. . . . However, the President's principal subordinates can come from the most diverse backgrounds. American executive leaders are drawn from the four corners of the nation, and at the close of the Administration they disperse to the four corners of the nation. No other major country draws its political executives from such diverse sources.[8] And in no other major country do individuals move back and forth so often between positions of leadership in the executive branch of the government and positions of leadership in the great institutions of society. In eighteenth-century societies, the social-economic leader, the aristocratic landowner, might also because of his status command a regiment in the army and a seat in the government. In the late nineteenth century, Americans reluctantly abandoned this reliance on amateurs in their army. In the late twentieth century, they still continue it in politics. . . .

The trend in the Soviet leadership is toward greater predominance by the professional apparatchiki, assisted on the one hand by the professional ideologues, and on the other by the experts. To think of an American analogy, one would have to imagine an Administration dominated by a combination of the old-time city-machine bosses and high civil servants, with Senator McCarthy or General Walker setting the ideological tone on one side, and a group of industrial executives providing the technical counsel on the other. The educational data (in several cases quite arbitrary classifications were made because of the imprecision of available information) also support the view that the composition of the leadership is becoming increasingly undifferentiated. Stalin's Politburo of 1949 involved a variety of institutional backgrounds and educational levels, with one-fourth of the Politburo lacking any formal education (the self-

---

[8] While diversity presents problems, it also has its advantages, as some British observers have become aware. See the comments on the British and American systems of recruitment by Max Beloff, "The Planner's Place in Foreign Policy," *The Times* (London), January 18, 1963, p. 9.

made man). Khrushchev's Presidium of early 1962 was four-fifths apparatchiki and almost four-fifths had a higher education. In that, too, its composition was in keeping with the trends inherent in modern professional bureaucracy.

While the Presidium and the Secretariat do not strive to "represent" the various institutional segments of the Soviet system or the varied geographical and national interests of the Soviet society, and some (for instance, the military) are currently altogether unrepresented, the members perforce do specialize in particular functions and in that sense may be said to reflect indirectly certain specific considerations. Furthermore, an effort is usually made to have two or three non-Russians in the top party organs. However, it is always important to bear in mind that the organizational tradition and discipline of the party inhibits the formation of a narrow, specialized outlook among the Presidium and Secretariat members. Like the cardinals on the Vatican Curia, they are predominantly professional politicians, sharing a common organizational outlook, common interests, and increasingly common background. . . .

A NEW PROFESSIONALISM?

The absence of a corps of professional bureaucratic politicians is the most important feature distinguishing political leadership in the United States from that in the Soviet Union. The top political leader in the Soviet Union is a politician and a bureaucrat. The top political leader in the United States is either a politician or a bureaucrat. John Kennedy had fourteen years in politics but none in bureaucracy. Dwight D. Eisenhower had thirty-five years in bureaucracy but none in domestic politics. Khrushchev, in a sense, combines the experience of both. Here is the crucial problem of political leadership in the United States. The modern society is a bureaucratized society: it needs bureaucratic politicians to run it. In the United States the traditional type of professional politician is retiring into the legislatures. To what extent is the United States likely to develop a type of professional bureaucratic politician to replace the declining electoral politician? Can the non-political leader from the Establishment become a successful bureaucratic politician and political leader in government? He is probably more likely to succeed in Administration posts, apart from the Presidency, than is the electoral politician.[9] But if his career has been primarily or exclusively in industry, banking, education, law, or the military, is he likely to bring into government the principal skills and experience required there? To some extent, of course, all bureaucratic organizations are similar, and the skills required to lead them are

---

[9] Cf. "By and large, the members of President Kennedy's Cabinet who have held elective office seemed to have had more difficulty in adjusting themselves to their Cabinet roles than did those previously associated with big business, big labor, or big foundations." E. W. Kenworthy, *New York Times*, July 16, 1962, p. 16.

the same. The successful military commander can transform himself—not entirely painlessly—into a successful corporation executive officer. But adjusting to shifts from one specialized bureaucracy to another may well be easier than shifting from any one specialized bureaucracy to leadership in the Administration. Within a specialized bureaucracy, advancement is normally a product of pull, influence, and contacts, on the one hand, and ability judged by fairly objective standards of technical knowledge and achievement, on the other.

In a political bureaucracy such as the Communist Party of the Soviet Union or any single American Administration, these two grounds become both more general and less distinguishable. Access and contacts are, in a sense, technical criteria for judging politicians. Achievement on the job is measured in terms of social, political, and ideological values which, unlike the standards in the specialized bureaucracy, are diverse, subjective, and controversial. The cabinet officer who is a success to a conservative may be a dismal failure to a liberal. Thus the factors which may bring a man to the top of a specialized bureaucracy do not necessarily prepare him for the wide-open competition in a political bureaucracy. Not having made a career of the struggle for governmental office and power, he may well have his problems in adjusting successfully to that struggle. In general, the more technical and specialized his experience in private life, the more difficulty he will have in government: hence the common observation that Wall Street bankers seem to do better in Washington than Midwestern industrialists. Inherent in the American amateur tradition has been the assumption that individuals who are leaders in one area can also be leaders in another area, that leadership consists of certain traits which some may develop while others do not. Leadership abilities, however, are not universal but specific to particular situations: the leader in one environment may be most inadequate in another.

Successful political leaders thus are likely to be those with experience in political bureaucracy. To some extent, the United States may be slowly developing such a group of bureaucratic politicians. The immense expansion of the federal bureaucracy has multiplied the number of "political offices" at the top of it. It is not inconceivable that a new type of American professional bureaucratic politician is emerging—a man who may have gotten his start in one of the private institutions of the Establishment, but moved into a junior position in government at a still relatively early age, and then worked himself up to a top position in the Administration. Apart from the normal risks of politics, the key problem in such a career is that no Administration lasts longer than eight years. Hence, a career as an Administration political executive is not likely to be a lifetime one. Three alternative patterns are possible. First, if one Administration is succeeded by another of the same party, undoubtedly many of the bureaucratic politicians in the first will also find places in the second. Second, even if the other party comes to power, a few individuals may still continue their governmental careers. (They would, under Galbraith's definition, be the true "Establishment men": Republicans serving a Democratic Administration or Democrats serving a Republican one.) Or, third, if the other party does come to power, many of the political bureaucrats from the previous Administration may temporarily return to private institutions and come back to government when the parties change once again. That the United States may be developing such a corps of "ministrables" is suggested by the fact that 13 per cent of the leaders of the Kennedy Administration had mixed governmental-private careers, as compared with 10 per cent of the leaders of the Eisenhower Administration and 3 per cent of those in the Truman Administration. The fact that almost 40 per cent of the leaders of the Kennedy Administration had held some post in the Truman Administration also suggests that in the future the elite of one Administration may frequently be recruited from the subelite of the last previous Administration of that party. Extensive governmental service interlaced with some private experience may be the pattern for the new American apparatchik.

It is unlikely, however, that the new professionalism of the American political leadership will result in the emergence of a type of leadership similar to the Soviet. The more ideologically oriented Soviet system requires much more selectivity in recruitment and far greater emphasis on personal commitment to a particular and overt orientation than can be justified by the purely functional requirements of a political system of an advanced industrialized society. But since that selectivity and commitment are vital to the elite's hold on power, it is likely that the ruling elite will continue to stress it, using the device of party membership to siphon off the politically oriented and ambitious elements of society into its own professional bureaucratic network. Lateral entry into political leadership from non-political posts of high responsibility will continue to be viewed as dangerous to the homogeneity of the leadership and hence to its power. In fact, it would be an important clue to change in the Soviet Union if at the political apex one saw the appearance in significant numbers of individuals whose careers had been primarily associated with a non-political bureaucratic profession. But until that happens, the exercise of power and the making of policy in the Soviet Union, unlike the United States, will remain a matter of bureaucratic professionalism and ideological homogeneity. The Soviet leadership still heeds closely Machiavelli's injunction (in which we substitute the word "politics" for "war"): "A prince should . . . have no other aim or thought, nor take up any other thing for his study, but politics and its organization and discipline, for that is the only art that is necessary to one who commands. . . . The chief cause of the loss of states, is the contempt of this art. . . ."

C. Nationalism

49. NATIONALISM AND POLITICAL DEVELOPMENT*

Rupert Emerson

IF IT WERE NECESSARY to select the most important single force behind the revolutionary drive of the rising peoples of Asia and Africa, the choice would inevitably go to nationalism. For none of its potential rivals can an effective case be made. Indeed, almost all of them contribute in one fashion or another to the mounting nationalist demand. Arnold Toynbee, profuse with capitals, may denounce Nationalism as a "disastrous corruption," "a perversion of Industrialism and Democracy," or "the monstrous outcome of the impact of our modern Western Democracy upon the Parochial State"; but to the peoples newly asserting their claim to equal status in the world, nationalism is the essence of what they seek.

In the debates in the United Nations on the Covenants on Human Rights the right of self-determination has frequently been considered the foundation on which all other rights rest; self-determination denied, no other right can be secure. It is in this light that peoples around the globe have viewed nationalism, assuming that the remaining goods they seek will flow from its attainment. The usual version of this goal is an acknowledged equality expressed in sovereign independence; more rarely, an adequate substitute may be found in free association with another country as is the case between Puerto Rico and the United States, or between British Togoland and Ghana, or perhaps within the French Community.

The prime rival to nationalism as a driving force is presumed to be the desire for an improved standard of living. From time to time it is asserted that the ordinary poverty-striken Asia and African is really interested only in seeing an end put to his poverty. This is a highly dubious proposition. The evidence indicates that he regards at least temporary economic privation as an appropriate price to pay for national salvation. It has also been contended that his real demand is for a transition to modernity, as manifested in economic and social development. In some part the pressure for economic development derives from the same root as the desire for an improved standard of living. However, it also has nationalist implications in its drive for equality.

However strong the urge toward better living conditions and economic development, it tends always to take second place to the political claims of

* From *The Journal of Politics,* Vol. 22, No. 1 (February, 1960). By permission of the *Journal* and the author.

nationalism. The individual who protects his economic position by refusing to undertake the sacrifices which patriotism demands reads himself
out of the community of right-minded, nation-fearing men. As one of the
standard phrases of nationalism has it: we would rather be governed like
hell by ourselves than well by someone else. Furthermore, the issue
between nationalism and material advancement here posed is seen as a
quite unreal one since the nationalist creed normally embraces the belief
that material improvement will surely follow in the wake of national
self-realization. Both well-being and economic development are considered unattainable in the shadow of imperialism. Only when the national
destiny is safely entrusted to national and not alien hands is it possible to
move confidently ahead on the path which leads to wealth, strength, and
modernity. Nationalism opens the way to a new economic era, and the
latter in turn lends new power to the nation.

Communism might be put forward as a contemporary threat to nationalism and undoubtedly, in certain cases, individuals and groups have
given to the Party a priority which they deny to the nation. More
frequently, however, and particularly in the revolt against imperialist
domination, Communism is seen as an alternative means of reaching
national goals. Although objective reality may contradict them, Asian and
African Communists are far more likely to view their Party membership as
a positive expression of their nationalism than as a negation of it. Official
Communist dogma itself puts self-determination in the forefront of its
doctrines (even though the small print always carefully reduces it to an
instrument to be used for Party purposes) and distinguishes between the
rightful patriotism of the unfree peoples and the proper devotion to
proletarian internationalism of those whose national identity is old-
established. It has often been contended that the success of the Communists in Asian countries hinges upon their ability to identify themselves
with the local nationalist cause.

The priority of nationalism has been vigorously affirmed by both
Jawaharlal Nehru and Kwame Nkrumah. In his opening address to the
IRP conference at Lucknow in 1950, the Indian Prime Minister described
nationalism as a war-cry which warms the heart of almost every Asian:
"Any other force, any other activity that may seek to function, must
define itself in terms of this nationalism. . . . No argument in any
country of Asia is going to have weight if it goes counter to the nationalist
spirit of the country, Communism or no Communism." Supporting much
the same theme, Ghana's Prime Minister cited the motto of the Convention
People's Party, which was his own creation. "We prefer self-government
with danger to servitude in tranquillity" and followed it up with what he
called the party's policy, "Seek ye first the political kingdom and all
things shall be added unto you."[1] It is to the attainment of the political

---

[1] The citation from Nehru is to be found in William L. Holland (ed.), *Asian Nationalism and the West* (New York, 1953), pp. 353–354; Nkrumah's statement appears

kingdom of the nation that the guiding spirits of the new states and their followers have looked, confident that the nation came first and that the rest would follow after.

It is a great deal easier to assert the priority given nationalism than to lay out with any measure of precision its content. Rarely does nationalism represent a coherent and positive body of doctrine and belief, reaching significantly beyond insistence on the establishment of an independent state. Freedom from partition or alien intrusion is normally a far better defined matter than are the uses to which freedom would be put. In the speech cited above, Nehru commented on the fact that a large element in nationalism is negative. "Nationalism is essentially an anti-feeling," he has written elsewhere, "and it feeds and fattens on hatred and anger against other national groups, and especially against the foreign rulers of a subject country."[2]

The negative or 'anti'-character of nationalism in a colonial setting is simple enough to explain, but it is by no means unique to colonialism. Everywhere the national "we" has been to a considerable degree defined by contrast to the alien and opposing "they," and in most instances no operationally significant statement of what the nation stands for can be expected. Indeed, this may be held to be a standard feature of all nationalism until one arrives at what Carlton Hayes called integral nationalism or what might today be called totalitarian nationalism. I take it to be characteristic of liberal nationalism that its particular content remains very largely unspecified, allowing for a multitude of sins as well as virtues. The Fourth of July oration of the past, praising America's blue skies and broad horizons, its heroes and its great achievements, reached an approximately acceptable level of specificity. It roused a glow of pride in being an American and yet did not rule out any significant number of Americans who were heretical on one or another point mentioned by the speaker. Tom Paine, George Washington, Alexander Hamilton, Thomas Jefferson, and Andrew Jackson must all fit within the American heritage; New England, the South, the Middle West and the Far West must find an equal place. If any of them are to be ruled out by authorized fiat we have come to the proto–Fascist phase when some body arrogates to itself the right to determine among Americans what is to be accepted as American. France must embrace the *ancien régime*, the Revolution, Napoleon, and

---

in his autobiography, *Ghana* (New York, 1957), pp. 162–163. In his opening speech at the Pan–African Conference in Accra on December 8, 1958, Prime Minister Nkrumah repeated this conviction: "My first advice to you who are struggling to be free is to aim for the attainment of the Political Kingdom—that is to say, the complete independence and self-determination of your territories. When you have achieved the Political Kingdom all else will follow. Only with the acquisition of political power real power through the attainment of sovereign independence—will you be in a position to reshape your lives and destiny; only then will you be able to resolve the vexatious problems which harass our Continent."

[2] *Toward Freedom* (New York, 1941), p. 74.

the twists and turnings of the last century and a half. To demand that each nation have a single positive content and program for nationalism is to ask that it select from a diverse history certain strands which alone will constitute its legitimate national heritage. Not far down this road lies the *Gleichschaltung* of the Nazis.

The new states are however, peculiarly divided within themselves by the gaps which separate different elements in the population. Not only do they have as diverse and internally contradictory a history as do other peoples, but they are also afflicted by an unusual degree of distance between the bulk of the population and the newly arisen leadership. The most notable gap is the one which divides the active, Western-educated urban group from the inert, uneducated, tradition-bound mass mainly composed of the peasantry. It is the first group from which the heirs of empire have been drawn to constitute the new élite, putting its stamp on the states which it has been largely responsible for bringing into being. Here are the makings of a fundamental dilemma. It is arguable that any nation's claim to a distinctive place in the sun must be derived from the past which has shaped it in this peculiar national fashion, yet the entire leadership of the new states tends to be made up of those most removed from the traditional society of their ancestors. Nationalism has characteristically been the property of the constantly expanding but still relatively slight minority most influenced by the West.

The social structure in Asian and African nations, then, is that a newly fashioned élite, oriented toward the West and modernization despite its passionate repudiation of Western imperial control, has taken a predominant lead in societies the bulk of whose members are still close to their ancestral past. In such a circumstance the definition of the national purpose must evidently be a hazardous process. We do not as yet have any accurate evidence or body of precedent by means of which to determine what course the new states are likely to take. We do not know whether the gaps which are now so apparent will be filled with greater or less speed, and whether the mass will tend to move in the Westernizing and modernizing direction of its currently ruling élite (which seems most probable) or the élite move toward re-absorption into the mass and the older patterns of life (which is highly unlikely as a general phenomenon). Against the current trend toward an optimistic view of the prospects for development must be set the general failure of almost all non-Western countries save Japan to swing into the modern stream during the last century. Furthermore, the record shows that many Latin American countries not only relapsed into lethargy but also made little headway in achieving the national integration of different elements of their population. It may be that a similar decline into stagnation on the part of Africa and Asia is precluded by the speed at which the world now moves and the new modes of production, transport and communication which work to break down old barriers and isolationisms. The precedents of the past have perhaps become irrelevant in the face of such developments as the deep penetration of virtually every society by Western forces and ideas, the inescapable pressure of outside events, and the presence of Communism, ready to exploit every difficulty or failure. Both what has already happened and the widespread expectations for a different kind of future render a return to the old ways impossible. The clear probability is that the West has loosed forces the forward sweep of which can only temporarily be diverted or checked, though no reliable estimate can be made either of the speed of change or of the form it will take. The nationalist movements have themselves been the spearhead of the demand for change.

The existence of great gaps in the society of the new states raises a further question. How real is the solidarity of a nation when it is so profoundly divided within itself? It is evident that no single and all-embracing answer can be given to such a question since the backgrounds and present situations of the different countries vary so greatly. What can be said of Egypt has no necessary bearing for Ghana or the Philippines, and India's prospects may be quite unrelated to those of its neighbors, Pakistan, Burma, Ceylon, and Afghanistan. Precisely the 'anti'-character of nationalist movements in colonial or quasi-colonial countries is likely to lend a deceptive sense of national unity. The fact that a people can stage a consolidated anti-imperial movement conveys no assurance that it will be able to maintain political coherence once the imperial enemy has vanished. It is, of course, true that the mere carrying on of an extended and concerted struggle is in itself a significant factor in the creation of national sentiment, but a more basic identity is necessary if the national unity is to endure. The sense of belonging together through the experience of a common history and of facing a common destiny is not something which can be created overnight.

How great importance should be attached to the gap between the Western-oriented élite and the mass is not a matter on which a precise estimate can now be given. When a nationalist movement has gotten into full swing, the people at large are likely to follow the lead of the active nationalist élite though they may have given little prior evidence of political interest. One commentator has remarked that there is no difference between African peoples which is as great as their collective difference from the Europeans who have ruled them. When India was aflame with nationalism in the 1930's, Gandhi and his lieutenants were able to win the support of many whose knowledge of what the struggle involved must have been slight. Similarly, when the euphemistically labelled police actions of the Dutch were carrying colonial warfare to the Indonesians, an unexpectedly broad segment of the population gave its backing to the nationalist forces. And yet the gap remains. The mass has so far demonstrated only meagre interest in taking an active part in day-to-day political life. The leaders, for their part, have often shown an inclination to see themselves as an élite, properly entrusted with the destinies of their untutored countrymen. "Guided democracy," which Sukarno considers suitable to the present state of development in Indonesia, also describes the élite conception of government in many other countries. Nor have the mass of the people up to this point been inclined to challenge the élitist claim of their new leaders, although the military have presented a decisive challenge in several countries. Where democratic institutions survive for an extended time and the people come to feel that political power is actually in their hands, the present relationship between mass and élite may take on a quite different cast. . . .

The social contract theorist, in his purer flights of fancy, pictured a world in which distinct atoms of human beings, impelled by reason and other pressures, came together to make a contract which brought state and government into being. In the contemporary scene, the nation-state, as the term indicates, assumes that the state is built upon, or is the institutional embodiment of, a community of men who are already joined by intimate and old-established links. The state is not the product of random particles arbitrarily joined in political co-operation, but the expression of the close prior bonds which has brought this "We" to a sense of difference from the alien "They." Society derives, so to speak, not from a contract but from natural and organic growth.

If political institutions are to be established, a first necessity is that the demographic and geographic limits which define the scope of those institutions should be laid down. In a tribal era they are as extensive as the tribe—which may, of course, be nomadic and thus have no spatial boundaries. When religion is predominant, the religious community sets the standard; at another time the city-state is the accepted unit; and in monarchical days the limits are set by the range of the ruler's jurisdiction. What is important in the latter system is not that a common history has brought the people to a sense of community but that they are all subjects of the appropriate majesty. We are just emerging from the imperial era in which a few of the states of the West, belatedly joined by Japan, extended their political sway to embrace most of the rest of the world.

With the coming of nationalism all these political systems move into the discard or at least make a suitable pretense of adapting themselves to the new demands. Henceforward it is not a king nor a religion nor imperial conquest nor even a contract which legitimizes a state, but the coincidence of state and nation. Where the state fails to be built upon the nation there is every presumption that the structure must be redesigned to approximate the ideal. Where empires embrace more than one nation, they must undergo the surgeon's knife, as has already happened in Europe and in Asia and is now rapidly under way in Africa. Only in the Soviet Union, successor to the empire of the Tsars, does the multi-national state survive on the grand scale. Where the state falls short of the nation, as in the partition of Germany, Korea, or Vietnam, and perhaps in the case of the Arab states, it is necessary to work toward reunification in order to satisfy the present criteria of legitimacy. Given the assumptions of the nationalist age, the first prerequisite is the determination of the national units which form the foundation of the state system. . . .

The nation establishes the demographic and geographic frontiers of the state. For the survival of the state nationalism furnishes another vital element in that it supplies the emotional cement which holds the members of the state together when disagreements threaten to pull them apart. What the social contract sought to provide by engaging men in formal obligations to each other came to be provided in the contemporary world by the social-historical fact of being born, brought up, and educated within the close-knit and emotion-laden confines of the nation. In the theory of the national era the state exists in order to realize the purposes of the nation, and, short of external attack, it can maintain its unity as long as the "We" of the nation takes priority over all the divergent pulls which might distract and disrupt.

Does nationalism have a clear tendency to produce one or another type of political institution? The answer to this question must be a slightly hesitant "No"; slightly hesitant because nationalism has in it democratic elements which cannot be ignored even where it has turned in ruthlessly authoritarian directions.

In fact, to assign to nationalism any particular political coloration is presumably impossible since it has been associated with almost every conceivable régime and attitude. Even though an impressive case can be made for the proposition that every true nationalism rests on democratic underpinnings of sorts, there are many ardent and unmistakable nationalisms in which democracy as a specific type of political system is either non-existent or is no more than a facade of outward conformity with current political fashions. Where the general constellation of forces has been such as to promote democracy, as most notably in Western Europe and the countries which it has settled overseas, nationalism has maintained a predominantly democratic outlook; where the foundations of democracy have been weak, as in most of the rest of the world, nationalism has betrayed the democratic promise which the nineteenth century liberal saw in it and has become an instrument of the established ruling groups or of totalitarianism. It is, of course, always the champion of self-government in the sense of national as opposed to alien rule, but it is only accidentally self-government in the sense of rule by the many as opposed to rule by the few. Reduced to its bare bones, nationalism is no more than the assertion that this particular community is arrayed against the rest of mankind. This sense of separate identity can by itself give no clue as to how the community may choose to manage its own affairs.

At a time when nationalism in the West has often drifted in reactionary or militarist directions and when the most dangerous and abhorrent elements in it have so recently been arrogantly paraded by the Fascists and

Nazis, it may appear paradoxical, or even outrageous folly to suggest the existence of an essential bond between nationalism and democracy; yet both in idea and in actual historical development there has been such a bond. Hans Kohn has put the matter in the extreme form of saying that "nationalism is inconceivable without the ideas of popular sovereignty preceding—without a complete revision of the position of ruler and ruled, of classes and castes."[3] On the face of the historical record no statement as uncompromisingly sweeping as this can be sustained . . . and yet it has more than a germ of fundamental truth.

Once full-fledged nationalism has appeared, a transformation of deep and lasting importance in the relations of people, rulers, and state tends to occur. Even in the Fascist variants the rôle which the people play is sharply distinguished from their rôle in the earlier type of dictatorship or monarchy, as witness the efforts of Fuehrer and Duce to carry the masses with them, to give at least the appearance of popular consultation through plebiscitary techniques, and to spread the tentacles of the Party down into every cranny of the society. This, certainly, is not democracy in any acceptable sense, and yet it is equally certainly a perverse offshoot from democratic roots. The Leader and the Party put themselves forward as emanations of the popular will, as a truer distillation of the national *volonté générale* than the people themselves can produce.

To reduce the question to its most basic terms, the argument linking democracy and nationalism would run something as follows. Nationalism is peculiarly a product of or a response to the distinctive forces which have gone into the shaping of the modern world. Those forces are inherently and inevitably "democratic" in the sense that they mobilize submerged elements and classes of society into new social rôles, eat away at traditional attachments and relationships, and work toward the building of a new great society into which, in principle, all men are actively drawn. Obviously what is involved here is by no means necessarily a democratic constitutional structure nor even an immediate approximation of a society striving toward egalitarianism, although both of these are likely to be present at least as active aspirations. Far more, it is the general conception, derived from the changing social scene, that the people, the mass of ordinary humans, are of consequence, that they are achieving a sense both of their own worth and of their right and ability to do something about it, and that the leaders must speak in their name. The national era comes to be an era of mass communications and mass production, inescapably headed toward mass politics.

The heart of the argument is the proposition that the rise of nationalism is normally associated with deep-running social ferment and change which disrupt the old order of society and bring about a rise in social consequence and awareness of ever-widening segments and classes of the

---

[3] *The Idea of Nationalism* (New York, 1941), p. 3.

people at large. On this basis nationalism is seen as one of the major and typical manifestations of what Karl Mannheim has spoken of as "the fundamental democratization of society," the stirring "into action of those classes who formerly played a passive part in political life."[4] As the peoples themselves—or, at least, a significant new element among them—begin to come of age and to a new consciousness of themselves, they demand a new place in a society in process of transformation. One of the characteristic forms which this demand has taken is insistence upon the centrality of the national community and upon the latter's right to make the state the sovereign organ of its identity and will. The people, after all, compose the nation, and it is not beyond the bounds of reason to suggest the revolutionary importance of the fact that the social-political community which has come to occupy the center of the contemporary stage—taking over the state in its own name and establishing a new criterion of legitimacy—should, therefore, be defined in terms of the people. In the new dispensation the state could no longer be seen as made up of the ruler and those who happened to be his subjects, but became in principle the emanation and instrument of the nation. The forward thrust of the bourgeoisie in Europe and later of the masses, has its close overseas parallel in the awakening rebellion of colonial people, in roughly similar circumstances and under similar leadership.

The rise of democracy as a political phenomenon has coincided too closely with the emergence of nations as conscious entities to be explained in terms of random chance. The lines of interconnection between the two are many. The most evident is the one which has already been briefly discussed: the fact that nationalism is one of the major manifestations of the modern social ferment which overturns traditional relationships and gives new consequence to formerly submerged elements of society.

A second line of interconnection is the immense prestige which democracy has achieved—even among those who have no serious intent of practicing it. Democracy is taken as an ultimate good to which all peoples must aspire, but which only the advanced peoples can hope to master. The imperial centers—Britain, France, the Low Countries, the United States—, which have so largely set the tone for the world as it has evolved in the last century and more, have established the pattern of democratic supremacy, and have, at least until recently, made no effort to conceal their belief that the "lesser breeds of man" could not be trusted to manage a democratic system. The imperial powers themselves, properly democratic at home, must impose a benevolently autocratic rule on the peoples whose tutelage they had undertaken. For the nationalists struggling to win their equality with the imperial masters here was a challenge: democracy was the political system whose realization would serve as a symbol that the bonds of inferiority had been broken.

---

[4] *Man and Society in an Age of Reconstruction* (London, 1940), p. 44.

Nor was the striving for democratic institutions only a matter of prestige. Assuming the nationalist leaders to be in almost every instance the product of Western education at home or abroad, the political philosophy and political history with which they were imbued pointed to democracy as the form of government which represented man's highest achievement and as the form which modern man naturally adopted. If they lived and studied abroad, they were likely to come in contact with democratic institutions, and in dependent countries the imperial authorities grudgingly introduced installments of democracy at which their wards were allowed to try their hand under close supervision. Political education in both a formal and a practical sense had the concepts and institutions of democracy in large part at its center, and other approaches to democracy were made in the new era through the upcoming political parties, trade unions, co-operative organizations, and other such bodies, all of which represented popular adaptation to the new Western forces coming in under the aegis of imperialism.

Furthermore, a swing in the democratic direction was a matter of vital political necessity for the nationalists. Their legitimacy in the eyes of their imperial opponents, and, no doubt, in their own as well, rested in very considerable part on their ability to demonstrate that they had the mass of their people behind them. If it could be established that they spoke for a nation with the blessing of its people, their moral claim to take over approached the irrefutable. To this moral aspect of their struggle must be added the hard political fact that if they were to represent enough of a political force to have a serious impact on the imperial power whose position they contested, they must be able to enlist the masses in battle behind them. Particularly in the colonial areas the effective strength of the nationalists rested upon their ability to have a larger hold on the loyalty of the people than could be exercised by the colonial officials. As the grandest example of all, when the Indian National Congress under Gandhi's guidance became a mass organization in the 1920's and 1930's the British authorities could no longer maintain the claim that the people at large really preferred alien rule nor could they count on having their orders generally obeyed. Prisons and bayonets still served to keep the system temporarily in operation, but they were an unacceptable substitute for consent.

In these and other fashions nationalism works to promote democracy, but it also contains ingredients which can with the greatest of ease turn in undemocratic or anti-democratic directions. Wherever nationalism is the main driving force, there is the temptation to give priority to the attainment of national unity, strength, and independence. In such circumstances the liberalism of democratic nationalism may yield to the demand for unity put forward in the name of the nation itself. The problem is always present of giving specific content to the national will and singling out those who formulate it. Rousseau's *volonté générale*, itself only precariously identified with the concrete wills of actual human beings, is sublimated by Hegel into a *Volksgeist* which manifests itself in a realm above that of ordinary mortals but must be brought down to earth. The national will speaks with irresistible authority, yet whose voice speaks for it? The national soul may reside in the simple peasant, villager, or worker, but his ignorance and lack of experience of the great world render him, it may be contended, unable to give it true expression. In his stead the élite or the charismatic leader takes over as the emanation of the national will. The nation is sovereign, but the exercise of that sovereignty, so the argument all too fluently runs, should, for the good for the nation itself, be entrusted to those who can use it rightly. By this time the national democracy is well on the way toward transformation into nationalist autocracy; and it was down this road that the Germans were stampeded into the disaster of Nazism.

If the nation is one entity with a single sacred destiny, how can it be allowed to dissipate its energies in internal disaffection and conflict, particularly when it is threatened by external danger and is embarked on basic internal reconstruction? In the actual situation of the new states the attraction of power and the estimate of national need combine to enhance the already strong élitist tendency of Western-oriented leaders who are amply aware of the illiteracy, backwardness, and inexperience of the bulk of their countrymen. And where the civilian élites do not themselves step in to furnish the "guided democracy," the military are likely to be standing by to impose their version of order and of the national will on peoples whose ability to manage the democratic constitutions they have decreed for themselves is minimal. Latin America and the Middle East furnish unhappy models which are already having their imitators elsewhere, often with explicit insistence that the democratic order is being overturned only in order to lay solider foundations for a return to democracy. At the next remove the Communists will gladly furnish their own improved rendering of democracy.

No great confidence can be placed in the general populace as the defender of threatened democratic institutions. Poverty-ridden peoples in a climate of rising expectations are not likely to make their first concern the preservation of political forms and liberties whose meaning is obscure to them and whose promise appears of less significance than other prospects that are held out to them. If democracy fails to produce results with adequate speed and if authoritarian methods seem to hold the remedy, the masses cannot be counted on to rise to the defense of unfamiliar political machineries. In general they lack not only the democratic tradition but also the more basic tradition of standing up to do battle for their rights against the remote and superior authorities who have through the ages pushed them around. Nothing in their experience has brought home to them the belief that they are the possessors of human rights and fundamental freedoms which they are entitled to and able to defend. The present array of democratic institutions has been imposed on them from above almost as much as any of the previous systems; certainly the constitutions have not been adopted in response to a demand from below. All too often it is probable that the people would feel more at home with a government which, in traditional style, tells them what to do.

Whatever their composition, the ruling authorities in this democratic or post-democratic age will seek popular consent or approval to establish the legitimacy of their title to power, but this can be handled through the familiar plebiscitary techniques without disturbing the people by placing alternatives before them.

In the West nationalism is now often denounced as being a divisive and anachronistic force—bad enough at any time and intolerable in the atomic era. From this the moral is drawn, most frequently in France, that the Asian and African peoples should resign themselves to recognition that the world has arrived at a time of interdependence which renders a demand for sovereignty absurd. Of the grievousness of nationalism's faults there can be no doubt. They can exact a high price, yet what is bought at that price is also of great value, particularly, perhaps, for those who are just entering into the modern national phase. The divisiveness of nationalism has a different bearing for the people of the new states than for those who are old established and even outgrowing their nationhood, and the element of anachronism is to be measured not only by the calendar but by the life-span of the particular nationalisms as well.

Even for the Western peoples whose reaping of the fruits of nationalism is of relatively old standing the undermining of the nation by insistence on its shortcomings could create a worse rather than a better situation unless preferable forms of community, acceptable to the people, were ready at hand. The brotherhood of man finds much of its present working expression within the nation, even though its other face is hostility to those outside. Whatever changes in the structure of the global society may lie just around the corner, they are still sufficiently concealed to make it impossible to see the form and nature of the nation's successors. We have, unhappily, no necessary reason to assume that if the nation were to lose its hold the next stage would mark any appreciable advance toward a more desirable world. France presented no pretty picture in the years just before World War II when the idea of the nation had lost its force for both the right and the left, and many in the center as well.

In the newly rising countries nationalism has functions to perform which it has largely exhausted in the West. While in the West the nation has come to represent the actual outer boundaries of communal allegiance for most men or has set limits which are already found too confining, in Asia and Africa it constitutes a great potential widening of the social and political horizons of most of the people. Far from forcing men to live within restricted quarters, it opens new doors and windows. Where men's lives have traditionally been bounded by family, tribe, or caste, by village, market town, or petty state, the emergence of nationalism creates pressures which force men into larger communities, as nationalism is itself a response to similar pressures. That lesser communities can put up strong resistance to full absorption into the nation, or what claims to be the nation, is demonstrated on a small scale by the existence in all countries of isolated pockets of people who have not effectively been drawn into the broader national society.. On a larger scale there are any number of evidences of growing pains such as the demands of linguistic communities in India, the revolts in different parts of Indonesia, and Nigeria's troubles with its tribes and regions. In some instances, as in Pakistan's split from India, even the assertion that there is a single nation embracing the peoples concerned may be successfully denied. For many individuals and groups considerable time will surely elapse before their social-political consciousness expands to the new national limits, but the forces of the modern world are on the whole conspiring to make man's age-old parochialism impossible.

For the leaders and organizers of national movements it is obviously a matter of the first importance to wean as many people as possible away from their more local attachments and bring them to active awareness of their national ties. In addition to ethical and religious considerations Gandhi was moved by a simple political calculation in pleading the case for the untouchables: if the latter remained outside the national fold, the Indian nation could bring that much less pressure to bear on the British in its struggle for independence. In taking the national cause to the masses, men like Gandhi, Sukarno, Nasser, and Nkrumah have not only immeasurably strengthened their political position but have also taken a creative part in shaping the nations they represent. All the agitation and propaganda associated with nationalist parties and upheavals dramatize the issues and serve to make the nation a living reality for people who have had no consciousness of its existence. To the extent that the new concept is grasped, the peasant isolated in his village becomes a citizen of a nation which takes its place in the world's councils. The nation is itself still far removed from meeting the needs of an age of jet planes, radio, and intercontinental ballistic missiles, but it is at least an advance in social magnitude over what preceded it.

To the national unity which it brings to the new states nationalism adds another vital ingredient for survival: a revolutionary zeal and a sense of devotion to the nation and the state which is to be its instrument. In the new states and in those which are in process of formation the nation is not something which can be taken casually for granted but an exciting new achievement, worthy of love and sacrifices. Independence has been won as the result of campaigns whose emotional momentum in some part carries over and may be utilized in dealing with the problems of the difficult years ahead. Particularly in colonial areas but also to some extent in any country still living under some variant of the *ancien régime*, the nation and nationalism open the possibility of tapping sources of popular energy and participation which no alien or old-style autocratic ruler could hope to tap. To carry on warfare, to put through major reforms, or to require present sacrifices for future benefits enlists a new dimension of popular support if it can be called for by national leaders as a part of the nation's due.

How long the zeal and devotion will last and how usefully they can be channeled into dealing with the post-independence tasks are questions the the answers to which the heirs to imperial power must anxiously seek. Certainly there can be no simple transference. At the extreme the youngster who has carried on years of guerrilla warfare against the Dutch in Indonesia or against the French in Indochina or Algeria is unlikely to be the most suitable candidate for a desk job in the Ministry of Reconstruction and not even perhaps for the routines of a peace-time army. More broadly, the demonstrated ability of the nationalist leadership to perform the political function of rallying the people against imperial domination can give no guarantee of ability to perform another and quite different job. A strong case can be made for the proposition that the sacrifices and basic social changes which development calls for can only be got across to the people by the political leader and not by the expert or bureaucrat, but the nationalist revolutionary who has been victorious in one setting may fumble badly in another. The dramatic and heroic temper of nationalist battle is far from being a wholly suitable mood in which to tackle the problems of managing a stable and progressive policy and a modernized and expanding economy.

Nationalism by itself gives the answer to virtually none of the particular problems arising from the ubiquitous demand for development and, indeed, to very few of the multitude of questions which confront peoples coming to independence. Its most vital contributions is in the realms of the intangibles of the spirit: the restoration of self-respect, the building up of morale, and the stimulation of social solidarity. It does not, however, determine the choice between alternative and often conflicting values, each legitimately put forward as embraced within the national destiny; it does not provide all the good things associated with independence; and it does not establish the institutions necessary for further advance. One must look elsewhere than to nationalism to decide even such over-all questions as whether a free enterprise system or Communism, liberal democracy or centralized authoritarianism, is most fitting and the vast majority of lesser decisions must also be taken primarily on other than nationalist grounds. In almost every instance, to hold up the concept of the national interest as the determinant of decision and action is to produce an empty symbol whose content is in dispute between different factions within the nation. Even in the realm of foreign affairs where nationalism most evidently comes into play, it is likely to give no conclusive answer to questions concerning entry into this alliance or that, neutralism or commitment. The danger is also real that nationalism may serve as an actual impediment to advance, as, for instance, in curtailing access to alien goods, skill, and capital, and it can always be paraded as a screen to hide domestic failures or abuses.

The dimensions of the task which lie ahead of the new states are staggering. They cannot rest content with taking their newfound sovereignty and enjoying it, as they might have at some earlier point in history. Both national pride and the imperatives of survival now demand that they move speedily into the modern world, rivalling the achievements of peoples who have long preceded them on the road. Despite illiteracy, inexperience, and tragic shortages of trained manpower, the latest model of the welfare state plus modernized armed forces is to be produced by governments equipped with all the trappings of parliamentary democracy. Economic systems are to be transformed and the remnants of backwardness wiped from the slate. The new national community is to take its place in the organized society of nations, be represented at a multitude of international conferences and meetings, and furnish an appropriate quota of personnel for international secretariats.

In moving toward goals such as these, nationalism can be of immense assistance if it is wisely and skillfully used by those responsible for the guidance of the new states. If it is used merely to inflame and obscure, its contribution can be disastrous.

Chapter XV. Revolution

Introductory Note

THE PATTERN of beliefs which justify a given system is subject to constant strain. When these beliefs are no longer accepted by the population, that is, when the legitimacy of the State is widely questioned, a revolutionary situation comes into being. Economic specialization gives rise to social groups whose interests may conflict with those of the existing ruling elite. Technological developments may undermine the economic position of the groups in power. Capitalists, workers, engineers, and merchants no longer may see the reason for continued rule by the aristocracy. Each social group generates its own ideology, and the political system as a whole is faced with the challenge of adjusting conflicting claims and integrating diverse views.

Among the social groups who play a key role in the processes of change and revolution are the intellectuals, the "keepers of the myths." The intellectuals manipulate the ideological symbols of a given society. The teachers, writers, editors, and priests transform power into legitimacy and link the governors with the governed. They are also the first group to reflect doubts and uncertainty about the ideology of the regime and, as such, are sensitive indicators of the stability or instability of a system. Intellectuals furnish the masses with a "consciousness" of injustice which is an indispensable element in any revolutionary situation. Comparative study could usefully be made of the social status of intellectuals, the degree and extent to which they are valued in their society, their political and economic status, and the responsibility they have for the performance and maintenance of the system.

The student should attempt to think of revolution in terms of some unifying concepts. Perhaps the most influential theory of revolution is the one put forth by Karl Marx, which is worth summarizing at length. Modern capitalism, according to Marx, encounters a basic contradiction between its mode of production and the social relations engendered. In order to secure a return on their investments, capitalists require the workers to produce "surplus value" (over and above what is required for mere subsistence). The social environment congenial to the continued functioning of capitalism is one in which the workers are divided and weak, and therefore unable to resist the demands of the capitalist.

When the workers come together in factories, they inevitably discuss their grievances; their revolutionary consciousness grows sharper. Eventually, capitalists find themselves confronted with a proletariat that is organized and militant, not dispersed and pliable. The productive forces (drive for profits under capitalism) come into conflict with productive relationships (development of a revolutionary proletariat that will no longer tolerate exploitation) and, at a point that can be objectively determined, a readjustment of forces and relationships takes place. Since the State represents the capitalists and controls all instruments of force, the change will have to take place by a workers' revolution.

Does the Marxist theory explain revolutionary developments in Russia, eastern Europe, China, and the "non-Western" nations? Have these revolutions all followed the same course? If not, what accounts for the variations? How has it happened that some countries have escaped these revolutionary upheavals, and managed to satisfy the demands of disaffected groups without recourse to violence? It may be suggested that revolutions are one among many manifestations of social change, which may also come about in other ways.

The Marxist view is most concisely formulated in N. Lenin, *State and Revolution*. An interesting, though not entirely convincing study of the strategy of seizing power, is in Curzio Malaparte, *Coup d'Etat, The Technique of Revolution* (tr. Saunders, 1923). In addition to Crane Brinton's book, systematic analyses include P. A. Sorokin, *The Sociology of Revolution* (1925). There are important reflections on revolution in Arnold J Toynbee's *Study of History* (6 vols., 1934–39). For the twentieth century revolutions see, among many, Hugh Seton-Watson, *The East European Revolution* (1950); Lucian Pye, *Guerrilla Communism in Malaya* (1956); Benjamin I. Schwartz, *Chinese Communism and the Rise of Mao* (1951).

Readings

50. THE ANATOMY OF REVOLUTION*

Crane Brinton

Some Tentative Uniformities

WHEN ALL necessary concessions are made to those who insist that events in history are unique, it remains true that the four revolutions we have studied [English, American, French, and Russian] do display some strik-

---

* Reprinted with permission of Prentice-Hall, Inc., from *The Anatomy of Revolution* by Crane Brinton. Copyright 1952 by Prentice-Hall, Inc.

ing uniformities. Our conceptual scheme of the fever can be worked out so as to bring these uniformities clearly to mind. We shall find it worth while, in attempting to summarize the work of these revolutions, to recapitulate briefly the main points of comparison on which our uniformities are based.

We must be very tentative about the prodromal symptoms of revolution. Even retrospectively, diagnosis of the four societies we studied was very difficult, and there is little ground for belief that anyone today has enough knowledge and skill to apply formal methods of diagnosis to a contemporary society and say, in this case revolution will or will not occur shortly. But some uniformities do emerge from a study of the old regimes in England, America, France, and Russia.

First, these were all societies on the whole on the upgrade economically before the revolution came, and the revolutionary movements seem to originate in the discontents of not unprosperous people who feel restraint, cramp, annoyance, rather than downright crushing oppression. Certainly these revolutions are not started by down-and-outers, by starving, miserable people. These revolutionists are not worms turning, not children of despair. These revolutions are born of hope, and their philosophies are formally optimistic.

Second, we find in our prerevolutionary society definite and indeed very bitter class antagonisms, though these antagonisms seem rather more complicated than the cruder Marxists will allow. It is not a case of feudal nobility against bourgeoisie in 1640, 1776, and 1789, or of bourgeoisie against proletariat in 1917. The strongest feelings seem generated in the bosoms of men—and women—who have made money, or at least who have enough to live on, and who contemplate bitterly the imperfections of a socially privileged aristocracy. Revolutions seem more likely when social classes are fairly close together than when they are far apart. "Untouchables" very rarely revolt against a God-given aristocracy, and Haiti gives one of the few examples of successful slave revolutions. But rich merchants whose daughters can marry aristocrats are likely to feel that God is at least as interested in merchants as in aristocrats. It is difficult to say why the bitterness of feeling between classes *almost* equal socially seems so much stronger in some societies than others—why, for instance, a Marie Antoinette should be so much more hated in eighteenth-century France than a rich, idle, much publicized heiress in contemporary America; but at any rate the existence of such bitterness can be observed in our prerevolutionary societies, which is, clinically speaking, enough for the moment.

Third, there is what we have called the desertion of the intellectuals. This is in some respects the most reliable of the symptoms we are likely to meet. Here again we need not try to explain all the hows and whys, need not try to tie up the desertion of the intellectuals with a grand and complete sociology of revolutions. We need state simply that it can be observed in all four of our societies.

Fourth, the governmental machinery is clearly inefficient, partly through neglect, through a failure to make changes in old institutions, partly because new conditions—in the societies we have studied, pretty specifically conditions attendant on economic expansion and the growth of new monied classes, new ways of transportation, new business methods—these new conditions laid an intolerable strain on governmental machinery adapted to simpler, more primitive, conditions.

Fifth, the old ruling class—or rather, many individuals of the old ruling class—come to distrust themselves, or lose faith in the traditions and habits of their class, grow intellectual, humanitarian, or go over to the attacking groups. Perhaps a larger number of them than usual lead lives we shall have to call immoral, dissolute, though one cannot by any means be as sure about this as a symptom as about the loss of habits and traditions of command effective among a ruling class. At any rate, the ruling class becomes politically inept.

The dramatic events that start things moving, that bring on the fever of revolution, are in three of our four revolutions intimately connected with the financial administration of the state. In the fourth, Russia, the breakdown of administration under the burdens of an unsuccessful war is only in part financial. But in all our societies the inefficiency and inadequacy of the governmental structure of the society come out clearly in the very first stages of the revolution. There is a time—the first few weeks or months—when it looks as if a determined use of force on the part of the government might prevent the mounting excitement from culminating in an overthrow of the government. These governments attempted such a use of force in all four instances, and in all four their attempt was a failure. This failure indeed proved a turning point during the first stages, and set up the revolutionists in power.

Yet one is impressed in all four instances more with the ineptitude of the governments' use of force than with the skill of their opponents' use of force. We are here speaking of the situation wholly from a military and police point of view. It may be that the majority of the people are discontented, loathe the existing government, wish it overthrown. Nobody knows. They don't take plebiscites *before* revolutions. In the actual clash—even Bastille Day, Concord, or the February Days in Petrograd—only a minority of the people is actively engaged. But the government hold over its own troops is poor, its troops fight half-heartedly or desert, its commanders are stupid, its enemies acquire a nucleus of the deserting troops or of a previous militia, and the old gives place to the new. Yet, such is the conservative and routine-loving nature of the bulk of human beings, so strong are habits of obedience in most of them, that it is almost safe to say that no government is likely to be overthrown until it loses the ability to make adequate use of its military and police powers. That loss of ability may show itself in the actual desertion of soldiers and police to the revolutionists, or in the stupidity with which the government manages its soldiers and police, or in both ways.

The events we have grouped under the names of first stages do not of

course unroll themselves in exactly the same order in time, or with exactly
the same content, in all four of our revolutions. But we have listed the
major elements—and they fall into a pattern of uniformities—financial
breakdown, organization of the discontented to remedy this breakdown
(or threatened breakdown), revolutionary demands on the part of these
organized discontented, demands which if granted would mean the virtual
abdication of those governing, attempted use of force by the government,
its failure, and the attainment of power by the revolutionists. These
revolutionists have hitherto been acting as an organized and nearly
unanimous group, but with the attainment of power it is clear that they
are not united. The group which dominates these first stages we call the
moderates. They are not always in a numerical majority in this stage—
indeed it is pretty clear that if you limit the moderates to the Kadets they
were not in a majority in Russia in February, 1917. But they seem the
natural heirs of the old government, and they have their chance. In three
of our revolutions they are sooner or later driven from office to death or
exile. Certainly there is to be seen in England, France, and Russia a process
in which a series of crises—some involving violence, street fighting, and
the like—deposes one set of men and puts in power another and more
radical set. In these revolutions power passes by violent or at least
extralegal methods from Right to Left, until at the crisis period the
extreme radicals, the complete revolutionists, are in power. There are, as a
matter of fact, usually a few even wilder and more lunatic fringes of the
triumphant extremists—but these are not numerous or strong and are
usually suppressed or otherwise made harmless by the dominant radicals.
It is therefore approximately true to say that power passes on from Right
to Left until it reaches the extreme Left.

The rule of the extremists we have called the crisis period. This period
was not reached in the American Revolution, though in the treatment of
Loyalists, in the pressure to support the army, in some of the phases of
social life, you can discern in America many of the phenomena of the
Terror as it is seen in our three other societies. We cannot here attempt to
go into the complicated question as to why the American Revolution
stopped short of a true crisis period, why the moderates were never ousted
in this country. We must repeat that we are simply trying to establish
certain uniformities of description, and are not attempting a complete
sociology of revolutions.

The extremists are helped to power no doubt by the existence of a
powerful pressure toward centralized strong government, something
which in general the moderates are not capable of providing, while the
extremists, with their discipline, their contempt for half measures, their
willingness to make firm decisions, their freedom from libertarian qualms,
are quite able and willing to centralize. Especially in France and Russia,
where powerful foreign enemies threatened the very existence of the
nation, the machinery of government during the crisis period was in part

constructed to serve as a government of national defense. Yet though modern wars, as we know in this country, demand a centralization of authority, war alone does not seem to account for all that happened in the crisis period in those countries.

What does happen may be a bit oversimply summarized as follows: emergency centralization of power in an administration, usually a council or commission, and more or less dominated by a "strong man"—Cromwell, Robespierre, Lenin; government without any effective protection for the normal civil rights of the individual—or if this sounds unrealistic, especially for Russia, let us say the normal private life of the individual; setting up of extraordinary courts and a special revolutionary police to carry out the decrees of the government and to suppress all dissenting individuals or groups; all this machinery ultimately built up from a relatively small group—Independents, Jacobins, Bolsheviks—which has a monopoly on all governmental action. Finally, governmental action becomes a much greater part of all human action than in these societies in their normal condition: this apparatus of government is set to work indifferently on the mountains and molehills of human life—it is used to pry into and poke about corners normally reserved for priest or physician, or friend, and it is used to regulate, control, plan, the production and distribution of economic wealth on a national scale.

This pervasiveness of the Reign of Terror in the crisis period is partly explicable in terms of the pressure of war necessities and of economic struggles as well as of other variables: but it must probably also be explained as in part the manifestation of an effort to achieve intensely religious ends here on earth. The little band of violent revolutionists who form the nucleus of all action during the Terror behave as men have been observed to behave before when under the influence of active religious faith. Indepedents, Jacobins, Bolsheviks, all sought to make all human activity here on earth conform to an ideal pattern, which, like all such patterns, seems deeply rooted in their sentiments. A striking uniformity in all these patterns is their asceticism, or if you prefer, their condemnation of what we may call the minor as well as the major vices. Essentially, however, these patterns are a good deal alike, and all resemble closely what we may call conventional Christian ethics. Independents, Jacobins, and Bolsheviks, at least during the crisis period, really make an effort to enforce behavior in literal conformity with these codes or patterns. Such an effort means stern repression of much that many men have been used to regarding as normal; it means a kind of universal tension in which the ordinary individual can never feel protected by the humble routines to which he has been formed: it means that the intricate network of interactions among individuals—a network which is still to the few men devoted to its intelligent study almost a complete mystery—this network is temporarily all torn apart. John Jones, the man in the street, the ordinary man, is left floundering.

We are almost at the point of being carried away into the belief that our conceptual scheme is something more than a mere convenience, that it does somehow describe "reality." At the crisis, the collective patient does seem helpless, thrashing his way through a delirium. But we must try to avoid the emotional, metaphorical appeal, and concentrate on making clear what seems to be the really important point here. Most of us are familiar with the favorite old Tory metaphor: the violent revolutionist tears down the noble edifice society lives in, or burns it down, and then fails to build up another, and poor human beings are left naked to the skies. That is not a good metaphor, save perhaps for purposes of Tory propaganda. Even at the height of a revolutionary crisis period, more of the old building is left standing than is destroyed. But the whole metaphor of the building is bad. We may take instead an analogy from the human nervous system, or think of an immensely complicated gridwork of electrical communications. Society then appears as a kind of a network of interactions among individuals, interactions for the most part fixed by habit, hardened and perhaps adorned as ritual, dignified into meaning and beauty by the elaborately interwoven strands of interaction we know as law, theology, metaphysics, and similar noble beliefs. Now sometimes many of these interwoven strands of noble beliefs, some even of those of habit and tradition, can be cut out, and others inserted. During the crisis period of our revolutions some such process seems to have taken place; but the whole network itself seems so far never to have been altered suddenly and radically, and even the noble beliefs tend to fit into the network in the same places. If you kill off *all* the people who live within the network, you don't so much change the network of course as destroy it. And in spite of our prophets of doom, this type of destruction is rare in human history. Certainly in none of our revolutions was there even a very close approach to it.

What did happen, under the pressure of class struggle, war, religious idealism, and a lot more, was that the hidden and obscure courses which many of the interactions in the network follow were suddenly exposed, and passage along them made difficult in the unusual publicity and, so to speak, self-consciousness. The courses of other interactions were blocked, and the interactions went on with the greatest of difficulties by all sorts of detours. The courses of still other interactions were confused, short-circuited, paired off in strange ways. Finally, the pretensions of the fanatical leaders of the revolution involved the attempted creation of a vast number of new interactions. Now though for the most part these new interactions affected chiefly those strands we have called the noble beliefs—law, theology, metaphysics, mythology, folklore, high-power abstractions in general—still some of them did penetrate at an experimental level into the obscurer and less dignified part of the network of inter-actions among human beings and put a further strain on it. Surely it is no wonder that under these conditions men and women in the crisis period should behave as they would not normally behave, that in the crisis period nothing should seem as it used to seem. . . .

Certainly none of our revolutions quite ended in the death of civilization and culture. The network was stronger than the forces trying to destroy or alter it, and in all of our societies the crisis period was followed by a convalescence, by a return to most of the simpler and more fundamental courses taken by interactions in the old network. More especially, the religious lust for perfection, the crusade for the Republic of Virtue, died out, save among a tiny minority whose actions could no longer take place directly in politics. An active, proselyting, intolerant, ascetic, chiliastic faith became fairly rapidly an inactive, indifferent, worldly ritualistic faith.

The equilibrium has been restored and the revolution is over. But this does not mean that nothing has been changed. Some new and useful tracks or courses in the network of interactions that makes society have been established, some old and inconvenient ones—you may call them unjust if you like—have been eliminated. There is something heartless in saying that it took the French Revolution to produce the metric system and to destroy *lods et ventes* and similar feudal inconveniences, or the Russian Revolution to bring Russia to use the modern calendar and to eliminate a few useless letters in the Russian alphabet. These tangible and useful results look rather petty as measured by the brotherhood of man and the achievement of justice on this earth. The blood of the martyrs seems hardly necessary to establish decimal coinage.

Yet those who feel that revolution is heroic need not despair. The revolutionary tradition is an heroic one, and the noble beliefs which seem necessary to all societies are in our Western democracies in part a product of the revolutions we have been studying. Our revolutions made tremendous and valuable additions to those strands in the network of human interactions which can be isolated as law, theology, metaphysics and, in the abstract sense, ethics. Had these revolutions never occurred, you and I might still beat our wives or cheat at cards or avoid walking under ladders, but we might not be able to rejoice in our possession of certain inalienable rights to life, liberty, and the pursuit of happiness, or in the comforting assurance that one more push will bring the classless society.

When one compares the whole course of these revolutions, certain tentative uniformities suggest themselves. If the Russian Revolution at the end of our series is compared with the English at its beginning, there seems to be a development of conscious revolutionary technique. This is of course expecially clear since Marx made the history of revolutionary movements of the past a necessary preparation for revolutionists of the present. Lenin and his collaborators had a training in the technique of insurrection which Independents and Jacobins lacked. Robespierre seems almost a political innocent when his revolutionary training is compared with that of any good Bolshevik leaders. Sam Adams, it must be admitted, seems a good deal less innocent. All in all, it is probable that this difference in the explicitness of self-conscious preparation for revolution, this growth of a copious literature of revolution, this increasing familiarity of revolutionary ideas, is not one of the very important uniformities we have to record. It is a conspicuous uniformity, but not an important one. Revolutions are still not a form of logical action. The Bolsheviks do not seem to have guided their actions by the "scientific" study of revolutions to an appreciably greater degree than the Independents or the Jacobins. They simply adapted an old technique to the days of the telegraph and railroad trains.

This last suggests another conspicuous but not very important tendency in our four revolutions. They took place in societies increasingly influenced by the "Industrial Revolution," increasingly subject to those changes in scale which our modern conquests of time and space have brought to societies. Thus the Russian Revolution directly affected more people and more square miles of territory than any previous revolution; its sequence of events compresses into a few months what in England in the seventeenth century had taken years to achieve; in its use of the printing press, telegraph, radio, airplanes and the rest it seems, as compared with our other revolutions, definitely a streamlined affair. But again we may well doubt whether such changes of scale are in themselves really important factors. Men's desires are the same, whether they ride toward their achievement in airplanes or on horseback. Revolutions may be bigger nowadays, but surely not better. Our prophets of doom to the contrary notwithstanding, the loudspeaker does not change the words.

Finally, at the risk of being tedious, we must come back to some of the problems of methods in the social sciences which were suggested in our first chapter. We must admit that the theorems, the uniformities, which we have been able to put forward in terms of our conceptual scheme, are vague and undramatic. They are by no means as interesting or as alarming as the ideas of revolution held by the late George Orwell, who really believed that totalitarian revolutionary leaders have learned how to change human beings into something wholly different from their immediate predecessors. They cannot be stated in quantitative terms, cannot be used for purposes of prediction or control. But at the very outset we warned the reader not to expect too much. Even such vague theorems as that of the desertion of the intellectuals, that of the role of force in the first stages of revolution, that of the part played by "religious" enthusiasm in the period of crisis, that of the pursuit of pleasure during Thermidor, are, one hopes, not without value for the study of men in society. In themselves they amount to little, but they suggest certain possibilities in further work.

In the first place, by their very inadequacies they point to the necessity for a more rigorous treatment of the problems involved, challenging those who find them incomplete and unsatisfactory to do a better job. In the second place, they will serve the purpose of all first approximations in scientific work—they will suggest further study of the *facts*, especially in those fields where the attempt to make first approximations has uncovered an insufficient supply of the necessary facts. Notably here the facts for a study of class antagonisms are woefully inadequate. So, too, are the facts for a study of the circulation of the elite in prerevolutionary societies. But there are a hundred such holes, some of which can surely be filled. Our first approximations will then lead the way to another's second approximations. No scientist should ask more, even though the public does.

A Paradox of Revolution

Wider uniformities will, to judge by the past of science, someday emerge from more complete studies of the sociology of revolutions. Here we dare not hazard much that we have not already brought out in the course of our analysis of four specific revolutions. After all, these are but four revolutions of what seems to be the same type, revolutions in what may be not too uncritically called the democratic tradition. So precious a word is "revolution" to many in that tradition, and especially to Marxists, that they indignantly refused to apply it to such movements as the relatively bloodless but certainly violent and illegal assumption of power by Mussolini or Hitler. These movements, we are told, were not revolutions because they did not take power from one class and give it to another. Obviously with a word in some ways as imprecise as "revolution" you can play all sorts of tricks like this. But for the scientific study of social change it seems wise to apply the word revolution to the overthrow of an established and legal parliamentary government by Fascists. If this is so, then our four revolutions are but one kind of revolution, and we must not attempt to make them bear the strain of generalizations meant to apply to all revolutions.

It is even more tempting to try to fit these revolutions into something like a philosophy of history. But the philosophy of history is almost bound to lead into the kind of prophetic activity we have already firmly forsworn. It may be that mankind is now in the midst of a universal "time of troubles" from which it will emerge into some kind of universal authoritarian order. It may be that the democratic revolutionary tradition is no longer a living and effective one. It may be that the revolutions we have studied could only have taken place in societies in which "progress" was made a concrete thing by opportunities for economic expansion which cannot recur in our contemporary world, with no more frontiers and no more big families. It may even be that the Marxists are right, and that imperialistic capitalism is now digging its own grave, preparing the inevitable if long-delayed world revolution of the proletariat. There are many possibilities, as to which it is almost true that one man's guess is as good as another's. Certainly a conscientious effort to study four great revolutions in the modern world as a scientist might cannot end in anything as ambitious and as unscientific as social prognosis.

We need not, however, end on a note of blank skepticism. It would seem that there are, from the study of these revolutions, three major conclusions to be drawn: first, that, in spite of their undeniable and dramatic differences, they do present certain simple uniformities of the kind we have tried to bring together under our conceptual scheme of the fever; second, that they point sharply to the necessity of studying men's deeds and men's words without assuming that there is always a simple and logical connection between the two, since throughout their courses, and especially at their crises, they frequently exhibit men saying one thing and doing another; third, that they indicate that in general many things men do, many human habits, sentiments, dispositions, cannot be changed at all rapidly, that the attempt made by the extremists to change them by law, terror, and exhortation fails, that the convalescence brings them back not greatly altered.

Yet one hesitant major generalization binding all four of these revolutions together may here be made from many anticipations earlier in this book. These four revolutions exhibit an increasing scale of promises to the "common man"—promises as vague as that of complete "happiness" and as concrete as that of full satisfaction of all material wants, with all sorts of pleasant revenges on the way. Communism is but the present limit of this increasing set of promises. It is not for us here to rail or protest, but simply to record. So far, these promises in their extreme form have been fulfilled nowhere. That they are made at all offends the traditional Christian, the humanist, perhaps even the man of common sense. But they are made, more vigorously perhaps today in China, in Southeast Asia, in the Near East, wherever Communism is still a young, fresh, and active faith. It is not enough for us Americans to repeat that the promises are impossible of fulfillment, and ought not to be made. It would be folly for us to tell the world that we Americans can fill these promises, especially since we have not filled them at home. Revolution is not a fever that will yield to such innocent and deceptive remedies. For a time, at least, we must accept it as being as incurable as cancer.

As to what the experience of a great revolution does to the society that experiences it, we cannot conclude here too widely without trespassing on wider fields of history and sociology. Yet it does seem that the patient emerges stronger in some respects from the conquered fever, immunized in this way and that from attacks that might be more serious. It is an observable fact that in all our societies there was a flourishing, a peak of varied cultural achievements, after the revolutions. Certainly we may not moralize too much about the stupidities and cruelties of revolutions, may not lift up our hands in horror. It is quite possible that wider study would show that feeble and decadent societies do not undergo revolutions, that revolutions are, perversely, a sign of strength and youth in societies.

One quiet person emerges from his study, not indeed untouched by a good deal of horror and disgust, but moved also with admiration for a deep and unfathomable strength in men which, because of the softer connotations of the word, he is reluctant to call spiritual. Montaigne saw and felt it long ago:

I see not one action, or three, or a hundred, but a commonly accepted state of morality so unnatural, especially as regards inhumanity and treachery, which are to me the worst of all sins, that I have not the heart to think of them without horror; and they excite my wonder almost as much as my detestation. *The practice of these egregious villanies has as much the mark of strength and vigor of soul as of error and disorder.*

Berkman the anarchist, who loathed the Russian Revolution, tells a story which may represent merely his own bias, but which may nonetheless serve as a brief symbolical epilogue to this study. Berkman says he asked a good Bolshevik acquaintance during the period of attempted complete communization under Lenin why the famous Moscow cabmen, the *izvoschiks,* who continued in diminished numbers to flit about Moscow and to get enormous sums in paper roubles for their services, were not nationalized like practically everything else. The Bolshevik replied, "We found that if you don't feed human beings they continue to live somehow. But if you don't feed the horses, the stupid beasts die. That's why we don't nationalize the cabmen." That is not an altogether cheerful story, and in some ways one may regret the human capacity to live without eating. But clearly if we were as stupid—or as sensible—as horses we should have no revolutions.

51. TWENTIETH CENTURY REVOLUTIONS*
Hugh Seton-Watson

THE FIRST half of the twentieth century is richer than any previous period of human history in the activities of revolutionary movements. Some have failed, others are still engaged in the struggle. A few have achieved revolutions of historic importance. But there is one important feature of the twentieth century revolutionary movements which distinguishes them from those of the nineteenth century. The earlier movements arose in culturally and economically advanced countries, while those of the present century have for the most part affected backward regions and peoples.

These movements are much discussed at present by journalists and politicians, but have received little attention from historians. In current discussions the main emphasis is usually placed on the mass aspect of the movements and on economic factors. It is assumed that their strength comes mainly from the unrest of subject nations, industrial proletariats and impoverished peasants. The victories which they have won are

* From *The Political Quarterly*, Vol. 22 (July–September, 1951), pp. 251–65. By permission.

usually attributed to mass support. The conclusion is that revolutions can best be averted if the wealthier nations invest large sums in the development of backward economies. Better food crops, new jobs in industry and more extensive trade will reduce the mass poverty and deprive the revolutionaries of their opportunity.

It would be absurd to deny that revolutionary movements thrive on mass poverty and mass discontent, or that improvement in the standard of living of the masses makes for political stability. But two further factors deserve consideration. The first is the origin and the nature of revolutionary leadership. The second is the political framework within which revolutionary movements develop. Both these factors have of course been minutely studied by historians of the revolutions of the eighteenth and nineteenth centuries in Western Europe and North America. They have, however, been somewhat neglected in connection with the twentieth century movements in Eastern Europe, Asia and Africa. Such attempts as have been made are too often the work of uncritical admirers or passionate adversaries. Yet even a brief examination of these two factors may make possible some significant conclusions about the twentieth century revolutionary movements of backward peoples.

West European and American political commentators and economists are too inclined to consider world problems from the point of view of the economics and political traditions of Western Europe and North America. But the "western society" on which their ideas are based is not the typical society of the world. It exists only in Scandinavia, north-west Europe, North America, and the British Dominions of the Pacific. If northern Italy and Germany are added, the whole area has a population of less than 400 million out of a world population of more than 2,000 million.

The society of this "north-western corner" of the world, which has grown up since the end of the Middle Ages, has certain specific features. The class structure is balanced. The level of skill and the standard of living of workers and farmers are on the whole high. There is a numerous and influential middle class, in which the three subdivisions of business, free professions and administration play their parts. Education is widespread and long established. The tradition of representative institutions, both national and local, is deeply rooted. Though there are great differences in wealth, all citizens belong to the same century. Class structure, education and constitutional forms vary considerably within different regions and countries of the north-west corner, but all share these general characteristics, in contrast to the lands outside the corner.

If the typical classes of the north-west corner are skilled workers, educated farmers and business men, the typical classes of the outside world are unskilled labourers, uneducated peasants and bureaucrats. In southern and eastern Europe, Asia, Africa and Latin America the great majority of the population are primitive and poverty-stricken peasants. In the last decades the rapid industrialization of certain regions has reduced the number of peasants and increased the number of unskilled workers in mines or factories, little if at all less primitive or poor. One reason for the poverty of the peasants has been the survival of great landed estates and of various semi-feudal legal forms. This was the case in Russia before 1917 and in Hungary until 1945. It is still the case in southern Italy, Spain, Egypt and large parts of Asia, Africa and Latin America. But experience has shown that the distribution of landlords' estates among the peasants—which was done in parts of Eastern Europe after 1918, in other parts after 1945, and in Japan, Korea and China after the Second World War—is not the end of the peasants' poverty. A more basic cause of poverty is rural overpopulation. The numbers of people in the villages have grown more rapidly than the output of the soil has been increased or than new jobs in industry have been created. Overpopulation means underemployment for the peasants, and a reserve of half-employed peasants keeps down the level of wages for all but the skilled minority among the urban workers.

For those sons of peasants who are able by ability or good fortune to rise in the social scale the best opportunities have usually lain in the state service. But the growing influx of recruits from below inflates the bureaucracy intolerably. As the numbers of bureaucrats grow faster than the national wealth, their material conditions deteriorate. An enormous underpaid civil service breeds corruption: only by bribery can the poor official feed his family. To corruption must be added a tradition of arrogance and brutality. The official is accustomed to despise and bully the human cattle whom it is his duty to push, pull or drive whither his masters bid. This has certainly long been the practice in Spain, Hungary, Poland, the Balkans and Russia. It is still more so in Turkey, Persia, China or Japan. In colonial countries the situation has been somewhat different. The West European administrators have tried, with varying success, to bring to their colonies the more civilized methods of administration prevalent in their own countries, and have also resisted the pressure to inflate the numbers of officials. But the lower ranks of their administration have been filled with local people who have imperfectly acquired the higher standards, while the limitation of numbers has contributed above all to the frustration of the subject nations. As soon as they attain independence the colonial peoples rapidly expand their civil services. The world must be shown that they are not "unfit to govern," and jobs must be found for the boys. Corruption increases faster than ever, and the new bureaucrats feel even more strongly than the old how distinct and superior a caste they are.

In this type of society, which until recently was typical of most of the world outside the north-west corner, the masses were too inert and the bureaucrats too powerful. If there was to be radical change, leadership must be found. The source of such leadership has been the small educated class—the "intelligentsia."

The intelligentsia is a product of western influence. Already in the eighteenth century western ideas and ways of life were known to the aristocracies of Poland, Hungary and Russia. During the nineteenth century schools and universities developed in these countries, slowly it is true, but with important effects. The professional class was formed from two directions, from the children of the landed gentry for whom there was no place on the family estate, and from the children of small officials, merchants and village shopkeepers who had just enough money, ability or "connections" to mount the educational ladder. Even the reactionary but incompetent Ministers of Education of mid-nineteenth-century Russia were unable either to reserve higher education to members of the nobility or to purge it of progressive ideas. In the Balkan countries liberated from Turkish rule no social hierarchy barred the way to education. The Balkan governments were keen to extend education: the obstacle was the meagre wealth of the states. Though the intention was education for all, the more prosperous families were in fact privileged. The children of the army officers, officials, inn-keepers, pig-merchants and village usurers from whom the ruling class of the new states was formed, had better chances than the children of peasant smallholders, miners, railwaymen or factory workers. In Asia the process started later. In the Middle East the Islamic system or education was open to comparatively poor children, but it was more or less unrelated to the needs of the nineteenth and twentieth centuries. The same was true of the Confucian system in China. The introduction of western ideas and influences was largely the work of such institutions as the French schools in the Levant, the American Robert College at Constantinople, the American University of Beirut, and European and American missions in China. Japan alone among Asiatic countries systematically copied European education and diffused it among her subjects. In Latin America considerable efforts had been made in education ever since the Spanish and Portuguese conquests.

The best education available at the most modern schools and universities in Eastern Europe, Asia and Latin America has been little inferior to that available at the same time anywhere in the western world. Some institutions in Africa have recently approached or attained the same standard. The best scientists, writers, doctors or engineers produced by this education have been as good at their jobs as their western counterparts. They have entered the twentieth century, while their peoples, suffering from social injustice and political oppression, have remained in the eighteenth, or fifteenth, or tenth century.

Many, probably most, members of the East European and Asian intelligentsias accepted this fact. Some believed that by becoming twentieth-century people, and doing twentieth-century jobs, they were working for their own nations' good, and would help to raise their nations to their level. Others were so engrossed in their special skill that the wider issues did not occur to them. Others simply enjoyed the life of a French lawyer or an American engineer, rather than that of a Hungarian worker, a

Lebanese peasant or a Chinese coolie. Their lives were more agreeable than those of their compatriots: let the latter fend for themselves.

But a minority, and in some countries a very numerous minority, rebelled. They were horrified by the contrast between themselves and their peoples, between the fifteenth and twentieth centuries. The social injustices were intolerable, and the political factors which perpetuated them—the dominance of a privileged class or a privileged nation—must be swept away. There were young Slovaks who were not content, by learning the Magyar language and so reaching a Magyar university, to merge themselves in the Hungarian ruling class, but insisted on fighting for the national and social liberation of the submerged Slovak nation. There were Russian or Chinese intellectuals, of both distinguished and humble birth, who could not ignore the landhunger in the villages, the maltreatment of peasants by landlords or police, the dead weight of a bureaucracy suspicious of every generous initiative.

To these idealist motives must be added personal motives for revolt. Semi-feudal legal survivals of foreign rule were not only socially or nationally unjust: they were also obstacles to the ambitions of the local intellectuals. Poles, Ukrainians, Balts and Caucasians in the Russian Empire; South Slavs, Slovaks and Roumanians in Hungary; the Asiatic and African subjects of European colonial empires found their way to power and wealth barred by members of the dominant nations. In Hungary, Roumania and Poland between the world wars many of the best posts in business and the free professions were held by Jews. University graduates who found no jobs attributed their difficulties to a sinister Jewish conspiracy. Idealism and interest alike led them to anti-semitic fascism. Chinese in Siam and Malaya, Indians in East Africa, Greeks in the Middle East, and Europeans throughout Asia, form a host of "Jewish problems," seem to the young intellectuals of each country to have robbed them of their birthright, and drive them to revolutionary nationalism. Balkan university students denounced their professors as "reactionary" because they failed in their examinations. Egyptian or Indian students have beaten or murdered invigilators who objected to their bringing cribs into the examination hall. To join an extremist party—fascist, nationalist or communist—was emotionally satisfying and required less sustained mental effort than plain hard work. For most of the revolutionary intellectuals of the backward countries the broader and the personal motives existed side by side. The personal motive is perhaps more powerful in colonial countries, where the presence of the foreign Power is a constant irritant, and where the level of education is lower than in Eastern Europe, Japan or even the Middle East. The half-educated are perhaps more frustrated, and more inclined to revolutionary short-cuts, than the fully educated.

It was through the intelligentsia, created by the development of western types of education, that the modern political ideas of Western Europe reached the countries of Eastern Europe, Asia and Africa. It should be noted that the ideas reached the backward countries ready-made, before the economic social and political conditions to which they were related had arisen. Examples are Russia in the 1870s, Bulgaria in the 1890s and China in the 1920s. Even nationalism was preached by the intelligentsia when national consciousness hardly existed among the masses. Examples from Europe are the Slovaks and the Ukrainians. In Asia and Africa this has been still more the case.

The relationship between the ideas of the intelligentsia and the social condition and consciousness of the masses has varied according to the stage of general economic and cultural development. This is well illustrated by the case of Russia. In the Russia of the 1870s, when the intelligentsia was separated by a chasm from the masses, the intelligentsia's best hope of victory for their ideas was to organize a secret conspiracy of professional revolutionaries. In the Russia of 1913, in which a middle class and a skilled working class were becoming important factors, the peasants were becoming educated, and even the intellectuals were beginning to find a legal outlet for their energies and abilities, political action by mass parties, as in Western Europe, was becoming possible. This was what the Menshevik faction of Russian socialism advocated, and every year after 1905 seemed to strengthen their case. Lenin, who clung to the older conspiratorial type of party, seemed a reactionary utopian. But in the Russia of 1917, when the Russian state collapsed and the europeanizing work of 50 years was undone, Lenin was the realist and the Mensheviks the utopians.

Between the world wars Hungary, Poland and Japan to some extent resembled the Russia of 1913. Large-scale industry was fairly well developed. Skilled workers, technicians and business men were numerous. Political power, however, did not belong to these classes, not even to a very large extent to the business men. It was held to some extent by landowning families, and to an increasing extent by a bureaucracy whose higher officials were descendants of landowners, who had succeeded in impressing even on its lower ranks—recruited from the poorer classes—the traditional outlook of the landowning class—gentry, szlachta or samurai. The peasants were still economically backward, had too little land, and were in many cases victims of exploitation.

The Balkan countries between the world wars had some points of resemblance to the Russia of the '70s. Industry was still backward, skilled workers were few and the middle class was weak. When dictatorships were installed in the 1920s the police were no less powerful, and probably more cruel, than the police of Tsar Alexander II. On the other hand, the Balkan nations had no landowning aristocracy or semi-feudal survivals; their education was making great progress; and they had far more experience of self-government than the Russians.

In Asia and Africa development was of course slower. The most modern provinces of Egypt, India and China bear some resemblance to the Russia of 1913, but in the backward provinces conditions remained as primitive as in the Europe of the Middle Ages. In large parts of Africa things are very much more primitive still. In these countries the local man who has received a twentieth-century education is cut off from his people by a deeper gulf even than were the Russian intellectuals of the mid-nineteenth century.

The impact of ready-made West European political ideas on these various types of backward societies had effects at least as far-reaching as the impact of West European trade and technique. The political ideas were reflected in political movements, in which inevitably the leadership came from the intelligentsia. In Russia, China, the Ottoman Empire and the Balkan states the radical intellectuals were forced by the repressive policy of dictatorial governments to resort to more or less revolutionary and conspiratorial methods. In Austria-Hungary, Japan and the British and French empires they enjoyed greater freedom of action, though this fell short of "western democracy" as understood in Britain and France. In general, the radicalism of the intellectuals and their importance in the revolutionary movements varied in inverse proportion to the economic and cultural development of their peoples. As the masses became more prosperous, more skilled and more educated, broadly based mass movements became more possible, the leadership of intellectuals became less essential, and it became more reasonable to hope for improvement by comparatively peaceful means. It is the combination of backward masses, extremist intellectuals and despotic bureaucrats which creates the most conspiratorial movements.

These movements may be, in European terminology, "extreme left" or "extreme right."

The earliest example of a "left" type were the Russian Populists of the 1870s. They held unrealistic views about the revolutionary potentialities of the Russian peasants, and about the possibility of transforming the traditional organs of village self-government into organs of a socialist society. But as conspirators they were efficient, at any rate judged by the technical standards of the time. They created a small but well disciplined organization, which assassinated several high officials and finally killed the Tsar himself. Their technique was later copied and improved by Lenin, whose Bolshevik party was from the first intended to be an organization of "professional revolutionaries." The Bolshevik technique of conspiracy has in turn served as the model for the Communist parties in all countries. Some of these have been forced by police persecution to operate "underground" during most of their existence. But even those which have enjoyed the political liberties of a democratic state were obliged by the Twenty-One Conditions of the Second Comintern Congress of 1920, to maintain, parallel with their "legal" organization, an "illegal" apparatus. The efficiency of Communist conspirators has varied greatly in the last 30 years. Among the more efficient were the illegal parties of Bulgaria and

Yugoslavia between the world wars. In both countries the intellectual youth was strongly attracted to Communism. Students and graduates of Belgrade and Sofia universities succeeded in popularizing Communism and the Soviet Union and built up cadres which were to prove valuable during the resistance movements in the Second World War. Another country in which Communism made a most powerful appeal to young intellectuals was of course China.

An interesting example of a "right" type of revolutionary movement in a backward country is the Roumanian Iron Guard. Led by university students and graduates, it was able during the slump of the early 1930s to exploit the misery of the peasants and the idealism of the intelligentsia. It promised vague social reforms, including a further distribution of land. Oppression was identified with the Jews, liberation and justice with the German Nazis. Like the Russian Populists, the Iron Guardists "went to the people," studying their living conditions more honestly and more thoroughly than the elder generation of liberal politicians have done, and at the same time propagating their ideas. Like the Communists, they infiltrated themselves into official organizations and into oppositional parties. Like the Communists, they were savagely repressed by the police. Parallels with the Roumanian Iron Guardists can be found among the nationalist movements of Asia and Africa. One example is the conspiratorial groups of young officers in Japan, who had more or less fascist ideas, wished to regenerate their country, were antiparliamentarian and anti-capitalist, and whose policy was a mixture of modernization and anti-western traditionalism. Another is the Moslem Brotherhood in Egypt, a combination of modern nationalism and Islamic conservatism. Like the Roumanian Iron Guardists and the Japanese secret societies, the Moslem Brothers make use of assassination as a political weapon.

Communism is to-day the most important of the revolutionary movements among the backward peoples, but it is not and will not necessarily be the only one. Communism, as developed by Stalin and Mao Tse-tung, is only the most important example of a wider phenomenon, the revolt of the backward peoples, led by a section of their intelligentsia, against the West.

*   *   *   *   *

The obstacle to the seizure of power by the revolutionary movements has been the bureaucratic state machine. Communist theory has paid much attention to this problem. But in fact no Communist movement in this century has, solely by its own efforts, captured or destroyed the state machine. In three cases only Communists have seized power—in Russia, Yugoslavia and China. But in all three cases the state machine was smashed not by the revolutionaries but by a foreign invading Power.

In the chaos of the collapse of Tsardom the Bolsheviks were more clear-headed, better disciplined and less scrupulous than their rivals. They were also more efficient demagogues. By promising the people at once the things they most needed, and which in fact they knew that they would not be able to give them, they won considerable popular support. Lenin, who for more than a decade had devoted himself to the study of power, built a new army and a new police machine. He made good use of the quarrels between his Russian rivals and between his foreign enemies. He was also able to some extent to exploit Russian patriotism against Poles and Japanese. His skill in all these matters gave him the victory, but he would not have had a chance to begin it Ludendorff had not crushed the armies of the Tsar. Nor would all his skill have availed him had not Russia possessed the advantages of geographical remoteness. The British, French and American publics were not convinced that it mattered to them what happened in distant Russia. Their governments, dependent on their votes at election time, soon abandoned their very small attempts at intervention. In Hungary, where the collapse of the old régime gave the Communists a similar opportunity, they were crushed. This was no doubt partly due to the fact that Bela Kun was not so good a leader as Lenin. But it was still more due to the geographical accessibility of Hungary to the armies of the victorious Allies and of their smaller protégés.

In Yugoslavia the old police régime which had kept down the Communists was destroyed by the German and satellite invaders. In China the same thing was done by the conquering Japanese. In both countries the Communists assumed the leadership of national resistance. The Chinese Communists had already acquired valuable experience of guerrilla warfare in their struggle against Chiang Kai-shek. The Yugoslav Communists had no guerrilla experience in their own country, but they possessed cadres of brave and disciplined underground organizers, and some of their leaders had learned the art of warfare as volunteers in the Spanish civil war. In both countries the Communist-led resistance forces liberated considerable areas, in which they set up a civil administration and conscripted the population into their armies. Thus by the time the Germans and Japanese were defeated by the Allied Great Powers, both the Chinese and Yugoslav Communists possessed disciplined military and civil bureaucracies, ready to take over power in the rest of their country. The factor of geographical remoteness also operated in their favour. If either the Germans or the Japanese had sent over-powering forces into the fastnesses of the Yugoslav and Chinese Communists, they could no doubt have crushed them. But the commitments on the main war fronts and the difficulty of the Communist-held terrain made it not worth their while to do so. After the defeat of the invaders, the two countries were outside the area of the western armies, which might have been expected to be unsympathetic to the Communists. Belgrade and Manchuria were "liberated" by the Soviet armies. The supply of American arms to the forces of Chiang Kai-shek was even less effective than the supply of arms from France and Britain to the Russian Whites in 1919–20.

In other areas also Communist-led resistance forces gained experience of military leadership and civil administration, but were not able to seize power. The European example is Greece, where a large "liberated area" was held in 1943–4 and again in 1947–9. In Asia there were similar areas in Malaya, Burma and Indo-China. These areas were not, however, geographically remote enough. British forces defeated the Greek Communists in 1944, and American aid enabled the Greek National Army to defeat them again in 1949. In Burma the Communists and nationalists came to blows, and the government of Burma, granted independence by Britain, gradually gained control of most of the country. In Malaya Communist guerrillas are still a very serious nuisance, but there is no prospect of their obtaining power over the country unless they are supported by an invading army. In Indo-China the outlook is uncertain. . . .

There have of course been numerous occasions when Communist régimes have been installed by the military intervention of Soviet Russian forces. This was done in Georgia in 1921, in Outer Mongolia in 1922 and in the Baltic states in 1940. An unsuccessful attempt was made in Finland in 1939. The "democratic government" set up in Terijoki under the Comintern veteran Otto Willi Kuusinen merely made itself and its patrons ridiculous. It was abandoned when peace was made with Finland, and it was not revived after the defeat of Finland in the war of 1941–4. Another failure took place in 1946 in Persian Azerbaidjan, where a puppet administration was created under the "Democrat" Pishevari, who had played the same role more than twenty years earlier. The Soviet government yielded because the Powers which it then still nominally regarded as its Allies were strongly opposed. But Pishevari, who with true Bolshevik self-criticism had publicly analysed the mistakes he had committed in 1920, repeated the performance in almost identical terms in 1946. These failures, however, seem small in comparison with the successes achieved in Eastern Europe after 1944. In Poland and Roumania the Russians put in their puppets by open display of force. In Bulgaria and Hungary they forced the removal from public life of political leaders whose courage and popularity were an obstacle to Communist victory. In Czechoslovakia the presence of Russian forces in 1945 made possible the seizure by the Communists of the key posts which enabled them to seize power three years later. In 1948 the signal for action was given by Moscow and the presence of Russian troops round four-fifths of Czechoslovakia's frontiers was a decisive factor. Gottwald's "February revolution" was made by the police. It can be compared with Mussolini's march on Rome by sleeping-car in 1922, and still more closely with Hitler's elevation to the German Chancellorship and subsequent elimination of his opponents in 1933. The roles of the ailing President Hindenburg and the ailing President Benes are strongly similar.

The establishment of Communist régimes in Eastern Europe has historic importance, for it has brought 100 million people under Moscow's control. If the Chinese Communist aggressors were to establish similar régimes in Korea and parts of South-East Asia, that too would be an important victory. But neither can tell us anything of the technique of revolution, for these régimes were not created by revolution. The imposition of puppet governments by imperialist Powers is nothing new in history, even if some of the details of its execution by Moscows' agents are original.

Certain tentative conclusions may perhaps be drawn from this survey.

Few revolutionary movements of the twentieth century have attained power solely by their own efforts. Two exceptions are the triumph of Kemal Ataturk in Turkey and of the Kuomintang in China in 1927. At least in the second case there can be doubt as to how complete was the triumph and how revolutionary the movement. The three most impressive revolutionary triumphs of the century (Russia, 1917–20, Yugoslavia, 1941–4, and China, 1945–9) were won only because a foreign enemy had smashed the state machine which the revolutionaries had previously been too weak to destroy or to capture. The triumphs of Asian nationalism (India, Burma, Indonesia) were won by the willing or reluctant surrender of the colonial Powers. Other Communist successes were won by Soviet or Chinese conquest. Fascism was set up in Italy and Germany, and Communism in Czechoslovakia, by consent of the civil and military authorities. The various violent changes of power that have from time to time taken place in the Balkans, Latin America and the Middle East have been *coups d'état*, not revolutions. If Communist and other revolutionary movements have won through Russian conquest, through defeat of their enemies in war, or through the surrender of the legal rulers, then their intended victims in the free world must make sure that they are not defeated in war and that they do not yield positions of power. This is a question of military strength, national unity and the enlightenment of the free peoples. It is the first priority, and seems at last to be recognized as such by the governments concerned. Even so, much remains to be done in revealing to the free nations the true nature and the urgency of the danger. . . .

Great financial sacrifices will have to be made by all the western nations for the development of the backward countries. The aim should be to reduce both poverty and corruption, the means should be to create the right industries, the right technicians and the right education. None of these tasks can be achieved unless the military power of the free world deters aggression. Nothing can be done in any direction unless the western governments not only make their plans but explain them to their own peoples and to that section of the backward peoples which is accessible to information—that is, to the educated section. None of these tasks will be completely achieved even in the most favourable conditions. But partial success is enough to save the free world. Neither the Communist nor any other revolutionary movements are invincible. The history of their seizure of power shows that their claims to scientific infallibility and predestined victory lack any serious foundation.

Chapter XVI. Politics of Modernization

Introductory Note

ONE OF THE most important historical developments of the twentieth century has been the achievement of independence by peoples who had been brought under the political control of European states in the course of the preceding two centuries. At least one third of the population of the world is involved in this surge toward national independence. Viewed in perspective, the Europeans were able to conquer and administer vast areas of Asia, Africa, and the Middle East because of their crushing superiority in military technology, in turn based on a vastly more developed economy. The Indonesians, Indochinese, Indians, and Africans simply were unable to resist the comparatively small but modern armed forces of the European powers intent upon expanding their influence in the world. The epoch of imperialism registered European advance and domination in all areas of human activity—economic, military, and even cultural. During the era of imperialism, political analysts confined their attention mainly to Europe and North America. Little attention was paid to other parts of the world, except by students of colonial administration.

The virtual monopoly of military and economic superiority, on which European domination depended, began to erode in the twentieth century. Japan showed the way by rapidly assimilating European technology and creating a new power center in Asia within fifty years of Commodore Perry's voyage. Economic and industrial development took place in all colonial areas, along with an awakening of the political consciousness of the masses. The European powers in effect were busily creating the instruments which would inevitably be used by the colonial peoples to achieve their independence. Arsenals, factories, hospitals, roads, schools, newspapers, and radio stations all served to strengthen the local economy and develop the political awareness of the people.

Colonialism exploded in the wake of World War II. The chief colonial powers—Great Britain, France, and Holland—were exhausted by the conflict and unable to engage in any new military ventures. Their rule over possessions in Asia and southeast Asia had been shattered by Japanese armies, which demonstrated to the world that the Europeans were not invincible. In order to gain the loyalty of India in the face of a threatened Japanese invasion, the British were compelled to promise independence. France and Holland were unable to reimpose their sovereignty in Indo-china and Indonesia by arms. The countries of western Europe lost their predominant position in 1945. Power shifted to two non-European states: the United States and the Soviet Union, both of whom began to court the support of former colonial peoples. The European powers were thus at a severe disadvantage in relation to their former colonies: They were not permitted by the new dominant world powers to attempt reconquest, and in any case they were no longer capable of doing so.

The changed nature of relations among the principal areas of the world is one of the most significant developments of our time, comparable in importance to the French Revolution, the industrialization of Europe and North America, and the triumph of Communism in Russia. Each of these world historical events changed the social and cultural environment, and led to new forms of political power and organization. The resurgence of the formerly subjugated peoples of Asia and Africa symbolizes a new kind of world crisis and requires a new focus of interest in our study of comparative politics.

For a general view of social change see: Robert M. MacIver, *The Modern State* (1926); Pitirim Sorokin, *Social and Cultural Dynamics* (one volume edition, 1957); B. F. Hoselitz and W. E. Moore (eds.), *Industrialization and Society* (1963); R. Braibanti and J. J. Spengler (eds.), *Traditions, Values, and Socio-Economic Development* (1961); and Wilbert E. Moore, *Social Change* (1963). Recent studies of individual non-Western systems include: Douglas Ashford, *Political Change in Morocco* (1961); James S. Coleman, *Nigeria: Background to Nationalism* (1958); R. L. Park and I. Tinker (eds.), *Leadership and Political Institutions in India* (1959); Lucian Pye, *Politics, Personality and Nation Building: Burma's Search for Identity* (1962); and Howard Wriggins, *Ceylon: Dilemmas of a New Nation* (1960).

Readings

52. COMPARATIVE POLITICS OF NON-WESTERN COUNTRIES*

George McT. Kahin, Guy J. Pauker, and Lucian W. Pye

THERE IS wide recognition that in the non-Western world[1] profound social and cultural changes are taking place as traditional societies have

* From *The American Political Science Review*, Vol. XLIX, No. 4 (December, 1955). By permission.

[1] [ED.—By the term "non-Western" the authors have in mind those areas of the Far East, Middle East, Africa, and Latin America which are in various stages of reaction to the introduction of Western institutions and practices.]

been exposed to the ideas and the ways of the West. There is also general agreement that new political patterns and relationships are evolving in these countries. However, with respect to most non-Western countries, it remains difficult to foresee whether the consquences of social change are to be stable, viable political practices or endemic instabilities in government. In many cases, it is still an open question whether the future will bring them a liberal democratic form of politics or some type of authoritarian rule such as communism.

This state of affairs can be a challenge to the comparative method of political analysis. This is particularly so because most of the non-Western political systems have many features in common. They are generally the product of a traditional past in which the administration of government was the preserve of a select few. Many show the influence of a previous colonial rule, some even that of the same country. More important, they are often quite self-conscious about the problem of moving from a definite past to an idealized future. In looking to the future, most of them see themselves developing in the same general direction: toward some variant of the Western model of government and politics. All of them feel it necessary to have in time parliaments, cabinets, political parties, and institutions which had their origin in the West. Even when not impressed by Western ideals, they seek to adopt concrete Western practices and techniques. To the student of comparative politics, this suggests such questions as: Why does one country tend to develop in one direction and another in a different one? Why are some Western practices or institutions more fully followed than others? And why in some case are there roughly congruent patterns of development?

The pace of change in most of these countries during the last decade has been such as to make these questions matters for empirical investigation and not just speculation. The fact that many of these societies have set for themselves targets of achievement makes more conspicuous the actual record of their progress. Of course, it is not for the student of comparative politics to set up the model of Western politics as the standard these countries ought to follow. However, he can find methodological advantages in the fact that many of these societies have accepted particular Western institutions and practices as their explicit goals for development. At the same time, the researcher must be aware that the Western model is far from an unambiguous one. His task, as will be seen, includes discovering the numerous ways in which the West has been perceived by different peoples.

The distinctive characteristic of the non-Western societies is not just that they are in a process of change. Indeed, the incidence of change in many fields may be far greater in Western industrial societies. The important fact is that outside the West the transitions are far more abrupt and the contrasts with the recent past are far sharper. For several generations, Western influences have been working on the traditional societies and the results are cultural conflicts that have as yet not been resolved. In most of the non-Western societies, there are spheres in which Western influences dominate, while there are others that have hardly been touched. Change has thus been a far from uniform process; it has produced divisions and cleavages which affect the political life of the entire country. An extreme example of such a division, to be found in most of these societies, is the attempt by people who speak and think in a Western language to share a common political destiny with tradition-bound peasants.

This is, of course, the problem that makes the politics of non-Western countries a distinct category for study. It is, however, only at the most general level that we can speak of the non-Western societies as having this common problem. At such a level of generality, it is necessary to ignore the rich varieties of traditional cultures and also to overlook the numerous different ways in which Western influences have been introduced into these societies. Thus, although the basic category of tradition-oriented societies can be of great help in posing the essential problem for comparative study, once analysis begins it is necessary to become sensitive to the difference among cultural heritages. Traditional forms have a life of their own and certainly by no means all of them have been weakened by Western influences. The old is not simply being replaced by the new; the resilient forces of tradition are capable of rejecting and modifying many Western patterns.

Likewise, the particular historical conditions under which Western methods and ideas have been introduced in the different non-Western societies are relevant in explaining comparative developments. There are, first of all, differences in the auspices under which Western influences were introduced. In some cases, the agent was Western rule in the form of colonialism; in others, it was the activities of private Western individuals and organizations. In still other cases, the Western impact was mediated through a native elite. There are, secondly, differences in the spheres of life in which the Western influences were most clearly felt. In some cases, it was directly at the level of government; in others it was mainly in such fields as education, commerce, or religion that Western practices and ideas made the initial inroads. Thirdly, there have been differences in the intensity and the duration of Western influences. Some traditional societies have been exposed to Western ideas for a long period of time, but only in a mild form, while in others the impact has been of a vigorous character over a short span of years.

Such differences as these must be respected in attempting comparative studies of the current politics of particular non-Western societies. They are the first factors that must be recognized in seeking to understand the different patterns of development.

THE POLITICAL PROCESS

We have suggested that the comparative method may be most fruitfully employed in the task of understanding differences in the developmental tendencies of non-Western countries. We would now like to suggest that the researcher concerned with this general problem can best proceed by viewing the politics of the different non-Western countries as a process in which definite groups and individuals have various political roles. The direction in which the politics of a country will develop over time is likely to be determined largely by the day-to-day interaction of the various elements that make up its political processes. This is not to deny the value of more specialized studies of particular institutions or political groups. However, in order to foresee the general direction of development in such countries, it is necessary to appraise the significance of such particular elements in the total complex of their political life.

In proposing that studies be made of the total political processes of non-Western countries, we are encouraging an approach that has been of value in understanding Western politics, and more especially American politics. At the same time, we would like to indicate that there are some differences between the political process in the West and that in the non-Western societies. These differences should guide the researcher and condition his expectations.

In the first place, the political process in most non-Western countries is characterized by a high rate of recruitment of new elements into political activity. These societies are developing out of a past in which their governmental activities were limited primarily to the actions of traditional autocratic rulers or the few practitioners of colonial rule. Under these conditions, there was restricted participation in the making of political decisions, at least above the village level. Popular discussion of the values and ends for which the administrative machinery might be legitimately used was not sanctioned. In the traditional autocratic societies, officials were guided primarily by inherited values and considerations. In societies with a colonial past, major decisions were made either in the mother country, by a government responsive to a different political process, or by colonial administrators who viewed themselves as technicians of government and not as politicians. In both cases, there was no formally recognized arena for the discussion of public policy or for the open clash of political forces. There was instead a quite informal and highly personal form of politics, characterized by family solidarity, a high degree of nepotism, forms of favoritism, intrigues, cliques, and "getting the ear" of officials who controlled the administration.

At present, these societies are experiencing an expansion of the area of recognized political activity. Increasingly, people who do not belong to the administrative apparatus are becoming involved in influencing public policy. Many of them have new ideas about the direction in which their societies should develop and on how the machinery of government should be employed. Differences in the conditions under which the new participants are being introduced to a political action can lead to differences in attitudes among them.

This leads to a second characteristic of most non-Western political processes: the lack of consensus about the legitimate forms and purposes of political activities. The fundamental cultural conflict between traditional beliefs and Western influences has gone far toward destroying the earlier bases of political consensus, and the increasing number of participants complicates the conscious attempts at developing a new consensus.

One of the basic problems for the researcher, then, is to analyze the forces that may be most significant in contributing to or disrupting the evolution of a new pattern of consensus. He will be concerned with discovering the distribution of attitudes and behavior which may in time become institutionalized, and which will provide compatible orientations on the appropriateness of means and ends of political activity.

It should be noted that in some non-Western societies having Westernized leaders there may appear to be a stronger basic consensus than actually exists. The disappearance of a particular leader may reveal that the people have been held together only by their common response to a charismatic personality. In several of the newly independent countries of South and Southeast Asia, we may be observing a high point of political stability now. In the future, as charismatic leaders die or their charisma wears thin, there may be a period of greater fluctuation before a more impersonal form of consensus can be achieved.

The prevalence of charismatic leaders is a third characteristic of most non-Western political processes. There are several reasons why charismatic leaders are likely to appear in such societies. The cohesive force in the nationalist movement in the newly independent countries often requires such a form of leadership. At a more fundamental level, the process of breaking from a traditional past creates attitudes that are strongly inclined toward accepting charismatic leaders. Indigenous ruling houses and aristocracies are rapidly losing, or have already lost, an authority sanctioned by supernatural beliefs. A withering of the deep emotional roots of respect for traditional authority is taking place which leaves habits of obedience free-floating, in search of new attachments. In the meantime, the slow spreading of education of a rational character and the scarcity of media of mass communication retard the development of a new consensus based primarily on intellectual persuasion. In such periods of transition, charismatic leaders are likely to fill the vacancy.

A fourth difference between the political process in the West and that in non-Western societies is that in the latter there is likely to be a lower degree of integration in the actions of the participants. Indeed, in some non-Western societies there appear to be several nearly autonomous political processes. In particular, there may be little relationship between the political activities that take place at the village level and those that occur at the national level. Communications may hardly exist between the national elite and the local leaders, and the great masses of the population may only vaguely comprehend the policies of the national government. However, as the scope of governmental activities broadens, more policies expressing the political roles of the urban elite are likely to have an impact on the life of the villagers. The area of decision-making that was previously based on local consensus may be narrowed. In the absence of direct participation of the masses in the political process at the national level, the pressures from the central government and the capital are likely to clash with the local forces. These clashes may, however, be absorbed and reconciled by an intermediate group of leaders, adept at understanding and mediating between the two sets of positions. The researcher should give particular attention to the role of these "middlemen."

A fifth general difference is that the actors in the political process in Western societies are likely to have more clearly defined and more specific roles than those in non-Western societies. In the latter, with less complete divisions of labor, there is generally a high degree of substitutability of roles. Thus, in some such countries military elites can become governments, while in others scholars—regardless of their field of competence—become rulers and administrators. The researcher should be aware that in non-Western societies many of the politically active people do not necessarily act according to a narrow definition of their functional roles. In non-Western societies, particular individuals may have many different and even apparently contradictory roles, and thus it is often difficult to predict how such individuals are likely to behave with respect to specific issues.

Another closely related difference is that the political process in the West is generally composed of more formally and explicitly organized interests than is the case in non-Western countries. For example, in American politics there are few interests that are not formally represented by some form of organization. In contrast, the researcher should expect to find in non-Western countries a far greater degree of informality and many interests unrepresented by concrete associations.

Finally, a general characteristic of the political process in non-Western countries is that all the potential political elements do not usually manifest themselves in a continuous manner. There is thus an element of latency in the politics of such countries, with many aspirant elites able to enter the political arena only in a sudden, erratic, and often violent way. The possibility of unorganized and generally inarticulate segments of the society suddenly finding expression contributes to the potentially explosive nature of politics in some non-Western countries. In the West, regardless of how weak they may be, most potential interests are manifest in the political process and thus a continuous form of adjustment of relative power is possible. In some non-Western countries, the peasants, for example, have no way of constantly indicating their political demands, and the result can be sporadic peasant revolts of great violence, reminiscent of the *Jacquerie* in earlier European political development. Similarly, mob action can occur in urban centers. Once these forms of political behavior have spent themselves, they may again disappear from the active political arena.

These, then, are some of the distinctive characteristics of the political process in non-Western countries. They may serve as helpful hypotheses for guiding the researcher. They suggest that, in general, he will find the political process in such countries less stable and less predictable than the form of politics he knows in the West. In his field work, he will be concerned with discovering how these systems tend to operate and what their future course of development is likely to be. . . .

As more field work is carried out in particular countries, it will be possible to get a better understanding of the total operations of their political processes. If we can say for any given country at any given time: these are the issues that matter, these are the potentially or currently active groups, these are the guiding values, this is the political style, much of significance will have been accomplished. We might then be able to relate all this to the actual functioning of the governmental apparatus, and perhaps even predict how this will affect the lives of individuals and the stability of the system.

As this is done with respect to more countries, it will then be possible to compare total political processes. This can be done by developing typologies that cover the various kinds of political processes that have been studied. These will be empirical typologies based on empirical analysis— not the product of speculation. At present, we are able to characterize the politics of non-Western countries only by such vague and general terms as "unstable" and "unpredictable." It may be expected that on the basis of research along the lines suggested here, we will be able to distinguish various kinds of "instabilities" and thus better predict the directions of political development.

Once we are in a position to compare the various non-Western systems with each other and with the different Western systems, we may have the basis for a more general theory of politics. Such a development could do much to reinvigorate the discipline of comparative politics.

In the nineteenth century, the comparative method was widely, though crudely, applied. The reason is fairly obvious. Social scientists worked with broad evolutionary schemes. Comparisons were used to illustrate developmental sequences. This came to an end with the accumulation of overwhelming evidence proving that unilinear evolutionism was not defensible. Deeper philosophical currents favored pluralism as against monism. An emphasis on the uniqueness of human events as contrasted with the repetitiveness of phenomena studied by the natural sciences reinforced the swing of the pendulum. Cultural relativism was only one result of this intellectual climate, although perhaps the most interesting. All this led to an excessively monographic approach. Tribes, communities, or nation-states were and still are studied as isolated entities. What were and still are presented as comparative studies or textbooks amount to little more than an editorial assemblage of discrete studies or the impressionistic use of comparisons and contrasts for purposes of illustration.

The traditional strength of comparative politics lay in its early development of such categories of governments as monarchies, aristocracies, and republics. Once these original typologies no longer seemed so meaningful, new ones were not developed. Attention shifted to particularistic studies or philosophical analyses of ideologies. Advances in the behavioral sciences have been accepted by students of comparative politics, but the result has not as yet been a major reorientation of the field.

As we said at the beginning, we feel that the study of the political process of non-Western societies can be a challenge to comparative politics. These are political systems that are undergoing conspicuous changes. While we no longer expect to arrange social and political systems in an evolutionary sequence, we are vitally concerned with the patterns of political development in societies that have set as their goal the liberal democratic model of politics. Thus both a scientific and a moral-political purpose may be served by the development of a systematic comparative politics.

53. THE TRANSITIONAL PROCESS*

M.I.T. Study Group

THE TRADITIONAL SOCIETY

A. The Range of Cases

THE NATURE of the transitional process which we are considering here—and which American policy confronts in many parts of the world—takes its start from the character of the traditional societies which are in the process of being superseded. We begin, therefore, with an effort to sketch briefly the major features of the traditional society.

History offers us a wide range of such societies. Some were relatively primitive tribes living within a narrow region, on a self-sufficient base,

---

* From *United States Foreign Policy: Economic, Social and Political Change in the Underdeveloped Countries and Its Implication for United States Policy.* A report submitted to the United States Senate Committee on Foreign Relations (Study No. 12) by the Center for International Studies, Massachusetts Institute of Technology, Cambridge, Mass. (Washington, D.C.: Government Printing Office, 1960).

with tribal rather than territorial political and economic organization, and tenuously connected if at all with other tribes and regions. In parts of Africa and in small areas elsewhere we can still find such isolated and primitive forms of social, political, and economic organization.

Other traditional societies have been made up of loosely organized regions, with fairly elaborate structures of political and social organization and quite sophisticated agricultural techniques, but weak or non-existent central governments. Medieval Europe, for example, could be described in some such terms, as well as India before the arrival of the European colonial powers.

But some traditional societies were very substantial empires with quite powerful centralized governments, manipulating a corps of civil servants and a military establishment, capable of collecting taxes and maintaining public works over large areas, capable of conquering and administering other regions and of generating a framework for elaborate patterns of trade and even significant industrial development. The Roman and Mayan Empires were such elaborate traditional organizations, as were certain of the Chinese dynasties at the peak of their effectiveness and some of the Middle Eastern empires at various stages of history.

B. Basic Features of the Traditional Society

What did these traditional societies have in common? One essential fact about them was that they developed within a limited technology. They sometimes exhibited high proficiency in certain directions, but they were incapable of generating a regular flow of inventions and innovations and of moving into a sustained growth process. It followed directly from this limitation that the bulk of their economic activity was taken up with acquiring food. Typically, some 75 percent or more of the working force was in agriculture.

However, the history of traditional societies—notably those which had reasonably strong centralized governments—was not static. In times of peace, acreage would be expanded, trade would increase, the population would rise; the government would collect taxes efficiently, maintain the irrigation works, and expand the opportunities for commerce. But the traditional society could not break through into sustained economic growth.

The periodic breakdowns in traditional societies were brought on by various immediate causes: population pressure, wars, the disintegration of central rule, etc. But behind these lay more fundamental facts. Basically, these societies lacked the adaptability to adjust their behavior to new circumstances. In the absence of a modern scientific attitude and a corps of inventors and technological innovators, for example, they could not produce the flow of new technology necessary to overcome the pressure of population and the natural limitation of arable land.

It followed from the preponderant role of agriculture that the ownership and control of land was a decisive factor in social prestige and, usually, in political influence. In some, the bulk of the land was owned by a relatively small number of nobles and the king, and it was worked by peasants who stood in a feudal, hierarchical relationship to these owners. This condition still exists, for example, in parts of the Middle East. In other cases landownership was quite widely spread, as it was in China, resulting in an endless struggle by the peasants to acquire more land, to establish an economic position relatively independent of the luck of the harvests, and thus to rise in the society. In many of the African tribes, land was owned communally, with no concept of individual tenure and thus little incentive for systematic investment in improvements.

In traditional societies, face-to-face relationships were extremely important, as were the ties to family and clan. Men tended to be bound together and be valued by one another in terms of such intimate connections rather than because of their ability to perform specific functional tasks.

Although traditional societies sometimes provided a channel for able men of the lower economic classes to rise in power and prestige (often through the civil service and the military establishment), there was a tendency for people to assume that the status of their children and grandchildren would be similar to that of their parents and grandparents. A kind of longrun fatalism pervaded traditional societies despite the ebb and flow of family fortunes and despite the slow evolution of the society as a whole.

The cultural and religious life of traditional societies, and the values they elevated, varied widely. Generally, however, they formed a coherent pattern, giving men a reasonably orderly rationale for the relatively stable round of life they faced, at whatever level in the society they found themselves. They provided a set of relationships of men to one another and to the world about them which gave them a degree of security in facing their appointed destiny within the traditional structure.

C. Disequilibrium in Traditional Societies

Well before some traditional societies moved into an active phase of modernization, they began to develop men, institutions, and attitudes which helped prepare the way for modernization. The requirements of conducting war, for example, led the central government to enlarge the military caste, which in some cases proved to be more willing to face the consequences of modernization of the society than the traditional landowners. This was true, for example, of Prussia before 1793, Japan before 1868, China in the second half of the 19th century, and Turkey before 1914. War also increased the requirements for credit and trade, tending to elevate somewhat the status of moneylenders and those who managed domestic and foreign commerce—men whose formal place in the traditional hierarchy was usually low. And in those traditional societies which assumed imperial responsibility, the management of empire itself strengthened the role and status of the civil servant and the technician.

Thus some traditional societies had undergone substantial changes toward modernization, out of their internal dynamics, before they were actually confronted with the shock of full-scale intrusion by more advanced societies. In other cases, however, more advanced nations moved in on traditional societies which were extremely primitive, with virtually no elements initially prepared to deal with the values and methods of modern life.

WHAT BREAKS UP TRADITIONAL SOCIETIES AND MOVES THEM TOWARD MODERNIZATION?

Leaving aside the gradual evolutions of Great Britain, Western Europe, and the United States, what forces have in the past broken up traditional societies? The broad answer is that they have been disrupted, their cohesion and prestige shattered by contact with societies which were more advanced economically and as social and political units.

The impact of more advanced societies took at least three distinguishable forms: physical intrusion, including in many instances colonial rule; economic example; and the communication of skills and ideas. We shall examine briefly the role of each in unhinging traditional societies and launching the modernization process.

A. Intrusion

Intrusion by a more advanced society most commonly was accompanied or followed by occupation and the setting up of colonial administrations, actions which had revolutionary effects on the traditional society in two ways.

First, in pursuit of its own interests (and often, too, in response to an impulse to spread the values and advantages of modern civilization) the colonial power executed specific policies which directly affected the economic, social, political, and cultural life of the traditional society. Ports, docks, roads, and, in some places, railroads were built. These were usually designed primarily for the economic or military advantage of the colonial power, but they had wider effects in creating national markets, commercializing agriculture, helping cities to grow, and bringing to backward areas contact with elements of modern life. Forms of central administration and centralized tax systems were usually set up, providing in some instances the initial framework for a modern government. Some colonials were drawn into the modern economic and administrative activities necessary to execute the purposes of the colonial power. Some modern goods and services were diffused, altering the conception of the level of life which men could regard as attainable. To at least a few colonials the opportunity for a Western education was opened. Perhaps most important, the colonial power usually brought to the traditional society some version of the Western tradition of law, a version of those rules and procedures for the dispensation of justice which transcend and limit the powers of the individuals who exercise political authority.

In short, it was of the nature of the colonial experience that at every level of life it brought to the traditional society contact with some degree of modernization.

The character and extent of modernization varied with the concept of colonial rule that each power brought to its various colonies. In India, for example, the British made special efforts to train men for both the civil service and the army: the Moslems on the whole opted for military training, the Hindus for the civil service, reflecting in that choice underlying differences in the culture of the two groups in the Indian peninsula. In Burma, on the other hand, the British did relatively little to train either soldiers or civil servants. The French, in their empire, made great efforts to bring a thin top layer of the indigenous leaders as fully as possible into French cultural, intellectual, and political life. The Belgians in the Congo concentrated, for economic reasons, on literacy and vocational training for the lower levels of the labor force and did nothing to prepare an elite for leadership. The Dutch in Indonesia and the Portuguese in East Africa by and large adopted policies designed to limit the extent and the pace of modernization.

But however colonial policy might vary, colonialism nevertheless had one first and universal direct effect. It set the static traditional societies in motion, so to speak, moving them into transitional status. That is, they lost the cohesion and integrity of the traditional system, but by no means did they attain the full status of modern societies.

The second effect of colonialism was indirect but perhaps even more profound than the direct infusion of modern elements. As time passed, and an increasing number of men in the colonial society became acquainted with the methods and ideas of the West, they reacted against the human and collective humiliation that inevitably accompanied colonial rule, and they sought independence. Many, it is true, were drawn imitatively toward the manners and mores of the colonial power (for example, colonials who were educated abroad or who had positions of privilege within colonial rule), and others found their positions strengthened by colonial rule (for example, African tribal chiefs and the Indian princes). But in the end a reactive nationalism emerged, spreading through elements in the colonial elite, catching up the urban populations, and reaching back even into the countryside. Of all the forces which have helped bring about the modernization of traditional societies, this reactive nationalism has probably been the most powerful.

Colonial rule was not the only form of intrusion that helped unhinge traditional societies. The defeat of the traditional society in war against a more advanced power often played an important role. This was so, for example, in Germany after the Napoleonic occupation; in Russia after the Crimean War; in Japan after its imposed opening to trade by the West in the shadow of modern naval cannon; in Turkey after the First World War; in China after the defeats by the British in the 1840's and by the Japanese in the 1890's. The demonstration that the traditional form of organization was incapable of maintaining the physical integrity of the nation tended to lower the prestige of the traditional rulers, their values, and their institutions. And it tended to strengthen the hand of those groups in the traditional society—soldiers, intellectuals, men of commerce, civil servants, lesser nobility—who for various, often differing reasons were already interested in moving toward some form of modernization.

B. Economic Example

Quite aside from the multiple impacts of colonialism and superior military power, contact with more advanced societies sometimes led to a spreading awareness of what modernization could do in terms of human welfare. Such contact demonstrated, for example, that public health could be improved; that food output could be increased; and that cheaper textiles could be provided to the peasant and the worker. In the 20th century the intimacy of communications, including the fact that modern armies have been based in many of these transitional societies, has peculiarly heightened an awareness of the gap between modern and traditional standards of life. Any awareness of this kind, creating as it does an increasing pressure for a rapid rise in popular welfare, undermines the traditional society.

The contrast between the traditional and the modern economy was not solely, or perhaps even most significantly, a contrast in standards of living and levels of consumption. The employment opportunities and the modes of life available in the new cities gave people new images of the roles they could play in society. In traditional societies the normal thing was to accept one's status and frequently one's occupation as determined by inheritance and custom. Modern economic activity, whether colonial or indigenous, has taken people out of their conventional roles and put them in new situations both of work and of life which have greatly broadened their perception of the range of alternative activities in which they might engage. This increased mobility and widened perception of alternatives has markedly weakened the most stabilizing elements in traditional society.

C. The Communication of Skills and Ideas

Contact with the more modern societies brought about, for some, a training in new skills. Those trained usually formed part of the transitional society's elite, with some access to instruments of political power. But until the local society was transformed in quite fundamental ways, these trained men found it difficult to exercise effectively their skills as, for example, doctors, engineers, economists, and soldiers. The problem of unemployed intellectuals troubles many parts of contemporary Asia and the Middle East. A part of the force which has tended to disrupt the transitional societies has been the frustration of those with modern training who found that they lacked adequate scope for the exercise of their newly developed talents and opportunities to play newly perceived roles.

Moreover, the more advanced societies of the West communicated not only skills but also ideas. Among these ideas were the quite revolutionary Western notions that all men stood equal before the law, that they should have equal opportunity to develop their talents, and that policies should be determined and political leadership selected on a one-man, one-vote basis. It is easy to forget how powerful and disruptive these long-accepted foundations of modern Western life still are in traditional or only partly modernized societies.

In addition to these democratic ideas, many of the new intellectuals from the transitional societies have been exposed during their formative years in the West to Marxist and other socialist notions. These have often had a great appeal because they purport to explain the forces at work in transitional societies. The theory of the class struggle, Lenin's theory of imperialism, and Communist doctrine on the organization of revolutionary movements have gained considerable currency and influence, and have helped generate dissatisfaction with traditional attitudes and values.

Although the traditional societies or those early in the transitional process were not technically prepared to install modern democratic processes, the disruption of the traditional society and the infusion of these new ideas sometimes led to strong movements toward increased popular participation in the political process. Among the peasants the spread of these ideas encouraged powerful movements for land reform, in which the peasant's ageless hunger for his own plot of land at last expressed itself. The modernization of Mexico, for example, took its start with just such a primitive agrarian drive.

The new ideas have not by any means been uniquely responsible for the pressure of the peasantry for land reform, for peasant revolts have been a periodic feature of the history of traditional societies. But from the French Revolution, through the Taiping Rebellion in China and the Russian revolution, down to the pressure for land reform in contemporary Egypt and Iran, the spread of egalitarian ideas has played a catalytic role of some importance. The impact of new ideas, moreover, is vastly heightened today by the existence of the mass media and the instrumentalities of mass organization. Revolutionary ideas can be diffused with extraordinary rapidity, reaching groups throughout the society.

D. The Dynamics of Modernization

Contact with more advanced societies has been, then, the principal force which has eroded the structure and values of traditional societies. Through physical intrusion, economic example, and the communication of skills and ideas, this contact has pushed the traditional societies into a transitional process. After a certain point, the energies of those colonial people who had acquired some modern skills have tended to focus around the goal of independence; and this objective has helped to unify elements in the society which in fact held quite differing views of the modernization process. Where the colonial problem did not exist, the transitional process has been furthered in different degrees by a sense of military inferiority and national danger; by the pressure of the peasants for their own land; by the pressure of the educated elite for a chance to exercise their new skills; by the spreading perception that higher standards of welfare were attainable.

But the process has also been advanced by the fact that the breakup of the traditional society opened the way for men who enjoyed the exercise of power to contend for the vacated or weakened places of authority. Transitional societies which did not experience colonial rule, or newly independent ex-colonial states, have generally experienced a period of unstable rule in which various individuals and groups have sought to seize and consolidate power. These struggles for power have often been just that: the contention of men for positions of prestige and authority, quite unrelated to movements toward or away from modernization. But over substantial periods of time these struggles for power have reflected and become suffused with the views and objectives of various specific groups in the society who wished to achieve, or forestall, various aspects of the modernization process. The raw struggle for power in succession to the traditional leaders or the colonial power, or both in combination, has thus been in itself an active element in the transitional process.

WHAT RETARDS AND DISTORTS THE PROCESS OF MODERNIZATION?

A. The Scope of Change

It is one thing for a traditional society to experience the intrusion of modern elements which set in motion new dynamic trends. It is quite a different matter for such a society to achieve a working modern system which moves toward peaceful objectives by increasingly democratic means. Before a modern society can be achieved—before the modern elements within a traditional society can become not only dominant but constructive—a succession of profound changes must take place at every level; for any established society has deeply rooted characteristics which yield only reluctantly, with pain and the passage of time, and only to strong and persistent pressure for change. And along the way there are many possibilities for distortion, frustration, and situations disruptive to world order and the American interest.

Historical experience indicates that modernization does not require the destruction of a traditional culture. On the contrary, the old culture almost always leaves permanent and significant marks of continuity on the fully modernized society. Nevertheless, the traditional culture must undergo drastic alteration.

Psychologically, men must transform the old culture in ways which make it compatible with modern activities and institutions. The face-to-face relations and warm, powerful family ties of a traditional society must give way to more impersonal systems of evaluation in which men are judged by the way they perform specialized functions in the society. In their links to the nation, to their professional colleagues, to their political parties, men must find a partial alternative for the powerful, long-tested ties and symbols of the traditional life centered on family, clan, and region. And new hierarchies, based on function, must come to replace those rooted in land ownership and tradition.

Politically, the people must come to accept new forms for the organization of political power. The balance of social and political power must shift from the village to the city, from the tasks and virtues of agricultural life to those of commerce, industry, and modern administration. And they must come to accept new forms for the transfer of political power. They must begin—in a process with many difficult stages—to judge politics and politicians in terms of policies rather than merely inherited status or even personality; and they must develop forms for transferring power by registering consent.

Economically, they must achieve a situation where the society regularly saves and productively invests a sufficient volume of its resources, and incorporates regularly new ways of doing things, so that the growth of the national economy outpaces population increase and continuing economic growth becomes the normal condition of the society—a process which, in itself, involves every dimension of the society and many sectors of the economy.

To achieve these conditions requires the passage of time: time for the social structure to be altered; time for new political attitudes and institutions to be created and consolidated; time for the creation of the skills and habits and institutions on which capital formation depends. Above all, time must pass for new generations to succeed one another, each finding the environment, techniques, and goals of modernization a bit more familiar and acceptable.

Moreover, there is nothing which decrees that the forces of modernization will win eventual or automatic victory. It is of the very nature of the transitional process that at every step of the way the impulses making for modernization live in active contention with powerful forces tending to retard and to frustrate the transformation of the traditional society into full constructive modernity.

The interplay between the new hopes and the old ways may yield bloody civil conflict susceptible to exploitation by external powers; there may be efforts to channel the modernization process into disruptive foreign adventures; there may be a seizure of the society's politics by dictators who exploit popular frustrations and the inevitable looseness of the transitional period for their own or for other purposes.

There are four principal areas in which elements of resistance must be overcome if the modernization of a traditional society is to be carried through successfully: human attitudes, politics, economics, social structure. . . .

B. The Pull of the Past

The modernization process requires that fundamental human attitudes must change in such ways as to make the efficient operation of a modern society not only possible but also psychologically congenial; and it may well be that, especially in the first generations of the transition, the commitment of men to the goal of modernization is more apparent than real.

Modern man is psychically mobile, his distinctive characteristic being the ability to imagine himself performing all manner of tasks and roles. Traditional man was so inhibited by the barriers of status that he believed it wrong and dangerous even to move mentally out of his place in the social order. Transitional man can imagine and hope for change, but in his mind the exciting possibilities are balanced against old doubts and fears. And so the literate elite in transitional societies may be quite skilled, and they may talk the language of modernization with fluency and apparent conviction; but latent within them is a conflict between the modes of action and the values which modernization requires and the ingrained habits and attachments of the traditional society.

The latent power of the traditional society—the pull of the past—may take many forms. It may lead men to gather around them in authority not the most competent colleagues but those most personally loyal, often members of their family. It may lead them to talk of industrialization while in fact harboring a profound reluctance to engage in the homely pursuits of production and the marketplace, which in the traditional society enjoyed so low a status. It may prevent them—as in contemporary India—from treating cattle as part of the material stock of agricultural capital rather than as religious symbols. It may lead them to continue to concentrate their attention and emotions on old familiar issues and feuds—sanctioned by the values and history of the traditional society—rather than on the new issues and tasks of modernization.

No matter how passionately in one part of their beings men may want to see their societies and themselves enjoy the benefits of modernization, they are capable of sustaining in tolerable psychological order only a limited rate of change; and they may cling more tenaciously than they are aware to elements in the traditional society as a source of security in a transitional situation where much else about them is changing.

C. Political Resistance

A society freed from colonial rule or one which has overthrown a traditional government must create a minimally effective national government, a task which confronts such problems as these:

It is almost certain to be the case that much energy and attention must be devoted to overcoming the residues of political authority derived from the traditional society which cannot be harnessed constructively to the purposes of the new modern national government. Examples are the sects in southern Vietnam, the Indian princes, the Chinese war lords, the African tribal leaders.

The new government must also develop a minimum core of technically trained men capable of maintaining order, collecting taxes, and organizing the staff work required for the inevitably substantial role of the government in the economy and in the educational process.

Modernization develops aspirations in the minds of various groups of citizens for progress toward many new goals, economic, educational, and cultural, which are not regarded by traditional governments as within their responsibilities. The new government must demonstrate effective leadership in establishing programs to promote these new objectives if it is to survive. Means of communication must be developed between the government and its citizens to convey to them a sense that the national goals being pursued are ones which they would sanction.

Political development thus must contend with vested power derived from the traditional society; the lack of trained men; the low literacy rate and the lack of other facilities permitting persuasive mass communication; and the absence of a widespread popular conviction that the new national government is an appropriate vehicle for furthering popular goals.

In the process of contention there are many occasions for frustration and backsliding, many ways in which political life may be diverted to sterile or disruptive goals. The Communist appeal to the underdeveloped areas is designed to exploit precisely these possibilities.

D. Lack of Basic Capital

The resistance to modernization also takes the form of certain basic initial economic weaknesses. A very considerable expansion must take place in the number of modern men and institutions, as well as in physical capital, before sustained growth is possible at rates which substantially outstrip population increase.

Regular growth requires that men learn to apply systematically and progressively to the production of goods and services what modern science and technology have created. It is this ability to absorb and to apply modern technology (to agriculture and raw materials as well as industry) which distinguishes a modern growing economy from a traditional economy.

In one sense, the most basic economic change required is, therefore, psychological. Men must cease to regard the physical world as fixed. They must learn that it is capable of being understood and manipulated in terms of stable and logical rules which men can master. But such a change in attitude is not enough. Before a society's economic capabilities can grow regularly at a rate higher than its population increase, large numbers of men must be trained in specialized techniques; and the economic institutions of the society, public and private, must be effectively geared to the process of regular innovation. The society must learn to mobilize and to use its surplus above minimum consumption not for high living for a few nor for war nor for traditional monuments but for productive investments. Moreover, the industrial process itself requires that important nonindustrial sectors be developed: notably, social overhead capital, agriculture, and foreign exchange earning sectors.

It will already be evident from this analysis that such wide-ranging economic change cannot occur unless there is prior or concurrent change in the social, political, and psychological dimensions of the society. But even on narrow economic grounds it is clear that a time interval will be required before the transitional society can acquire sufficient basic capital in human, institutional, and material forms to gather momentum. . . .

E. Social Conflict

The small elite groups who dominate the political process in a transitional society will at first be united in motives and purpose only in opposition to some external power or threat. By their very nature they will be of many minds as to the evolution of their own society.

Some, in fact, may be primarily concerned not with modernization but with the maintenance of their own economic and social prerogatives, granted by the traditional society, the colonial powers, or both. Some may seek to divert the national sentiment and the energies of the new national government into external adventure in hope of redressing old humiliations or exploiting newly perceived opportunities for national aggrandizement. Still other groups may strive primarily to consolidate the power of the new central government as against contending regional authorities. Others may be interested primarily in seeing quickly installed the political and legal forms of modern democracy; and still others—initially usually a minority of the elite—may be anxious to get on with the concrete tasks of economic and technical modernization of the economy.

The confusions and cross-purposes which result from this diffusion of objectives inevitably retard the process of modernization. They may tempt men to seek escape from the frustrations of internal differences and to unite in aggressive attitudes or action toward the outside world. Or they may tempt men to accept in desperation the unity and discipline which Communist or other totalitarian forms hold out to them.

Although the small westernized and literate elites play a disproportionately powerful role in the early stages of the modernization process, in the end the mass of citizens must be brought into the mainstream of change. Each person must begin to assume new functions and new relations to the economic and political process.

The transition to modernization usually begins with more than 75 percent of the population in the countryside and less than 10 percent literate. The round of life is tied to the rhythm of the harvests and to the narrow local scene; to a traditional system of land tenure and the assumption that life for the children and grandchildren is likely to be much as it is and has been in living memory. Social life is built around a close family; traditional political and social relations, long sanctioned by custom, tend to be passively accepted. The government—and the nation itself—is likely to seem a remote and distant entity, associated with the extraction of taxes and the arbitrary recruitment of sons for military service.

In the end all this must alter. There must be a radical shift in balance to urban life; literacy must increase; agricultural methods must change; and the markets must widen and become increasingly commercial. Land tenure arrangements are likely to require alteration. The idea must spread that the physical environment can be understood and controlled in ways which permit higher standards of welfare. The government must come to be identified with activities and objectives which conform to popular interests. And in the end, if democracy is to emerge, the citizen must come to accept the responsibilities as well as the power to determine who shall rule and in what direction public policy shall go.

Merely to list this array of fundamental changes is to suggest the massiveness of what is involved in modernization for the many hundreds of millions of human beings whose lives now are caught up at various intermediate points between the traditional society and one version or another of modern society. The scale and profundity of change suggest also why time must pass and the generations succeed each other. Even more important for an understanding of the policy problems we confront, this array suggests why we must expect inner conflict, frustration, and outbursts of violent popular feeling as modernization proceeds.

As the traditional society loses its authority and sanctions, men are made both insecure and at the same time more hopeful that their lot may be improved. The rapid spread of modern communications, including international communications, begins to make vivid what the fruits of successful modernization might be in material, social, and political terms. But the process of modernization intrinsically requires a long time, even if the society's leaders give to its constructive dimensions all their energy and attention. It is not surprising, therefore, that popular moods may at times turn backward, in an effort to recapture some of the lost security and order of the traditional society. In Burma, for example, U Nu recently waged a successful campaign to return to power on the basis of an appeal to Buddhism. It is not surprising that men and women caught up in the process of modernization can easily be led to turn their frustrations against foreigners. And it is not difficult to understand why, if frustration and chaos persist, communism may be accepted, in apathy or with eagerness, as a promised resolution of these conflicts and dilemmas.

But there is also evidence from the distant and recent past that if the processes of modernization are steadily extended, if the loss of elements from traditional life is balanced by evident, even if limited, progress, these multiple changes can take place without irreversible damage to the society and without its seizure by totalitarian dictatorship.

F. Strategic Dimensions of Modernization

It follows directly from the concept of modernization as a process of contention between modernizing and retarding elements, with many possibilities of frustration, diversion, and even regression, that the societies we call underdeveloped stand at various stages along the way from traditional to modern status.

It is, moreover, central to this analysis that every dimension of these societies is involved in the modernization process; that the progression cannot be defined simply in terms of psychological change or politics or social structure or popular attitudes or economics.

Nor do these elements in the process of modernization all move by some common law. In some societies the modernizing influence was initially felt in the realm of government and administration through colonial rule. In other societies the commercial, the educational, or the religious spheres were the first to be changed. There is thus no uniform pattern of development for all transitional societies.

Our knowledge about the uneven character of social change also suggests that not all changes will contribute equally to a general advance toward a more modern system. On the contrary, some innovations can create situations which make it more rather than less difficult for subsequent changes to occur in a smooth fashion. Improvements in public health standards, for example, can readily alter the death rate and produce a rapid growth in population, which will subsequently become a drain on all efforts to raise per capita incomes. Similarly, the expansion of educational facilities at a grossly faster rate than the openings of new career opportunities can produce well-recognized tensions and frustrations.

We can at this point reach certain broad conclusions: powerful and persistent forces are pressing all the transitional societies in the direction of modernization. Among these forces are the challenge of population pressure; the spread of literacy and modern skills; and the intensity of modern national and international communications. But while the direction of change is toward modernization in all these societies, the pace of movement will vary greatly, and so will their vulnerability to dangerous diversions—notably, aggressive behavior or acceptance of totalitarian government. . . .

SOME FACTORS IN SOCIAL CHANGE

A. Social Evolution in Transitional Societies

In the early period of transition, when a society begins to break out of its traditional structure, the most powerful social class generally consists of the men who own or control the land, a group likely to be deeply conservative in every respect. Feeling a deep attachment to the old ways of life, and sensing that social and technological change threatens their hegemony, they tend to resist all efforts to modernize.

Where their strategy has been to resist by partial incorporation of the new, the landowners often have survived as individuals while their power as a class waned. Where they have resisted all efforts at modernization, the landed class and its members have gone down together. The basic shift to urban and industrial life, which is the core process of modernization, must spell the end of hegemony by landowners as a class.

The traditional society is characterized by the absence of any indigenous middle class large enough or strong enough to challenge the landowners' power. In the early stages of transition, therefore, the decisive challenge to the landlords' supremacy generally comes not from any one social class but from a coalition, a group which varies considerably in specific composition from one country to another but whose leadership is almost invariably made up of men deeply affected by Western ways of thought and action.

In colonial countries those at the forefront of independence movements have often received a university education in the West, sometimes being trained for one of the professions like law or medicine, or they have been introduced to Western patterns of thought and organization through military corps, administration, and industrial and trade union organizations. In countries without colonial histories, such as Turkey, leadership has often been assumed by military officers whose sense of power combined with a strong sense of national pride created in them a desire to lead the way to modernity.

Whatever their particular background, those who lead the fight for independence, or in noncolonial societies the struggle to displace the landowning class, are likely to be more skilled in the political and military tasks of achieving power than in the arts of governing and modernizing a traditional society. Depending on the circumstances and problems of achieving independence, they may become skilled in communicating with and organizing peasants and workers for disruptive activity, in writing revolutionary tracts and editing revolutionary journals, or in conducting guerrilla warfare. Once independence or power is achieved, they often find it difficult to turn their minds and convert their skills to the tasks of modernization. As a result, the first generation of new leaders is often inadequately prepared by experience and training to deal with the problems confronting them when responsibility is attained. Thus progress toward modernization is inevitably slow in the early transitional period. Groups within the governing elite are likely to contend in an erratic and unstable manner, with frequent shifts of power from one to another. Moreover, the elite groups tend to rally around individuals, the substance of whose programs may be ambiguous and unclear even to themselves. Political activity revolves around issues of power and personality rather than around alternate national policies.

Nevertheless, during this period certain dynamic forces are at work in the society which tend to move the social structure and the political debate into a new phase. First, contacts with more modern societies are likely to increase the number of persons trained in the West or otherwise introduced to modern ideas and skills. Second, the very responsibility of managing a national government, even if conducted without great skill and purpose, tends to enlarge the number of men with modern attitudes and commitments. Third, even if sustained economic growth is unlikely at this early stage, commercial activity is apt to increase, cities to grow, and some experiments in industrialization to be undertaken. Finally, because progress is slow and the high hopes and optimistic slogans that accompanied the arrival of independence (or the proclamation of a modern-style government) remain still largely unfulfilled, there is a dynamic created by the sense of frustration on the part of members of the younger generation of the westernized elite.

This combination of forces may bring into being a new coalition determined to push forward with a more purposeful program of modernization. The balance of the social elements in such a coalition varies widely according to the initial structure of the traditional society and its experience during transition. In some instances the coalition has contained a large percentage of men from the military; in others (e.g., the Congress Party in India) the military has played no significant role. At some stage in the process, though not necessarily at the beginning, intellectuals and professionally trained men have been influential; occasionally men of commerce and industry have been in the forefront; and in a few cases landowners, drawn for one reason or another into a commitment to modernization, have played a constructive role. We can, then, make the general observation that the social basis for the modernizing coalition lies in the city and in the essentially urban skills of the elite, both military and intellectual, who have adopted Western attitudes.

We shall deal particularly with two of the groups which often join in the modernizing coalition. The first is the military, which is playing a decisive role in many transitional societies today. The second is the intelligentsia, the manipulators of symbols who shape the slogans and doctrines by which the new ways of life are rationalized and justified.

B. The Special Potential of the Military

The likely social origins of the military group in a transitional society, the nature of their profession, and the context in which they operate contribute important elements to their potential for leadership toward modernization.

The top officer group was traditionally from the landowning class and committed to the preservation of old privileges and social relationships. But lower officers sometimes came from other classes; their social status was not high, and they were not so firmly committed to defend the old social order. Moreover, in recent times, because the military has had to be expanded and thus officers have had to be recruited more widely, in many armies officers have increasingly come from less elite classes—even from craftsmen or peasant groups—and sometimes reflect dissatisfaction with the old order.

Moreover, a contemporary military organization is by its nature a modern rather than a traditional structure. In concept at least, men are arrayed according to function and advanced according to skill and reliability in the execution of their function. They are judged by individual performance rather than by their connection with other persons, family group, or clan. While these objective norms have not been fully and promptly recognized in all the armies that have emerged in transitional societies, they have exercised a powerful modernizing influence.

This influence has been strengthened by the care and resources often devoted by professionals from Western societies to the training of the military, and by traditional pride in military prowess, which has made it easy for restless individuals to find satisfaction in a military career. It is no accident that competent and distinguished military units have emerged in transitional societies well before modern institutions in the civil service, politics, or the economy; for example, the Indian Army, the Malay Regiments, the Philippine Scouts, the Arab Legion, the Gurkha Regiments, and the King's Own African Rifles. As long as these forces were controlled by foreign powers they were naturally conservative—or at least their feelings of rebellion at colonial policies were suppressed. But once independence was achieved, the military could acquire only through the national government the equipment and the professional stature they sought. It is of the nature of the military profession that something like patriotism in modern terms be accepted.

Finally, the officer corps is likely to face an easier set of problems in the transitional period than their civilian counterparts within the new leadership. They may have to undertake military operations, either against the colonial power or against residual traditional elements; but where successful, these exercises arouse confidence in their strength. Aside from combat itself, their tasks are to acquire new equipment, to train men in their use, and to maintain in tolerable order the peacetime round of military life—inherently an easier job than to get political, social, and economic programs organized on a wider basis in the society. Thus it is possible for the army to develop a group of confident officers with modern attitudes and modern skills, operating within a reasonably orderly modern institution administered on relatively modern lines.

Supplementing these broad influences on the officer corps is the fact that those who are recruited into the army are given with their training a certain minimum technical education for modern life. Historically, armies in transitional societies have been a vehicle for expanding literacy; and the handling of motor transport, guns, and other military equipment has spread—and usually quickly spread—elements of basic training in industrial skills. The Burmese Army, for example, in addition to the standard engineer corps and signal corps, has special chemical warfare and psychological warfare sections and even a historical and archeological section. In all the new armies attempts have been made to introduce specialized training schools and advanced techniques of personnel and procurement. Inevitably, then, a certain number of officers and men are being trained in industrial skills more advanced than those common to the civilian economy.

It is by no means foreordained—as the history of the military in Latin America amply demonstrates—that their potentials for modernization will automatically and constructively harness the military to the modernization process. The military leadership may for long periods build and maintain their modern units in a vacuum, drawing important resources from the society but keeping aloof from its civilian problems and making little contribution to their solution. The officer corps may develop a hypernationalism and throw its inevitably substantial political weight toward external adventure, diverting the society from modernizing tasks. It may exploit its unity and high degree of organization to seize power but bring to power little insight and sympathy for the complex civil tasks of modernization. In some instances its political weight has been used to preserve the status of groups rooted in the traditional society who conceived it to be in their interest to forestall the course of modernization.

But history has also demonstrated in numerous instances from the Samurai and the Prussian Army of the 19th century down through Ataturk and Magsaysay that the military can play a thoroughly constructive part in modernization.

A striking example is the unbroken maintenance of civilian supremacy in the Turkish Republic over the past 35 years despite the important role which the military played in founding that Republic. A major condition in this case was Ataturk's establishment and effective maintenance of a clear division between military and civilian leadership. The corps of officers who with him made the revolution and founded its republican institutions were obliged, like Ataturk himself, to resign their commissions when they took up posts of political authority; as a corollary, no officer who remained in uniform was permitted to be active in political life. An important consequence, once the principle and practice of civilian supremacy was firmly established, was that the Turkish Army could perform major functions in the modernization of Turkish society without compromising the civil authority.

At present, the Turkish Army recruits some 200,000 young civilians into its training program each year. These young men (and women) are often illiterate villagers, whose induction into the Army represents their first sustained exposure to other Turks in other areas of Turkey. They are taught to read and write, to handle tools and equipment; they are taught the fundamentals of personal hygiene and public health; they are taught the symbols and institutions of modern political life in a republic. As they complete their training and return to their villages, these young people become a permanent asset in the modernization of Turkey. They put their new knowledge to work; they teach other villagers at home some of what they have themselves learned; they remain a "relay point" for information and opinion emanating from the modernized section of Turkish society. Thus they speed the process of modernization while helping to stabilize it.

In summary, then, the military—the one traditional social order likely to survive the process of social change—may be able to play a key role in promoting mobility while maintaining stability, in facilitating charge while preventing chaos. Upon the efficiency with which the military sector can be made to perform this role may hinge the successful outcome of the transition in many societies.

C. The Secular Intelligentsia

While the military are strong in their capacity to manage violence, in their commitment to rational institutions based on functional criteria and efficient performance, in their sense of nationhood as a supreme value, they are often weak in other skills and attitudes needed in a modernizing society. Consider, for example, the basic process of economic growth. Military men are not generally trained economists, and their economic programs are likely to be inspirational rather than productive. In the Middle East, where military takeover has been virtually continuous over the past few decades, instances have multiplied in which new military regimes rapidly foundered on their own well-meant land reform programs. Virtually every new regime made some more or less serious gesture in the direction of land reform which won it popular plaudits for a time but which failed to solve the basic problem of raising agricultural productivity.

Military elites are liable to make dangerous errors in framing and administering laws, instituting and operating schools, devising and sustaining a communication network, unless they are guided by people with professional knowledge and experience in these activities. These people are the "secular intelligentsia"—the economists and engineers and agronomists, the lawyers and administrators, the doctors and public health officers, the deans and professors, the "communicators" who manage the flow of public news and views that no modernizing polity can do without. They are an "intelligentsia" because it is they who acquire and apply modern knowledge to the manifold tasks of running an urban, industrial, participant society efficiently. They are "secular" because their public roles and social functions are independent of, and usually hostile to, the sacred symbols and institutions of the traditional society.

Their first task as a class is to win preeminence over the sacred intelligentsia, who traditionally performed most of the legal and judicial, teaching and counseling, healing and helping, soothsaying and certifying functions that the secular intelligentsia now seeks to perform. In societies moving toward a modern division of labor—with increasing urbanization, industrialization, participation—the new men of knowledge steadily gain strength. But there are continuous frustrations. The doctor is unhappy when people go to the *shaman* for medical therapy, the lawyer when people go to the *shariya* for adjudication, the teacher when people go to the *imam* for learning, the agronomist when people go to their neighbor for weather forecasts, the communicator when people go to the village elder for guidance on moral judgment of public issues.

These frustrations mount as the number of modern specialists expands in an environment that remains highly traditionalized. The men of the secular intelligentsia become individually impatient and as a group extremist in their views of what must be done. They may form alliances of various sorts—with each other, with foreign agents, even with "deviants" among the traditionalist sectors of landowners and sacred intelligentsia. But ultimately, if they are to make more than a short splash, the secular intelligentsia ally themselves with the military sector.

The historical logic is clear. The military possess the coercive power needed to maintain stability; the secular intelligentsia have the knowledge needed to effect change. Military leadership alone usually has foundered because its perspective is too narrow to cope with the variety of problems that arise in modernizing societies; the secular intelligentsia alone usually has failed because its ideas outrun its capacity to develop institutions that are operational. Neither can manage the transition without the other, and so forms the "unholy alliance," which Western social scientists have described (and decried) since Pareto, Mosca, Michels, Lasswell.

D. Social Change under a Modernizing Coalition

If the modernizing coalition we have described meets with some success, and modernization actually begins to make a dent upon the society, the pace of social change steps up rapidly. New people begin to take over the shaping of public policy—people with the attitudes and technical skills needed to perform the manifold tasks of urbanization, industrialization, and monetization as well as the complex tasks produced by the rationalization of work and the secularization of beliefs.

In general, and with deference to the variety of specific forms which modernization has taken historically and in the contemporary scene, the central tendency of sociological change appears to be the multiplication of key social roles, in part new roles, in part adaptations of old ones. As life becomes more technically oriented, power and prestige shift away from the few dominant men in the traditional structure—the wealthy pasha, the wise priest, the village elder—toward men equipped to perform more specific functions in the modern division of labor. Professional and technical skills are required for the roles associated with the growth of cities and the spread of industries, the technical advances and moderniza-tion of agriculture, the growing dependence of public policy upon an informed and participant citizenry. The banker and the economist tend to replace the landowner and moneylender as sources of cash and managers of credit; the industrialist and manager replace the merchant and trader; the civil servant, the engineer, the agronomist, and others take over special functions that earlier were concentrated in village elders and other men of hereditary wealth or wisdom.

Significant for the long run is the replacement of the sacred in-telligentsia by the new secular intelligentsia; as the importance of tradi-tional religious outlook diminishes, attention shifts to new professions skilled in the secular learning demanded by people caught up in moderni-zation. Especially important among these are the teachers, since every society undergoing modernization exhibits a great increase in the numbers of people who go through formal public education as a way of learning their new careers. Another important group are those who manage the mass media of communication. Through these channels the bulk of the population, including the illiterate elders as well as the younger people destined for new lives, are brought into contact with the new ways and the new words by which these ways are rationalized. Involved here is the important process of increasing popular participation in a modernizing society.

E. The Peasants and Urban Workers

Our analysis thus far has focused on narrow elites—on men who acquire certain Western skills and are in a position to contend for power and to direct the course of events within their nation. We turn now to the evolution of attitudes and skills among the people as a whole, and to their slow change from a passive to an active role in the moderization process.

Here again the course of events depends substantially on the kind of traditional structure that existed; on whether the society underwent a period of colonial tutelage and on the kind of colonial policy that was pursued; on the particular setting and impulses that led to the overthrow of the traditional society, colonial rule, or both. Without excessive distortion, however, we can draw a general picture of the changing horizons of the peasant and the urban worker as modernization proceeds.

In the traditional society and in the early stages of transition something like 75 percent of the population lives in rural areas and up to 90 percent of the population may be illiterate. Mass media, if they exist at all, reach only a small number of people. There are no institutions which permit genuine popular participation in the political process. The peasants are likely to appear apathetic, accepting their traditional lot, but their apathy may well conceal extremely complex feelings. They may harbor, for example, a deep hunger to own their own land, or to see their children healthy, educated, and advanced, aspirations which find expression only when a realistic opportunity for change presents itself. On the other hand, as we have previously noted, they may simultaneously feel great reluctance to abandon the familiar way of life, which offers psychic security as well as a familiar protection from some of the crushing burdens of poverty.

In the early period of transition, as urban activity increases, the attractions of the city draw men away from the countryside, even though urban life itself is often impoverished and demands an almost revolutionary shift in social and cultural adjustments. In the cities the unskilled worker is generally left on his own, but in the trades of higher skill unions are organized at a relatively early stage of the modernization process. Literacy and technical training begin to spread. And so fairly early in the transitional stage the cities often develop a quite modern way of life, standing as advanced enclaves in a society still predominantly rural and primitive.

The coming to power of the modernizing coalition has direct effects on both the urban worker and the peasant. Their political role begins to change, for the new leadership feels impelled to make a direct appeal to the mass of citizens. The legitimacy of the new leadership, which has often won out by revolution against the colonial power or the old order, rests in large measure on a real or pretended commitment to advance the interests of the people as a whole and to achieve for all the citizens of the nation the fruits of modernization. At a minimum, the modernizing coalition is likely to take steps to establish means of communication between the government and the people as a whole. This is the stage at which politicians are likely to take to the airwaves and a popular press is apt to be created.

Whatever the substantive accomplishments of the modernizing coalition in its early period of power, and however deep or shallow its commitment to furthering popular interests, its very existence will probably increase the demand for modernization and for an increasing degree of participation in the society's decisions.

This is a point of maximum danger for the developing society. The mass media, bringing news and views of the world to illiterates in their urban slums and remote villages, introduce a new element into the process of modernization. People learn for the first time about the world outside their immediate environs, and their sense of life's possibilities begins to expand. We recall Nasser's statement:

> Radio has changed everything. . . . Leaders cannot govern as they once did. We live in a new world.

One danger is that people will learn the fashions of popular participation long before the institutions of representative government are properly functioning. Then "pseudoparticipation" takes command, i.e., plebiscites that offer the form of public election without its substance, mob politics of the street in which "popular will" can destroy people and property without constructing better public policy. When exposure to the mass media overstimulates a people to this point, the leadership is pressed to give radio propaganda primacy over political economy. While oratory resonates, development is likely to be shunted to the side and growth impeded. The result, for people led to impose demands which their transitional society cannot yet supply, may be a potentially explosive and spreading sense of frustration.

Whereas the West achieved a participant society as an outcome of the slow growth of physical, social, and psychic mobility over many centuries (the centuries our history textbooks now summarize as age of exploration, renaissance, reformation and counterreformation, industrial revolution, rise of democracy), the new societies seek to accomplish this sequence in decades. In this desire for rapid progress lies the danger that the effect of mass media will be to increase popular desires and demands faster than they can be satisfied by economic and social growth. Mossadegh in Iran fell victim to this imbalance, as did Shishakli in Syria.

To analyze such dangers is easier than to prescribe ways of overcoming them. What the new governments must do is to create institutions through which individual citizens can begin to take part in the decisions of the community. Fully as important as plebiscites, representative assemblies, and other instruments of participation on the national scale—indeed probably a vital prerequisite for the successful operation of national institutions—are local organizations of many sorts which can engage people actively in matters of immediate concern to them.

In the villages, community development and other programs for agricultural cooperation and reform; in the towns, trade unions and other organizations; in both town and country, institutions of local government which engage the interest and support of the people—such activities as these help to bridge the gap between government and people, help to introduce content into the forms of democracy which most of the underdeveloped societies have eagerly accepted.

In terms of social change the problems confronting the transitional societies which are led by modernizing coalitions are those posed by the very nature of democracy. Democracy is not adequately summed up in the formula of universal suffrage; the individual requires something more than a vote to guarantee that his interests will be taken into account in the society's decisions. A sound democracy depends heavily on the strength and number of the institutions which stand between the individual and the national government, defending his individual rights in the process of defending institutional interests. And, while the process of modernization creates some of the preconditions for democracy, its emergence is by no means foreordained. Democracy is a purposeful human achievement, not an automatic reflex of modernization.

54. SOCIAL MOBILIZATION AND POLITICAL DEVELOPMENT*

Karl W. Deutsch

SOCIAL MOBILIZATION is a name given to an overall process of change, which happens to substantial parts of the population in the countries which are moving from traditional to modern ways of life. It denotes a concept which brackets together a number of more specific processes of change, such as changes of residence, of occupation, of social setting, of face-to-face associates, of institutions, roles, and ways of acting, of experiences and expectations, and finally of personal memories, habits and needs, including the need for new patterns of group affiliation and new images of personal identity. Singly, and even more in their cumulative impact, these changes tend to influence and sometimes to transform political behavior.

The concept of social mobilization is not merely a short way of referring to the collection of changes just listed, including any extensions of this list. It implies that these processes tend to go together in certain historical situations and stages of economic development; that these situations are identifiable and recurrent, in their essentials, from one country to another; and that they are relevant for politics. Each of these points will be taken up in the course of this paper.

Social mobilization, let us repeat, is something that happens to large numbers of people in areas which undergo modernization, *i.e.*, where advanced, non-traditional practices in culture, technology and economic life are introduced and accepted on a considerable scale. It is not identical, therefore, with this process of modernization as a whole, but it deals with

* From "Social Mobilization and Political Development," *American Political Science Review* (September, 1961), 493–502. Article and footnotes abridged by the Editors. Reprinted by permission of The American Political Science Association and the author.

one of its major aspects, or better, with a recurrent cluster among its consequences. These consequences, once they occur on a substantial scale, influence in turn the further process of modernization. Thus, what can be treated for a short time span as a consequence of the modernization process, appears over a longer period as one of its continuing aspects and as a significant cause, in the well known pattern of feedback or circular causation.

Viewed over a longer time perspective, such as several decades, the concept of social mobilization suggests that several of the changes subsumed under it will tend to go together in terms of recurrent association, well above anything to be expected from mere chance. Thus, any one of the forms of social mobilization, such as the entry into market relations and a money economy (and hence away from subsistence farming and barter) should be expected to be accompanied or followed by a significant rise in the frequency of impersonal contacts, or in exposure to mass media of communication, or in changes of residence, or in political or quasi-political participation. The implication of the concept is thus to assert an empirical fact—that of significantly frequent association—and this assertion can be empirically tested.

This notion of social mobilization was perceived early in intuitive terms, as a historical recollection or a poetic image. It was based on the historical experiences of the French *levée en masse* in 1793 and of the German "total mobilization" of 1914–18, described dramatically in terms of its social and emotional impact by many German writers, including notably Ernst Jünger. A somewhat related image was that of the long-term and world-wide process of "fundamental democratization," discussed in some of the writings of Karl Mannheim.[1] All these images suggest a breaking away from old commitments to traditional ways of living, and a moving into new situations, where new patterns of behavior are relevant and needed, and where new commitments may have to be made.

Social mobilization can be defined, therefore, as the process in which major clusters of old social, economic and psychological commitments are eroded or broken and people become available for new patterns of socialization and behavior. As Edward Shils has rightly pointed out, the original images of "mobilization" and of Mannheim's "fundamental democratization" imply two distinct stages of the process: (1) the stage of uprooting or breaking away from old settings, habits and commitments; and (2) the induction of the mobilized persons into some relatively stable new patterns of group membership, organization and commitment. In this fashion, soldiers are mobilized *from* their homes and families and mobilized *into* the army in which they then serve. Similarly, Mannheim suggests an image of large numbers of people moving away *from* a life of local isolation, traditionalism and political apathy, and moving *into* a different

---

[1] Karl Mannheim, *Man and Society in an Age of Reconstruction* (New York, 1940).

life or broader and deeper involvement in the vast complexities of modern life, including potential and actual involvement in mass politics.

It is a task of political theory to make this image more specific; to bring it into a form in which it can be verified by evidence; and to develop the problem to a point where the question "how?" can be supplemented usefully by the question "how much?" In its intuitive form, the concept of social mobilization already carried with it some images of growing numbers and rising curves. In so far as the constituent processes of social mobilization can be measured and described quantitatively in terms of such curves, it may be interesting to learn how fast the curves rise, whether they show any turning points, or whether they cross any thresholds beyond which the processes they depict have different side effects from those that went before. Notable among these side effects are any that bear on the performance of political systems and upon the stability and capabilities of governments. . . . .

SOME IMPLICATIONS FOR THE POLITICS OF DEVELOPMENT

In whatever country it occurs, social mobilization brings with it an expansion of the politically relevant strata of the population. These politically relevant strata are a broader group than the elite: they include all those persons who must be taken into account in politics. Dock workers and trade union members in Ghana, Nigeria, or the United States, for instance, are not necessarily members of the elites of these countries, but they are quite likely to count for something in their political life. In the developing countries of Asia, Africa and parts of Latin America, the political process usually does not include the mass of isolated, subsistence-farming, tradition-bound and politically apathetic villagers, but it does include increasingly the growing numbers of city dwellers, market farmers, users of money, wage earners, radio listeners and literates in town and country. The growth in the numbers of these people produces mounting pressures for the transformation of political practices and institutions; and since this future growth can be estimated at least to some extent on the basis of trends and data from the recent past, some of the expectable growth in political pressures—we may call it the potential level of political tensions—can likewise be estimated.

Social mobilization also brings about a change in the quality of politics, by changing the range of human needs that impinge upon the political process. As people are uprooted from their physical and intellectual isolation in their immediate localities, from their old habits and traditions, and often from their old patterns of occupation and places of residence, they experience drastic changes in their needs. They may now come to need provisions for housing and employment, for social security against illness and old age, for medical care against the health hazards of their crowded new dwellings and places of work and the risk of accidents with unfamiliar machinery. They may need succor against the risks of cyclical or seasonal unemployment, against oppressive charges of rent or interest, and against sharp fluctuations in the prices of the main commodities which they must sell or buy. They need instruction for themselves and education for their children. They need, in short, a wide range and large amounts of new government services.

These needs ordinarily cannot be met by traditional types of government, inherited from a precommercial and preindustrial age. Maharajahs, sultans, sheikhs and chieftains all are quite unlikely to cope with these new problems, and traditional rule by land-owning obligarchies or long established religious bodies most often is apt to prove equally disappointing in the face of the new needs. Most of the attempts to change the characteristics of the traditional ruling families—perhaps by supplying them with foreign advisers or by having their children study in some foreign country—are likely to remain superficial in their effects, overshadowed by mounting pressures for more thoroughgoing changes.

In developing countries of today, however, the increasingly ineffective and unpopular traditional authorities cannot be replaced successfully by their historic successors in the Western world, the classic institutions of 18th and 19th century liberalism and laissez-faire. For the uprooted, impoverished and disoriented masses produced by social mobilization, it is surely untrue that that government is best that governs least. They are far more likely to need a direct transition from traditional government to the essentials of a modern welfare state. The developing countries of Asia, Africa and parts of Latin America may have to accomplish, therefore, within a few decades a process of political change which in the history of Western Europe and North America took at least as many generations; and they may have to accomplish this accelerated change almost in the manner of a jump, omitting as impractical some of the historic stages of transition through a period of near laissez-faire that occurred in the West.

The growing need for new and old government services usually implies persistent political pressures for an increased scope of government and a greater relative size of the government sector in the national economy. In the mid-1950s, the total government budget—national, regional and local—tended to amount to roughly 10 per cent of the gross national product in the very poor and poorly mobilized countries with annual per capita gross national products at or below $100. For highly developed and highly mobilized countries, such as those with per capita gross national products at or above $900, the corresponding proportion of the total government sector was about 30 per cent. If one drew only the crudest and most provisional inference from these figures, one might expect something like a 2.5 per cent shift of national income into the government sector for every $100 gain in per capita gross national product in the course of economic development. It might be more plausible, however, to expect a somewhat more rapid expansion of the government sector during the earlier stages of economic development, but the elucidation of this entire problem—with all its obvious political implications—would require and reward a great deal more research.

The relationship between the total process of social mobilization and the growth of the national income, it should be recalled here, is by no means symmetrical. Sustained income growth is very unlikely without social mobilization, but a good deal of social mobilization may be going on even in the absence of per capita income growth, such as occurs in countries with poor resources or investment policies, and with rapid population growth. In such cases, social mobilization still would generate pressures for an expansion of government services and hence of the government sector, even in a relatively stagnant or conceivably retrograde economy. Stopping or reversing in such cases the expansion of government or the process of social mobilization behind it—even if this could be done—hardly would make matters much better. The more attractive course for such countries might rather be to use the capabilities of their expanding governments so as to bring about improvements in their resources and investment policies, and an eventual resumption of economic growth. To what extent this has been, or could be, brought about in cases of this kind, would make another fascinating topic for study.

The figures just given apply, of course, only to non-Communist countries; the inclusion of Communist states would make the average in each class of government sectors higher. It would be interesting to investigate, however, whether and to what extent the tendency toward the relative expansion of the government sector in the course of social mobilization applies also, *mutatis mutandis*, to the Communist countries.

A greater scope of governmental services and functions requires ordinarily an increase in the capabilities of government. Usually it requires an increase in the numbers and training of governmental personnel, an increase in governmental offices and institutions, and a significant improvement in administrative organization and efficiency. A rapid process of social mobilization thus tends to generate major pressures for political and administrative reform. Such reforms may include notably both a quantitative expansion of the bureaucracy and its qualitative improvement in the direction of a competent civil service—even though these two objectives at times may clash.

Similar to its impact on this specific area of government, social mobilization tends to generate also pressures for a more general transformation of the political elite. It tends to generate pressures for a broadening and partial transformation of elite functions, of elite recruitment, and of elite communications. On all these counts, the old elites of traditional chiefs, village headmen, and local notables are likely to prove ever more inadequate; and political leadership may tend to shift to the new political elite of party or quasi-party organizations, formal or informal, legal or illegal, but always led by the new "marginal men" who have been exposed more or less thoroughly to the impact of modern education and urban life.

Something similar applies to elite communications. The more broadly recruited elites must communicate among themselves, and they must do so more often impersonally and over greater distances. They must resort more often to writing and to paper work. At the same time they must direct a greater part of their communications output at the new political strata; this puts a premium on oratory and journalism, and on skill in the use of all mass media of communication. At the same time rapid social mobilization causes a critical problem in the communications intake of elites. It confronts them with the ever present risk of losing touch with the newly mobilized social strata which until recently still did not count in politics. Prime Minister Nehru's reluctance to take into account the strength and intensity of Mahratti sentiment in the language conflict of Bombay in the 1950s and his general tendency since the mid-1930s to underestimate the strength of communal and linguistic sentiment in India suggest the seriousness of this problem even for major democratic leaders.

The increasing numbers of the mobilized population, and the greater scope and urgency of their needs for political decisions and governmental services, tend to translate themselves, albeit with a time lag, into increased political participation. This may express itself informally through greater numbers of people taking part in crowds and riots, in meetings and demonstrations, in strikes and uprisings, or, less dramatically, as members of a growing audience for political communications, written or by radio, or finally as members of a growing host of organizations. While many of these organizations are ostensibly non-political, such as improvement societies, study circles, singing clubs, gymnastic societies, agricultural and commercial associations, fraternal orders, workmen's benefit soceieties, and the like, they nevertheless tend to acquire a political tinge, particularly in countries where more open outlets for political activities are not available. But even where there are established political parties and elections, a network of seemingly nonpolitical or marginally political organizations serves an important political function by providing a dependable social setting for the individuals who have been partly or wholly uprooted or alienated from their traditional communities. Such organizations may serve at the same time as marshalling grounds for the entry of these persons into political life.

Where people have the right to vote, the effects of social mobilization are likely to be reflected in the electoral statistics. This process finds its expression both through a tendency towards a higher voting participation of those already enfranchised and through an extension of the franchise itself to additional groups of the population. Often the increase in participation amongst those who already have the right to vote precedes the enfranchisement of new classes of voters, particularly in countries where the broadening of the franchise is occurring gradually. Thus in Norway between 1830 and 1860, voting participation remained near the level of about 10 per cent of the adult male population; in the 1870s and 1880s this participation rose rapidly among the enfranchised voters, followed by extensions of the franchise, until by the year 1900, 40 per cent of the Norwegian men were actually voting. This process was accompanied by a transformation of Norwegian politics, the rise to power of the radical peasant party *Venstre,* and a shift from the earlier acceptance of the existing Swedish-Norwegian Union to rising demands for full Norwegian independence. These political changes had been preceded or accompanied by a rise in several of the usual indicators of social mobilization among the Norwegian people. . . .

As we have seen, the process of social mobilization generates strong pressures towards increasing the capabilities of government, by increasing the volume and range of demands made upon the government and administration, and by widening the scope of politics and the membership of the politically relevant strata. The same process increases the frequency and the critical importance of direct communications between government and governed. It thus necessarily increases the importance of the language, the media, and the channels through which these communications are carried on.

Other things assumed equal, the stage of rapid social mobilization may be expected, therefore, to promote the consolidation of states whose peoples already share the same language, culture, and major social institutions; while the same process may tend to strain or destroy the unity of states whose population is already divided into several groups with different languages or cultures or basic ways of life. By the same token, social mobilization may tend to promote the merging of several smaller states, or political units such as cantons, principalities, sultanates or tribal areas, whose populations already share substantially the same language, culture and social system; and it may tend to inhibit, or at least to make more difficult, the merging of states or political units whose populations or ruling personnel differ substantially in regard to any of these matters. Social mobilization may thus assist to some extent in the consolidation of the United Arab Republic, but raise increasing problems for the politics and administration of multilingual India—problems which the federal government of India may have to meet or overcome by a series of creative adjustments.

In the last analysis, however, the problem of the scale of states goes beyond the effects of language, culture, or institutions, important as all these are. In the period of rapid social mobilization, the acceptable scale of a political unit will tend to depend eventually upon its performance. If a government fails to meet the increasing burdens put upon it by the process of social mobilization, a growing proportion of the population is likely to become alienated and disaffected from the state, even if the same language, culture and basic social institutions were shared originally throughout the entire state territory by rulers and ruled alike. The secession of the United States and of Ireland from the British Empire, and of the Netherlands and of Switzerland from the German Empire may serve in part as examples. At bottom, the popular acceptance of a government in a period of social mobilization is most of all a matter of its capabilities and the manner in which they are used—that is, essentially a matter of its responsiveness to the felt needs of its population. If it proves persistently incapable or unresponsive, some or many of its subjects will cease to identify themselves with it psychologically; it will be reduced to ruling by force where it can no longer rule by display, example and persuasion; and if political alternatives to it appear, it will be replaced eventually by other political units, larger or smaller in extent, which at least promise to respond more effectively to the needs and expectations of their peoples.

In practice the results of social mobilization often have tended to increase the size of the state, well beyond the old tribal areas, petty principalities, or similar districts of the traditional era, while increasing the direct contact between government and governed far beyond the levels of the sociologically superficial and often half-shadowy empire of the past.

This growth in the size of modern states, capable of coping with the results of social mobilization, is counteracted and eventually inhibited, however, as their size increases, by their tendency to increasing preoccupation with their own internal affairs. There is considerable evidence for this trend toward a self-limitation in the growth of states through a decline in the attention, resources and responsiveness available for coping with the implicit needs and explicit messages of the next marginal unit of population and territory on the verge of being included in the expanding state.

The remarks in this section may have sufficed to illustrate, though by no means to exhaust, the significance of the process of social mobilization in the economic and political development of countries. The main usefulness of the concept, however, should lie in the possibility of quantitative study which it offers. How much social mobilization, as measured by our seven indicators, has been occurring in some country per year or per decade during some period of its history, or during recent times? And what is the meaning of the differences between the rates at which some of the constituent subprocesses of social mobilization may have been going on? Although specific data will have to be found separately for each country, it should be possible to sketch a general quantitative model to show some of the interrelations and their possible significance.*. . .

---

* Editors' note: The author's quantitative model has been omitted.

55. LEADERS, FOLLOWERS AND MODERNIZATION IN LATIN AMERICA*

K. H. Silvert

THE IDENTIFICATION of élite groups, leaders and followers is in certain respects an even more treacherous task in underdeveloped than in developed lands. By this time it is platitudinous—even though still valid—to state that underdevelopment is also asynchronous development. This statement means that we should expect to find within some 'national' boundaries hunting and fishing cultures, stable village patterns, other groups moulded in feudal organization and attitudes, and sometimes even highly industrial urban complexes verging on the megalopolis. This array exists within contemporary Brazil, for example. Clearly there can be no single élite group, no single set of leaders or masses of potential followers within such complicated systems of only partially interacting coexistence.

Here, I shall concern myself only with one of these relationships between social universes— that between persons of generally traditional and generally modern values in the Latin American city. This choice is not made because most Latin Americans are in one or the other group. Indeed, in such countries as Guatemala and Ecuador, persons of 'traditional' village culture (as distinct from 'traditional' persons of a Mediterranean feudal culture) predominate numerically. Instead, urban Latin Americans are emphasized here because these persons whether 'traditional' or 'modern' in attitudes—control the 'national' economies of Latin America, and comprise what we normally refer to as the effective 'nationals'. It is their revolutions, their diplomats, their presidents to whom we refer when we speak of 'Latin American governments'.

Few sociological or social psychological studies of under-developed lands do more than distinguish between industrial society and all others, which they label traditional.[1] The grossness of this dichotomy appears the moment one begins to join values and attitudes to institutions and social structure. Certainly there is an institutional gap as great between the organization of a village in Chiapas and a Hispanic feudal fief as there is between the fief and a modern Latin American capital city. The face-to-face relationships of the Maya village, the single-class system, and the intimately related religious and political structures define an area tiny

---

* From "National Values, Development, and Leaders and Followers," *International Social Science Journal*, No. 4, 1963, 560–70. Footnotes abridged by the editors. Reprinted by permission of the United Nations Educational, Scientific and Cultural Organization.

[1] This statement holds, for example, for Daniel Lerner's *The Passing of Traditional Society* (Glencoe, Ill.: The Free Press, 1958), and for *Urbanization in Latin America*, edited by Philip Hauser, from which I quote in this article.

both physically and intellectually. On the other hand, the fief is characterized by a rigidly defined bi-class structure, far-flung economic relationships sometimes of an international nature, complex religious ideas, and a rather sophisticated division of function of the political.

In this article, then, the word 'traditional' will refer only to the present-day heirs of the mediaeval Iberian world view, and not to village or other face-to-face cultures. Hauser and Medina Echavarría, citing Gino Germani, offer a statement of contrast between the traditional and the modern which can well serve us as standard and which will later be modified to sharpen the distinction between village and mediaeval culture being made here. They write:

> 1. In traditional societies, the prevailing type of action is fixed or prescribed more or less rigidly for every situation. In industrial societies, on the other hand, the type of action derives from what may be termed a deliberate decision . . . the choice itself—or deliberate decision—is essentially imposed by the social structure.
> 2. . . . . The former ['traditional' society] discourages it [change], tending, rather, to attach great value to its legacy from the past. Conversely, the latter [modern society] esteems and encourages any innovation [sic]; in other words, change is 'institutionalized'.
> 3. . . . . The majority of functions are concentrated in a small number of institutions in a traditional society, while specialized institutions, each with its limited and specific function, predominate in an industrial society. The family is the best known and most striking example of this antithesis.[2]

The authors add that these three points—'the selective natue of action, the institutionalization of change and the specialization of institutions'—lead to a changed personality structure, a shift from local to national community, a social stratification system based on ascription instead of merit, lessened family relationships, and new political organization. But just as Weber showed enormous weakness when attempting to deal with the question of 'party' or political power in his trichotomous approach to social structure, so too do Hauser and Medina suddenly weaken when they have to deal with political matters, even though their views are unexceptionable. Their statement is worth quoting in its full paucity:

> Changes no less fundamental are taking place in the field of political organization and activity. In the past, the industrial society was associated with a specific political form, namely, liberal democracy. Today this appears to be subject to revision, according to certain groups of opinion. Nonetheless, whatever the political structure, the industrial society seems to demand a more extensive political participation on the part of increasingly large population sectors.[3]

In at least two basic respects this statement can be refined for our use: by making more stringent and more appropriate to the Latin American city the concept of traditionalism; and by joining the concepts of national

---

[2] Philip M. Hauser (ed.), *Urbanization in Latin America*, Paris, Unesco, 1961, p. 47–8.

[3] *Ibid.*, p. 50.

community and political participation mentioned above as being separate results of industrialization.

Contemporary Urban Traditionalism

The traditionalist within the tradition of Romance politics has not remained unchanged before the stimuli of the last five centuries: prodded by mercantilism, capitalism, and the growth of mass societies, he has reacted to propose solutions which will at worst leave his *Weltanschauung* only slightly amended, and at best strengthen and ramify it. To state simply that the traditionalist opposes change and rational choice is not to prepare to discover how the traditionalist actually has changed, what choices he has exercised, and—not at all incidentally—how he has done so in order to preserve both his ethical values and his notion of the proper social stratification system. Some of the basic ideas of classical Mediterranean traditionalism are: (a) that class position is given and is unchangeable; (b) that all human actions must be simultaneously judged for their religious as well as secular meaning; (c) that all human actions should be doubly sanctioned by an ordered relationship of the civil and the religious institutions (the Doctrine of the Two Swords); (d) that loyalties must be vertically ordered in accord with authority, and that religious and primary loyalties supersede secondary ones in the determination of social actions. These views persisted through colonization, Iberian mercantilism, and the establishment of flourishing service cities throughout Latin America in independence as well as during colonial periods.

Persons who express these ideas in relatively unchanged form continue to be able to live and function in Latin America's many industrial centres, even though they act at least in part as do those who do not think as traditionalists. Such a division between avowed thought and action is not at all uncommon, of course. But there are yet other traditionalists who have modified both action and ideology to accommodate themselves positively to a certain kind of industrialization. They probably better define what the classical traditionalist holds than he himself can do. These 'modern' traditionalists think in syndicalist or corporativist terms, essentially but a complication of the hierarchical order of mediaeval society. In this view the Doctrine of the Two Swords is amended to become the Doctrine of the Six or Seven or Eight Swords, depending upon the number of institutional pillars created to become the fasces of the quasi-modern traditionalism, so to speak. Some such kind of formal adjustment of traditionalism to industrialism should be expected, of course, especially given the rather high order of technological development to be seen in Spain as well as in many countries of Latin America.

Marx wrote his attacks upon the evils of industrialism from the vantage point of the northern European heir to the Protestant and Rationalist traditions; later, southern Europeans, too, began to attempt to protect themselves against the fully revolutionary implications of industrialism and 'massification'. Mosca, Croce, and others were the intellectual scions of the period, reflected in Hispanic society by the work even of such persons as apparently alien to their thought as Ortega y Gasset, whose *Revolt of the Masses* was not a kind of early *The Lonely Crowd* in Spanish, but rather an appeal against mass man from the stance of a troubled universalist whose humanism was rooted deep in the mediaeval cultural base of his land. The good society pictured by the syndicalist would have the individual firmly rooted in his newly complicated institutional place. His representation in government would not be a result of his individuality or of his mere nationality, but rather a function of his place in the institutional order of events. Public decisions would then result from the interplay of the institutional oligarchs, and not from the deliberations of groups and men elected at large from a citizenry escaping its occupational and class bonds in an act of political selection and decision formally and somewhat substantively indicative of equality. The secular State could not become supreme in its area; mass man would be tamed by being herded into institutional kennels, safely under the tutelage of the leader. This school of thought also specifically rejects liberalism, together with all its equalitarian and socially universalistic content. The pluralism of liberalism, based on an individualism adjusted to social groups in accord with a secularized natural law, is replaced by a pluralism of an institutionalization sanctioned by rite. The corporativist may be considered on the left of the traditional scale of politics in Latin America; on the right are the 'standard' traditionalists, grouped into Conservative parties or their contemporary descendants.

The major social purpose of the syndicalist approach is to find a way of subsuming the new class complications of modernism to hierarchy, preserving a king of Latin *Führerprinzip*, leaving inviolate the privileges and powers of the traditional, and thus escaping the secularization and, to their eyes, immorality of the nation-State. Argentina, Brazil and Mexico are three important examples in Latin America of the varied uses of this kind of modified traditionalism.

Pluralism and the State

A primary function of the secular nation-State, too, is to channel and order class as well as other interest conflicts which threaten whatever may be the definition of the public welfare at given times and places. The acceptance of the institution of a totally secular State as the ultimate arbiter of civic dispute involves certain other crucial commitments:

1. The concept of 'market-place' in a political as well as an economic sense must be accepted. The market-place orders access to and participation in the national polity and economy in social procedures having much to do with the behavior associated with political freedom.

2. An at least interim suspension of religious judgment must be exercised with respect to public acts. Law must be accepted as ultimate until it can be changed, evidence of that juridical relativism without which equality before the laws cannot be effective.

3. The weighing of public acts must then be in part at least pragmatic. Empiricism and whether something 'works' are the form of the interim judgments of the limited relativism and secularism of the nation-State.

4. Participating citizenship in the nation-State must be extended with 'massification' in a move away from the 'bourgeois night-watchman' nation-State of the last century toward the universal nation-State of this century.

5. The nation-State must be impersonal in its actions if its functions as arbiter on the one hand and recipient of organized consensus on the other are to be sufficiently self-sustaining to permit it to act as governor of the "institutionalization of change'.

The secular nation-State thus channels and organizes class and other interest conflicts of the type engendered by industrialism, ensures that long-term decisions can be made, permits the diversification of the institutional structure by providing for secular ordering and control, and allows the proliferation of far-flung secondary relationships by the generation and application of apposite rules. The mere attitudes of modernism cannot be fruitful without the institutional framework for their expression; conversely, without such attitudes held at least in certain power centres, no government can muster the coercive power or claim the legitimacy to become national. The definition of social development for the emergent nations must then hinge largely on the question of national values and national institutions.

Corporativism has never proved a sufficient ideology or organizing device for self-sustaining development, even though at times it has introduced heightened levels of industrialization. Corporate States have administered partially industrial countries and even enlarged the industrial plant, but we have no historical examples of self-sustaining development under corporativist forms. Growing freedom of choice, nationalism and development thus far have been historical correlates in cases of self-sustaining growth, of the 'institutionalization of change'. Given the failure as yet of any Latin American country to reach modernity, so defined in terms of the dynamics of accommodation, the region does not seem to be immune to these general rules of development.

Some Modern and Traditional Men in Latin America

It is probable that any occupational group at any level studied in the industrial cities of Latin America will comprise at least some persons of an essentially modern mentality (defined as national persons, as indicated above), and others of a fundamentally traditionalist cast (also as defined above.) In seventeen groups in four countries (Brazil, Argentina, Chile and Mexico) ranging from slum-dwellers in Rio de Janeiro to members of the Mexican Congress, examined for these characteristics, sufficiently strong divisions were noted to invalidate any notion that Latin Americans share essentially the same value orientations concerning life in its public manifestations. A simple percentage distribution of the samples by those persons with high, medium and low scores on the index of national identification is sufficient to demonstrate this point (see Table 1).

The minimum demonstrated by these results—that there are very conflicting social values among groups in the Latin American industrial city—is an important clue toward an understanding of the nature of political conflict and its resolution in Latin America.[4] The vast difference

TABLE 1
NATIONAL IDENTIFICATION SCORES AMONG SELECTED LATIN AMERICAN GROUPS

	Percentage		
Country and group	*High*	*Medium*	*Low*
Brazil			
Managers	30	43	27
Skilled workers	20	41	39
Slum-dwellers	17	45	38
Argentina			
First-year medical students	37	42	21
Last-year medical students	46	30	24
Physicians	26	39	35
First-year mathematics and physics	36	40	24
Last-year mathematics and physics	41	34	25
Graduates	41	36	23
First-year economics	28	37	35
Last-year economics	38	28	34
Graduates	15	33	53
Chile			
Primary-school teachers	62	33	5
Secondary-school teachers	55	33	12
University of Chile professors	56	28	16
Catholic University professors	15	32	53
Mexico			
Members of Congress	15	32	53

Note: This index is composed of four parts, the first concerning Church and State loyalties, the second the respondent's occupational interests and the State, the third the economy as a whole and the State, and the last a measure of patriotic response to Independence Day observances. The index measures only the presence of national identification, of course, and does not tell us what exists in its absence.

between those persons who 'see' and accept a national community as a primary fact of social relationships and those others who consider only class, family and religious identifications worthy of basic loyalty is reflected in two different orders of 'national' politics in Latin America. This split was noted above in the example of the two different scales of left and right; it also is evidenced in differing meanings given to law, to political behavior, to questions of freedom, and to international relations. Traditional persons are consistently prone to authoritarian politics (as

---

[4] It will be noted that we are here speaking of 'values' and not 'ideologies'. The former were defined for the purpose of this study as implicit ways of seeing and defining the world. Ideologies were defined as explicit bodies of thought, written and expounded, concerning the nature of desirable and undesirable public action. This distinction is useful as an analytical device, and also reveals the depth at which the study hoped to probe in defining 'values of national identification'.

distinct from totalitarianism), exclusivist in their social attitudes concerning access to their professions, jealous of the extension of full social
participation to aspirant groups, and normally in favor of the forcible
application of œcumenical religious beliefs. Persons who rank high on the
national identification scale are not immune from authoritarian and especially totalitarian political ideologies, but they tend to clothe these
views—when they hold them—in more empirical robes, lean toward
welcoming all into the fold on the basis of personal and not ascriptive
group qualities, and are tolerant in the matter of religion. If these
conflicting attitudes are widespread within given class and occupational
sectors, as they appear to be, they offer an important clue to the politics of
frustration which have grown in such countries as Chile and Argentina.
What may very well be happening is that there is sufficient elasticity
among the traditional to permit them to co-operate with the moderns
during early and even intermediate phases of the industrialization process,
but that when the moment comes to make the decisive secular, national
commitments demanded for further growth, the schism obtrudes to
prevent continued non-revolutionary movement. The case of the Mexican
congressmen, who respond to ideological questions in a modern manner
for traditional reasons, is an excellent demonstration of flexibility on the
one hand, and resistance to full commitment on the other. The large
numbers of persons caught in the middle is also rich evidence of the
painfully transitional nature of Latin American politics in these most
fundamental respects.

This division concerning the nation should not be taken to mean,
however, that interaction between traditional and modern persons is
impossible; on the contrary, these studies—and the historical evidence—
suggest strongly that we must look for the specific manners in which these
two groups find the accommodation which clearly exists, even though it is
one which inhibits growth, wastes energies in internecine conflict, and
embitters many lives and family relationships. We must also seek those
cases in which modern men act as though they have traditional values, and
traditional men act as though they are modern ones. Clearly such transpositions must exist as a response to professional and other occupational
demands, as well as to the simple necessity for personal coexistence with
colleagues and relatives. Certainly in the more industrially developed
lands, too, there must be many persons whose social conduct is 'national',
but whose private values are 'traditional'. But the effect of such divisions
where the dominant values and modes of behavior are as well set as in
contemporary Great Britain, for example, will be very different from
where they waver and seesaw as in Argentina at this time.

The data from the studies being cited also show that the mere fact of
upward occupational mobility of an intergenerational type does not
appear to correlate with national values one way or another. The quality
of mobility, not its mere existence, is what counts; in no one of the study

groups was there a significant correlation between upward mobility of all kinds and national values. In the case of the Faculty of Economics in Argentina, the group with the highest mobility was also the lowest Argentine sample on the scale of national identification. Many persons, in their upward climb, were identifying with the values ostensibly held by the country's traditional oligarchy. In the bifurcated value situation of the Latin American city there is no reason why attitudes should not be molded by the striver in accordance with the traditional ideal model and not the modern one.

In Argentina and Brazil, where differing occupational groups were studied, there is a clear relationship between the type of occupation and the degree of national identification. The higher the individual's position on the social scale and the greater his involvement with the development process, the more closely he holds national values. In Chile, within the teaching profession, the striking split comes between those employed in publicly supported schools and the professors in the Catholic University of Chile, who share with Mexican congressmen the lowest positions in the ranking. These findings all fit widely-held stereotype views of the nature of the occupations concerned and of the location of radical and conservative groups, and thus of the kinds of opportunities open for aspirants to these occupations. In short, the group 'image' projected at large was found in all cases to be in reasonable conjunction with what was actually discovered inside the samples studied; recruitment or self-selection is thus a quite realistic process, providing a reinforcement which in turn makes the accepted candidate's prophecies self-fulfilling.

Even though most of the groups studied would be counted normally as 'élite', the conclusion cannot be drawn that the individuals concerned are highly or even uniformly 'politicized'. Brazilian managers, for example, show little inclination to political action, as might be expected. Nevertheless, from these groups more potential leaders will indubitably flow than from others at lower status levels. What is at least as important about them is that they provide followers. The competing value sectors produce their competing leaders; the leaders must also look for followers, of course. These studies strongly suggest where followers of certain types will be found, and why it is that Chilean primary-school teachers, for example, are so often accused of inculcating their students with Communist ideology, or that Argentine economics students are seen within the University of Buenos Aires as bulwarks of stolid conservatism. Certainly, the gulf between the Chilean primary-school teachers and the professors of the Catholic University, and also between Argentine students of exact sciences and economics, is immense—so immense that the erroneous notions of the opposition widely held by Latin Americans are easily understandable.

The relationships between the value split and the mobility effects underscore the profundity of a division which also has its class aspect. Some Latin American specialists—economists and anthropologists as well as sociologists—have contended that in reality there is a double class system in the region. Their argument usually points to a traditional upper class based on land and a modern upper class based on industry, to the old governmental and professional middle class as distinct from the new middle classes of industrialism; and to the land-bound peasant and city menial worker on the one hand, and the new industrial worker on the other. This view of class, based so solidly on occupation as it is, might well be usefully modified to involve questions of social status and political power, especially since we have seen how persons in the same occupations can have value systems so completely opposed. In any event, the Latin American value schism is in all probability reflected in and reinforced by institutionalization in a complex class structure. If this supposition is borne out by future research, the implications for the study of politics and for the potential costs of continued development in Latin America should be of major importance. This primary suggestion concerning social structure and values is the essential background against which other related hypotheses and research areas present themselves.

Other Implications for Research

To recapitulate, we need to know much more of the intricacies of the relationships among persons of traditional, modern and intermediate values. Data in this area should indicate the degree of distance separating such groups, the patterns of their interactions, the quality of what intransigence may exist, and the possibilities for their continued limited agreement in the pursuit of national developmental goals. The position of the transitional person should be closely examined to learn which way he leans and with what affective quality. To what is he politically most susceptible under given conditions? How does he act as follower? How does he act as leader? What has been and what can be his role at differing stages in the growth of industrial society?

The rational fomenting of change also depends in important measure upon identifying the loci of persons of modern mentality. Directed culture change might well intervene least—and, paradoxically, most—as a result of the continual expansion of the power base of persons with high national identification.

Further, the implications of the relationship between political activity both as follower and as leader in modern and traditional groups needs much more treatment. The complication of the matter is indicated by the apolitical views of many modern groups as well as by the previously noted lack of coherence at times between avowed personal values and actual public action. Thus the quality of the leader-follower relation in both modern and traditional groups also suggests itself as an important area of research, particularly given the importance to development of impersonal concepts of the market-place, contract and equality before the laws.

Not only is the relationship between modern and traditional groups important, but so too are the interclass identifications within each group. If our data are truly reliable concerning the existence of modern attitudes among groups of some size even among slum-dwellers, then how do they see élite moderns, and how are they seen in turn? How 'mobilizable' are these nationalists at various social levels? What 'play' is there between social values and ideologies, and how can such disjunction be employed for political recruitment to modernization?

These research suggestions, hasty and sketchy as they may be, also suggest how far we must go before we can speak with reasonable precision concerning the roots of the Latin American political process and its relationship to general development. Ideologically argued solutions, international aid programmes and the work of 'technicians' will all remain but poetic evocations of ignorance until we know more about the patterns and possibilities of the political uses and potential of Latin America's human resources. There really is no longer any excuse for writing books about urbanization in Latin America, development in Latin America, education in Latin America, or anything else social in Latin America, without taking into account power and politics in Latin America at a level of profundity appropriate to the intensity of the changes implied in social modernization.

Chapter XVII. Transplanting Democracy

Introductory Note

THE WESTERN democracies, whose peoples uniformly enjoy a high standard of living, constitute one of the "models" on which the development of the newly emerging nations might be based. But under what conditions may democracy—historically the product of European culture—be transplanted in "non-Western" countries?

The first condition is obviously that the people and the dominant social groups desire to introduce democratic institutions and practices. This desire does not exist universally. The leaders of Ghana, Guinea, Indonesia, Vietnam, Egypt, and many other countries, specifically reject the Western model of parliamentary democracy as unsuitable. Many new regimes, however, are ostensibly fashioned after the Western democratic nations. Throughout the former colonies of Great Britain, for example, attempts have been made to introduce the British political system: a head of State with mainly ceremonial functions designates a prime minister, who selects a Cabinet and secures a vote of confidence from Parliament; the members of the Cabinet in turn are "collectively responsible" for all decisions or actions by any of the ministers. The American presidential system has been widely copied in Latin America, the Philippines, and Vietnam; while the French influence is clearly evident in the administrative and political structures of her former colonies in Africa and Asia.

However, democracy involves more than the existence of formal institutions. British cabinet government, for example, in itself is easily adaptable to the requirements of dictatorship—in the absence of a vigorous opposition, a free press, and above all, historical traditions of individual freedom. The institutions function within a specific social, historical, and cultural context. Democracy can work only when democratic norms and values, particularly those relating to free expression and political organization, are understood and accepted by all the people. John Stuart Mill pointed out, in a classic analysis of the social conditions of representative government:

A people may be unwilling or unable to fulfill the duties which a particular form of government requires of them. A rude people, though in some degree alive to the benefits of civilized society, may be unable to practice the forebearance which it demands. . . . In such a case, a civilized government, to be really advantageous to them, will require to be in a considerable degree despotic: to be one over which they do not themselves exercise control, and which imposes a great amount of forcible restraint upon their actions.

In any case, the social structures of the developing nations are so different from those of Europe and North America, that some adaptation or modification of democratic institutions appears inevitable. The precise form which this modification assumes in the various nations of Africa, Asia, and Latin America makes an exciting subject for comparative study.

Some of the more comprehensive studies of institutional transfer, with all that it entails, are: Robert Scalapino, *Democracy and the Party Movement in Prewar Japan* (1956); Sir Ivor Jennings, *The Approach to Self-Government* (1956); David A. Apter, *Ghana in Transition* (1963); Henry L. Bretton, *Power and Stability in Nigeria* (1962); and B. P. Lamb, *India: A World in Transition* (1963). See also F. S. C. Northrop, *The Meeting of East and West* (1953), and Barbara Ward, *Five Ideas That Change the World* (1959).

56. MODERNIZATION AND DEMOCRACY IN JAPAN*
Robert E. Ward

I

THE TERM "political modernization" is of late encountered with increasing frequency in the literature of political science. Its antecedents are somewhat diffuse. In the most general sense, it seems to represent a specialized adaptation of scholars' long-standing concern with the question of whether the process of social change is determinate or variable, random or patterned, continuous or episodic, cyclic or evolutionary. Within this tradition "political modernization" is a concept opposed in tendency to the relativistic character of much modern scholarship in the field of politics. It would seem to be oriented more in the direction of a patterned and evolutionary—although not necessarily determinate or value-laden—interpretation of social change.

In a more restricted sense, this concept is perhaps more directly related to the search for new methodological principles which has been so notable an aspect of the discipline of political science for the past ten years. For at least this period, students of comparative politics have been systematically seeking analytic concepts and categories of inquiry broad enough in ambit and yet sufficiently sensitive and researchable to permit meaningful cross-national comparisons of political systems and their component parts. This concern has focused upon problems of both cross-sectional and

* From "Political Modernization and Political Culture in Japan," *World Politics* (July, 1963), 569–96. Abridged by the Editors. Reprinted by permission of *World Politics*.

developmental comparison and it is in the latter context that the concept of "political modernization" has seemed promising.

Third, the concept also finds a more practical provenance in the expanding commitments of the United States government to the "development" of many so-called underdeveloped areas. While initial efforts in this campaign were largely confined to the economic and military spheres, it was rapidly discovered that durable economic development required a comparable degree of political development. This circumstance has reinforced general professional interest in the process and determinants of "political modernization," and provided unusual opportunities for both study and experimentation in actual field situations.

Finally, the concept of "political modernization" is to some degree indebted to recent theorizing and writing in the analogous field of "economic development." This new concern within the profession springs, therefore, from a variety of sources. Since it has not as yet, however, gained general acceptance, it might be well at this point to provide a working definition for it.[1]

The concept of "political modernization" assumes and is intelligible only in terms of the existence of a "modern" society as the essential environment for a modern political system. A modern society is here viewed as a massive and new type of social development which has come upon the scene in mature form only in the course of the last century. It is characterized by its far-reaching ability to control or influence the physical and social circumstances of its environment, and by a value system which is fundamentally optimistic about the desirability and consequences of this ability. More specifically, in its non-political sectors it is also characterized by low birth, death, and morbidity rates and by high ratios, degrees, or levels of: (1) inanimate to animate sources of energy; (2) tool technology, mechanization, and industrialization; (3) specialization and professionalization of labor; (4) gross and per capita national product of goods and services; (5) urbanization; (6) differentiation, achievement orientation, and mobility in social organization; and (7) literacy, mass education, and mass media circulation.

No society, of course, possesses all of these qualities in a complete or polar sense. Even the most "modern" society contains substantial admixtures of what might be described as pre-modern or traditional elements and is, in this sense, mixed or dualistic in character. Despite the measure of commonality which this fact ensures to all societies, there obviously exist profound differences in the proportion and pattern in which modern and pre-modern elements are distributed or "mixed" in various societies. In some cases, the "mix" is such as to yield almost purely traditional types such as Yemen or Afghanistan; in others, it produces something as

---

[1] This definition is adopted from Robert E. Ward and Roy C. Macridis (eds.), *Modern Political Systems: Asia* (Englewood Cliffs, N.J., 1963), 445.

innovational, as "modern" as the United States or the USSR. In this sense judgments of modernity are more concerned with the central tendency or thrust of societies than with any undiluted conception of uniformly modern or traditional social characteristics.

A "modern" polity is a subsystem of a "modern" society. As such it has separable characteristics, the most important of which are a high degree of both functional differentiation and integration of political structure and political roles; a rational, secular, and scientific system of political decision-making; and the volume, range, authority, and efficacy of its output of political decisions and administrative actions. More specifically, it is also characterized by: (1) a reasonably general and effective sense of popular identification with the history, territory, myths, and national identity of the state concerned; (2) widespead popular interest and involvement in the political system, though not necessarily in the decision-making aspects thereof; (3) an allocation of political roles in accordance with standards of achievement rather than ascription; and (4) judicial and regulatory techniques based upon a predominantly secular and impersonal system of law.

Other attributes of importance to a definition of the process of political modernization can doubtless be adduced but, for present purposes, this may serve as a working list of central tendencies possessed by all political systems generally regarded as being "modern." It should be added that while political modernization is, of course, a continuing process—unachieved and probably unachievable in the ideal-type sense—it is not necessarily open-ended or permanent. It is quite possible to conceive of the emergence of other types of political systems differing in important respects from that defined above as "modern." In this sense—bizarre though the semantics may be—there may be point in speculating about the characteristics of post-modern polities, as we already do about those of pre-modern polities. Such speculation aside, however, the present utility of the concept of "political modernization" rests upon the hope that it validly and objectively defines the essential features of the political developments which have occurred in all so-called advanced societies and that it also represents the pattern toward which politically underdeveloped societies are now evolving.

Two other aspects of the concept should be noted. First, no political system is completely modern in this sense. Even those regarded as being the most modern have substantial admixtures of what are by definition pre-modern or traditional elements. These seem capable of coexisting with the dominant modern component for very substantial periods of time, perhaps indefinitely. In fact, their role is sometimes supportive of the political modernization process in important respects. Second, the concept of political modernization in its present form is neutral with respect to the philosophic or ethical orientation and particular form of government of political systems. It regards all such systems—whether democratic, totalitarian, or intermediate in type as either actually or potentially modern. The form of government is not a critical factor. Both the United States and the USSR represent politically modern societies in this sense.

II

This statement of the characteristics of a modern society and political system poses the question of Japan's current status. How modern are contemporary Japanese society and the Japanese political system? How do their performances compare with those of other Asian and Western states?

No single indicator can provide a satisfactory answer to this question, but by combining a variety of indices one can achieve helpful insights. For the present, let us confine ourselves to some of the more obvious statistical measures of modernity. In recent years Japan's birth and death rates per thousand of population (17.5 and 7.4 respectively in 1960) compare very favorably with those of the United States, the USSR, France, or Great Britain, as does her population's expectation of life at age 0 (65.2 for men and 69.8 for women in 1959). Approximately 98 per cent of her population is literate, a figure that places Japan among the world's leading societies in this respect. The school enrollment ratios at the primary and secondary level are fully the equal of those of the leading Western countries, while her college and university enrollment ratios are considerably higher than those of Great Britain or France. In circulation of daily newspapers per 1,000 of population, Japan's figure of 398 in 1958 was exceeded only by the United Kingdom, Sweden, Norway, and Luxembourg. Sixty-three per cent of her population is urban in residence, and secondary or tertiary in employment characteristics. In 1961 her steel output ranked fourth in the world, ahead of Great Britain's, while for the sixth straight year she led the world in shipbuilding. Her gross national product on a per capita basis, while still low by Western European standards ($399 in 1961), is the highest in Asia if one excepts Israel. And it is increasing rapidly as a consequence of an economy which has been expanding at a rate of 18 per cent in 1959, 14 per cent in 1960, and 10 per cent in 1961. These are among the world's highest rates of economic advancement where already developed societies are concerned.

Thus, judging by the common statistical measures of modernity, Japan's performance is outstanding. Viewed in terms both more qualitative and more specifically political, her record, while somewhat less unequivocal, is impressive. Her formal political structure is among the most modern, rational, and functionally differentiated in the world. Her decision-making system, while still displaying a considerable number of traditional characteristics, stands far in advance of the norms for Asia or the underdeveloped world in general. The same is true of her output of political decisions and administrative actions.

By any standards of modernity, therefore, Japan indubitably possesses developed and modern social and political systems. The distance which separates her from American or Western European performance in these spheres may still be appreciable, but it is far less impressive than the gulf which separates Japanese performance from that of practically all other parts of Asia.

Against this background, it is our purpose to examine in a quite general and selective way certain aspects of the political modernization process in Japan in an attempt to clarify at least some of the circumstances which contributed to a successful outcome in this one historical case. It is not claimed that Japan's path to political modernization can or should be the sole or complete model for Asian or other developing societies seeking a similar result. Some aspects of the Japanese experience are doubtless unique. But since Japan is the only indigenous Asian society that has succeeded in achieving types and levels of political performance which practically all other Asian states either desire or consider necessary, the nature of the Japanese experience inevitably becomes of extraordinary interest. It may not point to the only or the most effective path of political modernization for other developing societies, but it does represent the only mature specimen available for analysis. As a specific and concrete case it also affords opportunities for checking and enriching the types of relatively abstract and theoretical speculation which necessarily bulk large in the early stages of investigation in fields such as this.

III

As one looks back upon the history of political modernization in Japan, one might well be impressed first by the neatness of the manner in which it is usually periodized. In gross terms, for example, one is accustomed to distinguishing periods called Tokugawa (1603–1868) and post-Restoration (1868—) in Japanese political history. For somewhat more specific purposes, many distinguish an overlapping Restoration Period (ca. 1850–1890) when considering the beginnings of modern Japanese political development. Over the years these convenient denominators for the categorization of historical data have assumed an authority and potential for distortion which were never intended. . . .

In the Japanese case, this emphasis upon the Restoration and its aftermath as a time of revolutionary, i.e. discontinuous, new developments—especially in the political and economic spheres—acquired added force from a subsequent episode in Japanese historiography. This was the widespread practice of interpreting pre-Restoration Japan—the Japan of the Tokugawa Period (1603–1868)— in terms of a "feudal" model. Indeed, at a later period, this was compounded by the addition of the notion that the Tokugawa shoguns had in effect intervened in the normal course of Japan's historical development and succeeded in refeudalizing the country in the early seventeenth century at a time when its immanent tendencies were modernizing. Thus, pre-Restoration Japan came to be viewed not only as "feudal," but, in Professor J. W. Hall's apt phrase, as a "feudal throwback."

One can readily appreciate the consequences attendant upon so dichotomous a treatment of post-sixteenth-century Japanese history. For many the Restoration tended to become a watershed more formidable than the Rockies. What lay behind it was normally viewed as "feudal"; what lay on this side of it became either "modern" or a "feudal survival"—that is, an undesirable remnant of earlier practices or attitudes slated for eventual discard. This tendency was probably reinforced by real ignorance where the actual circumstances of life and society in Tokugawa times were concerned. It is only within the past few years that professional research in this period has become at all fashionable, and it is still seriously neglected in favor of more "glamorous" subjects drawn from the Restoration and later periods. As a consequence, the real beginnings of modernization in Japan have frequently been overlooked or attributed to much later periods than was actually the case.

The degree of literacy and of formal institutionalized education in pre-Restoration Japan provides a case in point. The educational preparation of at least sizable segments of a population is a basic factor in both the general and the political modernization process. Until recently it has been widely assumed that any really critical advances in this sphere waited upon the introduction of compulsory mass education in the 1870's. In fact, this was far from true. . . . Dore concludes that, despite the Confucian orientation of most of this pre-Restoration education, "the attitudes to popular education, the sense of the contingency of social institutions on the human will, the training in abstract analysis and the application of evaluating principles to policy, the development of a respect for merit rather than status, the stimulation of personal ambition and the strengthening of a collectivist ideology . . ."[2] represented important contributions to the modernizing process in Japan, and that all of these had undergone very considerable development long before the Restoration.

In a more specifically political sense, the same could be said of the origins and development of another major element in the modernizing process—the emergence of a professionally trained, rationally structured, and achievement-oriented bureaucracy. . . . In the light of insights such as these into what was actually taking place throughout the Tokugawa

---

[2] Ronald P. Dore, "The Legacy of Tokugawa Education" (unpublished paper prepared for the first seminar of the Conference on Modern Japan, January, 1962), pp. 1–2.

Period in Japan, one begins to appreciate the long, gradual process of institutional and attitudinal preparation for modernization which was well under way at least a century before the Restoration. Comparable "preparations" may readily be identified at the village level or in the economic sphere; there is nothing unduly selective about these examples. Japanese society during the Tokugawa Period may still be appropriately described by such terms as "centralized or nationalized feudalism" but, if so, it was feudalism with an important difference. Japan had come a long way from the hierarchic, personal, loyalty-focused relationships and the intricate structure of fiefs and practically enserfed villagers which had characterized the polity in the sixteenth and early seventeenth centuries. On balance the "feudal" attributes of the society perhaps still predominated. But mingled with and gradually subverting these were a number of the most salient and potent elements of "modern" society.

When evaluating the modernization of Japan, it is useful to keep in mind this long, complex history of covert preparation from which the society benefited. This still stands as a unique accomplishment in Asia, but its main roots are buried at least two hundred years deep in the country's social and political history. The florescence of national leadership during the early Meiji Period, combined with the international circumstances and opportunities of the times, had a great deal to do with the amazing speed at which Japan modernized, but in a more fundamental sense Japanese society seems to have been prepared for the experience to a degree still unmatched in some important respects among many contemporary Asian societies. In this context, the Japanese preparations for more modern forms of social, economic, and political organization may not be so completely different from their Western analogues as the apparent persistence of a "feudal" period until 1868 makes it seem.

IV

This extension in historical depth of the development of a modern society and polity in Japan also calls attention to what Professor Almond has termed the "dualism" of political institutions.[3] All modern polities contain substantial admixtures of traditional elements, and these are frequently not confined to isolated or backwater areas but may play a prominent and functionally important role in the modernization process.

In the Japanese case, this is well illustrated by our earlier account of the historical development of a professionally trained, rationally structured, and achievement-oriented bureaucracy in Japan. In this instance it was pointed out that what seemed to be a purely feudal institution performing functions of major importance in a predominantly feudal society was at the same time gradually acquiring more and more of the basic character-

---

[3] Gabriel A. Almond and James S. Coleman (eds.), *The Politics of the Developing Areas* (Princeton, 1960), pp. 20–25.

istics of a modern professional bureaucracy. In a historical sense, therefore, the late Tokugawa bureaucracy played a Janus-like role. It faced both backward toward the truly feudal institutions and times of the sixteenth century and forward toward the emergent modern society of the twentieth. It also served in gradually shifting proportions the purposes of both waning and emergent societies, and it continued to do this for upward of one hundred and fifty years. In other words, the capacity for peaceful coexistence—and even mutual supportiveness—of "feudal" or traditional with modern elements within a given institution, as well as within a society, is well demonstrated by the Japanese experience.

But the context has shifted since Tokugawa times. First, it was the existence of modern elements and tendencies within a feudal environment that seemed noteworthy. Now it is the "survival" of numerous so-called feudal or traditional traits within the predominantly modern context of present-day Japan which seems striking and gives rise to comments which are apt to be emotionally charged. To some these "survivals" represent the old, the "real," the quintessential Japan and are to be treasured and savored; to others they represent discreditable vestiges of an outmoded, or "Asian," or "feudal" past which should be given speedy burial.

The explanation of such reactions would seem to lie in the dichotomous way in which the terms "traditional" and "modern" are usually related in our thinking. They tend to be viewed as mutually exclusive or polar opposites. The institutions and attitudes associated with one come to be regarded as antipathetic to the other. From here, it is but a step to the conclusion that any given traditional "survival" is fated for elimination from a "modern" society through some inexorable process of social purgation impelled by a drive toward institutional self-consistency.

The history of the modernization of Japan challenges the tenability of any such thesis. It demonstrates in many ways not only the ability of "modern" institutions and practices to coexist with "traditional" ones for very substantial periods of time, but also the manner in which "traditional" attitudes and practices can be of great positive value to the modernization process.

The modernizing experience is a strenuous one for any traditionally organized society. If successful, it demands sacrifice, discipline, initiative, and perseverance in quantities and for periods of time which are certain to place the people concerned under very severe strains. One of the greatest problems of leadership under these circumstances is to devise conditions and motivations which will both liberate and focus an appropriate amount of popular energy, initiative, and resources and at the same time minimize dysfunctional behavior on the part of all significant elements in the population. Consider briefly some of the techniques used in Japan to achieve these goals and note the role played therein by traditional elements.

Most obvious of all, perhaps, was the use made of the emperor. This is not to say that there was not some measure of sincerity and philosophic or ethical commitment in the movement to restore the emperor to at least the semblance of temporal power. But the subsequent revival and institutionalization of Shinto and the cultivation of mass loyalty, obedience, and reverence for the emperor were too systematic and innovational to be anything but a deliberate and very clever attempt by the Meiji leadership to channel popular attitudes and conduct along lines which they considered constructive. In this instance the appeal was to an institutional complex that not only was traditional in terms of the circumstances of the 1870's, but would have been equally so in terms of those of 1603. The tradition of imperial rule, with very few exceptions, had possessed little validity since approximately the ninth century, while Imperial Shinto as a national cult had been moribund for at least as long, if indeed it had ever before existed in comparable form.

Again, one of the real keystones to the successful modernization of Japan was the device of holding constant, i.e. traditional, the circumstances of life in rural and agricultural Japan while at the same time using and exploiting the countryside as a means of building and rapidly developing the urban, commercial, industrial, and military sectors of the society. Modernization is an expensive undertaking and the costs must be borne by some segment of the population. In Japan in the early and critical years, it was the peasantry who, through the land tax, bore the bulk of this burden. A docile and productive agrarian labor force was, therefore, an element of crucial importance to the leaders of a modernizing Japan. In a social engineering sense, they strove to ensure this result by altering the actual socio-political circumstances of the pre-Restoration countryside as little as possible. Land reform was assiduously avoided; the existing political, social, and economic elites of the villages were insofar as possible confirmed in their status and authority; the traditional community and family systems were not only maintained but in a number of ways were reinforced and given new legal status and sanctions.

A systematic endeavor was made to ensure the tranquility, obedience, and loyalty of the countryside, and the control devices utilized were almost without exception traditional. This not only assured the government of a maximal flow of food, revenue, recruits, and urban-bound emigrants from the countryside, but also left them free to concentrate their attention and resources on the building of the more critical urban aspects of the national economy and defense establishment. This was a strategy of enormous importance to the rapid development of Japan, and its success rested ultimately on the effective enlistment of traditional institutions and appeals in the service of the modernizing process.

If one looks to the contemporary rather than the historical scene in Japan, many examples of this type of "reinforcing dualism" may still be discerned. The most reliable and important element in the long political dominance of the Liberal-Democratic Party in the post war period has been its control of the rural vote. Below the surface of this phenomenon, one will find a political support system compounded of largely personalized allegiance and loyalties reaching downward through the prefectures to roots in every farm hamlet in Japan. The ultimate approach of this apparatus to the voter is based upon a very shrewd admixture of appeals to personal and local advantage phrased in terms of traditional values and relationships. Again, the primacy of personal and hierarchical relations and loyalties in Japanese politics is obvious and well-known. The persistence of *oyabun-kobun* and similar forms of traditional fictive family relationships is but an extreme form of this trait. It would probably also be proper to regard the national predilection for consensual rather than adversary forms of decision-making and the dualistic nature of the national economy as other examples of the continued vitality and real functional importance of traditional attitudes and practices in the Japan of 1963.

In short, post-Restoration Japan has continuously represented a very complex amalgam of traditional and modern elements, a sort of mutually supportive or "reinforcing dualism" in which the relationship between the two sectors has often been symbiotic rather than antagonistic. This has been true to such an extent that it is probably accurate to claim that Japan could not have been successful in modernizing so rapidly and effectively had it not been for the many planned and unplanned ways in which traditional values and behavior positively contributed to and supported the process. Furthermore, there is a good deal of evidence indicative of the continued vitality of some segments of the traditional sector. It is still too early to predict even their gradual displacement by what we regard logically as more modern traits. . . .

V

The course of political modernization in Japan raises some interesting questions with respect to the form and organization of authority in modernizing societies. It was pointed out earlier that states which have achieved modernity may have democratic, totalitarian, or some intermediate type of political organization. The form of government does not seem to be a defining factor in mature cases of political modernization. The experience of Japan, however, makes one wonder if the same judgment applies with respect to forms of political organization in all earlier stages of the political modernization process. Is the process neutral in this respect throughout, or can one identify stages which demand authoritarian forms of government and which are antipathetic on grounds of developmental efficiency and potentiality to the introduction of democratic institutions on more than a very restricted basis? The question is of great importance from the standpoint of those who would prefer to see "backward" political systems develop along lines which are both modern and democratic. These are compatible but not necessary consequences of the developmental process. This poses the problem of how one can maximize the probability that developing polities will become both modern and democratic.

The experience of Japan alone certainly cannot provide definitive answers to either of the above questions. But neither is it irrelevant, and in circumstances where it represents the sole mature non-Western exemplar of the modernization process in all of Asia, it should be examined with unusual care and attention. The Japanese experience seems to suggest: (1) that authoritarian forms of political organization can be extraordinarily effective in the early stages of the modernization process; (2) that they need not debar the gradual emergence of more democratic forms of political organization; and (3) that some such process of gradual transition from authoritarian to democratic forms may be essential to the emergence of politics that are both modern and durably democratic. It should be emphasized again that these are no more than highly tentative hypotheses based upon the experience of Japan, but they do possess at least this much historical sanction and support. Let us then consider in a general way selected aspects of Japan's experience with the political modernization process which relate to the above three propositions.

First, authoritarian forms of political organization can be extraordinarily effective in the early stages of the modernization process. It is implied—though not demonstrable on the basis of the Japanese experience—that democratic forms are significantly less effective and that their early introduction may in fact result in conditions that will seriously inhibit the prospects of long-term democratic development.

This contention rests primarily on observations with respect to the relationship between the political modernization process and the process of social modernization in a general or total sense. The former is not autonomous, not a goal in itself. It is instrumentally related to the larger process and goal and should serve and expedite its purposes. This larger process of modernization entails for the society concerned, especially in the critical early or "take-off" stages, a series of shocks and strains of major proportions. It equally creates emancipations and new opportunities for some, but for major segments of the population this is apt to be a lengthy period of adjustment to new economic, social, and political situations and demands. Large-scale material and psychological stresses are invariably involved. One of the routine consequences of such a situation —at least in the non-Western world of the late nineteenth and the twentieth centuries—seems to be a greatly expanded role for government. A certain and perhaps very important amount of the modernization process may still take place under private auspices, but in recent times the needs and expectations which set the standards of modernization have been so urgent and expensive that national governments have had to assume a leading and dominant role. Only power organized at this level seemed capable of massing the resources and taking and enforcing the wide-ranging and difficult decisions involved.

This primacy of government in the modernizing process is more or less taken for granted throughout the underdeveloped world today. The situation was doubtless historically different in the case of the modernization of certain Western European societies and their offshoots, but in present-day underdeveloped societies there simply are no plausible and politically viable alternatives to the primacy of government as an agent of modernization. This was also true in the Japanese case at the time of the Restoration.

The overriding problems and goals of the 1870's and 1880's in Japan were well expressed by the popular political slogan of the day—*fukoku kyōhei* (a strong and wealthy nation). This captures the essence of the complex of forces and aspirations which underlay the Restoration movement and motivated its leaders in the difficult days that followed the initial successes of 1868. The greatest and most urgent needs were for national unity and the creation of armed strength sufficient to guarantee the national security against both real and fancied dangers of foreign imperialist agression and economic exploitation. Instrumental thereto, of course, was the creation of a strong and stable government to lead the nation along suitable paths. Fortunately for Japan, her leaders were wise enough to define these goals in broad and constructive terms. Military strength meant to them far more than a large army and navy well-equipped with Western armaments; it also meant the industrial plant to sustain and expand such a military establishment and appropriate training for the men who must staff it. National wealth came to mean a radical diversification of the predominantly agrarian economy, urbanization, systematic mass and higher education, planned industrialization, new commercial and financial institutions, and a variety of other commitments which were perceived as essential to survival and effective competitive status in a Western-dominated world. Not all of these commitments were either generally perceived or welcomed at the outset by the leadership group, but in their search for national unity, strength, and security they found themselves embarked upon a species of "modernization spiral" similar in some respects to the "inflationary spiral" of the economists. The most intelligent and able of them adapted to the general course set by the imperatives which these goals entailed; the others were eliminated from leadership circles.

The realization of national goals of this sort did not come easily to a society such as Japan's, even given the forms of covert preparation for modernization which had characterized the later Tokugawa Period. The really critical years between 1868 and 1890 must sometimes have seemed an unending series of crises. Civil war, the threat of international war and the fact of foreign economic exploitation, a series of economic crises, inflation and deflation, the recurrent threat of samurai conspiracies against the government, the embitterment of the peasantry at the failure of the government to improve their lot, the dearth of desperately needed technical knowledge and personnel, and all of the widespread fears and tensions which attend a time of new beginnings—these were merely some of the problems which constantly confronted the new political leadership. Yet, by 1890, policies capable of dealing with all of these problems had been developed and the country was firmly embarked on the path to modernization. The foreign threats had been faced and Japan's international position was secure; the menace of civil war had been permanently liquidated; the structural vestiges of feudalism had been eliminated and the country effectively unified; the position and authority of the government had been confirmed and regularized by constitutional arrangements; the economy had been stabilized and a promising start made upon its diversification and industrialization; a system of mass compulsory education had been inaugurated and mass media of communication established; in every critical category the strength of Japan showed remarkable and promising improvements.

Under such circumstances it may be that some measure of democratic participation could successfully have been introduced into the political system. There were those who advocated such changes. The *Jiyūminken Undō* (Freedom and Popular Rights Movement), for example, called for the establishment of a national parliament, a limited suffrage, and some dispersion of political authority. Had this been attempted during these years, the results need not have been fatal to the modernization of Japan. But under conditions of more or less constant political or economic crisis, widespread popular disaffection and lack of understanding of the necessity for the sacrifices entailed by many government programs, the unpredictable qualities and perils of the country's foreign relations, and what we have learned in general of the limitations of fledgling democratic institutions in largely unprepared contexts, it is difficult to envisage the feasibility or practicality of any very significant democratic innovations at this time.

These years from 1868 to 1890, or some similar period, would seem to be a time in Japan's modernization when an authoritarian form of political organization offered distinct advantages where rapidity of response, flexibility, planning, and effective action were concerned. This is said with full appreciation of the fumbling and shortcomings of authoritarian leadership groups and irresponsible bureaucracies—including the Japanese of this period—in all of these departments. It thus assumes the availability of some at least minimally competent and unified political leadership. If this is not available—and there are obviously cases where it is not—political modernization is not a practicable proposition for the countries concerned.

In the Japanese case, however, it seems on balance highly improbable that (1) the addition of any significant or effective democratic institutions to the decision-making apparatus at such a stage of national development could have had other than deleterious effects upon the speed and decisiveness with which urgent problems were handled; and that (2) this stage of the modernization process, beset as it inevitably was by so many and such desperate problems, would have been an appropriate time to launch so delicate an experiment as democratization.

Our second hypothesis was that the dominance of authoritarian forms of political organization in the initial stages of the political modernization process need not debar the gradual emergence of democratic forms of organization. This is not intended to imply any quality of inevitability in such a development, although in a secular sense some such tendency may exist.

In the Japanese case, no significant measures of democratization were introduced into the political system until the enactment of the Meiji Constitution in 1890, twenty-two years after the Restoration. Even then it is very doubtful if any of the authors of this document thought of their handiwork as an act of democratic innovation. It is certain that their so-called "liberal" opposition did not. Rather does it seem that the Meiji leadership group conceived of this constitution primarily as a means of regularizing the structure and operations of political authority—the absence of any rationalized or stable structure and the continual innovation and experimentation of the intervening years must have been very trying—and of further unifying and solidifying both the country and their own authority. As a consequence of this and a variety of later developments, there has been a tendency to undervalue both the degree of political change which the Meiji Constitution brought to Japan and the measure of democratic development which took place under it.

It is helpful to look at the Meiji Constitution and its attendant basis laws both in terms of the general political standards and practices of 1890 and in terms of its actual operations as well as its legal and political theory. If this is done, one will note that it makes public, explicit, and authoritative a particular theory of sovereignty and the state, and derives from this a functionally differentiated and rationally organized governmental structure; it establishes the legal status of citizens and specifies their political and civil rights and duties; it distinguishes legislative, executive, and judicial functions and, although establishing a dominant and protected position for the executive, does provide for their separate institutionalization; it specifies legal equality before the law and creates means for the assertion of popular against official rights; it establishes a restricted but expansible franchise and, in terms of this, a popularly elected house in the national legislature; it provides for some measure of decentralization in government, and renders inevitable the introduction of a much greater pluralism into both the Japanese oligarchy and the political system in general.

Against the background of Tokugawa and Restoration political practices, these are notable and democratic innovations. They did not, of course, put an end to the period of authoritarian political rule in Japan. But they certainly launched a process of democratization which has continued to play a major, although usually not dominant, part in Japanese politics ever since. In this sense the history of the democratization of Japan, viewed in the light of present circumstances, is a product of erosive and catalytic agents. Much of the story is told, until 1932 at least, in terms of the erosion of the authoritarian political forms and practices characteristic of the pre-constitutional period. This process never reached the point of establishing what the contemporary West would regard as an authentically democratic political system, but, by the 1920's, the degree of pluralism, responsibility, and popular participation characterizing Japanese politics would certainly have surprised, and probably appalled, the great leaders of the Restoration Period. Between the 1920's and the 1960's there intervened, of course, the resurgence of military and ultra-nationalist rule, the war, and the Allied Occupation of Japan. This last acted as a catalytic agent on the submerged but still vital forms of Japanese democracy and gave them institutional and legal advantages, authority, and prestige beyond what they could have hoped for on the basis of their own political position and strength. The consequence has been a great and apparently sudden florescence of Western-style democracy in Japan. In fact, however, the roots of this development lie deep in the political experience of post-1890 Japan.

There are two things about this gradual emergence of democratic politics from the authoritarian system of pre-1890 Japan which might have more general validity and interest. The first is that even the concession of a very carefully restricted and seemingly impotent governmental role to a popularly elected body can, over a period of time, have consequences well nigh fatal to sustained authoritarian rule. It would be hard to be optimistic about the influence or authority of the Japanese House of Representatives in terms of the provisions of the Meiji Constitution or the relevant basic laws. These faithfully reflect and implement the desire of the founders to make of the House an appealing but powerless sop to the demands of the opposition and public opinion. But the lessons to be learned from the subsequent history of the lower house are: (1) that it provides a means of institutionalizing and enlarging the role of political parties; (2) that, in modernizing circumstances, even vested powers of obstructing the smooth and effective flow of governmental decisions and actions can be critical—positive powers of initiation and control are not necessary; and (3) that in circumstances where a popularly chosen body can thus blackmail an authoritarian leadership, there is a fair possibility of forcing the latter into piecemeal but cumulative accommodations which are democratic in tendency.

The second generalization suggested by the history of democratic development in Japan relates to the conditions necessary to support an effectively authoritarian system of government. Japanese experience suggests the existence of a close relationship between effective authoritarian rule and the unity and solidarity of the oligarchy involved. The limits involved cannot be described with much precision, but authoritarian government in Japan began to disintegrate as the heretofore fairly solidary oligarchy began to split into competing cliques and factions. The probability of such rifts seems to be very high in modernizing societies. The development of role specialization and professionalization even at high levels is an essential part of the process of modernization, and this makes it hard for an oligarchy to maintain the degree of unity and cohesion feasible in revolutionary or in simpler times. Pluralism in this sense seems to be built into the process. And as an oligarchy breaks down into competing factions in this fashion, the terms of political competition in that society undergo an important change. Extra-oligarchic groups such as emergent political parties acquire new room for maneuver and new political leverages, and the ex-oligarchic cliques themselves acquire new incentives for broadening the basis of their support. Out of these altered political circumstances are apt to come new political alliances involving elements of the former oligarchy with elements of more popularly based bodies— in particular, with political parties. The total process is dilutive from the standpoint of authoritarian government and supportive of the gradual emergence of greater degrees of pluralism and democracy.

It is not intended to depict either of the foregoing generalizations on the basis of Japanese experience as controlling or inevitable. But they did occur within a fairly authoritarian context in Japan's case and there seem to be some reasons for regarding them as of more general validity. The conclusion would seem to be that an initial or early stage of authoritarian government on the path to modernization (1) does not commit a polity to long-term adherence to authoritarian forms; (2) does not necessarily make an authoritarian course of development probable; and (3) may even contain built-in elements calculated with time and development to break down and liberalize such authoritarian forms.

Our third hypothesis is even more tentatively stated and adds up to a feeling that some such process of gradual transition from authoritarian to democratic forms may be essential to the emergence of a political system which is both modern and durably democratic. In this connection Japan's experience suggests several notions of possible interest.

First, our commonly employed systems of periodization may involve serious distortions where the history of political modernization is concerned. Thus, in Japan's case, while the feudal-modern or Tokugawa-Restoration frameworks have a plausible amount of relevance to the emergence of a modern Japanese political system, they also serve to obscure important aspects of the process. They are calculated, as is the prewar-postwar framework, to produce an overemphasis on the significance of certain dramatic and allegedly "revolutionary" events in a country's history—in this case, the Restoration or the 1945 defeat plus the Occupation. This is conducive to a dichotomous view of the political development process which seriously overstates the enduring importance of alleged discontinuities in a national history at the expense of the less dramatic but fundamentally more important continuities.

Second, if the history of the development of democracy in Japan is weighted for this distorting effect of the commonly employed categories and system of periodization, the differences in preparation, timing, and depth of democratic experience which are often held to distinguish a democratic political system in Japan from its Western analogues would perhaps seem appreciably less valid and important than is usually assumed. The two patterns of development probably have more in common than is generally recognized.

Third, if the foregoing assumptions are valid, one is tempted to conclude that all practicing and at least ostensibly solid and durable democracies today are the products of lengthy and multifaceted evolutionary processes. In the Japanese case, if one looks only to the direct antecedents, seventy-three years intervene between the Meiji Constitution and the present. But far longer periods of preparation are involved if one looks to the less direct consequences of the introduction of mass literacy or a rationalized bureaucratic structure. In this sense it is questionable whether history provides any very encouraging examples of short-cuts to the achievement of a democratic political system.

Finally, such a train of argument suggests the importance of the relationship existing between a "modern" political system and a "democratic" political system. One hesitates to claim that all or a specific proportion of the attributes of a modern polity must be achieved before a society becomes capable of durably democratic performance or achievement, but Japan's experience at least suggests an important correlation between the two. It is hard to specify the proportions involved, but, in a rough and approximate way, one might say that perhaps only modern societies with modern political cultures of the sort defined in Section I are practical candidates for democratization.

57. AUTHORITARIAN TENDENCIES
IN AFRICAN POLITICS*

Martin L. Kilsen

WITH THE EXCEPTION of Libya, Egypt, the Sudanese Republic, and Ethiopia, where no political parties exist, some variation of the single-party political system or a distinctive tendency in that direction may be

* From "Authoritarian and Single-Party Tendencies in African Politics," *World Politics* (January, 1963), 262–94. Abridged by the Editors. Reprinted by permission of *World Politics*.

found in nearly all of the independent African states.[1] That this should have come to pass within the relatively short period of the rise of African states has been a surprise to some observers of African nationalist movements and parties during the colonial period—who were rather sanguine about the prospects of Western-type democracy and party systems in Africa—as well as to the colonial powers themselves (especially Britain and France)—who presumably assumed that their policies of decolonization in Africa were providing the institutional framework within which Western-type party systems and politics would prevail.

Inasmuch as African nationalist leaders attacked the colonial situation in their countries in democratic terms, it may be assumed that they too accepted the feasibility or applicability of Western-type party politics to African circumstances. However, much of the process of party competition adopted by African nationalists during the preindependence period was a function of the decolonization policies, which generally required free competition among political groups. In other words, since the colonial situation in its decolonization phase was strong enough to define the conditions and framework of the struggle for political power among African parties, the parties had little alternative but to function within this framework, irrespective of whether they accepted its principles and its feasibility as a framework for African development in the post-colonial period.

Our purpose in this article is to delineate and analyze the causes of the single-party tendency in African politics. Before proceeding, however, it is necessary to define what I mean by "single-party rule" in the African context. As I understand it, there are at least two usages of this term as applied to African party politics: (1) It may be used to denote a situation in which only one political party, the governing party, exists or is permitted to exist. This represents single-party rule properly so-called, and applies to the party situation in at least half of the nineteen African states in which the single-party tendency is dominant. For instance, it applies to the position of the *Parti Démocratique de Guinée* (PDG), the *Union Soudanaise* in Mali, the *Parti Dahoméen de l'Unité* (PDU), the

---

[1] My concern in this article is with independent African states in which the indigenous majority participates in government. Thus, Southern Rhodesia, which has had self-government since 1921, and the Republic of South Africa, independent since 1910, are not considered. It is noteworthy that though in these states a democratic system applies to parties and groups within the dominant white (minority) community, when viewed in reference to the overwhelming African majority these white parties constitute, for all practical purposes, *a single-party system—a single political community*—over and against the African majority. (Cf. Colin Leys, *European Politics in Southern Rhodesia* [Oxford, 1959].) They represent what may be termed an oligarchic single-party system, whose key feature is an alien minority that dominates political power, with a consequent absence of a meaningful franchise for the African majority. In this connection, Liberia is more akin to Southern Rhodesia and South Africa than to other African states, though its alien dominant minority is Negro, being of Negro-American slave origin.

Parti Démocratique de la Côte d'Ivoire (PDCI), the *Union pour le Progrès du Tchad* (UPT), and the True Whig Party in Liberia, among several others.

(2) A second usage of the term "single-party rule" is in reference to a situation in which two or more parties exist, but the governing party has both an overwhelming legislative majority and employs its legal, police, and political powers to restrict the competitive position of opposition parties and groups. This usage applies to the position of the Convention People's Party (CPP) in Ghana, the Sierra Leone People's Party (SLPP), the Tanganyika African National Union (TANU), the Northern People's Congress (NPC) in Northern Nigeria, and the *Union Progressiste Sénégalaise* (UPS), among others. In these situations, the direction or main thrust of the party system—that is, its dominant tendency—is single-party rule; and though it has not attained single-party rule properly so-called, the tenuous status of opposition parties, owing to restrictive measures by the governing party, is nearly tantamount to non-existence.

Common to the situations in Africa to which the foregoing usages of the term "single-party rule" apply is an authoritarian (extra-constitutional) use of political power as an essential fact in the continuance in office of a single party. Gosnell expressed the essence of an authoritarian party situation, viewed in its simplest form, when he observed that "without the possibility of a minority party becoming a majority party the democratic system could not exist . . . [and] an essential part of the system is the positive belief in the desirability of replacing one government with another by peaceful methods."[2] . . .

PATTERNS OF SINGLE-PARTY EVOLUTION AND PROSPECTS OF OPPOSITION

Patterns

. . . Let us abstract from [our] analysis of the causes of authoritarian and single-party tendencies in African politics the varied patterns of methods of single-party development, and appraise the prospects of opposition parties. Four rather distinct patterns may be delineated, though normally more than one of these is operative in any given state: (1) extra-parliamentary restrictions on opposition parties; (2) government dissolution or outlawry of opposition parties; (3) regroupment or a united-front process; and (4) a voluntary merger of the opposition with the ruling party.

Extra-Parliamentary Restrictions and Outlawry. The first two patterns of single-party evolution are best considered together because they in fact occur together, and they are more widespread than the other patterns. Extra-parliamentary or extra-legal restrictions against opposition

---

[2] Harold F. Gosnell, *Grass Roots Politics* (Washington, D.C., 1942), p. 7.

parties have occurred at one time or another in all of the 19 African states where the single-party tendency is dominant.[3] A variety of government measures have implemented these restrictions, among which have been imprisonment of opposition leaders, repression or censorship of newspapers, limitations on rights of assembly, and intimidation by police and/or party activists of the governing party. Imprisonment of opposition leaders has occurred in nearly all the African states noted above, and in three instances it involved charges of conspiracy to assassinate the head of state (viz., Ghana in 1958, Dahomey in 1961, Togo in 1961).

Restrictions on rights of assembly and the ability of opposition parties to agitate have also been relatively widespread. Indeed, if the claims of opposition parties themselves are accepted, such measures are well-nigh universal, not merely in states where the single party tendency is dominant but also in competitive situations like Western Nigeria, where opposition groups have complained of restrictions by government bodies. In some instances, government simply refuses permits for holding political rallies, as in Tanganyika, where in 1961 the Minister of Home Affairs banned political rallies of the opposition Tanganyika African National Congress (TANC) on grounds that, in the Minister's words, Congress's speakers "disregarded the conventions of public speaking." In this particular instance, another type of restriction on opposition parties was apparent in the TANU government's refusal to permit the Youth Wing of TANC to register as a political organization—a method of restricting political groups that is also used elsewhere in Africa. It should be noted, moreover, that this method of control over the formation of political groups (and also over non-political groups like welfare associations, tribal unions, etc., which often become *political* in African politics) is a continuation by African states of a power exercised by colonial governments. Given the peculiar problems of nation-state formation confronted by African states, some have utilized this power to prevent the establishment of particularistic parties—e.g., in Ghana or in Ivory Coast, where the Constitution holds any group whose purpose is "particularistic propaganda of racial or ethnic character" to be beyond the law. Ivory Coast and Ghana governments have even outlawed personal, physical acts of tribal identification, such as facial scarification, etc.

Restrictive measures involving the press have been less frequent than imprisonment of leaders and limitations on rights of assembly and agitation, but have been utilized in several states. In Tunisia, the opposition paper *al-Sabah* was suppressed in 1957 by the Neo-Destour government, presumably for its Pan-Arab tendency; in Ghana the *Ashanti Pioneer* Control Act of 1960 placed the main opposition paper under government censorship; and in Dahomey the PDU government passed a law in 1961

---

[3] These 19 states are: Congo (ex-French), Central African Republic, Dahomey, Gabon, Ghana, Guinea, Ivory Coast, Liberia, Mauritania, Mali, Niger, Northern Nigeria, Senegal, Sierra Leone, Tanganyika, Tchad, Togo, Tunisia, and Upper Volta.

permitting seizure of newspapers for incitement to misdemeanors and for other reasons.

As for outlawry of opposition parties, this has been a pattern of single-party evolution in all but five of the 19 states listed above, these five being Northern Nigeria, Sierra Leone, Mali, Tanganyika, and Gabon. An important feature of this pattern has been the simultaneous deportation or otherwise forced exile of leaders of outlawed organizations, even though they were citizens of the state concerned. Thus, in Ivory Coast, Ghana, Niger, Upper Volta, Liberia, Tchad, and Senegal, leaders of outlawed parties or unions have been deported.

One feature of the dynamic of the foregoing methods of single-party evolution is that there won't appear to be some relationship between the type of ruling party on the one hand and the specific government unit executing restrictive measures against opposition groups. Thus, in Ghana, Tanganyika, Guinea, and Ivory Coast, it has been the central government and its organs that execute these restrictions. This is partly due to the natural centralizing tendency of mass-type parties, reinforced in the case of Ghana or Guinea by the government's adherence to a variant of the Marxist pattern of development. On the other hand, in Sierra Leone and Northern Nigeria, where caucus-type parties rule, a major part of the restrictions against opposition has been executed by local government bodies, or more particularly by Native Authority Councils, Courts, and Police. Since the governmental consequence of a caucus-type ruling party has been a significant devolution of government power to local units associated with the traditional ruling elite, the latter has been capable of using this power to harass opposition groups.

Voluntary Merger and Regroupment Process. Voluntary merger has been the least current pattern of single-party evolution, the best examples being the merger of opposition parties in Guinea with the ruling PDG in 1958, and of the *Parti Soudanais du Progrès* with the *Union Soudanaise* in Mali in 1959. The regroupment or united-front process is somewhat similar to voluntary merger, especially insofar as both patterns have involved the grant of ministerial and other senior government posts to leaders of parties that merge or regroup with governing parties. However, in such instances of regroupment as occurred in Mauritania in 1961, Sierra Leone in 1960, Congo Republic in 1961, and Gabon in 1961, this pattern of single-party development has been preceded by a period of major restrictions against opposition groups by the government. Thus the extent to which the regroupment process has been "voluntary" would appear much less than the two instances of voluntary merger, properly so-called, in Guinea and Mali. Even in the latter states—and especially in Guinea—the post-merger period has witnessed government limitations (imprisonment and outlawry) upon groups tending or wishing to break away from the single-party system.

It should also be noted that the regroupment type of party merger has tended to occur in the context of a national election, taking the form of all parties establishing a national union electoral list that occasionally involves one candidate standing for a given office, and particularly the office of President. For instance, the Presidents of Ivory Coast, Mauritania, Gabon, Congo, and Togo were elected at national elections in which, through national union lists, they were the sole candidates for the office.

Prospects

Generally, the immediate future of effective opposition parties in African politics does not appear particularly bright. Even when they are not subjected to extra-parliamentary measures, they tend to be weak institutions, lacking the financial and other resources necessary for effectively competing with governing parties. The latter, on the other hand, in addition to their aura of nationalist legitimacy (a not inconsiderable advantage), have access to government apparatus as a means of perpetuating their rule, and African governing parties seldom hesitate to employ government funds, transport, and other equipment for electoral campaigns and other political activities. For instance, in February 1962 a Ghana government loan of £497,860 to the Guinea Press—which publishes all CPP organs—was written off for "services rendered by the Press." In Nigeria, where a relatively competitive party system prevails and formal expression is given to Western-type democratic procedures, government funds amounting to £2,000,000 have found their way into the service of the governing party in the Western Region, the Action Group, through the indirect method of transference to the party of a part of government loans to a private Nigerian firm (the Nigerian Investment Properties Corporation). Similarly, in the Ivory Coast the PDCI government grants subventions to folklore and youth groups connected with the party, as well as to an array of voluntary associations unrelated to it.

Another aspect of the use of government for party purposes that prevails in most French-speaking African states is the direct participation by civil servants in party politics as party members, officers, activists, etc., thus giving the governing parties a significant advantage over their rather weak opponents. In the Ivory Coast, this situation has even taken the form of organizing "une commission politique" of the PDCI in the departments and ministries of government in order, among other things, "to control the conformity of the authorities to the directives of the party. . . ." Ghana has moved along similar lines, commencing the formation of CPP branches in government ministries in January 1962. Thus, when these situations are combined with those I have analyzed as major causes of the tendency toward single-party rule, there would not appear to be very much in African politics to make one especially sanguine about the prospects of opposition parties.

As some observers have argued, it may be that such a prospect is neither necessary nor desirable at the present stage of African political systems, which function within nation-states still in process of becoming internally coherent. These observers also suggest that the single-party system is capable of sustaining an important measure of democracy, by which they mean widespread participation, active and free discussion, etc.—all of which constitute influence by the *demos* upon the decision-making process.[4] This proposition, however, has not been taken very much beyond the realm of assertion, still wanting empirical demonstration and conceptual definition. What *kind* of decisions, for instance, are influenced by participation and discussion in parties like PDG, CPP, TANU, and *Union Soudanaise?* How real is the choice of candidates for party and government office given to the masses in these single-party situations? What are the limits of opposition politics in these situations; that is, what is meant by "opposition" within a single-party when there is no assumption of a right to carry it to its logical conclusion (to *organize* one's opposition) when one's demands are not satisfied? It simply is not enough to say that one index of democracy in a single-party situation is the prevalence of "conditions in which opposition can be expressed."[5]

I should note here that my own reading and analysis of the single-party situations in African politics suggest a more sceptical view as to their democratic character, *but I am not particularly convinced that this is the most meaningful yardstick for appraising them.* Although I myself have used this measurement in much of this article (e.g., my characterization of methods of single-party development as "authoritarian"), I am inclined to look at other functions of African single-party systems besides the democratic one; and my analysis leads me to believe that the governing parties and their leaders do not consider it supreme. More specifically, I tend to concur with Mair's keen observation that "Since the unity of the new [African] States is so precarious, it may well be that their rulers cannot at present afford that tolerance of opposition which is the ideal of representative democracy. . . . The crucial problem for the new governments seems likely to be how to be authoritarian enough to maintain stability and carry through their modernizing policies, and yet not so obviously oppressive as to provoke active or passive resistance."[6]

I should point out, finally, that some observers hold that use of the term "authoritarian" in analyzing African single-party systems may not be

---

[4] Cf. Immanuel Wallerstein, *Africa:* The Politics of Independence (New York, 1961), 161–67, *passim.*

[5] Cf. Ruth Schacter, "Single-Party Systems in West Africa," *American Political Science Review,* LV (June, 1961), 304–7.

[6] L. P. Mair, "Social Change in Africa," International Affairs, XXXVI (October, 1960), 456; italics added. Cf. Carl J. Friedrich, *Constitutional Government and Democracy* (Boston, 1941), 8 ff.; "In the evolution of our Western World . . . national unification had to precede constitutionalism."

appropriate, especially where mass-type parties are concerned, given the large-scale participation provided by such parties, their role in national integration, etc. Thus, Professor Wallerstein maintains that "the one-party system in the African context is often a significant step toward the liberal state, not a first step away from it. . . . The one-party structure is an interim system of African states which they are maintaining for the present."[7] Interesting as this proposition is and *perhaps* true for the long run, it is not particularly apparent in the thinking of the leaders of single-party states, and certainly not among the leaders of Guinea, Mali, and Ghana, where an effort is being made to employ political power for a revolutionary reconstruction of society. Note, for instance, Touré's adumbration of his view of liberalism and thus, presumably, of the liberal state: "The enemy of revolutionary firmness is liberalism which, from compromise to compromise, drives a party into incriminations and anarchy. The best [liberal] arrangements and the most clever compromises only lead to general discontent and could not possibly preserve the higher interests of the people since they subordinate them, wholly or partly, to the selfish interests of groups or individuals; they could only maintain inequalities and increase antagonisms; they perpetuate confusion and doubt, distrust and discouragement."[8]

Nevertheless, whatever the correct term may be for classifying and measuring African single-party systems—as against other political arrangements—their reversal is not particularly imminent. And this appears true despite such developments as the grant of amnesty to political exiles on the part of the Ivory Coast and Ghana governments, overtures of such amnesty made by Niger and Upper Volta to their political exiles, the release of political prisoners in Ghana and Ivory Coast, or Ghana's revocation of the *Ashanti Pioneer* Act of 1960, censoring that newspaper. Such grants of amnesty to political exiles are primarily an astute response to the manner in which the keenly contested politics of Pan-Africanism may affect the internal political stability of participant states (e.g., the use of an exile for political purposes by the exile's host-state). The latter strategy—i.e., lifting of censorship laws, etc.—may be a unique feature of African politics whereby, once the purpose of a restrictive measure has been secured, its continuation as a formal legal measure is considered an unnecessary demonstration of restrictive intent. In other words, once the intent is accepted as second nature to the political system and its participants, statutory expression of the intent is not required. This does not, however, necessarily alter an African single-party system. It may well strengthen the system.

---

[7] I. Wallerstein, *Africa*, pp. 163, 166.

[8] Sékou Touré, "Message to the Nation . . . on the Occasion of the New Year, January 10th, 1962," in *The International Policy of the Democratic Party of Guinea*, VII (Conakry, n.d.), pp. 219–20.

58. DEMOCRACY IN SOUTH ASIA*

Werner Levi

THE LOT of democratic government in South and Southeast Asia in recent times has not been a happy one. Pakistan, which struggled for years to adopt a constitution and finally did so in 1956, never fully lived up to it and set it aside again in 1958. To the relief of large sections of the public and also of some political factions, a military leader took over power in the proudly announced and widely acclaimed conviction that democracy is not yet for Pakistan. Indonesia is torn by civil strife, elections are postponed, and parliamentary institutions replaced by advisory councils harmless enough not to interfere with "guided democracy." In Nepal, democracy serves largely as a pretext for selfish politicians to gain power and profit; the King has been ruling since the revolution of 1950 with a handful of advisers; it is too early to foresee the consequences of the recent elections. Burma, where democratic techniques never made as much progress as the democratic way of life, is under a "caretaker" government of the army and some democratic practices are suspended. Traditionally placid little Ceylon has been under martial law. India (with perhaps the Philippines) remains the showcase for parliamentary democracy in Southern Asia; yet there also strong doubts have arisen, for some of India's intellectuals question the suitability of democracy and many of her interest groups are dissatisfied with its functioning.

Former devotees of the democratic system—men like Jayprakash Narayan of India, U Nu of Burma, and prominent Indonesians—seem to be concluding from recent evidence that free Asia must evolve some other system of its own; Titoism, Nasserism, even de Gaulle's ideas are examined as possible alternatives. In all the countries of South and Southeast Asia which adopted democratic constitutions from the West, dissatisfaction with political democracy has grown, in several cases to the point where radical departures from it have taken place in proportion to its failure to bring the expected miracle of peace, order, and prosperity.

There is triumph among those who have always argued that a political system cannot be abstracted from its cultural context and then transferred in generalized form to a strange culture in the expectation that it will flourish on the strength of its own laws and inherent merits. The argument is cogent, but slightly beside the point. What is a country to do after its

* From "The Fate of Democracy in South and Southeast Asia," *Far Eastern Survey*, Vol. 28, No. 2 (February, 1959). By permission of the Institute of Pacific Relations.

escape from colonialism? A return to pre-colonial regimes is impossible, as reason would tell and as futile attempts in this direction by certain religious groups prove. A break in the continuity of political developments has occurred. In a new system some contrivance becomes indispensable.

Why democracy should have been given the first chance in these countries' search for a new system is fairly obvious. It was the legacy of the colonial powers, more because they preached it than because they practised it. Only some rudiments of parliamentary government had been established by some of the colonial powers, but apparently just enough to create some corresponding habits and vested interests to build upon when independence came. Western influence among important native leaders was strong and democracy appealed to them. Finally, to be recognized as Western and progressive (which included the need to profess democracy) facilitated admission to the coveted membership among the elite of the world. Democracy was thus established on a narrow basis of ruling groups; and for a variety of reasons which did not all reflect deep seated convictions about its superior qualities as a form of government. Nowhere did it come as the result of deliberate choice among carefully considered alternatives. Nowhere was the mass of its beneficiaries readied for its arrival and successful establishment.

The resulting problem is that the forms and mechanics of Western democracy are there now, but they do not have the backing of ideologies and social realities which gave them birth and make them viable in their homelands. Not that *all* prerequisites for a proper functioning of a democratic system are absent among the peoples of South and Southeast Asia; they possess them now in varying numbers and degrees of adequacy. But from the past they also retain beliefs, attitudes, and habits which interfere with democracy and are responsible for some of its difficulties in this region. Though they vary from country to country, of course, some generalizations about them and their relation to democracy can be made, with the usual risks, which apply to a greater or lesser extent to the whole region and which provide a clue to the decline of democracy from Pakistan to Indonesia.

This is true of individualism as the fundamental concept underlying democracy. While the worth of the individual is not an unknown value in Asia—Burma has been called a "community of individuals"—individualism as a doctrine formed by Europeans in the nineteenth century with all that it implies is strange to most of the peoples of South and Southeast Asia. The technological and social reasons which brought it forth in the West do not exist there. Its introduction without compensating rearrangements in customary social institutions has led to disturbing consequences in the communal life prevailing almost everywhere in this region. The individual has rarely been of primary concern; the joint family or the clan are the fundamental social units and the lower as well as the upper limit of loyalty. Loyalty to the national community has been as strange to most Asians as to the individual, causing a lack of solidarity with the state-wide community which has often been regretted by Asian leaders as a major cause for the weakness of democracy. Democracy as the tool of individualism, as the means for its political realization, can therefore not be very comprehensible to the Asian masses and might even appear sometimes as a threat to their social existence. A change could occur gradually as traditional individualism (and with it, democracy) becomes modified by the newer concepts of social responsibility and social coopera-tion—that is, as the interpretation of the ends of democracy corresponds more closely to Asian values and social organization.

The individual in subordination to the group; inequalities in power, status, and wealth; a hierarchical order of society (with greatly varying degrees of rigidity from country to country)—these things have char-acterized Asian societies for so long and have been rationalized so pro-foundly in systems of belief, that the masses must learn to question the system into which they were born before they can be expected to accept the values of individual dignity and rights and behave accordingly. They must be convinced that the order and values they and their forefathers have known are neither immutable nor necessarily the most beneficial. The corollary to this is, of course, a demonstration of the superior benefits of the new order and values they are to adopt in relation to their ambitions. Unfortunately for the cherished belief of many Westerners with their missionary zeal, the virtues of individualism are not self-evident. There should be no mistake in Western minds that the demand for national freedom in Asia implied demands for individual freedom. The two have little in common, except perhaps in the mind of the elite groups. There is no evidence that the expectations among the limited sections of the population who shared in the struggle for freedom included personal freedom in the form of Western individualism. There is, on the contrary, a point to be made that some nationalist leaders sublimated, for their own benefit, potential desires for individual freedom into the wider struggle for national independence—and that some are continuing to do so to this day.

Equally alien to most inhabitants of South and Southeast Asia is democracy's basic assumption that sovereignty rests in the people. As a device to pacify the Western conscience, which cannot easily reconcile power with freedom, it is not needed. Unlike the Westerner, the Asian has not yet turned this issue into a practical political problem. As an idea it has not found any support for hundreds of years in any major creed of the region and by some it is actually opposed. For long periods of time, theories of divine kingship have prevailed. Sooner or later all major creeds developed their own authoritarian ideologies. They all confirm, explicitly or implicitly, that the ruler is the embodiment of supreme political authority. Even where (as in Confucian China, Hindu theory, and certain early Islamic conceptions) the people's right was granted to determine whether the ruler possessed the mandate of heaven, the source of the mandate was heaven and the ruler monopolized sovereignty.

Some present leaders of Asia wish to read democratic features into these creeds, usually for internal or external political purposes, in an age when to be democratic carries the presumption of respectability; some of these creeds may indeed have been corrupted in the course of time to justify authoritarian rule; and the influence of these creeds, in their spoiled or unspoiled version, may be strong or weak today. The fact remains that because of these creeds (or in spite of them), the civilizations in which they prevailed have never had anything resembling democratic or even potentially democratic systems. This includes the often romanticized village systems of self-government which more often than not are run along authoritarian lines and which never affected the decidedly autocratic governments above them. On the contrary, and perhaps forcing the point somewhat, there is almost a direct relationship between the success of democracy in these countries of Asia and the extent to which either politics and religion could be separated, or religion could be reinterpreted to become compatible with democracy.

The practices and experiences of the peoples in the region correspond to their traditional doctrines—not surprisingly, since these were often developed to justify autocratic rule. Until the end of World War II, they knew only authoritarianism, native or foreign. Sometimes it was cruel, sometimes paternalistic. It had, at any rate, the advantage of being clearcut: one knew whom to worship, love, hate, or blame. One knew who the government was. Many Asian villagers continue to find it easier to understand a political system in which a recognized and recognizable leader personifies authority than one in which a vague mass, they included, represent it. This understanding is all the firmer and the system more desired because the traditional relationship between the citizen and his government has been antagonistic. Most of the time, government was the tax collector; much of the time it was a worse exploiter. It was therefore something to be suspicious of, to guard against. Government, in the words of former Prime Minister Suhrawardy of Pakistan, was to the people "something set against their own interests and purposes." There was rarely a mutually responsive relationship. The citizen, far from being the source of authority, was more likely its victim.

Consent was an unknown ingredient in government. Some Asians have a suspicion that vesting authority in the people is a subterfuge of unscrupulous rulers to evade responsibility for their actions; an open door to corruption; or a trick to exploit the people in the name of the people. Others, on a more rational level, argue that in the pluralistic societies of South and Southeast Asia such a diffusion of authority can have no reality and at the same time weakens the integrating effect of the national leader whose strong rule and symbolic role are sometimes the vital elements in holding such societies together.

There is little consolation for those who find government by representation unsuitable or suspect its implications in the fact that this (to them) nebulous relationship between ruler and ruled is made concrete through the accountability of the government. Delegation of authority is a mental process which requires training and for which there are few precedents in the social experience of Asia. Furthermore, and more important, the methods and institutions of accountability have not developed rapidly enough to make it real.

Notwithstanding justified pride felt by some observers in the success with elections in such countries as India and Ceylon, the fact remains that elections have limited value for making governments accountable, especially when they are a novelty to the voters. In many instances, where elections took place, candidates were nominated and elected because according to custom and tradition they had a right to be. Or candidates had themselves elected not on reasonable issues but by clever tricks appealing to ancient beliefs and superstitions. Further examples could be cited to indicate that many voters had no real conception of or interest in the motions they were going through at the ballot boxes. And it is questionable how much those governments really cared in those several countries which do not possess an effective opposition party. Elections have greatly reduced value where the real alternative to the present government is the same next government—or the army. More important, however, than these childhood diseases of the election process is the fact that an election is only one means of making government accountable, that accountabilty should be a continuous process whose performance requires additional means.

Political parties are important among these means, and parties, in this part of the world, are with few exceptions a sad chapter in the story of parliamentary democracy. The fundamental reason for this appears to be that parties have not developed as an integral part of the society in which they function. Most of them have been created from the top, more in response to the needs and desires of Westernized elites than to the basic concerns and views of large sections, especially rural sections, of the public. As a result, the parties usually float above the heads of the people. With some exceptions, such as the Indian Congress, they become active on the mass level only when the leaders, too often for personal reasons, need demonstrations of "popular" support. Few parties in this region can claim to be transmission belts between substantial numbers of the electors and the elected (few indeed have any organization reaching the village level). When there is any contact between the rural masses and the government—usually the great unknown far away in the big city—strong personalities are usually responsible for this rare situation.

Many parties are either factions or composed of factions. They are built around a leader or a grievance and disappear with the one or the other, leaving behind only a disturbing influence upon the growth of democracy. In these cases, the parties serve as instruments for individual leaders and their followers in the unending struggles for personal power and prestige, conducted by intrigue, corruption, violence. Constant mergers and dissolutions of "parties," switches in loyalty, splits and splinters are the external evidence of this unhealthy system. Nothing has discredited "democracy" more in the eyes of the Asian peoples, or has made them more cynical about politics, than this politicking in the worst sense of the word; nothing has produced more quickly calls for the strong man and the creation of "party-less democracy." It is this which has motivated some prominent Indians to urge Nehru and the Congress to quit party politics and become "a movement" which could harness *jan shakti* (the strength of the people) for the salvation of the country. "Democracy" has already become disreputable among large sections of the peoples in this region before they ever had a chance to experience it.

Great damage has thus been done. But luckily not all political leaders or all political parties fall into this evil category. They possess, however, characteristics which, though morally neutral, nevertheless form barriers to progress towards democratic government. The communal way of life of most of the citizens, their lack of loyalty to a national community, their preoccupation with local issues—all these have carried over into the party system. Parties have difficulty in reaching or maintaining themselves on a national level or, when they succeed, in retaining contact with the villages (or even the urban communities from which they usually sprang). Local problems could easily be taken up by some of the larger parties but frequently are not. Local politicians and enthusiasts turn them into ideological principles and create a party to defend them. Such a party lacks national concern; it is uncompromising, disrupts the political system and emphasizes the dangerously pluralistic nature of the society.

There are, on the other hand, all too many genuine and serious ideological splits in many countries of this region. They are founded on religious, racial, linguistic or similar fundamental facts and beliefs and do not lend themselves easily to the democratic processes of adjustment or compromise. These controversial issues, instead of being underplayed, became, in the absence of a higher loyalty to the national community, the foundation of political parties (and where the multiplicity of parties is based on such grounds, the stability and very existence of the state) is seriously threatened. Democracy cannot function for the dogmatic position of the parties, based on unadjustable ideologies instead of compromisable interests, makes it impossible for a government to serve them all; nor can the parties play their expected constructive role while in the opposition. In such circumstances, the government can make itself accountable to only one or the other side, and the opposition can only reciprocate by trying to make that government impossible. The prospect for democracy remains dim as long as all these matters of belief are expected by its believers to be reflected in the nature of the state and when it becomes the primary purpose of the parties to realize this goal. This dangerous situation was referred to by the Vice-Chancellor of Madras University, Dr. A. L. Mudalier, when he warned that democracy cannot function if emotional, spiritual, or other influences of this kind were brought to bear upon "purely" political issues.

The unfortunate fact is, however, that parties are too often considered by their founders and followers to be the proper outlets for such influences. They are considered movements more than political instruments. They perform more comprehensive functions than they do in the West. There is a dearth of other social organizations with specific functions which members could join to satisfy their needs—material, spiritual, psychological, or social—so that memberships in diversified organizations would overlap and the contrasts created by contradictory values and interests could be softened and play themselves out without endangering the whole foundation of the state at every turn. It may also be true that the chance to see ideologies realized in the form of the new states and maintained by political power has intensified the desire of their adherents to advance them as political issues. Perhaps, therefore, once the peoples of this region can take the existence of their states more for granted and their material existence as better assured, the present intense and disruptive debate about the nature of the state will become more relaxed. There might then be a growing inclination to subordinate ideological matters of this kind to an overriding desire for a smoothly functioning state which can serve a multiplicity of functions of which most Asians today can hardly conceive.

An increase in the social organizations would have the additional advantage of improving the formation and expression of public opinion as another important check upon government. Today, as an Indian editorial complained recently, the ideas holding nationwide sway are crude derivatives of class and caste antagonism, social jealousies, and individual cupidity. There is need for education for an understanding of the major national problems and a greater differentiation of the public along the lines of specific concerns and interests. Only then can leaders cease to appeal on the basis of broad and often emotional generalizations and turn to proposals for the solution of specific and manageable problems. Opinions are, of course, expressed every day in the market places of thousands of villages and they refer no doubt to local and specific problems, probably too much so. But they remain ineffective in the absence of adequate communication between them and with the government. The most efficient "grapevine" is a poor substitute for newspapers or nationally organized interest groups. It can lead only in the most exceptional circumstances to concerted action or influence upon the government. But newspapers and the few organizations are concentrated in the urban centers and serve only a minute fraction of the population. What passes as public opinion in a number of countries is the opinion of groups which may represent a diversity of interests but which are, by and large, composed of relatively homogeneous elites and tend to be identical with the actual or potential ruling groups. Public opinion lacks the representative and diversified character which make it valuable as a method of governmental accountability.

Altogether, government, parties, public opinion are too much the preserve of a relatively small group for a healthy democracy. The base of democracy is as yet too narrow, whatever the constitutions may say. It threatens to remain so for some considerable time, partly because some of the leaders have no interest in undermining their own positions by broadening it, partly (and more important) because there is poor communication between the Westernized, urbanized intellectuals and the masses of their fellow citizens on the land. The resistance of the technically backward and tradition-bound peasants to innovations has made the development-minded elites impatient. A deep gulf exists between the two groups. The democratic requirement of working with the acquiescence of those concerned and with respect for their culture is proving too much of a stumbling bloc to many of these restless and mostly well-meaning reformers. In a paternalistic and authoritarian mood they attempt to impose their own ideas upon the people instead of executing the people's wishes. They dare not risk the delays involved in exposing the masses to the education which has made them the reformers they are.

Democracy faces a dilemma here. The sense of superiority of Westernized Asians over their technically backward fellow citizens (which also leads them occasionally to despise these) is factually justified. They *are* superior. Yet the customary democratic methods of reconciling conflicting views and policies cannot easily be applied, even were they available, because they assume a certain degree of cultural homogeneity. Where there are such stark contrasts in cultural levels as can be found within several of the countries of this region of Asia, there is hardly common ground for agreement.

The counterpart to the superior attitudes among sections of the elites is a widespread attitude among the masses accepting these as natural. The class and caste systems and the authoritarian practices of native and colonial rulers have conspired to instil in the masses a great respect for the rulers, often simply because they occupy the ruling positions and regardless of how they got there. In return for this vast deference to the ruler, he is expected to solve the people's problems. Even in countries where this relationship is rapidly disappearing, its after-effects can still be seen in the extraordinary reliance of the people upon government initiative and direction. This mutual complementation of undemocratic attitudes delays the acceptance of fundamental democratic ideals of the equality of men and the sovereignty of the people.

Aggravating this condition among the elites is the incomplete moral and emotional satisfaction which democracy can give them in their present search for new values and new ways of life. While this problem should not be exaggerated—Asian youth being more interested in material welfare than philosophy, Asian "spirituality" notwithstanding—it has a bearing on the chances of democracy, if only because it has relevance also for the material progress of Asia. In the process of Westernization, the traditional way of life was destroyed, but Western education was too often formal and lacked social content or applicability. Western standards were rationally accepted, but emotions remained largely under traditional influences. Few Asians have achieved a synthesis, as Prime Minister Nehru implies when he refers to his personality as split between East and West. Furthermore, democracy (in contrast to Communism) as a philosophy and a political system is an incomplete substitute for the (at least partially) discarded integrated systems and practices of Asia. It does not offer a comprehensive view of the world or claim to provide an interpretation of history, an analysis of society, a knowledge of the future, and a timetable for action. It has few dogmas to cling to and no infallibility to rely upon. In other words, democracy does not provide the sense of security and the confidence in the future sought by a good many members of that Asian generation whose traditional beliefs have broken down because they do not fit a world they know or want. In day-to-day existence (of overwhelming concern is Asia today) democracy has few appeals because it does not supply prescriptions for the solution of economic problems any more than it does for the creation of conditions guaranteeing its successful functioning in the political sphere. One may hope that what appears as a trend away from democracy in South and Southeast Asia will in the end turn out to be the evolutionary process by which the values of democracy will be preserved in the forms best suited to the local environment.